# PSYCHOLOGY APPLIED TO WORK
## An introduction to industrial and organizational psychology

**The Dorsey Series in Psychology**

ADVISORY EDITORS

**Wendell E. Jeffrey**
University of California, Los Angeles

**Salvatore R. Maddi**
The University of Chicago

# PSYCHOLOGY APPLIED TO WORK

An introduction to industrial
and organizational psychology

PAUL M. MUCHINSKY
Iowa State University

1983 **⫼** THE DORSEY PRESS
Homewood, Ilinois 60430

ISBN 0-256-02862-1
Library of Congress Catalog Card No. 82–71974

*Printed in the United States of America*

4 5 6 7 8 9 0 M P 0 9 8 7 6 5

To Sam Mudd
Mentor and Friend

# PREFACE

I suppose that nearly all college professors have thought at one time or another that they had a better way than the author of their text book to explain material to students. So it was with me. After nearly 10 years of teaching industrial/organizational psychology, I decided to write a book which offered a scholarly and balanced portrayal of the profession. The discipline of industrial/organizational psychology represents a mix of science and practice. My dissatisfaction with previous texts is that I felt most were too slanted in one direction or the other. There is a rigorous scientific basis to industrial/organizational psychology, and I wanted to capture the essence of this foundation for the reader. Throughout the book, research studies bearing on the topics being discussed are presented. Most of what we know about our discipline is the product of research. Therefore, I feel it is impossible to truly understand industrial/organizational psychology without knowledge of empirical research. The world of work is exceedingly complex, and we need research to provide answers to some difficult and vexing questions. While pat solutions, oversimplifications, and slick generalities offer tempting explanations to our work problems, they are rarely accurate or sufficient. In this book, I have used the findings from research as the vehicle for presenting and explaining industrial/organizational psychology.

However, there is more to industrial/organizational psychology than a tedious compendium of research facts and figures. The discipline does not embrace ivory-tower topics far removed from reality. The substance of industrial/organizational psychology deals with everyday problems found in the work world. The content of the discipline is most certainly neither dull nor irrelevant. Accordingly, I have tried to present the material in a way which matches the vibrancy and significance of the issues addressed in the profession. In fact, I selected the title of this book, *Psychology Applied to Work*, to reflect the fact that industrial/organizational psychology represents the application of rigorous scientific principles of psychology to the domain of work. Most of us will spend the greatest single portion of our lives engaged in work. I can't think of a more salient area of life than what the field of industrial/organizational psychology addresses.

The world of work is continually changing. Exciting new advances and developments in industrial/organizational psychology are occurring continuously. While this book contains many classic topics and findings in the field, I also strove to include the most recent and emerging developments within the profession. I am sure the reader will be struck by the frequency of findings that have emerged in just the past 5 to 10 years. It is a challenge to remain current in one's discipline, and the ever-changing content of industrial/organizational psychology made this obligation both fascinating and enjoyable.

I must also confess to being enamored with my discipline. It has provided me with a very rewarding and satisfying vocation. I will be particularly gratified if the content of this book stimulates others to enter the profession. It has been written at a level for the student who has no previous exposure to the field. I once heard a eulogy in which a man was described as someone who "gave back to life more than he took out." This book represents a major attempt on my part to give something back to the profession which has given so much to me.

I am indebted to many people for making the writing of this book possible. Their generous contributions of time, effort, and support are deeply appreciated. First, I would like to thank my colleagues who served as reviewers of the book during its development. They were: Aaron W. Andreason (University of Montana); Alan A. Benton (University of Illinois–Chicago Circle); Lorraine Uhlaner Henrickson (Michigan State University); Neal Schmitt (Michigan State University); David Stimpson (Brigham Young University); and Sheldon Zedeck (University of California–Berkeley). Along with the reviews by the Consulting Editor, Salvatore R. Maddi (University of Chicago), these individuals contributed many valuable ideas and suggestions for improving the book. I would also like to thank two of my graduate students, Reneé Yerke and Jean Ann Woods, for their many helpful comments. I extend special thanks to Carlyn Monahan for her comments and encouragement over the past two years. My father, Michael W. Muchinsky, who has been practicing many of the principles of industrial/

organizational psychology in business for almost 40 years, also contributed many pertinent suggestions and ideas. My loyal and highly competent secretary, Martha Behrens, was a whiz at transforming illegible scrawls and numerous inserts into typed copy. Her efficiency and continual good humor made my job much easier. Finally, I would like to thank my two children, Andrea and Brian. On weary and frustrating days they were always there when I needed them.

Paul M. Muchinsky

# CONTENTS

## section 2          Personnel psychology

## 3   CRITERIA                                                                 67

## 4   PREDICTORS                                                              96

## 6  PERSONNEL TRAINING

## 7   PERFORMANCE APPRAISAL                                     242

## section 3       Organizational psychology

## 8   ORGANIZATIONAL INFLUENCES ON BEHAVIOR                      287

## 9  JOB SATISFACTION  317

## 10   WORKER MOTIVATION 357

## 11   LEADERSHIP 397

## section 4        The work environment

## 14   UNION/MANAGEMENT RELATIONS

## 15   WORK CONDITIONS

section 1    **Introduction**

# chapter 1

# INTRODUCTION

## PSYCHOLOGY

Psychology is defined as the scientific study of behavior. It is a complex discipline involving the study of behavior of both animals and humans. It is a science because psychologists use the same rigorous methods of research found in other areas of scientific investigation. Some of their research is more biological in nature (as the effects of brain lesions on a rat's food consumption). Other research is more social in nature (as identifying the factors that lead to bystander apathy). Because psychology covers such a broad spectrum of content areas, it is difficult to have a clear and accurate image of what a psychologist does. Many people think that every psychologist, "is a shrink," "has a black couch," "likes to discover what makes people tick," and so on. In fact, these statements usually refer to the specialty of clinical psychology—the diagnosis and treatment of mental illness or abnormal behavior. Most psychologists do not treat mental disorders, nor do they practice psychotherapy. In reality, psychologists are a very diversified lot with many specialized interests.

Professionally, many psychologists are united through membership in the American Psychological Association (APA), a national organization. As of 1979, there were almost 50,000 members, 71 percent men and 29 percent women. The diversification of interest among psychologists is reflected by the fact that there are 36 divisions of APA representing special-interest subgroups. Though some members have no divisional affiliation, others belong to more than one. The APA publishes several journals, vehicles through which psychologists can communicate their research findings to other scholars. (Psychologists can also publish their research in journals that are not under APA auspices.) The APA also holds regional and national conventions, sets standards for graduate training in certain areas of psychology (i.e., clinical, counseling, and school), develops and enforces a code of professional ethics, and helps psychologists find employment. The APA has three classes of membership. An *associate* has a minimum of either two years of graduate work in psychology or a masters degree in psychology. A *member* has a Ph.D. degree based in part on a psychological dissertation. A *fellow* has a Ph.D. degree and a minimum of five years of subsequent

**Figure 1–1**          **Employers of psychologists**

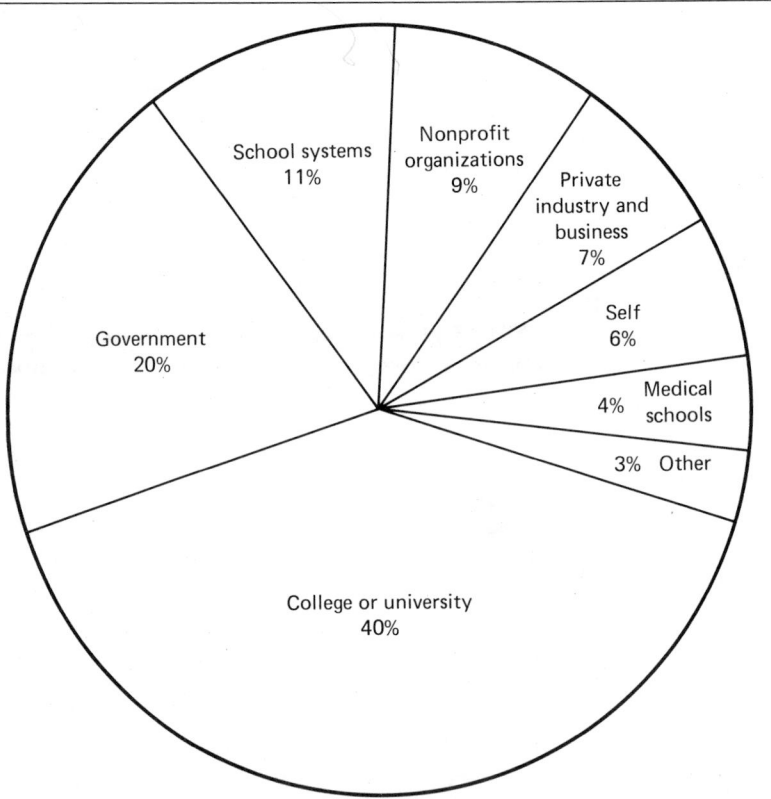

SOURCE: American Psychological Association, "Psychology as a Profession," *American Psychologist* 23 (1968), p. 196.

professional experience, and is judged to have made exceptional scientific contributions in his or her area of expertise.

Figure 1–1 shows areas where psychologists are employed. Colleges or universities employ the greatest number, followed by the government (federal, state, county, and municipal). Most psychologists who specialize in basic areas (e.g., experimental, social, developmental) are employed in colleges or universities. Many applied psychologists (those with training in clinical, counseling, industrial/organizational, school) work in nonacademic settings. In summary, psychology is a complex and varied profession whose members work in a wide variety of jobs.

## INDUSTRIAL/ORGANIZATIONAL PSYCHOLOGY

One of the specialty areas of psychology is industrial/organizational (I/O) psychology (represented by Division 14 of APA). As of 1979, there were about 1,800 members of Division 14, 92 percent male and 8 percent female. Schein (1971) commented that the area was greatly underrepresented by females, but recently more women have become members.

I wish I could say that becoming an I/O psychologist was my childhood ambition, but such was not the case; I originally wanted to be a chemist. But in college it soon became apparent that I lacked the skills and talents needed for that discipline. By accident I took an introductory psychology course taught by an I/O psychologist. I was so impressed by his teaching that I wanted to emulate him and was soon embarked on a new career. My happenstance entry into the field of I/O psychology places me in some distinguished company. Stagner (1981) reported that industrial psychology was the second career choice of many past presidents of Division 14 of APA. Like me, they gave circumstance or luck as the reason for "finding" I/O psychology. Perhaps this book will serve as a catalyst for some students to rationally select a career in I/O psychology rather than depending on fate.

A master's degree is necessary to qualify as an I/O psychologist (and for membership in Division 14 of APA). However, many obtain a Ph.D. degree, and this gives them more expertise and professional mobility. Unlike some areas of psychology, job opportunities are extremely good for I/O psychologists.

The distribution of psychologists in the major subfields is shown in Figure 1–2. According to the survey on which this figure is based, 10 percent of all psychologists are in the I/O area—and this represents a substantial number of people.

As a specialty area, I/O psychology has a more restricted definition than psychology as a whole. Guion (1965) defines industrial/organizational psychology as "the scientific study of the relationship between man and the world at work: the study of the adjustment people make to the places they

**Figure 1–2**                    **Distribution of psychologists by interest area**

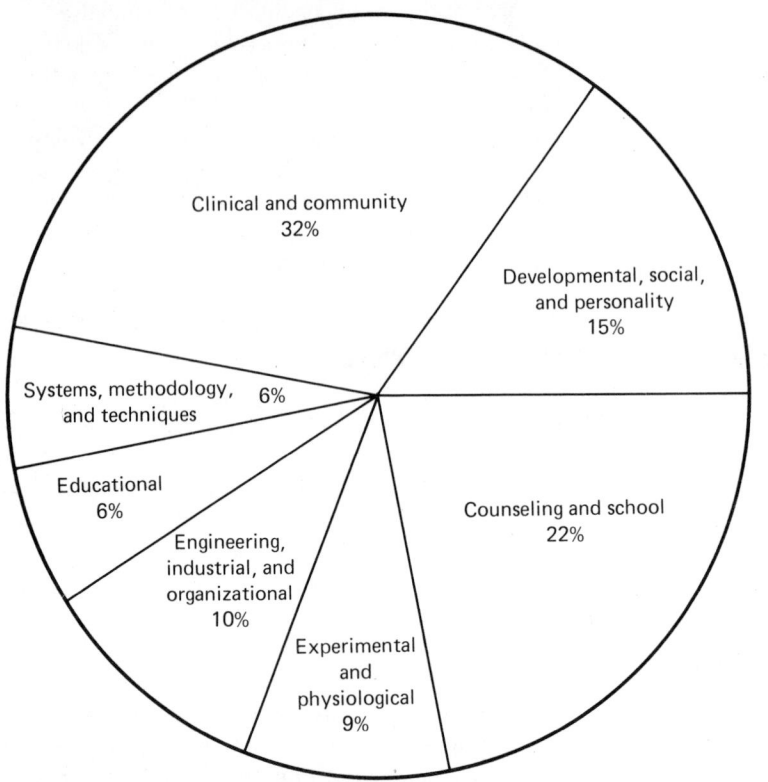

SOURCE: Data from a 1972 Survey of American Psychological Association members in the United States and Canada. *Careers in Psychology* (Washington, D.C.: American Psychological Association, 1975), p. 17.

go, the people they meet, and the things they do in the process of making a living" (p. 817). Blum and Naylor (1968) define it as "simply the application or extension of psychological facts and principles to the problems concerning human beings operating within the context of business and industry" (p. 4). Broadly speaking, the I/O psychologist is concerned with behavior in work situations.

There are two sides to I/O psychology: science and practice. I/O psychology is a legitimate field of scientific inquiry concerned with advancing knowledge about people at work. Like any area of science, questions are posed to guide the research, and scientific methods are used to help answer the questions. Researchers try to form the results of studies into meaningful patterns that are useful in explaining behavior. They seek to replicate findings to make generalizations about behavior. This area is I/O psychology as an academic discipline.

There is another side of I/O psychology, though—the professional side.

It is concerned with the application of knowledge to solve real problems in the world of work. I/O psychological research findings can be used to hire better employees, reduce absenteeism, improve communication, increase job satisfaction, and solve countless other problems. Most I/O psychologists feel a sense of kinship with both sides—science and practice.

As an I/O psychologist, I am pleased that the results of my research can be put to some practical use. But by the same token, I am more than a technician, someone who goes through the motions of solving problems without knowing why those actions "work" and what their consequences are. I/O psychology is more than just a tool for business leaders to use to make their companies more efficient. So the I/O psychologist has a dual existence. It is the realization that good application of knowledge can only come from *sound* knowledge. The well-trained I/O psychologist can do both—contribute to knowledge as well as apply it.

Figure 1–3 shows the main work settings of I/O psychologists. They are

**Figure 1–3**             **Principal work settings of I/O psychologists**

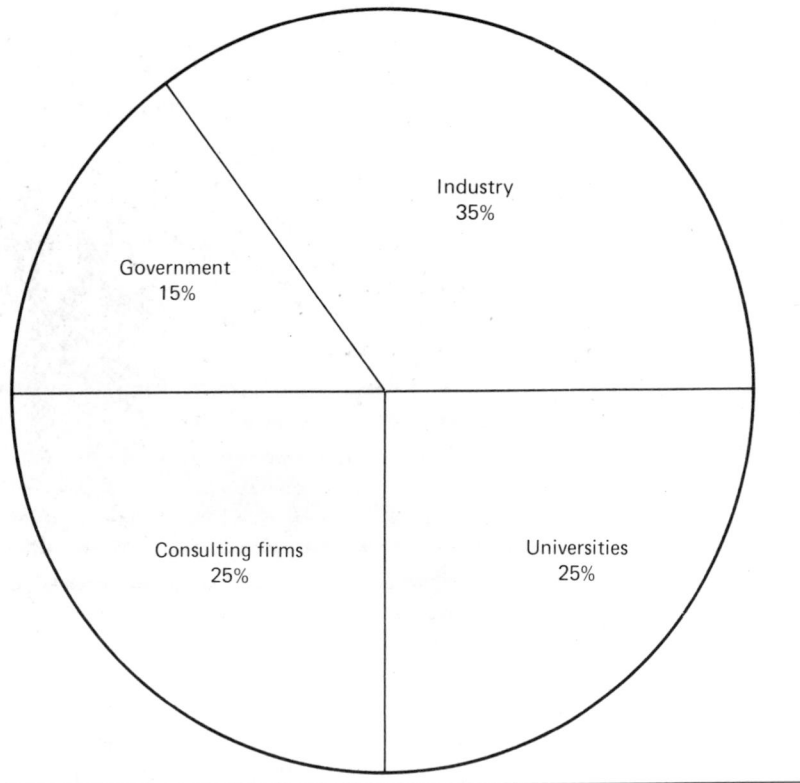

SOURCE: *A Career in Industrial/Organizational Psychology* (Washington, D.C.: American Psychological Association, Division of Industrial and Organizational Psychology, undated).

represented across the four areas, though industry is the primary employer. But across these four areas, I/O psychologists are unevenly split as to their scientist/practitioner orientation. Those working in universities are more involved as scientists; consulting firms employ more practitioners. Industry and government have a good mix of the two. This orientation difference has caused many problems in deciding the best way to train I/O psychologists. Should graduate programs train students as scientists or practitioners? This is an important question. Successful practitioners need certain skills the scientists do not need, and vice versa (Mayfield, 1975). Such noted I/O psychologists as Meyer (1972) and Naylor (1970) have discussed the consequences of poorly trained students, the product of unintelligent handling of this dualism issue (Muchinsky, 1973). While many "solutions" to the problem have been proposed (Task Force on the Practice of Psychology in Industry, 1971), no final blueprint has yet been devised. Some psychologists (Naylor, 1971) proposed adopting a strict "scientist" model of graduate training for all students. Others have proposed the separation of academic and professional training (Rodgers, 1964). I prefer the scientist end of the continuum for graduate training. But students who wish to become practitioners should have a chance to serve as interns in business or industry as part of their graduate training (Muchinsky, 1976). While training to become an I/O psychologist is an arduous process, the rewards in terms of challenging work, intellectual stimulation, and feelings of accomplishment are great.

## FIELDS OF I/O PSYCHOLOGY

Just as psychology is a diversified science, so is I/O psychology. Even within this specialty, there are subspecialties (see Figure 1–4).

**Personnel psychology.** The word *personnel* means *people*. So personnel psychology is concerned with all aspects of applied individual differences. Among other things, personnel psychologists determine what human skills and talents are needed for certain jobs, how to assess potential employees, how to grade employee job performance, and how to train workers to improve job performance. Personnel psychology is one of the oldest and most traditional activities of I/O psychologists. In fact, for many years personnel psychology and I/O psychology were synonymous. It was only after other topics caught the interest of I/O psychologists that personnel psychology became just a subspecialty of the total profession.

Personnel psychologists may belong to the American Society for Personnel Administration (ASPA). Also, the Academy of Management has a division called Personnel/Human Resources for people with interests similar to those of personnel psychologists. The academic boundaries between these areas are very loose. Members of these organizations have a common in-

**Figure 1–4**                          **Fields of industrial/organizational psychology**

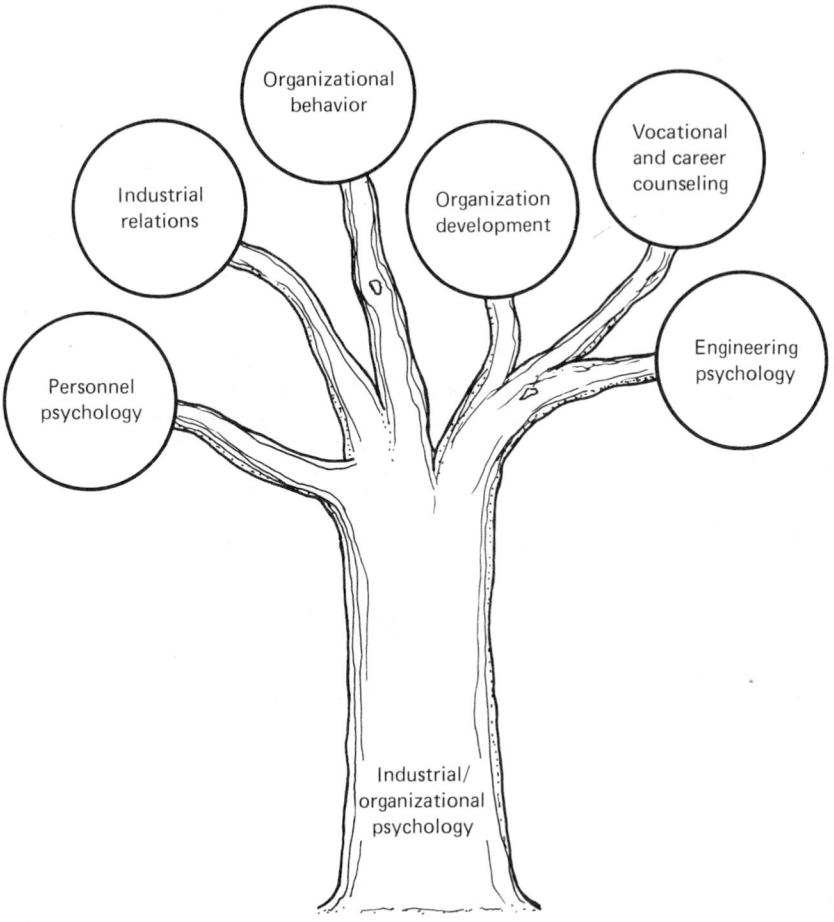

terest in personnel psychology, even though they come from a variety of academic backgrounds.

**Organizational behavior.** The subspecialty of organizational behavior is one of the newer areas of I/O psychology. Almost all employees work within some organizational context. We know that organizations can influence the attitudes and behaviors of people associated with them. Work in this area concerns such factors as role-related behavior, pressures that groups can impose on individuals, personal feelings of commitment to an organization, and patterns of communciation within an organization. There is a strong *social* influence in organizational behavior research because organizations are social collectivities. At the risk of overgeneralizing, personnel psychology is more concerned with *individual*-level issues (e.g., who gets hired and who doesn't); organizational behavior is more concerned with social and *group* influences.

Professionally, I/O psychologists in this area may be affiliated with other professionals in sociology and business administration, although their perspective may be somewhat different. Many I/O psychologists are members of the Academy of Management's Organizational Behavior Division. Traditional academic boundaries are also blurred in this area. Professional conventions may be attended by researchers in psychology, sociology, and business administration. Also business schools commonly hire I/O psychology graduates (Campbell, 1971, Schneider, 1971). While organizational behavior is a legitimate subspecialty of I/O psychology, it is also studied by people from other academic disciplines.

**Engineering psychology.** Engineering psychology concerns understanding of human performance in man-machine systems, including the design of equipment and machinery to enhance worker productivity and safety. Most tools, equipment, and machines are designed for a human to operate. However, humans have limitations in terms of strength, reaction time, coordination, sensory acuity, and so on. No one benefits if a machine's demands exceed the limits of human capabilities. Engineering psychology tries to modify the work environment to be compatible with human skills and talents. *Human factors psychology* and *ergonomics* are also names for this specialized field.

**Vocational and career counseling.** This subspecialty is a cross between counseling and I/O psychology; the counseling applies to people's problems at work. Industrial-oriented counselors help employees choose a rewarding and satisfying career path, resolve conflicts between work and nonwork interests, adjust to changing career interests, and prepare for retirement. I/O psychologists in this area may research these issues, or they may work for large organizations as in-house staff counselors.

**Organization development.** I/O psychologists in this area are concerned with improving or changing (i.e., "developing") organizations to make them more efficient. The I/O psychologist must be able to diagnose an organization's problems, recommend or enact changes, and then assess the effectiveness of the changes. Organization development involves the planned, deliberate change of an organization to resolve a particular problem; the change may involve people, work procedures, or technology. Organization development is the newest and least-structured subspecialty of I/O psychology.

Despite its relative embryonic state, organization development provides an exciting opportunity for some I/O psychologists to help organizations resolve or adapt to their problems.

**Industrial relations.** The final specialty area of I/O psychology is industrial relations. Industrial relations deals with problems between employers and employees and usually involves a labor union. I/O psychologists interested in industrial relations address such issues as cooperation and conflict between work parties, resolving disputes in the work force, and bargaining or negotiating agreements between various segments of the work force. I/O psychologists in this area have close contact with specialists in labor relations, i.e., people with knowledge of federal and state laws on employee rights, collective bargaining, and dispute settlement. Unlike some other areas of I/O psychology, industrial relations is heavily legislated, and a person who works in this area must have knowledge of these laws.

In summary, psychology as a discipline is composed of many specialty areas, one of which is I/O psychology. And I/O psychology consists of several subspecialties. While some of these subspecialities overlap, many are quite distinct from each other. Thus, I/O psychology is not really a single discipline. It is mix of subspecialties bonded together by a concern for people at work. Each of the subspecialties of I/O psychology will be explored to various degrees in this book.

## LICENSING AND CERTIFICATION OF PSYCHOLOGISTS

What makes a psychologist a psychologist? What prevents people with no psychological training from passing themselves off as psychologists? One way professions offer high-quality service to the public is by regulating their own membership. Selective admission into the profession helps protect the public against quacks and charlatans (who not only risk great damage to their clients, but also to the profession they allegedly represent). The practice of professional psychology is regulated by law in every state in the country. When both the title and practice of psychology are regulated, the law is called a *licensing law*. When only the title of psychologist is regulated, the law is called a *certification law* (Hess, 1977). The laws limit licensure to those qualified to practice psychology as defined by state law. Each state has its own standards for licensure, and these are governed by regulatory boards. The major functions of any professional board are to determine the standards for admission into the profession and to conduct disciplinary actions involving violations of professional standards.

Typically, licensure involves educational, experience, examination, and administrative requirements. Usually, a doctoral degree in psychology from an approved program is required as well as one or two years of supervised experience. Applicants must also pass an objective, written examination covering all areas of psychology. Specialty examinations (e.g., in I/O psychology) usually are not given. Currently, psychologists must pass a uniform national examination to attain a license (Hoffman, 1980). Finally, the applicant must meet citizenship and residency requirements and be of good moral character.

Psychologists disagree about how successful licensing laws have been in protecting the public. Some authors (Hess, 1977) are quite positive on the effects of licensing, some are pessimistic (Gross, 1978). Others have called for a greater separation between those involved in graduate education and those who serve on regulatory licensing boards (Matarazzo, 1977).

Licensing and certification are intended to ensure that clients receive services from qualified people (Fretz & Mills, 1980). However, scrupulous I/O psychologists can never guarantee results, and they should never try. Companies have been duped by consulting firms and individuals into believing a wide range of claims that simply cannot be guaranteed. The problems that the I/O psychologist faces are too complex for guarantees. Reasonable expectations on the part of both the I/O psychologist and the company are the best way to avoid such difficulties.

## THE HISTORY OF I/O PSYCHOLOGY

It is always difficult to write *the* history of anything. There are different perspectives with different emphases. It is also a challenge to divide the historical evolution of a discipline into units of time. In some cases, time itself is a convenient watershed (decades or centuries); in others, major events serve as watersheds. In the case of I/O psychology, the two world wars were major catalysts for changing the discipline. This historical overview will show how the field of I/O psychology came to be what it is and how some key individuals and events helped shape the discipline.[1]

### The early years (1900–1916)

In the early years, what we know today as I/O psychology didn't even have a name. In the beginning, it was a merging of two forces that gathered momentum before 1900. One force was the pragmatic nature of some basic psychological research. Most psychologists at this time were strictly scientific and deliberately avoided studying problems that strayed outside the boundaries of pure research. However, a psychologist named W. L. Bryan published a paper (Bryan & Harter, 1897) about how professional telegraphers develop skill in sending and receiving Morse code. A few years later (1903), Bryan's presidential address to the American Psychological Association (Bryan, 1904) touched on having psychologists study "concrete activities and functions as they appear in everyday life" (p. 80). Bryan did not advocate studying problems found in industry per se, but rather examining real skills as a base to develop scientific psychology. Bryan is not considered the father of I/O psychology, but rather a precursor.[2]

---

[1] I am indebted to David C. Edwards and Kimberley Abbey whose research provided much of the material for this section.

[2] The term *industrial psychology* was used apparently for the first time in Bryan's 1904 article. Ironically, it appeared in print only as a typographical error. Bryan (1904) was quoting a sentence he had written five years earlier (Bryan & Harter, 1899) in which he spoke of the need for more research in individual psychology. Instead, Bryan wrote *industrial* psychology and did not catch his mistake.

The second major force in the evolution of the discipline came from industry when industrial engineers wanted to improve efficiency. They were mainly concerned with the economics of manufacturing and thus the productivity of industrial employees. Two industrial engineers in particular (Frederick Taylor and Frank Gilbreth) redesigned jobs, developed training programs, and used selection methods to increase the efficiency of the employees. Thus the merging of psychology with applied interests and concerns for increasing industrial efficiency were the ingredients for the emergence of I/O psychology. By 1910, "industrial psychology" (the "organizational" appendage did not officially come into play until 1970) was a legitimate specialty area of psychology.

Three individuals stand out as the founding fathers of I/O psychology. They worked independently, and in fact their work barely overlapped. The major contributions of these individuals deserve a brief review.

**Walter Dill Scott.** Scott, a psychologist, was persuaded to give a talk to some Chicago business leaders on the need for applying psychology to advertising. His talk was well received and led to the publication of two books, *The Theory of Advertising* (1903) and *The Psychology of Advertising* (1908). By 1911, he increased his areas of interest and published two more books, *Influencing Men in Business* and *Increasing Human Efficiency in Business*. The first book dealt with suggestion and argument as means of influencing people. The latter book was aimed at improving human efficiency with such tactics as imitation, competition, loyalty, and concentration. In his later years, Scott was instrumental in applying personnel procedures in the Army during World War I.

Walter Dill Scott

*Courtesy Archives of the History of American Psychology*

**Frederick Taylor.** Taylor was an engineer by profession. His formal schooling was limited, but through experience and self-training in engineering, he went on to obtain many patents. As he worked himself up through a company as a worker, supervisor, and finally plant manager, Taylor realized the value of redesigning the work situation to achieve both higher output for the company and a higher wage for the worker. His best-known work is his book, *Principles of Scientific Management* (1911). The principles of scientific management were: (1) scientifically designing work methods for efficiency; (2) selecting the best workers and training them in new methods; (3) developing a cooperative spirit between managers and workers; and (4) sharing the responsibility of the design and conduct of work between management and worker. In perhaps the most famous example of his methods, Taylor showed that workers who handled heavy iron ingots (pig iron) could be more productive through the use of work rests. By training employees when to work and when to rest, average worker productivity increased from 12.5 to 47 tons moved per day (with less reported fatigue), and this resulted in increased wages for the employee. The company also increased efficiency drastically by reducing costs from 9.2 cents per ton to 3.9 cents per ton.

As a consequence of this method, it was charged that Taylor inhumanely exploited workers for a higher wage and that great numbers of workers would be unemployed because fewer were needed. Because there was rampant unemployment at this time, the attacks on Taylor were strident. Taylor's methods were eventually investigated by the Interstate Commerce Commission (ICC) and the U.S. House of Representatives. Taylor replied that increased efficiency led to greater, not lesser, prosperity. He also said

Frederick W. Taylor

*Courtesy Stevens Institute of Technology*

that workers not hired for one job would be placed in another that would better use their potential. The arguments were never really resolved. World War I broke out, and the controversy dissolved.

**Hugo Münsterberg.**   Münsterberg was a German psychologist with traditional academic training. He was invited to Harvard University by the noted American psychologist, William James. Münsterberg applied his experimental methods to a variety of problems including perception and attention. He was a popular figure in American education, a gifted public speaker, and a personal friend of Teddy Roosevelt. Münsterberg was interested in applying traditional psychological methods to practical problems of industry. His book, *Psychology and Industrial Efficiency* (1913), was divided into three parts: selecting workers, designing work situations, and using psychology in sales. One of Münsterberg's most renowned studies involved determining what makes a safe motorcar operator. He systematically studied all aspects of the job, developed an ingenious laboratory simulation of a motorcar, and concluded that a good motorcar operator could simultaneously comprehend all of the influences that bear on the progress of the car. Some writers consider Münsterberg *the* father of industrial psychology, although the contributions of Scott and Taylor are also highly significant.

When World War I broke out in Europe, Münsterberg supported the German cause. He was ostracized for his allegiance, and the emotional strain probably contributed to his death in 1916. Münsterberg's sudden departure from the field of industrial psychology created a scientific vacuum since he left no colleagues behind to continue in his work. Only America's involvement in World War I gave some unity to the profession.

Hugo Münsterberg

*Courtesy Archives of the History of American Psychology*

The primary emphasis of the work during the early years was the economic gains that could be accrued by applying the ideas and methods of psychology to problems in business and industry. Business leaders began to employ psychologists, and some psychologists entered applied research. However, World War I caused a shift in the direction of industrial psychological research.

## World War I (1917–1918)

World War I was a potent influence behind psychology's rise to respectability. Psychologists believed they could provide a valuable service to the nation, and some saw the war as a means of accelerating the profession's progress.

Robert Yerkes was the psychologist most instrumental in getting psychology into the war. As president of APA, he maneuvered the profession into assignments in the war effort. The APA suggested many proposals including ways of screening recruits for mental deficiency and of assigning them to jobs within the army. Committees of psychologists investigated soldier motivation, morale, psychological problems of physical incapacity, and discipline. Yerkes continued to press his point that psychology could be of great help to our nation in time of war.

The army, in turn, was somewhat skeptical of the psychologists' claims. It eventually approved only a modest number of proposals mostly involving the assessment of recruits. Yerkes and other psychologists reviewed a series of general intelligence tests and eventually developed one which they called the Army Alpha. When they discovered that 30 percent of the recruits were illiterate, they developed the Army Beta, a special test for those who couldn't read English. Meanwhile, Walter Scott was doing research on the best placement of soldiers in the army. Some of his work involved classifying and placing enlisted soldiers, performance ratings of officers, and developing and preparing job duties and qualifications for over 500 jobs.

Plans for testing recruits proceeded at a slow pace. The army instructed its camps to build special testing sites and ordered all existing officers, officer candidates, and newly drafted recruits to be tested. Both the Army Alpha and Beta group intelligence tests were used as were a few individual tests. The final order from the adjutant general's office (which gave complete authority to the testing program) did not come until August 1918. However, the Armistice was signed only three months later, and World War I was over. Testing was terminated just as it was finally organized and authorized. Because of this, the intelligence testing program didn't contribute as much to the war as Yerkes would have liked. Even though 1,726,000 individuals were ultimately tested in the program, actual use of the results was minimal.

While psychology's actual impact on the war effort was not substantial, the very process of giving psychology and psychologists so much recognition and authority was a great impetus to the profession. Psychologists were regarded as people who could make valuable contributions to society; who could add to a company's (and in war, a nation's) prosperity. Also in 1917, the oldest and most representative journal in the field of I/O psychology, the *Journal of Applied Psychology*, was published. Some of the articles in the first volume of that journal included "Practical Relations Between Psychology and the War" by Hall, "Mentality Testing of College Students" by Bingham, and "The Moron as a War Problem" by Mateer. The first article published in the *Journal of Applied Psychology* not only summarized the prevailing state of industrial psychology at the time, but also addressed the science-versus-practice issue that still faces I/O psychologists today.

> The past few years have witnessed an unprecedented interest in the extension of the application of psychology to various fields of human activity. . . . But perhaps the most strikingly original endeavor to utilize the methods and the results of psychological investigation has been in the realm of business. This movement began with the psychology of advertising. . . . Thence the attention of the applied psychologist turned to the more comprehensive and fundamental problem of vocational selection,—the question, namely, of making a detailed inventory of the equipment of mental qualities possessed by a given individual, of discovering what qualities are essential to successful achievement in a given vocation, and thus of directing the individual to the vocational niche which he is best fitted to fill.
> . . . . (E)very psychologist who besides being a "pure scientist" also cherishes the hope that in addition to throwing light upon the problems of his science, his findings may also contribute their quota to the sum-total of human happiness; and it must appeal to every human being who is interested in increasing human efficiency and human happiness by the more direct method of decreasing the number of cases where a square peg is condemned to a life of fruitless endeavor to fit itself comfortably into a round hole (Hall, Baird, & Geissler, 1917, pp. 5–6).

After the war, there was a boom in the number of psychological consulting firms and research bureaus. The birth of these agencies ushered in the next era in I/O psychology.

**Between the wars (1919 –1940)**

Applied psychology emerged from the war as a recognized discipline. Society was beginning to realize that industrial psychology could solve practical problems. Following the war, several psychological research bureaus came into full bloom.

The Bureau of Salesmanship Research was developed by Walter Bingham at the Carnegie Institute of Technology. There was little precedent for this kind of cooperation between college and industry. The bureau intended to solve problems with psychological research techniques—problems that had never been examined scientifically. Twenty-seven companies cooperated with Bingham. They contributed $500 annually to finance applied psychological research. One of the early products of the bureau was a book, *Aids in Selecting Salesmen*. For several years, the bureau concentrated on selection, classification and development of clerical and executive personnel as well as salesmen. Eventually, the bureau was disbanded since the Carnegie Institute stopped offering graduate work in psychology.

Another influential company during the period was the Psychological Corporation, founded by James Cattell in 1921. Cattell formed a business corporation and asked psychologists to buy stock in it. The corporation was established to advance psychology and promote its useful application. In addition to convincing industrialists of psychology's usefulness, the corporation also served as a clearinghouse for information. Quacks and charlatans were becoming more prevalent, especially those making extravagant claims. So the Psychological Corporation provided companies with reference checks on any prospective psychologist. Unlike many agencies, the Psychological Corporation did not go out of business. Over the years, it changed its early mission, and today it is one of the country's largest producers of psychological tests.

During the 1920s, the emphasis of industrial psychology was on testing. But the focus switched from mental testing of people in a laboratory setting to employment testing of industrial workers in field settings. The *Journal of Personnel Research* (later renamed *Personnel Journal*) began in this era, and it has remained a useful journal especially for practitioners. Also the term *industrial psychology* achieved its own identity, as witnessed by the book by Viteles (1932).

In 1927, a series of experiments began at the Hawthorne Works of the Western Electric Company. Although they seemed of only minor scientific significance at the beginning, they became classics in industrial psychology. In the opinion of many writers, the Hawthorne Studies "represent the most significant research program undertaken to show the enormous complexity of the problem of production in relation to efficiency" (Blum & Naylor, 1968, p. 306).

The Hawthorne Studies were a joint venture between Western Electric and several researchers from Harvard University (none of whom were industrial psychologists by training). The original study attempted to find the relationship between lighting and efficiency. The researchers installed various sets of lights in workrooms where electrical equipment was produced. Much to the researchers' surprise, productivity seemed to have no relationship to the level of illumination. The workers increased productivity (or maintained a level of satisfactory productivity) whether the illumination decreased, increased, or was held constant. In some cases, the light was intense; in other cases, it was reduced to the equivalent of moonlight. The results of the study were so bizarre that the researchers hypothesized some other factors were responsible for productivity.

The results of the first study initiated four other major studies that occurred over a 12-year period: (1) relay assembly test room; (2) mass interviewing program; (3) bank wiring observation room; and (4) personnel counseling. (For more information on these studies, see the original text by Roethlisberger and Dickson [1943].) In essence, the Hawthorne Studies revealed many, previously unrecognized aspects about human behavior in a workplace. Researchers hypothesized that the results of the study were caused by the employees' desire to please the researchers. The employees were impressed when distinguished investigators from Harvard University took the time to study them. In response to this perceived special treatment, the workers went out of their way to do what they thought would please the researchers; namely, be highly productive. They produced a lot whether the room was too light or extremely dark. The researchers learned that factors other than purely technical ones (i.e., illumination) influence productivity.

One of the major findings from the Hawthorne Studies was a phenomenon labeled the *"Hawthorne Effect"*. The workers' job performance began to improve following the start of the researchers' intervention. Performance continued to improve because of the novelty of the situation; e.g., the employees responded positively to the novel treatment they were getting from the researchers. Eventually, however, the novelty began to wear off, and productivity levels returned to their earlier level. This phenomenon of a change in behavior following the onset of novel treatment, which eventually culminates in a return to the previous level of behavior (as the effect of novelty dissipates) is called a Hawthorne Effect. A Hawthorne Effect is presented graphically in Figure 1–5. Its significance is that sometimes behavior change is due just to a change in the environment (e.g., the presence of the researchers) and not to the effect of some experimentally manipulated variable (e.g., the amount of illumination). The psychological literature indicates that Hawthorne Effects may last anywhere from a few

**Figure 1–5**  **Graphic portrayal of a Hawthorne Effect**

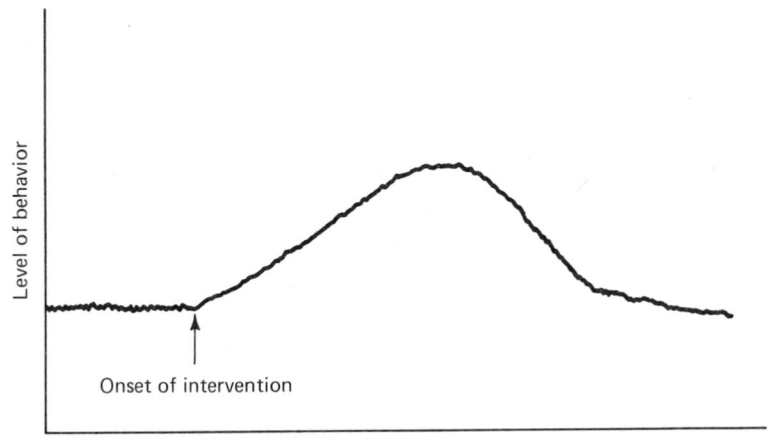

days to two years depending upon the situation. Throughout this book, research findings will be cited that appear attributable to Hawthorne Effects.

The Hawthorne Studies also revealed the existence of informal employee work groups and their controls on production. In addition, findings showed the importance of employee attitudes, the value of having a sympathetic and understanding supervisor, and the need to treat workers as people instead of merely human capital. The Hawthorne Studies open up new vistas for industrial psychology. For nearly 40 years previously, improving company efficiency was the dominant force behind industrial psychology. That theme was altered by the discovery of the complexity of human behavior in the Hawthorne Studies. Today the Hawthorne Studies are not considered "perfect" examples of field research. But they are the greatest single episode in the formation of industrial psychology. The Hawthorne Studies also show that sometimes researchers obtain results that are totally unexpected. The investigators were not tied to any one explanation, so their studies took them into areas never before studied by industrial psychology. They posed questions that otherwise might not have been asked, and industrial psychology was never the same again.

This era in industrial psychology ended with the coincidental conclusion of the Hawthorne Studies and the outbreak of World War II. Industrial psychologists were now faced with an immense task: helping to mobilize a nation for a two-continent war.

## World War II (1941–1945)

When the United States entered World War II, industrial psychologists were more prepared for their role in the war effort than they had been in 1917. Between the wars, psychologists had studied the problems of employee selection and placement, and had refined their techniques considerably.

Walter Bingham chaired the advisory committee on classification of military personnel, a committee formed in response to the army's need for classification and training. Unlike World War I, this time the army approached the psychologists first. One of the committee's first assignments was to develop a test that could sift new recruits into a few broad categories based on their ability to learn the duties and responsibilities of a soldier. The test that was finally developed was the Army General Classification Test (AGCT), a hallmark in the history of group testing. The committee also worked on other projects, such as methods of selecting people for officer training, trade proficiency tests, and supplemental aptitude tests.

Psychologists also worked on the development and use of situational stress tests, a project undertaken by the United States Office of Strategic Service (OSS) (Murray & MacKinnon, 1946). The purpose of this testing program was to assess candidates for assignment to military intelligence units. During a three-day session of extremely intensive testing and observation, the candidates lived together in small groups under almost continual observation by members of the assessment staff. Specially constructed situational tests, many modeled after techniques developed in the German and British armies, were used to assess candidates in nontraditional ways. For example, one test involved constructing of 5-foot cube out of a series of wooden poles, pegs, and blocks. It was impossible for one person to assemble the cube in the allotted time, so two helpers were provided. The "helpers" were actually psychologists who played prearranged roles. One helper acted very passive and contributed little; the other obstructed work by making impractical suggestions and ridiculing and criticizing the candidate. No candidate could complete the project with this kind of help. The real purpose of the test was not to see if the candidates could construct the cube (they couldn't), but to assess their emotional and interpersonal reactions to stress and frustration. In general, the OSS assessment program was judged to be quite successful.

Another area of work was in the selection and training of pilots to fly war planes. The committee on selection and training of aircraft pilots was formed consisting of psychologists, military personnel, and civilian pilots. The policy of the committee was to move the traditional experimental test setting from the laboratory to a cockpit. Airplanes were outfitted with recording and monitoring devices to assess the problems and reactions of student pilots. The products of this research were twofold. Good candidates were selected and trained as pilots (the traditional domain of personnel psychology). Second, equipment was redesigned to make the pilots' job easier and safer (a contribution of the new field of engineering psychology).

In 1943, sensing the need for a general psychological research organization, the military helped establish the Applied Psychological Panel. The panel worked on three broad areas of research: classification of personnel, training, and equipment design. Within these general fields, some 20 major research programs were undertaken. Most research began with a request for assistance from some branch of the military. All but a few of the projects were conducted in field settings with military personnel rather than in university laboratories.

Throughout the war, industrial psychology was also being used in civilian life. There was a great increase in the use of employment tests in industry. Because the nation needed a productive work force, psychologists were also called on to help reduce employee absenteeism (Pickard, 1945). Industry discovered that it could use many of the techniques of industrial psychologists, especially in the areas of selection, training, and machine design, and it was particularly interested in the applications of social psychology. New methods of measuring soldier attitude and morale also could be applied to industry. In short, the techniques developed during the war could be applied to business and industry in peace time. World War II was a springboard for refining industrial psychological techniques, and it honed the skills of applied psychology.

Each of the two world wars had a major effect on industrial psychology, but in a somewhat different way. World War I helped form the profession and give it social acceptance. World War II helped develop and refine it. In the last era in the history of I/O psychology, the discipline evolved into subspecialties, and attained higher levels of academic and scientific rigor.

**Toward specialization (1946 – present)**

In this era, industrial psychology evolved into a legitimate field of scientific inquiry, having already established itself as an acceptable professional practice. More colleges and universities began to offer courses in "industrial psychology," and graduate degrees (both M.S. and Ph.D) were soon given.

As with any evolving discipline, subspecialties of interest began to crystallize, and industrial psychology experienced a splintering effect. New journals emerged along with new professional associations. Engineering psychology, born during World War II, was recognized as a separate area, in part due to such seminal books as *Applied Experimental Psychology* (Chapanis, Garner, & Morgan, 1949) and the *Handbook of Human Engineering Data* (1949). Engineering psychology entered an explosive period of growth from 1950 to 1960. This was due mainly to research done in affiliation with the defense industries (Grether, 1968). Engineering psychology's heritage was a mixture of both experimental and industrial psychology, as seen in its early label, "applied experimental psychology."

That part of industrial psychology specializing in personnel selection, classification, and training also got its own identity—"personnel psychology." The journal *Personnel Psychology*, started in 1948, helped to establish that area as a legitimate specialty. In fact, most I/O journals were started in the last 35 years.

Sometime in the 1950s, interest grew in the study of organizations. Long the province of sociologists, this area caught the interest of psychologists. In the 1960s, there was a stronger "organizational" flavor to industrial psychology research. Investigators gave more attention to social influences that impinge on behavior in organizations. Terms such as *organizational change* and *organization development* appeared in the literature regularly. Industrial psychology addressed a broader range of topics. Classic text books of the 1950s such as *Personnel and Industrial Psychology* by Ghiselli and Brown (1955) gave way in title (as well as substance) to books with more of an organizational thrust. In 1970 the Division of Industrial Psychology of APA changed its name to the Division of Industrial-Organizational Psychology. In 1971 Korman published a book entitled *Industrial and Organizational Psychology*. The I/O psychologist had arrived!

Traditional academic boundaries between disciplines began to blur in this post-War period. Engineering psychology was a fusion of experimental and industrial psychology. Organizational behavior is a mix of industrial psychology, social psychology, and sociology. This melding of disciplines is healthy because it decreases the probability of narrow, parochial attempts to address complex areas of research. Today I/O psychology is multidisciplinary with regard to both its content and methods of inquiry. Upon reflection, it was the same at the turn of the century—a confluence of interest in advertising research, industrial efficiency, and mental testing. In a sense, the evolution of I/O psychology is the chronicle of mushrooming interests along certain common dimensions as molded by a few seismic events.

If the Hawthorne Studies were the biggest event in the middle period of the history of I/O psychology (if not the entire history), the latest period also was transformed by an event. The biggest single influence in this era was a piece of federal legislation called the Civil Rights Act of 1964. The act banned discrimination in such areas of life as housing, education, and employment. As part of the Civil Rights Act, the Equal Employment Opportunity Commission (EEOC) was created to investigate claims of discrimination in employment. This ultimately led to a close examination of many employment selection tests used in industry. Although the nature and implications of EEOC will be presented in greater detail later in the book, this action essentially put industrial psychological testing on trial. Psychologists became legally responsible to prove that the employment tests they administered did not unfairly discriminate against any subgroup of people. In addition, the new policy did not limit itself just to paper-and-pencil tests or to the personnel function of selection. It addressed *all* types of devices (e.g., interviews, tests, application blanks) used to make *all* types of personnel decisions (e.g., selection, placement, promotion, demotion, transfer, etc.). The intent of this policy was admirable; unfair discrimination is a social and economic injustice. To the extent that EEOC is successful in overcoming unfair discrimination in employment, the actions psychologists are now forced to take are certainly justified. The problem was, however, that psychologists disagreed with the standards the government imposed. Because these standards were contradictory, it was difficult for psychologists to comply. It wasn't until 1978 (14 years alter the Civil Rights Act was passed) that the government finally produced a *uniform* set of employment standards. In general, personnel testing was no longer the sole domain of I/O psychology. Government intervention arrived, for better or worse. (This topic will be discussed further in a later chapter.)

In 1976 the *Handbook of Industrial and Organizational Psychology* was published. Its 37 chapters are a tribute to the richness and diversity of I/O psychology. The field has come a long way since Münsterberg's *Psychology and Industrial Efficiency* (1913).

## SCOPE OF THE BOOK

This book explains the field of I/O psychology. While it does discuss some technical areas, it does not presume the student has an extensive background in psychology, applied measurement, or statistics.

There are four major sections to help the student identify homogeneous units of material. The first section (Chapters 1 and 2) will give the student some exposure to and appreciation of how scientists address research questions.

The second section (Chapters 3 through 7) involve personnel psychology. Chapter 3 addresses a crucial topic—evaluative standards or what I/O psychologists call "criteria". Criterion development is one of the oldest and most intriguing areas of research in I/O psychology. The next chapter discusses psychological tests and other measures used to predict how well people will do in some aspect of their work. Chapter 5 shows how psychologists make decisions about hiring employees and classifying them in certain jobs, and what factors influence their decisions. Chapter 6 concerns personnel training—how psychologists decide who needs training, on what aspects of their job they need it, types of training techniques, and whether or not training works. The last chapter in this section (performance appraisal) tells why a person's performance is evaluated, how it is done, and what problems arise in appraising different types of employees.

The third section of the book reflects the organizational influence in I/O psychology. Chapter 8 reviews the nature of organizations, how organizations are different from each other, and what effect they have on human behavior. Chapter 9 concerns employee attitudes and feelings of satisfaction at work. What makes for a good job? Do all people value the same kind of job? And what factors influence people's reaction to their work? The following chapter (worker motivation) explores the approaches investigators have used to understand why people behave as they do. Chapter 11 is concerned with leadership and supervision at work. What is the basis of leadership? Are some people just born to be good leaders? Chapter 12 addresses organizational communication and how it affects the way people behave at work.

The final section discusses the work environment. Chapter 13 is on work design and organization development. It shows how jobs can be designed (or redesigned) to make them more rewarding for both the company and the employee. The chapter also looks at how entire organizations can be "developed", or brought through a series of changes to meet some desired objectives. Chapter 14 examines union/management relations: the em-

**MISS PEACH**

ployer/employee relationship, collective bargaining and the resolution of industrial disputes, and recent behavioral research on unions. Finally, Chapter 15 (working conditions) explores the areas of environmental stress, accidents and safety, and research on work schedules.

In addition, brief case studies will show how the text material can be applied to problems in the workplace. When students have finished the book, they should have a much better understanding of human behavior in the workplace. Perhaps some people will be stimulated enough to continue work in I/O psychology. It is a most challenging, rewarding, and useful profession.

# REFERENCES

American Psychological Association. Psychology as a profession. *American Psychologist*, 1968, *23*, 195–200.

Bingham, W. V. Mentality testing of college students. *Journal of Applied Psychology*, 1917, *1*, 38–45.

Blum, M. L., & Naylor, J. C. *Industrial psychology: Its theoretical and social foundations*. New York: Harper & Row, 1968.

Bryan, W. L. Theory and practice. *Psychological Review*, 1904, *11*, 71–82.

Bryan, W. L., & Harter, N. Studies in the physiology and psychology of the telegraphic language. *Psychological Review*, 1897, *4*, 27–53.

Bryan, W. L., & Harter, N. Studies of the telegraphic language. *Psychological Review*, 1899, *6*, 345–375.

Campbell, J. P. Psychology in business schools. *Professional Psychology*, 1971, *2*, 6–11.

*A Career in Industrial/Organizational Psychology*. Washington, D.C.: American Psychological Association, Division of Industrial and Organizational Psychology, undated.

*Careers in psychology*. Washington, D.C.: American Psychological Association, 1975.

Chapanis, A., Garner, W. R., & Morgan, C. T. *Applied experimental psychology*. New York: John Wiley & Sons, 1949.

Dunnette, M. D. (Ed.). *Handbook of industrial and organizational psychology*. Skokie, Ill.: Rand McNally, 1976.

Fretz, B. R., & Mills, D. H. *Licensing and certification of psychologists and counselors*. San Francisco: Jossey-Bass, 1980.

Ghiselli, E. E., & Brown, C. W. *Personnel and industrial psychology*. New York: McGraw-Hill, 1955.

Grether, W. F. Engineering psychology in the United States. *American Psychologist*, 1968, *23*, 743–751.

Gross, S. J. The myth of professional licensing. *American Psychologist*, 1978, *33*, 1009–1016.

Guion, R. M. Industrial psychology as an academic discipline. *American Psychologist*, 1965, *20*, 815–821.

Hall, G. S. Practical relations between psychology and the war. *Journal of Applied Psychology*, 1917, *1*, 9–16.

Hall, G. S., Baird, J. W., & Geissler, L. R. Foreward. *Journal of Applied Psychology*, 1917, *1*, 5–7.

*Handbook of human engineering data*. Medford, Mass.: Tufts College & United States Naval Training Devices Center, 1949.

Hess, H. F. Entry requirements for professional practice of psychology. *American Psychologist*, 1977, *32*, 365–368.

Hoffman, P. J. On the establishment of an appropriate length for the EPPP. *Professional Psychology*, 1980, *11*, 784–791.

Korman, A. K. *Industrial and organizational psychology*. Englewood Cliffs, N.J.: Prentice-Hall, 1971.

Matarazzo, J. D. Higher education, professional accreditation, and licensure. *American Psychologist*, 1977, *32*, 856–859.

Mateer, F. The moron as a war problem. *Journal of Applied Psychology*, 1917, *1*, 317–320.

Mayfield, E. C. *Preparation for work in business and industry: The results of a survey of recent graduates*. Unpublished manuscript, 1975.

Meyer, H. H. The future for industrial and organizational psychology: Oblivion or millenium? *American Psychologist*, 1972, *27*, 608–614.

Muchinsky, P. M. Graduate training in industrial psychology: One more time. *Professional Psychology*, 1973, *4*, 286–295.

Muchinsky, P. M. Graduate internships in industrial psychology: A success story. *Professional Psychology*, 1976, *7*, 664–670.

Münsterberg, H. *Psychology and industrial efficiency*. Boston: Houghton Mifflin, 1913.

Murray, H. A., & MacKinnon, D. W. Assessment of OSS personnel. *Journal of Consulting Psychology*, 1946, *10*, 76–80.

Naylor, J. C. Training patterns in industrial psychology. *Personnel Psychology*, 1970, *23*, 192–198.

Naylor, J. C. Hickory, dickory, dock! Let's turn back the clock! *Professional Psychology*, 1971, *2*, 217–224.

Pickard, C. O. Absentee control plans. *Personnel Journal*, 1945, *23*, 271–276.

Rodgers, D. A. In favor of separation of academic and professional training. *American Psychologist*, 1964, *19*, 675–680.

Roethlisberger, F. J., & Dickson, W. J. *Management and the worker*. Cambridge, Mass.: Harvard University Press, 1943.

Schein, V. E. The woman industrial psychologist: Illusion or reality? *American Psychologist*, 1971, *26*, 708–712.

Schneider, B. Differences between prospective students of industrial-organizational psychology in psychology and nonpsychology departments. *Professional Psychology*, 1971, *2*, 11–16.

Scott, W. D. *The theory of advertising*. Boston: Small, Maynard, 1903.

Scott, W. D. *The psychology of advertising*. New York: Arno Press, 1908.

Scott, W. D. *Increasing human efficiency in business*. New York: MacMillan, 1911. (a)

Scott, W. D. *Influencing men in business*. New York: Ronald, 1911. (b)

Stagner, R. Training and experiences of some distinguished industrial psychologists. *American Psychologist*, 1981, *36*, 497–505.

Task Force on the Practice of Psychology in Industry. Effective practice of psychology in industry. *American Psychologist*, 1971, *26*, 974–991.

Taylor, F. W. *The principles of scientific management*. New York: Harper, 1911.

Viteles, M. S. *Industrial psychology*. New York: W. W. Norton, 1932.

# chapter 2

# RESEARCH METHODS IN I/O PSYCHOLOGY

We all have hunches or beliefs about the nature of human behavior. Some of us believe that red-haired people are temperamental, dynamic leaders are big and tall, blue-collar workers prefer beer to wine, the only reason people work is to make money, etc. The list is endless. Which of these beliefs are true? The only way to find out is to conduct *research*, the systematic study of phenomena according to scientific principles. Much of this chapter is devoted to research methods used in I/O psychology. Understanding the research process helps people solve practical problems, apply the results of studies reported by others, and assess the accuracy of claims made about new practices, equipment, etc. (Stone, 1978). I/O psychologists are continually faced with a host of practical problems. Knowledge of research methods gives us a better opportunity to find useful solutions to problems rather than merely stumbling across them by chance. An understanding of research methods will also help us apply the results of studies reported by others. Some factors promote the *generalizability* of research findings, while others retard it. Finally, people often claim the superiority of some new technique or method. Which of these techniques will actually turn out to be useful, and which is only a cheap gimmick? A knowledge of research methods will help determine which is which.

Kaplan (1964) suggests that there are three goals of science: description, explanation, and prediction. The descriptive function of science is like a photograph—a picture of a state of events. Descriptions may be made of levels of productivity, number of employees who quit during the year, average level of job satisfaction, etc. The explanatory function of science is perhaps the most difficult to unravel; it is a statement of why events occur as they do. It tries to find causes: why production is at a certain level, why employees quit, why they are dissatisfied, etc. The last function of science is prediction. Researchers try to predict which employees will be productive, who are likely to quit, and who will be dissatisfied. This information is then used to select those applicants who would be better employees.

This chapter will give the reader some insight into the research process in I/O psychology. There are a number of methods or strategies an investigator can use, so special attention will be given to specific research methods. The empirical research process is the major framework for this chapter. It begins with a statement of the problem and ends with the conclusions drawn from the research. This chapter should help you become a knowledgeable consumer of I/O psychological research.

## THE EMPIRICAL RESEARCH PROCESS

Figure 2–1 shows the steps that are followed in conducting empirical research. The research process is basically a five-step procedure with an important feedback factor. That is, the results of the fifth step influence the first step in future research studies. The research process begins with a statement of the problem. What question or problem needs to be answered? Next, how do you design a study to answer the question? Third, how do you measure the variables and collect the necessary data? Fourth, how do you apply statistical procedures to analyze the data? (In other words, how do you make some sense out of all the information collected?) Finally, how do you draw conclusions from analyzing the data. Let's look at each of these steps in more detail.

**Statement of the problem**

Questions that initiate research don't arise out of thin air. They are based on existing knowledge—your experience with the problem, someone else's experience with the problem, personal intuition, insight, or some formal theory. Most research begins with personal insight or intuition. As studies are conducted, the researcher becomes more familiar with the problem and may expand the scope of the questions being asked. One person's research may stimulate similar research by someone else; thus researchers often benefit from the studies done by their colleagues. After much research has been conducted on a topic, researchers may propose a theory about why the behavior occurs. The sequence that starts with data and culminates in theory is the *inductive* method of science. The opposite sequence is the

**Figure 2-1**                 **The empirical research cycle**

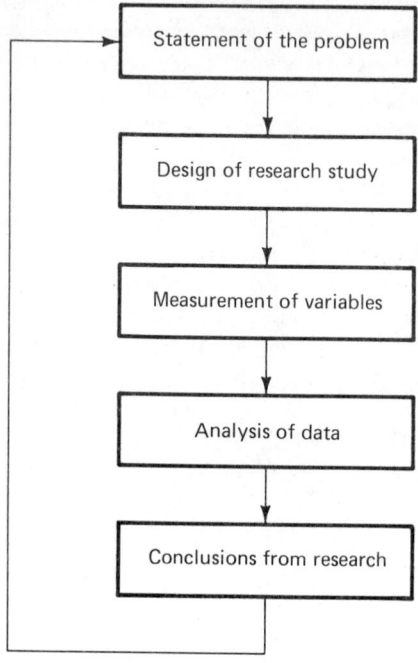

*deductive* method. In the deductive method, a researcher first forms a theory (perhaps by intuition or by studying previous research) and then *tests* the theory by collecting data. If the theory is accurate, the data will support it; if the theory is inaccurate, the data will not support it.

The value of theory in science is that it integrates and summarizes large amounts of information and provides a framework for the research. Despite the merits of theory, not all researchers agree on its value. The following quotes illustrate three different (yet valid) views:

1. "There is nothing quite so practical as a good theory."—Kurt Lewin, noted social psychologist.
2. "Research designed with respect to theory is likely to be wasteful."—B. F. Skinner, noted experimental psychologist.
3. "Theory, like mist on eyeglasses, obscures facts."—Charlie Chan, noted fictional detective.

Lewin's statement is often cited in psychology. Its essence is that a theory is useful for conducting research. A theory synthesizes information, organizes it into logical components, and directs the researcher's efforts in future studies. But Skinner believes that too much effort is spent on "proving" theories; that is, the theory is master of the research. Skinner feels that most theories eventually fall out of favor and that productive research does not require a theory. His position is an extreme case of empiricism. Charlie Chan thinks that researchers become too committed to proving their theory and become blinded to information that doesn't conform to what they want to believe. A good researcher doesn't let the theory obscure the facts.

Rather than thinking of theories as "right" or "wrong," try to think of them as being useful or not. A useful theory helps give meaning to the problem. It helps the subject matter make more sense.

The role of theory in I/O psychological research is quite mixed and depends on the subspecialty involved. Personnel psychology has been called "a lot of data but little theory"; organizational psychology has been called "a lot of theory but little data." Engineering psychology is almost completely devoid of theory, while organization development draws heavily on theories of social influence and change. As an entire discipline, I/O psychology is not as dominated by theories as other areas of psychology. In fact, I/O psychology has sometimes been referred to as the bastion of "dustbowl empiricism" by more theory-oriented psychologists. Such a statement is obviously a value judgment made by people who believe that theory is the best source for problem identification. Theory is only one way to formulate a research problem: but other methods can also result in high-quality research. This is especially true in a pragmatic area like I/O psychology where some research problems come from everyday experiences in industry. If 50 percent of a company's work force quits every year, you don't need a theory to realize that this is a serious problem. Developing a carefully thought-out research problem is far more important than which source (e.g., experience, theory, intuition) it came from.

## Design of the research study

A research design is a plan for conducting a study. There are a number of strategies a researcher can use; the choice of method depends on the nature of the problem being studied. The strategies can be compared along several dimensions, but the two most important dimensions are (1) the naturalness of the research setting and (2) the investigator's degree of control over the study. No one strategy is the best under all conditions; there are always trade-offs.

**1. Naturalness of the research setting.** In some research strategies, the problem can be studied in the environment in which it naturally occurs. This is desirable because we don't want the research strategy being used to destroy or distort the phenomenon under study. Some research strategies appear phony because the problem is studied in unnatural ways. For example, the Hawthorne Studies were done right in the plant with actual employees performing their normal jobs. However, there are studies that need not be conducted in a natural environment because the behavior under investigation is assumed to be independent of the setting. For example, an engineering psychology study testing whether people react faster to red or green lights could be done as appropriately in a laboratory as in a natural field setting.

**2. Degree of control.** In some research strategies, the researcher has a high degree of control over the conduct of the study. In others, very little control is possible. In the Hawthorne Studies the researchers could control the exact amount of lighting in the work area by installing (or removing) lights (though it turned out factors other than lighting affected the workers' performance). But suppose you want to study the relationship between peoples' age and their attitude toward I/O psychology. You are particularly interested in comparing the attitudes of people over 40 with those under 40. You develop a questionnaire that asks their opinions about I/O psychology (is it interesting, difficult to understand, etc.), and you distribute the survey to your classmates. But it turns out that every person in the class is under 40. You have no information on the over-40 group, so you can't answer your research question. This is an example of a low degree of control (you cannot control the age of the people in the study). Low control is particularly endemic to the survey questionnaire research strategy.

The following discusses the major research methods used in I/O psychology. Note that no one method is perfect: no one method offers both a high degree of naturalism *and* a high degree of control. The selection of method is a function of the nature of the research problem being studied. Each method will be described and evaluated, and an example will be given.

## LABORATORY EXPERIMENT

Laboratory experiments are conducted in contrived settings as opposed to naturally occurring organizational settings. In a laboratory, the researcher has a high degree of control over the conduct of the study, especially those conditions associated with the observations of behavior (Zelditch & Hopkins, 1961). The experimenter designs the study to test how certain aspects of an actual working environment affect behavior. The laboratory setting must mirror certain dimensions of the natural environment where the behavior normally occurs. A well-designed laboratory experiment will have some of the conditions found in the natural environment but have none of the conditions that would never be found in the natural environment (Fromkin & Streufert, 1976).

A laboratory experiment has several advantages.

1. It is the only method where causality can be inferred; i.e., the experimenter can eliminate or control for other explanations for the observed behavior. The experimenter can determine which variables influence other variables.

2. The measurement of behavior is usually very precise because it is observed under tightly controlled conditions.
3. Laboratory experiments can easily be replicated by other researchers because all the experimental conditions are measured and recorded.

But there are disadvantages.

1. Laboratory experiments may lack realism (i.e., a high degree of similarity between the experimental conditions and the natural environment).
2. Some phenomena cannot be analyzed in a laboratory (e.g., how riots affect individual behavior and attitudes).
3. Some variables may have a weaker impact in a laboratory than they do in a natural environment.

**Example of the method.**    Hegarty and Sims (1978) reported an example of a laboratory experiment in I/O psychology. In this study, researchers wanted to know what factors cause people to behave unethically in business decisions. Specifically, they wanted to examine under what conditions would people agree to make kickbacks, i.e., illegal payments of money in return for favorable treatment. The subjects in the study were 120 graduate students enrolled in a business college. They were told to pretend that they were sales managers for a large wholesaling company. Each subject had to decide how many salesmen to hire in their company because the number of salesmen directly affected the company's profits. If too few were hired, the company couldn't sell enough to be profitable. If too many were hired, the company would pay out more in salary than each salesman returned in profit. But, if a salesman paid a kickback to a purchasing agent, the sales for that salesman would increase and so would the company's profit.

Hegarty and Sims tested the effects of two factors on the practice of making kickbacks. One factor was the degree to which kickbacks increased the company's profits. Some subjects were told that they could stop their salesmen from making kickbacks purely on moral grounds, that kickbacks had no effect on profit. Other subjects were told that they could stop kickbacks, but it would probably decrease the company's profits. The second factor was a sense of competitiveness instilled in the subjects. Some subjects were not told how well other people were doing in the experiment (i.e., how much profit the other subjects were making). Other subjects were told that if their profit performance was among the best of all subjects in the study, they would each be paid an extra cash incentive (a few dollars) as a reward.

The results of the study showed that if unethical behavior (i.e., making kickbacks) is rewarded, it is more likely to occur. It appears that subjects can "learn" to be unethical if such behavior enhances their position. Also unethical behavior increased when competitiveness was intensified. Subjects who were offered money for performing better approved kickbacks more than other subjects.

In evaluating this study, you can see both the advantages and disadvantages of a laboratory experiment. First, the researchers showed that two factors (the degree of reward and interpersonal competitiveness) directly caused people to behave in unethical ways. They controlled the only two factors that were varied in the experiment and showed that increasing the reward for illegal behavior resulted in more illegal behavior. This is a big step toward showing why people engage in illegal behavior. It is also based on objective empirical evidence, not hunch or guesswork.

However, the study also shows the disadvantages of the method. The subjects were not really sales managers: they were students pretending to be sales managers. Would real sales managers act the same way? We don't know. Second, if this problem occurred in the real world, would the results have been the same? Would even more people approve of kickbacks if they were threatened with being fired for failing to reach a certain profit level? We can only speculate about this because the study was not done in an actual company with real sales managers.

## FIELD EXPERIMENT

A field experiment is a research strategy in which the manipulation of independent variables occurs in a natural setting (i.e., the people in the study do not perceive the setting as having been created in order to conduct the research). As in a laboratory experiment, the researcher tests the effects of a few variables on the behavior of the subjects; but there is less control than in a laboratory experiment. (In a laboratory experiment, all the variables are under the discretion of the researcher; they can be included or excluded according to the design of the study.) However in a field experiment, variables that occur in the natural setting are also part of the experiment. Though they add to the richness and realism of the field experiment, they also lessen the researcher's control.

The *advantages* of field experiments include the following.

1. Because field experiments are conducted in natural settings, they are very realistic, and the results are highly generalizable.
2. If the proper experimental design is used, the researcher may be able to *suggest* some causal inferences about the observed behavior.
3. Unlike laboratory experiments, field experiments can address broader research questions dealing with complex behavior in real-life contexts.

The *disadvantages* of field experiments include the following:

1. Because there is less control in field experiments, it is difficult to measure variables precisely.

2. Sometimes the individuals or groups of people may refuse to participate in the study.
3. Researchers often can't gain access to a business or industrial setting—the "natural environment" for a field experiment.

**Example of the method.** Latham and Kinne (1974) reported on a study that used the field experiment as a research method. It examined how a one-day training program on goal setting affected the job performance of pulpwood workers. The subjects in the study were 20 pulpwood logging crews. Their behavior was observed as they performed their normal job duties harvesting lumber in a forest. The experimenters split the subjects into two groups of 10 crews each. The two groups were matched on a number of factors so that they were equal in terms of ability and experience. One of the groups was given a one-day course in how to set production goals, i.e., how many cords of wood they wanted to harvest per hour. The other group was not given any special instructions, and they worked in the usual way. The experimenters then monitored the job performance of the wood crews over the next three months. Results showed that the crews who were trained to set production goals for themselves harvested significantly more wood than the other crews. The study supported the use of goal-setting in an industrial context.

The major strength of this study (in terms of demonstrating the field experiment method) was that the context was very real. Real workers were used in the context of their everyday job. The setting was a forest, not a laboratory where the subjects pretended they were in a forest. While the study's design was not complex enough to rule out competing explanations for the observed behavior, it did allow the researchers to conclude that the goal-setting technique *may* have caused the increase in job performance.

This study also illustrates some of the weaknesses of the field experiment method. Some workers who were supposed to participate in the goal-setting group decided not to. This caused some problems for the researchers who had to redesign part of the study. Also, few I/O psychologists would be able to influence a company to change their work operations for research purposes. (In fact, one of the authors of this study was employed by the lumber company, so this undoubtedly had some effect on the company's willingness to participate.)

## FIELD STUDY

Like field experiments, field studies involve the study of people in intact, naturally occurring environments as opposed to those specifically created for research purposes (e.g., laboratory experiments). Unlike the field experiment, the field study gives the researcher very little control over the study. That is, the researcher cannot select certain variables to manipulate (as the effect of goal setting in the Latham and Kinne field experiment) because variables are not manipulated at all. Rather, the researcher relies on self-reports of subjects or some other nonmanipulative measure. In some cases, research based upon field studies is exploratory in nature. After some ideas have been generated as a result of the field study, the ideas may be translated into hypotheses which are then tested formally in a field or laboratory experiment.

Because field studies occur in natural environments, they are high in realism. The researcher's presence may distort the nature of the variables being studied, so he or she must remain as *unobtrusive* as possible. In most cases, field study data are obtained through questionnaires or interviews. But while the researcher's presence can be minimized, it can never be totally eliminated.

The *advantages* of the field study are:

1. Field studies are very realistic because they are conducted in naturally occurring environments.
2. Data on a large number of variables can be collected at the same time.
3. The researcher's impact in the study is not nearly as great as in other research strategies.

The *disadvantages* of the field study include:

1. Variables cannot be manipulated by the researcher and their effects systematically studied. So the method does not permit causality to be assessed.
2. Companies may not give permission to conduct a field study.
3. The measurement of the variables is not as precise as in laboratory experiments.

**Example of the method.**    Muldrow and Bayton (1979) conducted a study to investigate the accuracy of decision making in male and female executives. One hundred male managers and 100 female managers working in federal agencies in Washington, D.C., completed a questionnaire. It assessed how people decide to hire a new person in an organization. The subjects were given descriptions of three hypothetical job applicants. Their task was to review the information on each applicant and then pick one of the three to hire. The questionnaire asked each subject to describe what information about the applicant led them to make the decision they did and how they felt about the decision they made.

After this, each subject completed additional questionnaires that assessed their personality, their willingness to take risks, and how strong their sex-role perceptions were (i.e., questions about what is "typical" male and female behavior). Their responses were analyzed to see if there was any relationship between the response to the decision-making problem and the other variables (personality of the subject, inclination for risk taking, etc.). The findings showed that the most accurate decision makers were those who were confident of their decision and took more time to reach it. They also showed that the male and female executives were equal in terms of their decision-making ability. But there were differences between males and females in how they went about making decisions. The female executives were more cautious or less willing to take risks. Also, female executives held stronger sex-role perceptions than did male executives. The researchers concluded that certain variables are consistently associated with making correct decisions, and that males and females are equally competent in making managerial decisions.

The task used in this study was "natural" for the subjects. The subjects answered the questionnaires in their own offices. And the decision-making task (hiring a new person) was something they perform as a normal part of their job. While the subjects in this study probably do not routinely complete questionnaires about their personality, they undoubtedly do a large amount of report writing, questionnaire-taking, and paperwork in general. Thus, the researchers were not asking the subjects to engage in behavior they typically would not perform as part of their job. Also, the study allowed the researchers to examine many variables at once: decision-making ability, personality, risk-taking propensity, and sex-role perceptions. It was not confined to examining the effect on behavior of only one or two variables.

This example also brings out the weaknesses of the field study. The researchers could not prove that how much confidence people have in their decision *"causes"* good decisions. Nor could they say that more accurate decisions are caused by taking a long time to reach a decision. Perhaps factors other than those examined in this study caused the results. The researchers can only say certain variables are associated with making accurate decisions. Causality cannot be directly determined on the basis of this study. To test for causality, some of the variables in this study (as the time to make a decision) could be manipulated in a future laboratory experiment. Second, a major reason why this study took place is that one of the authors worked for the federal government. This is probably why the government agreed to permit the study. An I/O psychologist does not *have* to be employed by a company to get permission for a study, but having some "contacts" in a company greatly helps in the conduct of field research.

## SAMPLE SURVEY

A researcher using the sample survey research strategy collects information directly from subjects in a standardized manner. The survey is conducted in a natural setting, not one contrived by the researcher. The data are usually collected by a questionnaire, interview, or observation. Whatever technique is used, the researcher must be sure that it is used systematically (i.e., each person in the study answers the same set of questions). Variables are simply measured (not manipulated) by the researcher. This method is a good way to generate ideas which may later be tested more formally in a field or laboratory experiment.

The *advantages* of the sample survey method include:

1. The method is high in realism since data are collected in a naturally occurring environment.
2. The results of sample surveys often yield new hypotheses that might be tested by another method.
3. A number of sample survey techniques (e.g., questionnaires, interviews, and observation) may be used alone or in combination.

The *disadvantages* of the method include:

1. The researcher has little control over the variables in the study. Because no variables are manipulated experimentally, the method does not permit any inferences about causality.
2. People are becoming less willing to respond to surveys. If a questionnaire is used, only a low proportion are usually returned. A typical questionnaire (with no follow-up reminder to the respondents) has a return rate of about 40 to 50 percent.
3. Because some people do not respond to surveys, the responses of those people who do may be biased or unrepresentative of the group as a whole.

**Example of method.**   Two Canadian researchers (Goodale & Aagaard, 1975) conducted a survey to assess workers' reactions to switching from a five-day workweek to a four-day workweek (with longer hours per day). The researchers sent a questionnaire to several hundred employees of a large company that had recently switched to the four-day workweek. Each employee was asked to rate several aspects of their job with the four-day work schedule compared to the former five-day schedule. Questions involved absenteeism, psychological reactions to the longer work day, work performance, attitudes toward work, changes in leisure life, and feelings of overall satisfaction.

Chemistry is one scientific discipline that relies primarily on a single research method—the laboratory experiment. Psychology, on the other hand, utilizes several methods in its research.

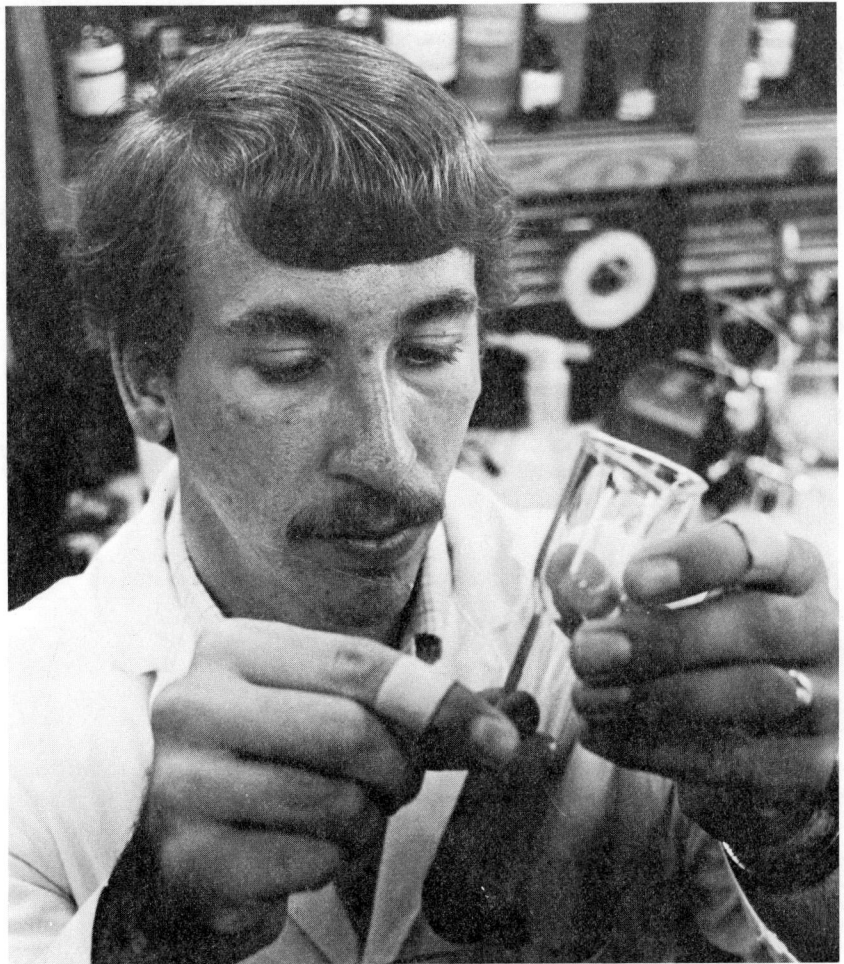

The results showed that most employees were enthusiastic and positive about the four-day workweek. Younger workers were more positive than older ones. Managers and supervisors were quite negative, both in their own attitudes and in how they perceived their employees' performance. The researchers concluded that the four-day workweek would be successful *except* where (1) employees must meet and work in groups, (2) customer service is provided five days per week, (3) supervisors feel the need to be available during all working hours, and (4) a majority of employees are relatively old.

One of the strengths of this study was that the data were collected in a very real environment. Employees were asked to evaluate a work schedule that affects their lives every day. Also, the data provided many ideas that might be pursued in future studies. For example, what changes could be made so that supervisors would like the four-day workweek? Are the positive reactions likely to continue, or are they the result of a Hawthorne Effect?

The disadvantages of the method are that the researchers could not experimentally manipulate any factors. They could not have half the employees work the four-day schedule and the other half five days and then compare the two sets of responses. Researchers could not test what causes older workers to dislike the four-day workweek. Are older workers more inflexible than younger workers, or are they just more used to working five days? What is not apparent from this study is the problem of the return rate and potentially biased results. Goodale and Aagaard had little trouble getting responses back. Other researchers are not always so lucky. The results of some well-planned and well-intentioned sample surveys have to be discarded because the return rate is too small to be meaningfully interpreted.

**Table 2–1**                    **Comparison of empirical research strategies**

|  | Laboratory experiment | Field experiment | Field study | Sample survey |
|---|---|---|---|---|
| Control (Potential for testing causal relationships) ..................... | High | Moderate | Low | Low |
| Realism (Naturalness of setting) ....... | Low | High | High | High |

Table 2–1 compares the four research methods on two major dimensions—researcher control and realism. No method is high on both factors. There is always a trade-off: a researcher may sacrifice realism for control or vice versa, depending upon the study's objectives. Choice of strategy should be guided by the purpose of the research and the resources available. A well-trained I/O psychologist is versed in all four of these research methods and knows the advantages and disadvantages of each.

# MEASUREMENT OF VARIABLES

After developing a study design, the researcher must next enact the design and measure the variables of interest. A *variable* is a symbol that can assume a range of numerical values. *Quantitative* variables (age, time, etc.) are those inherently numerical (21 years or 16 minutes). *Qualitative* variables (sex, race, etc.) are not inherently numerical, but they can be "coded" to give them numerical meaning—female = 0, male = 1, or white = 0, black = 1, Hispanic = 2, Oriental = 3, etc. For research purposes, it doesn't matter what numerical values are given to the qualitative variables since the number only identifies the sex or racial group for measurement purposes.

The term *variable* is often used in conjunction with other terms in I/O psychological research. Four such terms that will be used throughout this book are *independent, dependent, predictor,* and *criterion* (variables).

The terms *independent* and *dependent* variables are associated in particular with experimental (laboratory or field) research strategies. Independent variables are those that are manipulated or controlled by the researcher. They are chosen by the experimenter, set or manipulated to occur at a certain level, and then examined to assess their effect on some other variable. In the laboratory experiment by Hegarty and Sims (1978), two independent variables were used: (1) the degree to which kickbacks increased company profits and (2) the degree of competition among the subjects. In the field experiment by Latham and Kinne (1974), one independent variable was used: the effect of a one-day training program on goal setting.

Experiments assess the effects of independent variables on some other variable. This "other variable" is called the dependent variable. Dependent variables are the object of the researcher's interest. They are usually some aspect of behavior (though sometimes attitudes may be the dependent variable). In the study by Hegarty and Sims (1978), the dependent variable was the subject's willingness to engage in unethical behavior, i.e., accept kickbacks. In the study by Latham and Kinne (1974), the dependent variable was the number of cords of wood harvested by the lumber crews. The same variable can be selected as the dependent or independent variable depending upon the goals of the study. Figure 2–2 shows how a variable (employee performance) can be used as either an independent or dependent variable. In the former case, the researcher wants to study the effect

**Figure 2–2**                    **Employee performance used as either a dependent or independent variable**

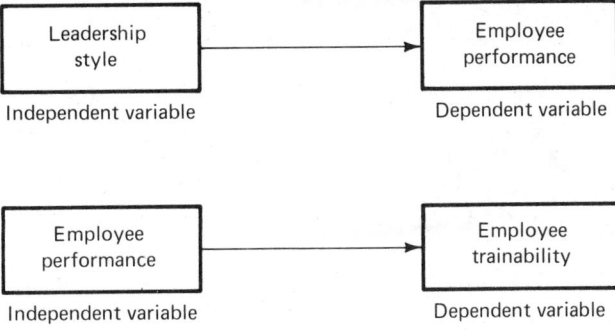

of various leadership styles (independent variable) on employee performance (dependent variable). The researcher might select two types of leadership styles (a stern, task-master approach versus a relaxed easy-going approach) and then assess their effects on job performance. In another study, a researcher might want to know what effect employee performance (independent variable) has on the ability to be trained (dependent variable). The employees are divided into "high performer" and "low performer" groups. Both groups then attend a training program to assess whether the high performers learn faster than the low performers. Note that variables are never *inherently* independent or dependent. Whether a variable is independent or dependent is up to the researcher's discretion.

The terms *predictor* and *criterion* variables are used often in I/O psychology. When scores on one variable are used to predict scores on a second variable, the variables are called predictor and criterion variables, respectively. For example, a student's high school grade-point average might be used to predict his or her college grade-point average. High school grades are the predictor variable; college grades are the criterion variable. As a rule, criterion variables are the focal point of our study. Predictor variables may or may not be successful in predicting what we want to know (the criterion). Predictor variables are similar to independent variables; criterion variables are similar to dependent variables. The distinction between the two is a function of the research strategy. Independent and dependent variables are used in the context of experimentation. Predictor and criterion variables are used in any research strategy where a researcher is interested in knowing the status of subjects on one variable (the criterion) as a function of their status on another variable (the predictor).

**Levels of measurement**

Variables must be measured as accurately and precisely as possible. Some variables can be measured very precisely, but others can be measured in only a coarse way. A *scale* is a measuring device to assess a person's score or status on some variable. While there are many scales used to measure people or objects, there are only four basic types: (1) nominal, (2) ordinal, (3) interval, (4) ratio (Stevens, 1958).

1. **Nominal scale.** A nominal scale, the crudest type of scale, classifies objects or people into categories. It simply shows that a person (or object) is a member of one of these categories. For example, a nominal scale could classify people by sex into one of two categories (male or female). Racial groups (Caucasian, Oriental, etc.) can also be categorized on a nominal scale. Note that a nominal scale does *not* arrange people or objects in some order or sequence.

2. **Ordinal scale.** An ordinal scale orders objects along some dimension. The most common type of ordinal scale is a rank order. If you were asked to rank order three foods (pizza, chicken, and steak) along a dimension of taste preference, you might rank them steak, pizza, and chicken.

We know you like pizza better than chicken and steak better than both pizza and chicken. But we don't know *how much* you like these foods. You may like all three or despise all three, or you may like only one. So an ordinal scale shows how things are ranked along a dimension but not the distance between the ranked items.

3. **Interval scale.**  An interval scale measures how much of a variable is present (there are equal distances between scale units). A thermometer represents an interval scale. The distance between 10° and 15° (5°) is the same as the difference between 87° and 92° (5°). An interval scale is more precise than an ordinal scale, because it not only shows relative preference (i.e., rank order), but also how much the objects are preferred. Suppose you rated the three foods on a 10-point scale (where a rating of 10 is high and 1 is low) and the results were steak 9, pizza 2, and chicken 1. The scale shows that you like steak a lot but not pizza or chicken. A person who had the same rank order but rated the foods as steak 10, pizza 9, and chicken 8 would obviously feel differently.

4. **Ratio scale.**  A ratio scale is the most precise type of scale. It has all the properties of the other three scales and one more. A ratio scale has a true zero-point. Measures such as length, weight, and age are all ratio scales. The true zero-point in the scale means that nothing can be shorter than 0 inches (or centimeters), lighter than 0 ounces (or grams), or younger than 0 seconds. A thermometer is not a ratio scale because it has no true zero-point ($-5°$ is a negative temperature). The term *ratio* means that a ratio can be formed between two objects; e.g., a person 20 years old is *twice* as old as a 10-year-old. But we cannot say that 20° is *twice* as warm as 10°.

These scales are important because how precisely the variables are measured affects how precisely they can be analyzed. More precise statistical analyses lead to more refined conclusions about the interrelationships of the variables.

## ANALYSIS OF DATA

After the data have been collected, the researcher has to make some sense out of them. Here's where statistics come in. Many students get anxious over the topic of statistics. While some statistical analytic methods are quite complex, most are reasonably straightforward. I like to think of statistical methods as golf clubs, tools for helping do a job better. Just as some golf shots call for different clubs, different research problems require different statistical analyses. Knowing a full range of statistical methods will help you better understand the research problem. It's also impossible to understand the research process without some knowledge of statistics. The following is a brief exposure to statistics.

**Table 2–2**       **One hundred IQ scores**

| | | | | |
|---|---|---|---|---|
| 133 | 141 | 108 | 124 | 117 |
| 110 | 92 | 88 | 110 | 79 |
| 143 | 101 | 120 | 104 | 94 |
| 117 | 128 | 102 | 126 | 84 |
| 105 | 143 | 114 | 70 | 103 |
| 151 | 114 | 87 | 134 | 81 |
| 87 | 120 | 145 | 98 | 95 |
| 97 | 157 | 99 | 79 | 107 |
| 108 | 107 | 147 | 156 | 144 |
| 118 | 127 | 96 | 138 | 102 |
| 141 | 113 | 112 | 94 | 114 |
| 133 | 122 | 89 | 128 | 112 |
| 119 | 99 | 110 | 118 | 142 |
| 123 | 67 | 120 | 89 | 118 |
| 90 | 114 | 121 | 146 | 94 |
| 128 | 125 | 114 | 91 | 124 |
| 121 | 125 | 83 | 99 | 76 |
| 120 | 102 | 129 | 108 | 98 |
| 110 | 144 | 89 | 122 | 119 |
| 117 | 127 | 134 | 127 | 112 |

**Figure 2–3**       **Frequency distribution of 100 IQ scores (grouped data)**

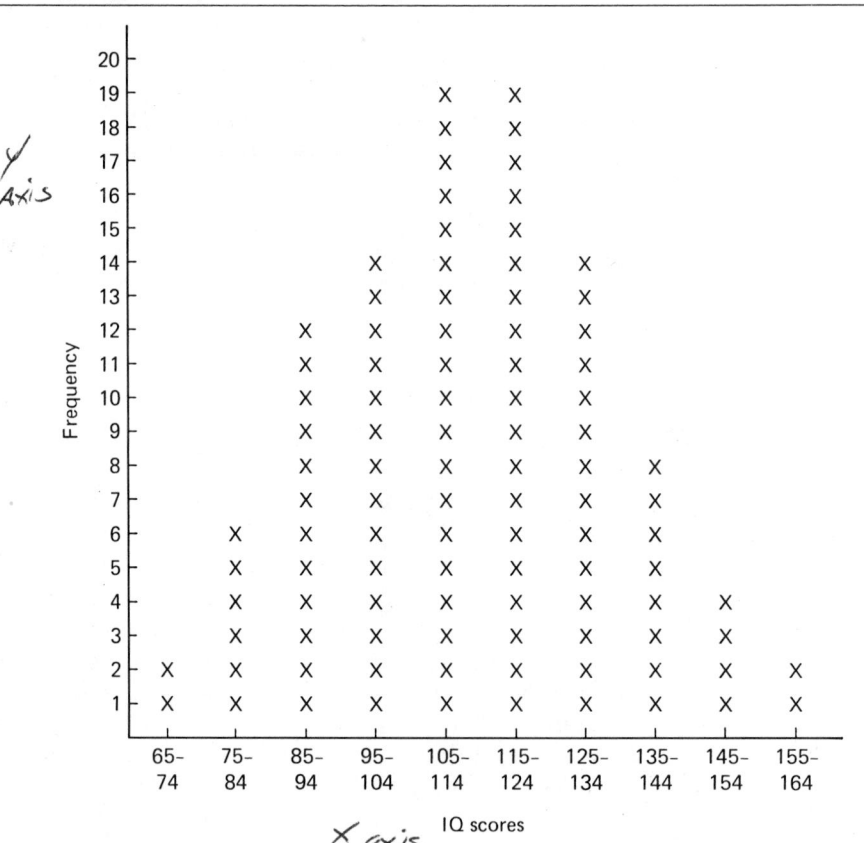

## Descriptive statistics

Descriptive statistics simply describe data. They are the starting point in the data analysis process; they give the researcher a general idea of what the data are like. Descriptive statistics can show the shape of a distribution of numbers, measure of the central tendency of the distribution, and measure the spread or variability in the numbers.

## Distributions and their shape

Suppose a researcher measures the intelligence of 100 people with a traditional IQ test. Table 2–2 shows those 100 scores. To make some sense out of all these numbers, the researcher arranges the numbers according to size and then plots them in a figure. Figure 2–3 shows what those 100 test scores look like. This is called a *frequency distribution*. Because so many scores are involved, the scores are grouped into categories of equal size with each interval containing 10 possible scores. If we recorded just the total number of IQ scores in each interval and graphed the results, we would have a *frequency polygon*. Figure 2–4 shows a frequency polygon for the data reported in Table 2–2. Both figures tell something about the

**Figure 2–4**

**Frequency polygon of 100 IQ scores (grouped data)**

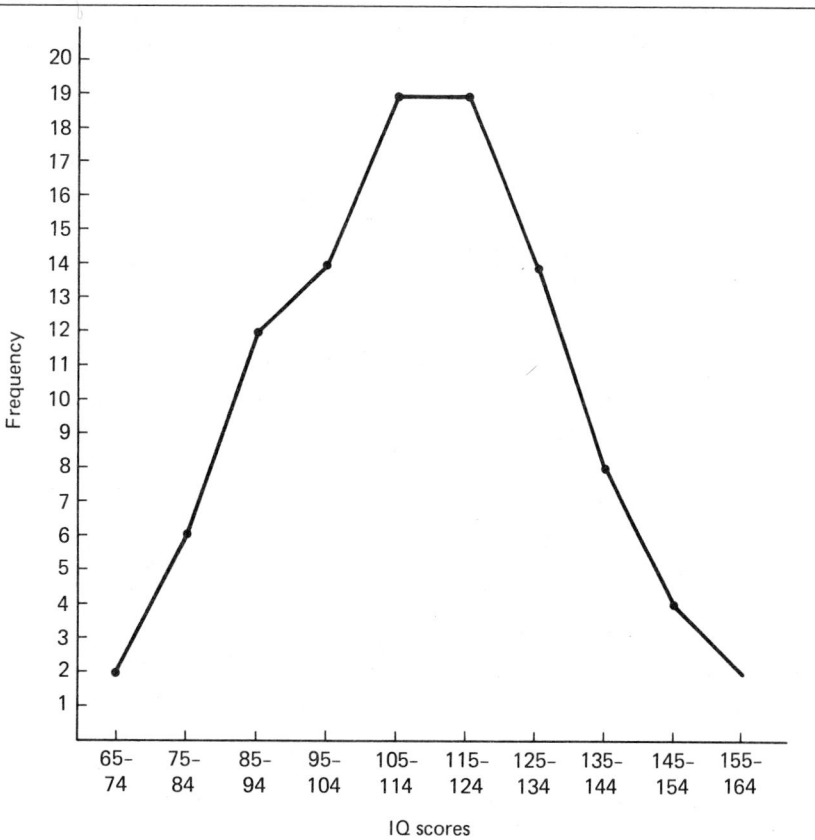

**Figure 2–5a**           **A normal or bell-shaped distribution of scores**

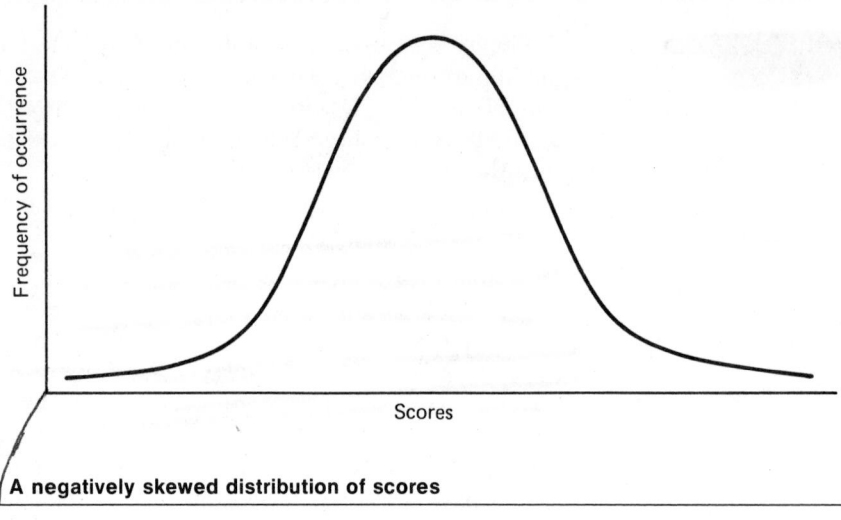

**Figure 2–5b**           **A negatively skewed distribution of scores**

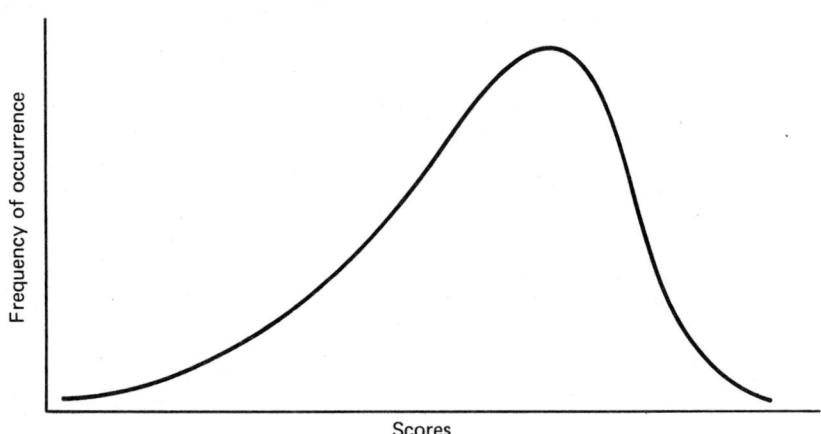

**Figure 2–5c**           **A positively skewed distribution of scores**

IQ data. We can see that the most frequently occurring scores are in the middle of the distribution; extreme scores (both high and low) taper off as we move away from the middle of the distribution. The general shape of the distribution in Figures 2–3 and 2–4 is called a *normal* or *bell-shaped* distribution. Many variables in psychological research are distributed normally; i.e., the most frequently occurring scores are in the middle of the distribution with progressively fewer scores at the extreme ends. Figure 2–5a shows a classic normal distribution. The smoothness of Figure 2–5a in comparison to Figures 2–3 and 2–4 is due to the fact that the occurrence of many test scores would take the "kinks" out of the distribution.

Not all distributions of scores are normal in shape. Some distributions are lopsided or pointed. If a professor gives an easy test, there will be a larger proportion of high scores. This would result in a pointed or *skewed* distribution. Figure 2–5b shows a *negatively* skewed distribution (the tail of the distribution is in the negative direction). The opposite would occur if a professor gave a difficult test; the result would be a *positively* skewed distribution (the tail of the distribution is in the positive direction). (See Figure 2–5c.) It is possible to have a distribution that is neither normal nor skewed. One example would be a *bimodal* distribution. This type of distribution would most likely occur if both men and women were tested for physical strength. Since most men are physically stronger than most women, the scores for most men would be in the top half of the total distribution. The scores for most women would be in the bottom half. But, some women would be physically stronger than some men, so the distribution of scores would blend or overlap in the middle. Figure 2–6 shows a bimodal distribution.

Thus, plotting the distribution of data is one way to understand it. Inferences can be made based on the shape of the distribution. (In the case

**Figure 2–6**          **A bimodal distribution of scores**.

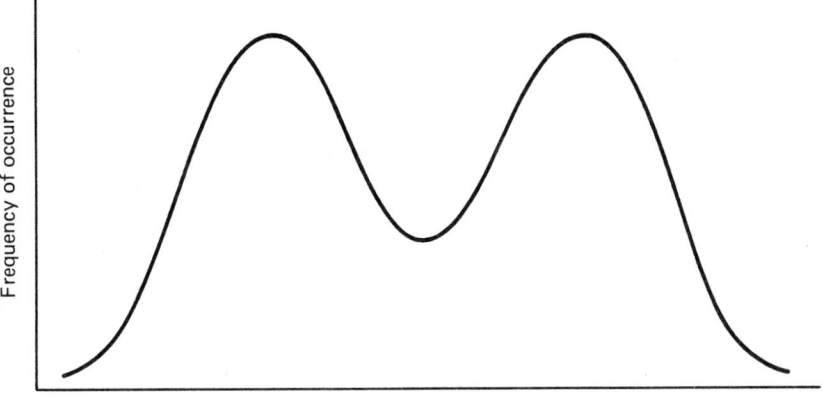

Physical strength scores

of the negatively skewed distribution of test scores, we infer that the test was easy.)

**Measures of central tendency**

After we know the shape of the distribution, the next step is usually to find the typical score. Three measures of *central tendency* are usually used for this, and the use of each measure depends upon the shape of the distribution. The *mean* is the most common measure of central tendency. The mean is the arithmetic average score in the distribution. It is computed by adding all of the individual scores and dividing by the total number of scores in the distribution. The formula for computing the mean is

$$\bar{X} = \frac{\Sigma X}{N}$$

where $\bar{X}$ is the symbol for the mean, $\Sigma$ is the symbol for summation, $X$ is the symbol for each individual score, and $N$ is the total number of scores in the distribution. The mean for the data in Table 2–2 is:

$$\bar{X} = \frac{11,322}{100} = 113.22$$

The average IQ in the sample of people tested is 113.22 (or 113 rounded). The entire distribution of 100 scores can be described by one number, the mean. The mean is a useful measure of central tendency and is most appropriately used with normally distributed variables.

The *median* is that point in the distribution that is the midpoint of all the scores. So 50 percent of all scores are above the median, and 50 percent are below the median. If we have a distribution of four scores and they are 1, 2, 3, and 4, the median would be 2.5. That is, half the scores (3 and 4) are above this point, and half (1 and 2) are below it. (The statistical procedure used to compute the median for graphed data is quite lengthy and will not be presented here. For point of information, the median for the data presented in Table 2–2 is 112.9.) The median is the best measure of central tendency for skewed distributions, because skewed distributions always contain some extreme scores. (The median is relatively insensitive to these extreme scores, but the mean would be affected by them.)

The *mode* is the least common measure of central tendency. The mode is the most frequently occurring score in a distribution. If *two* scores occur with the greatest frequency, the distribution would have two modes, as shown in Figure 2–6. The mode is not used for very many statistical analyses, but it may have a practical purpose. For example, if the modal number of selection tests used by a large number of companies was zero, we would then know that most companies did not use any selection tests. The mode for the data presented in Table 2–2 is 114. Although bimodal distributions do not occur often, the mode (or modes) is the best measure of central tendency for this shaped distribution.

In the normal distribution, the mean ($\overline{X}$), median ($Md$), and mode ($Mo$) are equal to each other as shown in Figure 2–7a. In a skewed distribution, the mean is pulled out the farthest toward the tail of the distribution, as shown in Figure 2–7b. In a bimodal distribution, the mean and the median are equal, but neither may be close to the two modes (as shown in Figure

**Figure 2–7a**     **Position of the mean, median, and mode in a normal distribution**

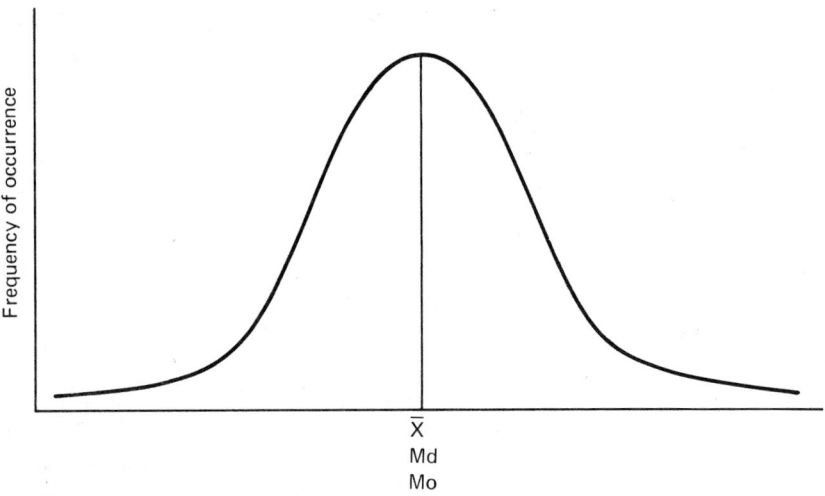

**Figure 2–7b**     **Position of the mean, median, and mode in a skewed distribution**

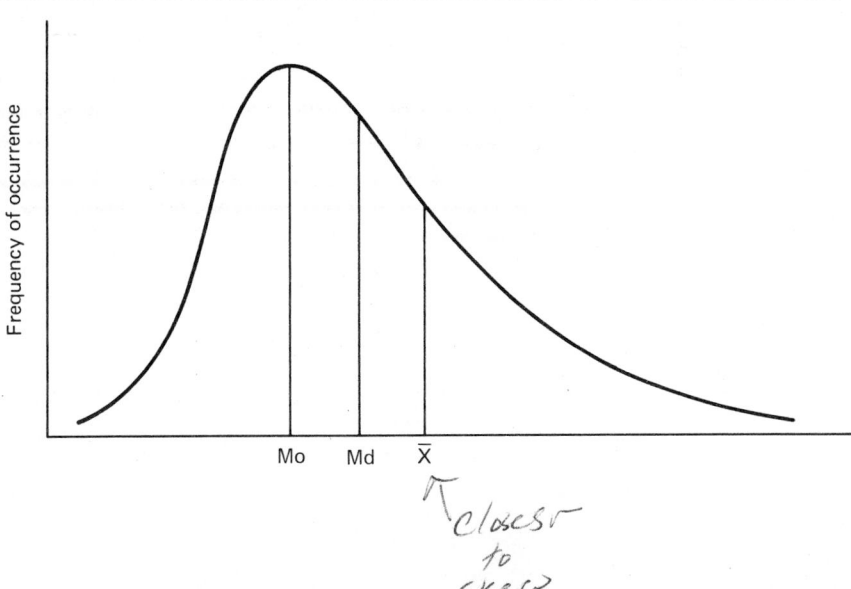

**Figure 2–7c**                    **Position of the mean, median, and mode in a bimodal distribution**

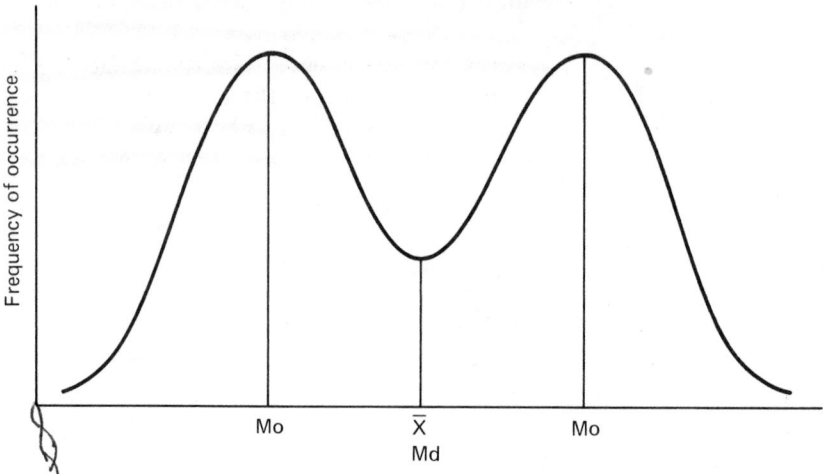

2–7c). Thus three measures of central tendency can be used to describe a typical score in a distribution. The measure used depends on the shape of the distribution.

## Measures of variability

In addition to describing a set of scores by the shape of their distribution and central tendency, we can also talk about the spread of the scores or their variability. Knowing the spread of scores or their variability is an indication of how *representative* the mean is as a measure of central tendency. There are several numerical indices to describe variability in scores. The simplest index is called the *range*. Subtracting the lowest score from the highest score gives the range. From the data in Table 2–2, the range would be $157 - 67 = 90$.

Consider Figure 2–8. Here there are two normal distributions with equal means but unequal variability. One distribution is very peaked with a small range; the other is quite flat with a big range. In addition to having different ranges, these distributions also differ with regard to another measure of variability, the *standard deviation*. The standard deviation is a measure of the spread of scores around the mean. The formula for the standard deviation is

$$s = \sqrt{\frac{\Sigma(X - \bar{X})^2}{N}}$$

where $s$ is the standard deviation, $X$ is each individual score, $\Sigma$ is the symbol for summation, $\bar{X}$ is the mean of the distribution, and $N$ is the total number of scores in the distribution. To compute the standard deviation,

**Figure 2–8**                              **Two distributions with the same mean but different variability**

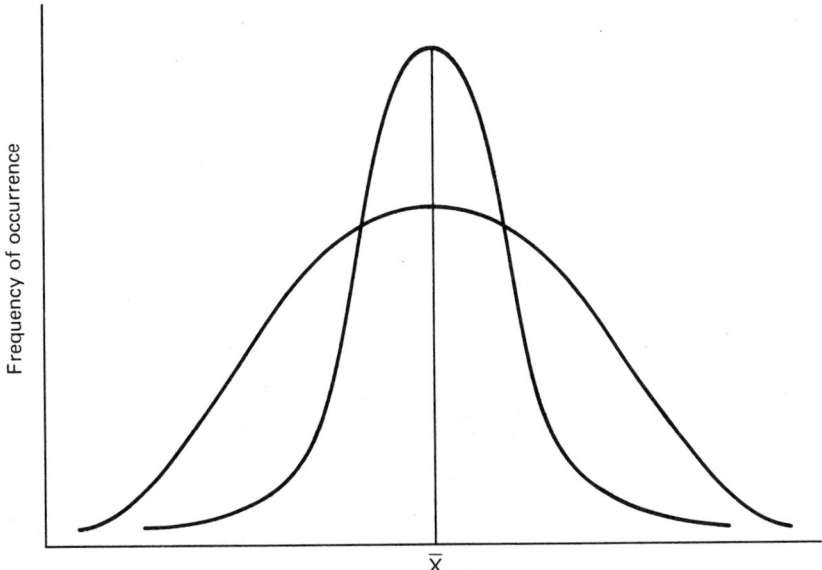

subtract the mean ($\bar{X}$) from each individual score ($X$) in the distribution, square that number, add up all the numbers, divide that total by the number of scores in the distribution, and then take the square root of the figure. By applying this formula to the data in Table 2–2, the standard deviation for that distribution is 19.96 (or 20 rounded off).

The standard deviation is particularly important in conjunction with the normal distribution. Given the mathematical properties of the normal curve, we know that theoretically 68 percent of all scores fall within ±1 standard deviation of the mean. So from the data in Table 2–2 (which has a mean of 113 and a standard deviation of 20) we know that theoretically 68 percent of all the scores should fall between 93 (113 − 20) and 133 (113 + 20). Furthermore, the mathematical derivation of the normal curve indicates that theoretically 95 percent of all the scores should fall within ±2 standard deviations from the mean, that is between 73 (113 − 40) and 153 (113 + 40). Finally, theoretically 99 percent of all the scores should fall within ±3 standard deviations from the mean, between 53 (113 − 60) and 173 (113 + 60). The actual percent of scores from the data in Table 2–2 is very close to the theoretical values; 69 percent of the scores fell within 1 standard deviation, 96 percent fell within 2 standard deviations, and 100 percent fell within 3 standard deviations. Figure 2–9 shows the percent of scores in a normal distribution encompassed by 1, 2, and 3 standard deviations, respectively. Other measures of variability besides the range and standard deviation are also used. But for the purposes of this book, these two measures will suf-

**Figure 2–9**          **Percentage of scores encompassed by 1, 2, and 3 standard deviations in a normal distribution**

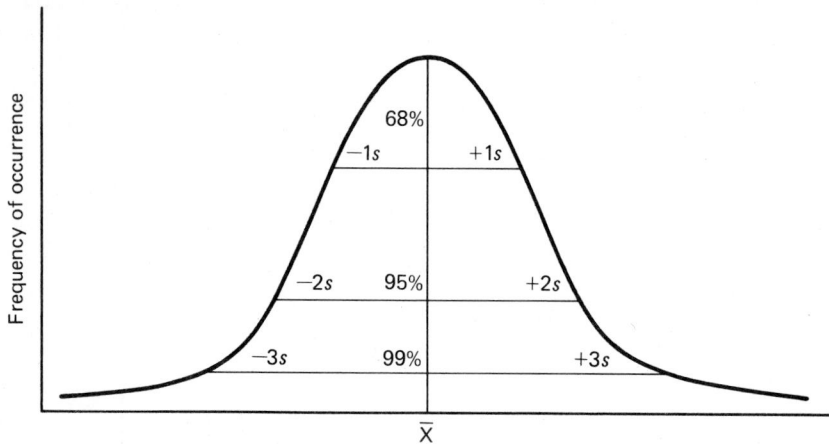

fice. Variability is important because it tells about the spread of scores in a distribution. And this can be just as important as knowing the most typical score in a distribution.

## THE CONCEPT OF CORRELATION

So far we have only been concerned with the statistical analysis of one variable—its shape, typical score, and dispersion. But in most I/O psychological research, we are concerned with the relationship between two (or more) variables. In particular, we are usually interested in the extent that we can understand one variable (the criterion or dependent variable) on the basis of knowing another variable (the predictor or independent variable). A statistical procedure useful in determining this relationship is called a *correlation coefficient*.

A correlation coefficient reflects the *degree of linear relationship* between two variables, which we shall refer to as $X$ and $Y$. The symbol for a correlation ir $r$, and its range is from $-1.00$ to $+1.00$. A correlation coefficient tells two things about the relationship between two variables: (1) the direction of the relationship and (2) its magnitude. The direction of the relationship is either positive or negative. A positive relationship means that as one variable increases in magnitude, so does the other. An example of a positive correlation would be that between height and weight. As a rule, the taller a person is the more the person weighs; increasing height is associated with increasing weight. A negative relationship means that as one variable increases in magnitude, the other gets smaller. An example of a negative correlation would be the correlation between a production worker's efficiency and scrap rate. The more efficient workers are, the less scrap is left. The less efficient they are, the more scrap they will leave.

The magnitude of the correlation is an index of the strength of relationship. Large correlations indicate greater strength than small correlations. A correlation of .80 indicates a very strong relationship between the variables, while a correlation of .10 would indicate a very weak relationship. Also, magnitude and direction are independent. A correlation of −.80 is just as strong as one of +.80.

Figures 2–10a, b, c, and d, show graphic portrayals of correlation coefficients. The first step in illustrating a correlation is to plot all pairs of variables in the study. For a sample of 100 people, record the height and weight of each person. Then plot the pairs of data points (height and weight) for each person. The stronger the relationship between the two variables, the tighter is the spread of data points around the line of best fit that runs through the scatterplot. Figure 2–10a shows a scatterplot for two variables that have a high positive correlation. Notice the slope of the line through the data points slants in the positive direction, and most of the data points are packed tightly around the line.

**Figure 2–10a**          **Scatterplot of two variables that have a high positive correlation**

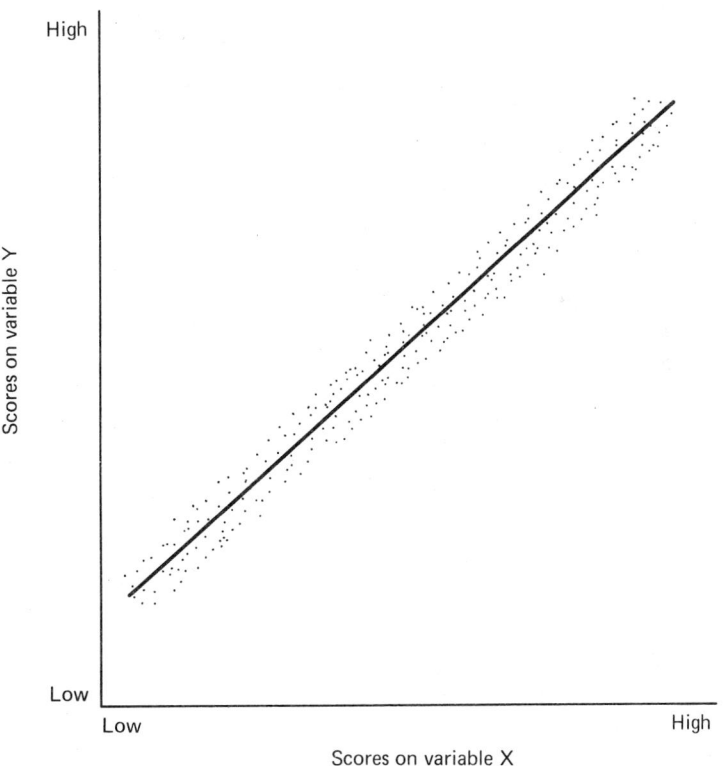

Scores on variable X

**Figure 2–10b**          **Scatterplot of two variables that have a high negative correlation**

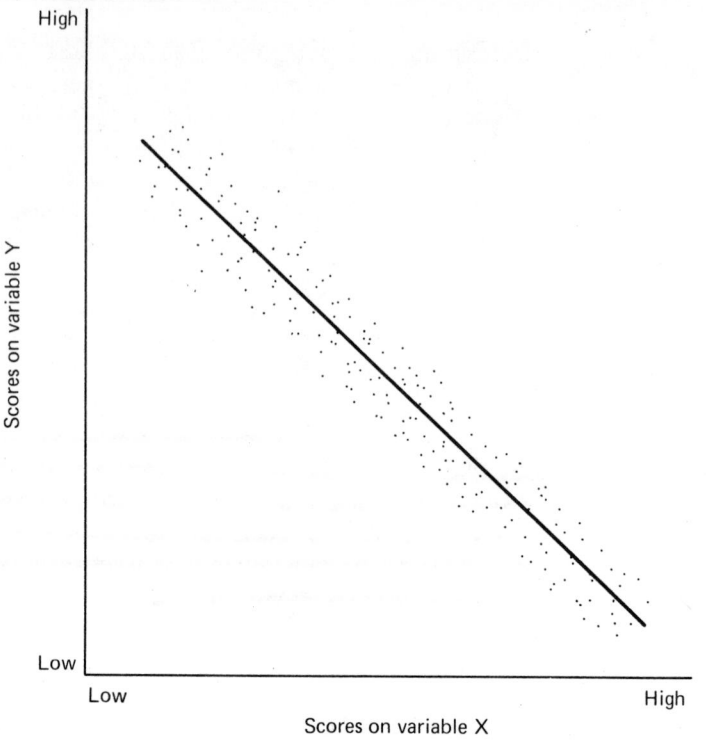

**Figure 2–10c**          **Scatterplot of two variables that have a low positive correlation**

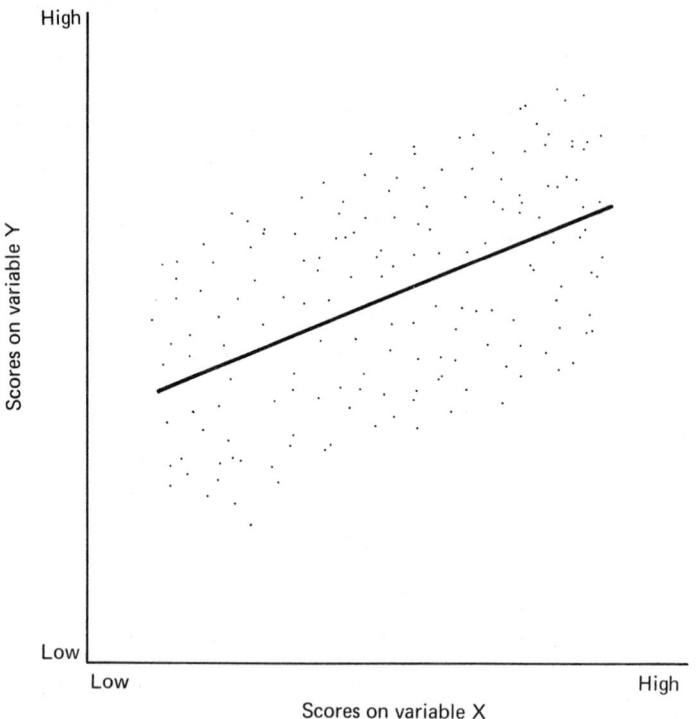

**Figure 2–10d**          **Scatterplot of two variables that have a low negative correlation**

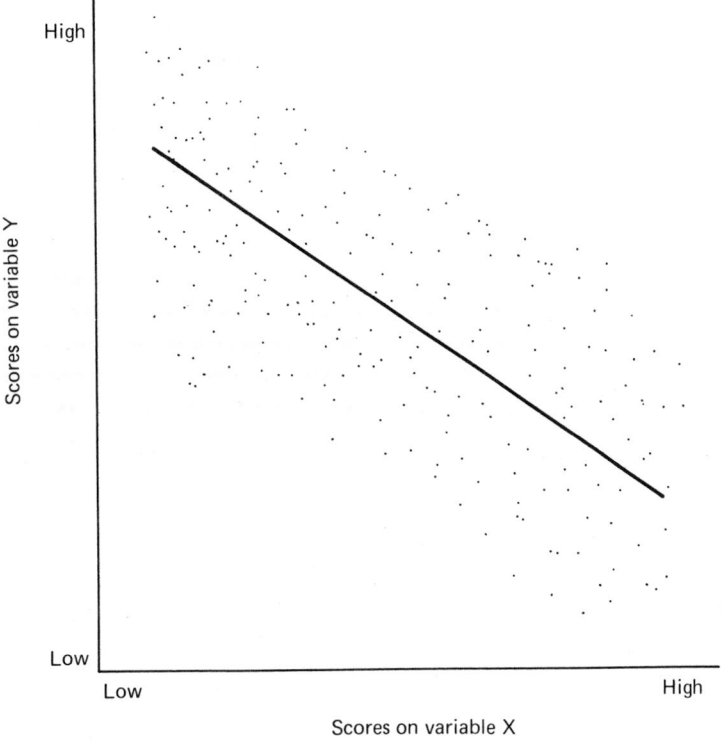

Figure 2–10b shows a scatterplot for two variables that have a high negative correlation. Again notice the data points are packed tightly around the line. But in this case, the line slants in the negative direction.

Figure 2–10c shows a scatterplot between two variables that have a low positive correlation. While the line slants in the positive direction, the data points are spread quite widely throughout the scatterplot.

Finally, Figure 2–10d shows a scatterplot between two variables that have a low negative correlation. The line of best fit slants in the negative direction, and the data points are not packed tightly around the line. The stronger the correlation between two variables (either positive or negative), the more accurately we can predict one variable from the other. The statistical formula used to compute a correlation will not be presented in this book since it is available in statistics books, plus the fact that it will not be necessary for the reader to compute any correlations. What is important is knowing what a correlation is and how to interpret one. However the reader should realize that the only way to derive the exact numerical value of a correlation is to apply the statistical formula. The eyeball inspection method of looking at a scatterplot will yield some idea of what the correlation is, though recent research has shown that people are generally not very good at inferring the magnitude of correlations just by looking at scatterplots (Bobko & Karren, 1979).

A few other issues are important to remember. A correlation is useful for describing the relationship between two variables when those variables are related in a linear or straight-line relationship. But not all variables are linearly related to each other. Figure 2–11 shows the relationship between two variables, arousal and performance. The figure shows that when a person is not aroused or motivated to work, performance is very low. As motivation increases to a moderate amount, performance increases accordingly. However, when a person's motivation level is too high, they get too anxious and performance suffers. There is a strong and clear relationship between these two variables, but it is not a linear one—it is *curvilinear*. When there is a curvilinear relationship between two variables, a typical correlation coefficient is an inappropriate statistic to measure the degree of association between the two variables. If a researcher were to compute a correlation between two variables that were curvilinearly related, the calculated correlation would be very small, leading the researcher to conclude

**Figure 2–11**        **Scatterplot of curvilinear relationship between arousal and performance**

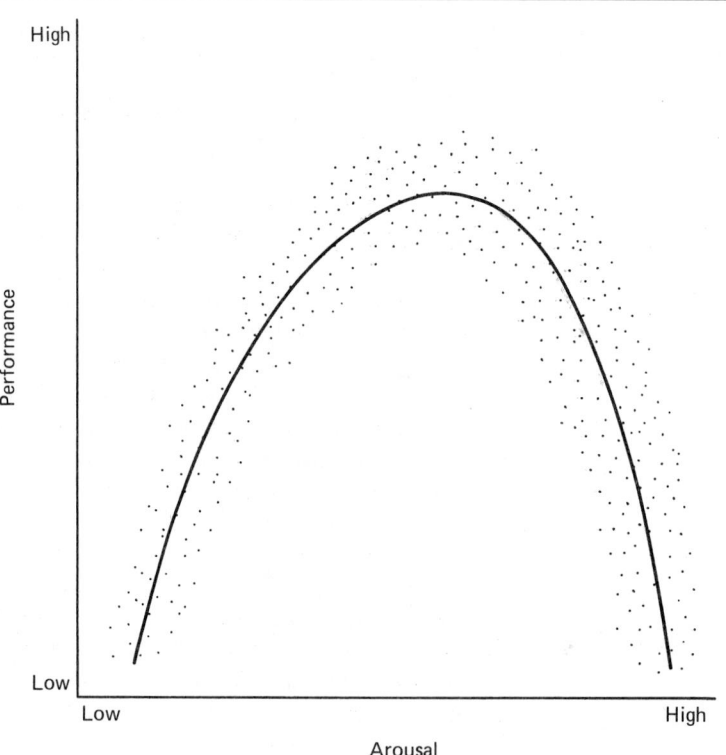

there is no relationship between the two variables. But this is wrong. There *is* a relationship between the variables, just not a linear one. So another statistical technique would have to be used.

Calculation of a correlation coefficient does not permit any inferences about causality, i.e., whether one variable caused the other to occur. While a causal relationship may exist between two variables, just computing a correlation will not reveal causality. Causality can only be ascertained through experimental research. Suppose you wish to compute the correlation between (1) the amount of alcohol consumed in a town and (2) the number of people who attend church there. You collect data on each of these variables in many towns in your area. The correlation turns out to be .85. On the basis of this high correlation, you conclude that because people drink all week, they go to church to repent (alcohol consumption causes church attendance). Your friends take the opposite point of view; they say that because people have to sit on hard wooden pews all cramped together, after church they "unwind" by drinking (church attendance causes alcohol consumption). Who is correct? On the basis of the existing data, no one is correct because causality cannot be inferred from correlation. One opinion may be correct, but proof of causality must await experimental research. (In point of fact, the causal basis of this correlation is undoubtedly neither of the above opinions. It is due to the fact that the various towns in the study have different populations, which produce a systematic relationship between these two variables along with many other variables, such as the number of people who eat out in restaurants, attend movies, etc.).

Because correlation is a common analytic technique in I/O psychological research, many of the empirical findings in this book will be expressed in those terms.

## Conclusions from research

After the data have been analyzed, the researcher draws conclusions. The conclusion may be that certain factors do indeed contribute to unethical behavior on the part of managers (Hegarty & Sims [1978]). If a company wants to diminish the likelihood of unethical behavior, they might remove any rewards associated with it. The study by Latham and Kinne (1974) concluded that goal-setting increased the rate of wood harvesting. So a company might decide to implement the goal-setting procedure throughout the firm. Generally it is unwise to implement any major changes based on the results of only *one* study. As a rule, we prefer to know the results from several studies. We want to be as certain as possible that any organizational changes are grounded in repeatable, generalizable results.

Sometimes the conclusions drawn from a study modify beliefs about a problem. Note in Figure 2–1 that a feedback loop extends from Conclusions from Research to Statement of the Problem. The findings from one study influence research problems in future studies. Theories may be altered if empirical research fails to confirm some of the hypotheses put forth.

While I/O psychology is not heavily dominated by theory, Ghiselli (1974) reports that most theories eventually fall out of favor rather than being *unequivocally* disconfirmed. But the major reason they do is that they repeatedly are not supported by data.

Research is a cumulative process. Researchers build on each other's work in formulating new research questions. They communicate their results by publishing articles in journals. A competent researcher must keep up to date in his or her area of expertise to avoid repeating someone else's study. The conclusions drawn from research can affect many aspects of our lives. Research is a vital part of industry; it is the basis for changes in products and services.

## ETHICAL PROBLEMS IN RESEARCH

Subjects in research have certain rights granted by law (Kelman, 1972). These rights pertain to their physical treatment in a study, confidentiality of information, privacy, and voluntary consent (no one can be forced to take part in a study). Researchers who violate these rights, particularly in studies that involve physical or psychological risk, can be subject to professional censure and possible litigation. The American Psychological Association (1973) has a code of ethics that must be honored by all APA members who conduct research. The code of ethics was created to protect the rights of subjects and to avoid the possibility of having research conducted by unqualified people.

The researcher is faced with additional problems with employees of companies. Argyris (1968) reports that while managers generally favor research, it can cause its own share of problems in an industrial context. Employees who are naive about the purpose of research often are suspicious when asked to participate. They wonder how they were "picked" for inclusion in the study and if they will be asked difficult questions. Some people even think a psychologist can read their mind and thus discover all sorts of private thoughts. Research projects that arouse emotional responses place managers in an uncomfortable interpersonal situation. Mirvis and Seashore (1979) have described some of the problems facing those who conduct research with employees. Most of the problems involve *role conflict*, the dilemma of being trained to be a good researcher, yet having to comply with both company and professional standards (London & Bray, 1980). For example, consider a role-conflict problem I faced in doing research with employees. I used a sample survey to assess the opinions and morale of industrial employees. The management of the company commissioned the research. As part of the research design, all employees were told that their responses would be confidential. One survey response revealed the existence of employee theft. Though I didn't know who the employee was, with the information given and a little help from management, that person could have been identified. Do I violate my promise and turn over the information to management? Do I tell management that some theft has occurred, but I don't have any way to find out who did it (which would not have been true)? Or do I ignore what I know and fail to tell management about a serious problem in their company? These types of problems are not unique to my study (Williams, Seybolt, & Pinder, 1975). The solution to a role-conflict problem is not always obvious. The pressures to conduct high-quality research, the need to be ethical, and the reality of organizational life sometimes place the researcher in a difficult situation. These demands place constraints on the I/O psychologist, constraints researchers in other areas do not always confront.

## RESEARCH IN INDUSTRY

While the empirical research process shown in Figure 2–1 portrays the conduct of most I/O psychological research, research conducted in industry (as opposed to universities or research centers) often has some additional distinguishing features. Boehm (1980) has observed that in industry, research questions arise inevitably from organizational problems. For example, problems of excessive employee absenteeism, turnover, job dissatisfaction, etc., may be the genesis for a research study designed to reduce the severity of such problems. Rarely in industry will research questions be posed just to "test a theory."

A second major difference involves how the results will be used. In industry, if the results of the study turn out to be positive and useful, the research unit of the organization will then try to "sell" (i.e., gain acceptance of) the findings throughout the rest of the organization. For example, if providing job applicants with a very candid and realistic preview of the organization reduces turnover, the researchers will try to convince the rest of the organization to use such procedures in recruiting new employees. If the results of a study turn out negative, the organization will look for side products or secondary ideas that will be of value. In research outside of industry, less attention is given to implementing the findings and convincing other people of their utility.

Finally, there are different motives for conducting research in industry as opposed to universities. Industrial research is conducted to enhance the efficiency of the organization. Among private sector employers, this usually translates into greater profitability. For example, research can be of vital importance in finding out consumer responses to new products and services, identifying ways to reduce waste, and making better use of the human talent within an organization. In university settings research may not have such an *instrumental* purpose. Research questions are posed that have relevance to industry, but the link between the findings and their implementation may not be as direct. I am reminded of a student who approached an organization with a research idea. The student was in need of a sample of managers to test a particular hypothesis. After patiently listening to the student's request, the organizational representative asked, "Why should we participate in this study? How can this study help us?" Industries that sponsor and participate in research do so for a reason; that reason is to enhance their welfare. University research is also conducted for a reason, but that reason may be nothing more than intellectual curiosity.

While academic and industrial research may be guided by somewhat different factors, both have contributed heavily to the I/O psychological literature. The infusion of research from both sectors has in fact been very healthy and stimulating for the profession. Jahoda (1981) has commented that more psychological research needs to be done in *anticipation* of future work problems as opposed to being a reaction to current problems. Seemingly industrial researchers may be in the best position to forecast future organizational concerns. Thus they may be able to find answers to problems before they become crises.

## FUTURE RESEARCH IN I/O PSYCHOLOGY

It is difficult to predict the future of I/O psychological research. Research topics can and do boom into existence for many reasons, and other topics fade.

Dipboye and Flanagan (1979) argue that research topics get studied either in laboratory *or* field settings. They feel that laboratory and field research strategies should be used in coordination rather than in competition with each other. The authors believe that each basic strategy has something to offer and that researchers can gain understanding by studying the problem with both methods.

Gordon, Kleiman, and Hanie (1978) are quite critical of I/O psychological research as a whole, claiming that much of the findings from I/O psychological research are "commonsensical," (i.e., could be predicted in advance by nonpsychologists). Gordon et al. argue for the development of more theory as a means of advancing the discipline beyond the investigation of commonsense problems. Dunnette (1966) has voiced similar concerns. He argued that psychologists are too easily influenced by fads and fashions in their research, and let their research methods dictate what problems get studied. ("I have a research method that is handy. Now what can I study with it?").

While it is easy to say that researchers should tackle big, socially important problems, such problems are much more complex. However, we should not be overwhelmed by them; otherwise, we will never study anything other than what can be handled. The contributions of I/O psychological research to such vast problems as the quality of life (Flanagan, 1978) and concern for the environment (Bass & Bass, 1976) have been proposed by some authors. An understanding of research methods is vital for psychologists to undertake the problems and issues confronting mankind in a world that is growing in complexity.

# CASE STUDY

Robin Mosier had just returned from her psychology class and was anxious to tell her roommate about an idea she had. Julie Hansen had taken the same class the previous semester, so Robin was hopeful that Julie could help her out. The psychology professor gave the class an assignment to come up with a research design to test some hypothesis. The basis for Robin's idea stemmed from the job she held the past summer.

Robin began to describe her idea. "Last summer I worked as a clerk in the bookkeeping department of a bank. Sometimes it wasn't always clear how we should fill out certain reports and forms. I was always pretty reluctant to go to my supervisor, Mr. Kast, and ask for help. So were the other female workers. But I noticed the guys didn't seem to be reluctant at all to ask him for help. So I got this idea, see. I think females are more reluctant than males to ask a male superior for help."

"Okay," replied Julie. "So now you have to come up with a way to test that idea?"

"Right" said Robin. "I was thinking maybe I could make up a questionnaire and ask students in my class about it. I think people would know if they felt that way or not."

"Maybe so," Julie said, "but maybe they wouldn't want to admit it. You know, it could be one of those things that you either don't realize about yourself, or if you do, you just don't want to say so."

"Well, if I can't just ask people about it, maybe I could do some sort of experiment" Robin commented. "What if I gave students some tasks to do but the instructions weren't too clear. If I'm right, more males than females will ask a male experimenter for help."

"Do you think you'd get the opposite effect with a female experimenter?" asked Julie.

"You mean would more females than males ask a female experimenter for help? I don't know. Maybe" answered Robin.

"If that's the case", said Julie, "you might want to test both male and female experimenters with both male and female subjects."

Robin scratched some notes on a pad. Then she said, "Do you think an experimenter in a study is the same thing as a boss on a job? You see your boss every day, but you may only be in an experiment for about an hour. Maybe that would make a difference in whether or not you sought help."

"I'm sure it could" replied Julie. "I know I would act differently toward someone I might not see again than someone I'd have to work with a long time."

"I know what I'll do" Robin responded. "I won't do the experiment in a lab setting, but I'll go back to the company where I worked last summer. I'll ask the male and female office workers how they feel about asking Mr. Kast for help. I saw the way they acted last summer, and I'd bet they tell me the truth."

"Wait a minute" cautioned Julie. "Just because some females may be intimidated by Mr. Kast doesn't mean that effect holds for all male supervisors. Mr. Kast is just one man. How do you know it holds for all men? That's what you want to test, right?

Robin looked disconsolate. "There's got to be a good way to test this, although I guess its more complicated than I thought."

Questions

1. What research method should Robin use to test her idea, and how would you design the study?
2. What other variables might explain the employees' attitude toward Mr. Kast?
3. If this idea were tested with a questionnaire or sample survey, what questions should be asked?
4. If this idea were tested in a laboratory or field experiment, what variables should be eliminated or controlled for in the research design?

# REFERENCES

Argyris, C. Some unintended consequences of rigorous research. *Psychological Bulletin*, 1978, *70*, 185–197.

Bass, R. M., & Bass, R. Concern for the environment: Implications for industrial and organizational psychology. *American Psychologist*, 1976, *31*, 158–166.

Bobko, P., & Karren, R. The perception of Pearson product moment correlations from bivariate scatterplots. *Personnel Psychology*, 1979, *32*, 313–326.

Boehm, V. R. Research in the "real world"—A conceptual model. *Personnel Psychology*, 1980, *33*, 495–504.

Dipboye, R. L., & Flanagan, M. F. Research settings in industrial and organizational psychology. *American Psychologist*, 1979, *34*, 141–150.

Dunnette, M. D. Fads, fashions, and folderol in psychology. *American Psychologist*, 1966, *21*, 343–352.

*Ethical principles in the conduct of research with human participants.* Washington, D.C.: American Psychological Association, 1973.

Flanagan, J. C. A research approach to improving our quality of life. *American Psychologist*, 1978, *33*, 138–147.

Fromkin, H. L., & Streufert, S. Laboratory experimentation. In M. D. Dunnette (Ed.), *Handbook of industrial and organizational psychology*. Skokie, Ill.: Rand McNally, 1976.

Ghiselli, E. E. Some perspectives for industrial psychology. *American Psychologist*, 1974, *29*, 80–87.

Goodale, J. G., & Aagaard, A. K. Factors relating to varying reactions to the 4-day workweek. *Journal of Applied Psychology*, 1975, *60*, 33–38.

Gordon, M. E., Kleiman, L. S., & Hanie, C. A. Industrial-organizational psychology: Open thy ears O house of Israel. *American Psychologist*, 1978, *33*, 893–905.

Hegarty, W. H., & Sims, H. P., Jr. Some determinants of unethical decision behavior: An experiment. *Journal of Applied Psychology*, 1978, *63*, 451–457.

Jahoda, M. Work, employment, and unemployment: Values, theories, and approaches in social research. *American Psychologist*, 1981, *36*, 184–191.

Kaplan, A. *The conduct of inquiry*. New York: Harper & Row, 1964.

Kelman, H. C. The rights of the subject in social research: An analysis in terms of relative power and legitimacy. *American Psychologist*, 1972, *27*, 989–1016.

Latham, G. P., & Kinne, S. B. Improving job performance through training in goal setting. *Journal of Applied Psychology*, 1974, *59*, 187–191.

London, M., & Bray, D. W. Ethical issues in testing and evaluation for personnel decisions. *American Psychologist*, 1980, *35*, 890–901.

Mirvis, P. H., & Seashore, S. E. Being ethical in organizational research. *American Psychologist*, 1979, *34*, 766–780.

Muldrow, T. W., & Bayton, J. A. Men and women executives and processes related to decision accuracy. *Journal of Applied Psychology*, 1979, *64*, 99–106.

Stevens, S. Problems and methods of psychophysics. *Psychological Bulletin*, 1958, *55*, 177–196.

Stone, E. *Research methods in organizational behavior*. Santa Monica, Calif.: Goodyear Publishing, 1978.

Williams, L. K., Seybolt, J. W., & Pinder, C. C. On administering questionnaires in organizational settings. *Personnel Psychology*, 1975, *28*, 93–103.

Zelditch, M., & Hopkins, T. K. Laboratory experiments with organizations. In A. Etzioni (Ed.), *Complex organizations: A sociological reader*. New York: Holt, Rinehart, & Winston, 1961.

# section 2 Personnel psychology

# chapter 3

CRITERIA

Each time you evaluate someone or something, you use criteria. *Criteria* (the plural of *criterion*) are best defined as *evaluative standards;* they are used as reference points in making judgments. We may not be consciously aware of the criteria that affect our judgments, but they do exist. We use different criteria to evaluate different kinds of objects or people. That is, we use different standards to determine what makes a good (or bad) movie, dinner, ball game, friend, spouse, or teacher. In the context of I/O psychology, criteria are most important for defining the goodness of employees, programs, and units in the organization, as well as the organization itself.

## DISAGREEMENT AMONG PEOPLE IN MAKING EVALUATIONS

When you and some of your associates disagree in your evaluation of something, what is the cause? Chances are good the disagreement is caused by one of two types of criterion-related problems. For example, take the case of rating Professor Jones as a teacher. One student thinks he is a good teacher, while another disagrees. The first student defines "goodness in teaching" as (1) class preparedness, (2) course relevance, and (3) clarity of instruction. In the eyes of the first student, Jones scores very high on these criteria and receives a positive evaluation. The second student defines goodness as (1) enthusiasm, (2) capacity to inspire students, and (3) ability to relate to students on a personal basis. The second student scores Jones low on these criteria and thus gives him a negative evaluation. Why the disagreement? Because the two students have different criteria for defining teaching effectiveness.

Disagreements over the proper criteria in decision making are quite common. Values and tastes often dictate people's choices of criteria. For someone with limited funds, a good car may be one that gets high gas mileage. But for a wealthy person, the main criterion may be physical comfort. Dyer, Schwab, and Theriault (1976) describe how managers and their bosses disagree on the criteria used in giving raises. Managers feel their performance is not given enough weight while budgets are given too much weight. The authors feel that such disagreements over the right criteria can adversely affect employee motivation and satisfaction.

However, not all disagreements are caused by using different criteria. Suppose that in our example, both students define teaching effectiveness as preparedness, course relevance, and clarity of instruction. The first student thinks Professor Jones is ill prepared, teaches an irrelevant course, and gives unclear instructions. But the second student thinks he is well prepared, teaches a relevant course, and gives clear instruction. Both students are using the same evaluative standards, but they do not reach the same judgment. The difference of opinion in this case is due to the discrepancies in the meaning attached to Professor Jones' behavior. This discrepancy may be due to perceptual biases, differential expectations, or operational definitions associated with the criteria which cause the difference. Thus, people who use the same standards in making judgments do not always reach the same conclusion.

The profession of I/O psychology does not have a monopoly on criterion-related issues and problems. They occur in all walks of life, ranging from the criteria used to judge interpersonal relationships (e.g., communication, trust, respect) to the welfare of nations (e.g., literacy rates, per capita income, infant mortality rates). Since many important decisions are made on the basis of criteria, it would be difficult to overstate their significance in the decision-making process. Because criteria are used to render a wide range of judgments, I define them as the "evaluative standards by which objects, individuals, procedures, or collectivities are assessed for the purpose of ascertaining their quality." Criterion issues have major significance in the field of I/O psychology.

## THE ULTIMATE VERSUS ACTUAL CRITERIA

Psychologists did not always feel that criteria were of prime importance. Prior to World War II, they were inclined to believe that "criteria were either given of God or just to be found lying about" (Jenkins, 1946, p. 93). Unfortunately, this is not so. A lot of careful consideration must be given to what is meant by a "successful" worker, student, parent, etc. We cannot plunge headlong into measuring success, goodness, or quality until we have a fairly good idea as to what (in theory, at least) we should be looking for.

A good point to begin is with the notion of the *ultimate criterion*. The ultimate criterion is a theoretical construct, an abstract idea that can never actually be measured. It is an ideal set of factors that constitute a successful person (or object or collectivity) as conceived in the psychologist's mind. Let's say we want to define a successful college student. We might start off with *intellectual growth;* i.e., better students should experience more intellectual growth than lesser-quality students. Another dimension might be *emotional growth.* A college education should help students clarify their own values and beliefs, and this should aid in emotional development and stability. Finally, we might say that a good college student should want to have some voice in civic activities, to be a "good citizen," and to contribute to the well-being of the community of which he or she is a part. As an educated person, the good college student will assume an active role in helping to make society a better place in which to live. We might call this dimension a *citizenship* factor.

These three factors thus become the ultimate criteria for defining a "good college student." We could apply this same type of process to defining a "good worker," "good parent," or "good organization." However, because ultimate criteria are theoretical abstractions, we have to find some way to turn them into measurable, real factors. That is, we have to obtain *actual criteria* to serve as measures of the ultimate criteria we would prefer to (but can't) assess. The decision then becomes what variables will be selected as the actual criteria. A psychologist might choose grade-point as a measure of intellectual growth. Of course, a grade-point average is not *equivalent* to intellectual growth, but it probably reflects some degree of growth. To measure emotional growth, a psychologist might ask the student's advisor to judge how much the student has matured over his or her college career. Again, maturation is not exactly the same as emotional growth, but it is probably an easier concept to grasp and evaluate than the more abstract notion of emotional growth. Finally, as a measure of citizenship, a psychologist might count the number of volunteer organizations (e.g., student government, charitable clubs, etc.) the student has joined over his or her college career. It could again be argued that the sheer number (quantity) of joined organizations is not equivalent to the quality of participation in these activities, and that "good citizenship" is more appropriately defined by quality rather than quantity of participation. Nevertheless, because of the difficulties inherent in measuring quality of participation, plus the fact that one cannot speak of quality unless there is some quantity, the psychologist decides to use this measure. Table 3–1 shows the relationship between the ultimate criteria and actual criteria of success as a college student.

| Table 3–1 | Ultimate criteria and actual criteria of a successful college student |
|---|---|

| Ultimate criteria | Actual criteria |
|---|---|
| 1. Intellectual growth ——————→ | Grade point average |
| 2. Emotional growth —————————→ | Advisor rating of emotional maturity |
| 3. Citizenship ————————————→ | Number of volunteer organizations joined in college |

In *theory,* how do we define a "good" college student? Using the ultimate criteria as the evaluative standard, a good college student should have a high degree of intellectual and emotional growth and should be a responsible citizen in the community. In *practice,* how do we operationalize a good college student? Using the actual criteria as the evaluative standard, we say a good college student has earned high grades, is judged by an academic advisor to be emotionally mature, and has joined many volunteer organizations throughout his or her college career. In reviewing the relationship between the two sets of criteria (ultimate and actual), remember "the goal is to obtain an approximate estimate of the ultimate criterion by selecting one or more actual criteria which we think are appropriate" (Blum & Naylor, 1968, p. 176).

## CRITERION DEFICIENCY, RELEVANCE, AND CONTAMINATION

The relationship between the ultimate and actual criteria can be expressed in terms of three concepts: deficiency, relevance, and contamination. Figure 3–1 shows the degree of overlap between the ultimate and actual criteria. The circle represents the conceptual content of each type of criterion. Because the ultimate criterion is a theoretical abstraction, we can never know exactly how much overlap occurs. The actual criteria selected are never totally equivalent to the ultimate criteria we have in mind, so there will always be a certain amount (although unspecified) of deficiency, relevance, and contamination.

**Criterion deficiency.** Criterion deficiency is the degree to which the actual criteria fail to overlap the ultimate criteria; that is, how deficient the actual criteria are in representing the ultimate criteria. There is always some degree of deficiency in the actual criteria. By careful selection of the actual criteria, we can reduce (but never eliminate) criterion deficiency. Conversely, criteria that are selected because they are simply expedient, without much thought given to their match to the ultimate criteria, will be grossly deficient.

**Criterion relevance.** Criterion relevance is the degree to which the actual criteria and ultimate criteria coincide. The greater the match between the ultimate and actual criteria, the greater is the criterion relevance. Again, because the ultimate criteria are theoretical abstractions, we cannot know the exact amount of relevance.

**Figure 3-1**        **Criterion deficiency, relevance, and contamination**

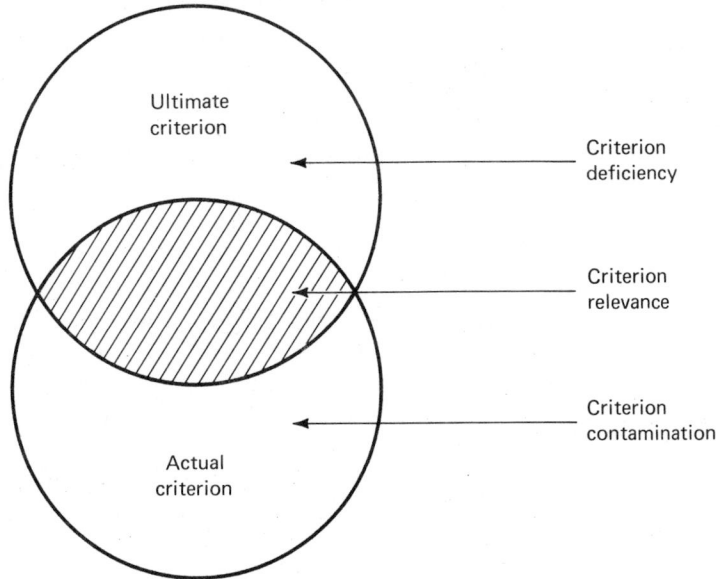

**Criterion contamination.** Criterion contamination is that part of the actual criteria which is unrelated to the ultimate criteria. It is the extent to which the actual criteria measure something other than the ultimate criteria. Contamination consists of two parts. One part, called *bias*, is the extent to which the actual criteria systematically or consistently measure something other than the ultimate criteria. The second part, called *error*, is the extent to which the actual criteria are not related to anything at all.

Both contamination and deficiency are undesirable in the actual criterion, and together they distort the ultimate criterion. This prompted Brogden and Taylor (1950b) to refer to them as *criterion distortion*. Criterion contamination distorts the actual criterion because certain factors are included that don't belong (i.e., they are not present in the ultimate criterion). Criterion deficiency distorts the actual criterion because certain important dimensions of the ultimate criterion are not included in the actual criterion.

Let's consider criterion deficiency and contamination in the example of setting criteria for a good college student. How might the actual criteria we chose be *deficient* in representing the ultimate criteria? Academic grades are a partially deficient measure of intellectual growth; the student might take easy courses and get high grades. Another student might take demanding courses that foster intellectual stimulation yet get only average grades. By using the grade-point average, we would conclude that the former student grew more intellectually. So the relationship between grades and intellectual growth is not perfect (i.e., it is deficient). A rating of emotional maturity by an academic advisor might be deficient because the advisor is not an ideal judge. He or she might have only a limited perspective of the student. Finally, it is not enough to just count how many volunteer groups a student belongs to. Quality of participation is as important (if not more so) than quantity.

How might these actual criteria be *contaminated?* If some academic majors are more difficult than others, grades will be a contaminated measure of intellectual growth; students in "easy" majors will be judged to have experienced more intellectual growth than students in difficult majors. This is a bias between earned grade-point averages and the difficulty of the student's academic major. The source of the bias effects the actual criterion (grades) but not the ultimate criterion (intellectual growth). A rating of emotional maturity by the student's advisor could be contaminated by the student's grades. The advisor might believe that students with higher grades have greater emotional maturity than students with low grades. Thus the grade-point average might bias an advisor's rating even though it probably has no relationship to the ultimate criterion of emotional growth. Finally, counting the number of organizations a student joins might be contaminated by the student's popularity. Students who join many organizations may simply be more popular rather than better citizens (which is what we wanted to measure.)

If we know that these criterion measures are contaminated in this way, why would we use them? In fact, when a researcher *knows* a certain form of contamination is present, its influence can be controlled through experimental or statistical procedures. The real problem lies in anticipating the occurrence of contaminating factors.

As Wallace (1965) has observed, psychologists have spent a great deal of time trying to discover new and better ways to measure actual criteria. Various analytical and computational procedures have been used to get more precise assessments. Rather than dwelling on finding new ways to measure an actual criterion, Wallace recommended that psychologists spend more time choosing actual criteria that are adequate measures of the ultimate criteria which are what we really seek to understand. The adequacy of the actual criterion as a measure of the ultimate criterion is always a matter of professional judgment—no equation or formula will determine the adequacy for us. As Wherry (1957) has said, "If we are measuring the wrong thing, it will not help us to measure it better" (p. 5).

## CRITERION DEVELOPMENT

I/O psychologists use several different means to identify or develop criteria. It is vital to determine the appropriate evaluative standards for making judgments. The adequacy and appropriateness of criteria set the limits for the quality of the judgments. Poor criteria beget poor judgments. But the issue of appropriate criteria is made more difficult by a time dimension. Short-term criteria for defining the goodness or quality of something may not be the same as long-term criteria. In deciding to buy a car, a short-term criterion may be initial cost; a long-term standard may be its resale value. Standards used to make short-term decisions about quality are *proximal* criteria. Standards used to make long-term decisions about quality are *distal* criteria. The following three studies of criterion development show different approaches to this topic.

Criterion may be developed *deductively* (from theory to data) or *inductively* (from data to theory). An example of the deductive approach was reported by Freeberg (1976). Freeberg wanted to define relevant criteria for judging the quality of youth work-training programs. The program's purpose was to train hard-to-employ teenagers in certain skills so they could get full-time jobs. Freeberg carefully examined the existing literature on training programs and arrived at 32 variables to indicate performance in the training program (proximal criteria). He found 40 variables to indicate post-program job performance (distal criteria). Trainees rated themselves on the 32 program-completion variables (e.g., their degree of vocational awareness and confidence, personal adjustment, and motivation). Former trainees who now held jobs rated themselves on the 40 post-program variables (e.g., their level of job performance, extent and level of employment, and vocational planning). A statistical procedure called *factor analysis* was used to identify the major dimensions of training and post-training success based on these ratings. The results showed that the 32 program-completion variables could be reduced to four major criteria of success in training: work motivation and social attitudes; social-community adjustment; training program adjustment; and competence in vocational planning. These four factors define the standards or the criteria for determining how well a person has done in the training program. The 40 post-program variables were reduced to five major criteria of success on the job: overall social and vocational adjustment; on-the-job success and satisfaction; job search motivation; competence in job planning; and short-range job orientation. These five factors represent the criteria for judging how well a person is doing on the job after training. This is a good example of the deductive approach to criterion development. It starts with a careful and rational identification of possible criterion variables, followed by an empirical assessment of their value.

Another example of using deduction to develop criteria was reported by Taber and Hackman (1976). These authors were interested in establishing the criteria of undergraduate college performance. Like Freeberg, they began their research with a rationally derived list of 67 aspects of student performance in college. The list covered both academic (e.g., general intelligence, analysis of ideas, etc.) and nonacademic (e.g., athletic involvement, participation in student organizations, etc.) areas. Faculty members and college students were asked to rate samples of "most successful" and "least successful" students on these variables. The purpose of the study was to determine what specific variables differentiate these two groups. Results showed that the criteria for success in college consisted of five academic factors (e.g., communication proficiency, career goals, etc.) and eight non-academic factors (e.g., ethical behavior, interpersonal sociability, personal growth, etc). The authors were able to establish that a "good" college student performs successfully in a number of specific academic and non-academic domains. In addition, both faculty members and students had similar views regarding the criteria of college success.

A study I conducted (Muchinsky, 1975b) is a final example of criterion development (in this case, the inductive approach). I was interested in establishing the criteria of consumer credit risk. I wanted to learn how people were judged to be good or poor credit risks. Unlike the two previous studies, I did not have any prior theoretical notions as to what constituted credit risk. I used the inductive approach, starting with data and culminating with some conceptual ideas, to establish the criteria of credit risk. I obtained the financial records of 500 people who had borrowed money from loan companies. Half of them were judged poor credit risks on the basis of how they repaid their loan, and the company would not grant them another loan. The other half were judged good credit risks on the basis of how they repaid the loan; they would be granted another loan by the company. I wanted to find out what aspects of loan repayment cause people to be judged good or bad credit risks. After comparing the two groups of people on several variables associated with loan repayment, I found two critical dimensions. These were how delinquent people were in making their monthly loan payments and whether they missed payments. Poor credit risks either missed several payments or were often late paying back the loan. So the concept of credit risk is defined by two criteria: missed payments and delinquency of payments. Working inductively, I then proposed an explanation of consumer credit risk (Muchinsky, 1975a).

What do we "do" with criteria once we have established them? They serve many purposes—both theoretical and applied. From a theoretical viewpoint, criteria are the basis for understanding a concept. In fact, the concept is best defined by the interrelationships among the criteria used to assess it. I was able to define the concept of credit risk after identifying its criterion dimensions. This procedure, called *construct validation*, will be discussed in more detail in a later chapter.

From a practical standpoint, the identification of criteria provides a rational basis for "treating" people, programs, or social collectivities. For example, as a loan company official, you would not give a loan to someone who has a history of missing payments or being delinquent. As a training program director, you would want the program to enhance trainee motivation and increase competence in vocational planning. As the director of a welfare agency, you would want to extend financial or medical aid to those communities at certain poverty or illness levels. Identifying criteria is the first step in initiating action (e.g., selecting, training, assisting, etc.) that is part of an organization's goals.

# JOB ANALYSIS

I/O psychologists often must identify the criteria of effective job performance. These criteria then become the basis to hire people (choose them on the basis of ability to meet the criteria of job performance), train them (to perform those aspects of the job that are important), pay them (high levels of performance should warrant higher pay), and classify jobs (jobs with similar performance criteria would be grouped together). A procedure useful in identifying the criteria or performance dimensions of a job is called *job analysis*.

Several authors (e.g., Nagle, 1953, Guion, 1961) have described how job analytic procedures may be used to develop criteria. After identifying the jobs to be analyzed, a job analysis dissects the work performed into component parts. A thorough job analysis will show the types of tasks that are performed on the job, the situation in which the work is performed (e.g., tools, equipment, working conditions), and the human qualities needed to perform the work. These data then provide the basic building blocks needed for many personnel decisions.

There are four major types of methods for analyzing jobs. The first type is a variation of an interview; employees are asked about the nature of their work. Employees may be interviewed individually, in small groups, or through a series of panel discussions. A second type uses structured questionnaires or inventories. Employees rate or describe their job by answering a series of questions about what activities are performed on the job, how often they are done, how important they are, etc. In a third technique, workers are observed as they perform their jobs, and information is recorded about the types of activities involved. Sometimes cameras or videotape equipment are used. The final type of procedure has workers record their own activities in a log book or work diary. The analyst then studies these books to infer the nature of the work performed. As a rule, variations of the interview and questionnaire methods are the most popular procedures. Though they differ in the quality of the information provided (Prien & Ronan, 1971), the methods are all useful for setting the criteria of job performance.

There is another distinction—"job-oriented" versus "worker-oriented" procedures. Job-oriented procedures normally study the tasks performed on the job and accordingly are referred to as "task analyses". Jobs are defined in terms of the tasks that are performed in them through the use of such job terminology as inspecting, repairing, hammering, etc. Figure 3–2 shows a task analysis inventory used in the Air Force. A worker-oriented procedure involves a study of the human behaviors that are performed on

**Figure 3–2**                    **Portion of a task analysis inventory for the Air Force**

| Listed below is a duty and the tasks which it includes. Check all tasks which you perform. Add any tasks you do which are not listed. Then rate the tasks you have checked.<br><br>A. Installing and removing aerial cable systems | Check √ if done | Time spent<br><br>1. Very much below average<br>2. Below average<br>3. Slightly below average<br>4. About average<br>5. Slightly above average<br>6. Above average<br>7. Very much above average | Importance<br><br>1. Extremely unimportant<br>2. Very unimportant<br>3. Unimportant<br>4. About medium importance<br>5. Important<br>6. Very important<br>7. Extremely important |
|---|---|---|---|
| 1. Attach suspension strand to pole. | | | |
| 2. Change and splice lasher wire. | | | |
| 3. Deliver materials to lineman with snatch block and handline. | | | |
| 4. Drill through-bolt holes and secure suspension clamps on poles. | | | |
| 5. Install cable pressurization systems. | | | |
| 6. Install distribution terminals. | | | |
| 7. Install pulling-in line through cable rings. | | | |
| 8. Load and unload cable reels. | | | |
| 9. Load lashing machine with lashing wire. | | | |

SOURCE: J. E. Morsh and W. B. Archer, *Procedural Guide for Conducting Occupational Surveys in the United States Air Force* (Lackland Air Force Base, Tex.: Personnel Research Laboratory, Aerospace Medical Division, September 1967).

the job, such as standing, sitting, talking, etc. Both of these procedures can be used to develop criteria. Job-oriented procedures define job success in terms of tasks performed; worker-oriented procedures define job success in terms of human attributes. Most job-oriented procedures have to be hand-made for each job to be analyzed because of the wide variation in jobs (McCormick, 1976). But worker-oriented procedures can use standardized questionnaires. One such worker-oriented procedure is the Position Analysis Questionnaire (McCormick, Jenneret, & Mecham, 1972). The Position Analysis Questionnaire (PAQ) consists of 189 statements used to describe the human attributes needed to perform a job. The statements are organized into six major categories of worker activity. Table 3–2 lists these categories along with examples of each category. A person called a *job analyst* uses the PAQ to analyze a job in terms of the worker activity involved. A job analysis does *not* indicate *how well* a person is performing the job (that procedure is *performance appraisal* and is the topic of Chapter 7). Likewise, a job analysis does *not* show how much money a given job is worth (that procedure is *job evaluation*). But job analytic information can help in appraising performance and evaluating jobs. A good job analytic procedure will yield accurate data regardless of who is doing the job or serving as the analyst. A study by Arvey, Passino, and Lounsbury (1977) showed that the PAQ gave job analytic information that was not strongly biased by either the sex of the employee or of the analyst. Similarly, Smith and Hakel (1979) found that samples of workers, supervisors, professional job analysts, and college students all arrived at comparable decisions about job content using the PAQ. These are highly desirable findings because job analytic methods should be sensitive to differences in jobs but insensitive to differences in people using the instrument.

A standardized technique like the PAQ can compare and contrast different jobs. It also permits grouping of jobs into similar clusters. Having clusters of like jobs helps determine wage rates, training needs, and other administrative functions. Indeed, Taylor (1978) reported that the PAQ helped reduce 76 insurance company jobs into six clusters based on similar performance criteria. Another example was reported by Arvey and Begalla

| Table 3–2 | Six major categories of the PAQ and illustrative job dimensions |
|---|---|

1. Information input:
   Visual input from devices/material
   Perceptual input from processes/events
2. Mental processes:
   Use of job-related knowledge
   Information processing
3. Work output:
   Control/equipment operation
   Use of foot controls
4. Relationships with other persons:
   Interpersonal communication
   Serving/entertaining
5. Job content:
   Unpleasant physical environment
   Hazardous physical environment
6. Other job characteristics:
   Job responsibility
   Work schedule

(1975). The authors analyzed the job of a homemaker and discovered that homemakers are often active physically and have to operate various pieces of equipment with hands and/or feet. The authors found that (on the basis of human attributes) the job of a homemaker is most like that of a patrol officer! Using a statistic called $D^2$ (a measure of similarity), the homemaker's job was compared to 20 other jobs. (See the results in Table 3–3.) The smaller the $D^2$ value, the more similar are the two jobs. A structured analysis of jobs can reveal similarities that are not apparent at first glance.

Still, the PAQ is not without some problems. Ash and Edgell (1975) reported that the PAQ requires reading ability between high school and college graduate level. This limits the type of people who could accurately use the procedure. Levine, Ash, and Bennett (1980) reported that users of the PAQ found it difficult to work with. They thought it gave less clear information than several other methods of job analysis. Finally, Cornelius, Carron, and Collins (1979) found some discrepancies between job clusters formed by the PAQ and other job analytic methods. Despite these problems (most involving user reaction), the PAQ has aided our understanding of jobs more than any other single job analytic method. Though complicated, it provides answers to some very complicated questions.

Another worker-oriented approach to job analysis can be seen in the *Dictionary of Occupational Titles* (DOT) (1977). The DOT describes many

**Table 3–3**                    **Jobs most similar to homemaker's job, based on similarity ($D^2$) scores**

| Job | $D^2$ |
|---|---|
| 1. Patrolman | 6.69 |
| 2. Home economist | 7.95 |
| 3. Airport maintenance chief | 9.96 |
| 4. Kitchen helper | 9.99 |
| 5. Fire fighter | 10.21 |
| 6. Trouble man | 10.23 |
| 7. Instrument-maker helper | 10.67 |
| 8. Electrician, foreman | 10.91 |
| 9. Maintenance foreman, gas plant | 11.12 |
| 10. Hydroelectric-machinery mechanic | 11.17 |
| 11. Transmission mechanic | 11.55 |
| 12. Lineman, repair | 12.25 |
| 13. Electric-meter repairman | 12.36 |
| 14. Instructor, vocational training | 12.43 |
| 15. Gas serviceman | 12.75 |
| 16. Inspector, motors and generators | 12.93 |
| 17. Lifeguard | 12.84 |
| 18. Fire captain | 13.05 |
| 19. Repairman, switch gear | 13.22 |
| 20. Home economist, consumer service | 13.47 |

SOURCE: R. D. Arvey and M. E. Begalla, "Analyzing the Homemaker Job Using the PAQ," *Journal of Applied Psychology* 60 (1975), p. 516.

jobs, each defined in terms of worker traits needed to perform the job. Eleven worker traits are given (e.g., intelligence, verbal ability, numerical ability, finger dexterity, motor coordination, etc.). The trait requirement ratings were made by job analysts who estimated how much of each of the 11 traits were needed on the job. The ratings were made on a five-point scale. They show the amount of each trait possessed by various segments of the working population, ranging from 1 (the top 10 percent of the population) to 5 (the lowest 10 percent). The jobs in the DOT are also described in terms of occupational groups based on similarity of job content.

The actual process of distilling criteria from job analysis data thus involves clustering similar work duties or attributes into criterion dimensions. Each cluster or group of work elements becomes the criteria to define success in that job. Using a job-oriented procedure, I studied an auto mechanic's job. I identified four criteria of job success: electrical, engine, transmission, and brake-repair work. The standards used to judge competence as an auto mechanic were performance in these four areas. Following Nagle's strategy of criteria development (1953), I then collected actual behavioral measures of the mechanic's performance on each of these four criteria. These measures included such variables as diagnosing mechanical problems, replacing damaged parts, and using tools. The criteria were later used (1) as a standard to hire future mechanics, (2) to appraise how well each mechanic was performing, and (3) to train apprentice mechanics. Note that there are many uses for the criteria developed from a job analysis.

## STANDARDS FOR CRITERIA

What should criteria be like? This listing by Blum and Naylor (1968) is most representative:

1. Reliable
2. Realistic.
3. Representative.
4. Related to other criteria.
5. Acceptable to the job analyst.
6. Acceptable to management.
7. Consistent from one situation to another.
8. Predictable.
9. Inexpensive.
10. Understandable.
11. Measurable.
12. Relevant.
13. Uncontaminated and bias-free.
14. Discriminatory.

This list might be reduced to three general factors; criteria must be appropriate, stable, and practical. The criteria should be relevant and representative of the job. They must endure over time or across situations. Finally, they should not be too expensive or hard to measure.

Other authors (e.g., Weitz, 1961) think other issues are important; e.g., the *time* when criterion measures are taken (after one month, six months on the job, etc.), the *type* of criterion measure taken (performance, errors, accidents, etc.), and the *level* of performance chosen to represent success or failure on the job (college students must perform at a C level before they can graduate). Weitz says the choice of criteria is usually determined either by history or precedent; but unfortunately, sometimes criteria are chosen because they are merely expedient or available.

# TYPES OF CRITERIA

Smith (1976) has documented several types of criteria that are used in I/O psychological research. She classifies criteria on the basis of whether they are "hard" or "soft." Hard criteria are taken from organizational records (payroll or personnel) and supposedly do not involve any type of subjective evaluation. "Soft" criteria are subjective evaluations of a person's performance (as a supervisor might render). While hard criteria may be devoid of subjective judgment, some degree of judgment must be applied to the hard criteria to give them meaning. Just knowing that an employee produced 18 units a day is not informative; this output must be compared with what other workers produce. If the average is 10 units a day, 18 units would clearly represent "good" performance. If the average is 25 units a day, 18 units is not good. Hard criteria appear to be objective, but some judgment is always involved. Soft criteria are judgmental.

## Hard criteria

**Production.**   Using units of production as criteria is most common in manufacturing jobs. If there is only one type of job in a whole organization, setting production criteria is easy. But in most companies, there are many types of production jobs, so productivity must be compared fairly. That is, if average productivity in one job is 6 units a day and in another job it's 300 units a day, productivity must be equated to compensate for these differences. Statistical procedures are usually used for this. The research of one psychologist (Harold Rothe) has focused on the production of various types of workers. Over the years, he has studied the work output of butter wrappers (Rothe, 1946), chocolate dippers (Rothe, 1951), welders (Rothe, 1970), coil winders (Rothe & Nye, 1958), machine operators (Rothe, 1947), and industrial employees (Rothe, 1978). His research has probably done more to increase understanding of production as a criterion of job performance than any other set of studies.

Other factors can diminish the value of production as a criterion of performance. In an assembly-line job, the speed of the line determines how many units get produced per day. Increasing the speed of the line increases production. Furthermore, everyone working on the line will have the same level of production. In a case like this, units of production are determined by factors outside the individual worker. So errors that *are* under the control of the worker may be measured as the criterion of job performance. However, this is no cure-all for the criterion problem either. Errors are not fair criteria if they are more likely in some jobs than others. Due to automation and work simplification, some jobs are almost "goof-proof". In such jobs, error-free work has nothing to do with the human factor.

**Salary.**    Salary has been used as a criterion of an employee's worth, but it is not a particularly "clean" measure of job performance. Salaries are based not only on job performance, but also on the value of the job to the organization. An efficient secretary earns less money than a poorly performing manager because managers (as a group) are paid more than secretaries (as a group).

One alternative is to make within-job comparisons; i.e., compare secretaries with each other, managers with each other, etc. The better performers should earn more money. But this approach also has its share of problems. While performance is a part of salary, it is not the only part. Seniority or tenure also affects salaries. Two equally performing managers may have different salaries if one has been on the job longer. Also some jobs have salary limits; no matter how well the person performs or how long they have been on the job, their salary cannot exceed a certain level. These problems limit the usefulness of salary as a criterion. But it can be used if statistical controls or corrections are used to account for some of the non-performance-based variations (e.g., Hulin, 1962).

**Job level and promotions.**    Supposedly, the more promotions people have, the better they are performing. But people get promoted for reasons other than good performance, and not all good performers get promoted. There may be "political" reasons (the worker is the son or daughter of the company president), seniority (everyone gets advanced after four years in the same job), as well as reasons relating to the organization's structure. Some organizations have "tall" structures; i.e., there are many different jobs between the lowest and highest levels. Thus, there are many possibilities for promotion. Other organizations have a "flat" structure, with few jobs between the top and bottom. Most college professors can only be promoted twice in their careers because there are only three job levels for them to be in: assistant, associate, and full professor. Promotions are best used as a criterion of job performance in companies where there is ample opportunity for promotions. Promotions are most often used as criteria for managerial and administrative personnel.

**Sales.**    Performance through sales is a commonly used criterion for wholesale and retail sales work. But there are a number of variations that must be considered. Using the sheer *number* of sales as a criterion is appropriate only if everyone is selling the same product(s) in comparable territories. A person who sells toothbrushes should sell more units than a person who sells houses. Also, someone selling tractors in Iowa should sell more than a person whose sales territory is Rhode Island. Not only is Iowa bigger than Rhode Island, but more farming is done proportionately in Iowa than in Rhode Island.

Total sales volume is equally fallible as a criterion. A real estate salesperson can sell a $100,000 house in one afternoon, but how long would it take to sell $100,000 worth of toothbrushes? The solution to these types of problems is to use norm groups to judge success. A real estate salesperson should be compared to other real estate salespersons in the same sales territory. The same holds for other sales work. If comparisons have to be drawn across sales territories or across product lines, statistical adjustments are needed. Ideally, any differences in sales performance would then be due to the ability of the salesperson, which is the basis for using sales as a criterion of job performance.

**Tenure or turnover.** Length of service is a very popular criterion in I/O psychological research. Turnover not only has a theoretical appeal (i.e., Mobley, Griffeth, Hand, & Meglino, 1979), but it is also a practical concern. Employers want to hire people who will stay with the company. Muchinsky and Tuttle (1979) reviewed over 100 studies that tried to predict (by a variety of means) what types of people are likely to quit. Voluntary employee turnover is related to individual personality as well as characteristics of the organization. But it is highly related to such economic factors as the availability of other jobs (Muchinsky & Morrow, 1980). For obvious, practical reasons, employers don't want to hire the chronic job hoppers. The costs of recruiting, selecting, and training new hires can be extremely high. Turnover is perhaps the most frequently used nonperformance criterion in the psychological literature. There appears to be no consistent relationship between those people who quit and their job performance (i.e., good performers quit as often as poor ones). But turnover is a valuable and useful criterion because it measures stability, and this can be as important to the company as performance.

**Absences.** Absence from work, like turnover, is an index of employee stability. While some degree of employee turnover is good for organizations, employee absenteeism always has bad consequences (Muchinsky, 1979). While there is no established relationship between absenteeism and productivity, absenteeism is often used as a criterion of job performance. Indeed, excessive absenteeism can be grounds for dismissal. Many companies try absence-reduction techniques (Pedalino & Gamboa, 1974) before taking the more drastic step of firing an employee. Also, since drug and alcohol abuse (Maxwell, 1959) are frequent causes of absenteeism, some companies sponsor counseling programs to help employees deal with their addiction.

Muchinsky (1977) and Steers and Rhodes (1978) have reviewed many studies on why people are absent from work. A consistent predictor of absenteeism was the extent to which people liked their work. Feelings of job satisfaction were negatively correlated with absenteeism (typical correlations being around −.30). Companies that provide more interesting and stimulating jobs reap the benefits of reduced absenteeism. Absenteeism is a pervasive problem in industry; it costs employers billions of dollars a year in decreased efficiency and increased benefit payments (e.g., sick leave) and payroll costs. A British psychologist (Nigel Nicholson) has conducted some of the best research on the causes of absenteeism and has proposed a theory to explain it (Nicholson, 1977). Absenteeism has social, individual, and organizational causes, and the results of absenteeism affect individuals, companies, and even entire industrial societies. Absenteeism is increasing (both nationally and internationally), so its importance as a criterion of job performance will increase in the years to come.

**Accidents.** Accidents are sometimes used as a criterion of job performance, though they have a number of limitations. First, they are mainly used as a measure for blue-collar jobs. (While white-collar workers can be injured at work, the frequency of such accidents is small.) So accidents are a measure of job performance for only a limited sample of employees. Second, accidents are hard to predict, and there is little stability or consistency in their occurrence. Third, accidents can be measured in many ways— number of accidents per hours worked, miles driven, trips taken, etc. Depending upon how accident statistics are calculated, different conclusions can be drawn. Employers don't want to hire people who, for whatever reason, would incur job-related accidents. But in the total picture of job performance, accidents are not used as a criterion as often as production, turnover, or absence.

## Soft criteria

Soft criteria refer to judgments made of an employee's performance. The judgment is usually a rating or ranking. For example, a supervisor might rate the employees in a department on the basis of overall effectiveness. This rating would then be the standard of job performance. Supervisor ratings are by far the most frequently used judgmental criteria. A study by Lent, Aurbach, and Levin (1971) reported that of the 1,505 criteria used in over 400 studies, 897 were supervisory ratings. But ratings may also be supplied by peers, subordinates, and the workers themselves. The ratings may be on a general factor, such as overall effectiveness, or specific factors, such as quantity of work, quality of work, creativity, practical judgment, etc. Many ratings judge performance on several factors (both general and specific). Some studies have even compared judgments made by two or

Sometimes the criterion of success is very straightforward. In marksmanship, the closer the bullets come to hitting the center of the bullseye, the better the performance.

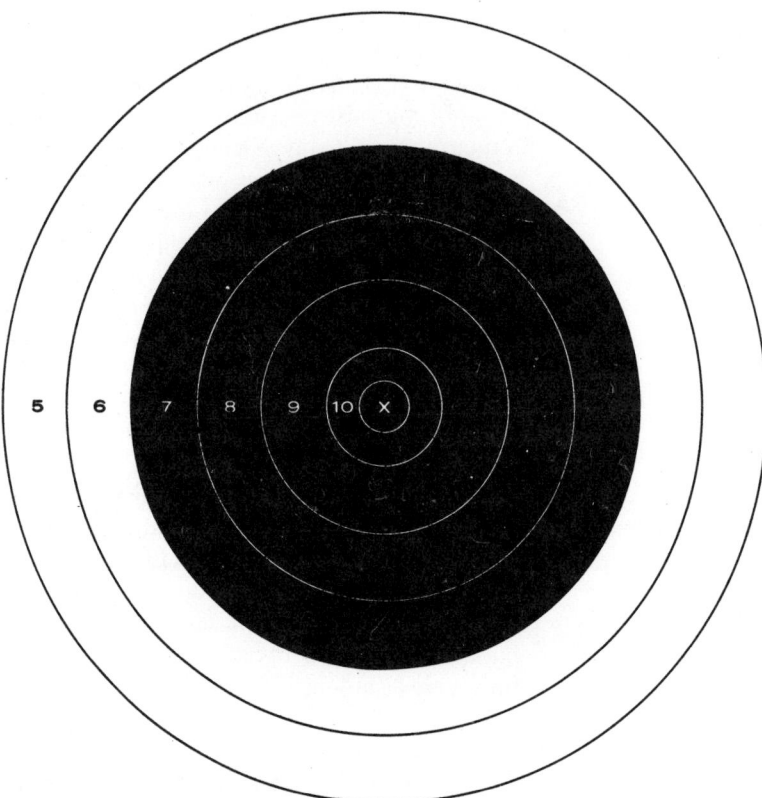

**NATIONAL RIFLE ASSOCIATION**

**OFFICIAL 50 YD. SMAI    BORE RIFLE TARGET**

FOR PRACTICE ONLY.   NOT FOR RECORD FIRING.

THIS TARGET IS OFFICIAL IN ALL DIMENSIONS BUT IS FOR PRACTICE ONLY.  FOR ALL OFFICIAL NATIONAL RIFLE ASSOCIATION COMPETITIONS, THE OFFICIAL N.  R. A.  TARGET CONTAINING 2 BULLS AND LITHOGRAPHED ON SPECIAL TAGBOARD, TO-GETHER WITH A BACKING TARGET IN A DOUBLE TARGET FRAME MUST BE USED.

SHOTS TOUCHING A SCORING RING
RECEIVE THE HIGHER VALUE.
SHOTS OUTSIDE OF SCORING RING
ARE SCORED AS MISSES.

COMPETITOR _____

LICENSE NO. 17          Mfg. By
                                          Outers Laboratories, Inc.
                                          ONALASKA, WIS.

NONE OFFICIAL
WITHOUT THIS SEAL

OFFICIAL

REGISTERED
U. S. PATENT OFFICE

A-9

more sets of raters (e.g., supervisors and peers) who evaluate several dimensions of behavior (Lawler, 1967). Such studies normally show that certain raters are more consistent in rating certain aspects of job performance. (Supervisors may agree in rating quality of work while peers agree in rating interpersonal relations.) A later chapter on performance appraisal will discuss this issue in greater detail.

Because judgmental criteria are used so often, a great deal of attention has been given to improving the quality of these judgments. If those people doing the judging don't know how to make such decisions, the quality of their decisions will be very low. Spool (1978) reviewed the research on training people to make more accurate judgments of behavior. He found that people can indeed learn to be accurate evaluators. People who are more involved and interested in evaluating behavior make more careful and accurate judgments. Research (e.g., Pursell, Dossett, & Latham, 1980) has revealed that a one-day training program can greatly enhance people's skills in observing and interpreting behavior.

From this discussion, it is clear that no single measure of job performance is totally adequate. While each criterion may have merit, it can also suffer from weakness along other dimensions. For instance, while few people would say that an employee's absence has *no* bearing on overall job performance, no one would say that absence is a *complete* measure of job performance. Absence, like production or job level, is but one piece of the broader picture. Readers should not be discouraged that no one criterion meets all our standards. It is precisely because job performance is multidimensional (and each single dimension is a fallible index of overall performance) that we are compelled to include many relevant aspects of work in establishing criteria.

## RELATIONSHIP AMONG JOB PERFORMANCE CRITERIA

While several job performance criteria can be identified for many jobs, the various criteria frequently assess different aspects of performance on the job. Job performance criteria are usually independent of each other. If they were all highly positively correlated with each other, say $r = .80$ or $r = .90$, there would be no point in measuring them all. Knowing an employee's status on one criterion would give his or her status on the others. Several studies have tried to identify interrelationships among the criteria. Studies by Turner (1960), Seashore, Indik, and Georgopoulos (1960), and Ronan (1963) revealed multiple job performance criteria and also showed that the criteria were relatively independent of each other. For example Seashore et al. studied 975 deliverymen on whom five job performance criteria were available. The criteria were: productivity (objectively measured by time standards), effectiveness (subjective ratings based on quality

Table 3–4

**Intercorrelations among five criterion variables for 975 deliverymen**

|  | Productivity | Accidents | Absences | Errors |
|---|---|---|---|---|
| Effectiveness ......... | .28 | −.02 | −.08 | −.32 |
| Productivity .......... |  | .12 | −.01 | −.26 |
| Accidents ........... |  |  | .03 | −.18 |
| Absences ........... |  |  |  | .15 |

SOURCE: Adapted from S. E. Seashore, B. P. Indik, and B. S. Georgopoulos, "Relationship among Criteria of Job Performance," *Journal of Applied Psychology* 44 (1960), pp. 195–202.

of performance), accidents, unexcused absences, and errors (based on the number of packages not delivered). The correlations among these five criteria are shown in Table 3–4. The data show that the five criteria are relatively independent of each other. The largest correlations were found among the variables of productivity, effectiveness, and errors (.28, −.26 and −.32). These results show that there really is no single measure of overall performance on the job; each criterion measures a different facet.

There is also a relationship between job level and the number of criteria needed to define job performance. Lower-level, relatively simple jobs do not have many dimensions of performance; more complex jobs have many. In fact, the number of job performance criteria can separate simple jobs from complex ones. Manual laborers who unload trucks might be measured by only three criteria: attendance (they have to show up for work), errors (they have to know how to stack the material), and speed. More complex jobs, as in the medical field (e.g. Taylor, Price, Richards, & Jacobsen, 1964, 1965), might be defined by as many as 15 independent criteria. The more complex the job, the more criteria are needed to define it and the more skill or talent a person has to have to be successful.

When a researcher collects criterion data on several aspects of job performance, it is common to have a mix of objective and subjective criteria. As was done by Seashore et al. (1960), intercorrelations are then computed. Sometimes this analysis is conducted separately for various subgroups of employees to see if there are differences among the criterion interrelationships. Bass and Turner (1973) conducted such a study. They found the employee's race greatly determined the relationships among the criterion dimensions. The study was done in a bank, and the subjects were black and white tellers. There were two objective criteria of performance for each teller: the number of shortages (having less cash in their drawer than they should) and overages (having more cash in their drawer than they should). Two subjective criteria of performance were also recorded: supervisor ratings of work quality and overall effectiveness. The relationship between the subjective and objective criteria were computed separately for each race. The results are reported in Table 3–5. Note that there is a much stronger relationship between the objective performance of *black* bank tell-

Table 3–5 **Correlations between supervisor ratings of performance and two objective criteria of performance for samples of black and white bank tellers**

|  | Supervisor ratings for black employees | | Supervisor ratings for white employees | |
| --- | --- | --- | --- | --- |
|  | Quality of work | Overall effectiveness | Quality of work | Overall effectiveness |
| Number of shortages . . . . . . . . . | −.62 | −.46 | −.22 | −.10 |
| Number of overages . . . . . . . . . | −.48 | −.36 | −.11 | −.11 |

SOURCE: A. R. Bass and J. N. Turner, "Ethnic Group Differences in Relationships among Criteria of Job Performance," *Journal of Applied Psychology* 57 (1973), pp. 101–109.

ers and supervisory ratings of their performance. For white tellers, the two types of criteria are more independent. Bass and Turner reasoned that the supervisors (who were white) tried to be "fair" in evaluating black tellers so they based their ratings heavily on the objective aspects of their job performance. But in evaluating white tellers, the supervisors gave them the benefit of the doubt and rated them on other aspects of their performance. This is an example of *criterion bias;* all the dimensions of overall job performance do not have the same weight for black and white employees. While some studies (e.g., Cascio & Valenzi, 1978) do not report such racial bias, the criteria of job success are not always uniformly applied to all types of people in the same job.

# COMPOSITE VERSUS MULTIPLE CRITERIA

There has been a long-running controversy in I/O psychology. Should criteria of job performance somehow be added together to yield a single performance score? Or should they remain as separate indicators of performance? Backers of the former believe in the *composite criterion* approach. Those who advocate the latter follow the *multiple criteria* approach. Each approach has merit, and only recently has a resolution been proposed.

**Composite criteria.** The composite criterion is the oldest approach to criterion conceptualization. Its premise is that the criterion should measure a person's "overall success" or "value to the organization." Advocates of composite criterion argue that a single index or number is needed to compare and make decisions about individuals (Toops, 1944; Thorndike, 1949). They argue that the criteria that define job performance (however many there are) must be combined in some way. Also, the various criterion elements should be weighted so that their difference in importance can be recognized. A student's grade-point average is a good example of a weighted composite criterion. The criterion elements for a student are the courses he or she is taking. Performance on these dimensions is measured by grades (A = 4.0, B = 3.0, etc.). The courses are "weighted" according to the number of credit hours each is worth. Let's say a student has taken four courses:

economics, psychology, art, and physical education. The credit hours for these courses are 4, 3, 3, and 1, respectively. The grades received are A, B, C, and D, respectively. The student's grade-point average (GPA) is:

GPA = Credit hours (economics grade) + Credit hours (psychology grade) + Credit hours (art grade) + Credit hours (physical education grade) / Total credit hours..
= 4 (4.0) + 3 (3.0) + 3 (2.0) + 1 (1.0)/11
= 2.91

The GPA of 2.91 would then be used to assess this person's "success" as a student. It may also be used as a basis for considering membership in an academic society, receipt of a scholarship, admission to graduate school, etc.

Weighting courses according to credit hours is relatively straightforward. However, in industry the weighting issue is not so clear-cut. If all the elements are equally important for job success, they all get the same weight, called *unit* weights. If the elements have different importance, they are weighted differentially. Various statistical procedures have been proposed to determine what the weights should be. The most elegant and sophisticated procedure has been proposed by Brogden and Taylor (1950a). They state that since employees work to enhance the economic standing of the organization, "the criterion should measure the contribution of the individual to the overall efficiency of the organization." They recommend that such contributions be measured in terms of dollars and cents by applying cost-accounting procedures to the employee's job behaviors. Thus, the weights for the criterion elements are dollar values; the more valuable elements (to the organization) receive a higher dollar weight. While such a procedure is workable in theory, it is extremely difficult to calculate the dollar value of some criterion elements.

So the advocates of the composite criterion favor it for practical purposes in making decisions about employees. The issue about weighting is concerned with making more accurate decisions on the basis of having more precise information.

**Multiple criteria.** The advocates of the multiple criteria approach base their arguments on two points. First, they argue that if the dimensions of job performance are relatively independent, they cannot be added up to form a composite (Ghiselli, 1956; Dunnette, 1963). A worker who has perfect attendance but makes a tremendous amount of errors in production cannot fairly be called an "average" worker. They say that a composite can be formed only when there are high positive intercorrelations among the criterion elements (thus indicating that a single dimension underlies performance). But the bulk of research shows that criteria rarely have a stable, unidimensional basis (Ghiselli & Haire, 1960; Bass, 1962). In response to this position, composite criterion advocates argue that despite the lack of statistical similarity among the criterion elements, when the elements are all relevant measures of economic variables, they can be combined into a composite without regard to their intercorrelations (Brogden & Taylor, 1950a).

The second argument in favor of multiple criteria is that when you lump all the criterion elements into a composite score, you lose understanding of the factors that contribute to job success. Since there are many ways a person can achieve a certain level of job proficiency (e.g., a C-average student can earn all C's or half A's and half F's), it is hard to separate a composite criterion into its various parts. Therefore, the best way to understand the ingredients of successful job performance is to keep the criteria separate to begin with.

**Resolution of the controversy.**   Schmidt and Kaplan (1971) proposed a resolution (of sorts) to the problem of composite versus multiple criteria. They argue that the selection of composite or multiple criteria should depend on their intended use. If the goal is a practical one (as in making personnel decisions), Schmidt and Kaplan advocate a weighted composite criterion. The criterion elements are weighted and added together to derive a composite value representing the overall value of the worker. However, if the goal is to *understand* the dimensions of job performance and how they contribute to job success, then multiple criteria should be used.

The basis for the resolution is in how the criterion will be used, and in many cases, both forms are helpful. If we want to promote the employee who is performing "best" on the job, a composite criterion will assess who is the "best". If we want to train people to improve their job performance in deficient areas, multiple criteria will help spot those areas. But the composite criterion approach is not without problems, even in cases of making personnel decisions. There can be the problem of compensating criteria. If two criteria of success as a brain surgeon are visual acuity and finger dexterity, a person with the eyes of a hawk who is all thumbs just won't do. In statistically computing a composite criterion, superior visual acuity may compensate for a lack of finger dexterity. But in actual practice, high score on one cannot make up for a deficiency in the other. In such a case, an alternative procedure would be needed to set minimal levels of performance on *each* criterion dimension. This point will be discussed again in the chapter on personnel decision.

## CONCLUDING COMMENTS

The issue of criteria in I/O psychology is complex and important. Nagle (1953) feels that the quality of research is only as good as the criteria. I agree. The perceptive reader will note that many of the references in this chapter are from the 1950s and 60s. The criterion problems and issues that confronted psychologists then continue to do so today. The quality of our judgments is only as good as the evaluative standards we use to make those judgments. If our goal is to improve the quality of the educational process as shown by the number of students elected to Phi Beta Kappa (a scholastic honorary), we could lower admission standards to this honorary. However, we are only deluding ourselves.

While new ways of thinking about criterion problems occasionally come along (e.g., James, 1973), students today still must understand the same criterion issues as their counterparts did many years ago. An understanding of criteria and their related problems is basic to I/O psychology.

# CASE STUDY

A panel of three high school teachers at Rippowam High School had been convened by the principal to make a most important decision. A local company was willing to award a $10,000 college scholarship to "the most outstanding senior" in the class, with the recipient to be determined by the high school. Walter Plant, Sandra Meltzer, and Jerry Driscoll were given the assignment to select the scholarship recipient. They agreed to meet at 2:30 to discuss their assignment.

Driscoll opened the meeting: "I wish we had more to go on than what they gave us. A student can be *outstanding* in many ways."

"Well, I assume grades are the most important factor," said Meltzer. "Why don't we start out with the ranking of all students based upon their grade-point averages. I'd be hard pressed to award $10,000 to any student other than the class valedictorian."

"I don't think its that easy," continued Plant. "I am far more impressed with a student who gets a B+ in honors physics than someone who gets an A in basketweaving. While a student's grade-point average is certainly a good measure of their academic accomplishments, it's tainted by the difficulty of the courses taken."

"That's not the only problem with the grade-point average," Driscoll warned. "I've got some students in my homeroom who will graduate with the minimum number of hours, and I've got some others who branched out and took more than the minimum. I think we should give some consideration to the total number of hours taken in the curriculum."

A deep frown appeared on Plant's face. "I don't see why we should penalize the student who did only what was required by the school. We specify what is needed for graduation, and the students have to comply. While I never discourage a student from sticking to the minimum, I don't think we should devalue their performance for having done so."

"Maybe we're getting too hung up with grades and hours," said Meltzer. "Suzanne Millord won first prize in the regional science fair competition. Shouldn't something like that count too? I'm more impressed with that than an A in any class."

"You know," Plant commented, "we are forgetting about some other things too. How about civic activities, as participation in student government or interest clubs. We encourage student involvement in these activities to make for a more well-rounded education. I don't feel we should ignore them when it comes time to make an award."

"I feel those activities have their own rewards," said Driscoll. "We want to give this scholarship to the best student, not the most socially active one."

"While we're at it," mused Plant, "how about athletic participation? We also stress physical education as well as social and intellectual development. Maybe we should also include interscholastic athletics. We've got some outstanding athletes in this school, and whose to say that 'most outstanding' can't be defined in terms of athletics."

"I hardly think this was designed to be an athletic scholarship," Meltzer grumbled. "If you want to make it more complicated, why not throw in financial need; $10,000 is a lot of money, and some families could use it more than others."

Driscoll stared out the window. He knew it would be a long afternoon.

Questions

1.  What do you think the ultimate criteria should be in making a scholarship determination?
2.  What are some sources of criterion deficiency and contamination in the actual criteria being discussed by the teachers?
3.  Would the criteria for selecting the "most outstanding student" be more biased or less biased by inclusion of financial need? Why?
4.  Do you think its more difficult to identify what the appropriate criteria are or to determine how to weight the criteria once they have been identified? Why?
5.  If you had been invited to this meeting, what suggestions would you make to help the teachers reach a decision?

# REFERENCES

Arvey, R. D., & Begalla, M. E. Analyzing the homemaker job using the PAQ. *Journal of Applied Psychology*, 1975, *60*, 513–517.

Arvey, R. D., Passino, E. M., & Lounsbury, J. W. Job analysis results as influenced by sex of incumbent and sex of analyst. *Journal of Applied Psychology*, 1977, *62*, 411–416.

Ash, R. A., & Edgell, S. L. A note on the readability of the PAQ. *Journal of Applied Psychology*, 1975, *60*, 765–766.

Bass, A. R., & Turner, J. N. Ethnic group differences in relationships among criteria of job performance. *Journal of Applied Psychology*, 1973, *57*, 101–109.

Bass, B. M. Further evidence on the dynamic character of criteria. *Personnel Psychology*, 1962, *15*, 93–97.

Blum, M. L., & Naylor, J. C. *Industrial psychology: Its theoretical and social foundations*. New York: Harper & Row, 1968.

Brogden, H. E., & Taylor, E. K. The dollar criterion—applying the cost accounting concept to criterion construction. *Personnel Psychology*, 1950, *3*, 133–154. (a)

Brogden, H. E., & Taylor, E. K. The theory and classification of criterion bias. *Educational and Psychological Measurement*, 1950, *10*, 159–186. (b)

Cascio, W. F., & Valenzi, E. R. Relations among criteria of police performance. *Journal of Applied Psychology*, 1978, *63*, 22–28.

Cornelius, E. T., Carron, T. J., & Collins, M. N. Job analysis models and job classification. *Personnel Psychology*, 1979, *32*, 693–708.

Dunnette, M. D. A note on *the* criterion. *Journal of Applied Psychology*, 1963, *47*, 251–254.

Dyer, L., Schwab, D. P., & Theriault, R. D. Managerial perceptions regarding salary increase criteria. *Personnel Psychology*, 1976, *29*, 233–242.

Freeberg, N. E. Criterion measures for youth-work training programs: The development of relevant performance dimensions. *Journal of Applied Psychology*, 1976, *61*, 537–545.

Ghiselli, E. E. Dimensional problems of criteria. *Journal of Applied Psychology*, 1956, *40*, 1–4.

Ghiselli, E. E., & Haire, M. The validation of selection tests in the light of the dynamic character of criteria. *Personnel Psychology*, 1960, *13*, 225–231.

Guion, R. M. Criterion measurement and personnel judgment. *Personnel Psychology*, 1961, *14*, 141–149.

Hulin, C. L. The measurement of executive success. *Journal of Applied Psychology*, 1962, *46*, 303–306.

James L. R. Criterion models and construct validity for criteria. *Psychological Bulletin*, 1973, *80*, 75–83.

Jenkins, J. G. Validity for what? *Journal of Consulting Psychology*, 1946, *10*, 93–98.

Lawler, E. E., III. The multitrait-multirater approach to measuring managerial job performance. *Journal of Applied Psychology*, 1967, *51*, 369–381.

Lent, R. H., Aurbach, H. H., & Levin, L. S. Predictors, criteria, and significant results. *Personnel Psychology*, 1971, *24*, 519–533.

Levine, E. L., Ash, R. A., & Bennett, N. Exploratory comparative study of four job analysis methods. *Journal of Applied Psychology*, 1980, *65*, 524–535.

Maxwell, M. A study of absenteeism, accidents, and sickness payments in problem drinkers in one industry. *Quarterly Journal of Studies on Alcohol*, 1959, *20*, 302–308.

McCormick, E. J. Job and task analysis. In M. D. Dunnette (Ed.), *Handbook of industrial and organizational psychology*. Skokie, Ill.: Rand McNally, 1976.

McCormick, E. J., Jenneret, P. R. & Mecham, R. C. A study of job characteristics and job dimensions as based on the Position Analysis Questionnaire (PAQ). *Journal of Applied Psychology*, 1972, *56*, 347–368.

Mobley, W. H., Griffeth, R. W., Hand, H. H. & Meglino, B. M. Review and conceptual analysis of the employee turnover process. *Psychological Bulletin*, 1979, *86*, 493–522.

Morsh, J. E. & Archer, W. B. *Procedural guide for*

**93**

*conducting occupational surveys in the United States Air Force*. Lackland Air Force Base, Tex.: Personnel Research Laboratory, Aerospace Medical Division, PRL–TR–67–11, September 1967.

Muchinsky, P. M. A comparison of three analytic techniques in predicting consumer installment credit risk: Toward understanding a construct. *Personnel Psychology*, 1975, *28*, 511–524. (a)

Muchinsky, P. M. Consumer installment credit risk: A need for criterion refinement and validation. *Journal of Applied Psychology*, 1975, *60*, 87–93. (b)

Muchinsky, P. M. Employee absenteeism: A review of the literature. *Journal of Vocational Behavior*, 1977, *10*, 316–340.

Muchinsky, P. M. Human resource management of employee absenteeism. In V. V. Veysey and G. S. Hall, Jr. (Eds.), *The new world of managing human resources*. Burbank, Calif.: North Hollywood Printing, 1979.

Muchinsky, P. M., & Morrow, P. C. A multidisciplinary model of voluntary employee turnover. *Journal of Vocational Behavior*, 1980, *17*, 263–290.

Muchinsky, P. M. & Tuttle, M. L. Employee turnover: An empirical and methodological assessment. *Journal of Vocational Behavior*, 1979, *14*, 43–77.

Nagle, B. F. Criterion development. *Personnel Psychology*, 1953, *6*, 271–289.

Nicholson, N. Absence behavior and attendance motivation: A conceptual synthesis. *Journal of Management Studies*, 1977, *14*, 213–252.

Pedalino, E., & Gamboa, V. U. Behavior modification and absenteeism: Intervention in one industrial setting. *Journal of Applied Psychology*, 1974, *59*, 694–698.

Prien, E. P., & Ronan, W. W. Job analysis: A review of research findings. *Personnel Psychology*, 1971, *24*, 371–396.

Pursell, E. D., Dossett, D. L., & Latham, G. P. Obtaining valid predictors by minimizing rating errors in the criterion. *Personnel Psychology*, 1980, *33*, 91–96.

Ronan, W. W. A factor analysis of eleven job performance measures. *Personnel Psychology*, 1963, *16*, 255–267.

Rothe, H. F. Output rates among butter wrappers: I. Work curves and their stability. *Journal of Applied Psychology*, 1946, *30*, 199–211.

Rothe, H. F. Output rates among machine operators: I. Distributions and their reliability. *Journal of Applied Psychology*, 1947, *31*, 484–489.

Rothe, H. F. Output rates among chocolate dippers. *Journal of Applied Psychology*, 1951, *35*, 94–97.

Rothe, H. F. Output rates among welders: Productivity and consistency following removal of a financial incentive system. *Journal of Applied Psychology*, 1970, *54*, 549–551.

Rothe, H. F. Output rates among industrial employees. *Journal of Applied Psychology*, 1978, *63*, 40–46.

Rothe, H. F., & Nye, C. T. Output rates among coil winders. *Journal of Applied Psychology*, 1958, *42*, 182–186.

Schmidt, F. L., & Kaplan, L. B. Composite vs. multiple criteria: A review and resolution of the controversy. *Personnel Psychology*, 1971, *24*, 419–434.

Seashore, S. E., Indik, B. P., & Georgopoulos, B. S. Relationship among criteria of job performance. *Journal of Applied Psychology*, 1960, *44*, 195–202.

Smith, J. E., & Hakel, M. D. Covergence among data sources, response bias, and reliability and validity of a structured job analysis questionnaire. *Personnel Psychology*, 1979, *32*, 677–692.

Smith, P. C. Behavior, results, and organizational effectiveness: The problem of criteria. In M. D. Dunnette (Ed.), *Handbook of industrial and organizational psychology*. Skokie, Ill.: Rand McNally, 1976.

Spool, M. D. Training programs for observers of behavior: A review. *Personnel Psychology*, 1978, *31*, 853–888.

Steers, R. M., & Rhodes, S. R. Major influences on employee attendance: A process model. *Journal of Applied Psychology*, 1978, *63*, 391–407.

Taber, T. D., & Hackman, J. D. Dimensions of undergraduate college performance. *Journal of Applied Psychology*, 1976, *61*, 546–558.

Taylor, C. W., Price, P. B., Richards, J. M., & Jacobsen, T. L. An investigation of the criterion problem for a medical school faculty. *Journal of Applied Psychology*, 1964, *48*, 294–301.

Taylor, C. W., Price, P. B., Richards, J. M., & Jacobsen, T. L. An investigation of the criterion problem for a group of medical general practitioners. *Journal of Applied Psychology*, 1965, *49*, 399–406.

Taylor, L. R. Empirically derived job families as a foundation for the study of validity generalization:

The construction of job families based on the component and overall dimensons of the PAQ. *Personnel Psychology*, 1978, *31*, 325–340.

Thorndike, R. L. *Personnel selection.* New York: John Wiley & Sons, 1949.

Toops, H. A. The criterion. *Educational and Psychological Measurement*, 1944, *4*, 271–297.

Turner, W. W. Dimensions of foreman performance: A factor analysis of criterion measures. *Journal of Applied Psychology*, 1960, *44*, 216–223.

U.S. Department of Labor, Employment, and Training Administration. *Dictionary of occupational titles* (4th ed.). Washington, D.C.: U.S. Government Printing Office, 1977.

Wallace, S. R. Criteria for what? *American Psychologist*, 1965, *20*, 411–417.

Weitz, J. Criteria for criteria. *American Psychologist*, 1961, *16*, 228–231.

Wherry, R. J. The past and future of criterion evaluation. *Personnel Psychology*, 1957, *10*, 1–5.

# chapter 4   PREDICTORS

A predictor is any variable used to forecast a criterion. In weather prediction, barometric pressure can be used to forecast rainfall. In medical prediction, body temperature may be used to predict (or diagnose) illness. In I/O psychology, we seek predictors of job performance criteria as indexed by productivity, absenteeism, turnover, etc. There is no limit to the variables we may use as predictors of job performance. While we don't use tea leaves and astrological signs like fortune-tellers, psychologists have explored a multitude of devices as potential predictors of job performance criteria. This chapter reviews those variables traditionally used, examines their success, and discusses some professional problems inherent in their use.

Before discussing predictor variables, we must remember that while their identification is valuable, they are always secondary in importance to criteria. If you think of criteria as being the objective or end-point of an empirical journey, predictors are the roads by which we reach the criteria. Predictors are merely means to an end. Nagle (1953) described the relationship between these two sets of variables:

> . . . predictors themselves can never be anything but subsidiary to the criterion, for it is from the criterion that the predictors derive their significance.

If the criterion changes, the predictors' validity is necessarily affected. If the predictors change, the criterion does not change for that reason. Likewise, it can be seen that if no criteria are used, one would never know whether or not the predictors were selecting those individuals likely to succeed. Research can be no better than the criteria used. One must, therefore, approach the prediction process in a logical fashion, developing criteria first, analyzing them, and then constructing or selecting variables to predict the criteria. When one or more variables show a satisfactory relationship to criteria, such variables may then be used as selection instruments (p. 273).

## ASSESSING THE QUALITY OF PREDICTORS

All predictor variables can be assessed in terms of their quality or goodness. They are measuring devices, and we can think of several features of a good measuring device. We would like it to be *accurate* and *consistent*. That is, it should repeatedly yield precise measurements. In psychology, we judge the goodness of our measuring devices by two *psychometric criteria:* reliability and validity. If a predictor is not both reliable and valid, it is useless.

## RELIABILITY

Reliability is the consistency or stability of a measure. A measure should yield the same estimate on repeated use. While that estimate can be inaccurate, a reliable measure will always be consistent. Three major types of reliability are used in psychology: all of them assess the consistency or stability of the measuring device.

**Test-retest reliability**

Perhaps the simplest way to assess a measuring device's reliability is to measure something at two points in time and compare the scores. We can give an IQ test to a group of people at one time and then give it to the same people at a later time. The two sets of scores are then correlated. This is called a coefficient of *stability* because it reflects the stability of the test over time. If the test is reliable, those who scored high the first time would also score high the second time, and vice versa. If the test is unreliable, the scores will "bounce around" between administrations, such that there will be no similarity in the scores for individuals between the two administrations of the test.

When we say a test (or any measure) is reliable, how high should the reliability coefficient be? The answer is, "the higher the better." A test cannot be too reliable. As a rule, reliability coefficients around +.70 are professionally acceptable, though some frequently used tests have test-retest reliabilities only in the +.50 range. "Acceptable" reliability is also a function of the test's use. A test used for *individual* prediction (to diagnose brain impairment) should be much more reliable than a test used for *group* prediction (to measure the attitudes of a work group).

## Equivalent form reliability

A second type of reliability is *parallel* or *equivalent form* reliability. Here a psychologist would develop two forms of a test designed to measure the same thing and give both to a group of people. The two scores for each person would then be correlated. The resulting correlation, called a coefficient of *equivalence*, reflects the extent to which the two forms are equivalent measures of the same concept. Of the three major types of reliability, this is the least popular. The reason is that it is usually challenging to come up with *one* good test, let alone two. Many tests do not have a "parallel form." However in the areas of intelligence and achievement testing (to be discussed shortly), equivalent forms of the same test are sometimes found. If the resulting coefficient of equivalence is high, the tests measure the same concept. If it is low, the tests are not equivalent and do not measure the same concept.

## Internal consistency reliability

The third major type of reliability measures the internal consistency of the test—the extent to which it has homogeneous content. Two types of internal consistency reliability are typically computed. One is called *split-half* reliability. Here a test is given to a group of people, but in the scoring of the test (not administering it), the items are divided or split in half. The odd-numbered test items comprise one half and the even-numbered items the other half. Each person thus gets two scores (for the two halves), and these two sets of scores are correlated. If the test is internally consistent, there should be a high degree of similarity in the responses (i.e., right or wrong) to the odd and even numbered items. Because this method of computing reliability divides a test in half (i.e., a 100-item test is reduced to two 50-item tests), we have really only computed the reliability of half the test. We must apply a statistical correction procedure to the resulting correlation to estimate the reliability of the entire (100 item) test. The most common procedure is the *Spearman-Brown formula*. If we compute the split-half reliability of 100-item test to be .70, the following Spearman-Brown formula would be used:

$$r = \frac{2r'}{1+r'}$$

where $r$ is the estimated reliability of the whole test, and $r'$ is the obtained reliability via the split-half method. We would have:

$$r = \frac{2\,(.70)}{1+.70} = .82$$

Thus, the best estimate of the internal consistency reliability of this 100-item test is .82.

A second technique for assessing internal consistency reliability is to compute a coefficient called Cronbach's alpha, or Kuder-Richardson 20 (KR20). Both of these procedures are similar (although not quite identical statistically). Conceptually, each item of a test is thought to be a minitest in itself. Thus a 100-item test is thought to consist of 100 minitests. The response to each item is correlated with the response to every other item. We thus have a matrix of interitem correlations, and all are averaged to get a general measure of the item similarity or homogeneity of the test. If the test is homogeneous (the item content is similar), the test will have a high internal consistency reliability. If it is heterogeneous (the test items cover a wide variety of things), the test is not internally consistent; the resulting coefficient will be low. Although there is some recent evidence that internal consistency reliability may not accurately assess a test's homogeneity (Green, Lissitz, & Mulaik, 1977), it is popular in I/O psychology.

It is possible to assess the reliability of a *single* test using two of the methods, and if a parallel form exists, all three methods can be used. The reliability of a single test can be assessed via the test-retest method as well as by internal consistency. Note that a test can be differentially reliable across the methods. For example, a test may be designed to measure a wide variety of abilities—quantitative ability, verbal ability, spatial ability, etc. In assessing the internal consistency reliability of the test, the test would be found to be quite heterogeneous in content (which indeed it would be), thus having low internal consistency reliability. However, the test may have very high test-retest reliability, meaning that it consistently measures the various abilities. The point is that the various methods are not interchangeable. The test-retest method is perhaps the most generic, while internal consistency should be used only with a test designed to measure similar or homogeneous content. A test might not have homogeneous content but still be a stable measure.

# VALIDITY

While reliability refers to consistency and stability of measurement, *validity* refers to accuracy and precision. A valid measure is one that yields "correct" estimates of what is being assessed. However, there is another factor that distinguishes validity from reliability. Reliability is inherent in a measuring device. Validity, on the other hand, depends on the use of a test. It refers to the *appropriateness* of a measuring device for predicting or drawing inferences about criteria. A given test may be highly valid for predicting employee productivity but totally invalid for predicting employee absenteeism. That is, it would be appropriate to draw inferences about employee productivity from the test but inappropriate to draw inferences about absenteeism from the same test.

There are several different types of validity (or, more accurately, ways of assessing validity). But they all involve determining the appropriateness of a measure (test) for drawing inferences.

## Criterion-related validity

Criterion-related validity refers, as its name suggests, to how much a predictor relates to a criterion. It is a frequently used and important type of validity in I/O psychology. The two major kinds of criterion-related validity are concurrent and predictive.

**Concurrent criterion-related validity.** In concurrent validity, we are concerned with how well a predictor can predict a criterion at the same time, or concurrently. Many examples abound. We may wish to predict a student's grade-point average on the basis of a test score. We collect data on the grade-point averages of many students, and then we give them a predictor test. If the predictor test is a valid measure of grades, there will be a substantial correlation between test scores and school grades. We can use the same method in an industrial setting. We can predict a worker's level of productivity (the criterion) on the basis of a test (the predictor). We collect productivity data on a group of current workers, give them a test, and then correlate their scores with their productivity records. If the test is valid, we can draw an inference about a worker's productivity on the basis of the test score. In concurrent validity, there is no time interval between collecting the predictor and criterion data. The two variables are assessed *concurrently,* which is how the method gets its name.

Because the criterion for concurrent validity is always available at the time of using the predictor, why bother to collect predictor data at all? The answer is that usually predictors provide a simpler, quicker, or less-expensive substitute for criterion data (Anastasi, 1976). For example, say the criterion is the yearly dollar volume of a salesperson. A predictor that could predict a certain level of sales volume would be much more efficient than having all job applicants serve as salespeople for a year.

**Predictive criterion-related validity.** In predictive validity, predictor information is collected and used to forecast criterion performance in the future. A college might use a student's high school class rank to predict the criterion of overall college grade-point average four years later. A company could use a test to predict if job applicants will pass a six-month training program.

While concurrent validity is used to diagnose existing status on some criterion, predictive validity is used to forecast future status. The only major distinction between the two is the time interval between collecting the predictor and criterion data. However, predictive validity is usually preferable to concurrent validity. In personnel selection, though, concurrent validity is used primarily as a substitute for predictive validity because of the practical constraints of obtaining criterion data for an entire set of job applicants. The conceptual significance between predictive and concurrent validity in the context of personnel selection will be discussed in the next chapter.

In both concurrent and predictive validity, predictor scores are correlated with criterion data. The resulting correlation is called a *validity coefficient*. While an acceptable reliability coefficient is in the .70–.80 range, an acceptable validity coefficient is in the .30 to .40 range. Validity coefficients less than .30 are not uncommon, but those over .50 are rare. Just as a predictor cannot be too reliable, it cannot be too valid. The greater the correlation between the predictor and the criterion, the more we know about the criterion on the basis of the predictor. By squaring the size of the correlation coefficient (*r*), we can estimate how much variance in the criterion we can account for by using the predictor. For example, if a predictor correlates .40 with a criterion, we can explain 16 percent ($r^2$) of the variance in the criterion by knowing the predictor. A correlation of 1.0 indicates perfect prediction (and complete knowledge). Some criteria are difficult to predict (no matter what predictors are used), and others are fairly predictable. Similarly, some predictors are consistently valid and are thus used quite often. Other predictors don't seem to be of much predictive value (no matter what the criteria are), and thus they fall out of use. Usually however, certain predictors are valid only for predicting certain criteria. Shortly, we will review those predictors typically used in I/O psychology and examine how valid they are for predicting certain criteria.

## Content validity

best
for
Achievement
(Performance) test

Content validity involves the degree to which a predictor covers a *representative sample* of the behavior being assessed. It is mainly limited to psychological tests, but it could also be extended to interviews or other predictors. Historically, content validity was most relevant in achievement testing. Achievement tests are designed to indicate how well the person has mastered a specific skill or area of content. A content valid achievement test on Civil War history, for example, should include a mix of questions on battles, military and political figures, etc. In order to be "content valid," the test must contain a representative sample or mix of test items covering the domain of Civil War history. If all of the questions were about the dates of famous battles, the test would not be a balanced representation of the content of the Civil War. If a person scores high on a content valid test of Civil War history, we would infer that the person is very knowledgeable about the Civil War.

How do you assess content validity? Unlike criterion-related validity, you do *not* compute a correlation coefficient. Content validity is assessed by experts in the field the test covers. Civil War history experts would first define the domain of the Civil War and then write test questions covering it. These experts would then decide how content valid the test was. Their judgments could range from "not at all" to "highly valid." Presumably the test would be revised and rewritten until it showed a high degree of content validity.

A similar type of validity based on the judgments of people is called *face validity*. This is concerned with the appearance of the test items—do they look appropriate for such a test? While estimates of content validity are given by test developers, estimates of face validity are given by test takers. Because test developers are more knowledgeable, content validity is far more important than face validity. It is possible for a test item to be content valid but not face valid, and vice versa. In such a case, the test developers and test takers would disagree over the relevance or appropriateness of the item for the domain being assessed.

Recently, content validity has increased in importance for I/O psychology. While it once was used mainly for academic achievement testing, it is now also relevant for employment testing. Employers develop tests that assess the knowledges, skills, and abilities needed to perform a job. How much the content of these tests is job related is assessed by content validation procedures. The domain of job behavior is first specified by employees and supervisors. Then test items are developed to assess the factors needed for success on the job. The content validity of employment tests is thus a function of the extent to which the content of the job is reflected in the content of the test. A procedure has been developed to *quantify* the content validity of an employment test, a feature previously unavailable in assessing content validity of achievement tests. More will be said about this issue in the next chapter.

## Construct validity

*(Theory)*

Construct validity is the most theoretical and complex type of validity. Examples of theoretical constructs are intelligence, motivation, anxiety, and mechanical comprehension. The construct validation process entails the following procedures. If we wish to assess whether a test measures a theoretical construct such as intelligence, we start out with known measures of intelligence such as numerical ability, verbal ability, and abstract reasoning. People take these tests along with the test we are developing. We then correlate scores on the new test with scores from the established tests. If the new test correlates highly with the other tests, we have a basis to believe that there is something common being measured by all of the tests. What is in common is the construct of intelligence. We would also correlate scores on the new test with other measures which we know do *not* assess intelligence, such as physical strength. There should be no correlation between the new test and these measures. That is, we can say that scores on the new test should *converge,*—it should show *convergent validity*—with known measures of the construct in question. Also it should *diverge*—test scores should show *discriminant* or *divergent validity*—with measures that do not assess the construct. Other statistical procedures may also be used to establish the construct validity of a test (e.g., Kalleberg & Kluegel, 1975). After collecting much data over a long period of time, we accumulate a body of evidence supporting the notion that the test measures a psychological construct. In turn, we would say the test manifests construct validity.

Construct validity is extremely important in I/O psychology. Many theoretical constructs have been proposed to explain human behavior in the workplace. Among them are job involvement, organizational commitment, self-esteem, organizational climate, and morale (these terms will all be explained at length in Chapter 8). Through this process, we identify the variables that define the construct. Just as we know that the construct of intelligence has both a verbal and mathematical component, we have also learned the "ingredients" of such work-related constructs as morale. We further establish that work groups with high morale feel and behave differently than work groups with low morale. When we say that a test or other measuring device has construct validity, we mean the items making up the test are conceptually interrelated. Test scores also relate to attitudes or behaviors external to the test. Establishing construct validity is difficult and is one of the highest accolades one can bestow upon a test. Tests in I/O psychology with high construct validity are among the most widely respected and frequently used assessment devices in the profession. For instance, the Job Descriptive Index (a measure of job satisfaction) now has such a reputation after many years of development and use. It will be discussed in Chapter 9.

Some psychologists have reexamined their thinking about the three main validity types and now believe all kinds of validational evidence support construct validity. While this is a matter of professional debate, most surely the different types of validity are not independent. Criterion-related validity can be used in part to demonstrate the construct validity of a test. That is, scores on a job satisfaction measure may well be related to a criterion, such as absenteeism. Similarly, content validity is one way to index the items comprising a construct. There is also some concern (e.g., Guion, 1978) that content validity is more of a *procedure* for ensuring relevance of test content than for assessing the accuracy of inferences. The fact that the different types of validity are related to each other can create confusion (e.g., Tenopyr, 1977), but we must not lose sight of their common meaning. They all involve the appropriateness of making inferences (about someone's intelligence, mechanical ability, capacity to succeed on a job, personality) based on a test score. If a test is highly valid, such inferences are warranted, though it would not be appropriate to draw inferences from a test that lacks validity.

**Criterion reliability and validity.** Before we leave this section on reliability and validity, note that they are as important to criteria as they are to predictors. The criteria we wish to predict must be stable measures of behavior, not will-o'-the-wisp variables that lack consistency. Similarly, the criteria must be appropriate and relevant. Shoe size is an invalid criterion of intelligence. That is, it would not be appropriate to make inferences about people's intelligence by measuring the size of their feet. However, it may be appropriate to make inferences about a person's height by measuring his or her shoe size. While the concepts of reliability and validity were introduced in this chapter on predictors, they are equally relevant to criteria.

## PSYCHOLOGICAL TESTS AND INVENTORIES

Psychological tests and inventories have been the most frequently used predictors in I/O psychology. The difference between the two is that in a test, the answers are either right or wrong; in an inventory, there are no right or wrong answers. Usually, though, the term *tests* or *psychological testing* represents the family of tests and inventories.

Testing has a long multinational history in the field of psychology. Sir Francis Galton, an English biologist, had an interest in human heredity. In the course of his research, he realized the need for measuring the characteristics of biologically related and unrelated persons. He began to keep records of people on such things as keenness of vision and hearing, muscular strength, and reaction time. By 1880, he had accumulated the first large-scale body of information on individual differences. He was probably the first scientist to devise systematic ways of measuring people. In 1890, the American psychologist Cattell introduced the term *mental test*. He devised an early test of intelligence based on sensory discrimination and reaction time. Ebbinghaus, a German psychologist, developed math and sentence-completion tests and gave them to school children, In 1897, he reported that the sentence-completion test was related to the children's scholastic achievement.

The biggest advances in the early years of testing were made by a French psychologist named Binet. In 1904, the French government appointed Binet to study procedures for the education of retarded children. In order to assess mental retardation, Binet (in collaboration with Simon) developed a test of intelligence. It consisted of 30 problems covering such areas as judgment, comprehension, and reasoning, which Binet regarded as essential components of intelligence. Later revisions of this test had a greater sampling of items from different areas. Binet's research on intelligence testing was continued by the American psychologist Terman, who in 1916 developed the concept of IQ (intelligence quotient). These early pioneers paved the way for a wide variety of tests that would be developed in the years to come, many of which were used by industrial psychologists to predict job performance. While most of the early work in testing was directed at assessing intellect, testing horizons expanded to include aptitude, ability, interest, and personality.

## TYPES OF TESTS

Tests can be classified by their administrative aspects or by their content. We will use both methods.

**Speed versus power tests.** Speed tests have a large number of easy questions. The questions are so easy that if you attempt to answer them, you will get them right. The test is timed (e.g., five-minute limit), and there are more items on the test that can possibly be answered in the allotted time period. Total score on such a test is the number of items answered and reflects your speed of work.

Power tests have questions that are fairly difficult; i.e., you cannot get them right just by trying. Usually, you have as much time as you need to answer all the questions. The total score on such a test is the number of items answered correctly. Most tests given in college are power tests. If time limits are imposed, they are done mostly for the convenience of the test administrator.

**Individual versus group tests.** Individual tests are given to only one person at a time. Such tests are not common because of the amount of time needed to administer the test to all applicants. For example, if a test takes one hour and 10 people are to take the test, 10 hours of administration time will be required. The benefits of giving such a test must be judged against the costs. Certain types of IQ tests are individually administered, as are certain tests for evaluating high-level executives. In these tests, the administrator has to play an active part (e.g., asking questions, demonstrating an object, etc.) as opposed to just monitoring the test.

Group tests are administered to a group of people simultaneously and are the most common type of test. They do not involve the active participation of an administrator. The Army Alpha and Beta tests were early group intelligence tests used in World War I. Most tests used in educational and industrial organizations are group tests. Group tests are used because they are efficient in terms of time and cost.

**Paper-and-pencil versus performance tests.** Paper-and-pencil tests are the most common type of test used in industrial and educational organizations. Such tests do not involve the physical manipulation of any objects or pieces of equipment. The questions asked in a paper-and-pencil test may require answers in either multiple choice or essay form. The physical ability of individuals to handle a pencil should not influence their score on the test. The pencil is just the means by which their response is recorded on a sheet of paper.

In a performance test, the individual has to manipulate an object or a piece of equipment. The score on the test is a measure of the person's ability to perform the manipulation. A typing test is an example of a performance test, as is a test of finger dexterity. Sometimes both paper-and-pencil and performance tests are used jointly. To get a driver's license, most people have to pass both a written and a behind-the-wheel performance test.

## ETHICAL STANDARDS IN TESTING

To prevent misuse of psychological tests, the American Psychological Association has developed guidelines for their use. The ethics of psychological testing are a major responsibility of psychologists, as seen in the APA code of professional ethics (*Standards for Educational and Psychological Tests*, 1974).

Tests users must have certain qualifications depending on the purpose of the testing. Sometimes, the test user must be a licensed professional psychologist. This is particularly true in the area of clinical psychology. But in industry, lesser qualifications are needed to administer employment tests. To prevent their misuse and to maintain test security, restrictions are also placed on who can buy the tests. Test publishers are discouraged from giving away free samples or printing detailed examples of test questions as sales promotions. This could invalidate future test results.

Other ethical issues involve the invasion of privacy and confidentiality (Anastasi, 1976). Invasion of privacy occurs when a psychological test reveals more information about a person than he or she would want. Tests should be used for precise purposes. They should not be used to learn everything about a person, whether or not it is related to the issue at hand. If a company uses a mechanical comprehension test to hire mechanics, it should not also use a personality inventory just to learn about potential employees' personal lives. Using a personality inventory, which has no relationship to job performance, could be an invasion of the applicant's privacy.

Confidentiality refers to who should have access to test results. When a person takes an employment test, he or she should be told the purpose of the test, how the results will be used, and what people in the company will need to see the results. Problems come up if a third party (another prospective employer, for example) wants to know the test results. The scores should be confidential. The only way the test scores should be given out is with a written release from the test-taker. Another problem in this area is the retention of records. Advances in computer technology have made it possible to store large quantities of information about people. Who has access to this information, and what guarantees are there that this information won't be misused? The results of an IQ test taken in seventh grade may become part of a student's permanent academic record. Should a potential employer get the results of this grammar school test? Furthermore, the test probably couldn't predict job performance, so why would anyone want it? These types of questions are central to problems of confidentiality.

## THE EQUAL EMPLOYMENT OPPORTUNITY COMMISSION

In 1964, the Civil Rights Act was passed as a major piece of federal legislation. The act was designed to reduce unfair discrimination in housing, education, employment, etc. Title VII is that portion of the law that deals with discrimination in employment. As part of the law, an agency called the Equal Employment Opportunity Commission (EEOC) was created to reduce discrimination in employment. In 1970, the EEOC published a brief guideline to be used by employers in selecting employees. The guidelines described perferred methods of test validation, spoke to the need for reducing *adverse impact*, and described procedures for documenting personnel records. *Adverse impact* is the name given to the results of a test that cause a disproportionate percentage of people being hired of a given sex, race, ethnic group, etc., compared to another group. That is, if a selection test results in 80 percent of the white applicants being hired but only 30 percent of the black applicants being hired, the test has an adverse impact on the hiring of blacks. Those (1970) employment guidelines were somewhat vague in defining adverse impact, and many psychologists found it hard to comply. Also, other federal agencies, such as the Civil Service Commission and the Department of Labor, had their own guidelines on fair employment practices. So even those federal agencies with authority to regulate employment practices could not agree among themselves as to what were "fair" hiring practices.

Over the years, the guidelines were revised. Finally in 1978, 14 years after the passage of the Civil Rights Act, a *uniform* set of employment guidelines endorsed by all of the appropriate federal agencies was enacted. The 1978 version was much longer, more precise, and more detailed than its predecessors. The government now regards these guidelines as "the Bible" of employment testing. However, many I/O psychologists feel that a set of testing guidelines developed by the Division of Industrial-Organizational Psychology (1980) are more technically precise.

As an initial reaction to the guidelines, many employers curtailed the use of psychological tests. But this was no way to avoid compliance with the guidelines because they dealt with *any* predictor used for selection, not just psychological tests. The guidelines were designed to determine the proper use of all selection procedures and to aid compliance with equal employment opportunity requirements with regard to race, color, religion, sex, and national origin. If a company's selection procedure systematically results in the disproportionate rejection of members of a certain group (e.g., race, religion, sex), a rejected applicant can file a complaint against the company with EEOC. EEOC then investigates the complaint and tries to reach an agreement with the company regarding use of the test. If the two parties cannot agree, the company can be sued for using unfair selection procedures. The company then has to prove in a courtroom that their tests are not unfair and their selection system is valid. Companies that lose such cases have been fined multimillion-dollar sums. The money is often used to pay those people who were the victims of the company's unfair tests. The financial settlements in such cases are called *class-action* (the person who is suing represents a class of similar people), *back-pay* settlements (the company has to pay a portion of what those people would have earned had they been hired.) The awards have reached $20 to $30 million in a single lawsuit. Needless to say, not everyone who fails an employment test has their day in court. A lawsuit must be predicated on "just cause" and not just the complaints of one disgruntled person who fails a test. Also, large employers who affect the lives of many people are more likely to be sued than small employers.

The EEOC guidelines did more to change personnel testing in this country than any other single event. If World War II was the stimulus for the boom in psychological testing, the EEOC guidelines were the stimulus for the reevaluation and reformulation of personnel selection procedures. The federal government is now involved in an area that used to be governed solely by the psychological profession. While many psychologists have commented on the difficulty in complying with federal law on personnel testing, it is generally acknowledged that there is less unfair discrimination in employment today than before the Civil Rights Act was enacted. To the extent that the EEOC guidelines were enacted to reduce discrimination in employment, they can be considered successful in meeting this important goal.

## SOURCES OF INFORMATION ABOUT TESTING

Because testing is a rapidly changing area, it is important to keep up with current developments in the field. Old tests get revised, new tests are introduced, and some tests are discontinued.

Fortunately, several key references are available. Perhaps the most important source is the series of *Mental Measurement Yearbooks* (MMY) edited by Buros. The MMY was first published in 1938 and has been revised in roughly a six-year cycle. Each yearbook includes tests published during a specified period, thus supplementing the tests reported in previous yearbooks. The *Eighth Mental Measurements Yearbook* (1978), for example, deals mainly with tests that appeared between 1970 and 1976. Tests may be reviewed again in later yearbooks as new information becomes available. Each test is critically reviewed by an expert in the field, and there is a complete list of references pertaining to each test. Information about price, publisher, and versions of the test is also given. The MMY series is the most comprehensive review of psychological tests available in the field.

Other, less detailed books have been prepared by Buros. They are *Tests in Print* (1974) and *Personality Tests and Reviews* (1970). Both of these books resemble bibliographies and help locate tests in the MMY. Some psychological journals also review specific tests.

Various professional test developers also publish test manuals. The test manual should give the information needed to administer, score, and evaluate a particular test as well as data on the test's reliability and validity. While these manuals are useful, they are usually not as complete and critical as reviews in the MMY.

The test user has an obligation to use the test in a professional and competent manner. Tests should be chosen with extreme care and concern for the consequences of using the tests. Important decisions are based on test scores, and the choice of test is equally important. Cronbach (1970) recommends that a test be thoroughly analyzed before it is considered for use.

## TEST CONTENT

Tests can be classified according to their content. While there are other types, the following tests are the major ones used in industry. Also presented is information on how valid the various types of tests have been in personnel selection as documented from their use in the psychological literature.

### Intelligence tests

Tests of mental ability or intelligence have long been used for personnel selection. Part of the reason for this is the belief that intelligence correlates with job performance. That is, all things considered, it is usually believed that if the worker is more intelligent, productivity will be higher, turnover will be lower, etc. While there is evidence that intelligence is correlated with performance, the relationship does not always hold. Research shows that some employees can be *too* intelligent for a job, particularly lower-level jobs. The employees want more stimulation than the job can provide, so they become bored and then quit. In such a case, it's better to hire less-intelligent workers.

Among the mental ability tests commonly used in industry are the Otis Self-Administering Tests of Mental Ability (1922–1929), the Wonderlic Personnel Test (Wonderlic & Hovland, 1939), and the Adaptability Test (Tiffin & Lawshe, 1942). Wonderlic chose the term *personnel* for the test title because it is less threatening than the term *intelligence*. Likewise, Tiffin (1970) said that while most people don't like to have their intelligence as-

**Figure 4–1**                    **Sample test questions from a typical intelligence test**

1. What number is missing in this series?
   3 – 8 – 14 – 21 – 29 – (?)
2. SHOVEL is to DITCHDIGGER as SCALPEL is to:
   (a) knife   (b) sharp   (c) butcher   (d) surgeon   (e) cut

sessed, few mind having their adaptability measured. All of these tests are quite short; they take only 12 to 15 minutes to administer. Reliabilities in the .90 range have been reported for all the tests. The tests seem to be most valid for selecting clerical workers and, to a lesser extent, first-line supervisors. Figure 4–1 shows some sample test questions from a typical intelligence test.

Ghiselli (1973) reported the results of studies that used many types of tests to predict job proficiency (measured in different individual studies) across multiple samples of employees. Table 4–1 summarizes the validity coefficients reported for four types of intellectual ability tests. Intelligence tests include all tests of mental alertness, such as the Otis test. Immediate memory tests list 5- to 10-place numbers, which the individual studies and must try to recall in a short period of time. Substitution tests involve learning and applying a code, and "substituting" the coded material for conventional letters or numbers. Arithmetic tests involve solving various kinds of math problems. These validity coefficients are based are large sample sizes (sometimes over 10,000 cases). The results show that intellectual abilities only modestly predict job proficiency. None of the coefficients exceed .31 (meaning that slightly more than 9 percent of the variance in job proficiency can be predicted by knowledge of intellectual ability); in fact, some coefficients are in the negative direction. Yet the results are quite similar across the seven samples of employees, giving some support to the notion that general intelligence is consistently related to job performance (although only at a modest level).

**Table 4–1**                    **Average validity coefficients of intelligence tests for predicting job proficiency in seven occupations**

|  | Managers | Clerks | Sales | Protective occupations | Service occupations | Vehicle operators | Trades and crafts |
|---|---|---|---|---|---|---|---|
| Intellectual abilities | .27 | .28 | .19 | .22 | .27 | .16 | .25 |
| Intelligence | .29 | .30 | .19 | .23 | .26 | .15 | .25 |
| Immediate memory | — | .31 | −.06 | .26 | — | — | .17 |
| Substitution | — | .24 | −.16 | — | — | — | .21 |
| Arithmetic | .23 | .26 | .25 | .18 | .28 | — | .25 |

SOURCE: E. E. Ghiselli, "The Validity of Aptitude Tests in Personnel Selection," *Personnel Psychology* 26 (1973), pp. 461–77.

**Mechanical aptitude tests**

There are two types of tests dealing with mechanical aptitude: those involving mechanical reasoning and those involving spatial relations. Mechanical aptitude tests generally require a person to recognize what mechanical principle is suggested by a test item. Tests of spatial relations are included because it is assumed that the ability to perceive geometric relationships between physical objects and to manipulate those objects are both parts of the larger construct of mechanical aptitude.

One of the most popular tests of mechanical reasoning is the Bennett Test of Mechanical Comprehension (Bennett, 1940). The test is a series of pictures reflecting various issues about mechanical facts and principles. Sample questions from the Bennett Test are shown in Figure 4–2. Reported reliabilities for the Bennett are in the .80 range.

Some of the more widely used tests of spatial relations include the Min-

**Figure 4-2**          **Sample test questions from the Bennett Test of Mechanical Comprehension**

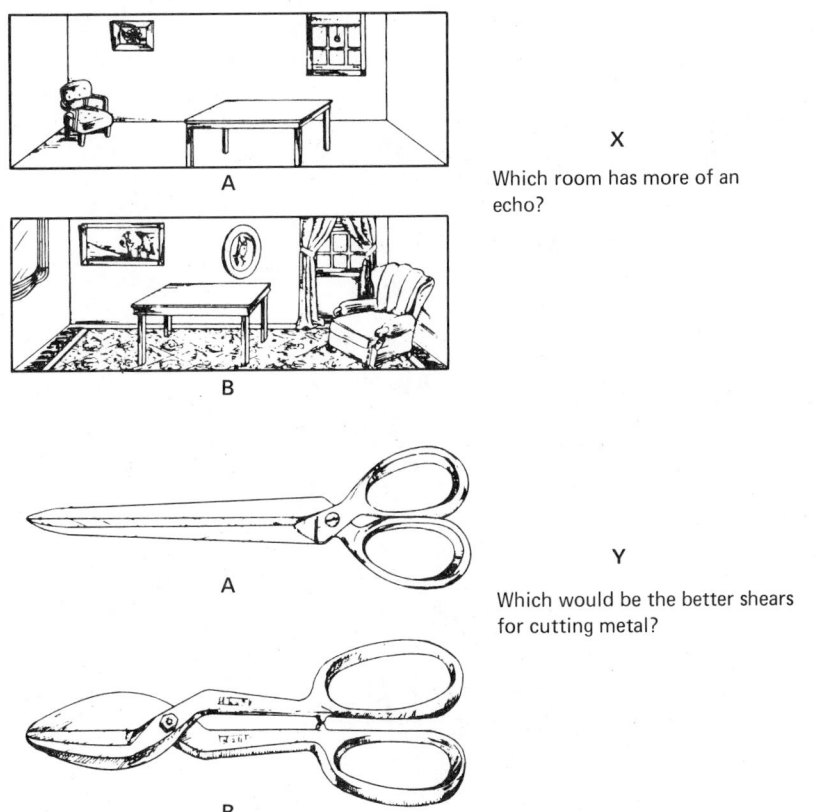

X

Which room has more of an echo?

Y

Which would be the better shears for cutting metal?

SOURCE: G. K. Bennett, *Test of Mechanical Comprehension* (New York: Psychological Corporation, 1940). Copyright 1941, renewed 1969 by The Psychological Corporation. All rights reserved.

nesota Spatial Relations Test (Paterson, 1930) and the Minnesota Paper Form Board Test (Likert & Quasha, 1941–1948). The Minnesota Spatial Relations Test measures both dexterity and spatial relations. A picture of the test is shown in Figure 4–3. In this test, 58 geometric shapes cut from a large board have to be placed into their appropriate slots as fast as possible. Both length of time and number of errors are counted.

The Minnesota Paper Form Board test does not involve dexterity as a variable in performance. It consists of 64 multiple-choice items. Each item shows the parts of a geometric figure which has been cut into pieces, followed by five assembled geometric forms. The test taker must pick which geometric form is the assembled version of the parts.

Ghiselli (1973) reviewed the validity of three sets of mechanical aptitude tests for predicting job proficiency. In addition to tests of spatial relations and mechanical reasoning, he also included location tests. In location tests, test takers must identify the location of a series of points and judge the

**Figure 4–3**          **The Minnesota Spatial Relations Test**

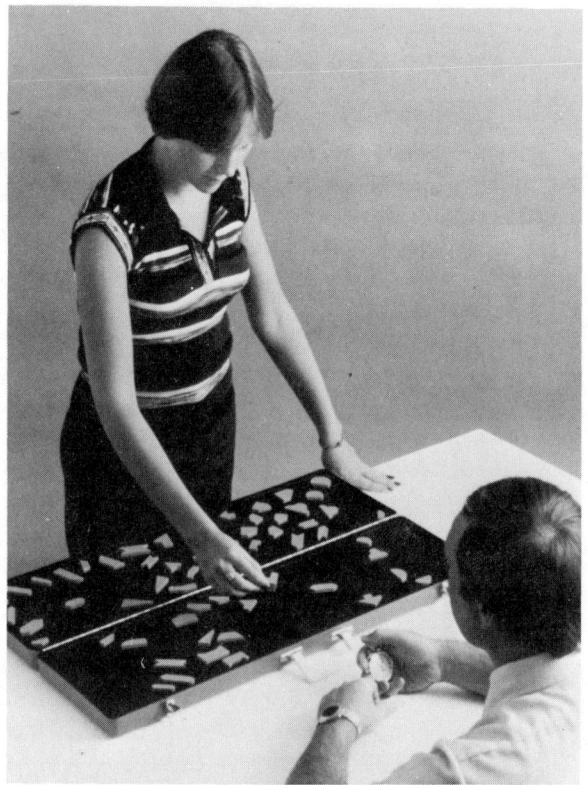

*Courtesy American Guidance Service, Inc.*

SOURCE: D. G. Paterson, *Minnesota Spatial Relations Test* (Chicago: Stoelting, 1930).

| Table 4–2 | Average validity coefficients of mechanical aptitude tests for predicting job proficiency in seven occupations | | | | | | |
|---|---|---|---|---|---|---|---|
| | Managers | Clerks | Sales | Protective occupations | Service occupations | Vehicle operators | Trades and crafts |
| Mechanical aptitude . . . . . . . . . . | .22 | .17 | .18 | .18 | .13 | .20 | .23 |
| Spatial relations . . . . . . . . . . . . | .21 | .16 | .18 | .17 | .13 | .16 | .23 |
| Location . . . . . . . . . . . . . . . . . . . | — | .16 | — | — | — | .18 | .20 |
| Mechanical reasoning . . . . . . . | .23 | .23 | .16 | .23 | — | .22 | .26 |

SOURCE: E. E. Ghiselli, "The Validity of Aptitude Tests in Personnel Selection," *Personnel Psychology* 26 (1973), pp. 461–77.

distances between them. The results of Ghiselli's study are shown in Table 4–2.

As can be seen, mechanical aptitude tests predict job proficiency most in the trades and crafts and least in the service occupations. None of the coefficients exceed .26. Keep in mind that these are *average* coefficients based on thousands of cases and that results from individual studies are more varied. On par however, results show that mechanical aptitude tests have modest validity for predicting industrial job proficiency.

## Ability tests

Ability tests usually cover two broad classes of tests: sensory ability and motor ability. Sensory ability tests assess visual acuity, color vision, and hearing sensitivity. These abilities are related to success in certain types of jobs.

Perhaps the best known test of visual acuity is the *Snellen Eye Chart,* a display with rows of letters that get increasingly smaller. The test taker stands 20 feet away from the chart and reads each row until the letters are indistinguishable. A ratio is then computed to express acuity:

$$\text{Acuity} = \frac{\text{Distance at which a person can read a certain line of print (usually 20 feet)}}{\text{Distance at which the average person can read the same line of print}}$$

For example, if the smallest line of print a person can read at 20 feet is a line most people can read from 40 feet, the person's score would be 20/40. Each eye is tested separately, and normal vision is 20/20.

The most common way to measure hearing sensitivity is with a machine called an *audiometer*. An audiometer produces tones of different frequencies and loudness. The tone is gradually raised in intensity. When the test taker signals that the note has been heard, the examiner records the level of intensity on an *audiogram*. This then shows the intensity of sound needed to hear tones of different frequency. An audiogram is prepared for each ear. Hearing loss is detected by comparing one person's audiogram with the results from a tested population.

**Figure 4–4**                              **Sample test question from a typical perceptual accuracy test**

Which pairs of items are identical?
17345290 — 17342590
2033220638 — 2033220638
WPBRAEGGER — WPBREAGGER
CLAFDAPKA26 — CLAPDAFKA26

Researcher's have also devised paper-and-pencil tests of perceptual accuracy. In these tests, two stimuli are presented, and the test taker must judge whether they are the same or different. The stimuli may be numbers or names (both are used in the Minnesota Clerical Test). Figure 4–4 shows the types of items in a perceptual accuracy test.

Tests of motor ability assess fine/or gross motor coordination. Frequently used motor ability tests include the Purdue Pegboard (Tiffin, 1941) and the Crawford Small Parts Dexterity Test (Crawford & Crawford, 1946). In the Purdue Pegboard, pins are placed into small holes in a pegboard, using the right hand first, then the left hand, and then both hands together. In the second part of the test, the pins are again placed in the holes but with the addition of collars and washers. The first part of the test measures manual dexterity; the second part measures finger dexterity. In the Crawford Small Parts Dexterity Test, pins are first placed in holes in the board and then metal collars are placed over the pins. In the second part of the test, a screwdriver is used to insert small screws after they have been placed by hand into threaded holes.

Ghiselli's (1973) review of test validities includes the results of several ability tests. Representative tests from that study are shown in Table 4–3. The results in Table 4–3 show that ability tests predict proficiency for clerks better than any other sample of workers. Ability tests have virtually no validity for predicting success in sales jobs. The validity coefficients for ability tests in some samples of clerks have exceeded .40.

**Table 4–3**                              **Average validity coefficients of perceptual accuracy and motor ability tests for predicting job proficiency in seven occupations**

|  | Managers | Clerks | Sales | Protective occupations | Service occupations | Vehicle operators | Trades and crafts |
|---|---|---|---|---|---|---|---|
| Perceptual accuracy | .25 | .29 | .04 | .21 | .10 | .17 | .24 |
| Number comparison | .31 | .30 | .05 | .16 | .14 | .37 | .14 |
| Name comparison | .21 | .30 | .05 | .23 | .15 | .15 | .25 |
| Motor abilities | .14 | .16 | .12 | .14 | .15 | .25 | .19 |
| Finger dexterity | .14 | .17 | .06 | .15 | .13 | .22 | .19 |
| Hand dexterity | .09 | .14 | .12 | .08 | .13 | .16 | .18 |

SOURCE: E. E. Ghiselli, "The Validity of Aptitude Tests in Personnel Selection," *Personnel Psychology* 26 (1973), pp. 461–77.

## Personality and interest inventories

Unlike the previously cited tests which have objective answers, in personality and interest inventories, the individual's responses are neither right nor wrong. Test takers answer questions about their personal likes ("I like to go swimming") or how much they agree with certain statements ("People who work hard get ahead"). Similar types of questions normally make up such a scale, as an "Interest in Outdoor Activity." Responses are tallied, and scores show the degree of interest in the activity. Similar procedures are used in personality inventories, which reflect a person's introversion, dominance, confidence, etc. These scale scores are then used to predict job success. The basic rationale is that successful employees have certain interests or personality patterns, and these patterns become the basis for selecting new employees.

Two of the commonly used interest inventories are the Strong Vocational Interest Blank (Strong, 1943) and the Vocational Preference Inventory (Holland, 1965). Both of these interest inventories have series of questions about vocational interests. A person's responses are then compared with the interests of members of various occupational groups. People can then know if their interests are more like certain groups (e.g., engineers) than others (e.g., pilots). It is assumed that the more similar the interest pattern, the more likely one is to succeed in that occupation.

Though many personality tests are available, the most well-known is probably the Minnesota Multiphasic Personality Inventory (MMPI), developed by Hathaway and McKinley (1943). The MMPI consists of 550 statements that must be answered true, false, or cannot say. The inventory has 10 clinical scales (e.g., Depression, Schizophrenia, etc.) A person's responses to these items are compared with the responses of normal individuals and of clinical patients. There are many other personality inventories, some of which are derived from the MMPI.

A big problem with using personality inventories in industry is that they may violate a person's privacy. Some scales of a personality inventory may be useful for personnel selection decisions, but information unrelated to employment success may be revealed in the other scales. Because of the EEOC's concern for fair employment practices, personality inventories are now used less often.

Ghiselli's (1973) study also included the results of personality and interest inventories as predictors of job success. The results are shown in Table 4–4.

Note that personality and interest inventories are most predictive of job proficiency in sales occupations. They are moderately predictive of proficiency in all samples, However, the number of cases these coefficients are based on is not nearly as large as for some of the other predictor tests. There is also some major disagreement in the literature on the value of personality inventories in predicting job success. Guion and Gottier (1965) reviewed the use of personality inventories in industry over a 12-year period. They concluded that evidence did not support their use for making

**Table 4–4**                        **Average validity coefficients of personality and interest inventories for predicting job proficiency in seven occupations**

|                | Managers | Clerks | Sales | Protective occupations | Service occupations | Vehicle operators | Trades and crafts |
|----------------|----------|--------|-------|------------------------|---------------------|-------------------|-------------------|
| Personality ........ | .21      | .24    | .31   | .24                    | .16                 | .26               | .29               |
| Interest ........... | .28      | .12    | .32   | −.01                   | —                   | .26               | .17               |

SOURCE: E. E. Ghiselli, "The Validity of Aptitude Tests in Personnel Selection," *Personnel Psychology* 26 (1973), pp. 461–77.

employment decisions. Questionable validity and the invasion of privacy issue have limited use of these inventories in recent years.

## Multiple aptitude test batteries

A final category of tests is based on their structural composition rather than item content. Test "batteries" consist of many of the types of tests already discussed: intelligence, mechanical aptitude, personality, etc. These tests are usually quite long; they may take several hours to complete. Each part of the test measures certain things: intellectual ability, mechanical reasoning, etc. The tests are useful because they yield a great deal of information. Such information can then later be used for hiring, placement, training, etc. The major disadvantages of the test are the cost and time involved. The two most widely known multiple aptitude batteries are the General Aptitude Test Battery (GATB) and the Differential Aptitude Test (DAT).

## Testing in retrospect

For many years, psychologists have used tests to forecast job success. The tests and the jobs under study are equally diverse. So psychologists have a lot of information on the value of tests as predictors of future behavior. Over the years, some tests have been found useful, while others have not. As an entire class of predictors, psychological tests have been modestly predictive of job performance. Single validity coefficients in excess of .50 are unusual; they were unusual in the early years of testing and they are still so today. As one reviews the findings reported in Tables 4–1 to 4–4, it can be seen that the modal range for the validity coefficients is in the .20s. That is, between 4 percent and 8 percent of the variance in job performance across a broad range of many jobs is predictable with psychological tests. While these coefficients are not as high as we would like, it is unfair to condemn the tests as useless. Some tests are very useful for predicting success in certain jobs. Also, keep in mind that validity coefficients are a function of both the predictor and criterion. A poorly defined and constructed criterion will produce low validity coefficients no matter what the predictor is like. But because of the limited predictive power of tests, psychologists have had to look elsewhere for forecasters of job performance. The balance of this chapter examines what other predictors psychologists have investigated.

# INTERVIEWS

In terms of sheer frequency, interviews are the most popular method of selecting employees (Dunnette & Bass, 1963). The popularity of the employment interview may also be due to increased legal problems with paper-and-pencil tests.

While most court cases regarding discrimination have involved paper-and-pencil tests, interviews are still regarded as a *test* by the EEOC (along with all other predictors). And as such, they are subject to the same judicial review. Unlike tests, interviews are highly subjective, so *chances* for unfair discrimination seem to be greater. Because interviews are used so often in employment decisions, many research studies have been conducted (especially recently). Some of the major issues inherent in the employment interview include the following.

## Format of the selection interview

The interviewer's purpose is twofold: (1) to gather relevant data and (2) to evaluate the data and decide to select or reject the applicant (Blum & Naylor, 1968). The nature and amount of information an interview generates is due to the type of interview and to the characteristics of the applicant and the interviewer. There are several types of interviews ranging from highly structured to highly unstructured. In a highly structured interview, the interviewer asks predetermined questions of all applicants in the same way. The interviewer then records each answer question-by-question. In an unstructured interview, the interviewer procedes on the basis of the applicant's answers to previous questions. The interviewer probes and explores the applicant's qualifications in a "play-by-ear" fashion. In theory no two applicants would be asked the same question. In practice, most interviews are half-way in between structured and unstructured. That is, the applicants get asked the same general questions, but their responses may cause the interviewer to question them more intensely.

Interviews can also be described in terms of the number of participants or trials. In most cases one applicant and one interviewer have one interview. The interviewer evaluates the applicant and makes a decision. An alternative is to have the applicant interviewed by several interviewers separately. This type of interview is usually conducted for individuals applying for higher-level jobs. The interviewers pool their separate opinions and reach a decision. A final format is for an applicant to be interviewed by a panel—perhaps as many as six or seven interviewers. Again, the interviewers pool their opinions and make a decision. This procedure is typical in government jobs where applicants are often interviewed by a Civil Service evaluation board.

Unlike a paper-and-pencil test, an interview is a dynamic selection device. Interviewers affect the behavior of applicants, and vice versa. While applicants try to impress interviewers and affect a favorable decision, it is also true that interviewers can affect applicants. The interviewer can knowingly or unknowingly alter the applicant's responses by saying such things as "you're right", "I agree", or "I disagree" (Verplank, 1955). Nonverbal responses (yawning, smiling, frowning, and the degree of eye contact) can alter the applicant's behavior too. Furthermore, the outcome of an interview can be affected by the interviewer's behavior. Thus, an interviewer's own behavior during the interview may be a determining factor as to whether the applicant is hired! Experienced interviewers learn a standard-

**Figure 4–5**     **Determinants of interview outcome**

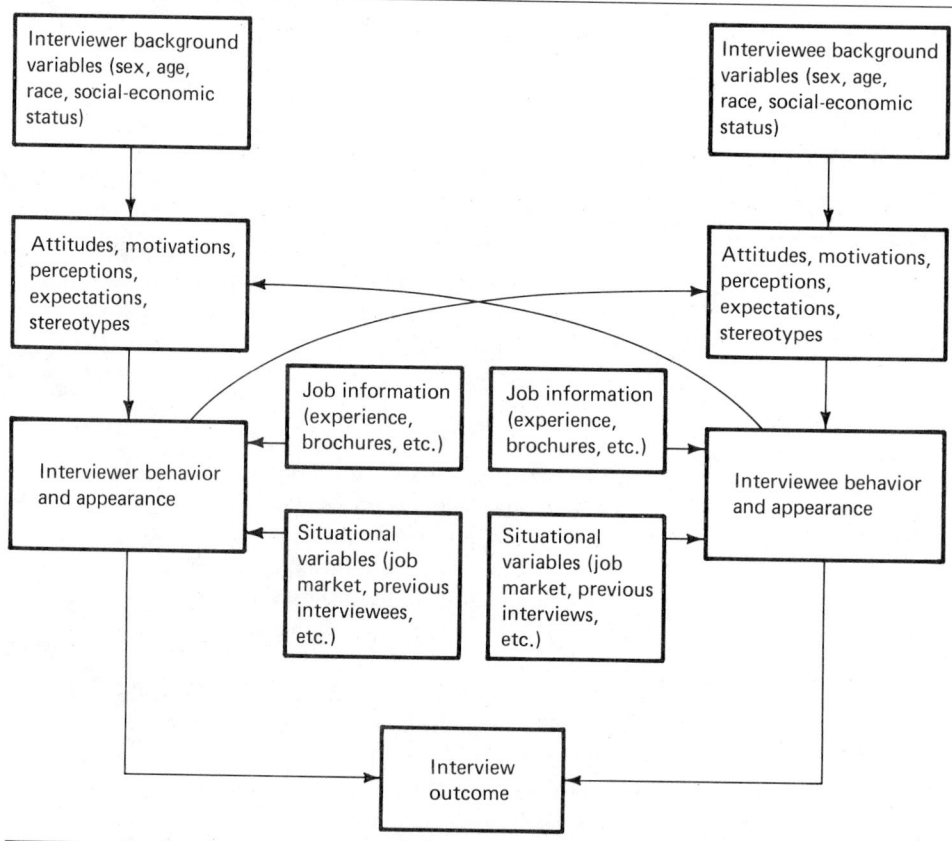

SOURCE: N. Schmitt, "Social and Situational Determinants of Interview Decisions: Implications for the Employment Interview," *Personnel Psychology* 29 (1976), pp. 79–101.

ized interview style to minimize the impact of their own behavior on the outcome of the interview.

Schmitt (1976) has developed a graphic model of the determinants of interview decisions. As can be seen in Figure 4-5, the interaction of the applicant and the interviewer determines the outcome. We will explore some of these factors in greater detail shortly. For the moment, note that many variables that affect the outcomes of interviews do not influence tests. For example, the interviewer's sex may influence who gets offered a job, but the sex of the test scorer would not influence the applicant's score.

## Evaluation of the interview

Interviews have been called "conversations with a purpose" (Bingham & Moore, 1941). The "goodness" of these conversations as predictors of job performance can be judged by the same criteria used to judge any predictor—reliability and validity.

**Reliability.** The reliability of an interview refers to the similarity of judgments made by the same interviewer over time (*intra*-interviewer reliability) or the similarity of judgments made by different interviewers about the same job applicant (*inter*-interviewer reliability). The two types of reliability address different issues.

Most of the research on *intra*-interviewer reliability indicates that interviewers are quite consistent in their evaluations. Whatever they like or dislike about applicants appears stable, so they make consistent evaluations. Carlson (1968) has shown that interviewer self-consistency increases when (1) the interviewer has a relative standard (i.e., a hypothetical ideal person) that can be used for comparisons, and (2) the applicants are quite diverse (i.e., some are good, some are bad).

While *intra*-interviewer reliability is typically high, this is not always true for *inter*-interviewer reliability. *Inter*-interviewer reliability assesses the extent to which different interviewers reach the same decision in evaluating applicants. A lot of research can be summarized by saying sometimes they agree, and sometimes they don't. Some studies report *inter*-interviewer reliabilities in the .80s; other studies report *inter*-interviewer reliabilities as low as .15. A crucial determinant of agreement among interviewers is what specifically they are being asked to evaluate. If the applicants are being judged in terms of how appropriate their past work history is for a given job, most interviewers would agree (*inter*-interviewer reliability would be high). If the applicants are judged on their personality and how it relates to the job, most interviewers would probably disagree (*inter*-interviewer reliability would be low). This occurs because interviewers have different ideas as to what the personality constructs mean and how they get translated into job performance. For example, if interviewers were asked if an applicant were "aggressive" enough to succeed in the job, each might have a different view on what aggressiveness was and how much of it was needed on the job.

**Validity.** Care must be exercised in evaluating the validity of the interview process as a whole versus the validity of the interviewer. The validity of the interview process refers to the extent that all of the information about an applicant brought to the attention of the interviewer is predictive of job performance. This would include not only the content of the interview itself, but also test scores, letters of reference, and records of past work history.

The validity of an interviewer is often tangled up in the validity of these other sources. It's hard to tell how much of the hiring decision was due solely to the interviewer's judgment and how much was due to the other information. Carlson (1972) reported that in reviewing 13 studies where the interviewer was the only source of information, 9 studies had validity coefficients in the .15–.25 range. (Note that this range is not too different for the validity coefficients of tests reported in Tables 4–1 to 4–4). When such ancillary information as test scores, letters of reference, etc., were added, the average validity coefficients were raised to the .30–.40 range. Finally, in those studies where the interviewers *rated* the applicants (as opposed to a simple hire/reject decision), the correlation between such a quantified judgment and the criterion was in the .40–.60 range. While relatively few studies report consistent correlations in this range, it is encouraging and refreshing to see such accuracy of prediction.

In summary, the interview process appears to be quite valid compared with other predictors of job performance. Keep in mind that the "interview-process" is an amalgam of individual predictors and that together they contribute to the prediction of job success. The validity of individual interviewers is a function of how adept they are at assessing applicant qualifications. Some interviewers are good, others are not. As Arvey (1979) has commented, interviews are subject to the same judgmental standards as any other predictor. As with any predictor, its utility rests on how much it fairly and accurately results in satisfactory applicants being hired and unsatisfactory applicants being rejected. Increasingly more cases involving interviews are being contested in the courts. Perhaps in the 1980s, interviews will have their "day in court" just as paper-and-pencil tests did in the 1970s.

## Factors influencing interview outcomes

Through extensive research involving hundreds of studies, psychologists now know that many factors can influence the outcome of an interview. Schmitt (1976) reviewed the literature on interviews and found a dozen factors (apart from the applicant's qualifications) that affect an interviewer's decision. (The criterion in this research is whether or not applicants are offered jobs, not whether they turn out to be successful employees.) We will examine some of the major findings from Schmitt's study.

**1. Negative-positive nature of the information.** Is it something positive that applicants say that results in being hired, or is it something negative that they say that causes their rejection? Research shows that negative information is more important than positive information. Many interviewers look for reasons (information) *not* to hire an applicant, and when they find it, the applicant is rejected. Suppose a high school graduate said she was on the honor roll for two years. This positive piece of information could be outweighed if she also said that she was expelled from school for two weeks for disciplinary reasons.

**2. Temporal placement of information.**   Does it make a difference *when* certain information is presented to the interviewer? If interviewers are most influenced by information given early in the interview, this is called a *primacy* effect. If they are most influenced by information given late in the interview, this is called a *recency* effect. The evidence for either is not clear-cut. Some interviewers are influenced by primacy effects, others by recency effects. But *what* gets said can interact with *when* it is said. In particular, a negative information-primacy effect results in unfavorable ratings. That is, if you start off the interview with something negative about yourself, you will more likely get rejected than if you "bury" it in the middle of the interview.

**3. Interviewer stereotypes.**   Do interviewers have an "ideal" candidate in mind when they interview applicants? The answer seems to be yes. But not all interviewers have the same ideal candidate in mind, even if they are interviewing for the same job. The "ideal candidate" probably contributes to high *intra*-interviewer reliability since interviewers are very consistent in evaluating applicants in comparison to their ideal applicant. Whether their conception of the ideal applicant is valid (would result in the best job performance) is another question.

**4. Contrast effects.**   Is one applicant's evaluation influenced by preceeding applicants? Will an applicant of average credentials appear worse if he or she was preceeded by someone with superior credentials? Research indicates that contrast effects do occur. Applicants with average credentials appear better to the interviewer if they follow someone with poor credentials. And they appear worse if they follow someone with superior credentials. A more controversial question is *how much* contrast effects influence interviewers. Some researchers think they exert substantial influence; others think their effects are minimal. It has been suggested that the interviewer's experience controls the impact of contrast effects; that is, more experienced interviewers are less influenced by contrast effects.

**5. Similarity of sex.**   Do interviewers prefer applicants of their own sex? The answer seems to be no. But what does appear to matter is whether male and female applicants are applying for traditional male and female jobs. Interviewers seem more likely to hire females for traditional female jobs than for traditional male jobs (and vice versa for male applicants). The *congruence* between the sex of the applicant and the traditional sex-orientation of the job is more influential than whether the applicant and interviewer are the same sex.

Some of the other factors reviewed by Schmitt include the experience of the interviewer, the effect of information about the job, and the degree of structure of the interview. Interviews are far more psychologically complex than many other predictors of job performance. With paper-and-pencil tests, what counts is whether the applicant got a passing score. The determinants of the passing score include such factors as knowledge of the test material, the applicant's motivation to pass, and the applicant's anxiety level. Interviews, on the other hand, are influenced by a far greater number of factors. While some factors are more important than others, they all influence the final decision. Their complexity aside, interviews must still conform to the same psychometric and legal standards as any other predictor of job performance. I concur with Arvey (1979) who said that a lot more research needs to be done on the interview as a selection device in I/O psychology.

## WORK SAMPLES AND SITUATIONAL EXERCISES

### Work samples

Work samples are a relatively new and exciting approach to personnel selection. Their rationale is simple. Rather than trying to identify predictors of job success that are usually quite different in nature from the criterion they are supposed to predict, why don't we create a "miniature criterion" and use that as the predictor? That is, our goal is to take the content of a person's job, shrink it down to a manageable time period, and let applicants demonstrate their ability in performing this replica of the job. This rationale was presented in an article by Wernimont and Campbell (1968), and has served as the blueprint for later empirical studies.

An excellent example of a work sample was reported by Campion (1972). Campion wanted to develop a predictor of job success for mechanics. Using job analytic techniques, he learned that the mechanic's job was defined by success in the use of tools, accuracy of work, and overall mechanical ability. He then designed tasks which would show an applicant's performance in these three areas. Through the cooperation of job incumbents, he designed a work sample that involved such typical tasks as installing pulleys and belts, taking apart and repairing a gearbox, etc. The proper steps necessary to perform these tasks were identified and given numerical values according to their appropriateness (e.g., 10 points for aligning a motor with a dial indicator, 1 point for aligning it by feeling the motor, 0 points for just looking at the motor). Using a concurrent, criterion-related validity design, each mechanic in the shop took the work sample. Their scores were correlated with the criterion of supervisor ratings of their job performance. The validity of the work sample was excellent: it correlated .66 with use of tools, .42 with accuracy of work, and .46 with overall mechanical ability. Campion showed that there was a substantial relationship between how well mechanics did on the work sample and how well they did on the job.

Subsequent research on work samples has been very positive and encouraging. Muchinsky (1975) and Schmidt et al. (1977) reported that work samples were the type of predictor device that readily conformed to EEOC standards for test fairness and lack of adverse impact. Mount, Muchinsky, and Hanser (1977) found that work samples gave highly desirable validity coefficients in both predictive and concurrent validity designs. Brugnoli, Campion, and Basen (1979) reported that work samples were relatively free of bias in the testing of black and white applicants. Finally, and perhaps most important, work samples have repeatedly been shown to be highly valid. Validity coefficients in the .40–.60 range are not uncommon.

But work samples do have limitations. They work primarily in blue-collar jobs that involve either the mechanical trades (e.g., mechanics, carpenters, electricians, etc.) or the manipulation of objects. They do not work very well when the job involves working with people as opposed to things. Second, work samples assess what a person *can* do; they don't assess potential. They seem best suited to hiring experienced workers rather than trainees. Finally, work samples are time-consuming and costly to administer. Because they are individual tests, they require a lot of supervision and monitoring. Few work samples are designed to be completed in less than one hour. If there are 100 applicants to fill five jobs, it may not be worth it to give a work sample to all applicants. Perhaps the applicant pool could be reduced with some other selection instrument (e.g., a review of previous work history). Yet despite their limitations, work samples are quite useful in personnel selection.

## Situational exercises

Situational exercises are roughly the white-collar counterpart of work samples. That is, they are used mainly to select people for managerial and professional jobs. Unlike work samples, which are designed to be replicas of the job, situational exercises only mirror part of the job.

Situational exercises involve a whole family of tests that in one way or another assess problem-solving ability. Two good examples of situational exercises are the In-Basket Test (Frederiksen, 1968) and the Leaderless Group Discussion (Bass, 1954). The In-Basket Test involves having applicants sort through an in-basket (of things to do). The contents of the in-basket are carefully designed letters, memos, brief reports, etc., which require the applicant's immediate attention and response. The applicant goes through the contents and takes the appropriate action to solve the problems presented. The applicant can make a phone call, write a letter, call a meeting, etc., as problem-solving approaches. A number of observers score the applicant in terms of such factors as productivity (how much work got done) and problem-solving effectiveness (versatility in resolving problems). The In-Basket Test is predictive of job performance of managers and executives—a traditionally difficult group of employees to select. But a major problem with the test is that it takes up to three hours and, like a work sample, is an individual test. Time needed to administer the In-Basket Test is prohibitive if there are many applicants.

The Leaderless Group Discussion (LGD) involves having a group of applicants (normally, two to eight) engage in a job-related discussion in which no spokesman or group leader has been named. Raters observe and then assess each applicant on such factors as "individual prominence", "group goal facilitation", and "sociability." Scores on these factors are then used as a hiring basis. The reliability of the LGD increases with the number of people in the group. The typical validity coefficient for the LGD is in the .25–.35 range.

While neither the In-Basket Test nor the LGD has the validity of a typical work sample, remember that the criterion of success for a manager is usually more difficult to define. If a mechanic installs a motor up-side-down, people know about it right away. If a manager picks the wrong people to do a job, it can be some time before the source of the problem is found. Thus the lower validities usually found in the selection of managerial personnel are as attributable to problems with the criterion and its proper articulation as anything else.

## BIOGRAPHICAL INFORMATION

If they gave an Academy Award for the "most consistently valid predictor," biographical information would be the winner. Of all the predictors used to forecast job performance, biographical information (as a general class) has consistently shown the greatest validity. What is more remarkable about this finding is that it occurs across wide differences in people, jobs, and criteria. Though in some cases, certain tests, interviews, work samples, etc., outperform biographical information, as a general type of predictor, it has the best overall track record.

Biographical information is frequently recorded on an application blank. The application blank, in turn, can be used as a selection device, where the information presented by the applicant is the basis for hiring the applicant. However, application blanks need not be used for personnel selection purposes. Sometimes the information is used just to facilitate record-keeping, so the company knows the applicant's home telephone number in case of an emergency, the applicant's home address, and so forth. One issue in developing application blanks is to decide what questions to ask. The answer is not too difficult. If the application blank is being used only for record-keeping purposes, ask only questions that are useful or meaningful for the company, such as address, telephone number, etc. Questions like "How many older brothers do you have?" would have no practical value and should not be asked. However, if the application blank is being used for selection purposes, those items that are predictive of job performance should be retained for making hiring decisions. While the maintenance of personnel record-keeping is important, we will focus on the latter use of application blanks—as a predictor of job success.

Application blanks (or personnel data forms, as they are sometimes called) are quite varied. Some ask as few as 15 to 20 questions; others, which are used for research purposes, may have as many as 800 items. Some questions can be verified: "Did you graduate from high school?" "What did your father do for a living?" Other questions are self-reports that cannot be verified: "Did you enjoy high school?" "Did you get along well with your father?". Most traditional application blanks contain only the former types. But some companies ask both types of questions (called "biodata"—a contraction for biographical data) for selection purposes.

In using biographical information for selection purposes, the following procedure is followed. A criterion of interest is chosen, usually productivity, turnover, or absenteeism. The sample of current employees may be divided into two groups (high productivity-low productivity, high turnover-low turnover, or high absenteeism-low absenteeism). Management usually decides what constitutes "high" and "low" performance. The next step is to see if the high and low criterion groups differ in terms of the characteristics of the people in the groups. If the responses to some biographical questions occur far more often in one group, that question is predictive of job performance. For instance, suppose 80 percent of the high-productivity group graduated from high school and only 30 percent of the low-productivity group did. That item ("Did you graduate from high school?") would be predictive of productivity and could be used to hire employees. Items that do not differentiate criterion groups would not be used for selection purposes.

It is common to assign scoring points to valid items. An item that greatly differentiated the criterion groups might be worth 3 points; an item that only marginally differentiated the criterion groups might be worth only 1 point. By adding the points, each applicant receives a total score. The company then sets a passing score based on the responses (and scoring weights) of their currently successful employees. All applicants that meet or exceed that passing score would be hired; others would not.

Some items may be predictive of performance in certain jobs, while other items may predict job performance in other jobs. It is possible to develop scoring *keys* to evaluate applicants for different jobs. Let's say that items 1, 3, 4, 5, 8, 9, and 10 were valid for predicting success as a clerk. A scoring key for a clerk's job would be a cardboard template with holes cut to show the responses to those questions. The administrator could quickly find the applicant's score based on the responses to those seven items. Other scoring keys would be developed for other jobs. Keep in mind that some items may be valid for all jobs. But items that are not valid for any job should be removed.

The literature is filled with examples of useful applications of biographical information. Cascio (1976) reported validity coefficients of .77 and .79 for predicting the turnover of white and black workers, respectively. While the magnitude of these validity coefficients is extremely impressive, what's also desirable is that the application blank method was fair to members of both racial groups. Other researchers have reported the success of application blanks in predicting salary earnings, absenteeism, and productivity. Lee and Booth (1974) showed that the proper use of an application blank resulted in a cost savings of $250,000 over a 25-month period. Also, the method is not complicated or too costly to develop. It takes time to identify the valid items (which is an on-going process), but after that, the method is quite efficient.

Two other issues are relevant to this type of predictor. One deals with how truthful people are. What little information we have on this topic is that most people don't lie. Cascio (1975) reported a correlation of .94 between self-reported information on an application blank and later verified answers to the same questions. This was taken as evidence of the truthfulness of such answers. Other researchers have reported less positive results. People seem to be more honest when they think their answers will be verified.

A second issue is the stability of the validity coefficients over time. Most studies show validity decay, and some report more than others. One application blank used to predict turnover had an initial validity of .74. Two years later, the validity fell to .61; three years later, it was .38; and five years later, it was .07. When the scoring key was revised, only 3 of the original 15 valid items were retained, so application blanks should be revalidated on a systematic, short-term basis. Changes in applicant pools, job market conditions, and the jobs themselves cause the validity coefficients to be unstable. Continually reassessing items is cumbersome. But, given the spectacular validity coefficients reported as well as the relative freedom from discrimination charges, the gains seem to far outweigh the problems.

As a final note, one might ask *why* biographical information is so valid. There is little in the way of theory to suggest an answer. I propose two answers. A detailed biographical form samples a large domain of activities and interests in a person's life. There is frequently a fair degree of consistency in the lives of people; individuals who played with mechanical toys as children often retain interest in manipulating mechanical objects as adults. The oft-used axiom in I/O psychology that "the best predictor of future behavior is past behavior of a similar kind" is perhaps the core of the validity of biographical information. Owens and Schoenfeldt (1979) have documented the validity of biographical information for a host of criterion variables ranging from selecting a major in college to performance on the job. A second explanation is psychometric in nature. Biographical information is very reliable. Since validity is limited by reliability, the high reliability of biographical information does not put any "ceiling" on its potential validity.

## PEER ASSESSMENT

Rather than having supervisors evaluate employees, an alternative is to have employees evaluate each other. This is the basis of *peer assessment* (Kane & Lawler, 1978). Though the peer assessment technique has some peculiar limitations, the method has yielded encouraging results when applicable.

Peer assessments are best used when the applicants for a job have known each other for some time. It is not employed for initial entry into an organization, but is used for selection into advanced positions. It has been used in the military to predict success as an officer and in industry to predict success after training. Applicants answer such questions as "Which of you do you think will make the best officer?" and "Who do you think will score the highest on the final exam in this course?" Responses are tabulated and then correlated with a criterion of performance. Hollander (1965) reported that peer ratings made in the third week of officer training correlated .40 with ratings of success as an officer three years later. Mayfield (1972) found that peer assessments made by life insurance salesmen in a training program correlated .29 with tenure and .30 with production. These ratings, made 18 days after the start of the training program, were predictive of those two criteria one year later.

By far the biggest limitation of peer assessments is that they cannot be used prior to hiring. Despite this practical limitation, it is apparent that candidates themselves, after a brief exposure to each other, have a fairly accurate sense of their own respective ability. It is likely that industrial use of peer assessments will continue in the future based on their validity and ease of administration.

## LETTERS OF RECOMMENDATION

One of the most commonly used and least valid of all predictors is the letter of recommendation. Letters of recommendation and reference checks are as widespread in personnel selection as the interview and the application blank. Unfortunately, they usually lack the same validity. Letters of recommendation are usually written in behalf of an applicant by either a current employer, professional associate, or personal friend. The respondent rates the applicant on such dimensions as leadership ability and written and oral communication skills, etc. The responses are then used as a basis for hiring. When validating the letter of recommendation as a predictor, the two most frequently used criteria are tenure and supervisory ratings.

Muchinsky (1979) completed a review of letters of recommendation, and discovered their *average* validity was .13. Some types of people even make recommendations that have an *inverse* relationship with the criterion; i.e., if the applicant is recommended for hire, the company would be best to reject him or her! One of the biggest problems with letters of recommendation is their restriction in range. As you might expect, almost all letters of recommendation are positive. Most often, the applicants themselves choose who will write the letters, so it isn't surprising that they pick people who will make them look good. Because of this restriction in range on the predictor (i.e., almost all applicants are described positively), the lack of predictive ability of the letter of recommendation is no surprise. While a few studies using specially constructed evaluation forms have reported moderate validity coefficients, the typical validity coefficient is close to zero. Because of their limited validity, letters of recommendation should not be taken too seriously in making personnel selection decisions. The only major exception to this statement would be the following condition. When applicants are described in positive terms, you won't know if they will be successful on the job or not. However, on those rare occasions when the applicant is described in negative terms (sometimes even only mildly), such an assessment is usually indicative of future problems on the job. Those types of letters should be taken seriously. On par though, the percentage of letters of recommendation that contain nonsupportive information about an applicant is very small.

## SUMMARY

In this chapter, we have examined six major types of predictors used in personnel selection: psychological tests (intelligence, aptitude, ability, personality and interest), interviews, work samples and situational exercises, biographical information, peer assessments, and letters of recommendation. These predictors have been validated against a number of different criteria for a variety of occupational groups. Some predictors have been used more extensively than others. Furthermore, certain predictors have historically shown more validity than others. Figure 4–6 shows the results of Ghiselli's (1966) study. He tabulated the proportion of validity coefficients of .50 or higher using job proficiency as the criterion. Not all of the predictors in this chapter were included in his review. But, note that the most consistently good predictors are biographical information and work samples. Over half (55 percent) of all studies using biographical information report validity coefficients over .50. Some predictors rarely demonstrate this validity (tests of spatial ability are only 3 percent). However, as the data indicate, in various proportions all predictors have reached that level of predictability.

At a horse race, odds represent predictions of who will win the race. The odds are determined by the horse's past performance and culminate in predictions ranging from "favorites" to "long-shots."

*photo by Lou Hodges*

**Figure 4–6**     **Proportion of validity coefficients .50 or higher with job proficiency as the criterion**

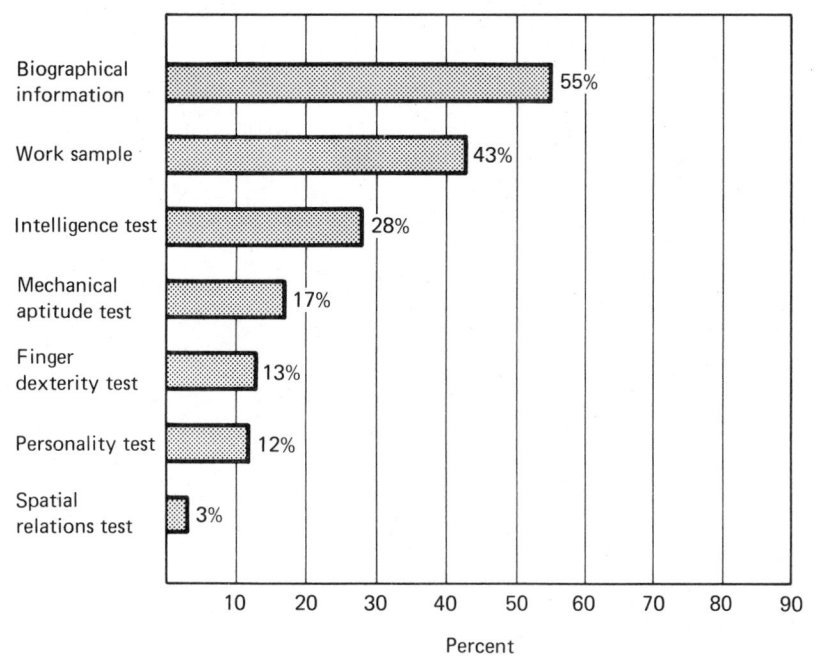

SOURCE: E. E. Ghiselli, *The Validity of Occupational Aptitude Tests* (New York: John Wiley & Sons, 1966).

In Chapter 3, we listed the attributes of good criteria. A similar list can be derived for predictors.

1. Reliable.
2. Valid.
3. Bias-free.
4. Consistent from one sample to another.
5. Inexpensive.
6. Not time consuming.

The ideal predictor would be an accurate forecaster of the criterion, equally applicable across different groups of people, and not too lengthy or costly to administer. But predictors rarely meet all these standards in practice.

Table 4–5 shows an integration of the content of Chapters 3 and 4. Across the top are the criteria of interest to I/O psychologists as discussed in Chapter 3. Down the column are the predictors that have been used to predict the criteria. Eight criteria and 11 predictors are listed. While occasionally other criterion and predictor variables have been used, personnel selection normally involves establishing these 88 ($8 \times 11$) predictor-criterion relationships. The entrees L, M, S in the table reflect whether a large (L), moderate (M), or small (S) amount of research has been devoted to the particular predictor-criterion relationship. Certain relationships have been studied far more extensively than others, while others may never have been established at all. The criterion of ratings has been used extensively in the psychological literature, as has the predictor of biographical information. Much less information is known about the criterion of acci-

**Table 4–5**      **Job performance criteria and predictors used in personnel selection and the frequency of their investigation**

| Predictors | Production | Absence | Turnover | Accidents | Salary | Promotions | Sales | Ratings |
|---|---|---|---|---|---|---|---|---|
| Intelligence tests | L | S | M | S | S | M | S | L |
| Aptitude tests | L | M | S | S | S | S | S | L |
| Ability tests | L | M | M | M | S | S | S | M |
| Interest inventories | S | S | M | S | S | M | S | M |
| Personality inventories | M | M | S | S | M | M | L | M |
| Interviews | S | S | M | S | M | M | M | L |
| Work samples | M | S | S | S | S | S | S | M |
| Situational exercises | S | S | S | S | L | L | M | L |
| Biographical information | M | L | L | L | M | M | M | L |
| Peer assessments | S | S | L | S | M | L | M | L |
| Letters of recommendation | S | S | M | S | S | S | S | M |

Note: L, M, and S indicate a large, moderate, or small amount of research directed toward a predictor-criterion relationship.

dents and the predictor of situational exercises, respectively. Finally, to the best of my knowledge, some predictor-criterion relationships have never been examined, such as using peer assessments to predict the criterion of absence. Table 4–5 provides an overview of the principal participants in the personnel selection process. The mechanics of that process and related issues are discussed in Chapter 5.

# CASE STUDY

Bay Ridge was a city with a population of about 125,000 people. The city experienced remarkable growth over a short period of time. There were two major reasons. First, several large industries had been attracted to the area, and with more jobs, there were more people. Second, due to a rezoning plan, several small townships were incorporated into Bay Ridge, and this caused a sudden burgeoning in the city's official population.

As a consequence of this growth, the city needed to expand its police force. For many years, the city had only a relatively small force and used only a brief interview to select the officers. Recently, however, there had been several complaints against the city's selection interview. Due to the complaints and the need to hire many more officers, the city council decided to abandon the old method of hiring. The city commissioned a job analysis for police officers and determined that three major factors contributed to success on the job. The next step was to develop selection measures to assess each of the three factors. The city council called a meeting with the city personnel director to get a progress report on the selection measures being proposed. Four city council members and Ron Davenport, the city personnel director, attended.

**Davenport:** I'm pleased to report to you that we have made substantial progress in our study. The job analysis revealed that the following factors determine success on the police force: (1) physical agility, (2) sensitivity to community relations, and (3) practical judgment. We are fairly pleased with the tests developed to assess two of the factors, although one of them is causing us some problems.

**Councilmember DeRosa:** Would you kindly elaborate on what these factors mean?

**Davenport:** Certainly. Physical agility is important in being able to apprehend and possibly disarm a suspect. It is also important in being able to carry a wounded officer out of the line of hostile fire. Sensitivity to community relations involves knowledge of racial and ethnic problems in the city, plus an ability to work with the community in preventing crime. Practical judgment entails knowing when it is advisable to pursue a criminal suspect and what methods of action to use in uncertain situations.

**Councilmember Flory:** How do you propose to measure physical agility?

**Davenport:** It looks like we'll go with some physical standard, as being able to carry a 150-pound dummy 25 yards, or something similar. We might also use some height and weight requirements. We could have some problems with sex differences in that females are not as strong as males, but I think we can work it out.

**Councilmember Reddinger:** Are all of these tests going to be performance tests?

**Davenport:** No, that's the only one so far. For the community relations factor, we're going to use a group interview. We'll ask the candidates how they would go about dealing with some hypothetical but realistic problem, like handling a domestic argument. The interviewers will grade their answers and give them a total score.

**Councilmember Hamilton:** What will be a passing score in this interview?

**Davenport:** We haven't determined that yet. We're still trying to determine if this is the best way to measure the factor.

**Councilmember Flory:** How do you plan to measure practical judgment?

**Davenport:** That's the problem case. We really haven't figured out a good test of that yet.

**Councilmember DeRosa:** How about a test of general intelligence?

**Davenport:** It appears that practical judgment is related to intelligence, but its not the same thing. A person can be very intelligent in terms of verbal and numerical ability but not possess a great deal of practical judgment.

**Councilmember Reddinger:** Hasn't some psychologist developed a test of practical judgment?

**Davenport:** Not that we know of. You also have to remember that the type of judgment a police officer has to demonstrate is not the same thing as the type of judgment, say, a banker has to show. I guess I'm saying there appears to be different kinds of practical judgment.

**Councilmember Hamilton:** Could you use some personality inventory to measure it?"

**Davenport:** I don't think so. I doubt if practical judgment is a personality trait. At least I'm not aware of any direct measures of it.

**Councilmember Flory:** How about using the interview again? A police officer has to demonstrate practical judgment in handling community relations. Can't you just expand the interview a bit?

**Davenport:** That's a possibility we're considering. Another possibility is to put candidates in a test situation where they have to demonstrate their practical judgment. It could be a pretty expensive method, all things considered, but it may be the best way to go.

**Councilmember DeRosa:** I have a feeling, Mr. Davenport, that your success in measuring practical judgment will determine just how many good officers we get on the force.

Questions

1. The city would have to validate whatever predictors they developed to select police officers. What method or methods of validation do you think they would use?
2. Do you think that biographical information might be useful in predicting success as a police officer? If so, what types of items might be useful?
3. Describe a work sample or situational exercise which might measure practical judgment.
4. What would be a problem in using peer assessments to select police officers?
5. Imagine the personnel department asked you to assist them in developing or selecting predictors of police officer performance. What advice would you give them?

# REFERENCES

Anastasi, A. *Psychological testing* (4th ed.). New York: Macmillan, 1976.

Arvey, R. D. Unfair discrimination in the employment interview: Legal and psychological aspects. *Psychological Bulletin*, 1979, *86*, 736–765.

Bass, B. M. The leaderless group discussion. *Psychological Bulletin*, 1954, *51*, 465–492.

Bennett, G. K. *Test of Mechanical Comprehension*. New York: Psychological Corporation, 1940.

Bingham, W. V. D., & Moore, B. V. *How to interview*, 3rd ed. New York: Harper & Row, 1941.

Blum, M. L., & Naylor, J. C. *Industrial psychology: Its theoretical and social foundations*. New York: Harper & Row, 1968.

Brugnoli, G. A., Campion, J. E., & Basen, J. A. Racial bias in the use of work samples for personnel selection. *Journal of Applied Psychology*, 1979, *64*, 119–123.

Buros, O. K. (Ed.) *Personality tests and reviews*. Highland Park, N.J.: Gryphon Press, 1970.

Buros, O. K. (Ed.) *Tests in print* II. Highland Park, N.J.: Gryphon Press, 1974.

Buros, O. K. (Ed.) *The eighth mental measurements yearbook*. Highland Park, N.J.: Gryphon Press, 1978.

Campion, J. E. Work sampling for personnel selection. *Journal of Applied Psychology*, 1972, *56*, 40–44.

Carlson, R. E. Employment decisions: Effect of mode of applicant presentation on some outcome measures. *Personnel Psychology*, 1968, *21*, 193–207.

Carlson, R. E. The current status of judgmental techniques in industry. Paper presented at the symposium "Alternatives to paper and pencil personnel testing." University of Pittsburgh, May 1972.

Cascio, W. F. Accuracy of verifiable biographical information blank responses. *Journal of Applied Psychology*, 1975, *60*, 767–769.

Cascio, W. F. Turnover, biographical data, and fair employment practice. *Journal of Applied Psychology*, 1976, *61*, 576–580.

Crawford, J. E., & Crawford, D. M. *Small Parts Dexterity Test*. New York: Psychological Corporation, 1946.

Cronbach, L. J. *Essentials of psychological testing*. New York: Harper & Row, 1970.

Dunnette, M. D., & Bass, B. M. Behavioral scientists and personnel management. *Industrial Relations*, 1963, *2*, 115–130.

Equal Employment Opportunity Commission. Adoption by four agencies of uniform guidelines on employee selection procedures. *Federal Register*, 1978, *43*, 38290–38309.

Frederiksen, N. *Organization climates and administrative performance*. Princeton, N.J.: Educational Testing Service, 1968.

Ghiselli, E. E. *The validity of occupational aptitude tests*. New York: John Wiley & Sons, 1966.

Ghiselli, E. E. The validity of aptitude tests in personnel selection. *Personnel Psychology*, 1973, *26*, 461–477.

Green, S. B., Lissitz, R. W., & Mulaik, S. A. Limitations of coefficient alpha as an index of test unidimensionality. *Educational and Psychological Measurement*, 1977, 37, 827–838.

Guion, R. M. "Content validity" in moderation. *Personnel Psychology*, 1978, *31*, 205–213.

Guion, R. M., & Gottier, R. F. Validity of personality measures in personnel selection. *Personnel Psychology*, 1965, *18*, 135–164.

Hathaway, S. R., & McKinley, J. C. *Minnesota Multiphasic Personality Inventory* (rev. ed.). New York: Psychological Corporation, 1943.

Holland, J. L. *Manual for the Vocational Preference Inventory*. Palo Alto, Calif.: Consulting Psychologists Press, 1965.

Hollander, E. P. Validity of peer nominations in predicting a distant performance criterion. *Journal of Applied Psychology*, 1965, *49*, 434–438.

Kalleberg, A. L., & Kluegel, J. R. Analysis of the multitrait-multimethod matrix: Some limitations and an alternative. *Journal of Applied Psychology,* 1975, *60,* 1–9.

Kane, J. S., & Lawler, E. E. Methods of peer assessment. *Psychological Bulletin,* 1978, *85,* 555–586.

Lee, R., & Booth, J. M. A utility analysis of a weighted application blank designed to predict turnover for clerical employees. *Journal of Applied Psychology,* 1974, *59,* 516–518.

Likert, R., & Quasha, W. H. *Revised Minnesota Paper From Board Test.* New York: Psychological Corporation, 1941–1948.

Mayfield, E. C. Value of peer nominations in predicting life insurance sales performance. *Journal of Applied Psychology,* 1972, *56,* 319–323.

Mount, M. K., Muchinsky, P. M., & Hanser, L. M. The predictive validity of a work sample: A laboratory study. *Personnel Psychology,* 1977, *30,* 637–645.

Muchinsky, P. M. The utility of work samples in complying with EEOC guidelines. *Personnel Journal,* 1975, *54,* 218–220.

Muchinsky, P. M. The use of reference reports in personnel selection: A review and evaluation. *Journal of Occupational Psychology,* 1979, *52,* 287–297.

Nagle, B. F. Criterion development. *Personnel Psychology,* 1953, *6,* 271–289.

Otis, A. S. *Otis Self-Administering Tests of Mental Ability.* Tarrytown-on-Hudson, N.Y.: World, 1922–1929.

Owens, W. A., & Schoenfeldt, L. F. Toward a classification of persons. *Journal of Applied Psychology,* 1979, *65,* 569–607.

Paterson, D. G. *Minnesota Spatial Relations Test.* Chicago: Stoelting, 1930.

*Principles for the validation and use of personnel selection procedures* (2nd ed.). Berkeley, Calif.: Division of Industrial-Organizational Psychology, 1980.

Schmidt, F. L., Greenthal, A. L., Berner, J. G., Hunter, J. E., & Seaton, F. W. Job sample vs. paper-and-pencil trades and technical tests: Adverse impact and examinee attitudes. *Personnel Psychology,* 1977, *30,* 187–198.

Schmitt, N. Social and situational determinants of interview decisions: Implications for the employment interview. *Personnel Psychology,* 1976, *29,* 79–101.

*Standards for educational and psychological tests.* Washington, D.C.: American Psychological Association, 1974.

Strong, E. K., Jr. *Vocational interests of men and women.* Stanford, Calif.: Stanford University Press, 1943.

Tenopyr, M. L. Content-construct confusion. *Personnel Psychology,* 1977, *30,* 47–54.

Tiffin, J. *Purdue Pegboard.* Chicago: Science Research Associates, 1941.

Tiffin, J. Personal communication, 1970.

Tiffin, J., & Lawshe, C. H., Jr. *The Adaptability Test.* Chicago: Science Research Associates, 1942.

Verplank, W. S. The control of the content of conversation: Reinforcement of statements of opinion. *Journal of Abnormal and Social Psychology,* 1955, *51,* 668–676.

Wernimont, P. F., & Campbell, J. P. Signs, samples, and criteria. *Journal of Applied Psychology,* 1968, *52,* 372–376.

Wonderlic, E. F., & Hovland, C. I. The Personnel Test: A re-standardized abridgement of the Otis S. A. test for business and industrial use. *Journal of Applied Psychology,* 1939, *23,* 685–702.

# chapter 5  PERSONNEL DECISIONS

Personnel decisions are decisions that affect people's work lives. They include hiring, promotions, training, placement, and termination of employment. These decisions can be evaluated in terms of *institutional* or *individual* criteria. Institutional criteria refer to the extent that the decision ultimately benefits the company or institution, as indexed by greater productivity and reduced costs. Individual criteria refer to the extent that the decision ultimately benefits the individual, as indexed by personal satisfaction and feelings of accomplishment. Institutional decisions aim to enhance the attainment of institutional objectives and are usually made on the basis of some objective standards. These objective standards reflect a person's predicted probability of success based on test scores, performance in an interview, or some other measure. Most companies do not offer a job unless there is a high probability that the person would succeed.

Individual decisions are designed to enhance the attainment of individual objectives and usually are made on the basis of both subjective and objective standards. Subjective standards involve individual preferences, likes, and tastes. A person might seek a career as a psychologist because he or she likes (or believes they would like) the work psychologists perform. An objective standard used to aid in vocational choices is a vocational interest inventory, such as the Strong Vocational Interest Blank discussed in the previous chapter. By taking the interest inventory, people can see if their vocational interests and values are similar to those of people already in a given profession. A vocational counselor might advise a person to pursue a career that is a good match between what they would like to do and what they seem to be most suited for on the basis of their aptitudes and abilities.

In almost all cases, there are limitations on both institutions and individuals with regard to personnel decisions. That is, a company cannot hire all applicants to discover which ones will succeed on the job. Likewise, individuals cannot try out 10 or 20 careers. Choices or decisions have to be made; some people are hired (or trained or promoted), and others are rejected. Likewise, some career is eventually selected, and others are ruled out. No one likes to make mistakes. Companies prefer to have the "right people," and people prefer to choose the "right career." This chapter examines the personnel decision process and explores the issues inherent in making good decisions.

Fortunately, there is a fair degree of overlap between personnel decisions that are "good" for the institution and those that are "good" for the individual. Decisions that benefit the company usually benefit the individual; decisions that hurt the company usually end up hurting the individual. A good match between a person's talents and a company's needs enhances the attainment of both individual and institutional goals.

Sometimes, however, legitimate conflict between individual and institutional goals does occur. A company may wish to promote an employee based on his or her abilities. It would benefit the company to have this person in that job. The employee, on the other hand, may not want the added responsibilities and pressures of the new job (especially if it entails a move to another city). So it would benefit the individual, all things considered, not to take the position. Here is a case of conflicting goals. Another, more frequent, case involves having too many qualified applicants competing for a few job openings. The company is in a "sweet" position; they can choose whomever they want knowing that their needs will be met. The rejected applicants, however, would not have their needs met. In such a case, the company must have legitimate and professionally sound reasons for hiring the people they did. The selection process must be valid and fair. This chapter, therefore, examines the process of making personnel decisions and the factors that help assess the degree of fit between the person and the job.

## PREDICTION OF JOB PERFORMANCE

Decisions made about people involve predictions—whether they will succeed on the job, pass a training program, be promoted, etc. The prediction may be based on a subjective judgment from an interview (i.e., the applicant passed), or on an objective, statistical factor. For example, a passing test score is set at 8 because it is predicted (via statistical techniques) that those applicants who score 8 or above will succeed on the job. It is important to understand how that passing score is determined.

**Regression analysis**

The statistical technique used to predict criterion performance on the basis of a predictor score is called *regression* analysis. While a correlation coefficient is useful to show the degree of relationship between two variables, it is not useful for predicting one variable from the other. Regression analysis, however, does permit prediction of a person's status on one variable (the criterion) based on their status on another variable (the predictor). If we assume that the relationship between the two variables is linear (as it usually is), the relationship between the variables can be described mathematically with a regression equation:

$$\hat{Y} = a + bX$$

where

$\hat{Y}$ = The predicted criterion score
$a$ = A mathematical constant reflecting where the regression line intercepts the ordinate (or $Y$ axis)
$b$ = A mathematical constant reflecting the slope of the regression line
$X$ = The predictor score for a given individual.

The values of $a$ and $b$ are derived through mathematical procedures which minimize the distance between the regression line (i.e., a line useful for making predictions) and the pairs of predictor-criterion data points. To develop a regression equation, you need predictor and criterion data on a sample of people. Let's say we have a sample of 100 employees. Supervisor ratings of job performance are the criterion, while the predictor test we wish to investigate is an intelligence test. We administer the intelligence test to the workers, collect the criterion data, and then see if we can predict the criterion scores on the basis of the intelligence test. On the basis of the predictor-criterion data, the following regression equation is derived:

$$\hat{Y} = 1 + .5X$$

The relationship between the two variables is shown in Figure 5–1. Note that the regression line crosses the $Y$ axis at a value of 1 (i.e., $a = 1$). Also, for every two-unit increase in $X$, there is a corresponding one-unit increase in $Y$. Thus, the slope of the regression line, defined as the change in $Y$ divided by the change in $X$, equals ½ or .5 (i.e., $b = .5$).

For any value of $X$, we can now predict a corresponding $Y$ score. For example, if someone scores 12 on the intelligence test, their predicted criterion rating would be:

**Figure 5–1**                    **Predictor-criterion scatterplot and regression line of best fit**

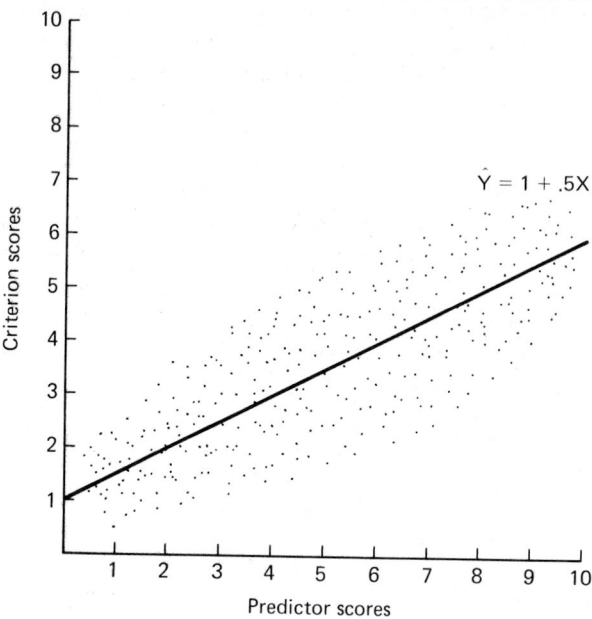

$$\hat{Y} = 1 + .5 \ (12)$$
$$\hat{Y} = 7$$

If a supervisor rating of 5 represented adequate job performance (and you don't want anyone with a lower rating), the regression equation can be worked backwards to get the minimum passing score.

$$5 = 1 + .5(X)$$
$$X = 8$$

So, if we use the intelligence test to hire, we would not accept any applicants who scored less than 8. Scores less than 8 would result in a predicted level of job performance lower than we want. There is also another way to find the passing score. In Figure 5–1, locate the value of 5 on the $Y$ axis (the criterion). Move horizontally to the regression line, and then drop down to the corresponding point on the $X$ axis (the predictor). The score is 8.

In addition to thinking about $b$ as the slope of the regression line, there is another way to view $b$ that shows the relationship between correlation and regression. Regression is based on correlation. That should make sense because if you can predict one variable from another, those two variables should be related. An alternative conceptualization for $b$ is the correlation between $X$ and $Y$, times the ratio of the standard deviation of $Y$, divided by the standard deviation of $X$. That is:

$$b = r_{xy} \left(\frac{s_y}{s_x}\right)$$

If the correlation between the intelligence test and the supervisor rating was .60, the standard deviation of the supervisor rating $(s_y)$ was 2.5, and the standard deviation of the intelligence test $(s_x)$ was 3, we would have:

$$b = .60 \left(\frac{2.5}{3.0}\right)$$
$$= .5$$

Using this way of thinking about $b$, you can see that if there were no correlation between the two variables, you couldn't predict one from the other. If $r_{xy} = .00$, then $b = 0$. If $b = 0$, the regression line would have no slope (it would be parallel to the $X$ axis), and every value of $X$ would yield the same predicted value of $Y$, thus making prediction of $Y$ pointless. Also, if the standard deviation of the criterion and predictor are equal, then the slope of the regression line equals the correlation coefficient, or $b = r$. To understand this relationship, Figure 5–2 shows three different regression lines. Note that the intercept and slope in the graph correspond to their expression in the equation.

**Figure 5–2**  **Three regression equations with their mathematical statements**

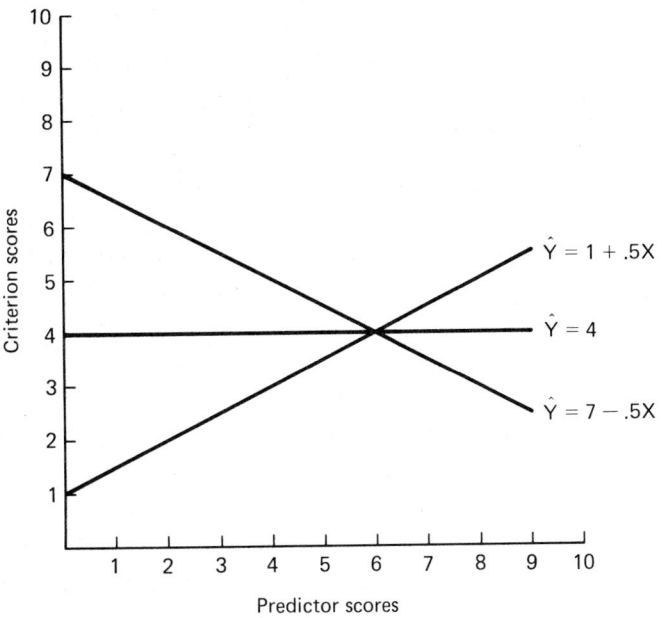

## Multiple predictors

To ensure better personnel decisions, many are made on the basis of more than one piece of information. How well two or more predictors combined improve the predictability of the criterion depends on their individual relationships to the criterion and their relationship to each other. Suppose two predictors both correlate with the criterion but do not correlate with each other. This relationship can be expressed in the following figure.

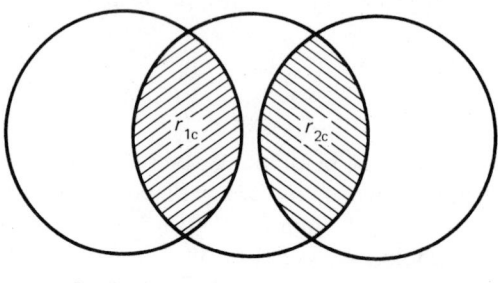

Predictor 1     Criterion     Predictor 2

The shaded area on the left shows how much the first predictor overlaps with the criterion. The overlap area is the validity of the (first) predictor, symbolized by the notation $r_{1c}$, where the subscript 1 stands for the first predictor, and $c$ stands for the criterion. The shaded area on the right shows the extent the second predictor overlaps with the criterion; its validity can be expressed as $r_{2c}$. As can be seen, a lot more of the criterion can be explained by using two predictors instead of one. Also note that the two predictors are unrelated to each other, meaning that they predict different aspects of the criterion. The combined relationship between two or more predictors and the criterion is referred to as a *multiple* correlation ($R$). The only conceptual difference between $r$ and $R$ is that the range of $R$ is from 0 to 1.0, while $r$ ranges from $-1.0$ to 1.0. When $R$ is squared, the resulting $R^2$ value represents the total amount of variance in the criterion that can be explained by two or more predictors. When predictors 1 and 2 are not correlated with each other, the squared multiple correlation ($R^2$) is equal to the sum of the squared individual validity coefficients, or:

$$R^2_{c.12} = r^2_{1c} + r^2_{2c}$$

For example, if

$$r_{1c} = .60 \text{ and } r_{2c} = .50$$
$$R^2_{c.12} = (.60)^2 + (.50)^2$$
$$= .36 + .25$$
$$= .61$$

The notation $R^2_{c.12}$ is "the squared multiple correlation between the criterion and two predictors." In this condition (when the two predictors are unrelated to each other), 61 percent of the variance in the criterion can be explained by two predictors.

In most cases, however, it is rare that two predictors which both relate to a criterion are unrelated to each other. Usually, all three variables share some variance with each other. That is, the intercorrelation between the two predictors $(r_{12})$ is not zero. Such a relationship is presented graphically in the following:

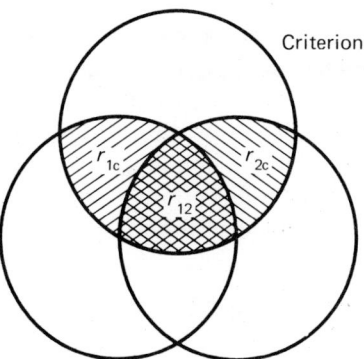

Criterion

Predictor 1    Predictor 2

In this figure, each predictor correlates substantially with the criterion $(r_{1c}$ and $r_{2c})$, but the two predictors also overlap each other $(r_{12})$. The addition of the second predictor adds more criterion variance than can be accounted for by one predictor alone. Yet all of the criterion variance accounted for by the second predictor is not new variance (part of it was explained by the first predictor). When there is a correlation between the two predictors $(r_{12})$, the equation for calculating the squared multiple correlation must be expanded to:

$$R^2_{c.12} = \frac{r^2_{1c} + r^2_{2c} - 2\,r_{12}\,r_{1c}\,r_{2c}}{1 - r^2_{12}}$$

For example, if the two predictors intercorrelate .30, given the validity coefficients from the previous example and $r_{12} = .30$, we have:

$$R^2_{c.12} = \frac{(.60)^2 + (.50)^2 - 2\,(.30)\,(.60)\,(.50)}{1 - (.30)^2}$$

$$= .47$$

As can be seen, the explanatory power of two intercorrelated predictor variables is diminished compared to when they are uncorrelated (.47 versus .61). This example provides a rule about multiple predictors: it is generally advisable to seek predictors that are related to the criterion but are uncorrelated with each other.[1] However, in practice, it is very difficult to find multiple variables that are statistically related to another variable (the criterion) but at the same time statistically unrelated to each other. Usually variables that are predictive of a criterion are also predictive of each other. Also note that the abbreviated version of the equation used to compute the squared multiple correlation with independent predictors is just a special case of the expanded equation, caused by $r_{12}$ being equal to zero.

## Suppressor variables

Suppressor variables are variables that enhance the prediction of the criterion even though they are unrelated to it. Usually when a variable is unrelated to the criterion, we think it is useless, and we discard it to search for better predictors. However, there is a case when such variables may be useful. The classic definition of a suppressor variable $(s)$ is a variable that is uncorrelated with the criterion $(r_{sc} = .00)$ but is correlated with another predictor $(r_{sp} \neq .00)$. Graphically that relationship would look like:

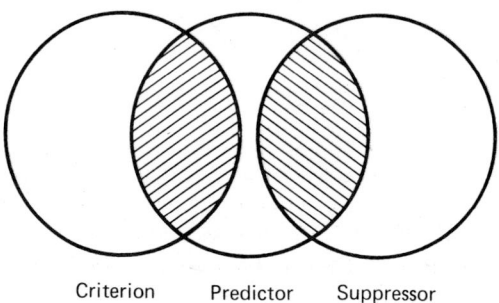

Criterion     Predictor     Suppressor

As can be seen, the predictor is correlated substantially with the criterion, but the suppressor is uncorrelated with the criterion. Yet the suppressor is correlated with the predictor, and the extent of the correlation is called the "suppressor effect." The suppressor effect removes a portion of the predictor variance that is uncorrelated with the criterion. You normally think of a useful predictor as one that increases common predictor-criterion variance. But a suppressor is useful because it decreases *uncor-related* predictor variance. Here is how a suppressor increases the multiple squared correlation. Suppose a predictor correlates .60 with the criterion, thus explaining 36 percent of the criterion variance. If a suppressor could

---

[1] In point of fact, the statistical relationship between the predictor intercorrelation $(r_{12})$ and the total predictability of a criterion $(R^2)$ is very complex. Dudycha, Dudycha, and Schmitt (1974) have shown that *negative* intercorrelations and *extreme* positive intercorrelations (.95 and greater) enhance predictability of the criterion beyond what would have been attained with independent $(r_{12} = .00)$ predictors. Of course, in reality, the likelihood of finding variables with such statistical properties is extremely small.

be found that correlated, say, .40, with the predictor (i.e., $r_{sp} = .40$), it would have this effect on $R^2$.

$$R^2_{c.12} = \frac{(.60)^2 + (.00)^2 - 2\,(.40)\,(.60)\,(.00)}{1 - (.40)^2}$$

$$= \frac{.36}{.84}$$

$$= .43$$

So by adding a suppressor variable to the prediction system, the percent of explained criterion variance goes from 36 percent to 43 percent, even though the suppressor shares no variance with the criterion. Suppressor variables are relatively rare, and when they are found, they are not always stable. Sorenson's (1966) research on predicting the job success of industrial mechanics is one example of how a suppressor variable enhanced prediction. Sorenson had a test of mechanical insight that stressed practical mechanics of the "nuts and bolts" type. It correlated .22 (i.e., $r_{pc} = .22$) with a criterion of job performance. He also had a test of mechanical principles that had a near-zero correlation with the criterion, (i.e., $r_{sc} = .00$) but a correlation of .71 with the other test (i.e., $r_{sp} = .71$). By adding the second test (which served as a suppressor), Sorenson could identify people with mechanical knowledge based on practical know-how (who would thus succeed on the job) as opposed to people with just traditional, academic knowledge (who would not succeed). The irrelevant contribution of academic knowledge about mechanical principles was thus ruled out by the suppressor variable.

## Moderator variables

Moderator variables affect or moderate predictor-criterion relationships without necessarily being correlated with either the predictor or criterion. A moderator variable is some characteristic of a person that makes it possible to predict the predictability of different individuals with a given test (Anastasi, 1976). Demographic variables, such as sex, age, or socioeconomic status, may act as moderators, as might scores on another test.

When computed for a total group of people, the validity coefficient of a test may be too low to be of much practical value. But when recomputed for subsets of individuals that differ on some identifiable characteristic (as sex, race, age, etc.), the validity may be high in one subset and low in another. Thus, the moderator variable would moderate the predictability of the criterion. In that subgroup where the predictor-criterion relationship is high, the predictor test would be useful. In the subgroup when the predictor-criterion relationship is low, the test would be inappropriate for making predictions, and some other test would have to be used.

The notion of a moderator variable that would differentiate subgroups of people on the basis of their predictability was proposed by Saunders (1956) and Ghiselli (1956a). Since that time, several empirical examples of moderators have been reported. In a study about predicting the job performance of taxi drivers, Ghiselli (1956a) found a modest correlation of .22 between an aptitude test and a criterion of job proficiency. When the taxi drivers were placed into subgroups on the basis of their occupational interest level, the correlation for drivers with high interest rose to .66. In this study, the level of occupational interest was the moderator of the aptitude test–job proficiency relationship. Seashore (1962) reported that the correlation between aptitude test scores and colleges grades was higher for women than men. In this study, sex of the student was the moderator variable.

But why does a moderator variable moderate a relationship? Sometimes the explanation seems to make sense in light of the data. In Ghiselli's (1956a) study, it makes sense that people who are more interested in their work would show a stronger relationship between aptitude and performance. In other cases, the explanation is more difficult. It is also hard to find *what* variable may be acting as a moderator. Although some elaborate statistical techniques have been developed to assess the effects of moderators (e.g., Bartlett, Bobko, Mosier, & Hannan, 1978), the identification of a moderator effect is not guided by any theory. In many cases, moderators are discovered by inspecting scatterplots, as in Figure 5–3.

Figure 5–3a shows a predictor-criterion scatterplot with a hypothetical correlation of .30 based on the total sample of subjects. Figures 5–3b and 5–3c show the results of dividing the total sample on the basis of some moderator variable. One scatterplot (5–3b) shows almost no relationship between predictor and criterion; the other (5–3c) shows a strong relationship.

**Figure 5–3a**                    **Undifferentiated predictor-criterion relationship**

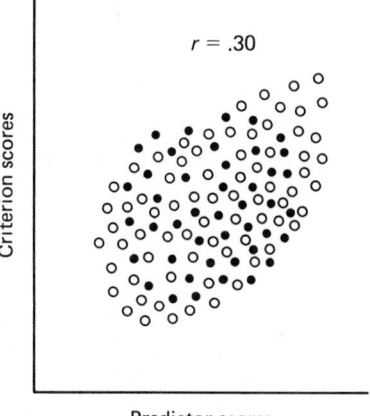

$r = .30$

Criterion scores

Predictor scores

**Figure 5–3b**                 **Predictor-criterion relationship illustrating low validity for a subgroup**

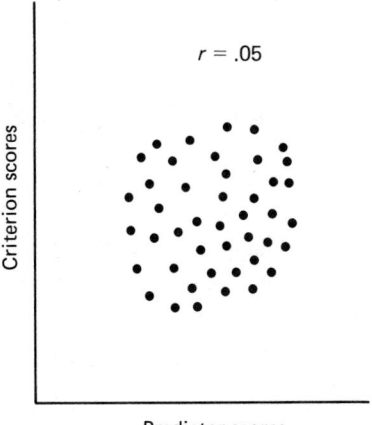

**Figure 5–3c**                 **Predictor-criterion relationship illustrating high validity for a subgroup**

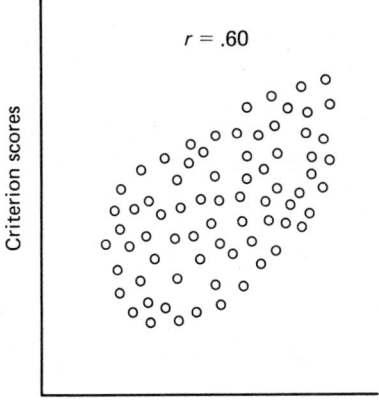

While the search for moderator variables has much intuitive appeal, moderators have not had much practical value in personnel selection research. In isolated studies, moderator variables have been identified, but as a general strategy of enhancing validity, they have met with limited success. Some researchers (e.g., Schmidt & Hunter, 1978) believe that their occurrence is strongly related to using small sample sizes. With a small sample size, the odds are greater of finding (moderator) variables which affect predictor-criterion relationships, but these effects dissipate with larger sample sizes. While there is strong evidence (e.g., Owens, 1978) that there are systematic differences among people based on certain variables (sex or age) associated with behavioral differences (i.e., scores on a test), few pervasive and stable moderators have been found.

## Multiple regression analysis

The relationship between correlation and regression is the foundation for the relationship between multiple correlation and multiple regression. Just as regression permits prediction on the basis of one predictor, multiple regression permits prediction on the basis of multiple predictors. The logic for using multiple regression is the same as the logic for using multiple correlation: it usually enhances prediction of the criterion.

As we noted before, the formula for a regression equation with one predictor is:

$$\hat{Y} = a + bX$$

When we expand this to the case of two predictors, we have

$$\hat{Y} = a + b_1 X_1 + b_2 X_2$$

where $X_1$ and $X_2$ are the two predictors and $b_1$ and $b_2$ are the regression weights associated with the two predictors. As before, the $b$ values are based in part upon the correlation between the predictors and the criterion. In addition, in multiple regression, the $b$ values are also influenced by the correlation among the predictors. However, the procedure for making predictions in multiple regression is similiar to the way predictions were made in one-predictor (or simple) regression. Suppose we have criterion data on a sample of industrial workers who then take two tests we think may be useful for hiring future workers. The data are analyzed to derive the values of $a$, $b_1$, and $b_2$, and we arrive at the following regression equation:

$$\hat{Y} = 2 + .4X_1 + .7X_2$$

If a person scores 30 on test 1 and 40 on test 2, that person's predicted criterion performance would be:

$$\hat{Y} = 2 + .4(30) + .7(40)$$
$$= 42$$

The degree of predictability afforded by the two predictors is measured by the multiple correlation between the predictors and the criterion. If the multiple correlation is large enough to be of some value for prediction purposes, we might use the two tests to hire future workers. The company would undoubtedly set a minimum predicted criterion score at a certain value (as 40). In this example, the person's predicted job performance score (42) was above the minimum score set by the company (40), so the person would be hired.

Multiple regression is not limited to just two predictors; predictors can be added to the regression equation until they no longer enhance prediction of the criterion. The $k$-predictor regression equation is simply an extension of the two-predictor regression equation, and all terms are interpreted as before. Such an equation would look like:

$$\hat{Y} = a + b_1X_1 + b_2X_2 + b_3X_3 + \cdots\cdots + b_kX_k$$

Usually, there comes a point where adding more predictors does not add to the prediction of the criterion. Four or five predictors usually do as good a job as regression equations with more numerous predictors. The reason is that the shared variance among the predictors becomes very large after 4 to 5 predictors, so adding more doesn't add unique variance in the criterion. If we could find another predictor that (1) was uncorrelated with the other predictors and (2) was correlated with the criterion, it should be a useful addition to the equation. Multiple regression is a very popular prediction strategy in I/O psychology; it is used extensively for a wide variety of research problems.

## Cross-validation

Cross-validation is a statistical technique involving regression analysis in general, but it is most commonly used with multiple regression (Mosier, 1951). Its purpose is to examine the stability of the regression weights, to test whether the predictive power of a regression equation is enduring or, alternatively, is not due to sample specific characteristics of the data (Cattin, 1980). Let's say that a company is interested in testing the validity of two tests that may be useful in hiring production workers. The company employs 200 production workers that can be used to test the tests in a concurrent criterion-related validity study. We give the two tests to all the workers, and then obtain criterion data on them reflective of their job performance. We then randomly divide the total sample into two groups of 100 workers each. We take the first sample of workers and develop a multiple regression equation on them, examining the extent to which the two tests are predictive of job performance. The resulting multiple regression equation might look like this:

$$\hat{Y} = 2 + .5X_1 + .6X_2$$

Let's assume the multiple correlation coefficient is .65. Using this regression equation, we then predict what the criterion scores will be for the second sample of workers based on the regression weights from the first. The first sample is the *validation* or *developmental* sample; the second sample is the *cross-validation* or *hold-out* sample. That is, the multiple regression equation is *developed* on the first sample, while the second sample is *held out* from the original analysis to test the stability of the regression weights.

If the regression equation is equally valid in making predictions in the second sample, the degree of predictability in the two samples should be equal. Applying the regression equation to the second sample, we discover the multiple correlation is .61. While .61 is quite good, it is not as good as the .65 in the first sample. We would conclude that the multiple regression equation did cross-validate fairly well because the two multiple correlation values were quite close to each other. A successful cross-validation means that the *a* and *b* values in the developmental sample are appropriate for making predictions in the hold-out sample. In other words, the *a* and *b* values are stable and can be used for prediction in another sample. Successful cross-validation adds confidence to our conclusions about the predictability of the criterion. The ultimate test of the goodness of cross-validation is a comparison of the multiple correlation coefficients. If the *a* and *b* values in the second sample were very different from the first sample (meaning the tests do not predict the criterion in the same manner), the resulting multiple correlation in the second sample would be very different. This implies that the *a* and *b* values are specific only to the developmental sample at the time the study was conducted. Therefore, we should be wary of the conclusions we draw regarding predictability and stability.

*Shrinkage* is the difference between the multiple correlation derived in the developmental sample and the multiple correlation derived in the hold-out sample. The amount of shrinkage in our problem was .65 − .61 = .04. The less the shrinkage, the more successful was the cross-validation. If the multiple correlation in the second sample had been .10 instead of .61, the shrinkage would have been .65 − .10 = .55, and our cross-validation would have been unsuccessful. Shrinkage is influenced by the similarity of the two samples, the number of predictors in the multiple regression equation, and the sample size. Large shrinkage is most likely when the two samples are quite different (e.g., the developmental sample had workers with a lot of experience, while the hold-out sample had mostly new employees) and when many predictors and few subjects are used. Little shrinkage is most likely when the two samples are comparable, few predictors are used, and many subjects are involved in the study. The proper ratio between the number of subjects and the number of predictors has been estimated around 10/1; i.e., there should be 10 subjects for every predictor in the equation. In our example, we had 100 subjects and two predictors (a ratio of 50/1), well within the proper bounds for cross-validation.

## DEVELOPMENT OF TEST BATTERIES

Because the predictability of a criterion is almost always enhanced by using multiple predictors, psychologists often employ several tests as predictors. The psychologist begins with several tests that he or she thinks may be predictive of the criterion. The tests that are used are referred to as a *test battery*. The initial test battery is experimental, because the psychologist does not know which tests will be predictive. Perhaps as many as 10 or 15 tests are included in the initial battery. The next step is to identify a subset of those tests that is predictive of the criterion. Several procedures have been proposed for creating an "optimal" test battery. One procedure is to start with the one test that is most predictive of the criterion. Then successively add predictors that will most increase the multiple correlation based on their individual validities as well as their correlations with the other tests. At some point, adding more predictors will not appreciably increase the predictability of the criterion. It is at that point where the final test battery is identified.

Table 5–1 is a list of 10 tests that might constitute a test battery, their individual correlation with the criterion, and the extent to which they add to the multiple correlation when added to the test battery. The tests are listed in order of their value to the battery. The first test, an intelligence test, has the largest single correlation with the criterion, so it is the first test in the battery. The second test, a test of mechanical aptitude, while *not* having the second largest correlation with the criterion, is added second to the battery because its incremental gain in the multiple correlation is greater than any other test. The remaining tests are added to the battery in order of the incremental increase in the multiple correlation. The value of the multiple correlation through adding new predictors is determined sequentially with multiple regression analysis. The final test battery would consist of the first six tests since the remaining tests don't add to the overall predictability of the criterion. While each of those four tests does correlate with the criterion, their intercorrelation with the other predictors is such that the variance in the criterion they account for has already been accounted for by the other tests. That is, the criterion variance accounted for is not unique. If psychologists were clairvoyant, they would have "known" that these six tests would comprise the final battery from the start. Because psychologists are not clairvoyant, it is only through the sequential testing of predictors that they arrive at the final battery.

Some other procedures (basically modifications of the above) have been

**Table 5–1**    **Sequential ordering of tests into a battery based on the incremental gain in the multiple correlation**

| Order of entry into battery | Test | Individual r | Cumulative $R^2$ |
|---|---|---|---|
| 1 | Intelligence | .50 | .25 |
| 2 | Mechanical aptitude | .31 | .32 |
| 3 | Spatial relations | .24 | .36 |
| 4 | Numerical ability | .45 | .39 |
| 5 | Verbal ability | .19 | .41 |
| 6 | Visual acuity | .21 | .43 |
| 7 | Abstract reasoning | .14 | .43 |
| 8 | Creative thinking | .09 | .43 |
| 9 | Finger dexterity | .26 | .43 |
| 10 | Eye-hand coordination | .22 | .43 |

proposed for developing test batteries. One such procedure is based on testing time, while another is based on cost. All other things being equal, the one preferred test out of several with equal validity is the one that (1) takes the least time to complete and (2) costs the least. These procedures not only attempt to arrive at a predictive test battery, but also one that is efficient in terms of time and money. These constraints add to the complexity of creating a test battery.

The final phase in developing a test battery is to examine it for shrinkage with cross-validation; a good test battery will not incur much shrinkage. Remember, one determinant of shrinkage is the number of predictors, so large test batteries are more likely to incur shrinkage, all other things being equal. We can place a lot of confidence in the generalizability of our test battery when shrinkage is small. So we could use the battery with different samples of employees, as opposed to coming up with a new battery for every different group of people.

## ASSESSING THE UTILITY OF A PREDICTOR

The *utility* of a predictor is the degree to which its use improves the quality of the people being selected beyond what would have occurred had that predictor not been used (Blum & Naylor, 1968). Several factors contribute to determining the utility of a predictor, some of which we will examine in close detail.

1. **Criterion reliability.** As we saw in the previous chapter, the measure of job performance against which a predictor is validated must be stable. Stability in the criterion is imperative; without it we cannot draw any accurate conclusions about predicted employee performance because that performance is too variable. It means little to talk about "average" job performance when performance fluctuates wildly. As was the case with predictor reliability, adequate criterion reliability would be in excess of .70.

2. **Criterion relevance.** Criterion relevance is analogous to predictor validity. It is important that the (actual) criterion that is selected to represent the ultimate criterion of job performance be an appropriate (i.e., *valid*) measure. The utility of a predictor is gauged by the improvement in the *quality* of the people being hired, so the criterion must be an accurate indicator of quality. If the criterion that is selected to represent job performance is lacking in relevance, it is highly unlikely that *any* predictor would systematically result in the hiring of better-quality people. While criterion relevance cannot be expressed in a quantitative way (and thus is somewhat elusive), it is necessary to have a "good" (relevant) criterion against which to validate a predictor.

3. **Predictor reliability.** As was stated earlier, a predictor must be reliable if it is going to have any value. But, high reliability alone is no guarantee that the predictor will be useful. It is possible for a predictor to have

*high reliability* but *low validity*. Remember, validity is not an inherent property of a test, but rather involves the appropriateness of inferences drawn from the test. A highly reliable clerical test may have no validity at all for hiring supervisors. However, the converse is not true. If a test has high validity, it must also have high reliability. The estimated upper limit of a test's validity is the square root of its reliability. That is, a test with a reliability of .80 would have as an upper limit a validity of .64. A test that has no reliability would, of course, also have no validity. Therefore, predictor reliability, like criterion reliability, is a necessary but not sufficient condition for predictor utility.

**4. Predictor validity.** While the first three factors are necessary for a predictor to have any utility, *predictor validity* is a factor that has a direct and highly visible effect. In fact, predictor utility is more influenced by predictor validity than any other factor.

To illustrate, consider Figure 5–4. It shows a scatterplot of a predictor-criterion correlation of zero. Along the predictor axis is a line, the *predictor cutoff*, that separates passing from failing applicants. People above the cutoff were accepted for hire, those below it were rejected. Along the criterion axis is a line (actually three lines all superimposed) that represents the average criterion performance of (1) the entire group of applicants, (2) the

**Figure 5–4**                    **Effect of a predictor test with no validity (*r* = .00) on test utility**

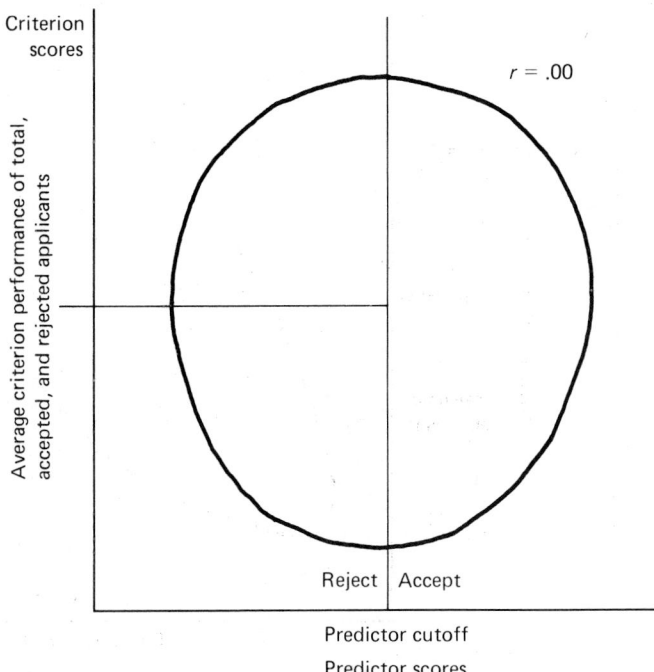

Criterion scores

*r* = .00

Average criterion performance of total, accepted, and rejected applicants

Reject | Accept

Predictor cutoff

Predictor scores

rejected applicants, and (3) the accepted applicants. Because the average criterion performance of the accepted group is no better than that of the rejected group, those two lines coincide with the third line—the average criterion performance of the entire group. Predictor utility is measured by the *difference* between the average performance of the accepted group minus the average performance of the total group. As can be seen, these two values are the same, so their difference equals zero. In other words, the predictor has no utility.

A different picture emerges for a predictor with substantial validity. Figure 5–5 shows a predictor-criterion correlation of .80. Again the predictor cutoff separates the accepted from the rejected applicants. This time, however, we see what effect a valid predictor has on criterion performance. The solid line is the criterion performance of the entire group, and it cuts the entire distribution of scores in half. The dashed line, the criterion performance of the rejected group, is *below* the performance of the total group. Finally, the dotted line, the criterion performance of the accepted group, is *above* the performance of the total group. Those people who would be expected to perform the best on the job are those above the predictor cutoff. In a simple and straightforward sense, that is what a valid predictor

**Figure 5–5**                    **Effect of a predictor with high validity (*r* = .80) on test utility**

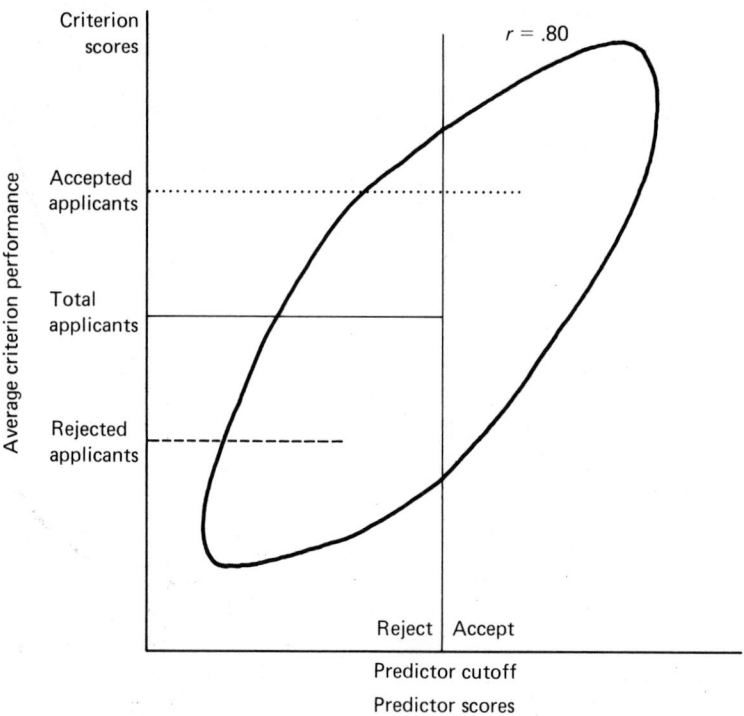

does in personnel selection—it identifies the more capable people from the total pool.

On the basis of this example, we see a direct relationship between predictor utility and predictor validity: the greater the validity of the predictor, the greater is its utility as measured by the increase in average criterion performance for the accepted group over that for the total group.

**5. Selection ratio.**  A fifth factor that determines the utility of a predictor is the selection ratio. The selection ratio (SR) is defined as the number of job openings (n) divided by the number of job applicants (N), or:

$$SR = \frac{n}{N}$$

When the SR is equal to 1.00 (there are as many openings as there are applicants) or greater (there are more openings than applicants), the use of any selection device has little meaning. The company can use any applicant who walks through the door. But most often, there are more applicants than openings (the SR is somewhere between 0 and 1.00), and thus, the SR has meaning for personnel selection.

The effect that the SR has on predictor utility can be seen in Figures 5–6 and 5–7. Let's assume we have a validity coefficient of .80 and the selec-

**Figure 5–6**                          **Effect of large selection ratio (SR = .75) on test utility**

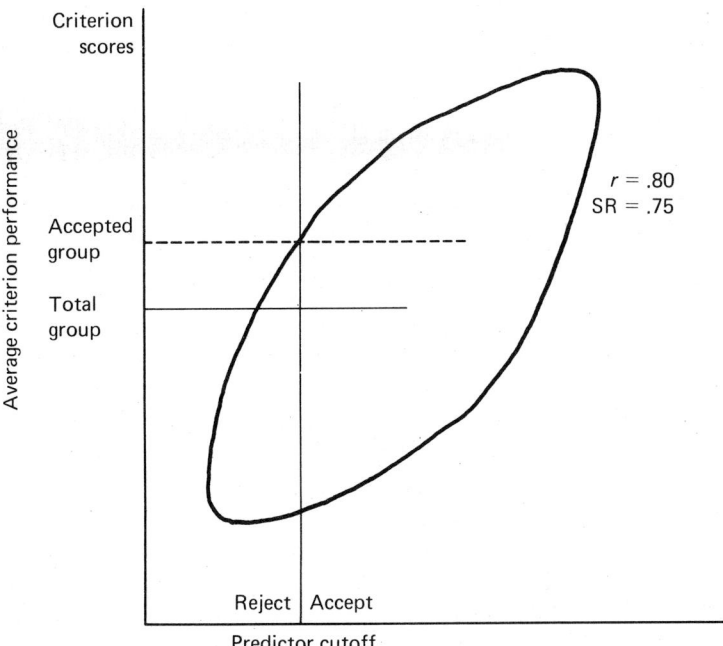

Predictor scores

**Figure 5–7**        **Effect of small selection ratio (SR = .25) on test utility**

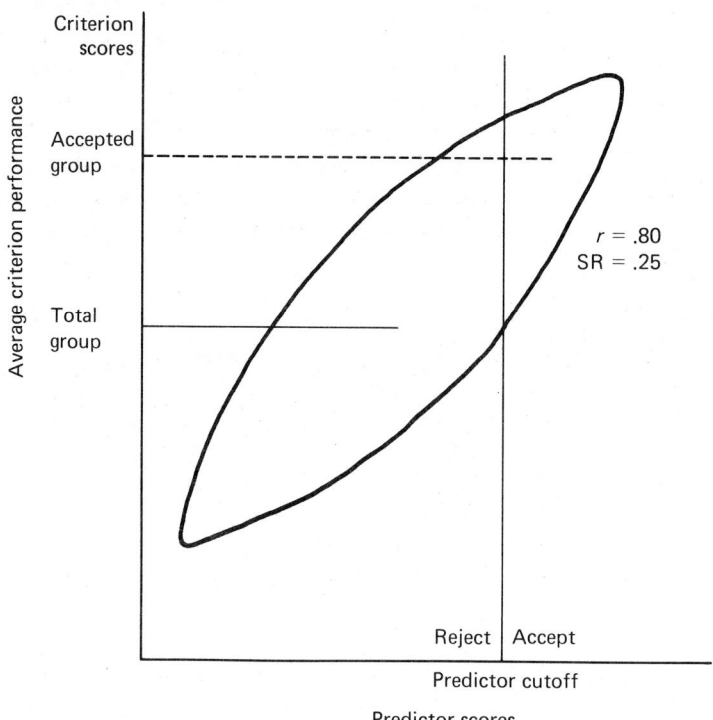

tion ratio is .75, meaning we will hire three out of every four applicants. Figure 5–6 shows the predictor-criterion relationship, the predictor cutoff that results in accepting the top 75 percent of all applicants, and the respective average criterion performance of the total group and the accepted group. By hiring the top 75 percent, the average criterion performance of that group is greater than the average performance of the total group (which is weighted down by the bottom 25 percent of the applicants). Again, utility is measured by this difference between average criterion scores. And by lopping off the bottom 25 percent (the one applicant out of four that is not hired), the average criterion performance of the accepted group will be greater than for the total group.

In Figure 5–7 we have the same validity coefficient ($r = .80$), but this time the SR is .25. That is, out of every four applicants, we will hire only one. The figure shows the location of the predictor cutoff that results in hiring only the top 25 percent of all applicants, and the respective average criterion performance of the total and accepted group. The average criterion performance of the accepted group is not only above the performance of the total group as before, but the difference is also much greater. That is, when only the top 25 percent are hired, their average criterion performance will be greater than the performance of the top 75 percent of the applicants, and both of these values will be greater than the average performance of the total group.

The relationship between $SR$ and predictor utility should be clear: the smaller the $SR$, the greater is the predictor's utility or value. This should also make sense intuitively. The fussier we are in admitting people (i.e., the smaller the selection ratio), the more likely it is that the people admitted (or hired) will be of the level of quality we desire.

**6. Percent of present employees who are successful.** The sixth factor that influences the utility of a predictor is the percent of present employees who are successful (also called the *base rate*). Management usually decides what constitutes successful job performance. They have a standard or critical value in mind that separates successful from unsuccessful workers. This critical value is the *criterion cutoff*. For example, in most undergraduate colleges, the criterion cutoff separating successful from unsuccessful students is a C average (2.0/4.0). The relationship between the base rate and predictor utility is somewhat deceptive since it depends on the way gains in average criterion performance are viewed. The possibility for the largest potential gain in criterion performance (in a *relative* sense) occurs for *low* base rates. If many people in a company are performing poorly (i.e., the base rate is low), the odds are fairly good that a new predictor will elevate the average performance of the group. For example, if the base rate of a company is 5 percent, a particular predictor may result in improving the quality of the work force to 10 percent, a 5 percent improvement in absolute terms but a 100 percent (5 ÷ 5 percent) improvement in relative terms. Conversely, if everyone in the company were performing successfully (i.e., the base rate was 1.00), it would be impossible for a new predictor to improve on this ideal state. Therefore, in relative terms, the lower the base rate, the larger will be the percentage increase in satisfactorily performing employees when a new predictor is used.

However, in *absolute* terms, the largest gains in average criterion performance will occur with a base rate of .50. That is, a new predictor will produce the greatest increase in the number of people who will attain satisfactory performance if the base rate is .50. For example, given a base rate of 50 percent, a particular predictor may result in improving the quality of the work force to 67 percent, a 17 percent improvement in absolute terms but a 34 percent (17 ÷ 50 percent) improvement in relative terms. As the base rate becomes more extreme (high or low), the utility of the predictor decreases. In other words, it is difficult for a predictor to change the actual number of workers who are performing successfully if the current group of employees is performing extremely well or poorly. Therefore, a base rate of .50 will produce the greatest change in the *absolute* percentage, while the greatest gains on a *relative* percentage basis occur with low base rates.

Therefore, the relationship between the percent of present employees who are performing successfully and predictor utility is as follows: the closer the base rate is to .50, the greater will be the gain in the *actual number* of new employees who will perform successfully.

**7. Cost.** All other things being equal, the predictor that costs the least to administer has the greatest utility. In many cases, however, all other things are usually *not* equal. For example, sometimes the most valid predictor also costs the most money to administer or score. In this case, is the increased cost of a predictor offset by its increased validity? As we will see later, increases in validity usually compensate for any increases in cost, unless of course the predictor is prohibitively expensive. Predictor validity has the greatest impact on utility, so in almost all cases, a more valid predictor is worth it.

While the seven factors listed here all influence predictor utility, the last four factors have the greatest impact. Also, they are more likely to be manipulated by the company. A company can alter its selection ratio (up or down) depending on staffing needs and the job market, and it can choose predictors based on their cost. Given these four factors, when is a predictor most likely to result in the hiring of higher-quality people? It will occur when the predictor is highly valid, the selection ratio is low, the base rate is .50, and the cost of the predictor is low. The relationship between all seven of the factors and test utility is summarized in Table 5–2.

## SELECTION DECISIONS

As long as the predictor used for selection has less than perfect validity ($r = 1.00$), we will always make some errors in personnel selection. The object is, of course, to make as few mistakes as is possible. With the aid of the scatterplot, we can examine where the mistakes occur in making selection decisions.

Figure 5–8a shows a predictor-criterion relationship of about .80 where the criterion scores have been separated by a criterion cutoff. The criterion cutoff is the point that separates successful (above) from unsuccessful (below) employees. Again, management decides what constitutes successful and unsuccessful performance.

| Table 5–2 | Effects of seven variables on test utility | | |
|---|---|---|---|
| Utility will be high when: | | | |
| 1. Criterion reliability | is | High | |
| 2. Criterion relevance | is | High | |
| 3. Predictor reliability | is | High | |
| 4. Predictor validity | is | High | |
| 5. Selection ratio | is | Low | |
| 6. Base rate | is | .50 | |
| 7. Cost | is | Low | |

**Figure 5–8**     **Effect of establishing (a) criterion cutoff, (b) predictor cutoff, and (c) both cutoffs on a predictor-criterion scatterplot**

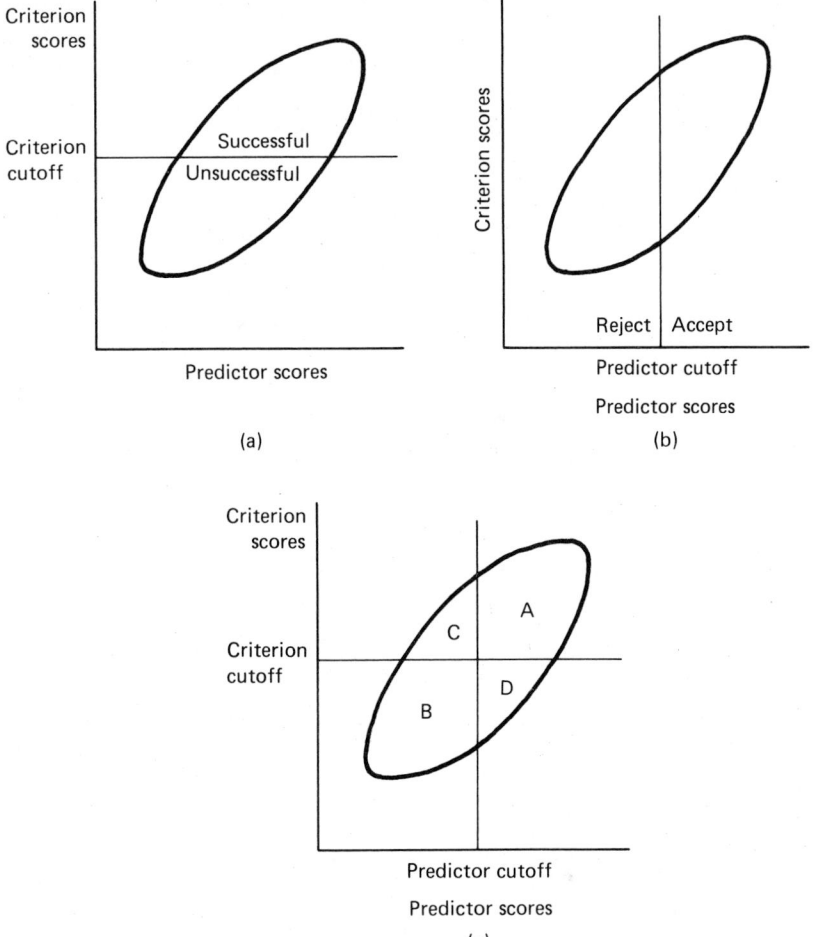

(a)

(b)

(c)

Figure 5–8b shows the same predictor-criterion relationship, except this time the predictor scores have been separated by a predictor cutoff. The predictor cutoff is the point that separates accepted from rejected applicants. Accepted applicants are above the cutoff, rejected applicants are below. What score constitutes passing the predictor test is determined by the selection ratio, cost factors, or occasionally by law.[2]

Figure 5–8c shows the predictor-criterion relationship intersected by

---

[2] In some public sector organizations (e.g., state government), the passing score for a test is determined by law. Usually a passing score is set at 70 percent correct.

both cutoffs. Each of the resulting four parts of the area is identified by a letter, and each part represents a different group of people.

**Part A.**    Those applicants who are above the predictor cutoff and above the criterion cutoff are called *true positives*. These are the people we think will succeed on the job because they passed the predictor test, and who in fact do turn out to be successful employees (vis-a-vis a predictive criterion-related validity paradigm). This group represents a correct decision—we correctly decided to hire them.

**Part B.**    The people in this group are those we thought would not succeed on the job because they failed the predictor test, and if we hired them anyway, they would perform unsatisfactorily. This group represents a correct decision; we correctly predicted they would not succeed on the job. These people are *true negatives*.

**Part C.**    Those people who failed the predictor test (and are thus predicted not to succeed on the job) but who would have succeeded if they were given the chance are called *false negatives*. We have made a mistake in our decision-making process with these people. They would really turn out to be good employees, but we mistakenly decided they would not succeed. These are "the good ones we let get away."

**Part D.**    Those people who passed the predictor test (and are thus predicted to succeed on the job) but who perform unsatisfactorily after they are hired are called *false positives*. We have also erred with these people. They are really ineffective employees who should not have been hired, but we mistakenly thought they would succeed. They are "the bad ones we let in."

Positive/negative refers to the result of passing/failing the predictor test; true/false refers to the quality (good/bad) of our decision to hire the person. In personnel selection, we want to minimize the false positives and false negatives.

If there is no difference between making false positive and false negative decisions (i.e., letting a bad worker in is no worse than letting a good one get away), it will do no good to "juggle" the cutoff scores. That is, by lowering the predictor cutoff in Figure 5–8c (moving the line to the left), we will *decrease* the space in part C, the false negatives. But, by reducing the number of false negatives, we *increase* the space in part D, the false positives. The converse holds for raising the predictor cutoff (moving the line to the right). Conceivably, we could juggle the criterion cutoff (with the same result), but in practice, it is unusual to "adjust" what constitutes successful job performance.

For many years, employers were *not* indifferent between making false positive and false negative mistakes. Most employers preferred to let a good employee get away (in the belief that someone else who is good could be hired) than to hire a bad worker. The cost of training, reduced efficiency, turnover, etc., made the false positive highly undesirable. While most employers still want to avoid false positives, false negatives are increasing in importance. The applicant who fails the predictor test and sues the employer on the grounds of using unfair tests can be devastatingly expensive. If people do fail an employment test, most employers want to be as sure as possible that they were not rejected due to unfair and discriminatory practices. Denying employment to a qualified applicant is tragic: denying employment to a qualified minority applicant can be both tragic and expensive. Recent EEOC legislation has accentuated the importance of this type of selection mistake. Both types of selection errors can be reduced by increasing the validity of the predictor test. The greater the validity of the predictor, the less the chance that people will be mistakenly classified.

## TAYLOR-RUSSELL TABLES

It is possible to compute the improvement in the quality of the work force by using a certain predictor if we know (1) its validity, (2) the selection ratio, and (3) the percent of present employees who are successful. And, it is possible to compute the additional improvement in work force quality if a test of greater validity is used or if the selection ratio is lowered. This information is given in the *Taylor-Russell tables*. The Taylor-Russell tables list what percentage of employees hired will be satisfactory under different combinations of test validity, selection ratio, and percentage of present employees considered successful. Let's say that 50 percent of a company's secretaries are performing successfully, a newly validated clerical test has a validity of .40, and the selection ratio is .60. How much of an improvement in the quality of the secretarial work force can we expect from using this test under these conditions? First, select the Taylor-Russell table with the percent of presently successful employees, in this case 50 percent. (See Table 5–3.) Then find the intersection of a validity coefficient of .40 and a selection ratio of .60. The value shown is .61 (61 percent). By using this new predictor, we can expect an 11 percent improvement (the difference between 50 percent successful employees before using the test and 61 percent successful after using the test). If the company were more selective in hiring and reduced the selection ratio from .60 to .30, the percent of successful employees would be .69, an improvement of 19 percent over the original 50 percent figure. Finally, if they could use a test with a validity of .60 *and* have a selection ratio of .30, the percentage of successful employees would be .79, a 29 percent improvement. The Taylor-Russell tables were developed in 1939 (Taylor & Russell, 1939), and have been useful in assessing the effects of various predictor validities and selection ratios on work force quality.

However, the tables do have some limitations. The major one is that the relationship between the predictor and the criterion must be linear (Smith, 1948). Nonlinearity occurs when increases in test score performance are

Table 5–3

**Example of a Taylor-Russell table: Percent of employees considered satisfactory (base rate = .50)**

| Test validity | Selection ratio | | | | | | | | | | |
|---|---|---|---|---|---|---|---|---|---|---|---|
| | .05 | .10 | .20 | .30 | .40 | .50 | .60 | .70 | .80 | .90 | .95 |
| .00 ...... | .50 | .50 | .50 | .50 | .50 | .50 | .50 | .50 | .50 | .50 | .50 |
| .05 ...... | .54 | .54 | .53 | .52 | .52 | .52 | .51 | .51 | .51 | .50 | .50 |
| .10 ...... | .58 | .57 | .56 | .55 | .54 | .53 | .53 | .52 | .51 | .51 | .50 |
| .15 ...... | .63 | .61 | .58 | .57 | .56 | .55 | .54 | .53 | .52 | .51 | .51 |
| .20 ...... | .67 | .64 | .61 | .59 | .58 | .56 | .55 | .54 | .53 | .52 | .51 |
| .25 ...... | .70 | .67 | .64 | .62 | .60 | .58 | .56 | .55 | .54 | .52 | .51 |
| .30 ...... | .74 | .71 | .67 | .64 | .62 | .60 | .58 | .56 | .54 | .52 | .51 |
| .35 ...... | .78 | .74 | .70 | .66 | .64 | .61 | .59 | .57 | .55 | .53 | .51 |
| .40 ...... | .82 | .78 | .73 | .69 | .66 | .63 | .61 | .58 | .56 | .53 | .52 |
| .45 ...... | .85 | .81 | .75 | .71 | .68 | .65 | .62 | .59 | .56 | .53 | .52 |
| .50 ...... | .88 | .84 | .78 | .74 | .70 | .67 | .63 | .60 | .57 | .54 | .52 |
| .55 ...... | .91 | .87 | .81 | .76 | .72 | .69 | .65 | .61 | .58 | .54 | .52 |
| .60 ...... | .94 | .90 | .84 | .79 | .75 | .70 | .66 | .62 | .59 | .54 | .52 |
| .65 ...... | .96 | .92 | .87 | .82 | .77 | .73 | .68 | .64 | .59 | .55 | .52 |
| .70 ...... | .98 | .95 | .90 | .85 | .80 | .75 | .70 | .65 | .60 | .55 | .53 |
| .75 ...... | .99 | .97 | .92 | .87 | .82 | .77 | .72 | .66 | .61 | .55 | .53 |
| .80 ...... | 1.00 | .99 | .95 | .90 | .85 | .80 | .73 | .67 | .61 | .55 | .53 |
| .85 ...... | 1.00 | .99 | .97 | .94 | .88 | .82 | .76 | .69 | .62 | .55 | .53 |
| .90 ...... | 1.00 | 1.00 | .99 | .97 | .92 | .86 | .78 | .70 | .62 | .56 | .53 |
| .95 ...... | 1.00 | 1.00 | 1.00 | .99 | .96 | .90 | .81 | .71 | .63 | .56 | .53 |
| 1.00 ...... | 1.00 | 1.00 | 1.00 | 1.00 | 1.00 | 1.00 | .83 | .71 | .63 | .56 | .53 |

SOURCE: H. C. Taylor and J. T. Russell, "The Relationship of Validity Coefficients to the Practical Effectiveness of Tests in Selection: Discussion and Tables," *Journal of Applied Psychology* 23 (1939), pp. 565–78.

not matched by increasing performance on the job. That is, there is a point at which job performance levels off no matter how high the predictor test score is. When such *nonlinearity* occurs, the Taylor-Russell tables are not accurate for forecasting work force quality. This statement should not come as a surprise. Recall from Chapter 2 that when a nonlinear relationship exists between two variables, a correlation coefficient is inappropriate to assess their degree of relationship. The Taylor-Russell tables are based on correlation coefficients to assess the degree of relationship between the variables. Nonlinearity nullifies the use of a correlation coefficient; so nonlinearity nullifies application of the Taylor-Russell tables.

## INDIVIDUAL VERSUS INSTITUTIONAL EXPECTANCY CHARTS

Expectancy charts are an alternative to the correlation coefficient as a means of showing a test's validity. There are two types of expectancy charts:

individual and institutional. The individual chart shows what percentage of employees in each test score category will meet a certain level of job performance. Job performance may be based on productivity, length of service, or any other criterion relevant to the company. The method works this way. First, all employees are evaluated on the criterion—let's say it's a rating of work quality. We want to hire people who will produce superior-quality work. Next, we administer a test, a scored application blank, or some other predictor to all employees. We then classify all the predictor scores into certain categories, as 0–20, 21–40, 41–60, 61–80, and 81–100. We then compute the probability or odds that a person with a predictor score in a given category (say, in the 41–60 category) will be a superior performer on the job. By tabulating the frequency with which certain predictor test scores are paired with the criterion of a superior rating, we can establish the likelihood of being a superior worker as a function of a given test score. Such an individual expectancy chart is shown in Figure 5–9. If an individual applicant scores in the 81–100 range, the odds are 91 chances out of 100 he or she will become a superior worker. As can be inferred, there is a sizeable relationship between test score and job performance. Applicants in the 0–20 test score range have virtually no chance (2 percent) of becoming a superior worker. The individual expectancy chart permits individual prediction—the likelihood that an individual will reach a certain level of criterion performance given a certain test score.

The *institutional* expectancy charts works a bit differently. As with the

**Figure 5–9**     **Individual expectancy chart showing percentage of workers rated "superior" for different ranges of test scores**

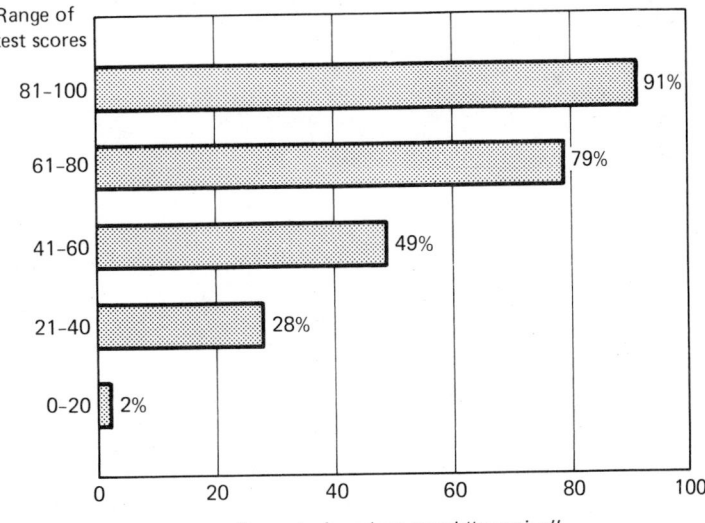

individual expectancy chart, all employees are first evaluated on the criterion. Next, they all take the predictor test. What is different is how the predictor-criterion relationship is tabulated. Certain critical test score values are selected, as 0, 21, 41, 61, and 81 (the beginning score of each range). The odds of reaching superior performance on the job are computed as a function of reaching a given test score or above. The institutional expectancy chart shows the percentage of superior employees that will result if all applicants above a certain score are employed. An example of an institutional chart is shown in Figure 5–10. The work force will have a greater percentage of superior employees if only high-scoring applicants are hired. If a company only hires applicants who score in the top group (81 and above), 91 percent of the new work force will reach superior performance. If the company cannot afford to be so selective and must hire those applicants who score 61 and above, 80 percent of the newly hired work force will reach superior performance. Institutional expectancy charts permit group predictions—the likelihood that a group of applicants will reach a certain level of criterion performance given that they all scored at or above a given test score. Individual and institutional expectancy charts are used according to the intentions of the hiring company. If a company wants to know the likelihood of an *individual* reaching a certain level of performance, the individual chart is used. If the company is concerned with the quality of a given *group* of applicants, the institutional chart is used. Note that if a predictor had no validity at all, all the horizontal bars would be of the same length for each test score range.

**Figure 5–10**          **Institutional expectancy chart showing percent of workers rated "superior" for different minimum test scores**

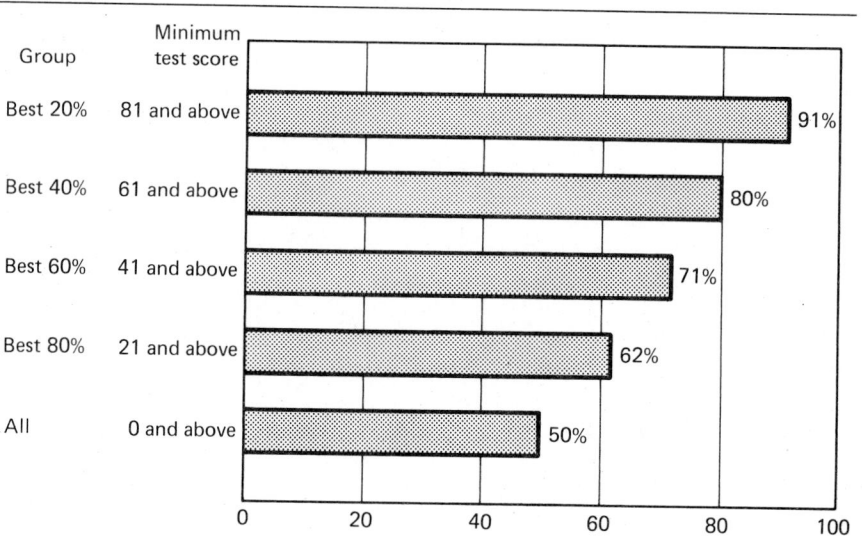

Percent of workers rated "superior"

Expectancy charts have one major advantage over the correlation coefficient as a means of expressing test validity. They are not limited to linear predictor-criterion relationships. If both high- and low-scoring applicants are likely to be successful on the job while middle-scoring applicants are not, the individual expectancy chart will clearly show the relationship. Such nonlinearity, however, would cause the correlation coefficient to yield an inaccurate assessment of the test's validity.

# SELECTION MODELS

For many years, there was a single model or framework to help I/O psychologists select personnel for hire. This model was called the *classic selection model*, and to a large extent it is still used today. But in recent years, some alternative models have been developed, all designed to get a better match between people and jobs. We will first examine the classic selection model. Then we will explore refinements in that model that led to the development of more elaborate models.

## Classic selection model

The classic selection model, like all selection models, is based on individual differences. The model tries to select those people that have the greatest amount of the attribute deemed important for job success. Figure 5–11 shows the six-step process of the classic selection model.

**Step 1: Analysis of the vacant job(s).** Using job analytic procedures, the vacant job(s) are studied to find the knowledges, skills, and abilities needed for job success. Many problems in personnel selection stem from the fact that there is often inadequate understanding of the job and its requirements. The "best" person is best only insofar as he or she optimally meets the requirements of the job. A person who is best for one job may not be best for another.

**Step 2: Selection of criterion and predictor.** This step involves two procedures. First, on the basis of the job analysis, a criterion of job success is chosen. As always, the criterion must be a sensitive indicator of worker quality.

Similarly, a predictor must be chosen. However, the choice of a predictor need not be as carefully considered as the choice of a criterion. If one predictor does not turn out to be useful, another one can always be selected. A psychologist could choose any of the predictors presented in Chapter 4. Predictors are chosen on the basis of an educated hunch. But actually verifying the predictor's value is done empirically.

**Step 3: Measurement of performance.** After the criterion and predictor have been chosen, the workers' performance is measured on both variables. This can be done in one of two ways. Current employees can have their job performance recorded and then take the predictor test (for the

**Figure 5-11**                    **The classic selection model**

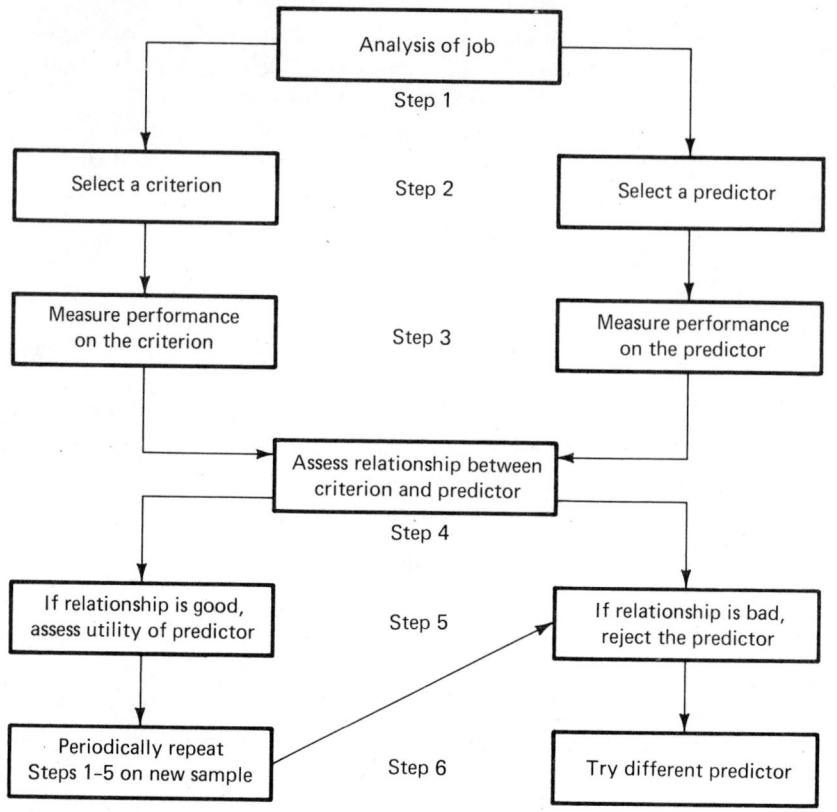

purpose of testing the test). The second way is to give the predictor to all job applicants, hire all the applicants, and then some time later collect criterion data on them. This is the difference between concurrent and predictive criterion-related validity. The significance of the difference between the two methods will be discussed shortly.

**Step 4: Assessing the predictor's validity.** The fourth step is to determine if differences in predictor scores correspond with differences in criterion scores. That is, does the predictor have validity? This procedure is done with statistical analysis, in most cases by computing a correlation coefficient. If the predictor has validity, there will be some appreciable relationship between predictor scores and criterion scores. If the predictor is lacking in validity, there will be no correspondence between the two sets of scores.

**Step 5: Determine the predictor's utility.** If the predictor has statistical validity, the next step is to determine just how useful it will be in improving the quality of the work force. Remember that the utility of a predictor is determined primarily by its validity, the selection ratio, the base rate, and its cost. If the predictor has no validity, there is no point in analyzing its utility since utility is most directly influenced by validity.

**Step 6: Reanalysis.** Over time, jobs can be changed, applicant pools can be altered, predictors can lose validity, invalid predictors can become valid, and so on. Any personnel selection program should be periodically reevaluated to see if changing employment conditions have altered the predictor-criterion relationship. This should be done at least every five years and preferably sooner.

**Concurrent versus predictive validity**

Criterion or job performance data can be collected in either a concurrent or predictive validity design. The difference between these two research designs has been the topic of much discussion in personnel selection research. The major distinction between concurrent and predictive criterion-related validity is the time interval between collection of the predictor and criterion data. While this distinction is technically correct, within the context of personnel selection and test validation, there are many significant implications. While the concurrent validity of a test is frequently established for practical reasons, some authors (e.g., Guion, 1965a) believe that concurrent validity should not be thought of as a substitute for, or even an approximation of, predictive validity. Guion feels the two methods are not even equivalent. Here are some of the reasons.

When a concurrent validity study is undertaken, usually the present workers take a predictor test (for the sake of testing the test). Their scores on this test are correlated with their job performance to obtain an estimate of the (concurrent) validity of the test. There are several problems with this method. First, employees who are secure in their jobs are less motivated to do well on the test than ambitious applicants who need work. Applicant scores are often higher than employees' scores. Rothe (1947) found that a predictor cutoff for a test that resulted in rejecting 15 percent of the actual applicants would have also resulted in rejecting 40 percent of the present employees had they been applying for their own jobs.

A second problem is one of experience. What an employee learns on the job may influence how he or she responds to a test item. The experience may increase the employee's test score, or it may decrease the test score if the employee reads too much into the question and thus gets the item wrong.

Finally, range in ability among present employees is restricted. Present employees are the "survivors" of some previous applicant pool. They are more homogeneous (and better) than the original pool of applicants from which they were drawn. The restriction in range causes a reduction in the variability of test scores, which serves to underestimate the validity of the test.

Some researchers have tried to establish the validity of a new predictor by giving the test to a group of selected applicants who were hired on the basis of some other predictor. No selection decisions are made on the basis of the new predictor score; they are just recorded for later use in a predictive validity study. This procedure has one major flaw. If scores on the new predictor (that is being tested) and scores on the other predictor (on which selection decisions were made) are substantially correlated, there will be the same restriction in range. Only if the two predictors are uncorrelated will there be no restriction in range.

For many years, the doctrine of the superiority of predictive validity over concurrent validity (for the reasons cited by Guion, 1965a) has been accepted by I/O psychologists. Recently however, this doctrine has been challenged. Barrett, Phillips, and Alexander (1981) feel the conceptual distinction between predictive and concurrent validity has been exaggerated. The ultimate test of the relative superiority of the two methods involves examining the quality of new employees hired with each method. If better-quality workers are hired with tests validated predictively than with tests validated concurrently, the former method would be superior. However, if both methods result in the same quality of new hires, neither method can be declared "better" than the other.[3]

While Barrett et al. do not present any data on the comparability of the two methods, they correctly comment that rarely have any data been presented showing the superiority of predictive validity. While on logical or conceptual grounds, predictive validity seems to be preferable, the authors point out that it has little *empirical* support. They also comment that predictive validity designs also have problems. It remains to be seen if I/O psychologists will revise their opinions of the long-held doctrine of deficiencies with the concurrent method. Because many validation studies rely on the concurrent method, it would be encouraging to know that the findings from such a design are not "poor substitutes" for or an "approximation" of results from predictive validity designs. Concurrent validity designs have long been used out of expedience. Predictive validity designs have many practical problems for the employer, as the hiring of all job applicants. If concurrent validity designs provide an accurate estimate of predictive validity, then they will be an extremely useful tool in personnel selection.

**Dunnette's selection model**

After many years of working with the classic selection model, Dunnette (1963) proposed a more complicated selection model. Dunnette wanted to show that several sets of variables can impinge on the predictor-criterion relationship. In essence, Dunnette proposed that several *intervening variables* can influence the relationship between test scores and job performance. His model is shown in Figure 5–12.

On the left side of the model are predictor (P) variables; on the right side are the consequences (C) of job behaviors as they relate to organiza-

---

[3]However, other factors, such as cost, may also enter into the decision. If two methods result in hiring of equally competent workers, the preferred method is the one that costs the least.

**Figure 5–12**                    **Dunnette's modified model of personnel selection**

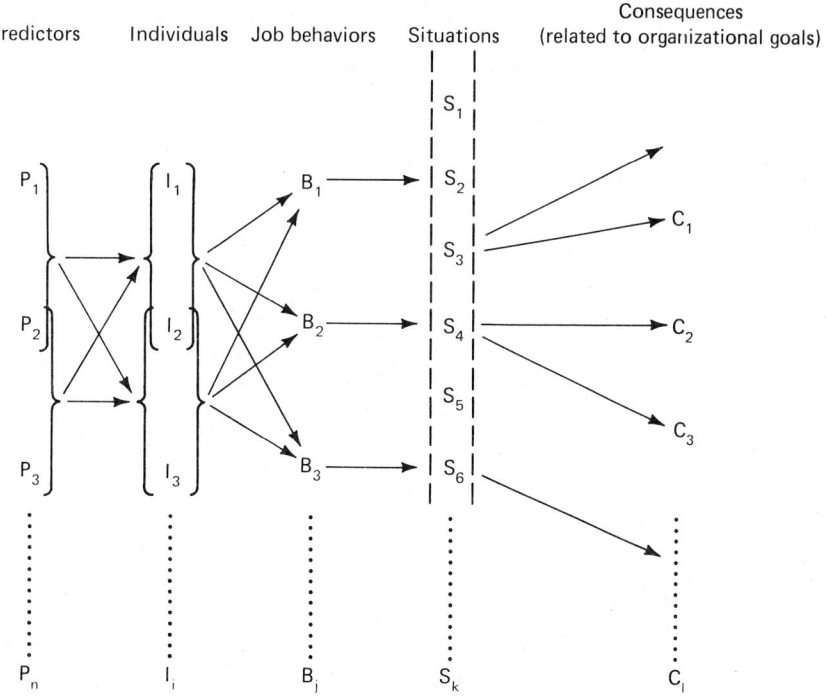

tional goals. In between these variables are factors that intervene in the $P$-$C$ relationship. There are differences among individuals ($I$) which causes differences in job behaviors ($B$). That is, certain subgroups of people behave differently at work than others. Finally, the relationship between job behaviors and consequences are influenced by situational ($S$) factors at work.

Dunnette's model is important because it shows the complexity of the selection process and where psychologists might look to improve the process. For example, applicants might be divided into predictable and unpredictable subgroups. Certain job behaviors might be stressed as opposed to overall job performance, which is the usual criterion. Finally, certain situational factors (whether workers are paid hourly or on an incentive system) might facilitate understanding the selection process. Dunnette believes that it is possible to identify segments of predictable variance with intervening variables that exist between the predictor and the criterion.

**Schmidt and Hunter's selection model**

Just as Dunnette took a stride toward increased *complexity* by advocating intervening variables in selection research, Schmidt and Hunter (1978, 1980) took a stride toward greater *simplicity* by rebuking the notion of intervening and moderating variables altogether. Although their position does not really constitute a "model" of selection per se, their arguments have wide-ranging implications. Schmidt and Hunter argue that for many years I/O psychologists believed in the situational specificity of test validity. That is, a test should be validated in each situation in which it is used. Also, there is the likelihood that the same test may be valid in one situation but not another. They argue that the problem of situational specificity of test validity is based on psychologists' erroneous belief in the "law of small numbers." The law of small numbers is the belief that whatever results hold for large samples will also hold for small samples. They think this belief is incorrect; that in small samples, results are highly unstable resulting in highly variable test validities. Schmidt and Hunter believe that in most cases psychologists settle for small samples ($N$s of 40 to 50) to validate tests. So situation-specific test validities are obtained. They argue that if tests were validated in large samples, the results would generalize (not be situation specific). They propose *validity generalization* as a basis for personnel selection. For instance, this notion means that there is *a* relationship between a test of clerical ability and performance as a secretary. Let's say that relationship is a correlation of .40, as based upon validity studies involving thousands of subjects each. In theory, we could generalize the validity of these findings from huge sample sizes to more typical employment situations with small samples. So companies with immense sample sizes would validate certain tests; the rest of the business world would simply "borrow" these validities as a basis to use the tests for hiring in their own companies.

In support of their position, Schmidt and Hunter (1978) present data based on a sample size of over 10,000 individuals. The sample was drawn from the army. Data are reported on 10 predictors that were used to forecast success in 35 jobs. The results indicated highly similar validity coefficients across different jobs, meaning that differences among jobs did *not* moderate predictor-criterion relationships. Subsequent validity generalization research on computer programmers (Schmidt, Gast-Rosenberg, & Hunter, 1980), oil industry employees (Schmidt, Hunter, & Caplan, 1981) and clerical employees (Pearlman, Schmidt, & Hunter, 1980) have all yielded consistent and similar findings. The researchers concluded that the effects of situational moderators disappear with (appropriately) large sample sizes.

While Schmidt and Hunter's validity generalization model is new and has not yet been extensively evaluated by others, it does have some interesting implications. On the one hand, tests would no longer have to be validated every time they are used. Companies could simply look up a test's validity in some "record book" (as based on a huge sample size) and then use the test for selection purposes. This is exactly the opposite of current personnel practices. As dictated by EEOC legislation, all selection devices must be validated (if they result in adverse impact). On the other hand, the nature of test validation research would certainly be different in the future. Test validation research would probably be conducted by only a handful of people who have access to large numbers of employees. Probably the only psychologists who would validate tests would be those working for the military, the federal government, or a consortium of private-sector employers within an industry. They would document *the* predictor-criterion relationships for the rest of the profession. A second approach would be that psychologists who worked with much smaller and typical sample sizes would have to "pool" their data to arrive at a large enough sample size to eliminate situation-specific effects. Someone or some agency would then have to coordinate and integrate the findings. In any case, it will be interesting to see what happens to the validity generalization model in the years to come.

## SELECTION STRATEGIES

The problem facing a psychologist in making personnel selection decisions is: Should this person be hired? Several selection strategies can be used to help with this decision. These strategies differ in complexity as well as in their assumptions about predictor-criterion relationships. Each strategy has its own strengths and weaknesses, and each strategy presents a rationale for selecting the "best person" for the job. Four such strategies are used: (1) multiple regression, (2) multiple cutoff, (3) multiple hurdle, and (4) profile matching.

**Multiple regression**

The multiple regression selection strategy is based on the statistical procedure of multiple regression analysis. Recall that the method involves the use of two or more predictors weighted and added together to enhance the prediction of a criterion. Using a two-predictor model and assuming $a = 0$, the multiple regression equation would be:

$$\hat{Y} = b_1 X_1 + b_2 X_2$$

This approach assumes that there is (1) a linear relationship between the predictors and the criterion (i.e., higher scores on the predictor will lead to higher scores on the criterion) and that (2) having a "lot" of the attribute measured by one predictor compensates for having only a "little" of the attribute measured by the second predictor. While the former assumption (linearity) is usually met, the latter assumption (compensating predictors) is a more serious limitation.

Given a two-predictor regression equation where $a = 0$, $b_1 = 4$, and $b_2 = 2$, the equation of

$$\hat{Y} = 4X_1 + 2X_2$$

| Table 5–4 | | | |
|---|---|---|---|
| **How four job applicants with different predictor scores can have the same predicted criterion score using multiple regression analysis** | | | |
| Applicant | Score on $X_1$ | Score on $X_2$ | Predicted criterion score |
| A . . . . . . . . . . . . . . . 25 | | 0 | 100 |
| B . . . . . . . . . . . . . . . 0 | | 50 | 100 |
| C . . . . . . . . . . . . . . . 20 | | 10 | 100 |
| D . . . . . . . . . . . . . . . 15 | | 20 | 100 |

Note: Based upon the equation $\hat{Y} = 4X_1 + 2X_2$.

would be used to select job applicants. Let's say that a predicted criterion score ($\hat{Y}$) of 100 is considered necessary for hiring. Scores on the two predictors which would result in a passing score for four hypothetical applicants are presented in Table 5–4. Applicant A has none of the attribute measured by $X_2$, but because of the high score on $X_1$, he or she meets the minimum passing score of 100. Applicant B is just the reverse, having none of the attribute measured by $X_1$ but a lot of the attribute measured by $X_2$. Applicants C and D have differing amounts of $X_1$ and $X_2$ which compensate for each other in reaching a score of 100.

As can be seen, there are many combinations of predictor scores that result in a passing score on the criterion. Is this notion of "compensating predictors" acceptable for predicting job success? Sometimes it is, and sometimes it isn't. For instance, in the case of a surgeon, a low score on one attribute (finger dexterity) cannot be compensated for by a high score on a second attribute (visual acuity). But for other jobs, it may be acceptable to trade off low levels of one attribute with high levels of another. Keep in mind that it is rare for a person to have absolutely *no* amount of any attribute, so the degree of compensation is usually not as extreme in practice as it could be in theory. An interesting discussion of compensating and noncompensating predictors has been presented by Einhorn (1970). Despite this limitation, the multiple regression strategy is a powerful and popular technique in personnel selection.

## Multiple cutoff

The multiple cutoff strategy is an alternative to the multiple regression selection strategy. The multiple cutoff method is not limited by either (1) a linear relationship between predictors and criterion or (2) the problem of compensating predictors. This straightforward and uncomplicated method assumes that a *minimal* amount of ability on *all* predictors is needed for job success. Minimal passing score cutoffs are set for *each* predictor. If an applicant is below the cutoff on *any* predictor, he or she is rejected. All applicants who have scores at or above the cutoff are hired. Having a high score on one predictor cannot compensate for having a low score on another.

The advantages of the multiple cutoff technique are that there are no

For some jobs, personnel selection decisions are based only on physical characteristics.

*Circus World Museum—Baraboo, Wisconsin*

limiting assumptions and the method is easy to use. No formulas are involved in determining who passes and who fails. The major disadvantage involves determining the cutting scores. Generally, cutting scores are set by trial and error, with different cutting scores set for each predictor. However, it is quite difficult to establish the *validity* of a cutting score with concurrent validation procedures when no one in the company hired with the method would have any scores *below* the cutoffs. (If they fell below the cutoffs, they wouldn't have been hired.) Thus, if it was felt that the cutoffs were set too high, it would be difficult to assess what effect lowering the cutoffs would have on job performance. This restriction in range problem is not limited just to the multiple cutoff method, however; it effects all concurrent validity studies.

The multiple regression and multiple cutoff methods can be used in combination. This would take the form of not hiring someone unless their predicted criterion score was above a certain level (from the multiple regression strategy) *and* they were above some cutoff on each predictor (from the multiple cutoff strategy). These techniques work best when the selection ratio is low and there are many job applicants. Large numbers of applicants are needed because many will be rejected for one of two reasons: (1) they fell below the cutoff on one or more predictors, or (2) even though they were above each individual cutoff, their predicted criterion performance was not high enough. This combined approach is often used in selecting students for graduate school. Applicants usually have to have minimally acceptable quantitative and verbal ability, as well as an acceptable predicted grade-point average in graduate school (a frequently used criterion of success in academia).

## Multiple hurdle

In the multiple hurdle strategy, applicants must get satisfactory scores on a number of predictor variables (or hurdles) which are administered over time. The successful applicant is one who passes each hurdle and is thus ultimately hired. The multiple hurdle approach is not used very often. But when it is used, it most frequently is found in management training programs and in the military. First, people who meet certain basic requirements (perhaps nothing more than interest in the job) are chosen to comprise a pool of applicants. The first hurdle is designed to eliminate the least qualified applicants. In an industrial training program, the first hurdle may be a knowledge test covering the first few weeks of specialized instruction. In the military, the first hurdle for prospective paratroopers may be some test of physical fitness. At various points in time, additional hurdles (i.e., evaluations) are presented. To survive in the program, applicants must pass each hurdle; and those who don't are dropped along the way. Eventually, a certain number pass all the hurdles, and these people become industrial managers, paratroopers, etc.

The advantage of the program is that unqualified people do not have to endure an entire evaluation program before they are rejected. It is best for the company and the applicant to discover as soon as possible if he or she won't make it on the job. Because many evaluations are made, the company can be more confident in the quality of their final decision. The odds of a false positive surviving multiple evaluations are much less than surviving one test. The method is used primarily for "important" jobs, where the job's significance to the company warrants such an extensive selection program. Lower-level jobs are rarely so critical to the company.

Disadvantages of the method are the time and cost involved. Again, the job's value to the company should be a major factor in deciding whether to use this type of program. A problem (although not necessarily a disadvantage) is that the final group of survivors are extremely similar to each other, so there is a major restriction in range in all their predictor scores. If their predictor scores were correlated with some criterion of job success taken later, the correlation would be very low. One interpretation is that the predictors lack validity. A more likely explanation is that because the survivors are so homogeneous, their lack of difference on the predictor scores rules out a high correlation with any criterion.

## Profile matching

The last major selection strategy is called profile (or pattern) matching. In this method, all the current employees take a number ($k$) of predictor tests. Test scores are correlated with measures of job performance. Of the $k$ tests that were administered, a subset ($n$) of them would probably show some relationship to job success, or be valid predictors. These $n$ valid predictors are plotted on a graph that would look something like Figure 5–13. In this example, six predictors are listed along the $X$ axis, while the average score for each of these tests is plotted on the $Y$ axis. Connecting the points creates a profile or pattern of the average successful employee. In using the method to hire future employees, we would administer the six valid predictors to the applicants, plot their scores, and then select the person whose profile best matched the standard profile. But finding which applicant "best matches" the standard is not as simple as it may seem.

Two analyses are used to determine the degree of match between the applicants' profile and the standard profile. What complicates the picture is that sometimes the two analyses yield different conclusions about whom to hire. One approach is to simply correlate the applicants' scores on the predictors with the average company scores on the predictors and then hire the person whose scores correlate the highest. While this may seem sen-

**Figure 5–13**    **A hypothetical standard profile and the profiles of two job applicants**

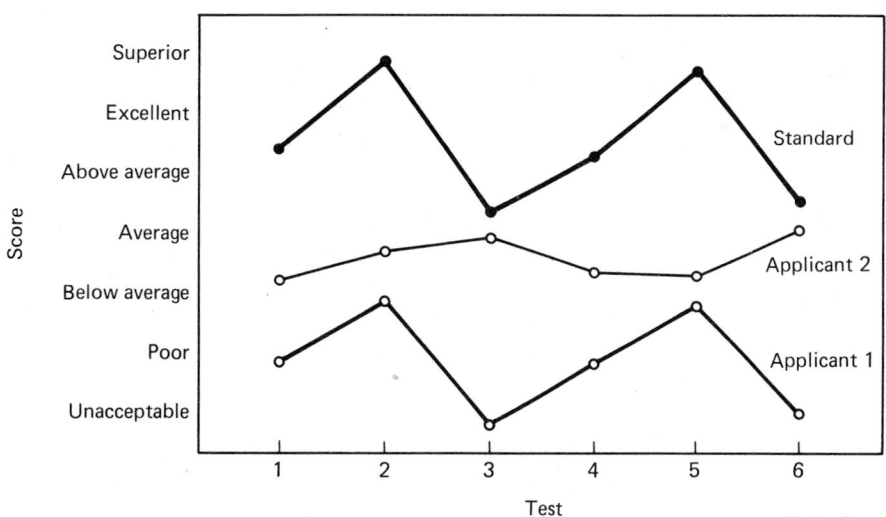

sible, there is one problem. Correlation is a measure of the degree of relationship between two variables. Two sets of scores may correlate highly, but there may be vast differences between the *magnitude* of the two sets of numbers. An applicant whose profile is similar to the standard (but whose scores are well below the standard in terms of magnitude) would appear to be a good candidate. Correlation reflects similarity of the *shape* of the two profiles, but not the degree of closeness. Using correlation as a measure of fit, applicant 1 in Figure 5–13 would be hired because her profile is more similar to the standard.

The second analytical procedure is to compute a measure of the differences between the applicant's scores and the standard scores. The difference $(d)$ is computed between each predictor and the standard. The differences are squared $(d^2)$ so that positive and negative differences can't cancel each other out, and then all the difference scores (six in our example) are added together. This figure, symbolized by $\Sigma d^2$, is a measure of the closeness of the applicant's predictor scores to the standard scores. The problem here is the reverse of the correlational method of determining a match. Similarity between the *shape* of the two profiles is ignored, while the difference between the levels is stressed. Using $\Sigma d^2$ as a measure of fit, applicant 2 in Figure 5–13 would be hired because of the lesser distance between her test scores and the standard.

Which method is best? The only way to answer that question is by comparing the two methods empirically. The best method is the one that results in better-quality people being hired. In practice, some people use a combination of the two methods. First, only those applicants whose scores are *above* the standard are considered (on the grounds that new applicants should be no worse than current employees on these predictors). Second, the applicant whose profile is most similar in shape to the standard is selected. This combination approach overcomes the deficiencies of the other two methods. But another problem is created; many applicants are needed to find a few people who will meet these criteria. In short, this variation of the method works only when the selection ratio is small and there are many applicants.

## ADDITIONAL ISSUES IN PERSONNEL SELECTION

**Synthetic validity**      In some small organizations where relatively few people are hired at a time, it is impossible to validate selection techniques using the traditional methods. That is, in criterion-related validity studies, minimal sample sizes are usually 30 to 50. Some authors (Schmidt, Hunter, & Urry, 1976) have suggested use of much larger samples to ensure stable findings. Small companies just don't hire in such quantities, so alternative means of validation must be used. One such procedure is called *synthetic* or job-component validity.

Synthetic validity was developed by I/O psychologists to deal strictly with the problem of small sample sizes. The term is a misnomer since validity cannot be synthesized or created; it can only be discovered. The concept has been useful over the years to select personnel for companies that lack the size usually needed in test validation (Lawshe, 1952; Guion, 1965b).

Here is how the method works. The jobs in a company are described in terms of such components as leadership, decision making, attention to detail, etc. After these components are identified, it is assumed that every job in the company consists of these job components in various degrees and combinations. Employees are evaluated in terms of their performance on each job component included in their particular job. Thus, performance in these job components constitutes the criterion, as opposed to the more traditional criterion of overall success on the job. Next, the employees take several tests that may turn out to be valid predictors of job component performance. The validity of each test to predict performance in each job component is calculated. Synthetic validity is also called "job-component" validity because we are predicting success in job components. Next, a matrix of predictor-job component validities is constructed (see Table 5–5). In this matrix, the two best predictors of each job component are marked with X's. Suppose someone were applying for a clerk's job and we know the job is defined by job components I and III. To predict how well the person would perform as a clerk, we would use predictors B, E, and F (valid predictors of those job components). Likewise, for the job of a security officer (defined by job components IV and VI), predictors C, D, and F would be used.

In essence, synthetic validation involves breaking down jobs into job components, assessing performance in those components, predicting performance in those components, and then recombining the components to constitute the jobs for which there are applicants. A limitation with the method is that the job components should not be highly correlated with each other. When the job components become substantially intercorre-

**Table 5–5**

**Relationships between predictors and job components in a synthetic validity study**

| Predictor test | Job component | | | | | |
|---|---|---|---|---|---|---|
| | I | II | III | IV | V | VI |
| A . . . . . . . . . . . . . . | | X | | | X | |
| B . . . . . . . . . . . . . | X | | X | | | |
| C . . . . . . . . . . . | | X | | X | | |
| D . . . . . . . . . . . | | | | X | | X |
| E . . . . . . . . . . . . . | X | | | | X | |
| F . . . . . . . . . . . . . | | | X | | | X |

Note: The two best predictors of each job component are marked with an X.

lated, the method of synthetic validity ceases to apply because the structure of jobs can no longer be clearly defined in terms of the combination of several different components. Despite this problem, synthetic validity has been a useful approach to personnel selection in certain situations (e.g., McCormick, DeNisi, & Shaw, 1979).

**Content validity**

While content validity is one of the generic types of validity described earlier, it has a special meaning in personnel selection. For many years, content validity was a subjective assessment of a test's content. Because it is qualitative, it is hard to estimate precisely just "how much" content validity a test has. In 1975, Lawshe developed a method to quantify content validity (Lawshe, 1975). His method also provided another means to validate personnel selection tests. The method is particularly relevant because the courts have stated that content validity is an acceptable means of demonstrating test validity. Unfortunately, though, the courts have not been consistent in their evaluation of content validity (Kleiman & Faley, 1978). Lawshe's method should provide greater uniformity in the assessment of this strategy. Like synthetic validity, content validity can also be used with small sample sizes.

Lawshe's method involves having a series of raters (usually job incumbents or supervisors) evaluate every item of a selection test. Each item is rated in terms of how essential the knowledges or skills that are measured in the item are to performance on the job. Items are rated as essential or nonessential to success on the job. Lawshe then proposes the calculation of a statistic called the Content Validity Ratio (CVR):

$$CVR = \frac{N_e - N_{ne}}{N_T}$$

where $N_e$ is the number (N) of raters who rate the item as essential (e) for job success, $N_{ne}$ is the number of raters who rate the item as nonessential (ne) for job success, and $N_T$ is the total number of judges. If eight raters evaluate an item as essential and two rate it as nonessential, the CVR for the item is:

$$CVR = \frac{8 - 2}{10} = .60.$$

Negative CVR values mean that more than half the raters judge the item as nonessential. The CVR is equal to zero if the judges are evenly split in their opinions. If a test has 100 questions, 100 CVR ratios are computed. Then a Content Validity Index (CVI), a measure of the content validity of the entire test, is computed by averaging the 100 CVR values. The CVI assesses the degree to which a selection test consists of questions about knowledges and skills that are really needed for success on the job. A test with a high positive CVI is a "good" test in the sense that the questions reflect important job duties. While other means of quantifying content validity may be developed, Lawshe's efforts are a major step toward having objective evidence of a test's worth. When sample sizes are too small for criterion-related validity designs, content validity and synthetic validity are the only recourses available.

**Differential prediction and test bias**

In recent years, no topic in I/O psychology has generated more discussion and controversy than differential prediction. Differential prediction literally means "different prediction" for various subgroups of people based on the same predictor-criterion relationship. The concept is limited mainly to criterion-related validity. Differential prediction is a complex topic, and it can take many forms.

Suppose samples of males and females take a predictor test and get their job performance evaluated. The two sets of scores are correlated for each group separately, and the results are plotted as in Figure 5–14. Note that the validity coefficient is the same for both males and females, $r = .50$. We also see that the average criterion performance for males $(\bar{Y}_M)$ is the same as for females $(\bar{Y}_F)$. However, the two groups do not have equal predictor scores; the average test score for males $(\bar{X}_M)$ is greater than the average test

**Figure 5–14**     **Example of intercept test bias for male and female predictor-criterion relationships**

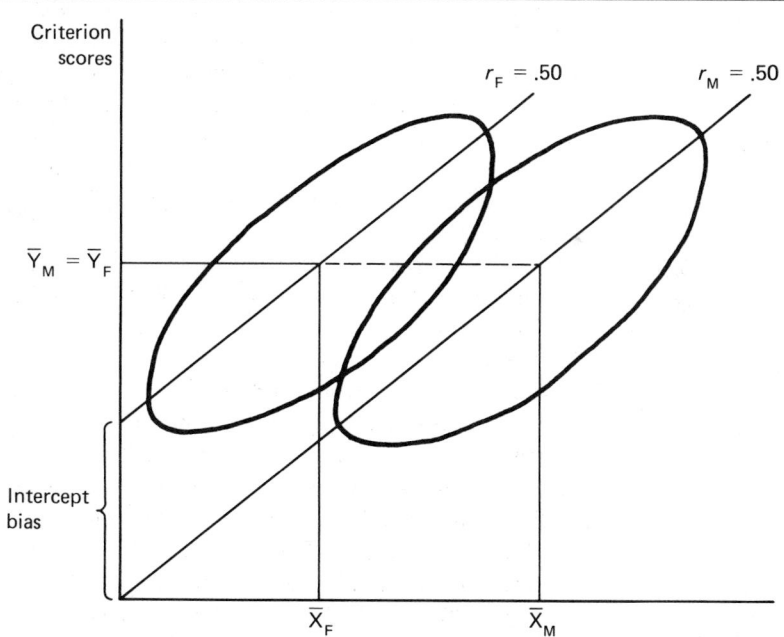

Predictor scores

score for females $(\bar{X}_F)$. If two regression lines were fit through these data, the slopes of the two regression lines would be equal (because the correlations are equal), but the intercepts would differ. If we used this test to hire future employees, we would probably end up hiring mostly males because males score higher on the average. But, this would be a mistake because males don't do any better on the job than females $(\bar{Y}_M = \bar{Y}_F)$. In this case, we have an example of *test bias* (Flaugher, 1978)—the test is biased against females. Males seem to be better test takers but not better workers. The best solution would be to set two passing scores, one for males and one for females. The hired females (who were above the female predictor cutoff) would be expected to do just as well as the hired males (who were above the male predictor cutoff). Requiring a higher passing score for males is *not* unfair or discriminatory. The two passing scores would be set to equalize chances for success on the job. In fact, having only one cutoff would discriminate against females, who do as well on the job as males when given the chance. The present example of test bias is called *"intercept bias"* because there is a significant difference between where the two regression lines intercept the $Y$ axis.

A more complex version of differential prediction is shown in Figure 5–15. In this case, the two groups have unequal validities. The test is valid for females $(r = .50)$ but not for males $(r = .00)$. In this case, sex is a moderator of test validity. Fitting a regression line through the scatter-plots would result not only in different intercepts but also in different slopes. The second type of test bias is called *"slope bias."* This is a significant difference between the slopes of the two regression lines caused by a significant difference between the two respective validity coefficients. Here is a dramatic case of differential prediction. In this case, it would be appropriate to use the test to hire females but inappropriate to hire males. That is, the test is valid for females but not for males. Another selection device would have to be found to hire males. This is an example of both intercept *and* slope bias.

Many other combinations of slopes and intercepts are possible with two subgroups (Bartlett & O'Leary, 1969). The subgroups here differed by sex. They could also differ by race, age, ethnic background, or any other meaningful factor. A major controversy in the literature is the extent to which differential prediction and test bias occur in practice. Differential prediction subsumes a topic called "differential validity." Differential validity literally means "different validities." Some authors (e.g., Katzell & Dyer, 1977) believe that differential validity is a fairly consistent finding in the literature, that tests frequently are valid for one group but not another. Other authors (e.g., Hunter, Schmidt, & Hunter, 1979) believe that differential validity is a by-product of basing test validities on small sample sizes. They argue that if the validation studies were done by professionally preferred methods (meaning large sample sizes and equal sample sizes for both groups), differential validity would occur no more often than chance would

**Figure 5–15**   **Example of both intercept and slope bias for male and female predictor-criterion relationships**

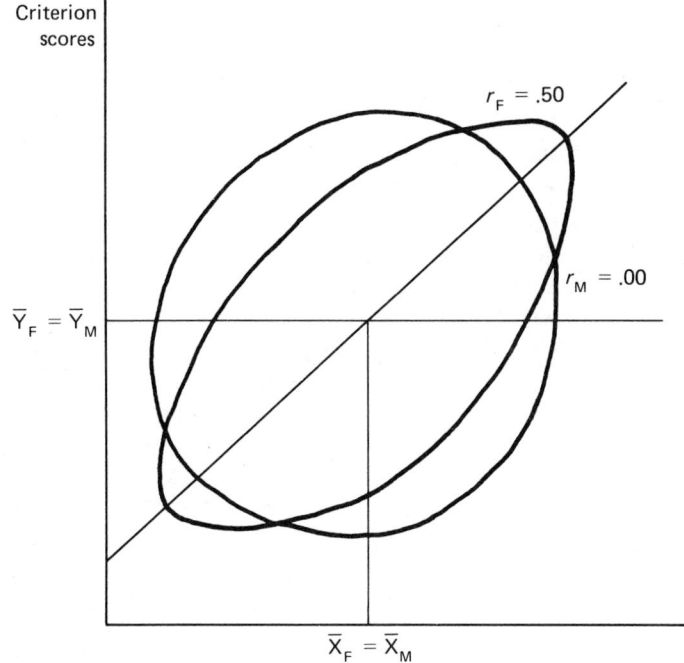

dictate. While the controversy continues (i.e., Linn, 1978), I agree with the latter position. In all likelihood, the occurrence of differential validity is due to questionable methodological practices. In particular, a study by Boehm (1977) shows that the frequency of differential validity is highly correlated with weak methodological practices. This is highly disparaging evidence for the viability of differential validity.

However, other aspects of differential prediction (apart from differential validity) are not so controversial. Few people argue over the occurrence of test bias, although its effects seem to be less obvious and smaller than we once believed (Cole, 1981). It is not uncommon for some groups of people to score higher on the predictor. Sometimes whites perform better than blacks on predictor tests. If there is a corresponding difference in job performance between the races, then the test is indeed valid. That is, differences in predictor scores correspond to differences in criterion scores. The only way such a situation would be discriminatory is if the criterion performance of blacks is unfairly judged. Examples of racial bias in the criterion have been reported, but it is not as common as racial bias in the predictor (Bass & Turner, 1973). In those cases where differences in test scores do *not* correspond with differences in criterion performance, the predictor test is biased against the lower-scoring group.

While the frequency of test bias is not agreed on, there are few arguments about the results of test bias. People in the lower-scoring group are the victims of unfair discrimination. They are denied the chance to work even though they would succeed if given the chance. Such applicants would be classified as false negatives. In addition to being a social injustice, it is illegal to use discriminatory tests as well as a poor business practice. Companies that use discriminatory tests can be sued by applicants who were unfairly denied employment. While there are several different, complex definitions of what is a discriminatory versus a "fair" test (Ledvinka, 1979), Guion's (1966) definition is still highly useful. He says discrimination occurs when people who have equal chances of job success do not have equal chances of being hired. Test bias and differential prediction are bound up in the notion of discrimination. They are important topics in personnel selection, and they have far-reaching social, economic, and legal implications.

## Test utility and organizational efficiency

Always remember that a company's personnel office is only one part of an organization. Each part must contribute to the overall success of the organization. If the company is a profit-making firm (as many are) or just wants to improve operating efficiency (as all organizations should), a basic question involves how much improved personnel selection techniques contribute to the company's overall profitability or efficiency. If we hire more productive workers as a result of a new selection technique, how much value or *utility* do these employees have to the company? A recent study did show just how much utility a valid testing program can provide.

Schmidt, Hunter, McKenzie, and Muldrow (1979) tried to find the dollar value to the company of using a valid employee selection program. The authors analyzed the job of a computer programmer. They asked supervisors to estimate the "worth" (in dollars) of a good, average, and poor quality computer programmer to the company. Supervisors considered such factors as work speed, number of errors, etc. The authors used the responses along with the following information they had collected: (1) a certain test useful in hiring computer programmers had a validity of .76; (2) it cost $10 to administer the test to each applicant; (3) over 4,000 computer programmers were employed by the company (which was, in this case, the federal government); (4) over 600 new programmers were hired each year; and (5) once on the job, the average programmer lasted about 10 years.

Using all this information, the authors compared the expected utility of the test (which had a validity of .76) to other tests that had been used in the past and that had validities ranging from .00 to .50. They also examined the effect of various selection ratios ranging from .05 to .80. The dollar value to the company of using the more valid test was astonishing. When the previously used test was assumed to have a validity of .50 and a selection ratio of .05, the incremental gain in efficiency (i.e., the result of hiring better-quality people) was $5.6 *million* in one year. This was the *smallest* dollar gain because the previous testing conditions were quite favorable ($r = .50$, $SR = .05$). Given the poorest testing condition (a previous test with no validity and a selection ratio of .80), the dollar gain was $97.2 *million* in one year. That is an amazing return on an investment of only $6,000 per year (600 applicants, $10 cost per applicant). Keep in mind that these dollar values pertain to using just one test to hire people in one job in one company for just one year. If you extend these principles to testing in general across many jobs and many companies (and also across time), the dollar value extends into the *billions*. Other studies have shown that the utility of valid tests enhances efficiency by reducing turnover, training time, and accidents. The key element in improved utility is test validity. The impact of test validity on subsequent job performance is dramatic: there is no substitute for using "good" selection techniques. The Schmidt et al. (1979) study shows convincingly that a valid testing program does indeed make a big difference in a company's operating efficiency.

## PLACEMENT AND CLASSIFICATION

The vast majority of research in personnel psychology is on selection—the process by which applicants are hired. Another personnel function (albeit less popular) involves deciding *what* jobs people should be assigned to after they have been hired. This personnel function is called either *placement* or *classification*, depending on the basis for the assignment. In many cases, selection and placement are not separate procedures. Usually, people apply for a certain, fixed job. If they are hired, they fill the job they were applying for. However, in some organizations (and at certain times in our nation's history) decisions about selection and placement have to be made separately.

Placement and classification decisions are usually limited to large organizations where there may be two or more jobs an applicant could fill. It must be decided *which* job would best match the persons's talents and abilities. A classic example is the military. Thousands of applicants were selected each year (either voluntarily or through the draft). Once "in," the next question was where to assign these people. Placement and classification procedures are designed to get the best match between people and jobs.

Placement differs from classification on the basis of the number of criteria used to make the job assignment. *Placement* involves allocating people to two or more groups (or jobs) on the basis of a single criterion score. Many junior high school students are placed in math classes on the basis of a criterion of math aptitude. The aptitude test is usually given during seventh grade. Students with high math aptitude are placed in an algebra class in eighth grade; students with average aptitude don't take algebra class until ninth grade. Students with low math aptitude don't take algebra until 10th grade, if at all. Applicants for secretarial positions may be placed into job grades (e.g., secretary I, secretary II, etc.) on the basis of a typing test. The point is that placement decisions are made on the basis of one criterion factor (math aptitude, typing speed, etc.).

*Classification* involves allocating people to jobs on the basis of two or more valid criterion factors. For this reason, classification is more complex. However, it results in a better assignment of people to jobs than placement. Classification uses smaller selection ratios than placement, which accounts for its greater utility. The reason that classification isn't used all the time (instead of placement) is that it is often difficult to find more than one valid criterion to use in assigning people to jobs. The military has been the basis of most classification research. Military recruits would take a battery of different tests covering such areas as intelligence, ability, and aptitude. Using these test scores, recruits would be assigned to jobs in the infantry, medical corp, military intelligence, etc. The procedure is also used by other organizations that have to assign large numbers of people to a large number of jobs. Given this constraint, relatively few companies need to use classification procedures. Nevertheless, Brogden (1951) has shown that the proper classification is just as important for organizational efficiency as the use of proper selection techniques.

Two sets of issues are particularly important in the areas of placement and classification. One has to do with the nature of the jobs that need to be filled. Placement and classification decisions are easier when the jobs are very different. It's easier to decide if a person should be assigned to the job of a janitor or a clerk than to decide between the job of a secretary or a clerk. The janitor and clerk jobs are very different, requiring different types of skills, while the secretarial and clerk jobs are more similar (thus having many similar job requirements). These decisions become more complex if the jobs in question require successive operations (as on an assemblyline) or if they involve coordination between workers. In these cases, we are also concerned about how well all of the people in the work unit will fit together to form a cohesive team (Cronbach & Gleser, 1965).

A second issue involved in placement and classification is the question of values. What is best in terms of satisfaction and productivity for the individual may not be the best for the company, and vice versa (Cascio, 1978). There can be conflicts between individuals and organizations as to which values underlie manpower allocation decisions. Basically three strategies are possible, and each reflects different values. The *vocational guidance* strategy aims toward maximizing the values of the individual in terms of his or her wants or preferences. College students select their own majors based on the careers they wish to pursue. That is, no college ever states that a student "must" major in a certain area—the decision is strictly an individual one. A second strategy, *pure selection*, maximizes organizational values. In this case, only the best-qualified people are placed in a job. While the placed people are indeed very good, the method is somewhat impractical. Large numbers of people would not get placed into any job because they are not the "best" of the applicants. The method is inherently wasteful because many applicants are unemployed. Both the vocational guidance and pure selection strategies have weaknesses. While the vocational guidance method may work well in educational institutions, it does not work well in industry. If all the applicants wanted to be the company president, large numbers of jobs would go unfilled. The third method, *successive selection*, is a compromise between the first two extremes. In this method (*a*) all jobs are filled by at least minimally qualified people, and (*b*) given available jobs, people are placed on those that make the best use of their talents. Successive selection is a good compromise because the jobs get filled (the organization's needs are met) and the individuals get assigned to jobs for which they are suited (the individual's needs are met).

At one time, placement and classification were as important (if not more so) as selection. During World War II, industry needed large numbers of people to produce war material. The question was not whether people would get a job, but what kind of job they would fill. A similar situation occurred in the military as thousands of recruits were inducted every month. It was of paramount importance to get the right people in the right jobs. Today, selection decisions are more numerous (Ghiselli, 1956b). While some research continues to be done on classification (e.g., Schoenfeldt, 1974), the volume on selection is much greater. However, the rationale behind placement and classification are still the same as before. They are based on the rationale that certain people will perform better in certain jobs than others. To this end, placement and classification are aimed at assigning people to jobs where their predicted job performance will be the greatest.

## EEOC AND AFFIRMATIVE ACTION

We conclude this chapter with a discussion of some legal problems inherent in personnel psychology. Affirmative Action and EEOC are two major influences on personnel decisions today. They have different objectives and different origins.

Strictly speaking, Affirmative Action is not a law but a voluntary agreement between employers and government agencies. It is basically a social policy directed at the personnel function of *recruitment* and aimed at righting previous wrongs in the work force. Employers are expected to recruit minority group members as vigorously as they do others. Recruiters may (1) visit colleges with mainly black or female students, or (2) advertise job openings in magazines or newspapers read by minority groups or on radio or TV programs favored by minorities. Affirmative Action programs require employers to recruit minority applicants who might not otherwise seek employment with the company. Also, companies must prepare Affirmative Action goals and timetables for employing a certain percentage of minority employees. This is done because many employers have a disproportionately small percentage of minorities in their work force compared to the population at large. Since Affirmative Action is not law, a company cannot be sued for not having an Affirmative Action program. But, economic pressures can be brought to bear against the company for lack of participation. If the company receives a portion of its business from government contracts, the government can withhold funds until the company develops an Affirmative Action program. Companies that rely heavily on federal contracts can be driven out of business for not having such a program.

Unlike Affirmative Action, EEOC is a law. Also, EEOC is directed at the personnel function of selection (among others) but not recruitment. Employers can be sued for not complying with EEOC law. Some companies have been sued for using discriminatory selection tests, and the financial settlements have been staggering. Compliance with EEOC is more technically complicated and precise than compliance with Affirmative Action programs. EEOC asserts that all selection tests which result in adverse impact must be validated. As we have seen, there are several ways to validate tests. Furthermore, personnel functions relating to layoffs, promotions, and transfers (as well as selection) must be grounded in empirical validity. Also, the technical requirements of validation studies are by no means routine or easy. To avoid expensive lawsuits, some companies are hiring employees just to meet certain quotas. Since the "green light" to prompt an investigation of a company's selection program is evidence of adverse impact, companies simply hire people (white/black, male/female) in proportions that match the government's standard. Adverse impact is determined by the "$4/5$ rule." The rule states that adverse impact occurs if the selection ratio for any subgroup of people (i.e., blacks) is less than four fifths of the selection ratio for the largest subgroup. Suppose 100 whites apply for a job and 20 are selected. The selection ratio is $20/100$ or .20. By multiplying .20 by $4/5$, we get .16. This means that if fewer than 16 percent of the black applicants are hired, the selection test has adverse impact. So if 50 blacks applied for a job, at least 8 ($50 \times .16$) would have to be hired. Rather than trying to hire people who will perform best on the job, some employers ignore validity and play a numbers game to reduce charges of discriminatory hiring. This is regrettable. Productivity declines, human talent is misused, and the unqualified worker who was hired often loses self-esteem from not succeeding on the job. Fear of federal investigations (and their financial consequences) has prompted some employers to take what seems to be an easy way out. The rationale is that in the long run it is less costly for the company to use quotas (and accept lower productivity but also avoid prosecution) than to hire people on the basis of strict merit (which requires evidence of validity if adverse impact results). Fortunately, not many employers adopt this posture. As Schmidt et al. (1979) have shown, valid selection procedures offer immense benefits to the company.

# TOWARD THE FUTURE

In the last few years, some major changes have occurred in how I/O psychologists view employment testing (Schmidt & Hunter, 1981). Researchers are challenging many doctrines, some of which have held for over 30 years. Among these new findings are the following:

1.  We need a minimum sample size of several hundred cases in criterion-related validity studies to accurately assess predictor-criterion relationships—not the 30 to 50 cases as we have long believed (Schmidt et al., 1976).
2.  All types of validity implicitly or explicitly relate to *construct* validity in the determination of the degree to which the results of a measurement (i.e., a test score) represent magnitudes of the intended attribute (Guion, 1980). Psychologists previously tended to view the three major types of validity (construct, criterion-related, and content) as distinct from each other.
3.  The validity of a particular type of test to predict proficiency in certain jobs may be generalized across different employment situations. That is, validity generalization may be tenable. This is opposed to the long-standing belief that moderator variables (type of company, nature of applicants, kind of work, etc.) produce situation-specific validity (Schmidt & Hunter, 1978).
4.  Valid testing programs have a major and measurable impact on an organization's profitability or effectiveness. Previously, we did not know how to totally assess the utility of valid test procedures and did not realize the magnitude of their effect on productivity (Schmidt et al., 1979)
5.  Concurrent criterion-related validity may not be a poor substitute for the long-preferred method of predictive validity in personnel selection. The two methods may not produce different conclusions regarding which applicants to hire (Barrett et al., 1981).

After many years of stagnation, the last decade (and, in particular, the last two to three years) has witnessed a major eruption in new methods, concepts, and ways of thinking about personnel decisions. While it remains to be seen if all the new ideas will attain professional acceptance, this is a most stimulating era in I/O psychology.

# CASE STUDY

Dennis McDermitt and John Fleming were meeting in McDermitt's office to discuss an important decision facing their company. McDermitt was the president of Excelsior Engineering, Inc., and Fleming was his vice president. The company manufactured and sold a variety of electronic products, but their biggest line was electronic readouts. They produced and sold electronic scoreboards used in high school and college basketball games as well as electronic time-and-temperature signs, which they often sold to banks. Their sales manager died unexpectedly the past week, and McDermitt and Fleming were meeting to select his replacement.

They were faced with three options. They could promote their best salesman, Reid Walker, into the position. Walker alone accounted for 20 percent of the company's sales and was extremely well-respected by his peers. However, Walker had expressed little interest in the sales manager's position. He considered his strength to be in sales, not management.

The second option would be to promote Ted LaPlante, another company salesman. LaPlante had adequate sales ability but lagged far behind Walker in sales volume. LaPlante had often expressed interest in a management position, and he told McDermitt he would like to be considered for the open position.

The third option would be to bring in an outsider for the position and thus leave Walker and LaPlante in sales. Neither McDermitt nor Fleming were too keen on this option. They both felt that the sales manager should be knowledgeable of the company's product lines and sales territories, so they favored an inside person.

Both McDermitt and Fleming were aware of the potential problems in promoting either Walker or LaPlante.

"I feel if we give it to Walker we may greatly jeopardize our sales," said Fleming. "He's clearly our best salesman, and I'm reluctant to take him out of his natural environment. I don't know how quickly we would recover our reduced sales volume if we pull him out of the field."

"The question is," McDermitt replied, "do we need him more as a manager or as a salesman? We need a competent sales manager, someone who knows our products and the market. I can't think of anyone more qualified for the position."

"He's a great salesman alright," responded Fleming, "but that doesn't mean he'll be a great manager. The fact that he's not hot on the position should tell us something too."

"I'm sure he could grow into it. His sales volume wasn't the greatest at first either, but he quickly learned what it took to do the job," McDermitt replied.

"If we pull LaPlante out of the field, it won't hurt us so much in sales. I also think because he wants the position, he may be a better manager than he is a salesman," said Fleming.

"I'm reluctant to reward an average salesman with such a promotion. It may give the message that the way to get ahead around here is to be just average," cautioned McDermitt.

"I hardly think you're rewarding somebody by giving them something they don't want," countered Fleming.

"Can't we just tell Walker we need him more in management?" asked McDermitt. "I'm sure he'd come around. He's not the type of person to tolerate mediocre performance in himself or anyone else for that matter. I like that in a manager."

"I wouldn't sell LaPlante short," replied Fleming. "He really wants the position. Since he's gunning for it, I'm sure he would rise to the occasion. I feel we can't ignore what these men want for themselves."

"I'm not down on LaPlante," noted McDermitt. "I just question whether he's the right man for the job."

The two men fell silent for a while.

McDermitt gazed into the distance and said: "This is an awful bind. I need Walker as a salesman, and I need him as a sales manager. I'd like to run him through our copy machine and have him in both places."

Fleming laughed and replied: "If you find a way to do that, we won't have to have so many meetings like this."

Questions

1. If you were in a position similar to that faced by McDermitt and Fleming, how would you weigh the preferences of individuals versus their abilities in making personnel decisions?
2. Do you feel that LaPlante's overall contribution to the company would be enhanced if he were made sales manager? Why?
3. If Walker were made sales manager, what would you predict his performance and satisfaction would be in his new position?
4. Does McDermitt think it's harder to get a good salesman or a good manager? Why?
5. McDermitt feels that Walker's performance as a salesman would generalize to his being a sales manager. Do you agree? Why or why not?

# REFERENCES

Anastasi, A. *Psychological testing* (4th ed.). New York: MacMillan, 1976.

Barrett, G. V., Phillips, J. S., & Alexander, R. A. Concurrent and predictive validity designs: A critical reanalysis. *Journal of Applied Psychology*, 1981, *66*, 1–6.

Bartlett, C. J., Bobko, P., Mosier, S. B., & Hannan, R. Testing for fairness with a moderated multiple regression strategy: An alternative to differential analysis. *Personnel Psychology*, 1978, *31*, 233–242.

Bartlett, C. J., & O'Leary, B. S. A differential prediction model to moderate the effects of heterogeneous groups in personnel selection and classification. *Personnel Psychology*, 1969, *22*, 1–17.

Bass, A. R., & Turner, J. N. Ethnic group differences in relationships among criteria of job performance. *Journal of Applied Psychology*, 1973, *57*, 101–109.

Blum, M. L., & Naylor, J. C. *Industrial psychology: Its theoretical and social foundations*. New York: Harper & Row, 1968.

Boehm, V. R. Differential prediction: A methodological artifact? *Journal of Applied Psychology*, 1977, *62*, 146–154.

Brogden, H. E. Increased efficiency of selection resulting from replacement of a single predictor with several differential predictors. *Educational and Psychological Measurement*, 1951, *11*, 183–196.

Cascio, W. F. *Applied psychology in personnel management*. Reston, Va.: Reston Publishing, 1978.

Cattin, P. Estimation of the predictive power of a regression model. *Journal of Applied Psychology*, 1980, *65*, 407–414.

Cole, N. S. Bias in testing. *American Psychologist*, 1981, *36*, 1067–1077.

Cronbach, L. J., & Gleser, G. C. *Psychological tests and personnel decisions* (2nd ed.). Urbana, Ill.: University of Illinois Press, 1965.

Dudycha, A. L., Dudycha, L. W., & Schmitt, N. W. Cue redundancy: Some overlooked analytical relationships in MCPL. *Organization Behavior and Human Performance*, 1974, *11*, 222–234.

Dunnette, M. D. A modified model for selection research. *Journal of Applied Psychology*, 1963, *47*, 317–323.

Einhorn, H. J. The use of nonlinear, noncompensatory models in decision making. *Psychological Bulletin*, 1970, *73*, 221–230.

Flaugher, R. L. The many definitions of test bias. *American Psychologist*, 1978, *33*, 671–679.

Ghiselli, E. E. Differentiation of individuals in terms of their predictability. *Journal of Applied Psychology*, 1956, *40*, 374–377. (a)

Ghiselli, E. E. The placement of workers: Concepts and problems. *Personnel Psychology*, 1956, *9*, 1–16. (b)

Guion, R. M. *Personnel testing*. New York: McGraw-Hill, 1965. (a)

Guion, R. M. Synthetic validity in a small company: A demonstration. *Personnel Psychology*, 1965, *18*, 49–65. (b)

Guion, R. M. Employment tests and discriminatory hiring. *Industrial Relations*, 1966, *5*, 20–37.

Guion, R. M. On trinitarian doctrines of validity. *Professional Psychology*, 1980, *11*, 385–398.

Hunter, J. E., Schmidt, F. L., & Hunter, R. Differential validity of employment tests by race: A comprehensive review and analysis. *Psychological Bulletin*, 1979, *86*, 721–735.

Katzell, R. A., & Dyer, F. J. Differential validity revived. *Journal of Applied Psychology*, 1977, *62*, 137–145.

Kleiman, L. S., & Faley, R. H. Assessing content validity: Standards set by the court. *Personnel Psychology*, 1978, *31*, 701–713.

Lawshe, C. H. What can industrial psychology do for small business (a symposium). 2. Employee selection. *Personnel Psychology*, 1952, *5*, 31–34.

Lawshe, C. H. A quantitative approach to content validity. *Personnel Psychology*, 1975, *28*, 563–575.

Ledvinka, J. The statistical definition of fairness in the federal selection guidelines and its implications for minority employment. *Personnel Psychology*, 1979, *32*, 551–562.

Linn, R. L. Single-group validity, differential validity, and differential prediction. *Journal of Applied Psychology*, 1978, *63*, 507–512.

McCormick, E. J., DeNisi, A. S., & Shaw, J. B. Use of the Position Analysis Questionnaire for establishing the job component validity of tests. *Journal of Applied Psychology*, 1979, *64*, 51–56.

Mosier, C. I. Problems and designs of cross validation. *Educational and Psychological Measurement*, 1951, *11*, 5–11.

Owens, W. A. Moderators and subgroups. *Personnel Psychology*, 1978, *31*, 243–247.

Pearlman, K., Schmidt, F. L., & Hunter, J. E. Validity generalization results for tests used to predict job proficiency and training success in clerical occupations. *Journal of Applied Psychology*, 1980, *65*, 373–406.

Rothe, H. F. Distributions of test scores of industrial employees and applicants. *Journal of Applied Psychology*, 1947, *31*, 484–489.

Saunders, D. R. Moderator variables in prediction. *Educational and Psychological Measurement*, 1956, *16*, 209–222.

Seashore, H. G. Women are more predictable than men. *Journal of Counseling Psychology*, 1962, *9*, 261–270.

Schmidt, F. L., Gast-Rosenberg, I., & Hunter, J. E. Validity generalization results for computer programmers. *Journal of Applied Psychology*, 1980, *65*, 643–661.

Schmidt, F. L., & Hunter, J. E. Moderator research and the law of small numbers. *Personnel Psychology*, 1978, *31*, 215–232.

Schmidt, F. L., & Hunter, J. E. The future of criterion-related validity. *Personnel Psychology*, 1980, *33*, 41–60.

Schmidt, F. L., & Hunter, J. E. Employment testing: Old theories and new research findings. *American Psychologist*, 1981, *36*, 1128–1137.

Schmidt, F. L., Hunter, J. E., & Caplan, J. R. Validity generalization results for two job groups in the petroleum industry. *Journal of Applied Psychology*, 1981, *66*, 261–273.

Schmidt, F. L., Hunter, J. E., McKenzie, R. C., & Muldrow, T. W. Impact of valid selection procedures on work-force productivity. *Journal of Applied Psychology*, 1979, *64*, 609–626.

Schmidt, F. L., Hunter, J. E., & Urry, V. W. Statistical power in criterion-related validation studies. *Journal of Applied Psychology*, 1976, *61*, 473–485.

Schoenfeldt, L. F. Utilization of manpower: Development and evaluation of an assessment-classification model for matching individuals with jobs. *Journal of Applied Psychology*, 1974, *59*, 583–595.

Smith, M. Cautions concerning the use of the Taylor-Russell tables in employee selection. *Journal of Applied Psychology*, 1948, *32*, 595–600.

Sorenson, W. W. Test of mechanical principles as a suppressor variable for the prediction of effectiveness on a mechanical repair job. *Journal of Applied Psychology*, 1966, *50*, 348–352.

Taylor, H. C., & Russell, J. T. The relationship of validity coefficients to the practical effectiveness of tests in selection: Discussion and tables. *Journal of Applied Psychology*, 1939, *23*, 565–578.

# chapter 6

# PERSONNEL TRAINING

Personnel training is somewhat of a paradox. On the one hand, it is an extremely important and popular activity in industry (Hinrichs, 1976)—and a multibillion-dollar a year expenditure for businesses. On the other hand, the training literature has been described as "nonempirical, nontheoretical, poorly written, and dull" (Campbell, 1971, p. 565). I think that personnel training in general lacks the empirical precision found in personnel selection. That is, it is not nearly as guided by an established array of scientific methodologies and paradigms as some other areas of I/O psychology. This is not a criticism, but rather an observation that many of the factors that contribute to the scientific rigor in other areas are not as manifest in personnel training. Among these factors are the following:

1. The field of personnel training is dominated by practitioners, most of whom are not psychologists (Hinrichs, 1976). So there is little creative interplay between scientists and practitioners. Without science's steady influx of new ideas, it isn't surprising that personnel training is quite static. Training programs are designed and implemented today in almost the same way they were 30 or 40 years ago.

2. Many industrial training programs are born out of an emergency. A company suddenly realizes that a portion of its work force lacks some skill it needs to work effectively. Management then orders the personnel office

to develop a training program to correct this problem. Under pressure to "do something," the personnel office may not have the time to carefully analyze the problem and develop an empirical rationale for the training program.

3. Training programs are, and have always been, dominated by fads and fashions. Some techniques are merely gimmicks, and some are indeed valuable. But few deliver on all of the sponsor's claims or user's expectations.

4. Despite the extensive amount of training conducted in industry, only a small amount of theory has evolved. One of the benefits of theory is that it permits us to build on our existing knowledge; we don't have to start at square one with every new study. Car manufacturers use existing knowledge of combustion, chemical bonding, aerodynamics, etc., in designing and building cars. We get new styles in cars every year only because the vast majority of a car's structure is carried over from preceding years. But training program designers rarely use such an *incremental* or *additive* strategy; often they do, in fact, begin each time at square one.

5. Finally, personnel training is complex and intricate. There are many forces that shape people's behavior. Personnel trainers have to earmark a few of these forces, modify them in some way, and then assess their effects on certain aspects of subsequent behavior. It's not easy to unravel a few strands from a skein, "treat" them, and then determine the effects of the treatment on the total skein. While more research would help, the problems are tremendous in conducting systematic, high-quality research in such a multifaceted area. The problems and limitations encountered in personnel training should not be attributed solely to weaknesses in the people who do the training. While as a profession we could do better work in personnel training, many of the problems stem from the inherent complexity of the issues that personnel trainers must confront.

## TRAINING AND LEARNING

In theory, the principles of learning make training work. That is, the factors that contribute to how a person *learns* should be the guiding principles in explaining how a person is *trained*. Such principles as practice, feedback, motivation to learn, similarity between the learning task and the final task, etc. have long been identified as instrumental for learning. But, in fact, training practitioners usually ignore these classic principles in designing training programs. And if they are incorporated, it is not necessarily on some a priori theoretical basis. Why aren't these learning principles formally incorporated into training? As Hinrichs (1976) has said, it's either because (1) the personnel trainer is stupid to ignore them, or (2) the principles don't work outside of a learning laboratory. Hinrichs feels there is some truth to both of these positions. A common finding is that new behaviors acquired in training don't persist on the job (i.e., people resort to their old ways of doing things). Perhaps a more complete study of the factors that contribute to learning persistence will help alleviate this problem. However, it is also true that many learning principles derived in sterile laboratory conditions cannot be generalized to complex field conditions. It is one thing to assess in a laboratory the effects of one variable (e.g., practice) when all other variables are controlled for; it is quite another to assess that variable in a field setting in the presence of many other variables. This is a prime example of where laboratory and field methods do not produce the same conclusions.

Classical principles of learning seem to have only marginal relevance for personnel training. But because they are relevant in some situations, they should not be ignored. I will describe these situations and discuss how successful training programs have been enacted.

## TRAINING DEFINED

Training in industry has been defined as "the formal procedures which a company utilizes to facilitate learning so that the resultant behavior contributes to the attainment of the company's goals and objectives" (McGehee & Thayer, 1961, p. 3). This definition has four noteworthy components. By "formal procedures" we mean that training is a systematic and intentional process, not random or haphazard. The "facilitation of learning" is the key psychological principle that accounts for the persistence of activity—that is, it is a *learned* skill. "Resultant behavior" means that training is designed to alter *behavior* (directly or indirectly). People should *do* things differently after training. Finally, "the attainment of the company's goals and objectives" refers to why training is conducted in the first place. It's purpose is to alter people's behavior in a way that contributes to organizational effectiveness. Fortunately, in most cases, the change in behavior also contributes to the *individual's* effectiveness at work, so people are rarely trained against their will.

Any behavior that has been learned is a *skill*. Within the area of training, the learning process is task-oriented: it enhances skills (Hinrichs, 1976). Training, therefore, is directed toward enhancing a specific skill which in turn enhances a person's proficiency in performing a certain task. For example, students in a driver education class are trained to shift gears, accelerate, brake, etc., to enhance their driving proficiency. Skills become the "target areas" of training, especially personnel training. In industry, training enhances three broad classes of skills. *Motor skills* are the manipulation of the physical environment based on certain patterns of bodily movements. *Cognitive skills* are the acquisition of mental or attitudinal factors. *Interpersonal skills* refer to enhancing interactions with other people. Though all three types of skills are the object of personnel training, their relative importance depends on the nature of the job. Machine operators need motor skills, while managers need cognitive and interpersonal skills.

## RELATIONSHIP TO ORGANIZATIONAL AND INDIVIDUAL GOALS

Personnel training should contribute to both the goals of the organization and the goals of the person. Training is a management tool designed to enhance the organization's efficiency. However, in the process of attaining organizational goals, many individual goals can also be attained. McGehee (1979) describes two issues that must be addressed when contemplating a training program. The first issue involves why the company should provide training—what *specific goals* are to be met as a result of training? If there are no apparent organizational goals that a training program can influence, there is no reason for the program. McGehee and Thayer (1961) list several specific ways that training can contribute to organizational goals:

1. Reduction of labor costs by reducing the amount of time it takes to perform the operations involved in producing goods or services; also reducing the time needed to bring the inexperienced employee to an acceptable level of job proficiency.
2. Reducing the costs of materials and supplies by reducing losses due to excess waste and the production of defective products.
3. Reducing the costs of managing personnel activities as reflected in turnover, absenteeism, accidents, grievances, and complaints.
4. Reducing the costs of efficiently servicing customers by improving the flow of goods or services from the industry to the consumer.

The second issue raised by McGehee is one of *cost effectiveness*. Cost effectiveness refers to the amount of money spent to attain organizational goals versus the amount of money spent on other activities in pursuit of those same goals. A cost-effective program attains organizational goals within a "reasonable" budget. Within the area of personnel training, an organization has to decide if the goal of increased productivity could most economically be reached by training employees to be more productive, by redesigning the task so that it is easier to perform, or by automating it. (This issue will be discussed in more detail later in this chapter.)

Obviously, employees must get some benefit from training or they wouldn't participate. The first benefit is that training provides an adequate opportunity to learn the job's duties and responsibilities. A structured approach is always preferable to a haphazard one. Adequate training gives the employee a chance to be successful at work, and helps avoid the psychological problems of failure or incompetence (or outright dismissal).

A second benefit involves pay. Employees paid on a piece-rate system (i.e., X amount per object produced) can earn more if they are well trained.

This benefit, though less obvious, still holds for hourly or salaried personnel. Merit pay increases are more likely for people who know their work (as a result of training).

Finally, trained employees are more marketable for higher-level jobs. Promotions are usually given to those who perform their current jobs the best. People can also become more marketable for other employers by enhancing their skills through training. Many organizations try to keep training "company specific" so they won't be training people for their competitors. (Some years ago, one company developed such an excellent management training program that other companies "raided" it for their own managerial talent. To reduce the turnover of young managers, the program had to be made more specific to the company.)

## STATING TRAINING OBJECTIVES IN BEHAVIORAL TERMS

*important*

Training objectives should always be expressed in behavioral terms, though it is not always easy to do so. If training objectives are stated in vague and general terms, two problems ensue. The objective or goal of the training is ill-defined; neither the trainers nor the participants fully understand what they are trying to accomplish. Second, assessing training effectiveness depends on the extent to which the *criteria* of effectiveness have been met. If the criteria are "fuzzy," the assessment will be fuzzy. As in personnel selection, success depends on a clear and comprehensive understanding of criteria. The success of any training program is a function of the degree to which employee performance on job-related criteria has been enhanced. The following pairs of training objectives are stated first in vague terms and next in behavioral terms.

---

**Training objectives**

---

| | |
|---|---|
| 1. To have more productive workers. | To increase output by 10 percent over current levels of production. |
| 2. To get more employees to show up for work. | To decrease the amount of employee absenteeism to less than 5 percent for the total work force. |
| 3. To give our managers a better understanding of financial matters. | To enable our managers to complete independently a profit-and-loss report. |

---

The behaviorally specified objectives are far more precise. Furthermore, they are not just another way of stating the more general objective. There could be *many ways* to increase a manager's knowledge of financial matters. Completing a profit-and-loss report is one way; developing a long-range budget proposal is another. Behaviorally specified objectives represent *training outcomes*. By using behavioral terms, differences in opinion about the overall goal of training can be identified and ironed out. Admittedly, some training results are more difficult to specify behaviorally than others. Some managers participate in training designed to enhance their understanding of the problems of black and female employees—a growing body of the work force. How do you translate "enhance the understanding" into more concrete behavioral terms? Training programs designed to enhance sensitivity and awareness are not nearly as grounded in their objectives. One way to operationalize such an objective might be "to decrease the number of voluntary resignations of blacks and females due to their perceived inability to fit into a predominately white male work force."

## DETERRENTS TO EFFECTIVE TRAINING

Several factors can block the effectiveness of training (McGehee & Thayer, 1961), and management must make a conscious effort to minimize their effect. First, training must be viewed as a means to an end rather than an end in itself. McGehee (1979) describes a hypothetical company vice president who is asked why his company has a training department. His answer is, "Of course, to train employees." Yet when asked why his company has a research and development department, his answer deals with the need to keep up with competition, to develop better and more attractive products, etc. Yet both departments have the same general goal, to improve corporate efficiency, though each one does it in its own way. The training department does it by enhancing employees' skills, while R&D does it by creating new products. Not until company executives view training as they do any other function (as a means to increased effectiveness), will it be considered more than a necessary nuisance.

Second, management must be responsible for training. Employees learn in many ways. Simply by being on the job, they learn something about their work (work flow, operating procedures, etc.). They pick up this information just by watching or asking a few questions. The effectiveness of this kind of learning can be contrasted with the more formal and structured approach a personnel training program would provide. The opposite of formal training is not the complete absence of training, but rather the acquisition of skills on an unstructured basis. While not all companies have formal training, all employees do indeed learn on the job. The question is, would they learn better, more, faster, etc., as a result of a formal training program? If the answer is yes (as it invariably is), management must develop and staff such a training program.

Third, management must have the knowledge and skill to develop and implement personnel training. If they don't, they should hire trainers who do. Training is a profession, and the trainer is an authority. Personnel training should not be turned over to someone who flunked out of the accounting department. Training is not something that anyone can do.

Last, the general climate of an organization should be one that favors (i.e., recognizes the benefits of) personnel training. Employees will be reluctant to participate in a training program (1) if more productive employees are not paid more, and (2) if more productive employees have no opportunity for advancement. If poor performers are treated the same in all respects as good performers (including job retention), the results of training won't seem to count for anything. In short, management must structure the organization so that personnel training has some meaning for employees.

In these four deterrents to training effectiveness, a consistent theme emerges: the role of management. Training is a management tool. Management can make personnel training a viable corporate activity. But through benign neglect, it can also relegate personnel training to the backburner of an organization's priorities. One key to the success of an organization is the quality of its employees. Personnel training can enhance that quality. To a large extent, the attitudes and actions of management determine the success of any training program.

## THE DESIGN OF PERSONNEL TRAINING

The entire personnel training process is predicated on a rational design which has a cyclical property (see Figure 6–1). It consists of seven steps or stages. The design of personnel training begins with an analysis of training needs and culminates with the assessment of training results. Important steps in between involve developing objectives, choosing methods, and designing an evaluation. Training directors must keep up with the current literature on training methods because previous successes or failures can help shape the selection or design of a training program. It is equally important to determine a means to evaluate the program before it is implemented. That is, evaluative criteria must be selected to serve as the program's score card. The bulk of this chapter will discuss the major steps in the design of personnel training.

## ASSESSING TRAINING NEEDS

If an organization uses training to achieve its goals, it must first assess its training needs. That is, which organizational goals can be attained through personnel training? Which people need training and for what purpose? And finally, what will the training cover? Goldstein (1980a) believes that assessing training needs is far more important than choosing particular training techniques (though trainers seem to have more interest in the latter). Assessing training needs usually involves a three-step process (McGehee & Thayer, 1961):

**Figure 6–1**    **Training design and evaluation model**

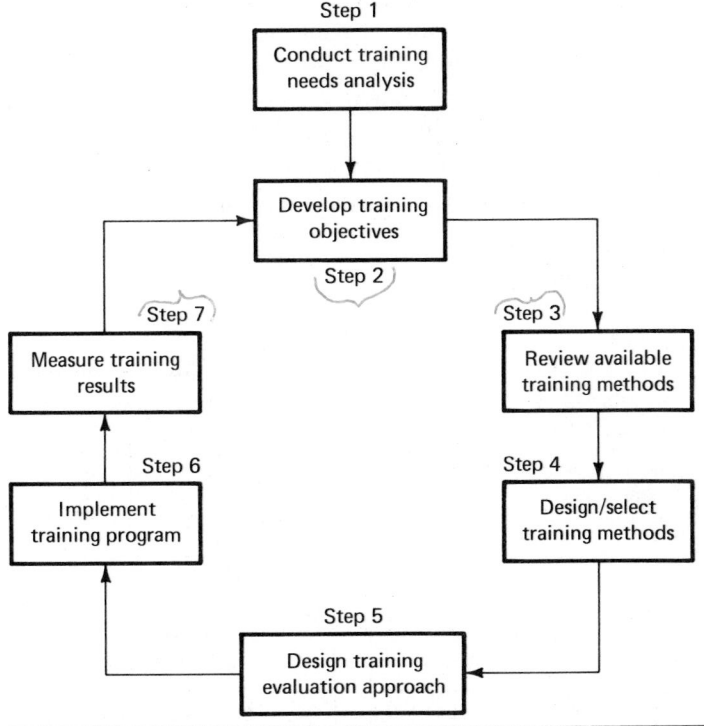

SOURCE: Adapted from T. C. Parker, "Statistical Methods for Measuring Training Results," in *Training and Development Handbook,* 2d. ed., ed. R. L. Craig (New York: McGraw-Hill, 1976). Copyright © 1976. Used by permission.

1. Organization analysis—determining where training emphasis can and should be placed within the organization.
2. Operations analysis—determining the content of training in terms of what an employee must do to perform a task, job, or assignment effectively.
3. Person analysis—determining what skills, knowledges, or attitudes an employee must develop to perform the tasks involved in his or her job.

**Organization analysis**

   Organization analysis is the study of an entire organization—its objectives, resources, and the way the resources are allocated to attain the organization's goals. At this level of analysis, we are not concerned with people's specific training needs; that function is addressed in operations and person analysis. Rather, the concern is with more global problems confronting the organization, which training may in some way help resolve.

Organization analysis can take several forms. One form is to conduct a *personnel audit* for manpower planning. A personnel audit is an inventory of the personnel assets of an organization and a projection of the kinds and numbers of employees that will be required in the future. Figure 6–2 shows a personnel audit for one division of a company. Information is usually collected by job and includes demographic data regarding age and turnover

**Figure 6–2**                    **Organization analysis personnel replacement chart**

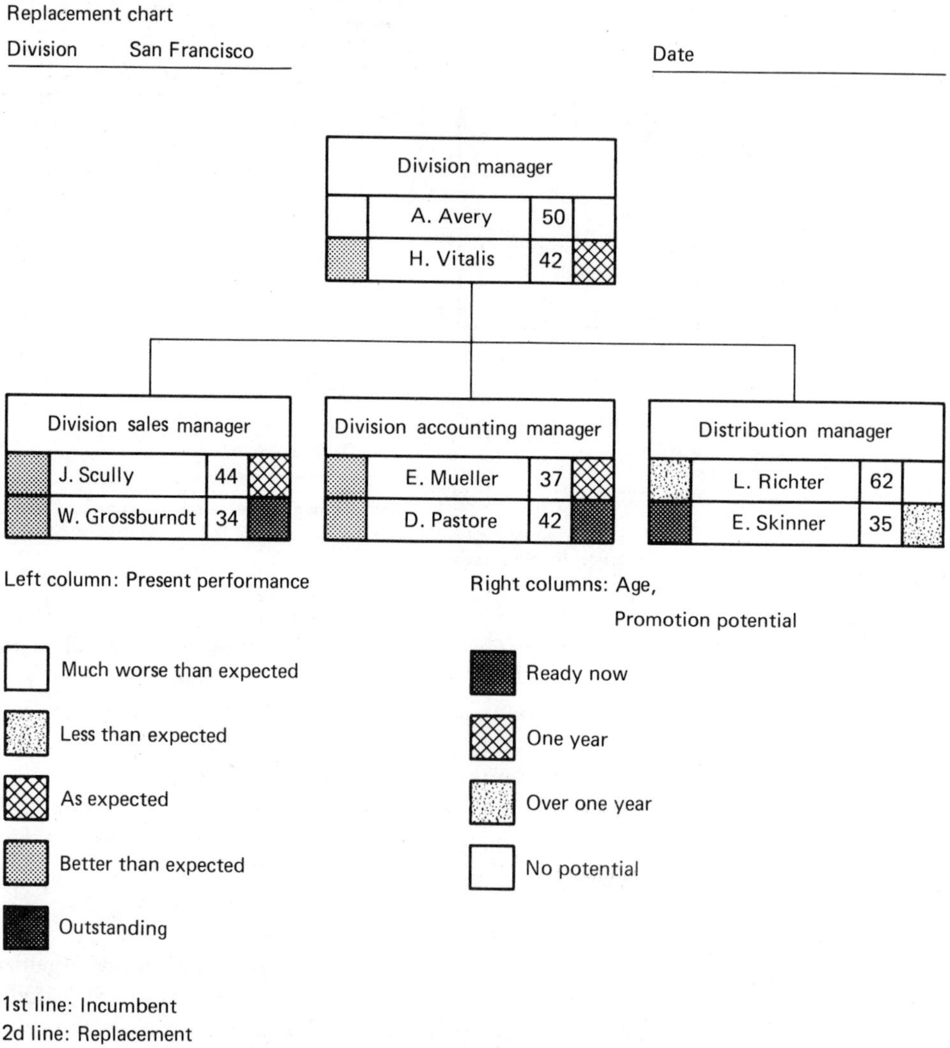

Replacement chart

Division        San Francisco                                    Date

Left column: Present performance

☐ Much worse than expected

▨ Less than expected

▨ As expected

▨ Better than expected

■ Outstanding

Right columns: Age,
                Promotion potential

■ Ready now

▨ One year

▨ Over one year

☐ No potential

1st line: Incumbent
2d line: Replacement

SOURCE: Adapted from J. H. Morrison, "Determining Training Needs," in *Training and Development Handbook*, 2d ed., ed. R. L. Craig (New York: McGraw-Hill, 1976). Copyright © 1976. Used by permission.

rates. A personnel audit might show that many of a company's managers are in their late 50s and early 60s. To this information is added the fact that most managers retire by 65, plus there are a certain number of deaths, resignations, and early retirements each year. So in five to seven years, many new managers will be needed. Based on these projections, the company decides to train current supervisors to fill these future positions. The personnel audit showed an organizational need and provided enough lead time for the company to plan a rational and orderly solution. These kinds of analyses are routine in large organizations and are the basis for many staffing decisions. However, organization analysis doesn't necessarily lead to a personnel training decision. New managers could be hired rather than promoted from the supervisors' ranks. Again, training is but one way to meet organizational goals; in this case, the goal of staffing the organization with capable people.[1]

A second approach to organization analysis involves indicators of organizational effectiveness. These are examined to see if training could improve the company's performance. Most companies measure effectiveness through a variety of indicators including labor costs, accidents, turnover, absenteeism, and the quality of their products or services. These indicators are not recorded just to identify training needs. Indeed, training alone may not be able to alter the company's status on a given indicator. But training may be one means to the end, and indicators do provide target objectives.

For example, due to the rising costs of raw materials, the dollar value of scrap and waste may reach a critical level. Management thus decides that something has to be done to reduce the amount of material waste. One approach to reduce waste might be a training program to teach employees to be more careful. Another approach, other than training, might be to redesign the work (i.e., with new equipment or a different production process). So the goal of reducing scrap might be met by either personnel training or work redesign.

Note that in both examples of organization analysis, the level of analysis is quite general. The analysis revealed problems (material scrap) or potential problems (manpower planning). These are not once-in-a-lifetime activities in the organization but activities that are performed on an on-going basis. In a general sense an organization analysis is an attempt to take the pulse of an entire organization. If the organization is "ill" in some regard, personnel training may be one type of remedy.

---

[1] Some research has involved combining both the personnel selection and training approaches to organizational staffing problems. Robertson and Downs (1979), for example, have described the development of *trainability testing*—the concept of selecting people into the organization on the basis of their ability to be trained to meet certain job requirements. Traditional personnel selection is usually based on the applicant already being competent to perform the job, while traditional personnel training often assumes no prior competence. Trainability testing is a cross between these two approaches. It assumes that those people who will succeed in training can be rationally selected with a test.

## Operations analysis

Operations analysis examines the task or job requirements, regardless of the person holding the job. It determines what an employee must do to perform the job properly. Operations analysis is most directly concerned with what training should cover. As Goldstein (1974) has observed, machinists don't choose their tools before they examine their job; builders don't order materials or plan schedules until they have blueprints. So why do trainers argue over training techniques without specifying what the technique is supposed to accomplish? Operations analysis should identify what training is to accomplish.

Operations analysis is the orderly and systematic collection of data about an existing or potential task, or a cluster of tasks which define a job (McGehee & Thayer, 1961). Its goal is to identify what an employee must be taught to perform the task or job. An operations analysis results in the following information:

1. The standards of performance for the task or job.
2. The identification of what tasks constitute a job.
3. Determination of how these tasks are to be performed.
4. Determination of what behavior is required of an employee in order to perform the tasks.

**Standards of performance.** Standards of performance are statements regarding work output. They are usually given in units of output of a specific quality in a specified amount of time. Management normally decides what level of performance constitutes a standard. So standards of performance are the measures that define job success. For example, typing 60 words per minute and selling $1 million worth of products per year might be the standard of performance for a typist and salesperson, respectively. These values, set by management, represent the level of job performance considered acceptable or standard. In some automated tasks, the standard of performance is determined by the machine. An example is an auto assembly line where a new car passes by a worker every few minutes. Without standards of performance, we wouldn't know whether training is successful; i.e., if it raises an employee's performance to an "acceptable" level.

**Identification of tasks.** To train an employee for a job, we must know what tasks are involved. We also need to know the relationship between these tasks and the job's standard of performance. That is, some tasks may be more strongly related to overall job success than others. An operations analysis lists each task and then indicates how critical it is to total job performance. For example, a secretary's tasks might include typing, filing, shorthand, and answering the phone. These tasks, in turn, can be broken down into more refined units (setting margins, centering the paper, etc.). Identifying tasks can be done through established job and task analysis procedures. These involve observing incumbents perform a job, asking them questions about their work duties, and perhaps recording job activities in some systematic way. The tasks are then related to overall performance by assessing the proportionate amount of time devoted to each task, the importance of the task to the job, and so forth.

**How each task is to be performed.** The previous stage identified *what* is done; this stage identifies *how* it is done. Time-and-motion studies are often used to determine the "best way" to perform a task. A time-and-motion study examines the amount of time it takes to perform a certain bodily motion and relates that activity to job performance. For example, one worker's job on an assembly line is to bolt a bumper to a car. If the worker drops a bolt on the floor while performing this task, should she or he pick it up or grab a new one? A time-and-motion study might show that it is more efficient to grab a new bolt rather than to scurry around looking for the dropped one. Thus the "best" method is determined by efficiency criteria.

Typing is one task in a secretary's job. But based on the amount of typing to be done, speed of work, importance of neatness, etc., either a manual or electric typewriter can be used. A clerical worker who does little typing needs only a manual typewriter. For a clerical job involving a heavy typing, an electric typewriter might be best; i.e., it would help in meeting the job's standards of performance.

Yet in other situations, workers have some latitude to develop their own methods for performing tasks. My work style is a case in point. As part of my job I have to compose many letters. As part of my secretary's job, she has to type the letters. I prefer to write out the letters, and my secretary prefers to type from a rough draft. We have developed a work method that is mutually satisfactory and efficient. Other secretary/boss teams may use a different method. The point is that while the task (letter composing) is a fixed part of my job, the method used to produce the finished product (a typed letter) was determined by mutual preference. As long as I am proficient in my task (letter composing) and my secretary is proficient in hers (letter typing), we will continue to use this method. If we are inefficient in this task, it would be better for both of us to be trained to use a new work method.

**Employee behavior.** The final stage of operations analysis is to identify the skills, knowledges, and attitudes that must be possessed or developed on the job. The nature of the job determines the amount of these skills, knowledges, and attitudes. Suppose a company produces 80-pound bags of cement. If manual laborers are needed to load the cement onto trucks and freight cars, the company will have to select or train people to have the physical skill (i.e., strength) to lift 80 pounds. If a secretarial job entails a great deal of typing, the typing demands of the job may be set at 100 words per minute. A person who couldn't type this fast would have to be trained to meet the standards of performance for that job. For jobs where the skill, knowledge, or attitude levels are constant, people must be trained to reach these performance levels. For jobs where the skill, knowledge, or attitude levels are increasing, the problem is more complex. In some areas like computer science, rapidly changing technology demands increasing levels of skill. So incumbents must be continually trained to keep up with the demands of the job. A similar problem occurs in medicine, where new procedures are being developed all the time. People in this field need constant retraining or updating. These issues will be discussed later in the chapter.

**Person analysis**

The final step, person analysis, is directed toward learning (1) whether the individual employee needs training and (2) what training he or she needs. It is focused directly on the individual employee. Person analysis is concerned, first, with ascertaining how well a specific employee is carrying out his or her tasks. Second, it is concerned with determining what skills must be developed, what knowledge acquired, and what attitudes engendered if the employee is to improve his or her job performance (McGehee & Thayer, 1961).

A large portion of person analysis involves *diagnosis*. We want to know not only how well people are performing, but *why* they are performing at that level. We try to determine if poor performance on a task is the result of not enough skill or knowledge, or whether it is caused by situational factors beyond the person's control. It's not easy to conduct a person analysis. The first part involves appraising an employee's performance. (Specific techniques are discussed in the next chapter.) Suffice it to say that performance appraisal can sometimes be imprecise. If a person's performance is judged to be uniformly positive, there is probably little need for "corrective" training. But, if their performance is deficient in some way, the next step is to diagnose *why* it is deficient.

Information about an employee's current level of performance is usually collected by traditional performance appraisal techniques. These involve both subjective evaluations as well as objective records. Supervisors may judge an employee's interpersonal skills, written communication skills, various types of job knowledges, etc. Figure 6–3 shows a person analysis based on a supervisor's evaluation. If the supervisor thinks the employee's skill or knowledge level is deficient, the reason must be explored. Objective records also supply information about an employee's performance (words typed per minute, units produced per hour, or sales made per month). These figures are then compared to the job's standards of performance, and any deficiencies are targets for improvement. But not all deficiencies in performance are due to deficiencies in skill, knowledge, or attitude. For example, substandard performance may be caused by using broken or antiquated tools or machinery. In this case, replacing worn-out equipment is a better solution than training.

Diagnostic achievement tests are another approach to person analysis. These tests determine whether the employee has the necessary knowledge to perform the tasks assigned. In many industrial jobs, an employee must

**Figure 6–3**        **Person analysis evaluation form**

TRAINING NEEDS ANALYSIS

EXPLANATION:

S = Outstanding Strength
M = Meets Requirements or
      Not Applicable to Job
D = Development Need

SUPERVISOR: Discusses strengths and weaknesses with subordinate during post-appraisal interview.
INCUMBENT: Discusses needs and goals with supervisor during postappraisal interview.

| | Management activity | S | M | D | |
|---|---|---|---|---|---|
| **PLANNING** | Promoting improvements | | | | |
| | Developing original ideas | | | | |
| | Applying new ideas | | | | |
| | Gathering information | | | | |
| | Analyzing information | | | | |
| | Planning objectives | | | | |
| **ORGA-NIZING** | Organizing ability | | | | |
| | Selecting people | | | | |
| | Utilizing people | | | | |
| | Delegation | | | | |
| **DIRECTING AND COORDINATING** | Coaching | | | | |
| | Training and developing people | | | | |
| | Oral expression | | | | |
| | Conducting meetings | | | | |
| | Written expression | | | | |
| | Keeping supervisor informed | | | | |
| | Keeping subordinates informed | | | | |
| | Achieving results through others | | | | |
| | Personal acceptance by others | | | | |
| | Setting standards for others | | | | |
| **CONTROLLING** | Maintaining control of operations | | | | |
| | Willingness to follow up | | | | |
| | Measuring results of operation | | | | |
| | Control of costs | | | | |
| | Control of quality | | | | |
| | Expanding income | | | | |
| | Improving net earnings | | | | |
| **OTHER** | | | | | |
| | | | | | |
| | | | | | |
| | | | | | |
| | | | | | |
| | | | | | |
| | | | | | |
| | | | | | |

Signed: _____ Date: _____
Incumbent

SOURCE: J. H. Morrison, "Determining Training Needs," in *Training Development Handbook*, 2d ed., ed. R. L. Craig (New York: McGraw-Hill, 1976). Copyright © 1976. Used by permission.

know certain facts. A secretary has to know grammar and punctuation; a design engineer has to know the principles of physical stress. An achievement test can help determine if a poorly performing employee needs more job knowledge. Furthermore, a worker's wrong answers pinpoint areas for training. If an employee does well on such a test but still performs poorly on the job, the problem may be in attitude, motivation, or situational (job) factors.

When job success involves "doing" as well as "knowing," paper-and-pencil tests only tell part of the story. Having a thorough knowledge of traffic laws doesn't necessarily make a good driver. Performance tests can assess an employee's motor skills in performing a certain task. Performance tests are most frequently used in the trades for carpenters, electricians, welders, plumbers, etc. Both skills and knowledges are measured in performance tests, making them a valuable diagnostic tool. A person who passes a job knowledge test but fails a performance test needs training in "how to do it" (motor skills) not in "what to do" (cognitive skills).

In general, person analysis is based more on assessing actual job performance than on achievement tests. Almost all employees get evaluated, either formally or informally. This then is a convenient basis to start a person analysis to determine individual training needs. Those companies that have developed diagnostic achievement tests can supplement them with performance appraisal. Both methods are designed to assess the training needs of the individual employee.

In summary, assessing training needs is a three-part process. Organization analysis identifies companywide goals, objectives, and problems. Operations analysis is concerned with the operations performed in a job: standards of operating performance, identifying tasks, and understanding of the methods and human attributes needed to perform the tasks. Finally, person analysis focuses on individual training needs.

Each phase involves a different level of analysis—the company as a whole, the work to be performed in jobs, and the needs of individuals. Assessing training needs has been described as "a grimy business, frustrating, and often carried on under increasing pressure to get something, just anything, going" (McGehee & Thayer, 1961, p. 25). However, it is vitally important for a training program's success. Moore and Dutton (1978) suggest that training needs analysis should be an ongoing process within the organization. Without such an assessment, training is conducted without any clear reason, continues with no purpose, and ends with no clear results.

## METHODS AND TECHNIQUES OF TRAINING

After determining an organization's training needs and translating them into objectives, the next step is to design a training program to meet these objectives. This isn't an easy task because each training method has its strengths, weaknesses, and costs. Ideally, we seek the "best" method—the one that meets our objectives in a cost-efficient manner. There are many training methods available. They can be classified in a number of ways, though probably the best way is according to *where* the training takes place.

## ON-SITE TRAINING METHODS

As the name suggests, on-site methods are conducted on the job site. On-site methods usually involve training in the total job, whereas off-site instruction often involves only part of the job (Bass & Barrett, 1981).

**On-the-job training**

On-the-job training is perhaps the oldest and most common form of instruction. Usually no special equipment or space is needed since new employees are trained at the actual job location. The instructors are usually more established workers, and the employees learn by imitation. They watch an established worker perform a task and try to imitate the behavior. One of the classic principles of training is maximized by this method—*transfer of training*. Transfer of training refers to the extent that the skills learned in training can be effectively transferred to the job. Since the training content (and location) are the same as the job content, there are usually few problems with transfer.

But on-the-job training has several limitations. Training is often brief and poorly structured. It may be little more than "watch me, kid, and I'll show you how to do it." Also many established workers find that teaching a new recruit is a nuisance, and the new employee may be pressured to master the task too quickly. On-the-job training is popular partly because it is so easy to administer. But since many new recruits make errors while training, the consequences of error must be evaluated. On-the-job training is far more feasible for custodians than for brain surgeons.

**Vestibule training**

Vestibule training is a type of instruction often found in production work. A vestibule consists of training equipment that is set up a short distance from the actual production line. Trainees can practice in the vestibule without getting in the way or slowing down the production line. These special training areas are usually used for skilled and semiskilled jobs, particularly those involving technical equipment. One limitation is that the vestibule is small, so relatively few people can be trained at the same time. The method is good for promoting *practice*, a learning principle involving the repetition of behavior.

Lefkowitz (1970) describes a study comparing vestibule training with on-the-job training for a sample of sewing machine operators. New employees were divided into four groups. The first three groups received one, two, and three days of vestibule training, respectively. The fourth group spent the first day in vestibule training, the second day in on-the-job training, and the third day back in vestibule training before actually starting work. Results showed that the longer the people were in vestibule training, the less likely they were to quit. But their average productivity was also slightly lower. The best overall results occurred for those people in the fourth group. Their productivity was at or above the other groups, and they had a relatively low quit rate. Lefkowitz concluded that a combination of the two methods was the most effective way to train sewing machine operators.

**Job rotation**

Job rotation is a method of training where workers rotate through a variety of jobs. They may be in the same job anywhere from a week to a year before they rotate. Job rotation is used with both blue-collar production workers and white-collar managers, and it has many organizational benefits. It acquaints workers with many jobs in a company and gives them the opportunity to learn by doing. Job rotation creates flexibility; during manpower shortages, workers have the skills to step in and fill open slots. The method also provides new and different work on a systematic basis, giving employees a variety of experiences and challenges. Employees also increase their flexibility and marketability because they can perform a wide array of tasks.

Like any method, job rotation also has its limitations. If workers are paid on a piece-rate or commission basis, they can earn more money on some jobs rather than others. That is, due to individual differences, people are not equally suited for all jobs. Workers are then reluctant to rotate out of their "best" job. Another problem is that the method weakens a worker's commitment to a given job (though it may increase loyalty to the company as a whole). Job rotation also challenges the basic principles of personnel placement: that workers are assigned to jobs that best match their talents and interests. Some employees are wary of a training system that puts them in jobs they're not good at or don't like. Willingness to learn new jobs is a key factor in the success of a job rotation system.

**Apprentice training**

Apprentice training is particularly common in the skilled trades. A new worker is "tutored" by an established worker for a long period of time (sometimes up to five years). The apprentice serves as an assistant and learns the craft by working with a fully skilled member of the trade called a *journeyman*. Apprenticeship programs are often used in the plumbing, carpentry, and electrical trades. At the end of the apprenticeship program, the person is "promoted" to a journeyman. Training is intense and lengthy. There is usually one apprentice assigned to one journeyman. A weakness of the method is that the amount of time an apprenticeship lasts is predetermined by the members of the trade. Individual differences in learning time are generally not allowed, so *all* apprentices have to work for a fixed time before they are upgraded. It has been argued that the apprentice program should be modified to allow more rapid rates of progression for fast learners (Franklin, 1976). The apprentice system is one of the oldest types of training programs in existence. Recently, the method has been modified for managerial positions. New workers serve under a "mentor," though the new employees are called "management trainees" rather than apprentices. But the principle of one-to-one tutelage is still the same.

## OFF-SITE TRAINING METHODS

There is more diversity in off-site training methods than on-site methods. Not only are there more methods, but they differ markedly in their content and approach to learning.

**Lectures**

As all students know, the lecture method is a popular form of instruction in educational institutions. It is also used in industry. With the lecture method, large numbers of people can be taught at the same time. In that sense, it is quite cost efficient. However, the more diversified the audience, the more general the content usually becomes. So, its utility for imparting specialized knowledge is more limited. A frequent reaction after a lecture on improving sales techniques is: "That idea sounds okay in principle, but how do I put it into operation in my company"? With a more homogenous audience, a trainer (or teacher) can direct the lecture to specific topics and techniques, which are often more beneficial than some broad-based lecture material. Lectures are an effective way to train large numbers of people at once, particularly if they have a specific training need.

On the negative side, lectures are usually one-way communication. There is little chance for dialogue, questions, individual problems, and special interests. Trainees themselves have to understand and personalize the content of the lecture. The lecture method is weak in such classic principles of training as practice, feedback, and transfer (Bass & Vaughan, 1966). While it is popular, it is not the best method to use for skill acquisition.

**Audiovisual material**

Audiovisual material covers an array of training techniques, such as films, slides, and videotapes. They allow participants to see as well as hear and are usually quite good at captivating trainees' interest. This underscores the importance of motivation and interest as a necessary condition for learning. After the initial expense of creating such a program, the cost of repeated use is usually minimal. Audiovisual material is particularly useful in training people in a work process or sequence. People can more readily trace the pattern of work flow when it is laid out graphically. Konz and

Dickey (1969) demonstrated that a slide presentation was superior to verbal and printed instructions in training employees to complete various work assembly operations.

On the negative side, it is difficult to modify these training methods to change the content. If the training content changes, a whole new film has to be made. Slide presentations are more modifiable since the outdated slides can be replaced with more current material. The production cost of training films can be quite substantial. A half-hour, color, sound-track film can cost $75,000 to produce. However, the costs are worth it if the task or job is very important to the company. With the aid of close-up images, stop-action, slow-motion, and instant replay, delicate and complex tasks can be broken down into discrete and understandable units.

Videotape is particularly useful in recording employees' job behaviors. Their performance can be taped and then observed (and evaluated) for effective and ineffective behaviors. The method is excellent for providing feedback. Feedback is a means to let people know how they are doing, and many studies (e.g., Ilgen, Fisher, & Taylor, 1979) suggest that feedback is an important part of the learning process. Kidd (1961) showed that videotape instruction was useful for training people as diplomatic overseas advisors. They learned more effectively and retained more than people who only read a training manual on the same material. Seeing yourself on videotape can also be a most enlightening (and unnerving) experience. The first time I saw a videotape of one of my lectures, my reaction was "I look like *that?!*" I quickly saw my weaknesses as a teacher. With new electronic recording equipment, the use of videotape as a training technique will probably increase in the future.

## Conferences

The conference method of training stresses two-way communication. It is particularly effective if the ratio of trainees to trainers is not very large. This method is useful when the material needs clarification or elaboration, where a lively discussion would facilitate understanding. Sometimes the lecture method can be followed up by a conference discussion, giving the participants a chance to share opinions about the material (Bass & Barrett, 1981). The trainer can call on people to see if they understand the material, and participants can ask questions. An effective trainer can get all the participants involved—even the less vocal ones. The success of this method depends heavily on the skills and personality of the discussion leader. A dogmatic, abrasive leader can stifle discussion. A good leader must know when to lead the discussion and when to allow others to lead. The conference method can draw on the learning principles of motivation and feedback. Stimulated participants readily join in the discussion and then receive feedback on their ideas from others in the group. The conference method is used to enhance knowledge or attitudinal development. The willingness of the participants to acquire new knowledges and explore attitude change (and the trainer's ability to facilitate such learning) influences the success of the conference method. Perhaps because this method doesn't usually involve any tangible assets other than people, more than any other training method, the attitudes, enthusiasm, and verbal communication skills of the participants affect the outcome.

## Programmed instruction

Programmed instruction (PI) is a newer method of training, but its origin goes back to the research of learning theorist B. F. Skinner. The method of PI may involve an actual piece of equipment (usually called a teaching machine), or it may involve a specially constructed paper booklet. In either case, the method has three main characteristics. First, the participants are active in the training process. In fact, they determine their own learning pace. Second, what is to be learned involves many discrete pieces of material, and the participants get immediate feedback on whether they have learned each piece. Third, the material is divided into an organized sequence.

It takes a lot of time to develop material for PI. Each piece of material has to facilitate understanding of the total material covered. Thus, the sequence of material is highly integrated. It is verified to see that each piece of material contributes to understanding and that the entire process covers a unified theme.

Bass and Barrett (1981) describe the common features of PI:

1. A single piece of information is presented at each stage, and each stage is called a frame. All of the frames together (however many it takes to present the material) are called a program. The first frame deals with the first step in some procedure; in industrial training, it is usually a work procedure (like operating a piece of equipment). The frames may involve only one question, or they may involve examining some information given in a figure or diagram. A question is then asked about the diagram. The answer is either a true/false answer or multiple choice.

2. The participant gives an answer to the question in the first frame. If the answer is correct, the participant proceeds to the next frame (by turning a knob on the teaching machine or turning the page in a booklet). If the answer is incorrect, the correct answer is given along with an explanation of why it is correct.

3. The frames are arranged in the exact sequence that occur in the work process. This step-by-step sequence in learning matches the step-by-step sequence followed in performing the task on the job.

4. The participants go through the program at their own pace. Emphasis is placed on correct answers, not work speed. Some people learn best at a slow pace, while others can learn more rapidly.

5. The participant proceeds through the entire program. After completing the program, the number of correct answers are tabulated (either automatically on the machine or by hand with the booklet). A criterion of

mastery is set prior to training, usually 90 or 95 percent correct. If the participant reaches that level, training on that program is ended for that participant. If the percent correct falls below the criterion, the participant repeats the program.

Figures 6–4 and 6–5 show example frames from two different PI programs—one to train workers on the proper way to lift heavy boxes, the other to teach people to play chess. While PI has been used in industry, it is also used for school children.

There are many advantages to PI as a training method. Participants get immediate feedback. Because the material is presented in a precise and systematic manner, there are no gaps in the presentation. The participants are active learners; there is a constant exchange of information between themselves and the program. When participants make mistakes, there is

**Figure 6–4**                    **Sample problem from A Programmed Instruction safety program**

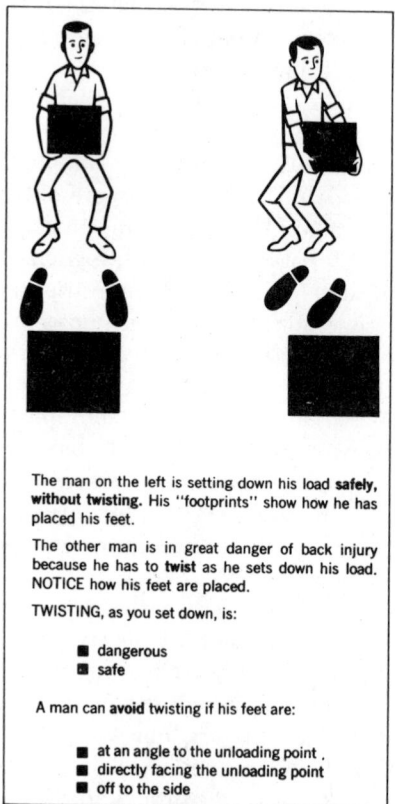

The man on the left is setting down his load **safely, without twisting.** His "footprints" show how he has placed his feet.

The other man is in great danger of back injury because he has to **twist** as he sets down his load. NOTICE how his feet are placed.

TWISTING, as you set down, is:

■ dangerous
▨ safe

A man can **avoid** twisting if his feet are:

■ at an angle to the unloading point .
■ directly facing the unloading point
■ off to the side

SOURCE: *A New Approach to Management's Role in Back Safety* (Hicksville, N.Y.: Advanced Learning Systems, 1966).

**Figure 6–5**                 **Sample problem from Programmed Instruction chess program**

6

Observe this position; then decide whether the Black King can capture
the checking White piece.

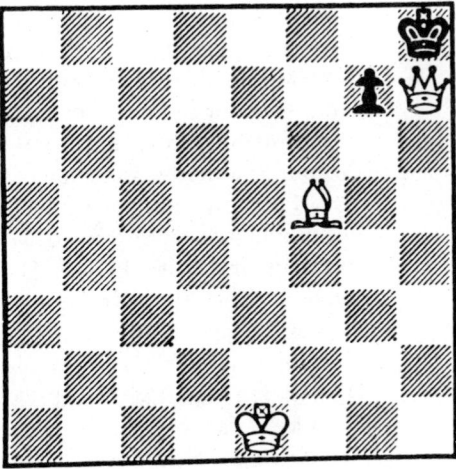

The White Queen is giving check.  The Black King:

☐  can capture

☐  cannot capture

FOR THE CORRFCT ANSWER TURN TO THE NEXT PAGE

SOURCE: B. Fischer, S. Margulies, and D. Mosenfelder, *Bobby Fischer Teaches Chess* (New York: Bantam Books, 1972).

no fear of embarrassment because they are the only one who knows they
erred. Fast learners don't have to wait for slow ones to catch up; slow
learners don't always have to try to catch up. Finally, PI is an efficient way
to train people on material that is structured and rote. It gives a trainer
more time to cover unstructured and ambiguous material with a different
method, usually the conference.

On the negative side, developing a PI program is time-consuming. The
material has to be broken down into a logical sequence. Each frame has
to be checked to be sure that it is accurate and contributes to overall
learning of the material. Some work procedures are hard to break down
into an exact sequence since there may be several correct ways to perform

the task. Also the stability or consistency of a structured task must be considered before developing a PI program. In a rapidly changing technological area, a PI program could be obsolete in a few months. Like any training method, PI has its place, but it is not a panacea for all training needs (Brethower, 1976).

Even with its limitations, PI has been a great asset to industrial training. Welsh, Antoinetti, and Thayer (1965) described the development of a 625-frame PI program designed to teach salespeople the fundamentals of selling life insurance. The authors reported that the PI method was as effective (but no more so) than more conventional training methods. But its major benefit was the amount of time (and thus money) it saved industrial trainers. Another example of the PI method was reported by Hughes and McNamara (1961). In this study, a company compared the PI and lecture training methods of teaching people to operate large, high-speed computers. Forty-two employees were trained with the classroom method, while 70 employees were trained with PI. The results of the study showed that training time with PI was 11 hours compared to 15 hours for the other method. The 90 percent criterion of mastery was attained by 89 percent of the employees trained with PI, compared to only 45 percent of the employees who learned in the classroom. Almost all the employees who had PI training reported that it was an exciting way to learn, and most wanted it to be a part of future training programs. Additionally, the initial cost of developing the PI material is almost all the cost involved.

Nash, Muczyk, and Vettori (1971) conducted a survey of industrial training programs in which PI was rated "practically superior" (defined as a

**Figure 6–6**   **Percent of training programs in industry in which Programmed Instruction was rated practically superior to conventional training methods on three training criteria**

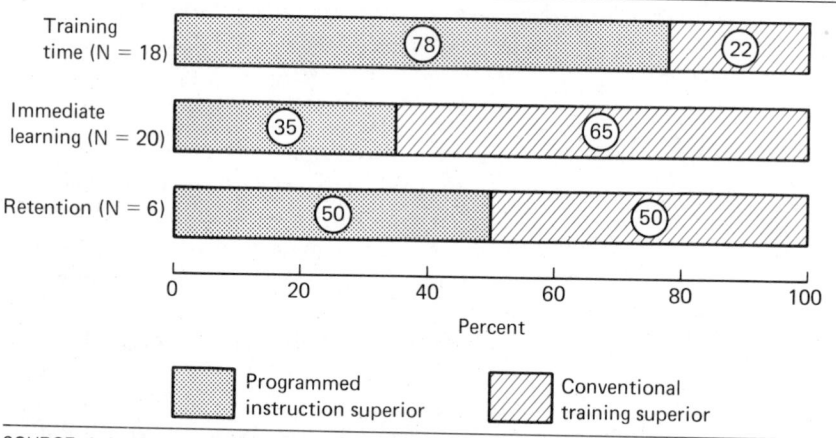

SOURCE: A. N. Nash, J. P. Muczyk, and F. L. Vettori, "The Relative Practical Effectiveness of Programmed Instruction," *Personnel Psychology* 24 (1971), pp. 397–418.

10 percent improvement in results over conventional training methods). Three criteria of training effectiveness were assessed: training time, immediate learning, and retention. The results are shown in Figure 6–6. On the basis of this study, it appears that PI does not enhance retention or immediate learning. Its primary advantage is training time. It takes less time to train employees with PI, and this reduces costs and allows the trainers time for other methods.

**Computer-assisted instruction**

The most recently developed training method is Computer-Assisted Instruction (CAI). It is a logical extension of PI and shares many of its benefits. But it has many more limitations, and because the method is so new, we don't know as much about it as the more established methods. CAI was born with the advent of large, complex computers. The computer is the

Computer-aided work operations are becoming increasingly common in organizations and require special training for employees.

*Courtesy NCR*

trainer and is programmed to teach a particular skill. Similar to PI, the task is broken down into its component parts. Questions are then asked about the material being covered. However, a major difference between CAI and PI is that computers can be programmed to ask questions of varying levels of difficulty. Furthermore, the computer can be programmed to "ask" why a person gave a wrong answer; e.g., was it because you didn't know the meaning of a term, thought the term meant something else, knew the term but didn't know how to apply it, etc. CAI is a sophisticated approach. It can teach a wide range of skills ranging from how to speak a foreign language to how to fly a helicopter.

CAI works as follows. The trainee sits at a console, usually a visual screen along with what looks like a typewriter. Both parts are connected to a computer programmed with the training material. The person communicates to the computer through the keyboard; the computer flashes its messages to the person on the screen. Questions and related information are displayed on the screen, and the person has to answer by pushing certain keys on the keyboard. One CAI program, when first turned on, begins by flashing the words "Good Morning" on the screen. If the person doesn't press a key that says "Good Morning" back to the computer in five seconds, the computer flashes a second message: "What's the matter—kind of grumpy today?" All this has been arranged (i.e., programmed) to make the trainee feel that the computer is not totally impersonal. This, in turn, is designed to enhance motivation.

Needless to say, access to a computer is extremely expensive. Not surprisingly, most CAI training in industry is done in companies that use large computers for their normal business operations. The banking and airline industries are two such examples. Once you have a complex computer, it can be programmed to perform another function—train employees. Hickey (1976) describes several advantages to CAI. Among them are (1) individualized instruction, (2) reduced training time, (3) elimination of travel for training, and (4) standardized training. The advantages to the trainee include (1) being able to work at his or her own pace, (2) being able to begin and end a lesson when convenient, and (3) being able to enter a program at his or her current level of achievement.

Koerner (1973) describes the disadvantages: (1) the high cost, (2) the fact that programming lags far behind the development of computers, and (3) programming for training purposes is still in its infancy. That is, if no new computers were made, we would still be challenged to develop good programs for the computers already here. But new computers are being produced all the time, so we are always behind in our ability to program them effectively.

As Cooley and Glaser (1969) and Suppes and Morningstar (1969) have discussed, CAI is a new and versatile approach to training. It is used in the military, in schools, and to some extent in industry. Since it is a new training technique, we have a lot to learn. As more industrial organizations come to rely on computers to assist them in their operations, greater use will be made of CAI in the years to come. At this stage of development, CAI probably has more potential for training in complex skills than any other technique.

## Simulation

Coppard (1976) defines simulation as "a representation of a real-life situation which attempts to duplicate selected components of the situation along with their interrelationships in such a way that it can be manipulated by the user." Simulations are carefully developed exercises. They try to model the important parts of the situation they are supposed to replicate. Simulations usually enhance cognitive skills, particularly decision making. They are a popular training technique for higher-level jobs where the employee must process large amounts of information.

Simulations have many forms. Some use expensive, technical equipment, while others are far less costly. Some simulations need only one participant; others may involve as many as 15 to 20 people working together as a team. Simulations are a broad-based training technique that can be adapted to suit a company's needs.

One example of a simulation is a training technique for managers called the in-basket (Fredericksen, 1962). The in-basket simulates how managers make decisions and allocate their time. As we saw in Chapter 4, the in-basket is an individual-level training technique. The manager sits at a desk in a room especially created for the training. The desk has a telephone, note pad, calendar, and so on. The most important feature is a manager's "in-basket" for incoming matters that need attention. But in this case, the contents of the in-basket are carefully developed and arranged in sequence. The manager proceeds through the in-basket and makes decisions about the matters that need attention. Usually, there are 10 to 15 items in the in-basket; the entire exercise may take 2 to 3 hours to complete. One item in the in-basket may be a request for information about the cost of a product. Another item may inform the manager of the possibility of disciplining an employee. The manager responds to these items in the same way he or she would on the job. Judges unobtrusively observe and evaluate the manager's performance. Performance is judged along certain dimensions, such as the quantity and quality of the work accomplished. The in-basket exercise may reveal deficiencies in the manager's work style (not delegating less important tasks to subordinates, spending too much time on certain matters and not enough on others, etc.). The manager gets feedback from the panel to enhance his or her performance on the job.

Many simulations use *games*. Business games train employees in certain skills. Within the rules of the game, participants try to meet the stated objectives of the exercise. Business games can be used to train individuals or groups. Games have been developed to simulate interpersonal relations problems, financial/budgeting issues, and resource allocation decisions.

Participants are told the objective of the game (e.g., to reach a certain profit level, to maximize financial return with a fixed budget, etc.). They are then evaluated on whether the game's objectives were met. Business games are popular for training managers and executives, particularly in financial matters. Raia (1966) reports that business games were superior to the lecture and conference methods in training managers in certain problem areas.

All simulations do not have involve games; some have been built to model a work process. In this case, the goal is to acquaint the employee with what the process will be like when it is done for real. Driving and flying simulators are examples. Flying simulators are used extensively in pilot training; a complex computerized system simulates how an airplane behaves under various operating conditions.

It is difficult to judge the utility of simulations because they cover such a broad range of training exercises. As a rule, the closer the simulation comes to modeling the job *in all respects*, the better the simulation will be as a training technique. Simulations that don't replicate crucial aspects of the job will not be very successful. A problem with simulations that have a game component is that the participants know it is only a game. Failing at a game is not the same as failing on the job. Participants sometimes behave differently than they would in real life. For example, in a marketing course, a business game was created to simulate marketing a product. The class was divided into work teams. The team that showed the greatest profit at the end of the semester received an award. Within the rules of the game (e.g., advertising the product, spending on research to improve the product, etc.), the "sales volume" of each work team was posted in the class weekly. As the weeks went by, some work teams gradually fell behind in profit. So members of the losing teams began to take unnatural risks with their companies, risks they probably wouldn't take on a real job. They didn't care if their actions failed (the company went bankrupt) because it was only a game. And if their wild risks came through, they received the award. In this case, the game did not include some key components found on the job. Unlike a semester, the life-span of a real company does not end on a predetermined date. The consequences of losing one's job (as well as destroying a company) are not the same as simply failing to win a class award. The best simulations are "best" because there is a high degree of transfer of training between the simulation and the job. Needless to say, some simulations are easier to construct to maximize this transfer than others.

## Role playing

Role playing is a training method often aimed at enhancing either human relations skills or sales techniques. As opposed to programmed instruction, which is deliberately geared to the individual, role playing involves many people. Wohlking (1976) defines role playing "as an educational or therapeutic technique in which some problem involving human inter-action, real or imaginary, is presented and then spontaneously acted out." The enactment is normally followed by a discussion to determine what happened during the enactment and why. Participants suggest how the problem could be handled more effectively in the future.

Participants in role playing are assigned roles in a scenario to be enacted. Unlike acting, where performers have to say set lines on cue, role playing is not so tightly structured. One scenario may be a department store. One person takes the role of an irate customer who is dissatisfied with a recently purchased product. A second person might be assigned the role of the clerk who has to attend to the customer's complaint. Aside from some general guidelines about the product, the participants are free to act out their roles however they wish. Their performance is judged by people who do not have an active part in the role-playing. In an educational setting, the observers may be other students in the class; in a business setting, the observers might be supervisors.

Many variations of role playing are possible. In some exercises, participants repeat the enactment several times but switch roles. In other cases, participants reverse the role they play in real life, e.g., the supervisor plays a union representative. Participants are forced (by the role) to adopt the position of the other side and then defend that position.

Goldstein (1980b) describes some recent advances with a technique called behavioral role modeling, which uses role playing as one of its parts. In behavioral role modeling, some points or principles to be stressed in training are identified. The participants watch a model use the principles (often on film). The participants rehearse the principles by role playing and then get social reinforcement from the trainer and other group members. Latham and Saari (1979) reported a study of behavioral role modeling that was designed to increase interpersonal skills in dealing with employees. Forty first-line supervisors were assigned to either the modeling group or a control group (which received another form of training to meet the same objectives). Results showed that the supervisors trained with behavioral role modeling were more impressed with the training, scored higher on a learning test six months after training, and were judged to perform better on the job a year later.

In another study, Moses and Ritchie (1976) evaluated the performance of 90 supervisors who participated in a behavioral modeling program compared to 93 supervisors in a control group. The supervisors were evaluated two months after training by a specially constructed assessment procedure. Each supervisor (in both groups) held a discussion with a trained individual who played the role of a subordinate. Three problem situations were role played involving absenteeism, discrimination, and theft. Each supervisor was evaluated by four raters on how effectively he interacted with the subordinate in trying to deal with the problems. Neither the "subordinate" nor the evaluators knew which supervisors had gone through behavioral

**Figure 6–7**                    **Average performance rating of supervisors trained with behavioral role modeling and a control group on three problem-discussion topics**

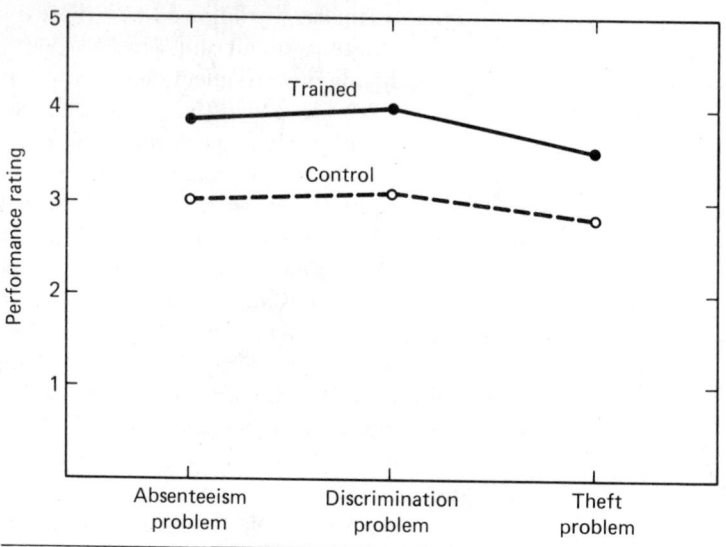

SOURCE: J. L. Moses and R. J. Ritchie, "Supervisory Relationship Training: A Behavioral Evaluation of a Behavior Modeling Program," *Personnel Psychology* 29 (1976), pp. 337–43.

modeling. The results are given in Figure 6–7. As can be seen, the trained supervisors were rated as more effective in discussing the problems than the untrained supervisors. Behavioral role modeling holds a lot of promise as a training method (Kraut, 1976), though some caution should be exercised in endorsing any new training technique (McGehee & Tullar, 1978). More research needs to be done on behavioral role modeling before we have a clear understanding of its strengths and weaknesses.

The advantages of role playing include the fact that participants are highly active. By "putting your feet in the other person's shoes," participants gain some understanding of what it is like to experience interpersonal conflict from someone else's position. Interpersonal relations skills are among the more difficult ones to enhance (with any method). Despite legitimate criticism that some people put more emphasis on acting than problem solving, the method has been quite useful.

## Sensitivity training

Sensitivity training is also called T-group (T for training) and human relations laboratory training. It is also probably the most controversial method of training. Its general goal is to enhance interpersonal relations skills. But specific sessions may be devoted to such themes as expressing anger, building trust, reducing conflict, etc. As the name suggests, its overall objective is to increase human sensitivity to others and their problems.

Sensitivity training has its origins in clinical psychology where it is used as a form of psychotherapy. In the last 20 years, it has been used as an industrial training technique.

Sensitivity training involves several participants at once—usually 10 to 12. The training is quite lengthy; it takes anywhere from several days to several weeks. Participants usually go to a retreat, a place removed from their place of work. The retreat can be held at a motel or hotel or a full-time social laboratory created for the training. Participants either know each other from work or come from different organizations. They are usually chosen by someone in their company who felt they needed training in human relations. The participants (under the direction of a staff of trainers) face an ambiguous situation. The normal factors encountered at work (an agenda, structure, norms, superior/subordinate relationships) are absent. Their task is to learn about themselves as people—their values, methods of behaving, and how they perceive others and are perceived by others. As people act, their behavior becomes the subject of learning. Activities then clarify, extend, and support the overall goal of becoming a more sensitive person.

There are many types of activities involved. Some situational exercises are designed to stress certain responses, such as trust. In one exercise, called a "trust walk," one person whose eyes are shut is led by another. The "leader" can lead the person around a room or out of a building and across a busy street. The followers can end the exercise at any time by opening their eyes. This exercise is observed by other people. The two participants are asked how they felt about trusting and being trusted, whether the leader "used" the follower to show off, whether the follower's trust bordered on gullibility, etc. People also have discussions, role play, and perhaps watch themselves on videotape.

According to Dupre (1976), the goals of sensitivity training are as follows:

1. Introspectiveness or awareness: the ability to reflect on feelings and ideas within ourselves.
2. Awareness of feelings: developing a high regard for the significance of feelings in living and working.
3. Recognition of, and concern about, feeling-behavior discrepancies: developing an ability to diagnose the relation between how we feel and how we behave, and to move toward greater congruence between these.
4. Flexibility: developing skill in behaving in new and different ways.

As can be seen by these goals, sensitivity training is aimed at the development of the entire person, not just one particular skill in that person.

Sensitivity training can be a very traumatic experience for some people. They may learn things about themselves they don't like. There are sharply divided opinions on the value of sensitivity training. Some psychologists like the method, others don't, and yet others conclude they don't know why the method produces the results it does (Smith, 1975). The mixed verdict on sensitivity training is perhaps best expressed by Cooper and Levine (1978). They say that sensitivity training can be a meaningful experience for certain people in certain circumstances. One of the problems with the method is transfer of training. Participants in sensitivity training learn new skills while in a very cloistered environment—one deliberately created so they feel free to express their feelings. Once they learn these skills (and have them reinforced by the group), participants return to the same environment that molded the very behavior they sought to change. Back on the job, they may not be reinforced by others for being more trusting, open, and sensitive. This can be a frustrating experience for some people, especially those who had positive feelings about their new-found behaviors. One person who experienced this problem summed up her reaction by saying, "My boss should have gone through that sensitivity training with me. He needs it more than I did."

## OVERVIEW OF TRAINING METHODS

Bass and Vaughan (1966) rated some of the off-site training methods in terms of their use of several learning principles and the types of training programs in which they are used. Their evaluation is shown in Figure 6–8. PI draws heavily on the various learning principles, while lectures and films are more limited in their use of these principles. Active participation of the subject is the most commonly used learning principle. Transfer of training

"If the coach says ballet will help our training, that's cool. But I've got my doubts about these new uniforms. . . ."

Reprinted courtesy of The Register and Tribune Syndicate

**Figure 6–8**    **Extent to which certain methods utilize certain learning principles and typical applications of training methods**

Legend: ● Yes  ○ Sometimes  ☐ No

| | Lecture | TV films | Conference | Laboratory training | Case method | Role playing | Management games | Programmed instruction |
|---|---|---|---|---|---|---|---|---|
| **USE OF PRINCIPLES OF LEARNING** | | | | | | | | |
| Motivation: active participation | | | ● | ● | ● | ● | ● | ● |
| Reinforcement: feedback | | | ○ | ● | ○ | ○ | ○ | ● |
| Stimulus: meaningful organization | ● | ● | ○ | | ○ | | ○ | ● |
| Response: practice, repetition | | | | ○ | ● | ○ | ○ | ● |
| S-R conditions favorable for transfer | | | | ○ | ○ | ○ | ○ | |
| **PROGRAMS IN WHICH TYPICALLY USED** | | | | | | | | |
| Orientation; introducing innovations | ● | ● | ● | | | | ● | ● |
| Special skill training | ● | ● | | | | | ● | ● |
| Safety education | ● | ● | ● | | | | | ● |
| Creative, technical, professional | ● | ● | ● | ● | ● | | ● | ● |
| Sales, supervisory, managerial | ● | ● | ● | ● | ● | ● | ● | ● |

SOURCE: B. M. Bass and J. A. Vaughan, *Training in Industry: The Management of Learning* (Monterey, Calif.: Brooks/Cole Publishing, 1966). Copyright © 1966 by Wadsworth Publishing Company. Reprinted by permission.

seems to be a consistently underutilized principle. This is particularly true for off-site training methods.

The 12 training methods we have discussed are used for different purposes. No one method is best. What is important is not the method per se but the change in behavior the method is designed to bring about. People who tout certain methods as panaceas for training needs have a misplaced sense of values. I concur with Goldstein's (1980a) opinion: greater emphasis should be given to identifying training needs rather than designing new training methods.

# TRAINING FOCUSED ON PARTICULAR POPULATIONS

Selected subgroups of the work force have special training needs. These needs have emerged due to the influx of different segments of the population into the work force and rapid changes in technology. Effective training procedures are directed at the tasks as well as the people themselves. Business organizations have been pressured by the government to hire minority-group members and women (especially in management positions). These companies also realize they are underutilizing a supply of talent, so they have been recruiting these groups more heavily. Thus, one function of training is to help assimilate these people into the work force.

## Hard-core unemployed

There is no good definition of the hard-core unemployed (HCU), but most definitions include the following: such people (1) are not regular members of the work force; (2) have been unemployed for the previous six months; (3) are typically young; (4) are members of a minority group; (5) lack a high school education; and (6) are below the poverty level specified by the Department of Labor (Goldstein, 1980a).[2]

The particular problem with this segment of the work force is lack of retention. After being on the job for a short period of time (and perhaps after earning more money then they had ever had at one time before), they frequently quit. Companies wanted to know what could be done to keep these people on the job. Early studies on HCUs (i.e., Friedlander & Greenberg, 1971) stressed the importance of the company's supportiveness and understanding. Later studies (Goodman & Salipante, 1976; Salipante & Goodman, 1976) examined the relationship between organizational rewards and the retention of HCUs. Five factors emerged as important determinants of retention: the type of pay system, promotional opportunities, type of job, type and degree of counseling, and type of training. With regard to the type of training, the results were mixed. Training that enhanced technical/job skills resulted in the retention of HCUs. But attitudinal training was negatively related to retention. Salipante and Goodman concluded that technical/job skill training was perceived by the HCUs to mean that a job was waiting for them. But they thought attitudinal training meant that something was "wrong" with them and that the training was some form of therapy. One study points out that training can have unintended consequences. O'Leary (1972) had 36 black females go through a 12-week training program involving role playing and group discussion. The training program was designed to acquaint the new employees with problems encountered on the job. The training helped the women develop much more positive feelings about themselves and their abilities. However, it also raised their aspirations, and they came to expect too much from the job. When their aspirations were not met on the job, they quit. Thus, the training program accomplished its immediate objective (i.e., acquaint employees with real-life job problems) but failed to meet the overall objective (minimize turnover of HCUs).

Triandis, Feldman, Weldon and Harvey (1974, 1975) tried to find greater

---

[2]Some authors feel that the term *hard-to-employ* is more appropriate than *hard-core unemployed*.

detail on *why* HCUs so frequently quit. They concluded that HCUs and traditional employees misunderstand each other's behavior. That is, across various cultures, people ascribe different meanings to the same behavior. HCUs were found to reject authority figures, were suspicious of others' motives, and in general viewed the work place as malevolent. The authors labeled this constellation of feelings and attitudes "ecosystem distrust." They discussed its potential for creating misunderstanding between supervisors and HCUs. Triandis et al. proposed the use of a "cultural assimilator"—a programmed instruction method that focuses on understanding incidents of intercultural conflict as a way of increasing communication.

Assimilating HCUs into the work force depends on training both the HCUs and the traditional employees. The cultures that produced these people are vastly different, so both groups must strive to better understand each other. Trainers of HCUs face some of the most vexing problems in the training profession.

## Women in management

While women have been a dominant force in the labor market for many years, only recently have greater strides been made to get them into management positions. Males who want to be managers must be trained to have administrative skills, but females have an even greater array of skills to master. Many of the problems facing women in management are attitudinal—attitudes women hold of themselves and attitudes about women held by others. These problems relate to role stereotypes, feelings of low self-esteem, and assessments of women's competence. O'Leary (1974) discussed how these factors are barriers for women. Among the objective problems women face in management are factors relating to role conflict and educational background. Role conflict is the tension caused when two or more roles must be filled at the same time but they do not blend well. Traditionally, females have had the main responsibility for homemaking and raising children. But a manager's job requires a big commitment of time and energy. Many women are caught in a bind. They feel they can't do both—be a competent manager and a competent homemaker. Also, many managers have either a business or technical educational background. Though more females are now entering these majors, in the past, they were quite male-dominated. Women who don't have this training find it hard to compete for managerial jobs with men who do.

A major type of training for women in management is assertiveness training. Assertive-skill training teaches people to stand up for their rights in such a way that the rights of others are not violated (Crane, 1979). It involves role playing and group discussion; people are trained to give certain assertive responses which then become a part of the behavioral response style. As with HCUs, many companies have to train their male managers to accept women as part of the managerial work force. Such training helps male managers be more aware of their own biases and stereotypical views of females. Thus, different types of training are directed at both females and males with the overall objective of assimilating females into a company's managerial ranks.

AT&T sponsors a training program called The Womanagement Process. It is a voluntary, ongoing, on-the-job program that provides career planning, educational seminars about the company, and workshops in confidence building. In one exercise, Alice in Corporationland, participants engage in simulated power plays and learn the rudiments of risk taking—an inherent part of management decisions. Larwood, Wood, and Inderlied (1978) suggest that the importance of training for women in management will continue as long as women enter these positions.

## Updating and retraining

People with scientific and technical backgrounds face the problem that their knowledge becomes outdated as new procedures are developed. Professional obsolescence is a serious problem in fields where there are continuous and rapid technological changes. Lukasiewicz (1971) estimated that in 1940, the knowledge of a newly trained engineer had a "half-life" of about 12 years; that is, in 12 years, half of this knowledge would be obsolete. And this half-life is surely less now than it was 40 years ago.

Professional obsolescence is not limited to engineers. Any profession (medical, dental, scientific) heavily linked to a technology is susceptible to obsolescence. New X-rays have eliminated some types of exploratory surgery that were common only a decade ago. Advances in hand-held calculators have taken place in only the past few years.

Sometimes the problem of obsolescence is so big it affects an entire industry. Engineers who were urged into the aerospace industry found themselves out of work (by the thousands) when the space program was cut back (Kinn, 1973). They were not only out of work, but they had specialized training in an area that shrank to a fraction of its original scope. Many had to be "retooled" to find other work in the engineering field.

The most common types of updating programs are either university or in-company training programs. Universities normally offer two types of courses to keep people abreast of current developments in a field. The first type, the standard semester course, is not the most effective. (Most courses cover more than just the latest developments in a field.) Employees can also take "short courses," workshops, and so on. These programs may last anywhere from a half day to two weeks. The instructors are usually college professors or paid consultants hired by the university. On a larger scale, some companies encourage employees to obtain graduate degrees. Obviously, this is broader in scope than a specialized workshop, but the benefits are also more broad-based. On the negative side, it may take several years to earn a graduate degree on a part-time basis.

In-company updating programs are far more company specific. Such programs run the gamut from lecture/conference formats to intensive CAI methods (Butman & Frick, 1973). The training method is chosen based on such factors as cost, availability, time, and the aptitude of the participants. Sometimes an industry or a profession will sponsor a training program for employees from many companies within the profession. Every year at the APA's national convention, the Division of Industrial and Organizational Psychology sponsors a one-day program. It consists of about 8 to 10 workshops for practicing I/O psychologists who want to know the latest ideas and techniques.

Individuals also differ in their willingness to be retrained. Some people think updating is a necessary part of their job; others with job security think it is a nuisance. Sometimes, a profession can pressure individuals to update their knowledge. To maintain a license in psychology, it is necessary to earn continuing education units (CEUs) by attending meetings and workshops. Companies can structure jobs to be more challenging (thus requiring updating), or they can phase out people with obsolete skills and channel them into less challenging positions. Established employees may have little motivation to update themselves if the more challenging jobs are given to younger (and more recently trained) employees.

Landy and Trumbo (1980) suggest a dual approach to the fight against professional obsolescence. First, continuing education should be a standard part of the job. Second, challenging work assignments should be given to employees commensurate with their newly developed skills. Again, training is but a means to an end. If the training doesn't count for anything, employees won't want to participate.

In conclusion, the importance of updating and retraining varies across professions and jobs. In some professions, updating is the difference between superior and mediocre performance; in others, it may be the difference between retention and termination.

In summary, training is a necessary part of any organization. However, for certain populations, the need for training is particularly acute. It is imperative that companies learn to understand the needs of their employees and, in turn, that employees learn how they fit into the company. Training is especially critical for HCUs and women in management positions. Where there is a rapid change in technology, it is equally critical that older employees update their knowledges and skills.

## THE EVALUATION OF TRAINING PROGRAMS

As is the case with any assessment or evaluation, some measure of performance must be obtained. Measures of performance refer to criteria, and the criteria used to evaluate training are just as important as those used in personnel selection. Relevance, reliability, freedom from bias, etc., are all important considerations. One distinction between criteria used in personnel selection and criteria used to evaluate training is that training criteria are more varied and are used to evaluate multiple aspects of a training program.

## Criteria

Kirkpatrick (1976) identified four levels of criteria used to evaluate training programs: reaction, learning, behavioral, and results. *Reaction* criteria are the participants' reaction to the program. They measure impressions and feelings about the training; e.g., was it useful, did it add to their knowledge, etc. Think of reaction criteria as a measure of the *face validity* of the training program. An evaluation form used to assess participant reactions is shown in Figure 6–9.

*Learning* criteria, when used, evaluate how much has been learned in the training program. A final exam given at the end of a training program would be an example of a learning criterion. With some training methods, such as Programmed Institution, the learning criterion is built right into the program; the participant must reach a certain level of proficiency (90 percent correct) before training is complete. With other methods, such as role playing directed at improving attitudinal skills, there may be no formal evaluation of how much was learned. Or participants might simply be asked if they changed their attitudes because of the training. Collectively, reaction and learning criteria are called "internal" criteria—they refer to assessments internal to the training program itself.

*Behavioral* criteria refer to actual changes in performance back on the job. They address the question "To what extent are the desired change in the job behaviors of the trainee realized by the training program" (Landy & Trumbo, 1980). If the goal of the training program is to increase production, the behavioral criterion involves assessing output before and after training. Other types of behavioral criteria include absenteeism, scrap rate, accidents, and grievances. All of these are hard criteria as discussed in Chapter 3. They can be measured easily and have relatively clear meaning. But if the goal of a training program is to increase managers' sensitivity toward hiring the handicapped, "increased sensitivity" has to be translated into some objective behavioral criteria. Also note that scores on learning criteria and on behavioral criteria do not always correspond to a great degree. Some people who perform well in training can't transfer their new knowledge or skills back to the job. This is particularly true with training programs aimed at changing attitudes or feelings.

*Results* criteria refer to the ultimate value of the training program to the company. It consists of assessing the costs of the training program compared to its benefits. Depending on the objective of the program, this can be quite difficult to do. Evaluating increased production output may not be too difficult. All the costs of the training (i.e., trainer time, employee time away from the job, training equipment and supplies, etc.) are calculated. Then the employees' level of productivity after training is calculated. The utility of the increased productivity is measured in terms of the com-

**Figure 6–9**                          **Participant evaluation form**

Acme Training Program

Trainer _____ Subject _____

Date _____

1. Was the subject pertinent to your needs and interests?
   ☐ No        ☐ To some extent        ☐ Very much so

2. How was the ratio of lecture to discussion?
   ☐ Too much lecture        ☐ OK        ☐ Too much discussion

3. Rate the leader on the following:

| | Excellent | Very good | Good | Fair | Poor |
|---|---|---|---|---|---|
| A. How well did he state objectives? | | | | | |
| B. How well did he keep the session alive and interesting? | | | | | |
| C. How well did he use the blackboard, charts, and other aids? | | | | | |
| D. How well did he summarize during the session? | | | | | |
| E. How well did he maintain a friendly and helpful manner? | | | | | |
| F. How well did he illustrate and clarify the points? | | | | | |
| G. How was his summary at the close of the session? | | | | | |

What is your overall rating of the leader?
☐ Excellent        ☐ Very good        ☐ Good        ☐ Fair        ☐ Poor

4. What would have made the session more effective? _____
_____
_____

_____
Signature (optional)

SOURCE: Adapted from D. L. Kirkpatrick, "Evaluation of Training," in *Training and Development Handbook*, 2d ed. R. L. Craig (New York: McGraw-Hill, 1976). Copyright © 1976. Used by permission.

pany's greater profit by having a more productive work force per the same unit of time (hour, day). If the benefits of training exceed the cost, the training program was worth it. But for some training programs aimed at improving attitudes, it is hard to quantify the value of employees with "better attitudes." Some attempts have been made to cost-account these variables (Mirvis & Lawler, 1977), but generally they are difficult to translate into dollars and cents. Also there can be many hidden benefits and costs. A well-trained employee is far more promotable. But that same employee can market these newly acquired talents to a competitor—a potential cost. In general, *results* criteria are the most important and the most difficult to develop. Collectively, behavioral and results criteria are called "external" criteria—they are evaluations external to the training program itself.

A survey conducted by Catalanello and Kirkpatrick (1968) revealed how companies evaluate their human relations training programs by these four types of criteria. Out of 110 organizations responding to the survey, 78 percent said they attempt to measure trainee reactions, and about 50 percent attempted to assess learning, behavior, and/or results criteria. The results of their survey are shown in Figure 6–10. A large portion of the companies tried to assess *learning* before and after training, but they were less involved with measuring change in *behavior*. Results of human rela-

**Figure 6–10**          **Responses from companies regarding their practices of measuring learning, behavior, and results of human relations training programs**

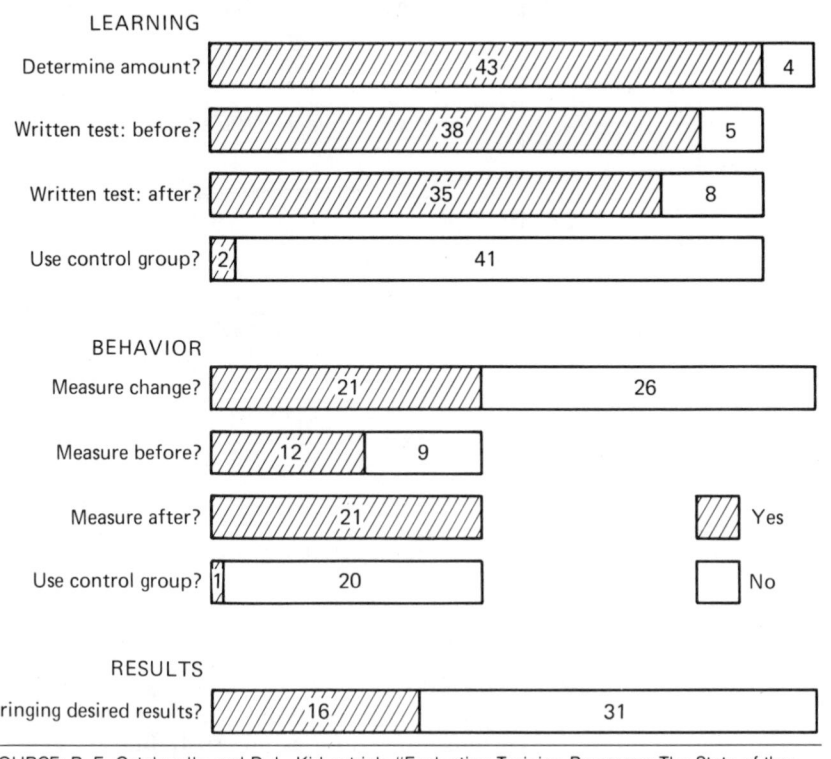

tions training are disappointing; 31 of 47 companies reported that they did not achieve the desired results. But note that control groups were rarely used, which indicates that companies seldom used adequate experimental designs. More will be said about experimental designs shortly.

I/O psychologists' interest in training criteria has blossomed recently. This interest is part of a general interest in "evaluation methodology," the technique of evaluating how well programs of all types (in medicine, criminal justice, social welfare) have worked. Within the area of training, Freeberg (1976) has stressed the need for multiple behavioral indices of training effectiveness, the need to have appropriate criteria to evaluate training, and the basic requirement of criterion relevance. Freeberg developed multiple criterion measures to assess the impact of job training programs created by federal manpower legislation. He defined training effectiveness in terms of how well individuals, communities, and occupations adjusted to the impact of these programs. He used these measures first at the end of the program and then six months later to show the interrelationships among the various sets of measures.

Goldstein (1978) illustrates the importance of assessing training effectiveness from multiple perspectives. He created some hypothetical complaints of people to show the many viewpoints by which the success of any training program can be judged.

From a trainee:

> There is a conspiracy. I just finished my training program. I even completed a pretest and a posttest. My posttest score was significantly better than the scores of my friends in the on-the-job control group. However, I lost my job because I could not perform the work.

From a trainer:

> There is a conspiracy. Everyone praised our training program. They said it was the best training program they ever attended. The trainees even had a chance to laugh a little. Now the trainees tell me that management will not let them perform their job the way we trained them.

From an administrative officer in the company:

> There is a conspiracy. My competition used the training program, and it worked for them. They saved a million. I took it straight from their manuals, and my employees still cannot do the job.

Each of these people claims that the program did not have the intended effect. Goldstein says that the validity of any training program can be assessed along four dimensions:

1. *Training validity.* Did the trainees match the criteria established for them in the training program? This dimension is concerned with what Kirkpatrick (1976) referred to as internal criteria and addresses the extent to which the trainees mastered the training.

2. *Performance validity.* Did the trainees match the criteria for success when they were back on the job? This dimension involves external criteria and addresses the extent to which employee performance on the job was enhanced by training.
3. *Intraorganizational validity.* Is the training program equally effective with different groups of trainees within the same organization? This dimension is concerned with the *internal generalizability* of the training, such as the effectiveness of sensitivity training for sales versus production workers in the same organization.
4. *Interorganizational validity.* Is the training program equally effective with different trainees in companies other than the one that developed the training program? This dimension involves the *external generalizability* of the training, such as the degree to which a training program successful for a manufacturing company would also be successful in a financial organization.

The question of training program success is not a simple one. I think that performance validity is the ultimate test of training program effectiveness. But depending on the company's objectives, the latter two types of validity can also be important.

**Research designs**

The basic issue in the design of training research is whether differences in criterion behavior are indeed the result of training. A *research design* assesses whether a training program has achieved its intended objectives. There are many research designs that can be used to measure training effectiveness. The more elaborate the design, the more confidence we have that the change in job performance is due to the effects of the training program.

The simplest research design is shown in Figure 6–11. One group of people are assessed before and after training. The difference between pre- and posttraining scores we attribute to training. But such a conclusion may be wrong; the change may be due to a Hawthorne Effect. Also, employees

**Figure 6–11**     **One-group pretest/posttest experimental design**

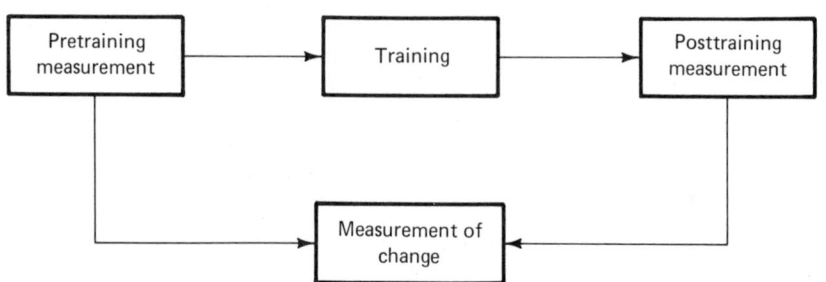

may change over time simply because they have more job experience, acquire new skills or knowledge, increase their self-confidence, and so on. These types of factors are called "history." That is, people may become more productive, make fewer errors, etc., just because they develop on the job, and this has nothing to do with training. For these reasons, simple pretest-posttest designs are usually inadequate.

A research design that can be used to address a Hawthorne Effect is shown in Figure 6–12. This is a two-group design. One group receives the experimental training, the other receives placebo training. Placebo training means that group receives *some* form of training but not the training method being studied. Placebo training is better than *no* training at all for that group since a Hawthorne Effect would still be possible. In this design, both groups experience the novelty of training. This design is preferable to the one-group design, but it too has limitations. The two groups are used as a basis for comparison, but we don't know if the groups were comparable to begin with. Perhaps one group of people was more intelligent, more motivated, had higher job skills, etc., from the start. So we have no *premeasure* of performance to indicate the initial comparability of the two groups.

The design shown in Figure 6–13 deals with the problems of the previous design. This is also a two-group design, but both groups are assessed before training as well as after. This is a "powerful" design. By careful analysis of the results, we can conclude with a high degree of confidence just how much of the difference in job performance is attributable to the experimental training.

Other, more complex research designs are also available (Solomon, 1949). They differ mainly in the use of multiple control groups. But they are not too practical in personnel training. It is sometimes difficult to divide intact employee work units into different groups. For example, if there is a lot of interaction among people in a work group, there are practical problems if

**Figure 6–12**             **Two-group experimental design with no pretest**

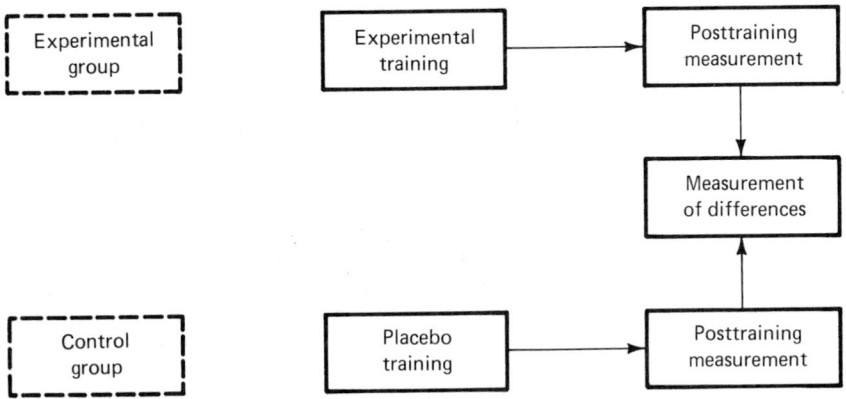

**Figure 6–13**        **Two-group pretest/posttest experimental design**

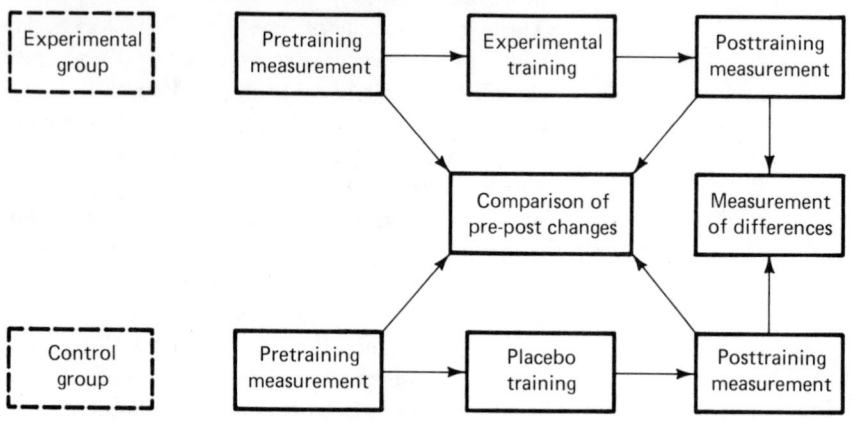

some of the people get experimental training and others get placebo training. If employees talk among themselves about their training, this can alter motivation and otherwise contaminate the design. In fact, some evidence (Hand & Slocum, 1972) suggests that experimental groups often out-perform control groups because people in the control group lose motivation; they are jealous or angry that *they* were not chosen for the experimental training.

The importance of having rigorous evaluation designs is well illustrated in a study by Bunker and Cohen (1977). The authors used a rather complex four-group design to assess the effectiveness of a basic electricity training program for telephone installers. The four groups were as follows:

1. Pretested—trained—posttested.
2. Pretested—untrained—posttested.
3. Unpretested—trained—posttested.
4. Unpretested—untrained—posttested.

Such a research design permits many comparisons: the effects of experimental training (groups 1 and 3) versus placebo training (groups 2 and 4) and the effects of using a pretest (groups 1 and 2) versus no pretest (groups 3 and 4). The findings show the importance of measurement contamination. After reviewing the results in increasing order of analytical sophistication, the authors saw that different conclusions were reached depending on the level of evaluation design selected. Different conclusions were reached by using a simple research design (Figure 6–11) compared to more sophisticated designs. The Bunker and Cohen study is a strong indictment against simple evaluation designs that lead to wrong conclusions and waste training and work time. The authors recommend that training researchers give as much care and thought to the evaluation of training as they do to its implementation.

The evaluation of training is vitally important. Without it, we don't know if the training is successful. In an era where more pressure is being brought to bear on departments to be *accountable* for their actions (if not their very existence), personnel departments too must prove that what they do is valuable to the company. Probably the two toughest questions that a training director has to answer are "Is the training program effective in bringing about desired changes in performance?" (behavioral criteria) and "If the training program is effective, is it worth it to the company?" (results criteria).

## EQUAL EMPLOYMENT OPPORTUNITY GUIDELINES AND TRAINING

Though far more lawsuits have charged unfair discrimination in the *selection* process, personnel training is subject to the same legal scrutiny. Employers must show the fairness and validity of their training procedures as well as their selection procedures. One major case before the U.S. Supreme Court involved charges of unfair discrimination in a company's training program. In *Weber* v. *Kaiser Aluminum*, Weber (a white male) alleged that he was denied the same access to a company training program as black employees. Without the training, employees were not promoted to a higher position. Kaiser's system of admitting employees to a training program involved taking the same proportion of black employees as white employees. Kaiser felt that they did not have enough black employees at higher levels in the company, so a racial quota system was set up to help resolve the problem. Weber alleged that this system represented unfair discrimination. He contended that admission to the training program was in part determined by race, and as the Equal Employment Opportunity Guidelines state, race cannot be a factor in making personnel decisions. The Supreme Court ruled in favor of Kaiser Aluminum. It said, in effect, that race can be used as a factor in personnel decisions when it is used to compensate for previous inequities in the composition of the company's work force. While the *Weber* case is best known as a test of reverse discrimination, it was based on a company's training program. It illustrates the importance of a company having a rational and defensible policy with regard to administering a training program.

Bartlett (1978) decomposed the training process into its constituent parts and showed how each part has a potential for discrimination. Possibilities exist with regard to whether training is a job prerequisite, who gets admitted to a training program, comparable treatment of individuals in the training program, who passes and who fails training, placement of employees into jobs as a result of training, and finally promotion, advancement, and compensation after training. Bartlett warns that a company must be prepared to defend its reasons at each stage of the training process. Personnel training, like personnel selection, must conform to fair employment practices.

## SUMMARY

Personnel training is an evolutionary process. The first step is to conduct an assessment of training needs using organization, operations, and person analysis. After this, training objectives are delineated in behavioral terms. Next, training methods are reviewed to see which method(s) seem best suited to meet the objectives. Those methods that appear to offer the most promise are then developed or selected. Then, the best approach for evaluating the program is considered. This decision depends on the nature of the training objectives and the feasibility of using various research evaluation designs. Next the training program is actually implemented. The results of training are then evaluated. Finally, the results from the evaluation then become the basis for developing future training objectives.

The training needs of selected populations of the work force must also be taken into account. In recent years, training of HCUs, women in management, and the updating of scientific/technical professionals has had greater importance. Training is a continuous process, not a once-in-a-lifetime experience. Finally, the training process that a company uses should be rational and legally defensible because the same legislation that governs personnel selection also applies to personnel training.

# CASE STUDY

Stan Rhodus, plant personnel director, was showing his new assistant the results of a job analysis. Rhodus was pointing to the findings from the accounting department and was in mid-sentence when the door to his office burst open. Andy Carey, the plant manager, was standing in the doorway with a red neck and glaring eyes. While Carey was known for his quick temper, he never seemed to lose his cool as much as today.

"Stan," bellowed Carey, "I've got a problem, and you're going to solve it! Our weekly staff meeting just ended with a lot of yelling, name calling, and vicious backbiting. I can't get the people in this plant to work together as a team. They're at each other's throats all the time. If I don't have enough trouble as it is with rising interest rates, competition, and delinquent accounts, now I have to put up with a running a zoo. And it just didn't start today. Internal dissension has been hurting us all along, but now its getting out of hand."

"You're in charge of personnel," Carey continued, "and its your responsibility to see that the staff gets along. I want to run our people through some human relations training. I don't care if you show them a film, give them a lecture, hold a discussion, or what. Frankly, I don't care if you bash a few heads together. But one way or another, our people are going to learn to respect each other, help each other, and work together. And if we don't do it and soon, we'll all be collecting unemployment checks together. Our competition won't have to do us in—we'll do it ourselves. I can't figure these people out. They act like they're playing survival games, and everyone is looking out for number one. Well, its going to stop—its got to stop, or we'll all lose."

Carey turned toward the door. He stopped only long enough to say he wanted some human relations training proposal on his desk by Monday.

Rhodus slumped in his chair. A dozen thoughts raced through his mind at once. He wondered what he would come up with for Carey. He could certainly produce something, but he didn't know if it would work in the long run. If it didn't, he knew Carey would be back in his office again, maybe only to give him his walking papers. Rhodus also wondered if he had the guts to tell Carey that *he* should be the first one to go through human relations training.

The hesitating voice of his assistant broke his concentration: "Is it always like this in personnel?"

Questions

1. Should we take it for granted that Carey is correct in his assessment of the need for human relations training? Why or why not?
2. If Rhodus wanted to corroborate the need for human relations training, what types of training needs analysis should be conducted?
3. If human relations training is needed, what training methods do you think might be effective?
4. How should Rhodus assess whether the proposed training has been effective?
5. Do you think that the personnel training approach is the most appropriate for addressing this problem? Why or why not?

# REFERENCES

Bartlett, C. J. Equal employment opportunity issues in training. *Human Factors*, 1978, *20*, 179–188.

Bass, B. M., & Barrett, G. V. *People, work, and organizations* (2nd ed.). Boston: Allyn & Bacon, 1981.

Bass, B. M., & Vaughan, J. A. *Training in industry: The management of learning*. Monterey, Calif.: Brooks/Cole Publishing, 1966.

Brethower, K. S. Programmed instruction. In R. L. Craig (Ed.), *Training and development handbook* (2nd ed.). New York: McGraw-Hill, 1976.

Bunker, K. A., & Cohen, S. L. The rigors of training evaluation: A discussion and field demonstration. *Personnel Psychology*, 1977, *30*, 525–541.

Butman, R. N., & Frick, F. C. Educational technology for teaching. In S. S. Dubin, H. Shelton, & J. McConnell (Eds.), *Maintaining professional and technical competence of the older engineer*. Washington, D.C.: American Society for Engineering Education, 1973.

Campbell, J. P. Personnel training and development. *Annual Review of Psychology*, 1971, *22*, 565–602.

Catalanello, R. E., & Kirkpatrick, D. L. Evaluating training programs: The state of the art. *Training and Development Journal*, May 1968, *22*, 2–9.

Cooley, W. W., & Glaser, R. The computer and individualized instruction. *Science*, 1969, *166*, 574–582.

Cooper, C. L., & Levine, N. Implicit values in experimental learning groups: Their functional and dysfunctional consequences. In D. L. Cooper & C. Alderfer (Eds.), *Advances in experimental social processes*. New York: John Wiley & Sons, 1978.

Coppard, L. C. Gaming simulation and the training process. In R. L. Craig (Ed.), *Training and development handbook* (2nd ed.). New York: McGraw-Hill, 1976.

Crane, D. P. *Personnel* (2nd ed.). Belmont, Calif.: Wadsworth, 1979.

Dupre, V. A. Human relations laboratory training. In R. L. Craig (Ed.), *Training and development handbook* (2nd ed.). New York: McGraw-Hill, 1976.

Fischer, B., Margulies, S., & Mosenfelder, D. *Bobby Fischer teaches chess*. New York: Bantam Books, 1972.

Franklin, W. S. Are construction apprenticeships too long? *Labor Law Journal*, 1976, *27*, 99–106.

Fredericksen, N. In-basket tests and factors in administrative performance. In H. Guetzkow (Ed.), *Simulation in social science: Readings*. Englewood Cliffs, N.J.: Prentice-Hall, 1962.

Freeberg, N. E. Criterion measures for youth-work training programs: The development of relevant performance dimensions. *Journal of Applied Psychology*, 1976, *61*, 537–545.

Friedlander, F., & Greenberg, S. Effect of job attitudes, training, and organizational climate on performance of the hard-core unemployed. *Journal of Applied Psychology*, 1971, *55*, 289–295.

Goldstein, I. L. *Training: Program development and evaluation*. Monterey, Calif.: Brooks/Cole Publishing, 1974.

Goldstein, I. L. The pursuit of validity in the evaluation of training programs. *Human Factors*, 1978, *20*, 131–144.

Goldstein, I. L. Training and organizational psychology. *Professional Psychology*, 1980, *11*, 421–427. (a)

Goldstein, I. L. Training in work organizations. *Annual Review of Psychology*, 1980, *31*, 229–272. (b)

Goodman, P., & Salipante, P., Jr. Organizational rewards and retention of the hardcore unemployed. *Journal of Applied Psychology*, 1976, *61*, 12–21.

Hand, H. H., & Slocum, J. W., Jr. A longitudinal study of the effects of a human relations training program on management effectiveness. *Journal of Applied Psychology*, 1972, *56*, 412–417.

Hickey, A. E. Computer-assisted and computer managed instruction. In R. L. Craig (Ed.), *Training and development handbook* (2nd ed.). New York: McGraw-Hill, 1976.

Hinrichs, J. Personnel training. In M. D. Dunnette (Ed.), *Handbook of industrial and organizational psychology*. Skokie, Ill.: Rand McNally, 1976.

Hughes, J. L., & McNamara, W. J. A comparative study of programmed and conventional instruction in industry. *Journal of Applied Psychology*, 1961, *45*, 225–231.

Ilgen, D. R., Fisher, C. D., & Taylor, M. S. Consequences of individual feedback on behavior in organizations. *Journal of Applied Psychology*, 1979, *64*, 349–371.

Kidd, J. S. A comparison of two methods of training in a complex task by means of a task simulation. *Journal of Applied Psychology*, 1961, *45*, 165–169.

Kinn, J. M. Professional future shock: Can engineers adapt? In S. S. Dubin, H. Shelton, & J. McConnell (Eds.), *Maintaining professional and technical competence of the older engineer*. Washington, D.C.: American Society for Engineering Education, 1973.

Kirkpatrick, D. L. Evaluation of training. In R. L. Craig (Ed.), *Training and Development handbook* (2nd ed.). New York: McGraw-Hill, 1976.

Koerner, J. Educational technology: Does it have a future in the classroom? *Saturday Review Supplement*, May 1973, *1*, 42–46.

Konz, S. A., & Dickey, G. L. Manufacturing assembly instructions: A summary. *Ergonomics*, 1969, *12*, 369–382.

Kraut, A. I. Developing managerial skills via modeling techniques: Some positive research findings—a symposium. *Personnel Psychology*, 1976, *29*, 325–328.

Landy, F. J., & Trumbo, D. A. *Psychology of work behavior* (rev. ed.). Homewood, Ill.: Dorsey Press, 1980.

Larwood, L., Wood, M. M., & Inderlied, S. D. Training women for management: New problems, new solutions. *Academy of Management Review*, 1978, *3*, 584–593.

Latham, G. P., & Saari, L. M. The application of social learning theory to training supervisors through behavioral modeling. *Journal of Applied Psychology*, 1979, *64*, 239–246.

Lefkowitz, J. Effect of training on the productivity and tenure of sewing machine operators. *Journal of Applied Psychology*, 1970, *54*, 81–86.

Lukasiewicz, J. The dynamics of science and engineering education. *Engineering Education*, 1971, *61*, 880–882.

McGehee, W. Training and development theory, policies, and practices. In D. Yoder & H. G. Heneman, Jr. (Eds.), *ASPA handbook of personnel and industrial relations*. Washington, D.C.: The Bureau of National Affairs, 1979.

McGehee, W., & Thayer, P. W. *Training in business and industry*. New York: John Wiley & Sons, 1961.

McGehee, W., & Tullar, W. L. A note on evaluating behavior modification and behavioral modeling as industrial training techniques. *Personnel Psychology*, 1978, *31*, 477–484.

Mirvis, P. H., & Lawler, E. E. Measuring the financial impact of employee attitudes. *Journal of Applied Psychology*, 1977, *62*, 1–8.

Moore, M. L., & Dutton, P. Training needs analysis: Review and critique. *Academy of Management Review*, 1978, *3*, 532–545.

Morrison, J. H. Determining training needs. In R. L. Craig (Ed.), *Training and development handbook* (2nd ed.). New York: McGraw-Hill, 1976.

Moses, J. L., & Ritchie, R. J. Supervisory relationship training: A behavioral evaluation of a behavior modeling program. *Personnel Psychology*, 1976, *29*, 337–343.

Nash, A. N., Muczyk, J. P., & Vettori, F. L. The relative practical effectiveness of programmed instruction. *Personnel Psychology*, 1971, *24*, 397–418.

*A new approach to management's role in back safety*. Hicksville, N.Y.: Advanced Learning Systems, 1966.

O'Leary, V. E. The Hawthorne effect in reverse: Trainee orientation for the hardcore unemployed women. *Journal of Applied Psychology*, 1972, *56*, 491–494.

O'Leary, V. E. Some attitudinal barriers to occupational aspirations in women. *Psychological Bulletin*, 1974, *81*, 809–826.

Parker, T. C. Statistical methods for measuring training results. In R. L. Craig (Ed.), *Training and development handbook* (2nd ed.). New York: McGraw-Hill, 1976.

Raia, A. P. A study of the educational value of management games. *Journal of Business*, 1966, *39*, 339–352.

Robertson, I., & Downs, S. Learning and the prediction of performance: Development of trainability testing in the United Kingdom. *Journal of Applied Psychology* 1979, *64*, 42–50.

Salipante, P. Jr., & Goodman, P. Training, counseling, and retention of the hardcore unemployed. *Journal of Applied Psychology;* 1976, *61*, 1–11.

Smith, P. B. Controlled studies of the outcome of sensitivity training. *Psychological Bulletin*, 1975, *82*, 597–622.

Solomon, R. L. An extension of control group design. *Psychological Bulletin*, 1949, *46*, 137–150.

Suppes, P., & Morningstar, M. Computer-assisted instruction. *Science*, 1969, *166*, 343–350.

Triandis, H. C., Feldman, J. M., Weldon, D. E., & Harvey, W. M. Designing preemployment training for the hard to employ: A cross-cultural psychological approach. *Journal of Applied Psychology*, 1974, *59*, 687–693.

Triandis, H. C., Feldman, J. M., Weldon, D. E., & Harvey, W. M. Ecosystem distrust and the hard-to-employ. *Journal of Applied Psychology*, 1975, *60*, 44–56.

Welsh, P., Antoinetti, J. A., & Thayer, P. W. An industry wide study of programmed instruction. *Journal of Applied Psychology*, 1965, *49*, 61–73.

Wohlking, W. Role playing. In R. L. Craig (Ed.), *Training and development handbook* (2nd ed.). New York: McGraw-Hill, 1976.

# chapter 7    PERFORMANCE APPRAISAL

Employees continually have their performance appraised on the job. Whether the appraisal process occurs on a formal or informal basis, it does occur. Appraisals may be made from haphazard observation, memory, hearsay, or intuition. Or a formal and rational system may be used. With the latter approach, appraisals are more accurate, fair, and useful to all concerned (Kujawski & Young, 1979). This chapter deals with formal programs, methods, and techniques for appraising employee performance.

Such appraisal can be defined as "a systematic review of an individual employee's performance on the job which is used to evaluate the effectiveness of his or her work." The purposes of appraisal programs fall into three categories (Barrett, 1966):

1. *Administrative:* involving personnel actions, such as raises, promotions, transfers, or discharge.
2. *Performance improvement:* using appraisal information to identify weaknesses in performance. This helps guide the employee in setting goals for improvement.
3. *Research:* Performance appraisal information is often used as a criterion to assess the validity of personnel selection and training procedures.

Just as organizations need to have a reason to conduct a training program, they must also have a rationale for conducting a performance appraisal program. The needs of the organization must be clearly stated so the appraisal program can be designed to meet them. Just as trainers have seemingly been more preoccupied with developing training methods than assessing training needs, it seems that many I/O psychologists have been more concerned with developing new appraisal techniques than with the more basic issue of what the appraisal program is supposed to accomplish. If the program has many purposes, care must be taken to ensure that each is met. Rarely does one technique meet all the desired objectives. Sometimes several are used at the same time or they are consolidated to meet the organization's major objectives. For example, the best appraisal technique for determining merit raises may not be the best for giving employees feedback on their performance.

## IMPLEMENTING A PERFORMANCE APPRAISAL PROGRAM

McGregor (1957) commented that people dislike formally evaluating others. So there is usually some resistance to participating in such a program. Managers have refused to conduct appraisal sessions, or they have conducted them in such a perfunctory way that they have little or no value. Some of the reasons behind this resistance are: managers don't like to criticize subordinates, they don't like to "play God" in appraising performance, and they lack evaluation skills. Therefore, an appraisal program should be developed that not only teaches supervisors how to evaluate, but also shows employees the need for appraisal. This reduces supervisor reluctance and employee anxiety.

**Training supervisors.** A comprehensive training program for supervisors who serve as appraisers is a major phase in an appraisal program. Like any skill, evaluating someone's performance and using that information can be enhanced with training. Without trained appraisers, evaluations may be invalid.

Having trained supervisors is important. But Lopez (1966) found that less than 50 percent of the organizations responding to a survey had formal training programs for supervisors on how to evaluate performance. Paradoxically, the same respondents rated ineptness of supervisors as the main obstacle to setting up an effective appraisal program. Lack of training of supervisors is not due to lack of training methods. Videotapes of how to appraise performance and how to communicate the results back to employees have been used, as have CAI methods designed to help supervisors identify major aspects of job performance. As one example of effective training, Latham, Wexley, and Pursell (1975) reported on an experiment in a large organization. Sixty managers who appraised performance were randomly assigned to three groups as follows:

1. *Workshop group.* This group was shown videotapes on evaluating individuals. They then discussed appraisal procedures and problems and practiced making appraisals, all with the intent of reducing certain common rating errors.
2. *Discussion group.* This group received training similar in content, but the main method was discussion.
3. *Control group.* This group received no training.

Six months later, the three groups were "tested." They were shown videotapes of several hypothetical job candidates along with job requirements. The managers were asked to evaluate the candidates' suitability for the jobs in question. They were scored on four types of rating errors. There were significant differences in the rating errors made by each of the three groups. Those in the workshop group had no rating errors. Those in the control group performed the worst—they made three types of errors.

As part of the performance appraisal program, the organization should develop a manual outlining the company's philosophy, objectives, and standards for the program. It can serve as a text during training and later as a handy reference.

**Orienting employees.**    Organizations should explain to all employees that their performance will be evaluated. Employees should also know the goals and objectives of the program as well as how they will benefit from the appraisal. Performance evaluations can be threatening, and such explanations help ease fears. To avoid problems, employees should also understand how the appraisal will be used. If employees believe the information will be used for pay raise and promotion decisions, they may be far more defensive about their weaknesses. On the other hand, if they believe the appraisal is a diagnostic aid to help them strengthen their weak areas, they may be far more accepting. In some organizations, appraisals are perfunctory. The company makes no use of them, so employees adopt a "who cares" attitude about the whole system. Open and honest communication about the intent of an appraisal cannot be overemphasized.

**Role of management.**    As in training, management plays a vital role in the success of any performance appraisal program. Appraisal is a management tool, so management has the main responsibility for making it work. Management must support the program strongly and tie it into the organization's overall goals. Clearly, appraisal has to "count" for something, and management has the authority to give it some clout. If pay raises are based on performance but every employee gets the same raise, the appraisal program will lose credibility. The same thing happens if promotions are supposed to be based on performance but they're actually awarded on seniority. In one organization, performance appraisals were supposed to be used to determine raises. But many managers didn't bother to evaluate their employees; they just gave everyone the same percentage increase. To get managers to conduct appraisals, the company stated that managers who failed to conduct appraisals would forfeit *their* annual pay increase. Not surprisingly, participation jumped to 100 percent. Like personnel selection and training programs, performance appraisal must be heavily backed by management to be effective.

**Monitoring and revising the program.** Monitoring and revising the appraisal program is a continuous process. Even the best designed and administered appraisal program is a time-consuming task for those involved. Typically, monitoring is done by the personnel department. The first concern is that the appraisals are actually done. Appraisals are usually conducted annually. They can be tied to: (1) the employee's birthdate, (2) the employee's employment anniversary date, (3) a fixed period for all employees, (4) by month for alphabetical groupings, and (5) by month for a department or group.

An even more important issue is how effectively the program meets its goals. If the program's goal is to identify those worthy of promotion, did these people in fact get promoted? If the program's goal is to give larger raises to more productive workers, was this accomplished? These questions and others all address the *validity* of the appraisal programs. As stated earlier, assessing validity is not always easy. A performance appraisal program may be valid for identifying weaknesses in employee performance. But a different appraisal system may have to be developed to make promotion decisions (or promotions could be made on other factors, such as seniority). Appraisal systems must meet organizational goals. If they don't or if goals change, then the system must be changed too.

# USING THE RESULTS OF PERFORMANCE APPRAISAL

Results of a performance appraisal program may be applied to many other management functions (see Figure 7–1). As discussed in Chapter 3, criteria are derived from job analytic procedures; the criteria, in turn, are the basis for appraisals. Expanding on Figure 7–1, the major uses of performance appraisal are as follows.

**1. Industrial training.** Perhaps the main use of performance appraisal information is for employee feedback. Feedback highlights employees' strengths and weaknesses. Of course, the appraisal should pertain to *job-related* characteristics only. Deficiencies or weaknesses are then the targets for training. Training should involve only those areas where poor performance can be attributed to the individual and not to aspects of the work environment. The supervisor plays a key role in helping develop the employee's skills. Though, by definition, performance appraisals are *evaluative*, in this context they serve more as *diagnostic* aids. Since some employees won't acknowledge their weaknesses, a supportive supervisor is

**Figure 7–1**  **Development of performance appraisal information and its applications**

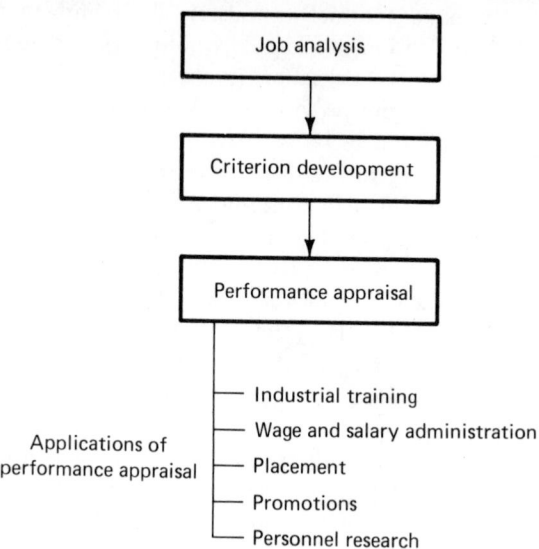

more effective than one who is threatening or critical. More will be said about this later in the chapter.

**2. Wage and salary administration.**   Perhaps the second most common use of performance appraisals is to make raises. Pay increases are often made, in part, on job performance. Appraisal programs can be designed so there is a direct relationship between the evaluation and the size of a raise. For example, an employee who is judged to be performing in the top 10 percent of the work force might get a 12 percent raise. Conversely, an employee who performs in the bottom 10 percent might get only a 2 percent raise.

Unfortunately, the "personnel development" and "salary administration" aspects of appraisal are often uncomfortable partners. Many employees attach far more meaning to raises because they are more immediate and real than learning about weaknesses on the job. If the two functions are combined in the same appraisal, employees can become defensive. When admitting weaknesses means getting a smaller raise, personnel development may take a back seat in importance. In a classic article, Meyer, Kay, and French (1965) talked about the need for "split roles" for supervisors in conducting appraisals. One is that of a counselor or coach in employee development or performance improvement. The other is that of a judge in making salary decisions. Evidence shows that most supervisors can't play both roles at the same time. The problem has been solved by having two appraisals; for example, one in January for employee development, the other in June for salary. Or the supervisor may handle development, and the personnel department, salary. Both functions are important, but it is best if they are not conducted at the same time by the same person.

**3. Placement.**   Performance appraisal information is vital for placement decisions. New employees (such as management trainees) are often exposed to many tasks or jobs at first. Over a 12-month period, a trainee might have jobs in marketing, finance, and accounting. After being appraised in each, the trainee might be permanently assigned to that area where he or she performed best. By identifying the employee's strengths, performance appraisal indicates where the person's talents might best be used.

**4. Promotions.**   Promotion may be based on how well an employee performs on his or her current job. Appraisals identify the better-performing employees, and an employee who can't perform well on his or her current job wouldn't be considered for promotion. However, performance is not the sole reason for promotion. Promotions are usually granted on a combination of seniority and merit. If made strictly on seniority, there is little way to assure that competent people get promoted. Promotions based strictly on performance are more defensible, but most experts agree that experience in a job is also worth considering.

**5. Personnel research.**   In many criterion-related validity studies, assessments of the criterion are derived from performance appraisals. Recall that the criterion is a measure of job success, and that is what performance appraisals are supposed to measure (how well people are doing on the job). When the personnel department wants to validate a new predictor test, scores are correlated with criterion measures, which are often exhumed from the company's performance appraisal files. The value of any selection device is only as good as the criterion it tries to predict. So the appraisal must be a relevant measure of job success. Research (e.g., Bass & Turner, 1973; Boehm, 1977) indicates that specially constructed performance appraisal instruments (for the purpose of personnel research) are more useful than "borrowing" performance appraisal information originally collected for another purpose (e.g., salary administration). In either case, appraisals can be used to assess job performance criteria. In turn, these are used for test validation research.

# PERFORMANCE APPRAISAL AND THE LAW

Federal law on fair employment practices also pertains to performance appraisal. Unfair discrimination can occur not only on the predictor (test) side of the equation, but also in the job behavior the test is trying to predict.

Holley and Feild (1975) discussed the relationship between performance appraisal and the law and raised concern about several possible areas for discrimination. Among them, the appraisal system must be relevant to the job. For example, security guards appraised on how pleasant their personality is could seriously question the relevance of the appraisal. Another factor is that supervisors should not evaluate aspects of an employee's performance that were not observable. This avoids the possibility of biases and misconceptions. Finally, evaluations should not be based on subjective and vague factors like "desire to succeed." This desire can take many forms for different people. The clearer the factors, the more likely the supervisor's attention will be centered on the pertinent aspects of job behavior.

Kleiman and Durham (1981) reviewed 23 court cases involving charges of discrimination in performance appraisal. They sought to determine the standards set by the courts in assessing performance appraisal systems. The authors discovered that the courts: (1) have a strong interest in appraisal systems regardless of their adverse impact; (2) emphasize job analytic procedures for identifying relevant appraisal criteria; and (3) want employers to demonstrate the *construct validity* of their performance appraisal evaluations. These legal findings support the results from empirical research on sex and race bias in performance appraisal (Schmitt & Lappin, 1980). Schmitt and Lappin demonstrated that raters of different races evaluate members of their own racial group differently than members of other racial groups. Black raters gave higher ratings to blacks than to whites; the opposite effect was observed for white raters. With such an empirical demonstration of race-linked bias in performance appraisal, it should be apparent that performance appraisal, like personnel selection and training, is another possible avenue for unfair discrimination in employment.

In summary, organizations must justify personnel decisions based on employee performance appraisal. EEOC Guidelines state that performance appraisal must not be discriminatory (Latham & Wexley, 1981). The number of court cases involving alleged discrimination in performance appraisal is not as great as those involving personnel selection. But the number is growing, and that trend is likely to continue.

## SOURCES OF PERFORMANCE APPRAISAL INFORMATION

As stated in Chapter 3, job performance can be characterized by many criteria. Guion (1965) identified three different measures: *objective data,* e.g., production output, *personnel data,* and *judgmental data.* Each of these job performance measures will be described, along with information about their reliability and validity.

**Objective production data**

Using objective production data as an index of how well an employee is performing on the job is limited in its frequency and value. For a person holding the job of a machine operator, job performance may be measured by counting the number of objects produced per day, per week, etc. Similarly, salespeople are appraised in terms of assessing (counting) their sales volume over a given period of time. It is also possible to evaluate the performance of firefighters by counting the number of fires they extinguish.

While each of these objective production measures has some degree of intuitive appeal, they are usually not complete measures of job performance. Two problems in particular affect each of these measures. First, we would like to assume that differences in performance across people reflect true differences in terms of how well these people perform their jobs. Unfortunately, variability in performance can be due to factors beyond the individual's control. One machine operator may produce more because he or she works with a better machine. A salesperson might have a large sales volume because his or her territory is better. Firefighters who put out few fires might be responsible for an area with relatively few buildings. This problem of variation in performance stemming from external factors should sound familiar. It represents a form of *criterion contamination,* a topic discussed in Chapter 3.

The second problem with objective performance measures is that they rarely tell the whole story. A machine operator who produces more objects per day but who also produces more defective objects wouldn't be described as the "best." *Quality* may be as important as *quantity,* but this can't be recorded in a simple count of objects produced. A salesperson spends a lot of time recruiting new customers, and this aspect must be weighed against simply making calls on established customers. Creating new customers can be as important as maintaining business with old ones. Sales volume might be less at first. But in the long run, the new customers would increase total sales volume. Finally, extinguishing fires is but one aspect of a firefighter's job; preventing fires is another one. Conceivably the "best" firefighter might not have put out many fires at all, but rather contributed heavily toward preventing the fires in the first place. In short, all of these actual criteria suffer from *criterion deficiency.* They are deficient measures of the ultimate criteria they seek to measure.

**Validity of objective production data.**   When we speak of a criterion's validity, we mean its *relevance.* For the jobs mentioned, objective production data has *some* relevance. It would be silly to say that sales volume has *no* bearing on a salesperson's performance. The salesperson's job is indeed to sell. The issue is one of degree of relevance. It is a mistake to give too much importance to objective production data in performance appraisal. This is sometimes a great temptation because such data are usually very accessible. But the meaning of those clear-cut numbers is not always so clear-cut. Finally, for many jobs, objective performance measures do not exist, or if they do, they have little relevance to actual performance. It would be difficult to argue that performance as a teacher can be appraised by counting the number of students in a class. In fact, this "body count" approach to teacher effectiveness can be argued either way. A teacher who is judged to be performing well can point to a large class enrollment as evidence of skill. Some students are sitting in the aisles just to partake in the learning experience. Another teacher who is judged to be performing poorly can point to a large class enrollment as evidence of a handicap against good teaching. How can anyone teach well with students crammed wall to wall? In summary, the issue of criterion relevance is a question of judgment. For some jobs, objective performance data are partially relevant measures of success; in many other jobs, such relevance is lacking.

**Reliability of objective production data.** Reliability of objective production data refers to its consistency over time. Some of the best work on production data reliability was done by Rothe and associates. They examined the output of workers in such jobs as butter wrappers (1946), machine operators (1947), and coil winders (1958). Their data indicate that there is great time variation in output. As a rule, output is not highly consistent. Correlations on production data reliability for different weeks ranged from .05 to .85. The average was about .45. In general, the correlation between weeks is higher for consecutive weeks than for widely separated weeks.

There is similar variation in other jobs. In retail sales, volume is usually heaviest the month before Christmas. In real estate, more houses are sold in the summer than in the winter. The point is that objective production data are not particularly stable or consistent; they tend to vary across time. Different conclusions might thus be made about an employee's performance depending on *when* the performance was appraised.

## Personnel data

The second type of appraisal information is *personnel data;* that is, data retained by a company's personnel office. The two most common indexes of performance are absences and turnover, though records may also be kept on accidents, grievances, and lateness. The critical issue with these variables is criterion relevance. To what extent do they reflect differences in job performance? Absence is probably the most sensitive measure of performance. In almost all jobs, employees who are often absent are judged as performing worse than others (all other factors being equal). Indeed, an employee can be fired for excessive absence. Most organizations have policies for dealing with absence, and this attests to its importance as a variable in judging overall performance. However, the measurement and interpretation of absenteeism are not clear-cut (Muchinsky, 1977). Absences can be "excused" or "unexcused" depending on many factors pertaining both to the individual (e.g., seniority) and the job (e.g., job level). An employee who has 10 days of excused absence may be still appraised as performing better than the employee with 5 days of unexcused absence. Whether the absence was allowed or not must be determined before performance judgments are made. Measuring absence is a thorny problem, but attendance/absence is seen as a highly relevant criterion variable in most organizations.

Turnover is also used to measure performance. It, too, involves measurement problems. Some turnover is voluntary (the employee quit), while some is involuntary (the employee was fired). An employee who quit would probably be appraised "better" than an employee who was fired. Some organizations will let an employee resign to improve his or her chances of getting another job. This clouds the value of turnover as a measure of performance. The meaning attached to a chronic job hopper has also changed over the years. At the management level, 20 years ago job hoppers were viewed with some suspicion; the person seemed unstable and unable to hold a job for long. Today, however, the job hopper is seen more positively. Exposure to different jobs is taken to mean the person has more breadth of experience. This is an example how the same behavior (turnover) acquires different interpretations over time.

Accidents can be used as a measure of job performance, but only for a limited number of jobs. Frequency and severity of accidents are both used as variables and so are accidents resulting in injury or property damage. Accidents are a more relevant criterion variable for blue-collar than for white-collar jobs. People who drive delivery trucks may be evaluated in part on the number of accidents they have. This variable can be contaminated by many sources, though. Road conditions, miles driven, time of day, and condition of the truck all contribute to accidents. While relevance is limited to certain jobs, accidents can contribute greatly to appraisal. Some companies give large raises to drivers with no accidents and fire those with a large number.

Grievances and lateness have the least relevance. But they may be of value in some situations. Grievances are formal written complaints submitted by an employee. They seem to be related more to how well employees *like* their jobs than to how well they are performing. However, it is possible that the "chronic complainer" with a high grievance rate would be viewed negatively. He or she might be coaxed into seeking employment elsewhere. Lateness is often caused by external factors (e.g., snow storms, sick children). Again, however, if the same employee is late repeatedly, the conclusion would be that it was the employee's fault, and this then affects appraisal. In general, being on time is not regarded as a virtue, but lateness (especially repeated lateness) is viewed as harmful to performance.

**Validity of personnel data.**    The validity of personnel data varies greatly. A problem common with all personnel information is accurate record-keeping. Sloppy record-keeping is common, and this is a source of error. Latham and Pursell (1975) found turnover recorded as (extended) absence. Similarly, recording accidents is notoriously poor (Blum & Naylor, 1968). Occasional lateness may not be reported until it becomes a consistent problem. Personnel data are indeed relevant in assessing job performance, though the accuracy of such data may be questionable.

**Reliability of personnel data.**    There is little information on reliability of personnel data. Most research is on absenteeism. The results (Huse & Taylor, 1962; Muchinsky, 1977) suggest that absenteeism is quite unstable.

Reliability coefficients reported by Muchinsky (1977) ranged from .00 to .74 for various indexes, with an average of .40. Hammer and Landau (1981) see the need for new means of categorizing absence data before it can be used as a sensitive and accurate index of performance. Little has been reported on the reliability of employee turnover, though it does seem that chronic job changers have some identifiable characteristics, such as low self-esteem (Cherry, 1976). The reliability of accident data is quite low (Hill & Trist, 1955). Research indicates that accidents are somewhat of a random phenomenon. There is not enough data on the reliability of grievances and lateness, but research suggests they are not consistent aspects of behavior. Personnel data, when accurately gathered and maintained, can be quite relevant in performance appraisal. However, research shows there is not much consistency among employees in behavior reflected by personnel data.

In the Olympics athletic performance in some events is appraised by judges or raters.

*Courtesy Daktronics, Inc.*

Because absences and accidents are lacking in ideal levels of reliability, we must be cautious not to overinterpret their value as measures of performance.

## JUDGMENTAL DATA

Judgmental data are usually used for performance appraisal. Guion (1965) reported that in 81 percent of the validation studies reported over a five-year period, some form of rated or judged performance was the criterion for job success. Lent, Aurbach, and Levin (1971) also reported that in 1,500 criterion measures used in I/O research, almost 900 (60 percent) were supervisory ratings of subordinates' performance. Judgmental data are popular in performance appraisal because finding relevant objective measures is difficult. Subjective assessments can also apply to almost all jobs. Those who do the assessments are usually supervisors, but some use has also been made of self-assessment, peer assessment, and subordinate assessment.

Performance appraisal has been addressed by researchers from several disciplines (e.g., those interested in organization, communication, and education). The contributions of I/O psychologists are particularly manifest in designing performance appraisal methods. A wide variety has been developed, all intended to provide accurate assessment of how people are performing. The major systems used in performance appraisal include:

1. Graphic rating scales.
2. Employee comparison methods.
   a. Rank order.
   b. Paired comparison.
   c. Forced distribution.
3. Behavioral checklists and scales.
   a. Critical incidents.
   b. Weighted checklist.
   c. Behaviorally anchored rating scale (BARS).
   d. Behavioral observation scale (BOS).
   e. Mixed standard scale.

**Graphic rating scales**

Rating scales are the most common system in performance appraisal. Individuals are rated on a number of traits or factors. The rater judges "how much" of each factor the individual has. Usually performance is judged on a five- or seven-point scale, and the number of factors ranges between 5 and 20. The more common dimensions rated are quantity of work, quality of work, practical judgment, job knowledge, cooperation, and motivation. Examples of typical graphic rating scales are shown in Figure 7–2.

| Figure 7–2 | **Examples of graphic rating scales for various performance dimensions** |

Job knowledge

High | X | | | | | Low
5   4   3   2   1

Quality of work

| | | X | | |

Superior   Above average   Average   Below average   Unacceptable

Dependability

Rate this employee's dependability by assigning a score according to the following scale:
  9   (Score)
1 to 5 (Poor). Gives up quickly.
6 to 10 (Average). Does the routine work.
11 to 15 (Good). Rarely gives up.

Quality of work

☐ Consistently exceeds job requirements   ☒ Frequently exceeds job requirements   ☐ Meets job requirements   ☐ Frequently below job requirements   ☐ Consistently below job requirements

Practical judgment

5   ④   3   2   1

In reality, these aspects of performance are rarely independent of each other. As an example, Muchinsky (1974) had the performance of a sample of professional engineers rated by their supervisors. The ratings on 10 criteria were intercorrelated, and the average degree of relationship was a correlation of about .50. These 10 dimensions thus assessed related aspects of performance. Using a statistical method called factor analysis, ratings on the 10 criteria were condensed to identify the underlying dimensions of performance as an engineer. Successful performance was shown to be a function of two factors: interpersonal relations ability and technical ability. The competent engineer knew the "facts and figures" and was able to relate to other people in a cordial manner.

**Rating errors.** In making appraisals with rating scales, the rater may (unknowingly) commit errors in judgment. These can be placed into three major categories: leniency errors, halo errors, and central tendency errors. All three stem from rater bias and misperception.

*Leniency errors.* Some teachers are "hard graders" and others "easy graders." So raters can be characterized by the leniency of their appraisals. Harsh raters give evaluations that are *lower* than the "true" level of ability (if it could be ascertained). This is called *severity or negative leniency.* The easy rater gives evaluations that are *higher* than the "true" level—called *positive leniency.* These errors usually occur because the rater applies personal standards derived from his or her own personality or previous experience.

*Halo errors.* Halo errors are evaluations (good or bad) based on the rater's general feelings about an employee. Thus the rater generally has a favorable or unfavorable attitude toward the employee, which permeates all evaluations of the employee. Typically, the rater has strong feelings about at least one important aspect of the employee's performance. This is then generalized to other performance factors, and the employee is judged (across many factors) as uniformly good or bad. The supervisor impressed by an employee's idea with might allow feelings about this one incident to carry over to evaluation of leadership, cooperation, motivation, etc. This occurs even though the "good idea" is not related to other factors. The converse also holds. The supervisor displeased with an employee's idea might allow this to spread to other aspects of performance. It might be said that the employee who can do no wrong in the eyes of the supervisor and the employee who is chronically in the supervisor's "doghouse" are the victims of halo error on the part of the supervisor. Raters who commit halo errors don't distinguish the many dimensions of employee performance.

*Central tendency errors.* Central tendency error is the rater's unwillingness to assign extreme—high or low—ratings (Landy & Trumbo, 1980). Everyone is "average," and only the middle (central) part of the scale is used. This may happen when raters are asked to evaluate unfamiliar aspects of performance. Rather than not respond, they play it safe and say the person is average in this (unknown) ability.

Despite the fact that we have long been aware of leniency, halo, and central tendency errors, there is no clear consensus on how these errors manifest themselves in ratings. Saal, Downey, and Lahey (1980) observed that researchers define these errors in somewhat different ways. For example, leniency errors are sometimes equated with *skew* in the distribution of ratings. That is, positive skew is evidence of negative leniency, and negative skew of positive leniency. Other researchers say that if the average rating on a particular scale is above the midpoint, this indicates positive leniency. The exact meaning of *central tendency* is also unclear. Central tendency errors occur if the average rating is around the mid-point of the scale but there is not much variance in the ratings. The amount of variance that separates central tendency errors from "good" ratings has not been defined. Saal et al. (1980) feel more precise definitions of these errors must be developed before they can be overcome.

All three errors can lead to a restriction in range. That is, the ratings are concentrated at the ends (or middle) of the rating scale. When the range of variability is restricted on the criterion, the validity coefficient for this criterion will be greatly curtailed. Thus, when supervisor ratings are used in personnel research and validity coefficients are low, the conclusion that the predictor lacks validity may be wrong. Restriction in range on either the predictor or criterion (or both) can lead the researcher astray in assessing the validity of the predictor. Similarly, the value of appraisal systems meant to identify an employee's strengths and weaknesses are questionable if aspects of performance are not differentiated. To help combat the errors discussed, other appraisal methods have been developed, as discussed below.

**Employee comparison methods**

Rating scales provide for evaluating employees against some defined standard. With employee comparison methods, individuals are compared to each other. By comparing individuals, variance is forced into the appraisals. Thus, the concentration of ratings at one part of the scale, caused by rating error, is avoided. However, all methods of employee comparison involve the question of whether variation represents true differences in performance or whether it creates a false impression of large differences when, in fact, differences in performance may be small. There are three major employee comparison methods.

**Rank-order method.** The rater ranks employees from high to low on a given performance dimension. The person ranked first is regarded as the "best," and the person ranked last is "worst." However, because rank-order data have only ordinal scale properties, we do not know how good the "best" is or how bad the "worst" is. We don't know the *level* of performance. For example, the Nobel Prize winners in a given year can be ranked in terms of their overall contributions to science. But we would be hard pressed to conclude that the Nobel laureate ranked last made the worst contribution to science. Rank-order data are all relative to some standard; in this case, excellence in scientific research. Another problem is that it becomes quite tedious and perhaps somewhat meaningless to rank order large numbers of people. What usually happens is the rater can sort out the people at the top and bottom of the pile. However, for the rest with undifferentiated performance, the ranks may be somewhat arbitrary.

**Paired comparison method.** With this method, each employee is compared to every other employee in the group evaluated. The rater's task is selecting which of the two is better on the dimension being rated. The method is typically used to evaluate employees on a single dimension—overall ability to perform the job. The process can also be repeated for several performance aspects (e.g., Campion, 1972). The number of evaluation pairs is computed by the formula $n(n-1)/2$, where $n$ is the number of people to be evaluated. For example, if there are 10 people in a group, the number of paired comparisons is $10(9)/2 = 45$. At the conclusion of the evaluation, the number of times each person was selected as the better of the two is tallied. The people are then ranked by the number of tallies they receive.

A major limitation of the method is that the number of comparisons made mushrooms dramatically with large numbers of employees. If 50 people are to be appraised, the number of comparisons is 1,225. This would obviously take too much time. Some procedures were developed to reduce the number of evaluations necessary with a large sample. The original group is either divided into smaller groups (Lawshe, Kephart, & McCormick, 1949), or a patterned sample of pairs is drawn (McCormick & Bachus, 1952). But the paired comparison method is still best for relatively small samples.

**Forced distribution method.** This is most useful when the other employee comparison methods are most limited—when the sample size is large. It is typically used when the rater must evaluate employees on a single dimension, but it can also be used when multiple dimensions are required. The procedure is based on the normal distribution and assumes that employee performance is normally distributed. The distribution is divided into five to seven categories. Using predetermined percentages (based on the normal distribution), the rater evaluates an employee by placing him or her into one of the categories. All employees are evaluated in this manner. The method "forces" the rater to distribute the employees in all categories (which is how the method gets its name). It is thus impossible for all employees to be rated excellent, average, or poor. An example of the procedure for a sample of 50 employees is shown in Figure 7–3.

Some raters react negatively to the method, saying that the procedure creates artificial distinctions among employees. This is partly because they feel that performance is not normally distributed. Rather it is negatively skewed (i.e., most of their employees are performing very well). The dissatisfaction can be partially allayed by saying that those in the lowest 10 percent are not necessarily performing poorly, just not as well as the others. The problem (as with all comparison methods) is that performance is not compared to a defined standard. The *meaning* of the differences among employees must be supplied from some other source.

**Figure 7–3**     **Forced distribution method of performance appraisal using five performance categories with a sample of 50 employees.**

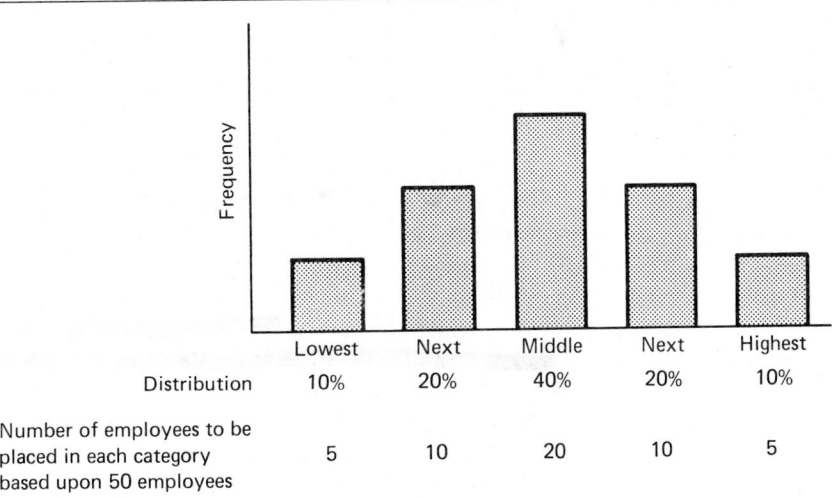

"Barkley, I perceive my role in this institution not as a judge but merely as an observer and recorder. I have observed you to be a prize boob and have so recorded it."

*Reprinted by permission of Tribune Company Syndicate, Inc.*

## Behavioral checklists and scales

Most recent advances in performance appraisal have involved behavioral checklists and scales. The key term is *behavior*. Behaviors are less vague than other factors. With more agreement on the meaning of the performance appraised, the greater the chance that appraisals will be accurate. All of the methods in this group have their origin (directly or indirectly) in the critical incidents method.

**Critical incidents.** Critical incidents are behaviors that result in good or poor job performance. Flanagan (1954) developed the critical incidents method. Supervisors record behaviors of employees that greatly influence their job performance. The supervisors are either to keep a running tally of these critical incidents as they occur on the job, or they are to recall them at a later time. Critical incidents are usually grouped by aspects of performance; job knowledge, decision making, leadership, and so on. The end product is a list of behaviors (good and bad) that constitute effective and ineffective job performance. The original method did not lend itself to quantification (i.e., a score reflecting performance). It was a method of guiding employees in the specifics of their job performance. Each employee's performance can be described in terms of the occurrence of these critical behaviors. The supervisor can then counsel the employee to avoid the bad and continue the good behaviors. For example, a negative critical incident for a machine operator might be "leaves machine running while unattended." A positive one might be "always wears safety goggles on the job." Discussing performance in such clear terms is more understandable than such vague statements as "poor attitude" or "careless work habits."

**Weighted checklist.**  A weighted checklist is simply an attempt to quantify performance using the critical incident technique. The procedure for developing a weighted checklist begins with a list of critical incidents. Once the list has been developed, a panel of "experts" (usually supervisors) then rate each critical incident in terms of just how "good" the good ones are and just how "bad" the bad ones are. Thus, a scale value is derived for each incident, reflecting the relative degree of its importance to the job. The scale values are usually derived by averaging the ratings made by the supervisors. Table 7–1 shows some examples of items from a weighted checklist for the job of secretary.

Supervisors then evaluate employee performance by checking off observed behaviors. The values for all behaviors checked off are added to yield the employee's score. The ideal employee would exhibit all the positive and none of the negative behaviors. The method gives information that can be used in many ways, including counseling employees on how to improve their performance. Employees can be ranked on total scores, thus providing information on the range of performance. The scores can be averaged for a measure of "typical" performance, which can serve as a standard for judging individual employees.

**Behaviorally anchored rating scales.**  Behaviorally anchored rating scales (BARS) are a combination of behavioral incident and rating scale methods. Performance is rated on a scale, but the scale points are anchored with

| Table 7–1 | Checklist of weighted critical incidents for a secretarial job | |
|---|---|---|
| | Critical incident | Scale value |
| | 1. Knows the difference between correcting the grammar in the boss's letter and correcting the writing style. | +6.5 |
| | 2. Knows various postal rates and mails material in a cost-efficient manner. | +4.2 |
| | 3. Knows what typing is to be done on plain paper versus dittos. | +3.1 |
| | 4. Keeps a running count on the use of office supplies. | +2.5 |
| | 5. Opens all mail whether or not it is marked "confidential." | −1.9 |
| | 6. Confuses priorities on typing that needs immediate attention and projects that have no established deadline. | −3.8 |
| | 7. Files away correspondence so that it can rarely be found for later reference. | −5.2 |
| | 8. Leaves many mistakes in typing from failing to proofread the typed copy. | −7.1 |

behavioral incidents. The development of BARS is time-consuming, but the benefits make them worthwhile. BARS are developed in a five-step process:

1.  The first step involves the generation of a list of critical incidents in the same manner that was discussed previously.
2.  Next a group of people (usually supervisors, either the same people who generated the critical incidents initially or another group) cluster the incidents into a smaller set of performance dimensions (usually 5 to 10 in number) which they typically represent. Thus, we have 5 to 10 performance dimensions each containing several critical incidents illustrative of the dimensions.
3.  The third step involves another group of knowledgeable people who are instructed to perform the following task. The critical incidents are "scrambled" in such a way as they are no longer listed under the dimension in which they were placed in step 2. The critical incidents might be written on separate note cards and presented to the people in random order. The task of the raters is to reassign or retranslate all the critical incidents back to the original performance dimensions from which they came. The step is a variation of the procedure developed by Smith and Kendall (1963), where the goal is to have critical incidents that clearly represent the performance dimensions under consideration. Usually a critical incident is said to be successfully retranslated if some percentage (usually 50 to 80 percent) of the raters reassign it back to the dimension from which it came. Those incidents that are not retranslated successfully (i.e., there is ample confusion as to which dimension it represents) are discarded.
4.  In this step, the people who retranslated the items are asked to rate each "surviving" critical incident on a scale (seven- or nine-point scales are most often used) in terms of just how effectively or ineffectively it represents performance on the appropriate dimension. This rating phase is similar to the process used to derive the scale weights in the weighted checklist. The ratings given to each incident by the raters are then averaged. The standard deviation for each item is then computed. Low standard deviations indicate high rater agreement as to the value of the incident. Large standard deviations indicate low rater agreement. A standard deviation criterion is then set for deciding which incidents will be retained for inclusion in the final form of the BARS. Typically, incidents that have a standard deviation in excess of 1.50 are discarded, because the raters could not agree on their respective value.
5.  The final form of the instrument consists of critical incidents that survived both the retranslation and standard deviation criteria. These incidents serve as behavioral anchors for the performance dimension scales. The final BARS instrument consists of a series of scales listed vertically (one for each dimension) anchored by the retained incidents.

The incident is located along the scale, depending on its established rating (Schwab, Heneman, & DeCotiis, 1975). An example of a BARS for patrol officer performance is shown in Figure 7–4. As can be seen, behaviors are listed as what the employee is *expected* to do at various performance levels. For this reason, BARS are sometimes referred to as "behavioral expectation scales" (BES).

One of the major advantages of the method does not involve performance appraisal. It is based on the high degree of involvement of those developing the scale. The participants must carefully examine specific behaviors that lead to effective performance. In so doing, they may reject false stereotypes about ineffective performers. The method has face validity for both the rater and ratee. It also appears to be useful for training raters.

Research on reducing rating errors with BARS is mixed. Some studies (e.g., Campbell, Dunnette, Arvey, & Hellervik, 1973) report fewer leniency errors with BARS. Other studies (e.g., Borman & Vallon, 1974) report the reverse. Generally, it seems that BARS are not much better than graphic rating scales in reducing rating errors. However, Landy and Trumbo (1980) commented that the scale development process ensures understanding of performance determinants. This alone is a benefit over simple graphic rating scales.

**Behavioral observation scales.** A recent development in appraisal is the behavioral observation scale (BOS). Like BARS, they are based on critical incidents. With BOS the rater must rate the employee on the *frequency* of critical incidents. The rater observes the employee over a period of time, such as a month. An example of a five-point critical incident scale used in appraising salespeople, as provided by Latham and Wexley (1977), follows:

**Knows the price of competitive products**

| Never | Seldom | Sometimes | Generally | Always |
|-------|--------|-----------|-----------|--------|
| 1     | 2      | 3         | 4         | 5      |

Raters evaluate the employees on several such critical incidents, recording how often the behavior was observed. The total score is the sum for all of the critical incidents. The final step is correlating the response for each incident (a rating of 1, 2, 3, 4, or 5) with the total performance score. This is called "item analysis." It is meant to detect the critical incidents that most influence overall performance. Those incidents that have the highest correlations with the total score are the most discriminating factors that influence performance. They would be retained to develop criteria for job success.

Latham, Fay, and Saari (1979) suggested advantages to performance appraisals with BOS. Like BARS, BOS are developed by those using the

**Figure 7–4**                    **Example of a behaviorally anchored rating scale for appraising patrol officers**

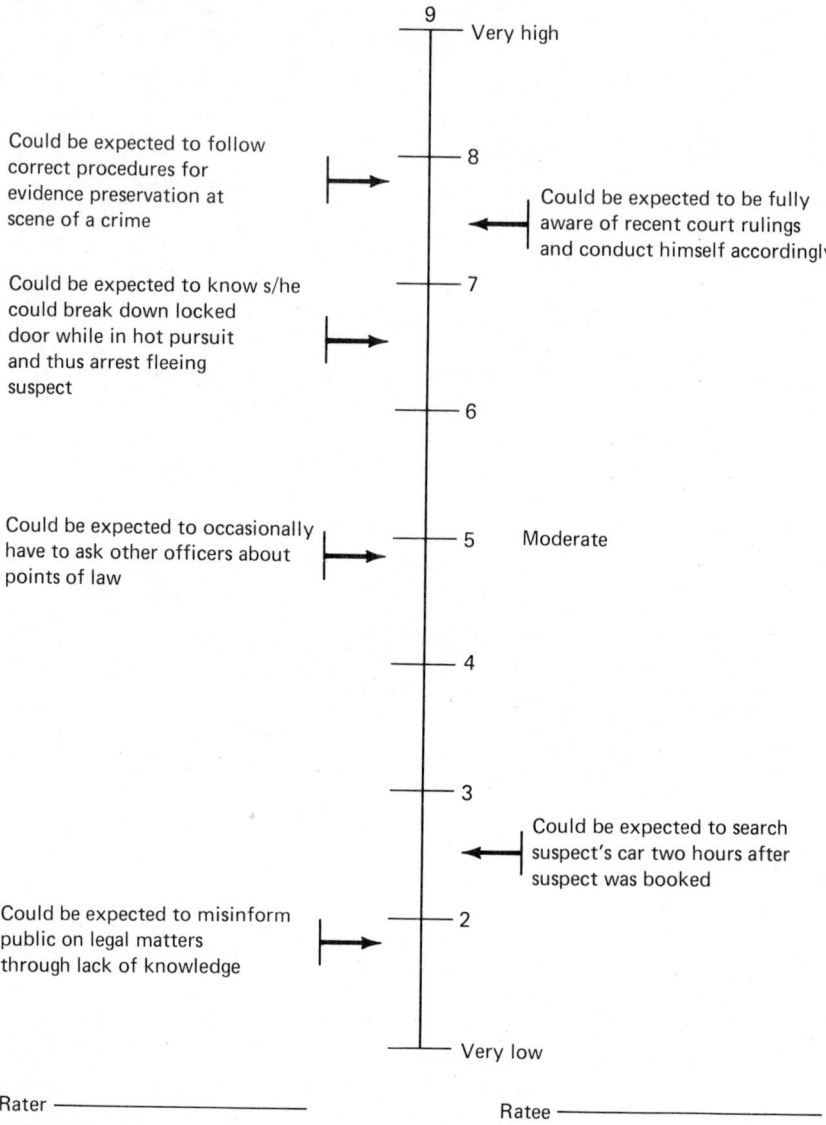

Job knowledge: Awareness of procedures, laws, and court rulings
and changes in them

9 — Very high

Could be expected to follow
correct procedures for
evidence preservation at
scene of a crime                    → 8

                                              Could be expected to be fully
                                          ← aware of recent court rulings
                                              and conduct himself accordingly

Could be expected to know s/he      — 7
could break down locked
door while in hot pursuit
and thus arrest fleeing           →
suspect

                                    — 6

Could be expected to occasionally
have to ask other officers about  → 5   Moderate
points of law

                                    — 4

                                    — 3

                                          Could be expected to search
                                      ← suspect's car two hours after
                                          suspect was booked

Could be expected to misinform      — 2
public on legal matters           →
through lack of knowledge

                                    — Very low

Rater ——————————              Ratee ——————————

SOURCE: F. J. Landy and D. A. Trumbo, *Psychology of Work Behavior*, rev. ed. (Homewood, Ill.:
Dorsey Press, 1980), p. 128.

method for evaluation. They understand they are committed to using the scales. Second, BOS information can be used to teach new employees the behaviors most critical to the job. Finally, BOS are content valid; the aspects of performance appraised are derived directly from the job. The authors believe this satisfies the EEOC requirement that appraisal methods be job relevant.

Few data are available on reducing rating errors with BOS versus BARS. There is some controversy (e.g., Bernardin & Kane, 1980; Latham, Saari, & Fay, 1980) over the merits of BOS as proposed by Latham et al. (1979). At this stage, we don't know enough about BOS for adequate evaluation. As more research is done, we will have a better understanding of its strengths and weaknesses.

**Mixed standard rating scale.** The final method we will consider is one that is still experimental—the mixed standard rating scale. It was developed by Blanz and Ghiselli (1972). The dimensions of performance (e.g., practical judgment) to be appraised are identified. *Three* critical incidents illustrating good, average, and poor performance for each dimension are obtained as described earlier. The incidents for each performance dimension are *randomly* presented to the rater so that a sequence (good, average, poor) *cannot* be detected. The rater also doesn't know the value (good, average, poor) of the incidents.

The rater is asked to evaluate each employee on whether he or she is "better than," "worse than," or "the same as" each critical incident in the random list. An example of this kind of scale is shown in Figure 7–5. In this example, the scale was used for police officer performance. Three dimensions were identified: judgment (J), job knowledge (K), and relations with others (R). Given three performance dimensions with three critical incidents each, nine statements are presented. There are poor (P), average (A), and good (G) examples for each dimension. The rater must decide whether performance is better than, worse than, or the same as each statement. It is proposed that the "mixed" nature of the rating form helps to minimize leniency errors as well as causing the rater to give careful consideration to each performance dimension and thus minimize halo effects. The method is also useful for identifying careless raters who give inconsistent evaluations. Though the method has not been used very much, one study (Saal & Landy, 1977) reported that the mixed standard rating scale reduced leniency and halo effects. But the reliability of the method was not impressive. However, Saal (1979) developed a coding system that was useful in correcting for inconsistency. This may make the scale more reliable.

Dickinson and Zellinger (1980) found that the mixed standard scale was not very popular among raters. As part of a larger study, they compared the reactions of teachers and students who used three rating scales: mixed standard, BARS, and a variation of the graphic scale. The raters were asked which scale was easiest to use, most preferred, and so on. The results are

**Figure 7–5**

**Example of the mixed standard rating scale for appraising the performance of police officers**

|  |  |  | Rating |
|---|---|---|---|
| (K) | 1. | The officer could be expected to misinform the public on legal matters through lack of knowledge. (P) | _____ |
| (R) | 2. | The officer could be expected to take the time to carefully answer a rookie's question. (G) | _____ |
| (K) | 3. | This patrol officer never has to ask others about points of law. (G) | _____ |
| ( J) | 4. | The officer could be expected to refrain from writing tickets for traffic violations that occur at a particular intersection which is unusually confusing to motorists. (G) | _____ |
| ( J) | 5. | The patrol officer could be expected to call for assistance and clear the area of bystanders before confronting a barricaded, heavily armed suspect. (A) | _____ |
| (R) | 6. | The officer could be expected to use racially toned language in front of minority group members. (P) | _____ |
| (K) | 7. | The officer follows correct procedures for evidence preservation at the scene of a crime. (A) | _____ |
| ( J) | 8. | The patrol officer could be expected to continue to write a traffic violation in spite of hearing a report of a nearby robbery in progress. (P) | _____ |
| (R) | 9. | This officer is considered friendly by the other officers on the shift. (A) | _____ |

SOURCE: F. J. Landy and D. A. Trumbo, *Psychology of Work Behavior,* rev. ed. (Homewood, Ill.: Dorsey Press, 1980).

presented in Table 7–2. As shown, the mixed standard scale was not rated highest on any of the five questions asked. In particular, it was difficult to use.

## Validity of judgmental data

The validity of judgmental data in performance appraisal, as is true of the validity of any type of performance appraisal data, refers to the extent that the observed data are accurate measures of the "true" variable being measured. The "true" variable can refer to a global construct, such as overall job performance, or a dimension of job performance, such as interpersonal relations ability. One method of assessing the validity of judgmental data is to correlate them with appraisals of performance with another method such as objective production data or personnel data. In those studies which have conducted this type of analysis, the resulting correlations have been only moderate in magnitude. While these results may be interpreted to mean that judgmental data have only moderate validity, the key question is whether the objective production data or the personnel data can be assumed to represent "true" ability. Those types of data might be just as incomplete or partially relevant as judgmental data. Since we never obtain measures of the ultimate criterion (i.e., "true" ability), we are forced to

**Table 7–2**        **Percentage of preferences for three rating formats**

| | Format | | |
|---|---|---|---|
| Questions asked of raters | MSS | BARS | GT |
| Instructions for this form were clear and easily understood. | 22% | 18% | 60% |
| This form was most successful in meeting assessment goals. | 24 | 52 | 24 |
| This form was easiest to use. | 13 | 31 | 56 |
| This form would provide the best feedback to students and faculty members. | 34 | 47 | 19 |
| Which form do you prefer? | 23 | 47 | 30 |

Note: MSS = Mixed standard scale; BARS = Behaviorally anchored rating scale; GT = Graphic type.
SOURCE: Adapted from T. L. Dickinson and P. M. Zellinger, "A Comparison of the Behaviorally Anchored Rating and Mixed Standard Scale Formats," *Journal of Applied Psychology* 65 (1980), pp. 147–54.

deal with imperfect measures which, not surprisingly, yield imperfect results.

Borman (1978) had another approach to assessing the validity of judgmental data. He made videotapes of two employment situations: a manager talking with a problem employee and a recruiter interviewing a job candidate. Sixteen videotapes were made, eight of each situation. Each tape showed a different degree of performance—e.g., from a highly competent recruiter to a totally inept one. Similar degrees of performance were shown in the tapes of the manager/subordinate meeting. Professional actors were used in the tapes. The same actor played the recruiter in all eight tapes, but a different actor played the new employee in each tape. Thus, the performance level (the "true" ability of the manager or recruiter) was "programmed" into the scripts. Raters were asked to rate the performance of the manager and recruiter with a series of rating scales. The evaluations were correlated with the performance levels depicted. Correlations between ratings and level of performance across several job dimensions (organizing the interview, establishing rapport, etc.) ranged from .42 to .97. The median was .69. Although this study used a simulation as opposed to actual job performance, the study did show that various types of rating procedures were susceptible to differences in validity. The study also revealed that certain dimensions of performance were more accurately evaluated ("answering recruitees questions," $r = .97$) than others ("reacting to stress," $r = .42$). Borman was led to conclude that raters are limited in their ability to appraise performance in that the raters could not accurately evaluate the levels of "true" performance which were acted out in the scripts. He suggested a practical upper limit to validity that is less than the theoretical limit ($r = 1.0$).

**Reliability of judgmental data.** Two basic types of reliability can be computed with judgmental data: the extent that raters agree (*interrater* reliability) and the extent that the same rater would make the same evaluation at a later time (called *rate-rerate* reliability). Interrater reliability is computed by correlating the evaluations given by two (or more) raters of the same employees to assess the degree of *agreement* in their judgments. Rate-rerate reliability is computed by correlating the evaluations given by the same rater to a set of employees at two points in time to assess the degree of *consistency* in the judgments.

Reliability of judgmental data is influenced by many factors. These include rater experience, the type of scale used, and dimensions of performance that are being evaluated. By and large rate-rerate reliabilities are quite high (correlations frequently in the .90s): raters are quite consistent in the evaluation they make. Whether these evaluations are *accurate* is a question of validity. Interrater reliability is more variable. Bernardin (1977) reported interrater reliability of .74 with BARS, and .72 and .70 with two graphic rating scales. Other studies have found far lower coefficients, with correlations in the .30 to .50 range.

Interrater reliability using employee comparison methods is similar. Lawshe et al. (1949) reported average reliability with the paired comparison method to be .83. Berkshire and Highland (1953) reported a range of .59 to .74 for the forced distribution method. These assessments are quite satisfactory. It seems that raters basically agree in what they evaluate, although there are exceptions. As mentioned earlier, if a measure has no reliability, it also has no validity. However, the fact that raters agree does not mean their evaluations are correct. It is easier to assess reliability than validity. We can only hope that when judges agree and when the evaluations correspond with other assessments, we are being fair and accurate appraisers of performance. Many important decisions are made on performance appraisal data. To the extent that our evaluations are in error, we create a form of injustice that harms both the organization and the individual.

## SELF AND PEER APPRAISALS

Most research on judgmental performance appraisal deals with evaluations made by a superior (supervisor, foreman, manager). However, there is information on the value of performance appraisals made by colleagues or peers. Self-evaluation has also been discussed. Our knowledge is somewhat limited, but these methods do offer added understanding of performance appraisal.

**Self-assessment**

With self-assessment, as the term suggests, each employee appraises his or her performance. The procedure most commonly used is some type of graphic rating scale. Meyer (1980) reported a study in which 92 engineers rated their performance against their view of the performance of other engineers in the company. On average, each engineer thought he or she was performing better than 75 percent of the rest of the engineers in the study. Statistically, this is quite a trick to have 75 percent of the work force feel that they are in the top 25 percent of job performers. This underscores the biggest problem with self-assessment—positive leniency. Most people have higher opinions of their own performance than do others. This has both negative and positive results. Negatively, there can be personal adjustment problems because the rest of the world doesn't see the person as he or she does. On the positive side, people who hold themselves in high regard (or have high self-esteem) have been found to be better motivated and to take more pride in their work than people with low self-esteem.

Thornton (1980) reports that, despite leniency problems, there are *fewer* halo errors with self-appraisals. It appears that people recognize their strengths and weaknesses and appraise themselves accordingly. Thornton also reported little agreement in most studies comparing self- and supervisor assessments. Superiors don't evaluate employees in the same way that employees evaluate themselves. This doesn't mean that one appraisal is "right" and the other "wrong." It just means that the two groups don't agree in evaluating the same performance. Thornton suggests this may be healthy because it provides a basis for discussing differences and may foster an exchange of ideas.

A study by Levine, Flory, and Ash (1977) showed self-assessments of clerical employees in such areas as spelling, grammar, reading speed, and word meaning correlated fairly well with two criteria of job performance. There were correlations as high as .74 between self-assessments, written tests, and supervisor ratings. Furthermore self-assessments of typing speed correlated .62 with typing test scores. However, these were *concurrent* criterion-related validity coefficients, as these people already held jobs. Among job *applicants* there may be more incentive to distort information. While the *predictive* validity of self-assessments awaits further research, the concurrent validity coefficients reported by Levine et al. (1977) are as good as the predictions made by other types of variables. As Heneman (1980) has said, we must do more research to determine conditions where self-assessments are useful.

## Peer assessments

In peer assessment, members of a group appraise the performance of their fellows. According to Kane and Lawler (1978), three techniques are commonly used. One is *peer nomination*—each person nominates a specified number of group members as being highest on a particular dimension of performance. *Peer ratings* have each group member rate the others on a set of performance dimensions using one of several kinds of rating scales. The third technique is *peer ranking*—having each member rank all others from best to worst on one or more performance dimensions.

Reliability of the method is determined by assessing the degree of interrater agreement. Most studies report high reliabilities (coefficients in the .80s and .90s), indicating that peers agree about the job performance of group members. Validity of peer assessments is determined by correlating the peer assessments with criterion measures usually made later; e.g., who successfully completed a training program, who got promoted first, the size of raises, etc. What is uncanny is that group members who have known each other a relatively short time (two to three weeks) can be quite accurate in making long term predictions about each other. Validity coefficients are fairly impressive, commonly in the .40 to .50 range. The peer *nomination* technique appears to be the best in identifying people with extreme levels of attributes compared to other members of the group. Peer *ratings* are most applicable but have only marginal, empirical support. It has been suggested that their use be limited to giving feedback to employees as to how others perceive them. Relatively little data are available on the value of peer *rankings*, though they may be the best method for assessing overall job performance.

There is some evidence that peer assessments are biased by friendship (i.e., employees evaluate their friends most favorably). But friendships may be formed on the basis of performance. Also, many work group members don't like to evaluate each other, so part of the method's success hinges on impressing participants with the value of the technique. Indeed, a study by Cederblom and Lounsbury (1980) showed that lack of user acceptance may be a serious obstacle in using this otherwise promising method. The authors found that a sample of college professors felt peer assessments were heavily biased by friendship. They thought peers would rate their friends (and be rated by their friends) more favorably than would be justified. Problems with knowing the people to be rated and fostering a "mutual admiration society" caused the professors to question the value of peer assessment. They also felt that the method should be used for feedback, not for raises and promotions.

Peer assessment, like self-assessment, is part of an overall performance appraisal system. The information generated cannot be isolated from information gained using other methods. Holzbach (1978) showed that superior, peer, and self-assessments all contribute information about performance. But information from each source involved halo errors. Borman (1974) showed that peers, superiors, and subordinates (if any) hold unique pieces of the puzzle that portrays a person's job performance. Thus, rather than having raters at just one level of the organization perform the entire performance appraisal, it is better to have each level contribute to the assessment the portion that it is able to perform more effectively than any other level. Each performance dimension should be defined precisely enough to obtain the information unique to the relevant source. And overlap with dimensions better assessed by other sources should be avoided. The appraisal system should include compatible and mutually supporting segments. Each segment should be assigned the role to which it is best suited

(Kane & Lawler, 1978). Performance appraisal should not be seen as simply selecting "the best" method. What is best varies with the use made of the information, complexity of the performance appraised, and the people capable of making such judgments.

## FACTORS AFFECTING PERFORMANCE RATINGS

Landy and Farr (1980) developed a model illustrating the complexity of performance appraisal. The model (Figure 7–6) shows the factors that can influence performance appraisal. Eight factors can affect what they call "Performance Description"—the goal of appraisal. In turn, Performance Description directly influences "Personnel Action"—e.g., raises, promotions, firing, etc.

**1. Rater characteristics.** This refers to rater biases that may influence evaluations, such as a dislike for younger employees, blacks, or those seen as overly aggressive.

**Figure 7–6**　　　　　　　**Process model of performance rating**

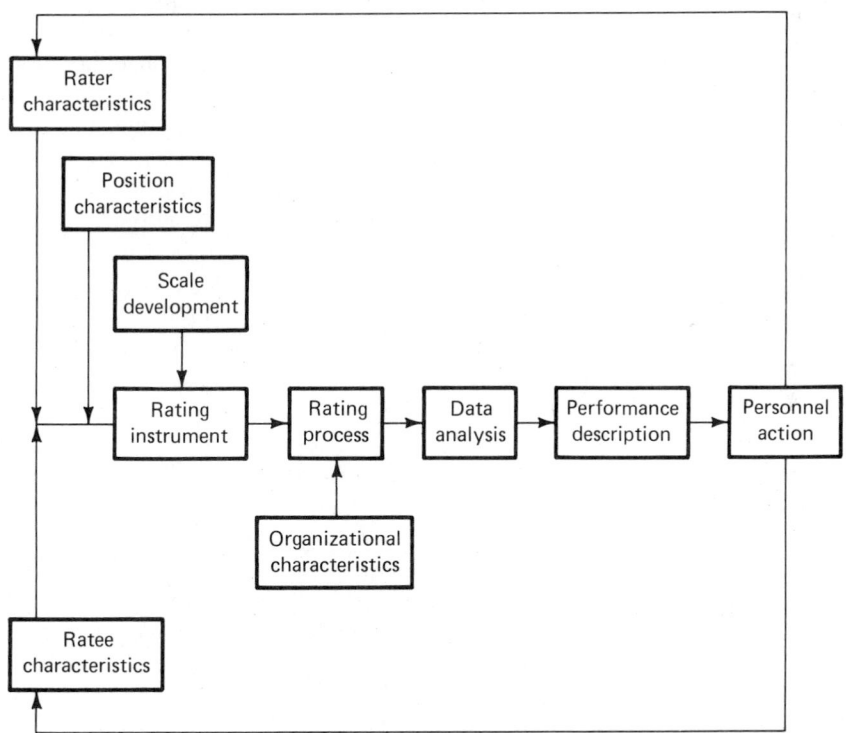

SOURCE: F. J. Landy and J. L. Farr, "Performance Rating," *Psychological Bulletin* 87 (1980), p. 94.

**2. Ratee characteristics.**    Ratees have characteristics that may influence performance appraisals, even though they may have nothing to do with the job. These might include sex, age, and physical attractiveness.

**3. Position characteristics.**    The position of the ratee may influence appraisal. This might involve upper versus lower level jobs or line (e.g., production worker) versus staff (e.g., payroll clerk) positions.

**4. Rating instrument.**    The rating scale used may bear on the evaluation. For example, graphic rating scales might provoke more lenient responses.

**5. Scale development.**    This is mainly the degree of rater involvement in developing the rating scale. One of the supposed advantages of behavioral scales is the people who use them also helped to develop them. Thus, they have more knowledge of the performance they evaluate.

**6. Rating process.**    This refers to such factors as when the evaluations are conducted (e.g., once a year at the same time for everyone or a staggered schedule) and whether the ratings must be justified with a great deal of documentation.

**7. Organizational characteristics.**    Characteristics of the organization that might influence ratings include size, production versus service, union/nonunion, public sector/private sector, etc.

**8. Data analysis.**    There is a question of how to analyze data. Ratings on various dimensions of performance could be kept separate, or they could be summated for an overall performance measure. Evaluations from several raters could be totaled or left independent.

Landy and Farr (1980) don't say which factors most influence ratings. However, all of them deal with ancillary factors which might affect the evaluation rather than actual performance itself. Stated another way, if rated performance were identical to actual performance, the effect of these eight factors on appraisals would be zero. Unfortunately, they do have an effect, and they distort our ability to accurately appraise performance.

The model also has some feedback properties. Personnel actions resulting from appraisal can affect characteristics of both the rater and ratee. The employee who gets a raise as a result of the appraisal may be more motivated and more committed to the organization. This, in turn, may influence the rater's opinion of the employee in the future.

We seem to know more about the effects of some of these factors than of others. Studies have compared the relative validity of different types of rating instruments. But we know relatively little about the effect of position characteristics, for example, on the accuracy of performance ratings. I/O psychologists might well spend some time on these neglected factors. The Landy and Farr model shows that there is more to performance appraisals than simply making check marks on a rating form. We have come a long way in appraising performance since the 1813 Department of Army document shown in Figure 7–7. But we have a great deal more to understand about the factors influencing performance evaluation.

**Figure 7–7**                    **Excerpts from a U.S. Army document regarding performance appraisal**

Lower Senaca Town
August 15, 1813

Sir:

I forward a list of the officers of the 27th Regt. of Infty. arranged aggreeably to rank. Annexed thereto you will find all the observations I deem necessary to make them.

Respectfully,
I am, Sir,
Yo. Cot. Servt.

Lewis Cass
Brig. Gen.

*27th Infantry Regiment*

Alex Denniston—Lieut. Col., Comdg.     —a good natured man.

Clarkson Crolins—First Major           —a good man, but no officer.

Captain Shotwell                       —a man of whom all unite in speaking ill, a knave despised by all.

      ″    Allen Reynolds         —an officer of capacity, but imprudent and a man of most violent passions.

First Lieut. Wm Perrin     )     —low vulgar men, with exception of Perrin,
    ″    ″   Danl. Scott     )    Irish and from the meanest walks of life—
    ″    ″   Jas. I. Ryan    )    possessing nothing of the character of offi-
    ″    ″   Robt. McElwrath  )    cers or gentlemen.

    ″    ″   Robt. P. Ross           —willing enough—has much to learn—with small capacity.

2nd Lieut. Nicholas G. Carner          —a good officer but drinks hard and disgraces himself and the services.

SOURCE: The First Recorded Efficiency Report in the Files of the War Department, August 15, 1813.

# ASSESSMENT CENTERS

*Assessment centers* involve appraising multiple dimensions of performance using several methods and several raters. Assessment centers are a group-oriented, standardized series of activities that provide a basis for judgments or predictions of human behaviors believed or known to be relevant to work performed in an organizational setting (Finkle, 1976). They may be a physical part of some organizations, e.g., special rooms designed for assessment. Or they may be located in a conference center away from the normal workplace. These centers are expensive, so they have been mainly used by large organizations that can afford them. However, some private organizations conduct assessment-center appraisals for smaller companies. The centers are used to appraise management personnel. The earliest systematic approach to assessment-center evaluation was developed in 1956 by AT&T and is described by Bray, Campbell, and Grant (1974). Since the pioneering efforts of AT&T, hundreds of other organizations have developed centers for the appraisal of upper-level employees.

There are several characteristics of the assessment-center approach.

1. Those selected to attend (the assessees) are usually management-level personnel the company wants to evaluate for possible promotion, transfer, or training. Occasionally organizations will send management *applicants* to the center, and appraisal information is then used for selection.

2. Assessees are evaluated in groups of usually 10 to 20. They may be divided into smaller groups for various exercises, but the basic strategy is to appraise individuals against the performance of others in the group.

3. Several raters do the evaluation. They work in teams and collectively or individually recommend personnel action (e.g., selection, promotion). Raters may be psychologists, but they are usually company employees unfamiliar with the assessees. Raters are usually trained in how to appraise performance. The training may last from several hours to a few days.

4. Performance is appraised using a wide variety of methods. Many involve group interactions, e.g., leaderless group discussions in which leaders "emerge" by their degree of participation in the exercise. Other methods include the In-Basket test, projective personality inventories, personal history information forms, and interviews. The program typically takes from at least one day to several days.

Given the variety of tests, the person assessed provides a lot of information about his or her performance. Raters evaluate the assessees on a number of performance dimensions judged relevant for the job in question. These involve leadership, decision making, practical judgment, interpersonal relations skills—the typical performance dimensions for managerial jobs. Based on these evaluations, a summary report is prepared for each assessee. Portions of the report are fed back to the assessee by a rater. Recommendations for personnel action are forwarded to the organization for review and consideration.

Conclusions about assessment-center effectiveness are mixed, though most evidence is quite positive. Since the evaluations are mainly rater judgments, reliability of these judgments is very important. Hinrichs and Haanpera (1976) reported interrater reliability coefficients for 15 performance dimensions from .23 to .92. The average was .52. It is clear that raters agree more on some dimensions than others. In a similar study, Schmitt (1977) found interrater reliability for 17 dimensions from .46 to .88, based on evaluations *before* raters discussed the candidates. *After* they "compared notes" and tried to iron out some differences of opinion, they rerated the candidates. The range then rose to .74 to .95. The practical implication is that companies shouldn't draw conclusions about employee performance on dimensions with low reliability. Personnel actions should be based only on those aspects where there is satisfactory agreement.

The validity of assessment-center evaluations is determined by comparing the judgments of performance in the center with some criterion of performance back on the job, usually rated job performance, promotions, or salary (Huck, 1973). Validity studies on assessment center evaluations are quite positive. Byham (1970) reported that correlations of center evaluations of managers with subsequent job performance rated by superiors ranged from .47 to .64. Moses and Boehm (1975) analyzed center evaluations for male and female employees, and concluded that assessment centers predicted the future performance for females as accurately as for males. Huck and Bray (1976) reported a similar finding regarding the fairness of assessment centers in predicting the future job performance of white and black employees. It seems that assessment center evaluations do not have the racial or sex bias of other job-performance predictors.

Long-term validity of assessment center evaluations is also encouraging. Mitchel (1975) reported an average multiple correlation of .42 between assessment-center judgments and a criterion of salary growth after one, three, and five years for a sample of managers. Hinrichs (1978) examined the predictive validity of 12 assessment-center evaluations in forecasting managers' positions one and eight years later. The results are shown in Table 7–3. Eleven of the 12 predictors *increased* in validity between the first and eighth year. Self-confidence was the strongest predictor ($r = .46$) after one year; aggressiveness was the strongest ($r = .69$) after eight years. Some predictors were uniformly valid. Others (e.g., risk taking) were not predictive of later performance. These validity coefficients are extremely impressive, not only

**Table 7–3**     **Correlations of assessment-center characteristics with promotional criterion**

| Characteristics | Promotional level | |
|---|---|---|
| | Year 1 | Year 8 |
| Aggressiveness | .27 | .69 |
| Persuasive and selling ability | .29 | .59 |
| Oral communication | .35 | .50 |
| Self-confidence | .46 | .60 |
| Interpersonal contact | .34 | .48 |
| Decision making | .36 | .42 |
| Resistance to stress | .41 | .42 |
| Energy level | .17 | .34 |
| Administrative ability | .20 | .22 |
| Written communications | .02 | .22 |
| Planning and organization | .11 | .20 |
| Risk taking | .16 | .01 |

SOURCE: Adapted from J. R. Hinrichs, "An Eight-Year Follow-up of a Management Assessment Center," *Journal of Applied Psychology* 63 (1978), pp. 596–601.

in size, but also because the criterion was assessed many years after collection of the assessment evaluation. However, as a study by Cascio and Silbey (1979) indicated, one need not have very high validity coefficients for assessment-center evaluations to have *utility*. As discussed in Chapter 5, the validity of a predictor has the most impact on utility. However, those who go through assessment centers usually hold important jobs where the consequences of making errors are expensive to the company. Validity coefficients as low as .1 can produce significant gains in overall criterion performance compared to random (i.e., $r = .00$) selection. That is, the utility of valid evaluations is increased because of the value of the assessee's job to the organization.

Assessment centers offer promise for identifying those with potential for success in management. Assessment centers seem to be successful in their major goal of selecting high-talent people.

However, these evaluations are particularly susceptible to criterion *contamination* from several sources. One is that overall judgments of performance are based on many evaluation methods (tests, interviews, life history forms, etc.). Validity of the evaluations may stem from the validity of these separate appraisal methods, quite apart from the assessors' evaluation. That is, a valid interview or test might be just as capable of forecasting later job success as the assessment-center evaluation. But because the incremental value of these methods is "buried" in the overall assessor judgments, it is debatable how much assessors' ratings contribute to predicting future performance beyond these separate methods (Howard, 1974). Some research attests to the predictive value of assessor judgments. Other studies find traditional predictions of job success based on test scores superior (e.g., Wollowick & McNamara, 1969).

A second source of contamination is far more subtle and was proposed by Klimoski and Strickland (1977). They contend that the reason assessment center evaluations are predictive is that both assessors and company supervisors hold common stereotypes of the "effective employee." Assessors give higher evaluations to those who "look" like good management talent. Superiors give higher evaluations to those who "look" like good "company" people. If the two sets of stereotypes are held in common, then (biased) assessment-center evaluations would correlate with (biased) job performance evaluations. The danger is that organizations will hire and promote those that fit the image of the successful employee. The long-term effect would be an organization staffed with people who are mirror images of each other. Opportunity for creative people who "don't fit the mold," but might be effective if given the chance, would be greatly limited. Klimoski and Strickland (1977) suggest looking for other criteria to validate assessment-center evaluations. This may make us reexamine who is really contributing to the organization. And it might make us rethink the type of people desired. Assessment centers are a new and comprehensive approach to performance appraisal. We clearly have much to learn about their utility. Given the cost (from \$500 to \$2,000 a day per person depending on level), the benefits should be carefully examined.

# FEEDBACK OF APPRAISAL INFORMATION TO EMPLOYEES

In the final step of appraisal, the employee and his or her superior review and discuss the evaluation. This is usually referred to by the misnomer "performance appraisal interview." Performance was appraised before the interview; the interview is a means of giving the employee the results. Both superior and subordinate are usually very uneasy about the interview. Employees often get defensive about negative performance aspects. Superiors are often nervous about having to confront employees face-to-face with negative evaluations. However, for an appraisal system to be effective, interview objectives must be met with the same rigor as the other system objectives.

The interview typically has two main objectives. The first is feedback on how well the employee is performing. This often means reviewing major job responsibilities and how the employee met them. The second objective is future planning. This means identifying goals the employee will try to meet before the next review. Both employee and superior should provide input in setting goals.

There has been much research on factors that contribute to success in meeting the two objectives of the interview. Feedback on job performance has two properties: information and motivation. That is, feedback can tell the employee how to perform better. It can also increase an employee's desire to perform well. Ilgen, Fisher, and Taylor (1979) showed that how the employee perceives the superior can greatly influence his or her response to feedback. They feel *credibility* and *power* are the most important aspects here. Credibility is the extent that the superior is seen as someone who can legitimately evaluate performance. It is enhanced when the superior is seen as having expertise about the employee's job and being in a position to evaluate performance. Power is the extent that the superior can control valued rewards. Ilgen et al. believe that credibility and power influence: (1) how the employee understands feedback; (2) the extent the feedback is seen as correct; and (3) how willing the employee is to alter behavior as suggested by the feedback.

Other factors can also influence employee reactions to the performance appraisal interview. Kay, Meyer, and French (1965) studied the relationship between criticism and employee defensiveness. They found that the more critical the superior, the more defensive the employee became. However, praise, per se, did not make employees more at ease. Most criticism was buried in a "praise sandwich" (i.e., praise/criticism/praise). The superior would praise the employee to ostensibly make him or her feel more at ease, then criticize some aspect of the employee's performance, then praise the employee again so he or she "left with a good feeling." But employees became conditioned to the fact that when they were praised, it was a signal that some criticism was just around the corner.

Another area of research, but largely untested in this context, is nonverbal communication. People give messages with a variety of nonverbal cues like frowning, smiling, eye contact, twitching, etc. Extensive research (e.g., Vetter, 1969) has shown that people do attribute meaning to these nonverbal cues, though the meaning attributed to them may not be accurate in assessing the affective state of the cue sender. For example, if an employee slouches in the chair during the interview, the superior can interpret this behavior to mean the employee is indifferent or bored with the interview. The superior who doesn't smile during the meeting may be perceived by the employee as having a rejecting feeling about the employee. Both people could be wrong in their attributions of meaning. The slouching employee may be very nervous, not bored. The unsmiling superior may only be trying to avoid the image that the interview is a light-hearted affair and one that should not be taken seriously. Sometimes nonverbal cues are seen as complementing the verbal message. ("I got praised up and down, and he never quit smiling the whole time.") At other times, they may be a mixed signal. ("I can't quite figure it out—he said I was doing great, but he didn't smile at me once.") The extent to which nonverbal cues are perceived to provide feedback in an interview relative to verbal responses is a matter that awaits further research.

The most effective way to conduct the appraisal interview from the perspective of setting target performance objectives has also been the subject of considerable research. Much of the research is based on addressing the degree of employee participation in the interview. Maier (1976) proposed three interview styles: tell and sell, tell and listen, and problem solving. In the tell and sell style, the employee has very little involvement in the interview; the superior "tells" the employee what to do and tries to "sell" the employee on how to improve performance. In the tell and listen style, employees are told their strengths and weaknesses. But they are allowed to express their feelings about how they can improve their performance. The problem-solving style allows employees the most participation. Job-related plans and goals are set based on the ideas of both parties. Maier's research indicates that employee satisfaction with the interview and motivation were most enhanced by the problem-solving style. Increased satisfaction and motivation, and actual improvements in performance were identified (Burke & Wilcox, 1969) as the most important consequences of the appraisal interview. Furthermore Burke, Weitzel, and Weir (1978) found that different aspects of the appraisal interview were related to the outcomes of employee satisfaction and subsequent improvements in job performance. Increased participation by the employee in the interview resulted in greater satisfaction (but not increased job performance). Discussion of problem solving and goal setting did result in subsequent job performance improvements.

The apparent superiority of the problem-solving style of interview seems to hold regardless of the personality of the employee. Wexley, Singh, and Yukl (1973) found that two personality variables—authoritarianism and need for independence—did not affect the amount of participation the employee desired in the performance appraisal interview. Their results indicated it was desirable to allow an employee to have substantial participation in appraisal interview decisions since it increased employee satisfaction with the interview and motivation to improve subsequent job performance. While Latham and Yukl (1975) concede that attitudes, education, and cultural background may affect an employee's response to mutual goal setting, we do not know the effect of these variables on the problem-solving style.

In any case, the appraisal interview, however conducted, is a vital last link in the total performance appraisal system. Most research has focused on methods of collecting appraisal information. But getting that information back to employees is critical. Without the interview, performance appraisal can appear to be a perfunctory operation which has no real impact on employees. Research on the performance appraisal interview indicates this concluding phase of the evaluation process can greatly influence the subsequent behavior of employees on the job.

## CONCLUDING COMMENTS

As noted, the major contribution of I/O psychologists to performance appraisal is the design of methods. The value of such methods is great, but I also feel that such heavy emphasis on "technique" is somewhat misplaced. Feldman (1981) observed that the psychological aspects of appraisal are complex. Evaluators must organize and store a great deal of information about subordinates, information produced through daily interaction. Attention and recognition are involved because certain aspects of behavior are judged more noteworthy than others. About once a year, an evaluator must appraise an employee's performance. The information then must be recalled, categorized, integrated, and evaluated. Finally, a check mark is made on a rating sheet reflecting the culmination of all the information processed. There is clearly more to performance appraisal than deciding if the check mark is to be made on a graphic rating scale, forced distribution, BARS, BOS, or the mixed standard scale. Because I/O psychologists are deeply concerned with problems of measurement, it is easy to see how our infatuation with rating scales came to be. Despite the legitimate need to understand "technique," we should also expand our horizons to other issues in performance appraisal. The cognitive processes used by raters such as Feldman (1981) proposed are one avenue. Another larger issue is demonstration of the *utility* of performance appraisal for the organization. If we believe that performance appraisal is a valuable tool for enhancing the welfare of both individuals and the organization (as we do), we should be able to demonstrate its actual worth, just as we did with personnel selection procedures. Another fertile area for research is how performance appraisal information is *used* after it is collected (by whatever means). Questions regarding exactly how administrators use performance appraisal information to make promotions, determine pay raises, and guide employees are just as important as whether performance appraisal information is biased or accurate. In summary, performance appraisal covers a broad array of substantive issues, ranging from how the human brain processes information to interorganizational differences in how performance appraisal information is used. We must not lose sight of the diversity of issues facing us in our pursuit of knowledge, and we should not fix most of our attention on but one part of the entire process.

# CASE STUDY

Franklin Community College employed a staff of 40 teachers. It was a new college offering a two-year associate of arts degree in a variety of areas. The teachers reported to Louise Medwick, who was in charge of faculty personnel. Economic conditions at the college were not good. The college had to fight for its yearly budget from the state education association, and lately, education had not been a high-priority item. The college had been told that due to cutbacks, 20 percent of the teachers must be laid off.

Part of Medwick's job was to conduct an annual performance appraisal of the teachers. She did not like this part of her job, but she knew it was critical. Her evaluations would be the main basis for the layoffs. Her boss, college president Fred Schweiker, was adamant about keeping the "best" faculty, and it was her job to determine who was best. There was also the usual concern over raises, as part of a teacher's raise was based on merit. This year, though, the stakes were a lot higher. It's one thing to get a 6 percent raise when you felt you deserved 8 percent; its quite another to get laid off. Medwick knew her decisions would directly and intimately affect the lives of eight teachers. She personally knew and liked the teaching staff, which didn't help matters either. The ax was going to fall, and it was just a case of whose heads were going to roll.

Medwick also faced a somewhat peculiar situation that made matters more easy and more difficult at the same time. The faculty at the college was not unionized. Thus, there was no formal labor contract covering layoffs. Some organizations used seniority as the basis for layoffs—the last person hired was the first laid off. While the college was not compelled to consider seniority in making layoffs, they could always do so if they wished. The problem was Schweiker didn't want to consider seniority—he wanted those laid off to be the poorest performers, not just the newest staff members.

The other oddity was that because the college was less than three years old, none of the staff had tenure. Tenure could preclude the dismissal of those teachers that had it, but no one did. Medwick saw the situation as a curse and a blessing. Seniority and tenure couldn't be used to reduce the pool of teachers who could be laid off, and this made her task more difficult. At the same time, poorly performing teachers couldn't hide behind seniority and tenure as reasons for their retention. Thus, everyone was thrown in the same pot. It was her job to give them all a fair shake.

Medwick knew all about the usual methods of appraising teacher performance, but she was very aware of the limitations when so much was on the line. She had used student ratings in the past. However, many teachers felt they were little more than a popularity contest. At least that's what the teachers who got low ratings said. She also used peer ratings, but only to help teachers improve, not for administrative decisions. Just about everyone taught the same number of classes, so there was no point in simply counting classroom hours. Besides, it would be hard to convince Schweiker that the best teachers also taught the most classes. Last year she wanted to start a behavioral measure of teacher performance—critical incidents, rating scales, the whole bit—but the idea got scratched because of time and financial problems. She wished she had forced this issue, but now it was too late.

Whatever method she used, she would have to be able to explain it and defend it. She also knew she would take a lot of heat from those who got laid off. While Medwick accepted her task as part of the responsibility that comes with the job, she wished she had more solid information to go on. Picking the best from the rest was complicated and she wasn't totally sure in specific terms what the "best" was. Best lecturer, best grader, best advisor? Medwick also knew that while some appraisals simply got filed away, this one wouldn't. The lives of 40 teachers and their families were riding on her decision.

Questions

1. Do you see any relationships between the topic of criteria discussed in Chapter 3 and the issue of performance appraisal? What are some of these relationships?
2. Can you think of any objective performance indexes or personnel data that might help Medwick make her decisions? Do you feel the best teachers would be identified with these indexes?
3. If the method used involves *ratings*, who do you think would best serve as raters?
4. One method Medwick could use is some type of forced-choice technique. What problems might Medwick face in ranking the teachers?
5. Suppose Medwick were allowed to use some other factors along with merit performance. What might some of those factors be?

# REFERENCES

Barrett, R. S. *Performance ratings*. Chicago: Science Research Associates, 1966.

Bass, A. R., & Turner, J. N. Ethnic group differences in relationship among criteria of job performance. *Journal of Applied Psychology*, 1973, *57*, 101–109.

Berkshire, J. R., & Highland, R. W. Forced-choice performance rating: A methodological study. *Personnel Psychology*, 1953, *6*, 355–378.

Bernardin, H. J. Behavioral expectation scales versus summated scales: A fairer comparison. *Journal of Applied Psychology*, 1977, *62*, 422–427.

Bernardin, H. J., & Kane, J. S. A second look at behavioral observation scales. *Personnel Psychology*, 1980, *33*, 809–814.

Blanz, F., & Ghiselli, E. E. The mixed standard rating scale: A new rating system. *Personnel Psychology*, 1972, *25*, 185–199.

Blum, M. L., & Naylor, J. C. *Industrial psychology*. New York: Harper & Row, 1968.

Boehm, V. R. Differential prediction: A methodological artifact? *Journal of Applied Psychology*, 1977, *62*, 146–154.

Borman, W. C. The rating of individuals in organizations: An alternative approach. *Organizational Behavior and Human Performance*, 1974, *12*, 105–124.

Borman, W. C. Exploring upper limits of reliability and validity in performance ratings. *Journal of Applied Psychology*, 1978, *63*, 135–144.

Borman, W. C., & Vallon, W. R. A view of what can happen when behavioral expectation scales are developed in one setting and used in another. *Journal of Applied Psychology*, 1974, *59*, 197–201.

Bray, D. W., Campbell, R. J., & Grant, D. L. *Formative years in business*. New York: John Wiley & Sons, 1974.

Burke, R. J., Weitzel, W., & Weir, T. Characteristics of effective employee performance review and development interviews: Replication and extension. *Personnel Psychology*, 1978, *31*, 903–920.

Burke, R. J., & Wilcox, D. S. Characteristics of effective employee performance review and development interviews. *Personnel Psychology*, 1969, *22*, 291–305.

Byham, W. C. Assessment centers for spotting future managers. *Harvard Business Review*, July–August 1970, *48*, 150–167.

Campbell, J., Dunnette, M., Arvey, R., & Hellervik, L. The development and evaluation of behaviorally based rating scales. *Journal of Applied Psychology*, 1973, *57*, 15–22.

Campion, J. E. Work sampling for personnel selection. *Journal of Applied Psychology*, 1972, *56*, 40–44.

Cascio, W. F., & Silbey, V. Utility of the assessment center as a selection device. *Journal of Applied Psychology*, 1979, *64*, 107–118.

Cederblom, D., & Lounsbury, J. W. An investigation of user acceptance of peer evaluations. *Personnel Psychology*, 1980, *33*, 567–580.

Cherry, N. Persistent job changing—Is it a problem? *Journal of Occupational Psychology*, 1976, *49*, 203–211.

Dickinson, T. L., & Zellinger, P. M. A comparison of the behaviorally anchored rating and mixed standard scale formats. *Journal of Applied Psychology*, 1980, *65*, 147–154.

Feldman, J. M. Beyond attribution theory: Cognitive processes in performance appraisal. *Journal of Applied Psychology*, 1981, *66*, 127–148.

Finkle, R. B. Managerial assessment centers. In M. D. Dunnette (Ed.), *Handbook of industrial and organizational psychology*. Skokie, Ill.: Rand McNally, 1976.

Flanagan, J. C. The critical incident technique. *Psychological Bulletin*, 1954, *51*, 327–358.

Guion, R. M. *Personnel testing*. New York: McGraw-Hill, 1965.

Hammer, T. H., & Landau, J. Methodological issues in the use of absence data. *Journal of Applied Psychology*, 1981, *66*, 574–581.

Heneman, H. G., III. Self-assessments: A critical analysis. *Personnel Psychology*, 1980, *33*, 297–300.

Hill, J. M., & Trist, E. L. Changes in accidents and other absences with length of service: A further study on their incidence and relation to each other in an iron and steel works. *Human Relations*, 1955, *8*, 121–152.

Hinrichs, J. R. An eight-year follow-up of a management assessment center. *Journal of Applied Psychology*, 1978, *63*, 596–601.

Hinrichs, J. R., & Haanpera, S. Reliability of measurement in situational exercises: An assessment of the assessment center method. *Personnel Psychology*, 1976, *29*, 31–40.

Holley, W. H., & Feild, H. S. Performance appraisal and the law. *Labor Law Journal*, 1975, *26*, 423–430.

Holzbach, R. L. Rater bias in performance ratings: Superior, self-, and peer assessments. *Journal of Applied Psychology*, 1978, *63*, 579–588.

Howard, A. An assessment of assessment centers. *Academy of Management Journal*, 1974, *17*, 115–134.

Huck, J. R. Assessment centers: A review of their external and internal validities. *Personnel Psychology*, 1973, *26*, 191–212.

Huck, J. R., & Bray, D. W. Management assessment center evaluations and subsequent job performance of white and black females. *Personnel Psychology*, 1976, *29*, 13–31.

Huse, E. F., & Taylor, E. K. The reliability of absence measures. *Journal of Applied Psychology*, 1962, *46*, 159–160.

Ilgen, D. R., Fisher, C. D., & Taylor, M. S. Motivational consequences of individual feedback on behavior in organizations. *Journal of Applied Psychology*, 1979, *64*, 349–371.

Kane, J. S., & Lawler, E. E., III. Methods of peer assessment. *Psychological Bulletin*, 1978, 85, 555–586.

Kay, E., Meyer, H. H., & French, J. R. P., Jr. Effects of threat in a performance appraisal interview. *Journal of Applied Psychology*, 1965, *49*, 311–317.

Kleiman, L. S., & Durham, R. L. Performance appraisal, promotion and the courts: A critical review. *Personnel Psychology*, 1981, *34*, 103–121.

Klimoski, R. J., & Strickland, W. J. Assessment centers—Valid or merely prescient? *Personnel Psychology*, 1977, *30*, 353–361.

Kujawski, C. J., & Young, D. M. Appraisals of "peo-

ple" resources. In D. Yoder & H. G. Heneman, Jr. (Eds.), *ASPA handbook of personnel and industrial relations.* Washington, D.C.: The Bureau of National Affairs, 1979.

Landy, F. J., & Farr, J. L. Performance rating. *Psychological Bulletin*, 1980, *87*, 72–107.

Landy, F. J., & Trumbo, D. A. *Psychology of work behavior* (rev. ed.). Homewood, Ill.: Dorsey Press, 1980.

Latham, G. P., Fay, C. H., & Saari, L. M. The development of behavioral observation scales for appraising the performance of foremen. *Personnel Psychology*, 1979, *32*, 299–311.

Latham, G. P., & Pursell, E. D. Measuring absenteeism from the opposite side of the coin. *Journal of Applied Psychology*, 1975, *60*, 369–371.

Latham, G. P., Saari, L. M., & Fay, C. BOS, BES, and baloney: Raising Kane with Bernardin. *Personnel Psychology*, 1980, *33*, 815–821.

Latham, G. P., & Wexley, K. N. Behavioral observation scales for performance appraisal purposes. *Personnel Psychology*, 1977, *30*, 255–268.

Latham, G. P., & Wexley, K. N. *Increasing productivity through performance appraisal.* Reading, Mass.: Addison-Wesley Publishing, 1981.

Latham, G. P., Wexley, K. N., & Pursell, E. D. Training managers to minimize rating errors in the observation of behavior. *Journal of Applied Psychology*, 1975, *60*, 550–555.

Latham, G. P., & Yukl, G. A. A review of research on the application of goal setting in organizations. *Academy of Management Journal*, 1975, *18*, 824–845.

Lawshe, C. H., Kephart, N. C., & McCormick, E. J. The paired comparison technique for rating performance of industrial employees. *Journal of Applied Psychology*, 1949, *33*, 69–77.

Lent, R. H., Aurbach, H. H., & Levin, L. S. Predictors, criteria, and significant results. *Personnel Psychology*, 1971, *24*, 519–533.

Levine, E. L., Flory, A., & Ash, R. A. Self-assessment in personnel selection. *Journal of Applied Psychology*, 1977, *62*, 428–435.

Lopez, F. M., Jr. The blood, sweat, and tears of employee performance evaluation. Paper presented at annual conference of the Public Personnel Association, 1966.

Maier, N. R. F. *The appraisal interview.* La Jolla, Calif.: University Associates, 1976.

McCormick, E. J. & Bachus, J. A. Paired comparison

ratings: I. The effect on ratings of reductions in the number of pairs. *Journal of Applied Psychology*, 1952, *36*, 123–124.

McGregor, D. An uneasy look at performance appraisal. *Harvard Business Review*, May–June 1957, *35*, 89–94.

Meyer, H. H. Self-appraisal of job performance. *Personnel Psychology*, 1980, *33*, 291–296.

Meyer, H. H., Kay, E., & French, J. R. P., Jr. Split roles in performance appraisal. *Harvard Business Review*, January–February 1965, *43*, 123–129.

Mitchel, J. O. Assessment center validity: A longitudinal study. *Journal of Applied Psychology*, 1975, *60*, 573–579.

Moses, J. L., & Boehm, V. R. Relationship of assessment center performance to management progress of women. *Journal of Applied Psychology*, 1975, *60*, 527–529.

Muchinsky, P. M. Performance ratings of engineers: Do graduates fit the bill? *Engineering Education*, 1974, *65*, 187–188.

Muchinsky, P. M. Employee absenteeism: A review of the literature. *Journal of Vocational Behavior*, 1977, *10*, 316–340.

Rothe, H. F. Output rates among butter wrappers: I. Work curves and their stability. *Journal of Applied Psychology*, 1946, *30*, 199–211.

Rothe, H. F. Output rates among machine operators: I. Distributions and their reliability. *Journal of Applied Psychology*, 1947, *31*, 384–389.

Rothe, H. F. Output rates among coil winders. *Journal of Applied Psychology*, 1958, *42*, 182–186.

Saal, F. E. Mixed standard rating scale: A consistent system for numerically coding inconsistent response combinations. *Journal of Applied Psychology*, 1979, *64*, 422–428.

Saal, F. E., Downey, R. G., & Lahey, M. A. Rating the ratings: Assessing the psychometric quality of rating data. *Psychological Bulletin*, 1980, *88*, 413–428.

Saal, F. E., & Landy, F. J. The mixed standard rating scale: An evaluation. *Organizational Behavior and Human Performance*, 1977, *18*, 18–35.

Schmitt, N. Interrater agreement in dimensionality and combination of assessment center judgments. *Journal of Applied Psychology*, 1977, *62*, 171–176.

Schmitt, N., & Lappin, M. Race and sex as determinants of the mean and variance of performance ratings. *Journal of Applied Psychology*, 1980, *65*, 428–435.

Schwab, D., Heneman, H. G., III, & DeCotiis, T. Behaviorally anchored rating scales: A review of the literature. *Personnel Psychology*, 1975, *28*, 549–562.

Smith, P. C., & Kendall, L. M. Retranslation of expectations: An approach to the construction of unambiguous anchors for rating scales. *Journal of Applied Psychology*, 1963, *47*, 149–155.

Thornton, G. C., III. Psychometric properties of self-appraisals of job performance. *Personnel Psychology*, 1980, *33*, 263–272.

Vetter, H. J. *Language behavior and communication.* Itaska, Ill.: F. E. Peacock Publishers, 1969.

Wexley, K. N., Singh, J. P., & Yukl, G. A. Subordinate personality as a moderator of the effects of participation in three types of appraisal interviews. *Journal of Applied Psychology*, 1973, *58*, 54–59.

Wollowick, H. B., & McNamara, W. J. Relationship of the components of an assessment center to management success. *Journal of Applied Psychology*, 1969, *53*, 348–352.

# Organizational psychology

# chapter 8  ORGANIZATIONAL INFLUENCES ON BEHAVIOR

As I/O psychologists expanded their scope of inquiry, we gained more appreciation for the organizational context in which work occurs. The Hawthorne Studies showed dramatically that employee behavior and attitudes are influenced by more than personal ability and disposition. The O in I/O psychology testifies to the influence that organizations have on behavior. While psychologists have traditionally studied *individuals,* it is obvious that we can't understand employee behavior apart from the social or organizational context in which employees work. This chapter will examine some characteristics of organizations, as well as discuss some individual attitudes and behaviors resulting from work.

It is beyond the scope of this book to discuss the theory of organizations. Interested readers may refer to several excellent works on the subject.[1] For our purposes, we simply acknowledge that an organization consists of many interrelated systems. One system is structural; it includes such concepts as size, technology, physical setting, and the interrelationships of jobs. This system has no human elements—the *structure* exists apart from its

---

[1]An informative article on organizational theory has been written by Scott (1974), whereas a more in-depth presentation can be found in the book by Scott, Mitchell, and Birnbaum (1981).

members. A second system consists of the people comprising the work force; their skills, attitudes, motives, personalities, and interests. These variables influence what people expect to receive from participating in the organization. They are most subject to change depending on the nature of the individuals who staff an organization. The third system involves the status and role concepts that exist in any organization. Their impact on the individual involves both the organization's formal structure and the particular people who are members of the organization. What people do (i.e., their behavior) and how they feel (i.e., their attitudes) are a product of these three systems. Furthermore, these three systems *interact* to shape attitude and behavior. We cannot understand behavior in organizations by examining just one system.

Thus, "organizational psychology" tends to deal with a broader range of variables than "personnel psychology." This does not mean that personnel psychology is simplistic, but rather that personnel selection, training, and performance appraisal embrace a narrower range of issues. Many of the topics addressed in personnel psychology involve techniques (such as techniques to hire, train, or appraise performance). There are relatively few *theories* in personnel psychology. Conversely, there are many theories in organizational psychology concerning job satisfaction, motivation, and leadership. Because there are many influences that shape behavior in organizations, it is an imposing task to integrate them into a theory of organizational behavior. Recently, however, researchers have made strides in this direction (e.g., Naylor, Pritchard, & Ilgen, 1980).

In this chapter, we will concentrate on those variables that influence employee attitudes and behavior in an organization. The systems have an interactive effect. We will also examine some constructs identified as a result of these interactions between individuals and organizations. Collectively, these constructs represent the emerging properties of interacting systems, and they set the stage for the remaining chapters in this section.

## COMPONENTS OF SOCIAL SYSTEMS

A *social* system is a structuring of events or happenings; it has no formal structure apart from its functioning. Physical or biological systems (cars or human beings) have structures that can be identified even when they are not functioning (an electrical or skeleton structure). That is, these systems have both an anatomy and a physiology. There is no anatomy to a social system in this sense. When a social system stops functioning, no identifiable structure remains. It is hard for us to think of social systems as having no tangible anatomy because it's easier to understand concepts with concrete and simple components (Katz & Kahn, 1978). Social systems do indeed have components, but they are not concrete. We will examine some of them while recognizing that they are more abstract.

**Roles**

When an employee enters an organization, there is much for that person to learn. This includes expected performance levels, who's important, dress codes, and time demands. Roles ease the learning process. Roles are usually defined as the expectations of others about appropriate behavior in a specific position (Scott et al., 1981). Each one of us plays several roles at the same time (parent, employee, club member, etc.), but we will focus on job-related roles.

Scott et al. (1981) listed five important aspects of roles. First, they are impersonal; the position itself determines the expectations, not the individual. Second, roles are related to task behavior. An organizational role is the expected behaviors for a particular job. Third, roles can be difficult to pin down. The problem is defining who determines what is expected. Since "other" people define our roles, opinions differ over what our role should be. How we see our role, how others see our role, and what we actually do may differ. Fourth, roles are learned quickly and can produce major behavior changes. Fifth, roles and jobs are not the same—a person in one job might play several roles.

We learn our role through a *role episode*, as Figure 8–1 shows. Group members have expectations about job performance. These are communicated either formally or by having the role occupant observe others in similar roles. In Stage 3, the role occupant behaves as he or she believes is appropriate. If the behavior (Stage 4) differs widely from the group's ex-

**Figure 8–1**            **The role episode**

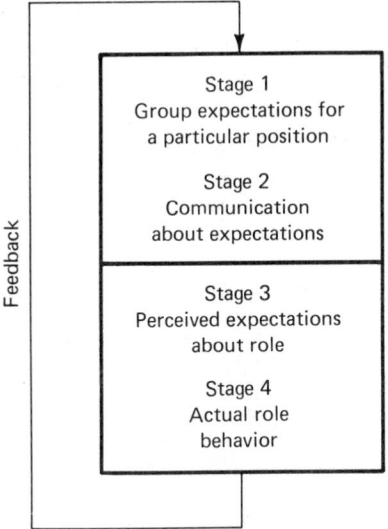

SOURCE: W. G. Scott, T. R. Mitchell, and P. H. Birnbaum, *Organization Theory: A Structural and Behavioral Analysis* (Homewood, Ill.: Richard D. Irwin, 1981).

pectations (Stage 1), the occupant gets feedback from the group regarding the discrepancy. This is intended to alter behavior toward group expectations. The role episode is ongoing. Expectations may change over time, as might the employee's behavior.

Another aspect is *role differentiation*. This is the extent that different roles are performed by employees in the same subgroup. One person's job might be maintaining good group relations (as a work unit coordinator). His or her role might thus require providing emotional or interpersonal support to others. Another's role might be setting schedules, agendas, and meeting deadlines. Such a person is usually an administrator. When all roles in a work group fit together like the parts of a puzzle, a smoothly running, effective group results. However, all parts may not fit together. Later in the chapter, we will examine the way some organization pressures produce role problems.

## Norms

Norms are shared group expectations about appropriate behavior. While roles define what is appropriate for a particular job, norms define acceptable *group* behavior. Roles differentiate positions; norms establish behavior expected of everyone in the group (Scott et al., 1981). This might concern when employees take coffee breaks, how much they produce, when they stop for the day, and what they wear. Norms are unwritten rules that govern behavior. A no smoking sign is not a norm but a formal written rule of behavior. If employees smoke despite the sign, there is a norm that sanctions such behavior in spite of the formal rule.

Norms have several important properties. First, there is "oughtness" or "shouldness." They are prescriptions for behavior. Second, they are usually more obvious for behavior judged to be important for the group. A norm might exist for *when* employees stop work before lunch. But there probably would not be a norm about *what* employees eat. Third, norms are enforced by the group. Much expected behavior is monitored and enforced through formal rules and procedures. With norms, group members regulate behavior. Sometimes formal rules and group norms clash. The no smoking rule and the group norm sanctioning smoking is an example. Unless the organization imposes sanctions on smokers (i.e., rule breakers), the group norm would probably prevail. Finally, the degree that norms are shared and the degree that deviation is acceptable vary (Scott et al., 1981). Not all smokers might smoke in proscribed areas, and those who don't might be as accepted by the group just like those who do.

There is a three-step process for developing and communicating norms. The norm must first be defined and communicated. This is either explicit ("Here is the way we do things around here") or implicit (the desired behavior is observed). Second, the group must be able to monitor behavior and judge whether the norm is followed. Third, the group must be able to reward conformity and punish noncomformity. Conformity enhances predictability of behavior within the group, which in turn promotes feelings of group cohesion.

Compliance with norms is enforced by positive or negative reinforcement. Positive reinforcement can be praise or inclusion in group activities. Negative reinforcement can be a dirty look, a snide remark, or actual physical abuse. (Workers who exceeded the group norm for productivity in the Hawthorne Studies were hit on the arm, which was called "dinging.") Another form of negative reinforcement is exclusion from group activities. The group will often try to convince the nonconforming employee (referred to as a *deviant*) to change his or her behavior. The group will try to alter the deviant's opinion through increased communication—verbal or nonverbal. This becomes more intense and explicit over time. The clearer and more important the norm, the more cohesive the group, the greater the pressure will become. Eventually, the deviant will either change or be rejected. If rejection occurs, the deviant becomes an *isolate,* and pressure to conform stops. Because the group may need the isolate to perform work tasks, a truce is usually reached; the isolate is tolerated in work, but is excluded from group activities and relations. Obviously, the isolate can quit the job and try to find a better match between his or her values and the group.

Finally, norms are not always *contrary* to formal organization rules or *independent* of them. Sometimes norms greatly aid organization goals. For example, there may be a norm against leaving for home before a certain amount of work is done. Although quitting time is 5 PM, the group may expect employees to stay until 5:15 or 5:30 and finish a certain task. In this case, the deviant is one who conforms to the formal rules instead of the group norm. When group norms and organization goals are complementary, high degrees of effectiveness can result.

## Power

In an organization, members give up some individual freedom in order to form an aggregate that can help them obtain their goals. In deference to the pursuit of the desired goals, individuals enter into a relationship with an organization whereby the organization (and parts of it) can control aspects of members' lives. The source of the control is the *power* the organization exerts over its members. Power is a complex topic; there are many variations or bases of power. It also works in both directions: employees (individually and collectively) can exert power over the organization. We will examine power in this section and in a later chapter.

Perhaps the best analysis of power in an organization is that of French and Raven (1960). They proposed five sources or bases.

**1. Reward power.** This is the capacity of an organization (or a member in a specified role) to offer positive incentives for desirable behavior. Incentives include promotions, raises, vacations, good work assignments and so on. Power to reward an employee is defined by formal sanctions inherent in a superior's role.

**2. Coercive power.** The organization can punish an employee for undesirable behavior. Dismissal, docking pay, reprimands, and unpleasant work assignments are examples. This capacity to punish is also defined by formal sanctions inherent in the organization.

**3. Legitimate power.** Sometimes referred to as authority, it means that the employee believes the power the organization has over him or her is legitimate. Norms and expectations help to define the degree of legitimate power. If a boss asks an individual to work overtime, this would likely be seen as legitimate, given the boss's authority. However, if a co-worker made the same request, it might be turned down. The co-worker has no legitimate authority to make the request. The individual might agree out of friendship, but not because the co-worker has legitimate power.

**4. Expert power.** The employee believes that some other individual has expertise in a given area and that he or she should defer to the "expert's" judgment. Consultants are called on for help in handling problems because they are seen as experts in certain areas. The source of expert power is the perceived experience, knowledge, or ability of a person. It is not formally sanctioned in the organization. There are also differences in the perceived boundaries of expertise. One employee may be seen as the expert on using tools and equipment. Others will turn to him or her for help with technical problems. However, that expertise may not be seen as extending to other areas, like interpersonal relations.

**5. Referent power.** This is the most abstract type of power. One employee might admire another, want to be like that person, and want to be liked by him or her. The other worker is a referent, someone the employee refers to. The source of referent power is the personal qualities of the referent. Cultural factors may contribute to the personal qualities of a referent. Younger people will often defer to an older person partly on the basis that age per se is a personal quality that engenders deference. Norms can also generate referent power. An employee may wish to identify with a particular group and will bow to their expectations.

Organizations differ in the extent to which they use the various bases of power. Authoritarian managers rely on reward and coercive power. Managers with a participative style rely on expert and referent power. The military seems to rely heavily on the legitimate power inherent in military rank. Educational organizations have a high degree of expert power over their members.

Employees (individually and collectively) can also attain and use power in dealings with the organization. Power is not only a "top down" affair. A secretary can have much power over her boss by knowing where things are filed, whom to call to get things done, and so forth. I am very aware of this when my secretary goes on vacation. I am then forced to do things on my own that she could do far more efficiently. A highly competent employee can exercise power by demanding a raise or threatening to quit. Unless the organization is prepared to lose the employee, they might have to agree to the raise.

Unions typify a major source of employee power. They can often obtain goals (better working conditions, greater pay) more effectively than members could on their own. Workers forming a union must forego some individual freedom (such as paying union dues), but in return they may have greater job security. Unions also have power in that members can strike if the organization (i.e., management) presents the union with "unreasonable" demands. However, the converse is also true. If management feels that the union is "unreasonable," they can prevent employees from working (a lockout). Power in union/management relations is a fascinating topic and will be discussed in greater detail in Chapter 14.

## Climate

Climate is a recently identified component of a social system. Hellriegel and Slocum (1974) define climate as "a set of attributes which can be perceived about a particular organization and/or its subsystems, and that may be induced from the way that organization and/or its subsystems deal with their members and environments" (p. 256). There is debate over whether climate is an attribute of an organization or merely the views of people working in the organization (Guion, 1973). Most researchers agree that organizations differ by climate, which suggests that climate is an organizational attribute. Such things as structure, standards, reward policies, etc., (the "set of attributes" mentioned by Hellriegel & Slocum, 1974) are dimensions of the organization that create its climate. They are identified through employee responses to questionnaires (samples are shown in Table 8–1). Based on employees' judgments, some organizations are seen as high in structure (great emphasis on rules and policies, clear channels of authority and responsibility). Others are seen as having little formal structure. Some organizations strongly emphasize performance standards (little tolerance for mistakes, all work is double-checked for accuracy, etc.). In others, the standards are not so exacting. Another attribute that distinguishes organizations has to do with reward policies. Raises and promotions may be tied directly to performance or to seniority or personal favoritism. Re-

**Table 8–1**         **Sample items from the Litwin and Stringer organizational climate questionnaire**

The jobs in this organization are clearly defined and logically structured.

We don't rely too heavily on individual judgment in this organization; almost everything is double-checked.

A friendly atmosphere prevails among the people in this organization.

In this organization we set very high standards for performance.

People are proud of belonging to this organization.

Note: Individuals mark responses to these items ranging from "strongly agree" to "strongly disagree."
SOURCE: From George H. Litwin and Robert A. Stringer, Jr., *Motivation and Organizational Climate* (Boston: Harvard University Division of Research, Graduate School of Business Administration, 1968). Items selected from Organizational Climate Questionnaire, Exhibit 1–B, pp. 204–7.

searchers discovered about six dimensions or attributes that can differentiate organizations (e.g., Sims & LaFollette, 1975; Muchinsky, 1976).

There is a lot of confusion over climate, particularly whether it is "good" or "bad." In and of itself, climate is neither good nor bad. An organization's climate only assumes some value when certain outcomes relate to it. For example, as in meteorological climate, a sunny day is "good" for a picnic but "bad" if crops need water. Thus, the judgment applied to the weather (climate) is a function of the outcomes or events associated with it. The same is true of organizational climate. Schneider (1975) has suggested that climate may foster or deter certain outcomes like creativity, interpersonal harmony, professional growth, and so on.

Furthermore, research (Lawler, Hall, & Oldham, 1974) has shown that an organization's climate can influence both the job performance and the satisfaction of its employees. In this study Lawler et al. proposed that climate was a construct that intervened between organizational structure and process (e.g., frequency of performance appraisals, professional autonomy, etc.) variables and employee behavior and attitudes on the job. This is shown schematically in Figure 8–2. Climate was measured by five attributes. These included how much responsibility the organization assumed, tendency to take risks, and degree that management was seen as impulsive. The dependent variables were employee satisfaction and how effectively the organization was performing. There were better correlations between climate and organization performance $(r = .25)$ and employee satisfaction $(r = .47)$ than between any other pairs of variables. This suggests that employee satisfaction and performance are directly related to perceptions of certain aspects of the work environment.

Unlike meteorological climate that we are unable to control, it seems that

**Figure 8–2**      **Proposed model showing organization climate as an intervening variable between structure and process variables and performance and satisfaction variables**

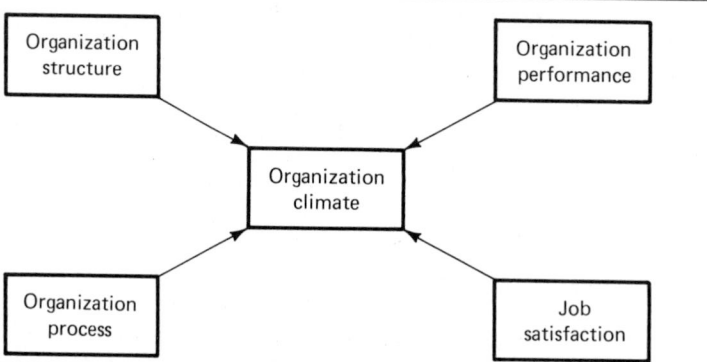

SOURCE: E. E. Lawler, D. T. Hall, and G. R. Oldham, "Organizational Climate: Relationship to Organizational Structure, Process, and Performance," *Organizational Behavior and Human Performance* 11 (1974), pp. 139–55.

organizational climates can be promoted to facilitate organizational goals. The problem is, however, that some organizational goals may not be mutually compatible. An organization that desires a climate which facilitates high standards of quality can create such a climate by double-checking work for accuracy, giving larger raises for high-quality work, firing employees whose work was poor, and so on. In the process, the organization may also make work very stressful. Under constant pressure to avoid errors, employees may feel they are under tremendous stress. This, in turn, can cause some negative consequences, such as absenteeism and chronic tension. Attaining one goal (high work standards) may come at the expense of another goal (a healthy work force). While organizations certainly do differ in their climates, we have more to learn about creating climates that will best serve the total needs of the organization.

**Summary of social system components**

Organizations have a physical structure, but structural features alone do not define an organization. The social fabric—norms, roles, power, and climate—are a significant influence on the conduct of organization members. These are not tangible entities, but they are as much attributes of an organization as its size. Organizations differ in norms, roles, use of power, and climate. Norms influence behavior, increasing consistency and predictability. Roles prescribe the boundaries of acceptable behavior and enhance conformity. Organizations exert many forms of power over their members to get them to behave in certain ways. These three variables all help produce uniformity and consistency in individual behavior. This is necessary in part to ensure that all organizational members are pursuing common goals. Individuals give up some freedom in joining an organization, and these constructs represent three ways freedom is limited. The climate of an organization is roughly like an individual's personality. Individuals differ in personality, organizations in climate. Similarly, just as certain personality types are better suited for some jobs, certain climates foster certain behaviors. Together, these four constructs define an organization's social system; they are intangible but potent determiners of behavior.

# PERSON-ENVIRONMENT CONGRUENCE

Almost all I/O psychology can be viewed as the interrelationship between people and work. Not all jobs are the same, as major differences exist in tasks, responsibilities, and working conditions. I/O psychologists try to get a good match or "fit" between people and jobs, believing that all people are not equally suited for all jobs. We go about this in several ways. In personnel selection and placement, we assume the job is fixed or constant. We try to identify (e.g., select and place) individuals who can best meet the demands of the job. In personnel training, we try to improve the

fit by upgrading the skills of individuals to better match the job requirements. We can also go about this process in reverse. As we will discuss
later, we can assume the people are fixed. Our goal is then to restructure
work to match the talents of the people. In short, we try to either find (or
shape) "pegs" (people) to fit existing "holes" (jobs), or we try to reshape
the holes to fit existing pegs. This matching process is called *person-environment congruence* (or fit).

There are several approaches to what makes a good fit between people
and environments. Pervin (1968) proposed that some environments more
or less match the individual's personality. A match of individuals and environments is reflected in high performance, satisfaction, and little stress.
Lack of fit results in decreased performance, dissatisfaction, and stress in
the system. Pervin reviewed psychological research in many areas to substantiate the importance of person-environment congruence for individual
performance and satisfaction. One study found that students who were not
very sociable performed better in lecture sections, while more sociable students performed better in leaderless discussion groups. The significance of
person-environment congruence is very evident in the academic performance and satisfaction of college students. Rather than speaking of bright
or dull students and good or bad colleges, it is more fruitful to focus on the
relationship between students, curricula, and schools. The key is the interaction of the person and the environment, not one factor or the other.
Research has shown that students who had authoritarian personalities had
a very high drop-out rate from colleges with a "liberal" attitude toward
education. Those students complained about the college permitting smoking in class, not requiring attendance, and expecting students to answer
their own questions. The converse has also been found to be true. Students
with highly flexible personalities dropped out of colleges whose policies
were seen to be "repressive," i.e., many required courses and required
attendance in class. According to Pervin, then, it is the personality of the
individual that determines the degree of fit with various environments.

O'Reilly (1977) conducted a laboratory study showing that certain types
of people perform better in certain types of environments. He identified
two types of people based on personality. One wanted a sense of achievement and personal growth in work; the other was more concerned with job
security and financial reward. Two types of work tasks were created, one
challenging, the other not. O'Reilly found that those wanting a sense of
achievement and personal growth were far more satisfied with the challenging task. Those seeking job security were more satisfied in the less
challenging task. Similar to Pervin, O'Reilly found that satisfaction with an
environment (in this case, type of task) was influenced by the congruence
between the individual's personality and that environment.

**Vocational choice.**    John Holland is a leading proponent of the importance of person-environment congruence. Holland (1973) developed a theory of vocational choice based on the match between people (as measured

by their interests and aspirations) and vocations (as measured by the types of activities performed). He proposed a scheme for classifying people according to their interests. Six categories, labeled Realistic, Investigative, Artistic, Social, Enterprising, and Conventional are used. Each type has different interests and preferences. For example, an Investigative *person* enjoys solving problems, the challenge of ambiguous situations, and so on. A Social *person* is one who especially enjoys interacting with other people, being in a position where interpersonal relations are important, etc. Holland developed several scales which were found to be reliable in classifying people in these six categories.

Holland also proposed that environments (e.g., vocations) can be classified on the basis of the tasks and activities performed. He uses the same terms to classify vocations. For example, an Investigative type *vocation* is one where tasks and activities are conducted to answer certain unknown questions. The jobs of a scientist and of a newspaper reporter would be classified as Investigative vocations. A Social type *vocation* would be one where tasks and activities are performed primarily involving relationships with other people. The jobs of social welfare worker and receptionist would be classified in the Social vocation. Holland has developed a scale which has been found to be reliable in classifying jobs according to their underlying vocational type.

Holland's thesis is that people will be happier, more productive, have longer tenure, etc., if there is a good fit between their interests and the requirements of their vocation. In short, Holland advises Social people to pursue Social vocations, Enterprising people to pursue Enterprising vocations, and so on for the other four categories. There is quite compelling evidence to support his theory. Mount and Muchinsky (1978) measured satisfaction of people with jobs congruent with their interests (e.g., Realistic-Realistic) or incongruent with their interests (e.g., Realistic-Artistic). As Holland's theory predicted, those in vocations that were congruent with their interests were much more satisfied with their work than people who were "mismatched", i.e., in vocations that were incongruent with their interests. Another criterion variable predicted by person-environment fit is turnover. Using Holland's general theory, Vaitenas and Wiener (1977) discovered that a sample of mid-life career changers were mismatched with their jobs as indexed by developmental, emotional, and interest variables. In summary, studies supporting Holland's theory are strong evidence for the significance of person-environment congruence.

**Life experience theory.** Another approach to person-environment congruence is the research of Owens. Owens studied early life experiences involving such factors as relationships with parents, interest and performance in school, relationships with members of the opposite sex, involvement in athletics, and many more. He grouped those people with similar life history experiences. He discovered that some 15 factors could be used to classify people. Owens then examined how these different groups of people performed in a wide variety of activities, such as academic performance, selection of a major, participation in civic affairs, etc. Owens and Schoenfeldt (1979) presented extensive data indicating that different types (based on early life history experiences) do indeed engage in, and succeed at, a wide variety of different activities. For example, Owens identified the "types" likely to flunk out of college, chronically switch majors, and have adjustment problems. His data provide a basis for identifying these types when they arrive on campus as freshmen. They also make it possible to give special guidance and counseling to those who will probably have difficulties.

A graphic portrayal of Owens' approach is presented in Figure 8–3. Owens (1976) described how his model works as follows: The circle at the left represents a large sample of people, as all the freshmen at a given university. These people are first administered a comprehensive life history questionnaire designed to cover the salient dimensions of their prior life experiences. On the basis of their responses, they are put in subgroups

**Figure 8–3**      **A conceptual model for life history research**

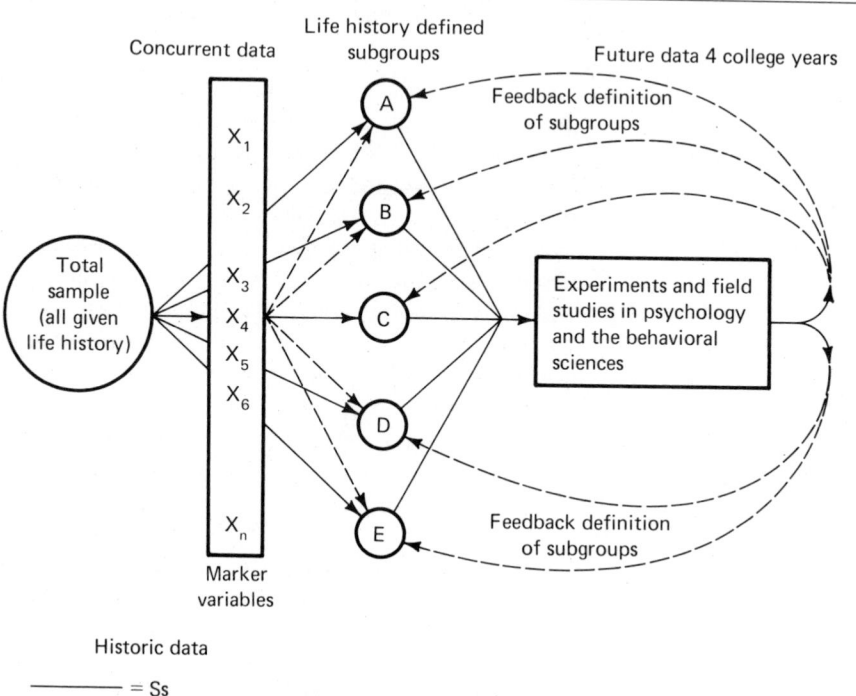

SOURCE: William A. Owens, Figure 3. A conceptual model for life history research, "Background Data," in Marvin D. Dunnette (ed.) *Handbook of Industrial and Organizational Psychology* (Chicago: Rand McNally, 1976). By permission of the editor.

representing similar patterns of prior experience. These subgroups are the smaller circles lettered $A$ through $E$. The tendency of those in each subgroup to behave similarly is measured in several ways. First, the letters $X_1$ to $X_n$ are reference variable tests useful in characterizing the subgroups. Distinctiveness of subgroup behavior is initially looked at in terms of the different scores on these reference measures (such as personality inventories). Second, the college career of these individuals may be regarded as a series of field studies in which different behavior of the subgroups is revealed and evaluated. Differences may be expected in academic achievement, major chosen, activities selected, etc. Finally, feedback is collected and summarized by subgroups. This feedback is given to those entering the university with the same characteristics as their predecessors. Thus, Owens has found a way of identifying, for example, those who will incur academic difficulties and may recommend special advising to them when they start college. This approach has also been useful for identifying those who will later have various types of employment problems.

The basis for person-environment fit in Owens' model is the consistent similarity of people given their life experiences and the recommended assignment of these people to various "environments."

As with all such classification schemes, we must be successful in measuring people and in measuring environments. Once we have these measurements, we can recommend strategies for matching the two. For the most part, we have been more successful in measuring differences in people than in environments. If efforts to obtain person-environment fit continue, we must become more skilled in measuring environmental differences.

"Environment" inevitably refers to some aspect of an organization. Organizations are complex. Our knowledge of organizational differences is not nearly as thorough as our knowledge of personal differences. Over time, we will become more successful in person-environment fit as we learn more about organizations. We do know some of the consequences of a "good" or "bad" fit between people and organizations. We will now look at how individuals respond to organizational environments.

## INDIVIDUAL RESPONSES TO PERSON-ENVIRONMENT INTERACTIONS

In organizations, two major forces are at work. One has to do with the individual. This includes personal factors (e.g., age, sex, race), abilities, knowledges, skills, interests, and personality. These are all the things a person brings to the organization. The second major force has to do with the organization. It includes organizational factors (e.g. location, size, technology), task and job demands, role expectations, norms, and climate. An individual will have to adjust to these factors if he or she accepts a job with the organization. There are a number of employee responses to this interface of individual and organization. We can think of them as reactions to the organization. They are not inherent in the individual or the organization, but emerge from the interaction. These emergent responses have been widely studied because they influence a variety of criterion variables that are important to the organization, such as productivity, absenteeism, turnover, and satisfaction.

## Stress

For many years, stress was studied mainly by medical researchers interested in physiological measures. Recently, however, stress has become of particular interest to I/O psychologists. We are just beginning to understand its effect on work behavior. Stress is difficult to define—it is not strictly an independent, dependent, or intervening variable. Rather, it is a collective term denoting demands which "tax" a system (physiological, social, or psychological) and the responses of that system. Job stress involves complicated interactions between the person and the environment, particularly as they occur over time. Beehr and Newman (1978) provide the following definition: "job stress refers to a situation wherein job-related factors interact with a worker to change (i.e., disrupt or enhance) his or her psychological and/or physiological condition such that the person (i.e., mindbody) is forced to deviate from normal functioning" (pp. 669–670).

These authors developed a detailed set of the major dimensions or *facets* of job stress. These facets are all valid areas of research in job stress; they underscore the breadth and complexity of the area. The authors listed seven facets (summarized below) and developed a model of the interrelationships among them.

**1. Environmental facet.** This includes job demands and characteristics (pace of work, responsibility), role demands and expectations, organizational characteristics (job security, hours of work), and external demands and conditions (laws and regulations).

**2. Personal facet.** Psychological conditions (personality traits, behavioral characteristics), physical condition (eating habits), life-stage characteristics (family and career stages), and demographics (education, race, age) are included here.

**3. Process facet.** This refers to how an individual adjusts to stress either psychologically or physically.

**4. Human consequences facet.** The psychological (anxiety, tension, depression, fatigue), physical (heart attacks, cancer, arthritis, death), and behavioral (drug abuse, aggression, vandalism, attempted suicide) consequences are involved here.

**5. Organizational consequences facet.** This involves how employee stress affects the organization. It includes changes in job performance, profits or sales, strikes, and grievances.

**6. Adaptive response facet.** This refers to how the individual and the organization can cope with stress. Individual responses include religious activity, biofeedback techniques, physical activity, and getting more rest.

**Figure 8–4**          **A general model of job stress**

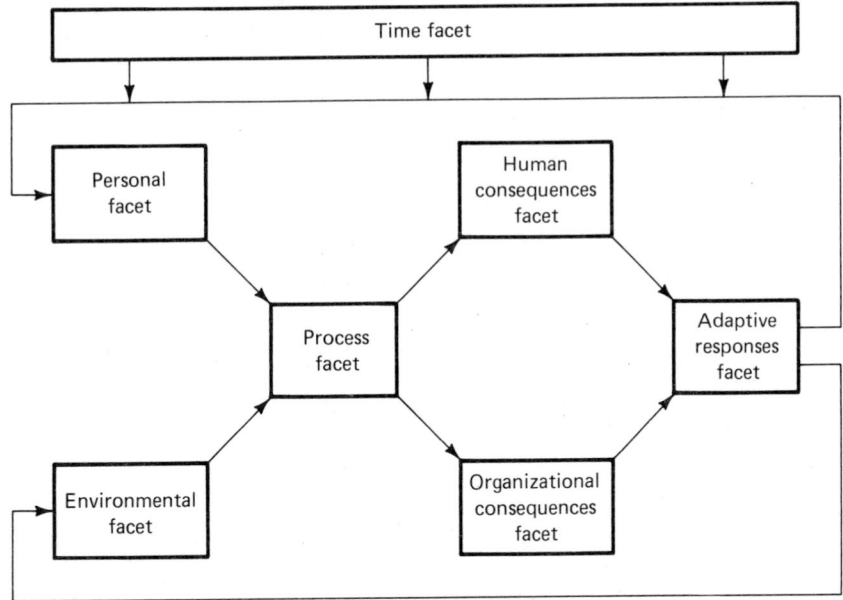

SOURCE: T. A. Beehr and J. E. Newman, "Job Stress, Employee Health, and Organizational Effectiveness: A Facet Analysis, Model, and Literature Review," *Personnel Psychology* 31 (1978), pp. 665–99.

Adaptive responses of the organization include redesigning jobs, changing work schedules, changing evaluation and reward systems, and providing counseling and social support services to employees.

**7. Time facet.** This involves time as a variable in the development of and response to stress.

Figure 8–4 shows the relationship among these facets proposed by Beehr and Newman (1978). As shown, the personal and environmental facets interact through the process facet to produce human and organizational consequences. Adaptation (reducing undesirable effects of stress) begins. The adaptive responses may, in turn, affect the personal and environmental facets. There are a variety of adaptive responses to job stress, but we know little about their effectiveness (Newman & Beehr, 1979). Newman and Beehr (1979) feel that I/O psychologists should further study stress and ways of coping with it. Job stress may be thought of as a result of trying to force "a round peg in a square hole." The peg won't fit, and the hole (environment) puts pressure on the peg (person)—a typical poor fit.

**Role problems**

Beehr and Newman (1978) listed three role problems contributing to the environmental facet of stress. We will examine each in some detail.

**Role ambiguity.** This refers to the difference between what people expect of us on the job and what we feel we should do. This causes uncertainty about what our role should be. There can be three reasons for this. One is that the employee doesn't understand what is expected. Second, the employee may not know how to meet expectations. (It is one thing for a salesperson to know annual sales volume should be $1 million; it is another thing to know how to do it.) Finally, an employee may think the job should be different.

Role ambiguity can cause significant problems on the job. It is related to stress, tension, and lower satisfaction. Medical data reveal that ambiguity may increase heart problems and lead to anxiety and depression. However, the effects of role ambiguity are not uniform, and role ambiguity seems to be more of a problem at higher organizational levels. Schuler (1975) reported that it was more strongly correlated with job satisfaction $(r = -.43)$ for upper-level employees than for lower-level employees $(r = -.23)$. Schuler (1977a) also found that employees with high ability coped better with role ambiguity. Finally, Schuler (1977b) reported that organization structure can interact with task duties to produce role ambiguity. He found that ambiguity was less when *simple tasks* were to be performed in an organization with very formalized rules and procedures, little intergroup communication, and strict adherence to the chain of command. This was compared to *complex tasks* performed in the same type of organization. Less role ambiguity was found when *complex tasks* were performed in an organization with low formalization of rules, high intergroup communication, and low adherence to the chain of command. Schuler (1977b) discussed the importance of congruence or fit between task complexity and organization structure in reducing role ambiguity. In this case, fit between two aspects of the organization (technological complexity and structure) can benefit the employee.

**Role conflict.**    When two or more pressures occur together so that complying with one would make doing the other more difficult, role conflict arises (Kahn, Wolfe, Quinn, Snoek, & Rosenthal, 1964). There are a variety of causes. It may be a function of conflicting messages (e.g., "I need this report finished by tomorrow and I want it done well"). The conflict is between the deadline and the request for high-quality work. Role conflict can also occur with promotion. A new manager may feel a conflict between new responsibilities and loyalty to former co-workers. For some women, there may be role conflict between the demand of home and job. An individual's personal values and beliefs may clash with role requirements. A used-car salesman may be torn between telling the truth about a car and trying to make a sale.

The effect of role conflict on employee attitudes and behavior has been studied. Rizzo, House, and Lirtzman (1970), and House and Rizzo (1972) studied the relationship between role conflict and job satisfaction, turnover, anxiety, and perceived threat. However, the results are not simple or clear-cut. Role conflict produces job dissatisfaction. But the strength of

Some people earn a living by mastering role overload.

*Circus World Museum—Baraboo, Wisconsin*

the relationship is affected by the employee's position. Role conflict is more strongly related to dissatisfaction for lower-level jobs, the reverse of the findings for role ambiguity (Hamner & Tosi, 1974). Keller (1975) found that role conflict was more strongly related to dissatisfaction with the boss; role ambiguity was more strongly related to dissatisfaction with the work itself. There is also evidence that role conflict diminishes performance. Szilagyi, Sims, and Keller (1976) found that role conflict was significantly related to poor performance among professional, technical, and clerical employees in a large medical center.

The effect of level is particularly interesting. Upper-level employees seem better able to cope with role conflict (vis-à-vis feelings of job satisfaction).

Perhaps upper-level employees expect conflicting demands as part of the price they pay for the job. Lower-level employees are more negative because they may feel role conflict is not a valid part of the job. In any case, there are no documented *benefits* of either role conflict or role ambiguity.

**Role overload.**   This occurs when a job's expectations and demands exceed the employee's ability. Overload is often seen with roles that are also ambiguous. Because expectations are unclear, demands made on the individual increase. Empirical evidence indicates that role overload takes its toll particularly in physiological response. Caplan (1971) measured overload objectively (number of telephone calls, interruptions) and subjectively (by questionnaire). He found both measures related to heart rate and cholesterol level (a correlate of heart attacks) among employees of a government agency. Cobb (1973) studied the effects of two types of role overload with employees responsible for people or for things. He found both types were associated with cigarette smoking. Responsibility for others was associated with high blood pressure and cholesterol level. Cobb also identified a pattern with those responsible for others and the occurrence of ulcers and heart attacks.

We know less about role overload than either ambiguity or conflict. It seems that role overload is internalized and has physiological effects. There are also no known benefits of role overload. As Beehr and Newman (1978) have stated, it's time that I/O psychologists worked jointly with organizational theorists and the medical profession to design work in a way that will not be so stressful.

## Morale

Morale loosely refers to "group spirit" and has been most commonly used in time of war. However, morale is not limited just to the military. It has also been used in athletics (e.g., the morale of a football team) and in industry, where it has long been thought vital to meeting organization goals. Blum and Naylor (1968) define morale as follows: "The possession of a feeling, on the part of the employee, of being accepted and belonging to a group of employees through adherence to common goals and confidence in the desirability of these goals" (p. 391). This definition stresses (1) feeling accepted by the work group; (2) sharing common goals, and (3) feeling these goals are desirable.

In an industrial organization, there are many work groups employees could use as a point of reference to assess morale. An employee might be part of a work team that is part of a larger group, like a department. Various departments comprise a division, and all divisions then constitute the organization. Various levels of morale might exist in each of these groups. Morale may be high in a work team where all members pursue a common goal. Yet there could be dissension between departments as different goals are pursued. Feelings of belongingness could be high within the work team but low within the division.

Morale is different from satisfaction, though the two concepts are often confused. Satisfaction is the attitudes of an *individual* toward job-related factors, while morale is the combined attitudes of all work-group members. Morale is generated by the group, reflects group unity, and can best be viewed as a by-product of person-environment interaction.

Guion (1958) feels that with high morale, there is little aggression or frustration-induced conflict, the work force is euphoric, and well-adjusted employees have become ego-involved in their work. Stagner (1958) expands this view saying morale is high when each member of the work group sees his or her own goals as contiguous with group goals. Morale can be measured by questionnaires and surveys. It can also be assessed less obtrusively (though less precisely). When members use terms like "we," "us," and "the group," there is cohesiveness. It is this process that transforms isolated individuals into a single unit. Morale is a product of this coalition formation. There are four major determinants of morale, though all four don't have to be present. The strongest is a "feeling of togetherness" or group cooperation. The second is agreement on goals. Third, there must be progress toward the goal. Finally, each member should have a specific, meaningful task that is necessary for goal achievement.

Depending on the organization, morale can support or detract from larger organization goals. In an industrial context, high morale can aid in pursuing productivity or effectiveness goals. However, there can also be group support for a strike. In this case, management might try to break group spirit. Management of prisons and prisoner-of-war camps may try to break morale if they perceive the group's goal to be an escape attempt. If the group's goals coincide with the organization's goals, morale is a virtue the organization nurtures. When the goals conflict, attempts can be made to weaken morale.

Motowidlo and Borman (1977) developed eight behaviorally anchored rating scales to assess morale in the military. The scales involved such aspects as community relations, teamwork and cooperation, performance and effort on the job, and pride in the unit, army, and country. Using standard scale-construction techniques, nine-point scales were developed. Sample items from one scale are shown in Table 8–2.

| Table 8–2 | **Sample items from one Motowidlo and Borman morale scale (performance and effort)** | |
|---|---|---|
| | Item | Scale value |
| | While clearing the brush from an approach to an airport, these dozer operators never shut the dozer off, running in shifts right through lunch. | 8 |
| | Many troops in this unit would leave the post as quickly as possible after duty hours to avoid doing any extra work. | 4 |
| | The men in this section signed out weapons to be cleaned but sat around and shot the bull until it was time to turn the weapons back in. | 2 |

SOURCE: S. J. Motowidlo and W. C. Borman, "Behaviorally Anchored Scales for Measuring Morale in Military Units," *Journal of Applied Psychology* 62 (1977), pp. 177–83.

*Interrater* reliability coefficients for the eight scales ranged from .34 to .70. Reliability of the performance and effort scale was .54. Overall reliability for the entire set was a correlation of .72. Given the difficulty of getting raters to agree, .72 is a fairly high degree of interrater reliability. When scores on these morale scales were correlated with criterion variables, results were encouraging. Morale correlated $-.48$ with reported dissent among the soldiers, $-.47$ with drug abuse, $-.68$ with attempts at destruction and sabotage, and .87 with unit effectiveness. In short, the morale scale appears reliable and *construct valid.*

Motowidlo and Borman (1978) also investigated the relationship between morale in two military units (platoon and company) and various indexes of effectiveness. They found platoon morale significantly correlated with individual satisfaction with aspects of military life. Soldiers were more satisfied with the army as a whole when morale within their platoon was high. The morale of entire companies (i.e., larger military units) was related to the number of reenlistments $(r = .53)$ and the number of congressional inquiries of complaints from individual soldiers $(r = -.44)$. There were more reenlistments and fewer inquiries in companies with high morale. The studies provide some firm evidence that morale is related to individual attitudes as well as to the effectiveness of organization subunits.

## Job involvement

Job involvement is the extent that individuals are ego-involved in their work, though there appears to be more here than just ego-involvement. Lodahl and Kejner (1965) define job involvement as "the degree to which a person is identified psychologically with his work, or the importance of work in his total self-image" (p. 24). They also say that involvement is internalizing values about the goodness of work or the importance of work in the worth of the person. There is some confusion over whether job involvement is a product of person-environment interaction or is simply an individual personality variable (Rabinowitz & Hall, 1977). However, most research indicates that job involvement can be altered by the work environment, thus supporting the notion that it is a product of person-environment interface.

Job involvement was found to be related to three sets of variables: demographic, situational, and work outcome. Saal (1978) has shown that job involvement is positively correlated with age and endorsement of the protestant work ethic (i.e., the belief that hard work is itself rewarding). Involvement is also related to job characteristics. Workers who have a greater variety of tasks, feel a sense of autonomy on the job, and deal with other people at work are more job-involved. Finally, involvement is consistently related to various types of job satisfaction, particularly satisfaction with work itself $(r = .52)$. That is, employees who really like what they do are more job involved. Job involvement is negatively related to absenteeism. Curiously, there is no relationship between job involvement and productivity. Workers who are not job involved are no less productive than workers who

| Table 8–3 | **Sample items from the Lodahl and Kejner job involvement questionnaire** |
|---|---|

I'll stay overtime to finish a job even if I'm not paid to do it.

For me, mornings at work really fly by.

Sometimes I lay awake at night thinking ahead to the next day's work.

SOURCE: T. M. Lodahl and M. Kejner, "The Definition and Measurement of Job Involvement," *Journal of Applied Psychology* 49 (1965), pp. 24–33.

are. The results of the Saal (1978) study are representative of all the research done on job involvement.

Lodahl and Kejner (1965) developed a 20-item questionnaire to measure job involvement. Several items from it are presented in Table 8–3. People respond to these items by indicating their degree of agreement with each statement. The internal consistency reliability of the questionnaire has been measured with several samples of employees, and an average reliability coefficient is around .80. This is adequate, but it appears some items assess aspects of job involvement that are not as clearly central to the concept as others.

While we are quite certain of the relationship between job involvement and several other variables, most of the variance in job involvement remains unexplained. People certainly do differ in how involved they are, but we don't really know *why* such differences exist. More work remains to be done on the *process* that generates involvement. Is some degree of job involvement necessary or desirable in all workers? Do certain jobs inspire more involvement than others? Can people be too involved for their own good? Perhaps workaholics, people who live only to work, suffer from too much involvement. Answers to these questions await further research.

If organizations want to employ highly involved people and job involvement is strictly an individual variable, then the issue is one of personnel selection. Organizations would use a job-involvement questionnaire and hire those who score high. However, if organizations can "do" something to make employees more involved (as the job characteristics correlates of involvement suggest), then the issue also becomes one of job design. Work should be designed in such a way as to facilitate feelings of job involvement.

Given our current level of knowledge, we must answer many questions before we can implement policies (regarding personnel selection and/or work redesign) to increase job involvement. Furthermore, we must know whether there is an upper limit—where too much involvement can have negative consequences.

## Organizational commitment

Organizational commitment is "the relative strength of an individual's identification with and involvement in a particular organization" (Steers, 1977, p. 46). It is characterized by: (1) strong belief in and acceptance of the organization's goals and values; (2) willingness to exert effort for the organization; and (3) desire to maintain membership in the organization (Porter, Steers, Mowday, & Boulian, 1974). Organizational commitment has both antecedent causes and consequences (as shown in Figure 8–5). Steers (1977) proposed three sets of antecedents: personal characteristics, job characteristics, and work experiences. Personal characteristics include age and education. Job characteristics involve challenge, opportunities for social interaction, and the amount of feedback provided on the job. Finally, work experiences include such factors as attitudes toward the organization, organization dependability, and the realization of expectations within the organization.

Steers tested the *antecedents* of organizational commitment with a sample of hospital employees. He used multiple regression analysis to assess the predictive power of each variable within each of the three antecedents. He obtained multiple correlations ($R$) of: personal characteristics (.55); job characteristics (.64); and work experience (.71). When the three sets were combined in a multiple regression analysis to collectively predict organizational commitment, the multiple correlation ($R$) was .81. If we square this, we get $R^2 = .65$, meaning that 65 percent of the variance in commitment is explained by the three types of predictor variables. This is most impressive. It indicates that we know more about organizational commitment than job involvement.

Steers tested the *consequences* by correlating commitment with a variety of outcome variables—attendance, performance, etc. With the same sample of hospital employees, Steers found that commitment correlated most strongly with three variables: desire to remain with the organization ($r = .44$), intent to remain with the organization ($r = .31$), and turnover ($r =$

**Figure 8–5**     **Hypothesized antecedents and outcomes of organizational commitment**

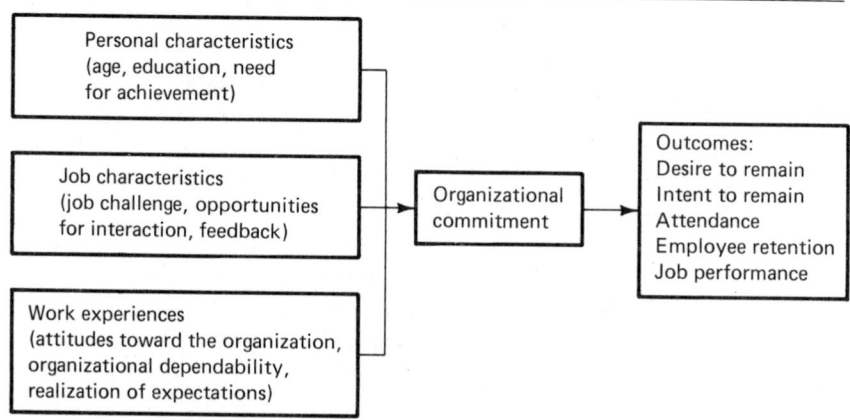

SOURCE: R. M. Steers, "Antecedents and Outcomes of Organizational Commitment," *Administrative Science Quarterly* 22 (1977), pp. 46–56. Reprinted by permission of *The Administrative Science Quarterly*.

**Table 8–4**          **Sample items from the Mowday et al. organizational commitment questionnaire**

I am proud to tell others that I am a part of this organization.

I really care about the fate of this organization.

I am willing to put in a great deal of effort beyond that normally expected to help this organization succeed.

SOURCE: R. T. Mowday, R. M. Steers, and L. W. Porter, "The Measurement of Organizational Commitment," *Journal of Vocational Behavior* 14 (1979), pp. 224–47.

.17). Like job involvement, organizational commitment was not related to any measures of productivity. In general, we know more about the antecedents of organizational commitment than we know about its consequences.

Mowday, Steers, and Porter (1979) developed a questionnaire measuring organizational commitment. It consisted of 15 items, with responses indicating degree of agreement. Table 8–4 contains three items from the questionnaire.

Internal consistency reliability of the questionnaire was very high; the average figure was around .90. Mowday et al. also correlated scores on the questionnaire with selected outcome variables. The results indicated that organizational commitment correlated with intent to leave the organization at −.45, and with intended length of service at .51. These results, in part, suggest that the questionnaire had an acceptable degree of construct validity and that organizational commitment appears to be a useful concept for organization research.

As with job involvement, we have more to learn about organizational commitment. What can an organization do to increase commitment? Can a person be overcommitted? Would an overly committed person refuse to retire? What is the conceptual relationship between job involvement and organizational commitment? (Empirically they correlate around .50.) What is a person "like" if committed to the organization but not involved in the job? Conversely, what is a person "like" if deeply involved in the job but not committed to the organization? Answers to these questions await further research.

**Self-esteem**

Korman (1970) proposed a theory of work behavior based on *self-esteem*. Self-esteem is the extent that a person sees himself or herself as competent and need satisfying. People with high self-esteem feel good about themselves, feel they are competent, and anticipate success. People with low self-esteem are the opposite. According to Korman (1970), there are three sources of self-esteem. The first, *chronic* self-esteem, is a persistent personality trait relatively consistent across situations. Second, there is *task-specific* self-esteem. This is an individual's feeling of competence in a particular task. It is likely a function of past experience with the same or similar tasks. Third is *socially influenced* self-esteem. This is a function of other's expectations. When others expect a person to perform well and communicate this, feelings of competence will increase. For the purposes of our person-environment analysis, we will focus on the last two types of self-esteem.

Korman's theory presents some interesting ideas about job performance. It suggests that there are hints of self-fulfilling prophesy in job performance. People who think they will fail and believe others think they will fail, will, according to the theory, indeed do poorly. The opposite is also true. Korman suggests that a reason some minority group employees perform poorly is that they were socialized to fail and believe the organization expects them to. If this is valid, then the organization's role in aiding job performance is very important. If the organization can convey expectations of success, the pattern of "failure begets failure" may be broken.

There have been many tests of Korman's theory, particularly as it relates to employee satisfaction and performance. Many of the studies are laboratory experiments. The subjects are led to believe by the experimenter that they are expected to do well or poorly on a task used in the experiment. The results of such studies (e.g., Greenhaus & Badin, 1974) indicate that the expectations of the environment (i.e., the experimenter) do indeed affect how well people will do on the job. One of the problems with the theory however, is that a portion of one's self-esteem (chronic self-esteem) cannot be changed; it is seen as an enduring personality trait. The organization only has the capacity to influence task-specific and social self-esteem. A crucial issue is, which of the three types of self-esteem is most dominant or important? Research indicates that the sources of self-esteem vary in importance for different people. Organizations will be most successful in inducing effective job performance among those not dominated by chronic self-esteem. The most successful people should, in theory, be those with high chronic self-esteem who are made to feel high task-specific and social self-esteem by the organization. The implications of Korman's theory are that through carefully developed personnel selection and training programs, an organization can be staffed with employees high in self-esteem who will be effective on the job.

Dipboye (1977) criticized Korman's theory because there are other explanations for why those low in self-esteem behave as they do. Specifically, Dipboye believes that people with low self-esteem are used to failure and will not put out much effort so that expected future failures are easier to accept. A person who fails because of a lack of effort can rationalize the failure more readily than a person who tries very hard and still fails. While Korman (1977) did not agree with Dipboye's criticisms regarding the causal basis of why low self-esteem produces the behavior it does, it is evident that self-esteem does play a role in a person's job performance. To the extent that an organization can influence an individual's expectations of performance, and that expectations do affect performance, self-esteem is another aspect of person-environment interface that warrants our attention.

**Overview of individual responses to person-environment interactions**

In this section, eight individual responses to person-environment interactions were presented: stress; role ambiguity; role conflict; role overload; morale; job involvement; organizational commitment; and self-esteem. Three (role ambiguity, conflict, and overload) are clearly "bad" for the individual. No benefits have yet been identified with them. Under certain conditions, stress might be beneficial; momentary or temporary stress may motivate a person to better performance. However, repeated stress is clearly unhealthy, as the research of Beehr and Newman (1978) has shown. We can view these four responses as the painful price that some people have to pay for certain person-environment interactions.

The remaining four concepts have no inherent value. Their value (i.e., good or bad for the individual and/or organization) is a function of their level. High morale, job involvement, organizational commitment, and self-esteem appear to be beneficial. Low levels seem harmful. It may also be possible for a person to be too involved or committed. Thus, both very low and very high levels may be harmful. It is also interesting that each of the last four responses is related to a different unit of analysis. Self-esteem, while influenced by environmental factors, is most directly tied to a person's own personality. Job involvement involves a person's feelings for his or her job. Morale is how a person relates to, and feels about, a work group. Finally, organizational commitment is a person's sense of identity with an entire organization.

## SUMMARY

This chapter dealt with organizational influences on behavior. It sought to explain a number of psychological constructs relating to people working in organizations. Organizations are composed of several interacting systems that shape the way people behave and feel. Such things as norms, roles, power, and climate are attributes of organizations, even though they are not concrete. They influence employee conduct in ways which aid organization goal attainment. They stem from organization structure; (e.g., technologies demanding high-quality performance will foster a climate stressing high standards) and personal factors (i.e., individuals will fill specified roles based on their skills and talents).

Person-environment congruence is the match between individuals and organizations. Researchers have proposed that such variables as personality, vocational interests, and life history directly influence the fit between people and organizations. When the fit is good, individuals are more productive, satisfied, and usually don't change jobs. When the fit is not good, dissatisfaction and stress result. To assess the degree of fit, it is necessary to accurately measure both. Research is currently being done on ways of obtaining precise measures of different "pegs" and "holes."

Finally, researchers here identified a number of responses to person-environment interaction. Three involve role (conflict, ambiguity, and overload). Each of these is related to a number of criterion variables. Morale is feelings of group solidarity and is a product of coalition formation. It is predictive of several behavioral variables. Job involvement and organizational commitment relate to attachment to work. There are wide differences among individuals in these factors. At this time, we do not fully understand the relationships between them and other organizational variables. Finally, feelings of self-esteem are influenced by the degree of success people have at work. Self-esteem, like job stress, is an index of the quality of person-environment fit.

This chapter illustrates how organizations can influence individual behavior and attitudes. It sets the stage for later chapters on job satisfaction, motivation, leadership, and communication. Each of these topics is a focal point of person-environment interactions.

# CASE STUDY

Paula Scott was examining the notes she had taken on three applicants for a management position. Paula was a manager herself and had worked her way up from a clerical job. She was the only female manager in a staff of seven and was acutely aware of her gender in her corporate position. Paula was highly respected by her peers, and her boss often praised the quality of her work. She took pride in her work, and she had the satisfaction of knowing she had made it on the basis of competence. Yet, she felt that being a woman had been a handicap to her over the years. She really thought she would have been promoted to her current position sooner if she had been a man. It was tough to break into an all-male management staff, and she questioned whether some of her male colleagues would have endured the same frustrations she had accepted. Paula demanded and got high performance from her staff. Her subordinates regarded her as a no-nonsense type of manager, someone who set high standards for them as well as herself. They admired her tenacity and perseverance in the company. Many felt she was the most talented manager on the staff.

Paula perused her notes. The management staff had interviewed each applicant, and at 3:00 they would meet to make their selection. The person chosen would become the eighth manager on the staff. Two of the candidates were male, the third female. The applicant selected must step in and assume a great deal of responsibility quickly. Paula knew if a bad choice were made, it would only mean more work for her and the other managers. A lot was riding on the decision, and nobody wanted to blow it.

On the basis of the interview and past work experience, Roger Morgan appeared to be the most qualified. Paula was sure the other managers would support him. A close but definite second was Claire Hart. Hart came across very well in the interview, but her academic training wasn't in business even though she had several years of business experience. Finally, Kevin Joyce seemed a distant third. His background training and experience weren't as strong, and his interview performance didn't help his case either.

Paula was torn between Morgan and Hart. Morgan appeared to be the stronger candidate, but his career had been handed to him. He was a business major from an excellent university and had six years of experience in his uncle's company. Hart got her degree in sociology, but she worked her way up to a responsible position after five years with the same company. Paula figured Hart got few breaks along the way, and whatever she got, she undoubtedly earned. Paula saw some of herself in Claire Hart. She would like to have another female manager on the staff since she was tired of being the company token. If the company was going to be more responsive to the talents of women, the candidacy of Claire Hart would be a good test case. Paula believed she and Claire could be two role models for other women in the company.

Yet Roger Morgan was also truly qualified. It shouldn't be held against him that he went to work for a relative. He came very highly recommended, and nothing about his credentials or personal conduct was objectionable. If Paula plugged Hart too strongly, she feared she would lose some of her reputation for being objective and performance-oriented. She could ill afford to lose her credibility by backing Hart primarily because she was a woman. If Hart had been a man, her choice of Morgan would be fairly clear-cut. Yet if she didn't take a stand on Hart, she saw little chance for change.

Paula thought maybe she should support Morgan and secretly hope he wouldn't take the position. Surely they would then offer it to Hart. No, she concluded, that's too much of a gamble. If she wanted Hart to join the company, and she knew she did, she would just have to support her outright from the start.

Questions

1. What is the source of role conflict in this case?
2. Do you think Paula Scott is justified in considering Claire Hart partly on the basis of gender?
3. Do you think she would have given as much thought to Hart's candidacy if Paula weren't the only woman on the management staff?
4. Do you think there is a way for Paula to reduce her role conflict without jeopardizing her personal values and professional integrity?
5. On the basis of the information presented, which candidate would you support for the position?

# REFERENCES

Beehr, T. A., & Newman, J. E. Job stress, employee health, and organizational effectiveness: A facet analysis, model, and literature review. *Personnel Psychology*, 1978, *31*, 665–699.

Blum, M. L., & Naylor, J. C. *Industrial psychology.* New York: Harper & Row, 1968.

Caplan, R. D. Organizational stress and individual strain: A socio-psychological study of risk factors in coronary heart disease among administrators, engineers, and scientists. Unpublished doctoral dissertation. Ann Arbor, Mich.: University of Michigan, 1971.

Cobb, S. Workload and coronary heart disease. *Proceedings of the social statistics section*, American Statistical Association. December 1973.

Dipboye, R. L. A critical review of Korman's self-consistency theory of work motivation and occupational choice. *Organizational Behavior and Human Performance*, 1977, *18*, 108–126.

French, J. R. P., & Raven, B. The bases of social power. In D. Cartwright & A. F. Zander (Eds.), *Group dynamics* (2nd ed.). Evanston, Ill.: Row & Peterson, 1960.

Greenhaus, J., & Badin, I. Self-esteem, performance, and satisfaction: Some tests of a theory. *Journal of Applied Psychology*, 1974, *59*, 722–726.

Guion, R. M. Industrial morale: I. The problem of terminology. *Personnel Psychology*, 1958, *11*, 71–78.

Guion, R. M. A note on organizational climate. *Organizational Behavior and Human Performance*, 1973, *9*, 120–125.

Hamner, W. C., & Tosi, H. L. Relationship of role conflict and role ambiguity to job involvement measures. *Journal of Applied Psychology*, 1974, *59*, 497–499.

Hellriegel, D., & Slocum, J. W. Organizational climate: Measures, research, and contingencies. *Academy of Management Journal*, 1974, *17*, 255–280.

Holland, J. L. *Making vocational choices: A theory of careers.* Englewood Cliffs, N.J.: Prentice-Hall, 1973.

House, R. J., & Rizzo, J. R. Role conflict and ambiguity as critical variables in a model of organizational behavior. *Organizational Behavior and Human Performance*, 1972, *7*, 467–505.

Kahn, R. L., Wolfe, D. M., Quinn, R. P., Snoek, J. D., & Rosenthal, R. A. *Organizational stress: Studies in role conflict and ambiguity.* New York: John Wiley & Sons, 1961.

Katz, D., & Kahn, R. L. *The social psychology of organizations* (2nd ed.). New York: John Wiley & Sons, 1978.

Keller, R. T. Role conflict and ambiguity: Correlates with job satisfaction and values. *Personnel Psychology*, 1975, *28*, 57–64.

Korman, A. Toward a hypothesis of work behavior. *Journal of Applied Psychology*, 1970, *54*, 31–41.

Korman, A. An examination of Dipboye's "A critical review of Korman's self-consistency theory of work motivation and occupational choice." *Organizational Behavior and Human Performance*, 1977, *18*, 127–128.

Lawler, E. E., Hall, D. T., & Oldham, G. R. Organizational climate: Relationship to organizational structure, process, and performance. *Organizational Behavior and Human Performance*, 1974, *11*, 139–155.

Litwin, George H., & Stringer, Robert A., Jr., *Motivation and organizational climate.* Boston: Harvard University Division of Research, Graduate School of Business Administration, 1968

Lodahl, T. M., & Kejner, M. The definition and measurement of job involvement. *Journal of Applied Psychology*, 1965, *49*, 24–33.

Motowidlo, S. J., & Borman, W. C. Behaviorally anchored scales for measuring morale in military units. *Journal of Applied Psychology*, 1977, *62*, 177–183.

Motowidlo, S. J., & Borman, W. C. Relationships between military morale, motivation, satisfaction, and unit effectiveness. *Journal of Applied Psychology*, 1978, *63*, 47–52.

Mount, M. K., & Muchinsky, P. M. Person-environment congruence and employee job satisfaction: A test of Holland's theory. *Journal of Vocational Behavior*, 1978, *13*, 84–100.

Mowday, R. T., Steers, R. M., & Porter, L. W. The measurement of organizational commitment. *Journal of Vocational Behavior*, 1979, *14*, 224–247.

Muchinsky, P. M. An assessment of the Litwin and Stringer organization climate questionnaire: An empirical and theoretical extension of the Sims and LaFollette study. *Personnel Psychology*, 1976, *29*, 371–392.

Naylor, J. C., Pritchard, R. D., & Ilgen, D. R. *A theory of behavior in organizations*. New York: Academic Press, 1980.

Newman, J. E., & Beehr, T. A. Personal and organizational strategies for handling job stress: A review of research and opinion. *Personnel Psychology*, 1979, *32*, 1–43.

O'Reilly, C. A. Personality-job fit: Implications for individual attitudes and performance. *Organizational Behavior and Human Performance*, 1977, *18*, 36–46.

Owens, W. A. Background data. In M. D. Dunnette (Ed.), *Handbook of industrial and organizational psychology*. Skokie, Ill.: Rand McNally, 1976.

Owens, W. A., & Schoenfeldt, L. F. Toward a classification of persons. *Journal of Applied Psychology*, 1979, *65*, 569–607.

Pervin, L. A. Performance and satisfaction as a function of individual-environment fit. *Psychological Bulletin*, 1968, *69*, 56–68.

Porter, L. W., Steers, R. M., Mowday, R. T., & Boulian, P. V. Organizational commitment, job satisfaction, and turnover among psychiatric technicians. *Journal of Applied Psychology*, 1974, *59*, 603–609.

Rabinowitz, S., & Hall, D. T. Organizational research on job involvement. *Psychological Bulletin*, 1977, *84*, 265–288.

Rizzo, J. R., House, R. J., & Lirtzman, S. I. Role conflict and ambiguity in complex organizations. *Administrative Science Quarterly*, 1970, *15*, 150–163.

Saal, F. E. Job involvement: A multivariate approach. *Journal of Applied Psychology*, 1978, *63*, 53–61.

Schneider, B. Organizational climates: An essay. *Personnel Psychology*, 1975, *28*, 447–479.

Schuler, R. S. Role perceptions, satisfaction, and performance: A partial reconciliation. *Journal of Applied Psychology*, 1975, *60*, 683–687.

Schuler, R. S. The effects of role perceptions on employee satisfaction and performance moderated by employee ability. *Organizational Behavior and Human Performance*, 1977, *18*, 98–107. (a)

Schuler, R. S. Role conflict and ambiguity as a function of the task-structure-technology interaction. *Organizational Behavior and Human Performance*, 1977, *20*, 66–74. (b)

Scott, W. G. Organization theory: A reassessment. *Academy of Management Journal*, 1974, *17*, 242–254.

Scott, W. G., Mitchell, T. R., & Birnbaum, P. H. *Organization theory: A structural and behavioral analysis*. Homewood, Ill.: Richard D. Irwin, 1981.

Sims, H. P., & LaFollette, W. R. An assessment of the Litwin and Stringer organization climate questionnaire. *Personnel Psychology*, 1975, *28*, 19–28.

Stagner, R. Industrial morale: II. Motivational aspects of industrial morale. *Personnel Psychology*, 1958, *11*, 64–70.

Steers, R. M. Antecedents and outcomes of organizational commitment. *Administrative Science Quarterly*, 1977, *22*, 46–56.

Szilagyi, A. D., Sims, H. P., & Keller, R. T. Role dynamics, locus of control, and employee attitudes and behavior. *Academy of Management Journal*, 1976, *19*, 259–276.

Vaitenas, R., & Wiener, Y. Developmental, emotional, and interest factors in voluntary mid-career change. *Journal of Vocational Behavior*, 1977, *11*, 291–304.

# chapter 9

# JOB SATISFACTION

Job satisfaction is one of the most researched areas in I/O psychology. Locke (1976) estimated that over 3,000 articles have been written on the topic, and that figure is probably low. Why has the subject aroused so much interest? There are three reasons which, at the risk of over-simplifying, I shall call *cultural*, *functional*, and *historical*. They are implicit rather than explicit because few researchers ever formally state their reasons. However, these reasons can be distilled from the research.

The first is *cultural* in the sense that as a nation, we value individual freedom, personal growth, and "opportunity." Such values stem from formal documents, such as the Bill of Rights, a doctrine which has guided the political and social evolution of this country for over 200 years. The values also flow from the belief that America is the "land of opportunity," as millions of emigrants left their native countries for a chance at a new life style in this country. A work ethic was also developed as part of the fabric of American life style, a work ethic formulated on the "pursuit of happiness" to which work contributes. Thus, concern over whether people like their jobs, their freedom to express feelings, and their freedom to alter their destiny through work are hallmarks of American tradition. We believe implicitly that everyone has a right to a rewarding, satisfying job. I know of *no* Russian studies on job satisfaction. In the Russian culture, feelings about work are not important. In certain European countries, like Germany, Sweden, and Holland, there has been a long-standing concern for industrial democracy in which the feelings of workers are of major importance. However, in some other European countries (deWolff & Shimmin, 1976) and in other parts of the world, interest in the quality of work life is just emerging.

The second reason for interest in job satisfaction is *functional.* The concept of job satisfaction has intrinsic value. But research has shown that satisfaction is also related to other important variables like absence, turnover, and performance. We will examine these relationships in more detail later. Though we don't know if job satisfaction has a *causal* relationship with these variables (e.g., feelings of high job satisfaction will cause a worker to be absent less often from the job), we do know that feelings of high job satisfaction are *associated* with certain levels of these variables. Because we want less absenteeism, less turnover, and better performance, job satisfaction might help in meeting these objectives. Indeed, Mirvis and Lawler (1977) applied cost-accounting procedures to the consequences of employee attitudes. The authors measured the attitudes of bank tellers and their absenteeism, turnover, and performance (as indexed by cash shortages). They again measured these variables later. Results showed that as teller attitudes improved, there were changes in job behavior. The authors calculated how much these changes were worth to the bank in dollars and cents. The results were impressive. For all bank tellers over a one-year period, if their scores on the job satisfaction questionnaire could be elevated by one-half of a standard deviation (through the efforts of the bank to make their work more satisfying), the estimated improvements in performance on the job led to a *direct* saving of $17,664. The potential *total* cost savings (including savings from not having to recruit, hire, and train new employees) came to over $125,000! The results definitely show a functional relationship between increased job satisfaction and improvement in organization effectiveness.

Finally, there is a *historical* basis to job satisfaction research. The Hawthorne Studies began in the 1920s as a study of the effects of work breaks and illumination on productivity. But the emphasis soon shifted to *attitudes.* Research revealed that employees had strong feelings about work. The Hawthorne Studies dramatically shifted the work variables studied by psychologists. Economic and structural variables became less important, and interpersonal and attitude factors were emphasized. A few years after the first report of the Hawthorne Studies was published, the first intensive study of job satisfaction appeared (Hoppock, 1935). He examined the factors contributing to satisfaction on the job (fatigue, working conditions, supervision, and achievement). During World War II, interest in leadership was aroused, and the results of many studies emphasized the importance of satisfaction with a leader. In the late 1950s and early 1960s, attention was given to designing jobs that were more satisfying. This early research was the nucleus for current work on changing the environment (designing jobs) to improve work life.

The cultural, functional, and historical bases of interest in job satisfaction resulted in a vast amount of research. In this chapter, we will examine job satisfaction from many perspectives. These include theories of what makes people satisfied, measuring job satisfaction, and the relationship of job satisfaction to other concepts. It is useful to think of job satisfaction as another example of person-environment congruence (Seybolt, 1976). As we will see, there are differences in people and in jobs (environments) that result in varying degrees of job satisfaction.

## THE CONCEPT OF JOB SATISFACTION

Like any feeling of satisfaction, job satisfaction is an emotional, affective response. *Affect* refers to feelings of liking or disliking. Therefore, job satisfaction is the extent to which a person derives pleasure from a job. Locke (1976) defines it as "a pleasurable or positive emotional state resulting from the appraisal of one's job or job experiences." Job satisfaction is strictly an *individual* response, unlike morale, which is a group response. The morale of a group could be high, while a person in that group could be dissatisfied. The converse could also be true. Similarly, satisfaction is distinct from job involvement. People who are highly involved in their jobs take their work seriously, and their feelings are strongly affected by job experiences. Involved individuals will probably feel very satisfied or dissatisfied with their jobs, depending on their degree of success on the job. Individuals who are not involved will probably experience less extreme responses.

It was initially thought that people would have an overall feeling of liking for a job, ranging from very low to very high. This is known as *global* job satisfaction, and it reflects a general feeling. We later learned that many factors contribute to how a person feels about a job. People can have dif-

**FRANK AND ERNEST**

Reprinted by permission. © 1978 NEA, Inc.

ferent feelings about their co-workers and their pay, and both contribute to overall feelings about a job. Thus, two people could feel the same level of global job satisfaction but for different reasons. One might be very pleased with her co-workers but unhappy with her pay. This would result in "moderate" global job satisfaction. A second person might be moderately pleased with both his co-workers and his pay and thus also have a moderate level of satisfaction.

Psychologists realized that people can feel differently about various aspects of a job, so these feelings are thus masked by assessing only global satisfaction. This led to examining job *facet* satisfaction. This involves measuring how people feel about various parts of a job. As Locke (1976) said: "A job is not an entity but a complex interrelationship of tasks, roles, responsibilities, interactions, incentives, and rewards. Thus a thorough understanding of job attitudes requires that the job be analyzed in terms of its constituent elements" (p. 1301).

What are the facets of a job, and how many are there? There is no one number that holds for all jobs. Jobs differ, and certain facets are more prevalent in some jobs than others. Identifying facets has proceeded along two lines: statistical and conceptual. The *statistical* approach involves analyzing employee responses to job attitude questions (e.g., "How much do you like your boss," "How satisfied are you with your pay," etc.). Responses are intercorrelated, and clusters or factors are created based on similarity of response. These factors thus become the facets of a job as perceived by the employees.

The *conceptual* approach involves specifying the facets to be examined, depending on the research goals. The facets are identified from the researcher's intuition, perhaps from a theoretical perspective.

No matter which method is used, results usually reveal from 5 to 20 facets contributing to satisfaction. Some facets are common to all jobs. Others are job specific. Locke (1976) summarized the facets contributing to employee satisfaction as shown in Table 9–1. The facets shown are fairly common to all jobs. Most employees quickly form impressions about the nature of their work, pay, promotion opportunities, etc. Locke distinguishes Events (conditions at work) and Agents (people). Events are ultimately caused by someone or something, and Agents are liked or disliked because they are seen as doing (or not doing) something. Employees can be satisfied with certain Events (pay) but dissatisfied with certain Agents (supervisors). Similarly, they can be dissatisfied with work (the Event) because their abilities are not fully used (the Agents are themselves). Locke classified the facets into logical groupings, providing an understanding of how and why some facets are liked or disliked.

Since there are many facets to job satisfaction, it seems logical that some facets are more important to an individual than others. For some people, pay may be more important than working conditions. Indeed, Kraut and Ronen (1975) showed systematic differences in the importance of 14 facets

| Table 9-1 | Effects of various events, conditions, and agents on job satisfaction |
|---|---|

| Source | Effect |
|---|---|
| Events or conditions: | |
| Work itself: challenge .............. | Mentally challenging work that the individual can successfully accomplish is satisfying. |
| Work itself: physical demand ........ | Tiring work is dissatisfying. |
| Work itself: personal interest ........ | Personally interesting work is satisfying. |
| Reward structure ................... | Just and informative rewards for performance are satisfying. |
| Working conditions: physical ........ | Satisfaction depends on the match between working conditions and physical needs. |
| Working conditions: goal attainment .......................... | Working conditions that facilitate goal attainment are satisfying. |
| Agents: | |
| Self ............................. | High self-esteem is conducive to job satisfaction. |
| Supervisors, co-workers, subordinates ..................... | Individuals will be satisfied with colleagues who help them attain rewards. |
| | Individuals will be satisfied with colleagues who see things the same way they do. |
| Company and management .......... | Individuals will be satisfied with companies that have policies and procedures designed to help the individual attain rewards. |
| | Individuals will be dissatisfied with conflicting roles and/or ambiguous roles imposed by company and/or management. |
| Fringe benefits ................... | Benefits do not have a strong influence on job satisfaction for most workers. |

SOURCE: Adapted from E. A. Locke, "The Nature and Causes of Job Satisfaction," *Handbook of Industrial and Organizational Psychology*, M. D. Dunnette (Ed.), by F. J. Landy and D. A. Trumbo, *Psychology of Work Behavior*, rev. ed. (Homewood, Ill.: Dorsey Press, 1980).

among samples of salesmen and repairmen in five countries. Importance was quite constant among employees across the five countries.

When psychologists attempt to *weight* facets by degree of importance, the results have generally *not* improved understanding of satisfaction. Several studies (e.g., Ewen, 1967; Mikes & Hulin, 1968) showed that weighting facets by importance to the individual does not improve prediction of certain criterion variables (like turnover) beyond what is attained by weighting all facets equally. The best explanation is that when people rate satisfaction with a single facet, they also indirectly judge its importance (Dachler & Hulin, 1969). Having strong feelings of satisfaction or dissatisfaction indicates that the facet is important enough to feel strongly about it. Conversely, neutral feelings of satisfaction typically mean that the facet really doesn't matter much. Therefore, weighting satisfaction ratings does not add any unique information; thus, it does not improve predictive ability.

## THEORIES OF JOB SATISFACTION

Several theories have been proposed to explain why people are satisfied with their jobs. None of the theories have garnered a great deal of empirical confirmation, which suggests that job satisfaction is a complex phenomenon with many causal bases and that no one theory to date has been successful in incorporating all of the bases into a single theory. As is usually true with multiple theories of a single phenomenon, each theory seems to explain a piece of the puzzle, but a complete understanding is beyond their scope. We will examine four very different approaches to job satisfaction. This is by no means a comprehensive review of all theories, but it will give some insight into the ways in which job satisfaction has been examined. The interested reader can refer to Locke (1976) for a more exhaustive review.

**Comparison processes**

According to McCormick and Ilgen (1980), "the most widely accepted view of job satisfaction assumes that the degree of affect experienced [by a person] results from some comparison between the individual's standard and that individual's perception of the extent to which the standard is met" (p. 306). Degree of satisfaction is the difference between the standard and what is received from the job. *Comparison process* theories compare what a person wants (the standard) with what he or she receives. The less the difference, the greater the feeling of satisfaction.

The standard and how it is derived must be defined. Some researchers believe the standard consists of human *needs*. Needs are inborn, and it is believed that everyone has the same basic needs. Needs are generally classified in two categories: *physical needs* required for bodily functioning (air, water, food); and *psychological needs* required for mental functioning (stimulation, self-esteem, pleasure). A satisfying job would fulfill the basic physiological needs (e.g., adequate income), and provide self-esteem and personal recognition. The research of Schaffer (1953) and Porter (1962) exemplifies the view of job satisfaction as a function of need fulfillment.

Other researchers believe the standard is derived from human *values* not needs. Values are what a person desires, wants, or seeks to attain. They are learned or acquired over time. All people have the same basic needs, but they differ in what they value. Values determine the choices people make as well as their emotional responses to those choices. A satisfying job would then provide an opportunity to attain outcomes that a person values. The research of Locke (1969) and Mobley and Locke (1970) supports this view.

It seems that value-based theories are more flexible than need-based theories. All people have the same needs. It could thus be argued that affective reactions to jobs would be uniform based on how jobs meet constant human needs. Clearly this is not the case. There are great differences in individual satisfaction with the same job. In defense of need theories, it can be argued that people may have the same needs, but they differ in the *strength* of these needs. Thus, a person with a strong need for self-esteem might be dissatisfied with a certain job. Another, with a weaker self-esteem need, might be quite satisfied with the same job. On the other hand, people certainly have different values, which explains differences in job satisfaction. Someone who values monetary rewards and personal challenge would probably not be satisfied with a low-paying, routine job. However, someone who values earning just enough to make ends meet without being mentally taxed might be quite satisfied with such a job.

Comparison process theories are based on the extent to which a job is perceived to meet a person's needs or values. If there is a wide discrepancy between what is needed or desired and what is obtained, job dissatisfaction results. A job could become dissatisfying if the strength of a person's needs were to change or if new values were acquired. To carry the theory to an extreme, if a person worked in a social vacuum (no other people) but needs or values were met, satisfaction would result. This *intra*person comparison process is distinctly different from the next theory of job satisfaction, which involves *inter*personal comparisons.

## Social comparison

The basis of the social comparison theory is the belief that people compare themselves to others in assessing their own feelings of job satisfaction. Rather than a *within* or intraperson comparison (based on needs or values), comparisons are made within a social system, interpersonally. An individual observes others in similar jobs and infers how satisfied they are. The person compares himself or herself to other people and then derives feelings of satisfaction based upon how others feel about their jobs (Salancik & Pfeffer, 1977).

Weiss and Shaw (1979) conducted a study illustrating the influence of individual perceptions of others' satisfaction. They developed a training film showing people working on an electrical assembly. Two types of tasks were shown, one routine and boring, while the other interesting. Throughout the film, actors made comments reflecting negative or positive feelings. Participants in the study then worked on one of the tasks (either the boring or interesting one). They then rated their satisfaction with the task. Results indicated that their feelings were influenced by the reactions of the people performing the same task in the film. Weiss and Shaw (1979) thus suggested that a sense of satisfaction is derived by observing others.

What the social comparison theories of job satisfaction have in common with the need or value-based comparison process theories is the belief that affective feelings about work are comparative. The two sets of theories differ in the basis on which comparisons are made. If a hypothetical individual worked in a social vacuum, social comparison theories would say that he or she couldn't assess job satisfaction.

That social factors influence feelings of satisfaction is intuitively appealing. Certainly a lot of research in social psychology indicates we assess ourselves by our perceptions of others, so it isn't unreasonable to assume that social comparisons operate in job satisfaction.

**Opponent-process theory**

Landy (1978) proposed a radically different job satisfaction theory. He said that the causal basis of satisfaction is physiological, involving the central nervous system. An individual's satisfaction will change over time even though the job remains constant. As an example, a job tends to be more interesting during the first few weeks than it is after several years. This reaction had been simply dismissed as "boredom," but no explanation was provided. Landy suggested that there are mechanisms within individuals that help them maintain emotional equilibrium. Since satisfaction and dissatisfaction are, in part, emotional responses, these mechanisms are thought to play a role in job satisfaction.

*Opponent-process* refers to opposing processes for dealing with emotion. For example, if a person is very happy, there is a physiological response opposing this emotional state and attempting to bring the person back to a neutral level. Extreme emotion (positive or negative) is seen as damaging to individuals. Physiological mechanisms are designed to protect a person from these extreme states. Landy suggests that the reason people differ in job satisfaction is because they differ in terms of the stage of their protective physiological function.

When a stimulus (a job) is introduced, it produces an emotional reaction, either positive or negative. Once the emotion exceeds a certain level, an opponent process automatically brings it under control. When the stimulus disappears (a person stops work for the day), the emotion stops and the opponent process recedes. In theory, each time the protective mechanism is activated, it becomes stronger. Thus, it is more intense in reducing extreme emotion over time. That is, a person becomes more neutral about a job the longer he or she is in it. If Landy's theory is right, we have an explanation for boredom on the job. Many people assume that a job loses its stimulating effect over time, resulting in boredom. Opponent-process theory suggests that the degree of stimulation is unchanged, but the opponent process becomes stronger. Therefore, it is not jobs per se that are boring but people's repeated exposure to the same job which results in a very strong physiological response that prohibits elation or pleasure.

Virtually no data exist on the validity of Landy's theory. The theory offers an explanation for boredom, but it doesn't explain why people become *more* satisfied or dissatisfied (not bored) with their jobs over time.

Also, we know that some people who have been on the same job for a long time are very pleased or displeased. It's too early to judge the theory for explaining job satisfaction. It seems useful in explaining some aspects deficient in explaining others. But this criticism can be leveled at any theory of job satisfaction. Landy's is a fresh approach. It illustrates how I/O psychologists might draw on other sciences to explain phenomena of interest.

## Two-factor theory

No theory has generated as much research and controversy as Herzberg's two-factor theory. Herzberg, Mausner, and Snyderman (1959) originally dealt with job satisfaction among engineers and accountants. They did individual interviews, asking subjects to describe when they felt very good or bad about their jobs. The worker described incidents that led to feelings of satisfaction and dissatisfaction. The interviews were *content analyzed* for common themes or ideas in the responses. This was done to determine (1) what kinds of things were mentioned when people described the times they were very satisfied, (2) what kinds of things were mentioned when people described times they were very dissatisfied and (3) whether what was described in the two circumstances was different.

Results showed that certain factors were associated with high satisfaction, others with dissatisfaction. The authors found that descriptions of good times included such things as achievement, recognition, advancement, and responsibility. All relate to the content of a job, so they were called *content* factors. Descriptions of bad times were characterized by factors dealing with company policy, supervision, salary, and working conditions. These factors all relate to the context of a person's job, and were therefore labeled *context* factors.

Herzberg proposed two classes of work variables: (1) *satisfiers*—content factors that result in satisfaction, and (2) *dissatisfiers*—context factors producing dissatisfaction. Because the theory proposed two general classes of work factors, satisfiers and dissatisfiers, the theory has come to be known as Herzberg's two-factor theory. Herzberg then went on to propose what is perhaps the most controversial aspect of his theory. He said that when a job provides a lot of content factors, i.e., a sense of recognition, achievement, etc., the employee will feel satisfied at work. When these factors are absent from a job, i.e., there is no sense of recognition, advancement, etc., the employee will *not* be dissatisfied but will feel neutral or indifferent. Alternatively, when a job provides a lot of context factors, i.e., a good salary, pleasant working conditions, etc., an employee will *not* feel satisfied but will feel neutral or indifferent toward the job. When these factors are absent from a job, i.e., the salary is poor, working conditions are unpleasant, etc., an employee will feel dissatisfied. Thus, with a high degree of reward *satisfiers* will result in satisfaction, and a low degree of reward will result in indifference. Conversely, with a high degree of reward *dissatisfiers* will result in indifference, and a low degree of reward will result in dissatisfaction. This relationship, which is the most controversial part of Herzberg's theory, is shown graphically in Figure 9–1. Thus according to Herzberg, jobs should be designed so there is a high degree of reward provided by *context* factors (to avoid dissatisfaction) and *content* factors (to ensure satisfaction).

Herzberg's theory has been criticized on two points. The first is the method of data collection. Herzberg assumed that those interviewed could and would accurately report the conditions that make them satisfied or dissatisfied with their jobs. Unfortunately, when a person describes something favorable, there is a tendency to attribute it to the person's own accomplishments (content items). Conversely, in describing an unpleasant experience, a person is more apt to blame others (context items) rather than accept the blame personally. Many critics attribute the "two factors" to this tendency. It means the results are really only artifacts of the method used.

The second major criticism is that many studies failed to replicate Herzberg's findings (e.g., Ewen, 1964; Hinrichs & Mischkind, 1967). Such studies showed that content and context factors both contribute to satisfaction *and* dissatisfaction. If people feel no sense of achievement or recognition, the response is likely dissatisfaction, not indifference. Similarly, people can get pleasure from salary and working conditions. At best, these factors do not have to result in indifference. Thus, the validity of Herzberg's classification is suspect. In summarizing tests of Herzberg's theory, King (1970) found little evidence to support it.

**Figure 9–1**          **Herzberg's effects of content and context factors on job satisfaction**

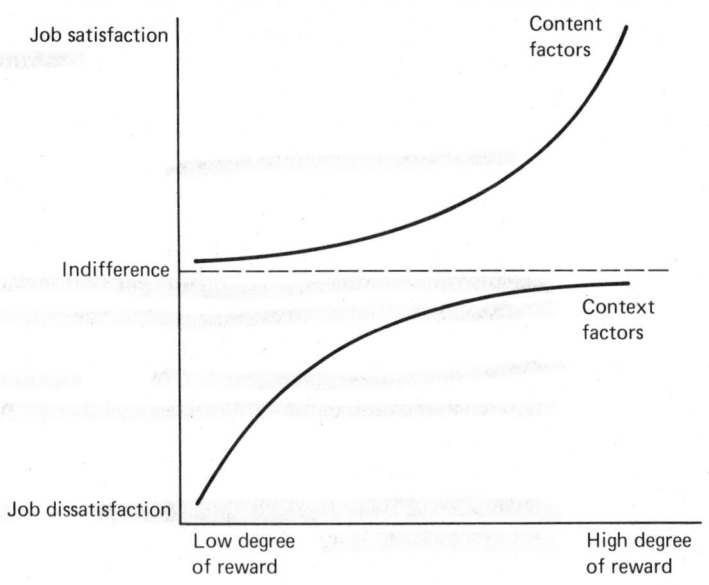

The reaction of I/O psychologists to Herzberg's theory is mixed, but more evaluations are negative. McCormick and Ilgen (1980) strongly reject it: "The two-factor theory no longer deserves consideration" (p. 308). Landy and Trumbo (1980) are more positive: "On the whole, Herzberg has had a positive effect on the research on job satisfaction" (p. 407). The theory is popular among practitioners because it is certainly elegant and straightforward. There are no references to intangible values or needs, no comparative others are needed to explain satisfaction, and certainly there are no references to mysterious functions of the nervous system. According to Herzberg, satisfaction derives from conditions of work. I'm sure that much of the theory's appeal is its simplicity. Unfortunately, however, the theory hasn't received much empirical support.

## REVIEW OF THE FOUR THEORIES OF SATISFACTION

After reading about the four theories, you should have some understanding and appreciation of the approaches to job satisfaction. According to the need- and value-based theories, satisfaction is the extent a job meets needs or fulfills values. It is an individual process. Social comparison theories postulate that satisfaction is derived from a comparison with others in similar jobs. This is a social process. The opponent-process theory indicates satisfaction is physiological. The central nervous system is responsible for satisfaction, particularly with regard to protecting a person from extreme emotions. Finally, with the two-factor theory, the sources of satisfaction are the conditions of work. Content and context factors determine how satisfied a person will be.

The most popular theory of job satisfaction (in terms of the amount of research generated) has been the two-factor theory, though the comparative process theories are currently seen as the most defensible. Each theory has, in its own way, contributed to our understanding of satisfaction. It seems unlikely that researchers will develop *the* theory of job satisfaction. Such a theory would be an integration of the existing theories, each of which explains a portion of job satisfaction.

## THE MEASUREMENT OF JOB SATISFACTION

Surveys have been developed to measure job satisfaction, as they have been developed for other attitudes. Some have been used extensively. Others were developed for a single study. There is nothing "wrong" with each researcher developing a measure, but the measurements must be reliable and valid. However, comparing studies that used different measures may be a problem. Some surveys measure global satisfaction, others facet satisfaction (and not always the same facets). Thus, the literature on job satisfaction is confusing. In recent years, more researchers are using standardized surveys. This permits across-study comparison, which is of value in making generalizations about job satisfaction. Three surveys are particularly popular, and each has been the object of intensive research. We will examine each of them in some detail.

## Job Descriptive Index

The Job Descriptive Index (JDI) developed by Smith, Kendell, and Hulin (1969) is the most often used and most researched measure of job satisfaction. The questionnaire measures five facets: satisfaction with work itself; supervision; pay; promotions; and co-workers. Each facet consists of 9 or 18 items. These are either words ("routine") or short phrases ("gives sense of accomplishment"). The employee indicates whether the item describes the job or not. An employee can also give a response of "uncertain." Each item has a scale value indicating how descriptive it is of a satisfying job. Sample items are given in Table 9–2. Five scale scores are tabulated that reflect satisfaction for each of the facets. The total score on the JDI has also been used to reflect overall job satisfaction.

Research showed the questionnaire to be useful. Smith, Smith, and Rollo (1974) found the JDI measured satisfaction equally well for blacks and whites. The authors also confirmed that it successfully measured different facets of satisfaction. Schneider and Dachler (1978) reported that test-retest reliability of the JDI over a 16-month interval was .57. They felt this was high enough to use the JDI in longitudinal studies, because satisfaction can change over time. McCabe, Dalessio, Briga, and Sasaki (1980) found a Spanish version of the JDI was of comparable quality to the English version. However, Yeager (1981) suggested that the JDI may measure more than five facets. Some of the original scales seem to consist of multiple dimensions. For example, the supervision scale could be broken into satisfaction with the supervisor's ability/performance and interpersonal skills. Nevertheless, the JDI seems to deserve its reputation as the best measure of satisfaction presently available.

**Table 9–2**    **Sample items from the Job Descriptive Index**

Think of your present job. In the blank beside each word or phrase, write
  Y for "yes" if it describes your job
  N for "no" if it does *not* describe your job
  ? if you cannot decide

| Work | Pay | Promotions | Co-workers | Supervision |
|------|-----|------------|------------|-------------|
| __Routine | __Bad | __Dead-end job | __Talk too much | __Up-to-date |
| __Satisfying | __Highly paid | __Promotion on ability | __Ambitious | __Hard to please |
| __Good | __Less than I deserve | __Infrequent promotions | __Lazy | __Asks my advice |
| __On your feet | __Income provides luxuries | __Good chance for promotion | __Loyal | __Around when needed |

SOURCE: P. C. Smith, L. M. Kendall, and C. L. Hulin, *The Measurement of Satisfaction in Work and Retirement* (Skokie, Ill.: Rand McNally, 1969). Copyright © 1975, Bowling Green State University, Department of Psychology, Bowling Green, Ohio, 43403.

## Minnesota Satisfaction Questionnaire

The Minnesota Satisfaction Questionnaire (MSQ) was developed by Weiss, Dawis, England, and Lofquist (1967). It is the second most popular measure of satisfaction. Like the JDI, the MSQ also measures satisfaction with facets of a job. Twenty are included, such as creativity, independence, supervision-human relations, supervision-technical, and working conditions. Each facet is composed of five items. The individual responds on a five-point scale ranging from "very satisfied" (5) to "very dissatisfied" (1). Sample items are presented in Table 9–3.

With 20 scales and 5 items per scale, the MSQ takes more time to com-

| Table 9–3 | Sample items from the Minnesota Satisfaction Questionnaire | | | | | |
|---|---|---|---|---|---|---|
| | | Very dissat-isfied | Dissat-isfied | Neutral | Satis-fied | Very satis-fied |
| | On my present job, this is how I feel about: | | | | | |
| | 1. Being able to keep busy all the time . . . . . . . . . . . | ——— | ——— | ——— | ——— | ——— |
| | 2. The chance to work alone on the job . . . . . . . | ——— | ——— | ——— | ——— | ——— |
| | 3. The chance to do different things from time to time . . . . . . . . . . . . . . . . . | ——— | ——— | ——— | ——— | ——— |
| | 4. The chance to be somebody in the community | ——— | ——— | ——— | ——— | ——— |
| | 5. The way my boss handles his men . . . . . . . . . . | ——— | ——— | ——— | ——— | ——— |
| | 6. The competence of my supervisor making decisions . . . . . . . . . . . . . | ——— | ——— | ——— | ——— | ——— |
| | 7. The way my job provides for steady employment . . . . . . . . . . | ——— | ——— | ——— | ——— | ——— |
| | 8. My pay and the amount of work I do . . . . . . . . . . | ——— | ——— | ——— | ——— | ——— |
| | 9. The chances for advancement on this job . . | ——— | ——— | ——— | ——— | ——— |
| | 10. The working conditions | ——— | ——— | ——— | ——— | ——— |
| | 11. The way my co-workers get along with each other . . . . . . . . . . . . . . . . . | ——— | ——— | ——— | ——— | ——— |
| | 12. The feeling of accomplishment I get from the job . . . . . . . . . . . . . . . . . | ——— | ——— | ——— | ——— | ——— |

SOURCE: D. J. Weiss, R. V. Dawis, G. W. England, and L. H. Lofquist, *Manual for the Minnesota Satisfaction Questionnaire*, Minnesota Studies on Vocational Rehabilitation 22 (Minneapolis: University of Minnesota Industrial Relations Center, Work Adjustment Project, 1967). From *Contemporary Approaches to Interest Measurement,* ed. Donald G. Zytowski (Minneapolis: University of Minnesota Press). Copyright © 1973 by the University of Minnesota.

plete than the JDI. However, research showed that 4 of the MSQ's 20 scales (satisfaction with advancement, compensation, co-workers, and supervision-human relations) correspond roughly to 4 of the 5 scales of the JDI (satisfaction with promotions, pay, co-workers, and supervision, respectively). Gillet and Schwab (1975) administered the MSQ and the JDI to a sample of production workers and intercorrelated the responses. These four pairs of scales seem to measure the same facets. Thus, responses were expected to be similar. Validity coefficients converged in a range from .49 to .70. These coefficients are not very high. They suggest that satisfaction with co-workers, for example, measured by the JDI is not equivalent to the same facet measured by the MSQ. So questionnaires that seem to measure the same dimensions of a job may in fact not have a great deal in common. The study underscores the difficulty of making comparisons based on different measures.

How many facets of job satisfaction a questionnaire should measure is debatable. The JDI measures 5, the MSQ 20. Data clearly indicate that these facets are not independent. As discussed, the number and kind of dimensions should be determined by the issues of interest to the researcher. In both the MSQ and the JDI, two dimensions of satisfaction with supervision are measured. In the MSQ, the two dimensions (satisfaction with the supervisor's human relations and technical abilities) are listed as two separate scales. They were established by the researchers before data were collected. The JDI contains only one satisfaction with supervision scale. However, research (e.g., Yeager, 1981) indicates that this one scale involves two dimensions of leadership. Thus, these dimensions were identified *after* the data were collected and analyzed. Similar conclusions can be drawn about an issue (in this case, satisfaction with supervision) via two different routes. This reflects the differences between the inductive and deductive modes discussed in Chapter 2.

## Faces Scale

The third most common satisfaction measure is the Faces Scale developed by Kunin (1955). This single-item scale is very different from the others. It measures global job satisfaction. And, as opposed to words or phrases, the scale points are drawings of a human face (see Figure 9–2).

Don't think that Kunin simply took a few minutes to sketch some faces. Actually, a series of scale construction procedures were used to create equal scale intervals. The Faces Scale is a good measure of overall satisfaction and is widely applicable. Words are not used, so there is less ambiguity about the meaning of the scale points. The person simply checks the face that reflects how he or she feels about the job in general. Kunin's Faces Scale is applicable for both males and females, though Dunham and Herman (1975) developed a version showing female faces.

Many researchers have used one of the three scales (JDI, MSQ, Faces) to assess job satisfaction. However, as Wanous and Lawler (1972) state,

**Figure 9–2**                        **The Faces Scale of job satisfaction**

**Put a check under the face that expresses how you feel about your job in general, including the work, the pay, the supervision, the opportunities for promotion and the people you work with.**

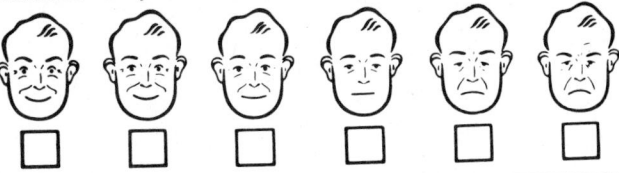

SOURCE: T. Kunin, "The Construction of a New Type of Attitude Measure," *Personnel Psychology* 8 (1955), pp. 65–77.

there is no one best measure of job satisfaction. Certain measures relate more strongly to certain variables than others. Indeed, the research we will review indicates that different facets have differential correlations with various criterion variables. The selection of a satisfaction questionnaire should therefore be guided by two things. First it should provide reliable and valid assessments. Second, it should measure the facets of satisfaction of greatest interest to the researcher.

## RELATIONSHIP BETWEEN JOB SATISFACTION AND PERSONAL VARIABLES

Several studies dealt with the relationship between job satisfaction and such personal variables as age, race, and sex. The results are only moderately consistent. That is, we can't say that males are always found to be more satisfied than females, or whites more than blacks. In one study a given group will be found to be more satisfied than another group, yet these findings may be reversed in another study. However, we will examine some findings in detail and try to explain the results.

**Age**

The results from some studies (e.g., Hulin & Smith, 1965; Gibson & Klein, 1970) suggest that *global* satisfaction increases with age, especially for males. Thus, the most dissatisfied workers are the youngest; the most satisfied are those nearing retirement. Glenn, Taylor, and Weaver (1977) reported similar findings for females.

The relationship between job *facet* satisfaction and age is not so uniform. Hunt and Saul (1975) reported that satisfaction with work, supervision, working conditions, and co-workers increased with age in a sample of males, but the only significant positive relationship for females was for satisfaction with work. Satisfaction with promotion opportunities was negatively related to age for both sexes. There was no relationship between age and satisfaction with pay for males; a negative relationship was found for females. Muchinsky (1978) reported somewhat different results. He found that older employees were least satisfied on four of the five scales of the JDI (supervision, pay, promotions, and co-workers). Both studies did report similar relationships between satisfaction with promotion opportunities and age.

There are several explanations for the relationship between age and job satisfaction. One is that younger, dissatisfied workers eventually quit and find jobs that will satisfy them. Employees who like their jobs remain; hence, the relationship between age and job satisfaction. A second explanation is that growing older promotes satisfaction. Over time, individuals become more realistic about what they can expect from a job, and this maturation results in greater satisfaction. A third explanation is based on the notion of cohorts. Here, cohorts are groups of employees who enter the labor force at the same time. Each succeeding generation of cohorts may be less inclined to enjoy their jobs, perhaps due to a decline in the work ethic or some other change in formative influences. If this is true, there will be a positive relationship between age and satisfaction. Employees don't become more satisfied over time, but rather, there are group differences in satisfaction. Employees in the 50 to 55-year-old cohort, for example, are more satisfied than employees in the 20 to 25-year-old cohort. Longitudinal (as opposed to cross-sectional) analyses would determine which theory is correct. In the cohort explanation, patterns of satisfaction would be stable over time. In the aging explanation, satisfaction should increase. However, aging and cohort effects might also interact to produce feelings of increased satisfaction with age. Whatever the explanation, the empirical results are far more consistent for global than for facet satisfaction.

## Race

Studies comparing racial-group satisfaction have mainly been limited to black-white differences. The results are fairly consistent, but black-white differences in satisfaction are not very great.

Some of the early studies compared blacks and whites in terms of which needs were satisfied on the job. Slocum and Strawser (1972) reported that black certified public accountants were less satisfied than their white counterparts along a number of dimensions, including needs for esteem, autonomy, self-actualization, and compensation. Similar results were reported by Bloom and Barry (1967) and O'Reilly and Roberts (1973).

Weaver (1977) found that whites were more satisfied with their jobs overall. Results were based on a national opinion poll of full-time employees. However, the difference, while statistically significant, was not very large. Weaver (1978a) extended his research to correlates of job satisfaction and found little difference between blacks and whites in satisfaction with various job aspects. For example, the correlation between satisfaction and autonomy was .12 for whites and .13 for blacks. While some differences between races were found, it appears that blacks and whites are more similar in their feelings about work than they are different. This suggests that though blacks may be somewhat less satisfied in *level* of job satisfaction (Weaver, 1974), the *degree of association* between satisfaction and other variables is comparable for the two races.

Jones, James, Bruni, and Sells (1977) suggested that black-white differ- .ences in satisfaction are not as important as understanding why they occur. Only one study (Moch, 1980) systematically dealt with explanations. Moch investigated two potential determinants of satisfaction: structural and cultural. Structural explanations state that systematic differences in the way employees are treated account for racial differences in satisfaction. An example would be black employees having fewer promotion opportunities. Cultural explanations attribute satisfaction differences to beliefs, values, or psychological states. Moch tried to assess the effects of these two types of variables on the global satisfaction of blacks, whites, and Mexican-Americans. Structural variables, such as work group assignments and position in the organization, were measured. So were cultural factors like the importance of interpersonal relations, intrinsic rewards, and extrinsic rewards. Moch then determined to what extent satisfaction was related to these factors. The results indicated that structural and cultural factors play a small but significant role. The findings are also somewhat discouraging about what organizations can do to improve feelings of satisfaction. Certainly promotion opportunities and work assignments which modestly influence satisfaction can be improved. However, cultural factors cannot be altered. As Moch (1980) states, "It may be that the differential satisfaction by race . . . can only be erased through broad racial and cultural change rather than through conscious management policy. If so, it may be a long time before people of different races report relatively equal degrees of satisfaction" (p. 305).

More research should be done on why such differences do (or do not) occur. If structural factors are a cause of differential satisfaction, an organization would have the power to alter these inequities. However, if cultural factors are a major cause of satisfaction differences, we have few options in improving the situation. The effects of years of discrimination cannot be erased quickly. As Moch stated, it may take a long time to reach equity in satisfaction among different races. At the very least, research on the causes of racial effects helps in identifying what can be done to improve satisfaction as well as identifying factors that cannot be controlled.

## Sex

Research on the relationship between job satisfaction and sex is inconsistent. Some studies report that males are more satisfied than females, some report the opposite, yet others report no differences. Hulin and Smith (1964) think sex differences are due to differences in education, pay, and tenure and that males and females are equally satisfied with their jobs when these factors are controlled for. Sauser and York (1978) found this to be correct in their study of government employees. Males were more satisfied in global terms and also with regard to such facets as promotions, supervision, and work. When differences between the sexes in education, pay, and tenure were considered, there were no significant differences between males and females. The only significant finding was that women were more satisfied than men with pay. It appears that male/female differences per se do not account for much variance in job satisfaction. Rather it is other variables (such as education) that are correlated with sex which best explain male/female differences in job satisfaction.

Several studies have tried to find the sources of job satisfaction for men and women. Andrisani and Shapiro (1978) reported that females derived satisfaction from both content and context factors. Results were similar to studies that tested the validity of Herzberg's theory with men. Women derive satisfaction from both intrinsic and extrinsic factors. Weaver (1978c) directly compared sources of satisfaction for samples of men and women. He found that both sexes derived satisfaction from the same factors. Prestige, income, autonomy, and education exerted comparable influences for men and women. Weaver (1978c) concluded, "It should be unnecessary, therefore, for researchers to distinguish between the sexes when investigating the functional relationships between job satisfaction and the determinants included in this study; nor should management expect male and female workers to differ in the way their morale is affected by changes in the conditions of work which are related to these determinants" (p. 271).

It would be a mistake, however, to conclude that women and men are equal in their feelings about work. Traditionally, married males have been the principal wage earners in a family, and females have had the main responsibility for child rearing. As more married women return to work, they experience role conflict that influences their feelings about a job. Andrisani and Shapiro (1978) state, "[The] conflicting responsibilities at work and at home among those [females] with dual careers may prevent such working women from utilizing their productive talents to the best advantage. As a consequence, many may be compelled to accept unfulfilling jobs in order to keep market work from too seriously interfering with family responsibilities" (p. 30). To reduce role conflict, some married women and mothers have to take jobs that don't fully use their skills and abilities. They may also be forced to give less importance to work (compared to males) given the demands of their personal lives. Therefore, for at least some parts of the female labor force, feelings of satisfaction and the importance of work must be weighed against responsibilities in other aspects of their lives. Most males, on the other hand, do not experience such conflicting role pressures.

## REVIEW OF PERSONAL CORRELATES OF JOB SATISFACTION

In considering the relationship between personal variables (age, race, sex) and job satisfaction, keep several points in mind. While there are age, race, and sex differences, they are not large. The variance in satisfaction caused by these variables was estimated at between 2 and 5 percent (Landy & Trumbo, 1980). Furthermore, when other variables (status, education, and pay) are held constant or controlled for, their effect is even less.

It is very difficult to find two groups of people that differ only with regard to age, race, or sex. Statistical methods can be used to control for variables known to affect satisfaction (like pay). But we assume that variables not controlled for don't influence satisfaction, and this may be incorrect. For example, if systematic differences (like cultural factors) exist between two groups, they, and not race, per se, determine differences in satisfaction. Moch's study (1980) showed that cultural differences did affect satisfaction, so perhaps racial differences should be seen as cultural differences.

Landy and Trumbo (1980) make the point that lower satisfaction of females and blacks may simply be a case of the "have nots" versus the "haves." White males have usually held better jobs, while females and blacks have held lower-paying, lower-status ones. Thus, it isn't surprising that people in "good" jobs (white males) like what they do more than those in "bad" jobs (blacks and females). Saying that all white males have good jobs and all blacks and females have bad jobs is an oversimplification. But job satisfaction data make more sense if we talk about differences in types of jobs rather than types of people. Under ideal conditions, we would match people on all relevant variables except for age, race, and sex. We could then see what percent of the variance in satisfaction these variables explain. Some researchers think the effect would vanish under such conditions. Since we can never have such an experiment, at best, we must be aware of possible contamination by other uncontrolled variables.

## RELATIONSHIP BETWEEN JOB SATISFACTION AND EMPLOYMENT CONDITIONS

Many researchers have been interested in the relationship between people's feelings about their jobs and employment conditions. The set of variables that comprise "employment conditions" is very large. I won't try to provide an exhaustive review of the relationships of all of them to job satisfaction. Instead, we will look at three sets of work-related variables: status, unions, and pay.

**Status**

Weaver and Holmes (1975) examined the work satisfaction of women employed full-time and full-time homemakers. They analyzed data from a national survey of 629 females, 331 with full-time jobs and 298 who reported their full-time activity was keeping house. The women responded to the question: "On the whole, how satisfied are you with the work you do—would you say that you are very satisfied, moderately satisfied, or a little dissatisfied?"

Information was also collected on demographic variables like age, marital status, education, family income, etc. Fifty-two percent of the respondents with full-time jobs and 53 percent of the homemakers reported being very satisfied with their work. The difference between the two groups (1 percent) was not significant. The responses were reanalyzed by demographic characteristics of the respondents. The only significant difference occurred in families with an annual income they perceived as below the national average; in this case, women who were homemakers were more satisfied than women who held full-time jobs. Apparently, the latter were dissatisfied because they were still below the national average in spite of their financial contribution. Weaver and Holmes (1975) felt their findings cast doubt on the hypothesis offered by some authors that satisfaction of women with full-time jobs would be less than that of full-time homemakers.

Ronen (1977) examined the job-facet satisfaction of paid and unpaid industrial workers. In the United States, it is difficult to think of industrial workers who are not paid. But in Israel, such a condition can exist among members of a *kibbutz*. Ronen offers this description: "A kibbutz is a voluntary collective settlement operating as a single economic unit and governed by a general assembly composed of all their members. Kibbutz members' needs are provided on an egalitarian basis and include food, clothing, housing, medical care, recreation, and equal pocket money, all of which are based on need and not on the level or style of their work or participation" (p. 585). Ronen administered the JDI (translated into Hebrew) to a sample of 135 unpaid kibbutz workers and 187 paid city workers. The pay scale of the JDI was not given to the kibbutz workers. Ronen wanted to see whether the general pattern of job-facet satisfaction scores was comparable for the two groups. He correlated the JDI scores with overall measures of job satisfaction. Levels of importance for the facets of job satisfaction were identical for the JDI scores. The most important facet (strongest correlate with overall job satisfaction) was satisfaction with supervision, followed by work, promotions, and co-workers. Ronen concluded that the nonmonetary aspects of satisfaction could be distinguished as clearly for unpaid as for paid workers, and that nonmonetary aspects could be studied independent of attitude toward pay. It would be interesting to know whether the *level* of satisfaction with each facet was also comparable for the groups. Perhaps workers who are unpaid derive more (or less) satisfaction from the work itself. Unfortunately, Ronen did not deal with this.

Miller and Terborg (1979) measured facet satisfaction of 665 part-time and 399 full-time employees of a general retail store. The results revealed that full-time employees were significantly more satisfied overall and with their work and benefits than were part-time employees. The two groups did not differ on satisfaction with supervision, pay, and advancement. Part-time employees were no more satisfied with any facet of their jobs than full-time employees. Miller and Terborg explained the results on the basis of the partial inclusion of part-time employees in the work force. Part-time employees may tolerate organization demands differently. Part-time work may be chosen because other commitments limit the amount of time they can devote to work. Part-time employees may be less satisfied because they are less included in the organization. They may be dissatisfied with benefits (insurance, vacation) because they receive fewer benefits due to their status.

## Unions

Schriesheim (1978) studied the relationship between satisfaction and voting in a union election. The sample was 59 production workers who had recently voted in a union election where union representation was defeated by two votes. Schriesheim wanted to see whether attitudes could be used to predict how employees voted. Using the MSQ, he collected data on four noneconomic facets of satisfaction (independence, variety, creativity, and achievement) and four economic facets (security, company policy, pay, and working conditions). Information was also collected on employee attitudes toward the local union and unions in general. The findings from the study are reported in Table 9–4.

The more positive the attitude toward the local union ($r = .57$) and unions in general ($r = .51$), the more likely the employee was to cast a vote in favor of the union. However, more potent predictors of the union vote were satisfaction with economic facets. The correlation for individual economic facets ranged from $-.41$ (for security) to $-.76$ (for working conditions). As a group, all four economic facets correlated $-.74$ with the prounion vote.

| Table 9–4 | Variable correlations with prounion voting |
| --- | --- |

| Variable | r |
| --- | --- |
| Attitude toward the local union | .57 |
| Attitude toward unions in general | .51 |
| Total noneconomic satisfaction | −.38 |
|    Independence satisfaction | −.36 |
|    Variety satisfaction | −.04 |
|    Creativity satisfaction | −.17 |
|    Achievement satisfaction | −.36 |
| Total economic satisfaction | −.74 |
|    Security satisfaction | −.41 |
|    Company policy satisfaction | −.55 |
|    Pay satisfaction | −.60 |
|    Working conditions satisfaction | −.76 |
| Total noneconomic and economic satisfaction | −.64 |

SOURCE: C. A. Schriesheim, "Job Satisfaction, Attitudes toward Unions, and Voting in a Union Representation Election," *Journal of Applied Psychology* 63 (1978), pp. 548–52.

Satisfaction with noneconomic facets was not as strong a predictor. The correlation for these facets was −.38 with the prounion vote. Schriesheim was able to show that a tendency toward unionization was mainly a function of dissatisfaction with economic facets. So to avoid unionization, an organization would be wise to improve economic factors (job security, pay, benefits). Schriesheim's study provided support for the adage that workers "vote their pocketbooks."

A second study on work attitudes as predictors of union activity was done by Hamner and Smith (1978). The authors sampled over 80,000 employees in 250 units of a large organization. In 125 of these units, some union activity had occurred shortly after the survey was taken; in the other 125 units there was no union activity. The study was meant to see whether satisfaction could predict the degree of union activity (ranging from no activity at all to holding an election which the union won). A 42-item satisfaction questionnaire was used, and responses were correlated with degree of union activity. Thirteen of the items correlated significantly with the criterion. These involved supervision, co-workers, company identification, amount of work, physical surroundings, and kind of work. When 13 items were combined in a multiple regression equation, the resulting squared multiple correlation was .30. In other words, approximately 30 percent of the variance in union activity could be explained by the responses to these 13 items. The results showed that attitudes can predict behavior. They also indicate that satisfaction surveys can be used by management to make changes that reduce dissatisfaction with work. Without such changes the likelihood of unionization probably increases.

The purpose of the study of unions and job satisfaction by Odewahn and Petty (1980) was different. The authors compared satisfaction of 102 unionized and 76 nonunionized employees of a residential mental health care facility. All were given the JDI. Responses were statistically adjusted for differences between the two groups in education and tenure variables relating to job satisfaction. Nonunionized employees were significantly more satisfied with work and pay. Differences in satisfaction with promotion, co-workers, and supervision were not significant. Odewahn and Petty believe their results should be of particular interest to union leaders. They feel that employee attitudes toward the company and the union may predict the outcome of union elections. Certainly the results of the previous two studies support their position.

## Pay

Two noteworthy studies investigated satisfaction with one particular facet of a job—pay. Why people are dissatisfied with pay has long interested I/O psychologists. Such dissatisfaction may affect performance, work stoppages, absenteeism, turnover, and overall satisfaction (Lawler, 1971). Dyer and Theriault (1976) studied pay satisfaction in three samples of U.S. and Canadian managers with the JDI pay scale. The managers also provided information on their current pay level, the personal inputs they brought to the job (as training and experience, seniority, effort, and performance), the importance they felt should be given to several factors in making salary decisions, and their supervisor's accuracy in assessing their performance. Each of these variables was correlated with the JDI pay scale. The best predictors were combined in a multiple regression equation. Satisfaction with pay was a function of many factors. But the results also differed somewhat for the three samples of managers. The best single predictor was level of pay; the more people are paid, the more satisfied they are with their pay. Another important factor was the perceived accuracy of the superior's assessement; the more accurate it was, the greater was satisfaction with pay. Finally, managers who felt that not enough importance was given to the cost of living in making salary decisions were dissatisfied with their pay. All the variables accounted for between 34 and 45 percent of the variance in pay satisfaction for the three samples. The authors concluded that their study adds to our understanding of why people are satisfied with pay. However, we still have more to learn; over half the total variance in pay satisfaction remains to be explained.

A second study in this area was conducted by Weiner (1980). It assessed pay satisfaction in a sample of public service employees by using the pay scale of the MSQ. Information was also collected on attitudes toward unionization, turnover, and absenteeism. All variables were intercorrelated. Results showed that the more satisfied people are with pay, the less favorable is their attitude toward a union. Weiner also showed that the more dissatisfied employees were with pay, the more likely they were to be absent and to quit. As in the previous study, a great deal of variance in pay satisfaction remains unexplained; but attitudes toward pay relate to important job behaviors as well as other attitudes.

## REVIEW OF EMPLOYMENT CONDITION CORRELATES OF JOB SATISFACTION

As shown, employment factors do influence feelings of satisfaction. Feelings of satisfaction are, in turn, related to subsequent behavior. The Miller and Terborg (1979) study showed that part-time employees were more dissatisfied. Therefore, we might expect less productivity, more absenteeism, or more turnover in this group. The studies relating job satisfaction to unions reported significant results. In the Schriesheim (1978) and Hamner and Smith (1978) studies, employee attitudes about their jobs were good predictors of their vote in union elections. The appeal of unions seems to be based on the belief that they can change the causes of dissatisfaction. If the employees are satisfied with their jobs, the union has much less of a chance of representing the employees since fewer benefits are attributed to the presence of a union. The Dyer and Theriault (1976) study showed that pay satisfaction is a function of many variables; the Weiner (1980) study illustrated that dissatisfaction with pay can lead to a number of undesirable behaviors. In general, it seems that there are some fairly strong relationships between work conditions and employee attitudes toward their jobs.

# RELATIONSHIP BETWEEN JOB SATISFACTION AND JOB BEHAVIOR

Job satisfaction has long been seen as a major criterion variable in I/O research. Other important variables are absenteeism, turnover, and performance. This section reviews the relationships among these variables, recognizing that the satisfaction-performance relationship is one of the most intriguing and oft-studied topics in I/O psychology.

## Absenteeism

It makes sense that employees who don't like their jobs are absent more often. However, research (e.g., Muchinsky, 1977; Porter & Steers, 1973) has shown that rarely does the correlation between satisfaction and absenteeism exceed $-.35$. We will examine three studies that offer insight into the relationship.

Smith (1977) took advantage of a natural occurrence to study how predictive job attitudes are of absenteeism. Smith examined attendance in one Chicago company on the day after a major snow storm when it took special effort to get to work. He had previously collected data on a number of satisfaction facets like supervision, work, future with the company, and pay. Smith then correlated these scores with attendance. He also conducted the same analysis with a sample of New York employees unaffected by the snow storm. Average attendance on that day in Chicago was much less (70 percent) than in New York (96 percent). The results are shown in Table 9–5. Every measure of job satisfaction predicted attendance in Chicago, but none predicted attendance in New York. The best predictor was the career future scale, suggesting that those who were most satisfied with their pros-

**Table 9–5**

**Correlations between job satisfaction levels and attendance levels on individual days for the Chicago and New York groups**

| Scale | Chicago* | New York† |
|-------|----------|-----------|
| Supervision | .54 | .12 |
| Amount of work | .36 | .01 |
| Kind of work | .37 | .06 |
| Financial rewards | .46 | .11 |
| Career future | .60 | .14 |
| Company identification | .42 | .02 |

*Group following storm.
†Group following no storm.
SOURCE: F. J. Smith, "Work Attitudes as Predictors of Attendance on a Specific Day," *Journal of Applied Psychology* 62 (1977), p. 18.

pects put out the special effort needed to get to work that day. Smith concluded that satisfaction measures can predict job behavior (in this case attendance) when that behavior is under the employee's control. The results reported by Smith for the Chicago sample are certainly above the averages reported for the satisfaction-absenteeism relationship. Without mitigating circumstances (as in the New York sample), the relationship between satisfaction and absenteeism is quite modest.

Ilgen and Hollenback (1977) investigated the relationship between satisfaction and absenteeism over a 20-month period with a sample of secretaries. Satisfaction was measured with the MSQ. The resulting correlation was only −.09. The authors proposed two reasons. One is that if the company allows frequent absences (e.g., sick days, excused absences), employees will take advantage of them regardless of satisfaction. In fact, Ilgen and Hollenback argue, company policies that permit absence should *increase* satisfaction. The second explanation is that if few rewards or sanctions are tied to absenteeism, no relationship would probably exist between satisfaction and absence. That is, if employees are neither rewarded nor punished for absence, what employees feel about their jobs will be independent of attendance. A correlation of −.09 indicates that the two aspects are nearly independent statistically if not conceptually. The authors believe that significant satisfaction-absenteeism relationships will occur only if rewards (promotions, raises) are based on attendance.

Finally, Steers and Rhodes (1978) proposed a model of attendance in which satisfaction plays a major role. The model is shown in Figure 9–3. Note that several factors intervene between satisfaction (Box 4) and attendance (Box 8). Such factors as pressure to attend (economic factors, work group norms, and incentive/reward systems), motivation to attend, and ability to attend (including family responsibilities and transportation problems) intervene. Given the many variables between satisfaction and attendance, it is not surprising that both strong and low relationships between satisfaction and absence were reported. A person who likes his job but has no pressure to attend, has low motivation to attend, and has limited ability to attend would probably have more absences despite higher satisfaction. Steers and Rhodes do an excellent job outlining the factors affecting attendance. They show that the link between satisfaction and attendance is neither simple nor direct.

**Turnover**

Muchinsky and Tuttle (1979) summarized 39 studies of the relationship between satisfaction and turnover. In all but four the relationship was negative. It appears then that the more people dislike their jobs, the more likely they are to quit. The magnitude of the satisfaction-turnover relationship, on average, is about −.40.

As an example of such work, Hulin (1966) matched clerical employees who quit with those who didn't via several demographic variables. Hulin

**Figure 9–3**                **Major influences on employee attendance**

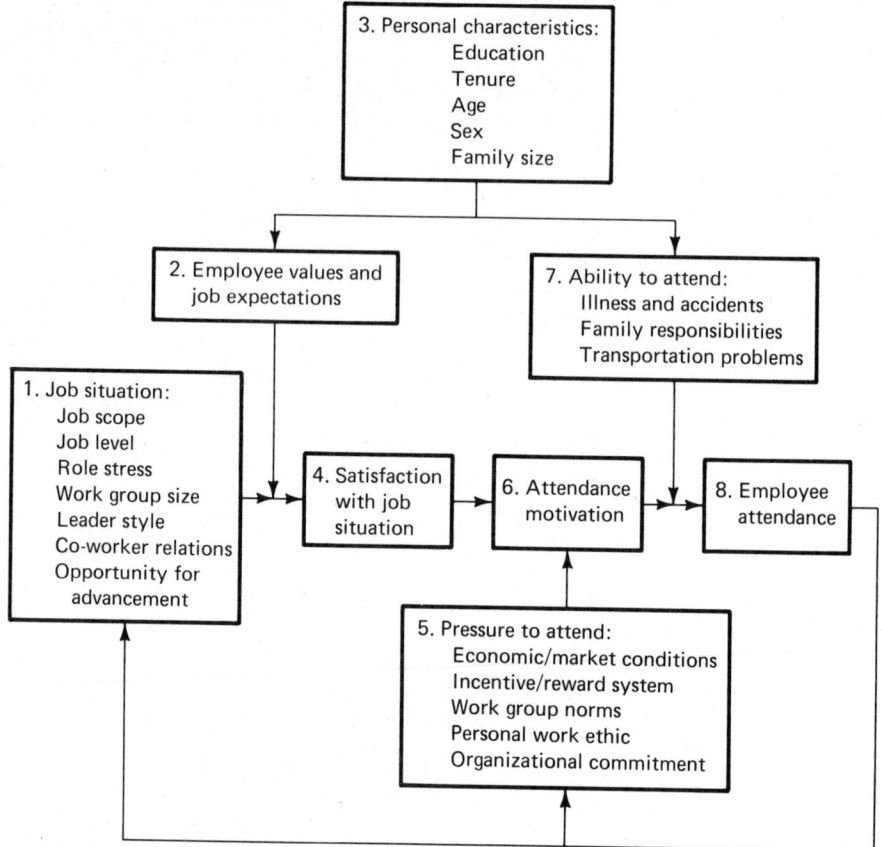

SOURCE: R. M. Steers and S. R. Rhodes, "Major Influences on Employee Attendance: A Process Model," *Journal of Applied Psychology* 63 (1978), pp. 391–407.

obtained satisfaction measures for all employees before any quit. He found that the mean satisfaction score for those who eventually did quit was significantly lower than for those who stayed with the company. Thus, it appeared that turnover could be predicted on a group basis, though the data did not permit individual prediction. A year later Hulin (1968) repeated the study in the same company and got the same results. Changes in company practices meant to reduce turnover by improving satisfaction were also successful.

Mobley (1977) proposed a model of employee turnover based on several hypothesized links between satisfaction and quitting. Such links include thinking of quitting, looking for another job, intending to quit (or stay), and finally the decision to quit (or stay). Mobley contended that feelings of dissatisfaction provoke thoughts of quitting, which in turn prompt the search for another job. If the costs of quitting are too high, the person may re-evaluate the job (producing a change in satisfaction), think less about quitting, and/or use other responses like absence or passive behavior. If the costs are not too high and the other job looks good, this will stimulate the intention to quit, followed by actual quitting. If the alternative job is not good, the situation may stimulate the intention to stay. Mobley's model was a major step forward in thinking of the process from job dissatisfaction to turnover, instead of repeatedly assessing the direct relationship between satisfaction and turnover.

Mobley, Horner, and Hollingsworth (1978) tested the model, which is presented in Figure 9–4. They measured the satisfaction of 203 full-time hospital employees. The authors also obtained measures of the other variables in the model. Turnover data were collected for 47 weeks after collection of the satisfaction data. Using correlation and multiple analysis, Mobley et al. tried to predict turnover from the variables in the model. Overall job satisfaction was found to correlate −.54 with thinking of quitting, −.54 with intention to search, −.49 with intention to quit/stay, and −.21 with actual turnover. When all the variables in the model as shown in Figure 9–4 were combined to form a multiple regression equation, the multiple correlation for intention to quit was .75, while the multiple correlation for actual quitting was .51. Mobley et al. were able to demonstrate that cog-

**Figure 9–4**   **A representation of the intermediate linkages in the employee turnover process**

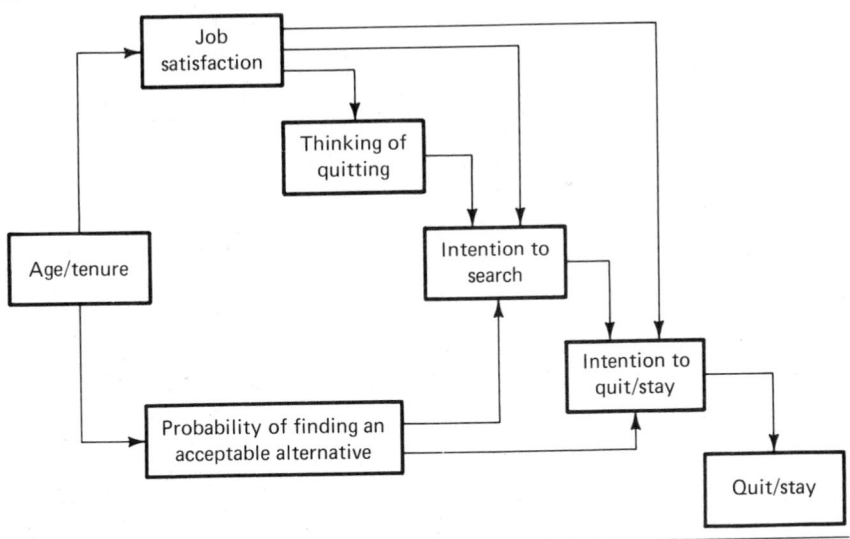

SOURCE: W. H. Mobley, S. O. Horner, and A. T. Hollingsworth, "An Evaluation of Precursors of Hospital Employee Turnover," *Journal of Applied Psychology* 63 (1978), pp. 408–14.

nitive and behavioral phenomena intervene between feelings of job satisfaction and actual quitting. Clearly, employee turnover is predicated on
more than feelings of unhappiness about a job.

Satisfaction is a determinant of turnover. But the economic context must
also be considered. Muchinsky and Morrow (1980) believe that satisfaction
will be a better predictor of turnover in good economic times. Under
conditions of high unemployment, they postulate that employees would
rather endure feelings of dissatisfaction rather than being out of work. Under good economic conditions with plentiful jobs, dissatisfaction could readily
result in turnover if other jobs are available. Mobley et al. make the point
when they say that turnover research should be longitudinal to accommodate economic changes.

## Performance

Probably no other topic has generated as much interest as the relationship between satisfaction and performance. The reason is obvious. We would
like employees to be happy *and* productive—both criteria are important.
Early research determined whether there was a relationship between the
two. Two major studies (Brayfield & Crockett, 1955; Vroom, 1964) reached
the general conclusion that they were either not related or only slightly so.
Vroom (1964) reported a median correlation of .14 across 23 studies of the
satisfaction-performance relationship. Subsequent research revealed that
certain types of performance were more related to satisfaction than others.
A controversy then arose over whether satisfaction caused performance or
performance caused satisfaction. The satisfaction-causes-performance view
led to the belief that the way to have productive workers was to *first* make
them happy. The opposite view is held today: people get pleasure from
their work after finding they are good at it—performance leads to satisfaction. It is difficult to establish causality between any two variables. But
through some careful laboratory research (e.g., Wanous, 1974) the latter
view seems more defensible. The case is not closed completely. Organ
(1977) has described some conditions supporting the former position. As
Lorenzi (1978) commented, the implications of which view is correct are
significant. If performance-causes-satisfaction is correct, managers should
base rewards on past performance in the belief that rewards will reinforce
desired performance. If the satisfaction-causes-performance view is correct,
managers should reward regardless of performance so that employees will
show their gratitude by performing better in the future. Most evidence
favors performance-causes-satisfaction. But the controversy continues (e.g.,
Sheridan & Slocum, 1975), and given its implications, it will probably never
be totally resolved.

Some efforts have been made to study the satisfaction-performance relationship in certain types of jobs. One approach has been to create boring
and stimulating jobs in a laboratory paradigm or to find such jobs in a field
paradigm. A reason for making jobs more stimulating is to enable job hold-

ers to experience satisfaction when they perform well. Thus it has been hypothesized that the satisfaction-performance relationship will be stronger in a stimulating job than in a boring one. The research results on this issue have produced conflicting conclusions. Baird (1976) obtained just the opposite result from what was hypothesized, namely that satisfaction with work was correlated with performance only in the boring job. Opposite and mixed results for the same type of study have been reported by Ivancevich (1978; 1979).

Other studies investigated the conditions under which satisfaction and performance are related. Jacobs and Solomon (1977) found that the relationship is stronger when rewards are based on performance. Thus, people whose pay is based on performance (like salespeople on commission) should be more satisfied with their performance than others paid on an hourly rate (Cherrington, Reitz, & Scott, 1971).

In general, however, the performance-satisfaction relationship is not very large, and certainly not consistent across different samples of jobs. Fisher (1980) pointed out that low performance-satisfaction relationships often emerge because researchers try to relate a *general* attitude (overall satisfaction) with a *specific* behavior (performance of some task). Fisher contends that researchers should use attitude measures as specific as the performance measures. Without such a "fit," the two variables will probably never correlate highly. The effect of Fisher's contention remains to be seen. What is clear is that performance and satisfaction are popular and important criterion variables in I/O psychology. Thus, research on the conditions under which they are related or dissimilar will continue.

## REVIEW OF JOB SATISFACTION–JOB BEHAVIOR RELATIONSHIPS

Job satisfaction is slightly correlated with absenteeism; low negative correlations are most often reported. Though the magnitude of the relationship is not great, the results are quite consistent for many studies. Nicholson, Brown, and Chadwick-Jones (1976) concluded that many other factors intervene in the satisfaction-absenteeism relationship. The Steers and Rhodes (1978) model indicates some of these mediating factors, particularly the importance of pressure to attend and ability to attend.

The relationship between dissatisfaction and turnover is fairly substantial; correlations in the .40s are not uncommon. However, as with absenteeism, the relationship is not direct. People don't quit their jobs simply because they are dissatisfied. Mobley (1977) and Mobley et. al (1978) described some factors which intervene between satisfaction and turnover. The attractiveness and relative cost of other employment influence the decision to quit. The relationship between satisfaction and turnover is also limited by economic conditions. Mild dissatisfaction may lead to turnover when

In some jobs feelings of satisfaction are very intense.

*Larry Morris/NYT Pictures*

jobs are plentiful; feeling of strong dissatisfaction may be endured if the only other option is unemployment.

The relationship between satisfaction and performance is of great interest to I/O psychologists. Most research indicates the two are only slightly related. Research favors the argument that performance causes satisfaction rather than vice versa. Some studies tried to identify the conditions that made the two more strongly related. Employees who are paid based on performance experience stronger satisfaction-performance relationships. Given the salience of satisfaction and performance as criterion variables, research on their interrelationship will probably continue.

## RELATIONSHIP BETWEEN JOB SATISFACTION AND LIFE SATISFACTION

Our final set of studies examines the relationship between job satisfaction and satisfaction with life in general. To what extent are work and nonwork attitudes related? Is work more important to some people than to others? These types of questions guided the research in this area.

On theoretical grounds, Kabanoff (1980) discussed three different explanations for the relationship between work and nonwork satisfaction. The first is *compensation*. High satisfaction in one domain (work) may *compensate* for less satisfaction in the other domain (nonwork). The second explanation is *spillover*. High satisfaction (or dissatisfaction) in one area will *spill over* into the other area. Thus, one would expect roughly equal satisfaction in both areas as the feelings generalize. The third explanation is *segmentation*. Segmentation theory postulates that social experiences in life are *segmented* or kept separate by individuals. That is, the worlds of work and leisure are essentially psychologically separate. Thus, the amount of satisfaction a person feels with these two areas need not be related at all.

There is no definite empirical support for any of the explanations. Kabanoff attributes this to methodology problems, particularly in measuring nonwork satisfaction. However, each theory has received some empirical support. We will now examine some studies testing the relationship between work and nonwork satisfaction.

Dubin (1956) proposed the concept of central life interest. He defined this as an expressed preference for behaving in a given locale. Some people see work as a central life interest. Dubin calls them *job oriented*. Such people should have a high evaluation of work and would score relatively high on satisfaction measures. Other individuals have central life interests other than work (church, family, or community). Dubin calls them *non-job oriented*. A smaller portion of this group should have strong feelings of job satisfaction. A third group may express no clear preference. They have a *flexible focus* central life interest. For this group, we would expect a small relationship between central life interests and job satisfaction.

Dubin and Champoux (1977) tested these hypotheses with samples of male blue-collar and female clerical workers. Each person in the study completed a measure of central life interests assessing their environment preference (job, nonjob, no preference). They also completed the JDI measure of job satisfaction. When satisfaction scores were computed for each group, the general level of job satisfaction was highest among these with a job-oriented central life interest. Satisfaction was lowest among workers with a non–job-oriented central life interest. Those with a flexible focus were intermediate. The results supported the hypothesis for job-oriented people. But the results for people with flexible focus were not as originally proposed. The authors concluded that this was reasonable. Some of the environment preferences for this group would include the world of work. Therefore, their job satisfaction scores should fall between those of the other groups.

Several studies examined how job satisfaction contributes to overall life satisfaction and general mental health. Gechman and Wiener (1975) sampled elementary school teachers using a job satisfaction questionnaire and a self-report assessment of mental health. The correlation between job satisfaction and general mental health was .48. The authors were led to conclude that "positive feelings toward work role may reach out and carry over into other sectors of life" (p. 523).

London, Crandell, and Seals (1977) used national survey data to investigate how much job and leisure satisfaction contributed to the quality of life. The latter was measured by the question "How do you feel about your life as a whole?" Questions were asked about all major facets of job satisfaction. Leisure satisfaction was measured using items involving friends, entertainment, recreation, and social gatherings. The total set of items was combined in a multiple regression equation to predict the evaluation of quality of life. Twenty-five percent of the variance in quality of life ($R = .50$) could be explained by responses to the job and life satisfaction questions. The job satisfaction items as a group accounted for a unique 4.3 percent of the variance in quality of life; the leisure satisfaction items accounted for a unique 13.6 percent. The findings revealed that non-job-related variables can be more important to a full life than job satisfaction for many subgroups of the population.

Orpen (1978) correlated measures of job and life satisfaction in a sample of first-line managers. Two questionnaires were administered at two different times, and the correlations between the two variables were .31 and .24. The design of Orpen's study suggested some causal relationship between job and life satisfaction. He concluded that differences in job satisfaction cause differences in fulfillment of life outside the job. He also concluded that satisfaction in one area spills over into the other area. Near, Rice, and Hunt (1978) conducted a similar study and arrived at roughly the same correlation between life and job satisfaction ($r = .30$).

In one of the more definitive studies Weaver (1978b) analyzed data from a national survey of over 1,500 people. Happiness with life in general was defined by items covering satisfaction with the community, nonwork activities, family, friendships, health, marriage, and financial condition. Similar to the London et. al (1977) study, Weaver discovered that job satisfaction was related to overall happiness in only 2 of 12 occupational groups studied. Thus, among many subgroups, feelings about work are not strongly related to feelings about life in general.

Weaver also found that satisfaction in one area is related to satisfaction in other areas. Weaver states, "Thus, happiness seems to be a generalized phenomenon, according to which employees are either generally satisfied or generally dissatisfied across a broad totality of life, with relatively few employees experiencing a significant satisfaction-happiness relationship in only one of a few aspects of life. . . . [T]he happiness of most employees would rarely come entirely from a satisfying job, with little or no support from satisfaction in other domains of life" (p. 839).

## REVIEW OF JOB SATISFACTION – LIFE SATISFACTION RELATIONSHIP

Job satisfaction is but one aspect of feelings of satisfaction with life in general. Among those for whom work is a central life interest, feelings of job satisfaction are more pronounced. Feelings of job satisfaction also contribute to general mental health. The relationship between job satisfaction and life satisfaction varies for different groups. The results of Weaver's (1978b) study suggest that degree of happiness is fairly pervasive; people are either generally satisfied or dissatisfied with the many factors which contribute to overall happiness. For most people, it is unlikely that a satisfying job can compensate for dissatisfaction in other areas of life.

## CONCLUDING COMMENTS

A question often raised in the popular press is whether job satisfaction is increasing or decreasing. The answer is difficult given the many facets of job satisfaction and the difficulties in drawing accurate inferences from longitudinal studies. Two studies have tried to address this issue with somewhat conflicting results. Weaver (1980) assessed the job satisfaction of over 4,000 workers examined from 1972 to 1978. He reported no significant changes in global satisfaction among full-time employees (see Table 9–6). The responses are highly consistent over the seven-year period. Furthermore, over 85 percent of the respondents in each year were satisfied with

**Table 9–6** **Reported job satisfaction among full-time workers in the United States, 1972–78**

| Attitudes | Year of survey | | | | | | | $\bar{X}$ |
|---|---|---|---|---|---|---|---|---|
| | 1972 | 1973 | 1974 | 1975 | 1976 | 1977 | 1978 | |
| Very satisfied ........ | 48.8% | 50.0% | 51.2% | 56.8% | 55.8% | 49.5% | 52.0% | 51.8% |
| Somewhat satisfied .. | 36.6 | 37.4 | 36.7 | 31.8 | 32.6 | 39.2 | 37.2 | 36.1 |
| A little dissatisfied ... | 11.2 | 9.0 | 8.5 | 8.1 | 8.5 | 9.6 | 7.9 | 9.0 |
| Very dissatisfied ..... | 3.4 | 3.6 | 3.6 | 3.3 | 3.1 | 1.7 | 2.9 | 3.1 |
| Total satisfied* ...... | 85.4 | 87.4 | 87.9 | 88.6 | 88.4 | 88.7 | 89.2 | 87.9 |

*The combined percentage who responded "very satisfied" or "somewhat satisfied."
SOURCE: C. N. Weaver, "Job Satisfaction in the United States in the 1970s," *Journal of Applied Psychology* 65 (1980), pp. 364–67.

their jobs. Weaver thus concluded that the global measure of job satisfaction is very stable, and as a measuring device, it may be unresponsive to changes in society.

However, a massive study by the Opinion Research Corporation (1981) reached a somewhat different conclusion. The attitudes of more than 25,000 workers from 400 companies were sampled over a 28-year period. This study differed from Weaver's (1980) in that attitudes about many facets of work were collected. Feelings of job security among managers were found to be lower now than they have ever been. However, clerical and hourly employees feel more secure than at any time in the past 20 years. Most employees now feel more dissatisfaction with intracompany communication. The results were quite complex. In general, it seems that job satisfaction is falling for some groups of employees but rising for others. Perhaps the differences between the two studies stem from the more varied sample, longer period of time, and use of facet (as opposed to global) satisfaction in the latter study. A complex question warrants a complex answer. The question of rising feelings of job dissatisfaction is difficult to answer in a simple manner. Though workers may complain more now, maybe they are just more willing to *voice* their complaints than ever before.

Nord (1977) made the point that I/O psychologists can improve our understanding of job satisfaction if we direct our research efforts toward helping improve employee satisfaction. He feels that too often scientists address esoteric issues and lose sight of the groups that could benefit from their research. Job satisfaction is certainly a valid area of inquiry since it affects the lives of millions of workers on a day-to-day basis. Nord contends that by making research more relevant for practitioners, we will develop a healthier and more balanced perspective. A similar idea was expressed by Wiggins and Steade (1976). They feel that job satisfaction is a social concern. We must consider it as our culture tries to improve the quality of life. Job satisfaction, therefore, has important practical implications for workers as well as being a topic of scientific investigation. We should never lose sight of our mission as scientists. But we should also not fail to grasp the importance of satisfaction for workers.

# CASE STUDY

Gil McKee contemplated his drink. After a hectic day, he was trying to unwind in a bar frequented by business people. Gil looked up to notice a friend from college coming through the door. It had been almost two years since he had seen Barry DeNisi when they were in the same marketing class.

"Barry," Gil yelled out over the din in the bar. "Have a seat. I haven't seen you in ages. I didn't know you were in town."

"I've been at Allied Insurance as a management trainee for the past 18 months," replied DeNisi. "How about you?"

"I'm with Stoner and Young, an advertising agency. I've been with them for almost a year," said McKee.

"What's it like?" asked DeNisi. "I hear they're a pretty high-pressure outfit."

"I don't know where you get your information," McKee responded, "but you're right. The pay is really good, but they get their pound of flesh from us every day. The people I work with are very sharp, but they're real competitive. I think Stoner and Young has an unwritten policy. They like to pit all the new people against each other, and the 'winner' gets promoted. People who don't get promoted don't seem to last very long. They either look elsewhere or get asked to look elsewhere, if you know what I mean."

A sympathetic look crossed DeNisi's face. "I have my own hassles at Allied, but they're different. My salary is pretty low, but I think I'm close to a promotion. I'd better be. When I started, they said we'd be moving up after nine months of training. Those 9 months became 12, then 15. I've been there 18 months now, and nobody in my group has moved up yet. We've had two resignations in the positions above mine, so they'll be moving two of us up soon. I hope I'm one of them. Their policy is to bring you along slowly. There's a lot of legal stuff to learn. I've picked up a lot, but I'm getting anxious to use it. My boss is terrific. Right when I feel really frustrated, he takes me aside and says I'm doing great. He shows me the corporate staffing projections and says he'll recommend me highly for an opening. I guess I'm just too impatient."

McKee stared back at his drink. "My boss is a dunce, but he's a slick dunce. He surrounds himself with people that make him look good. They do all the work; he gets all the credit. I've learned more from my peers than I have from him. I don't understand how someone like that survives in Stoner and Young.

**351**

You'd think by now they'd be on to him. He must be a better actor than I give him credit for."

"You like what you do?" asked DeNisi.

"Yeah, it's interesting stuff," answered McKee. "A lot more complicated than what we learned in college. Some of our professors ought to go out in business for a while as a refresher course. They didn't teach us about company politics. I never had a course in making my boss look good, but that's what I do."

They both fell silent for a while. Finally DeNisi said, "Say, the Yankees are in town on Friday night. You want to catch the game with me?"

"I'd like to Barry," said Gil, "but Rita has really been on my back lately about bringing a lot of work home. I promised her we'd go dancing Friday night. Maybe later, okay?"

"Sure," DeNisi replied, "right after we both get promoted."

They both laughed, and DeNisi reached for his coat to leave.

Questions

1. How would you assess the job *facet* satisfaction of both DeNisi and McKee?
2. Which person feels the most *overall* satisfaction with his job, and why?
3. Do the two men attach different degrees of importance to the various facets of their jobs? If so, which facets seem most important for whom?
4. Does any one theory of job satisfaction seem particularly useful in explaining McKee's feelings about his job?
5. Is there any information in the case that would lead you to speculate on the relationship between job and life satisfaction?

# REFERENCES

Andrisani, P. J., & Shapiro, M. B. Women's attitudes toward their jobs: Some longitudinal data on a national sample. *Personnel Psychology*, 1978, *31*, 15–34.

Baird, L. S. Relationship of performance to satisfaction in stimulating and nonstimulating jobs. *Journal of Applied Psychology*, 1976, *61*, 721–727.

Bloom, R., & Barry, J. Determinants of work attitudes among negroes. *Journal of Applied Psychology*, 1967, *51*, 287–292.

Brayfield, A. H., & Crockett, W. H. Employee attitudes and employee performance. *Psychological Bulletin*, 1955, *52*, 396–424.

Cherrington, D. J., Reitz, H. J., & Scott, W. E. Effects of contingent and non-contingent reward on the relationship between satisfaction and task performance. *Journal of Applied Psychology*, 1971, *55*, 531–536.

Dachler, H. P., & Hulin, C. L. A reconsideration of the relationship between satisfaction and judged importance of environmental and job characteristics. *Organizational Behavior and Human Performance*, 1969, *4*, 252–266.

de Wolff, C. J., & Shimmin, S. The psychology of work in Europe: A review of a profession. *Personnel Psychology*, 1976, *29*, 175–195.

Dubin, R. Industrial workers' worlds: A study of "Central Life Interests" of industrial workers. *Social Problems*, 1956, *3*, 131–142.

Dubin, R., & Champoux, J. E. Central life interests and job satisfaction. *Organizational Behavior and Human Performance*, 1977, *18*, 366–377.

Dunham, R. B., & Herman, J. B. Development of a female faces scale for measuring job satisfaction. *Journal of Applied Psychology*, 1975, *60*, 629–632.

Dyer, L., & Theriault, R. The determinants of pay satisfaction. *Journal of Applied Psychology*, 1976, *61*, 596–604.

Ewen, R. B. Some determinants of job satisfaction: A study of the generality of Herzberg's theory. *Journal of Applied Psychology*, 1964, *48*, 161–163.

Ewen, R. B. Weighting components of job satisfaction. *Journal of Applied Psychology*, 1967, *51*, 68–73.

Fisher, C. D. On the dubious wisdom of expecting job satisfaction to correlate with performance. *Academy of Management Review*, 1980, *5*, 607–612.

Gechman, A. S., & Wiener, Y. Job involvement and satisfaction as related to mental health and personal time devoted to work. *Journal of Applied Psychoology*, 1975, *60*, 521–523.

Gibson, J. L., & Klein, S. M. Employee attitudes as a function of age and length of service: A reconceptualization. *Academy of Management Journal*, 1970, *13*, 411–425.

Gillet, B., & Schwab, D. P. Convergent and discriminant validities of corresponding Job Descriptive Index and Minnesota Satisfaction Questionnaire scales. *Journal of Applied Psychology*, 1975, *60*, 313–317.

Glenn, N. D., Taylor, P. A., & Weaver, C. N. Age and job satisfaction among males and females: A multivariate, multisurvey study. *Journal of Applied Psychology*, 1977, *62*, 189–193.

Hamner, W. C., & Smith, F. J. Work attitudes as predictors of unionization activity. *Journal of Applied Psychology*, 1978, *63*, 415–421.

Herzberg, F., Mausner, B., & Snyderman, B. B. *The motivation to work*. New York: John Wiley & Sons, 1959.

Hinrichs, J. R., & Mischkind, L. A. Empirical and theoretical limitations of the two-factor hypothesis of job satisfaction. *Journal of Applied Psychology*, 1967, *51*, 191–200.

Hoppock, R. *Job satisfaction*. New York: Harper & Row, 1935.

Hulin, C. L. Job satisfaction and turnover in a female clerical population. *Journal of Applied Psychology*, 1966, *50*, 280–285.

Hulin, C. L. Effects of changes in job satisfaction levels on employee turnover. *Journal of Applied Psychology*, 1968, *52*, 122–126.

Hulin, C. L., & Smith, P. C. Sex differences in job satisfaction. *Journal of Applied Psychology*, 1964, *48*, 88–92.

Hulin, C. L., & Smith, P. C. A linear model of job satisfaction. *Journal of Applied Psychology*, 1965, *49*, 209–216.

Hunt, J. W., & Saul, P. N. The relationship of age, tenure, and job satisfaction in males and females. *Academy of Management Journal*, 1975, *18*, 690–702.

Ilgen, D. R., & Hollenback, J. H. The role of job satisfaction in absence behavior. *Organizational Behavior and Human Performance*, 1977, *19*, 148–161.

Ivancevich, J. M. The performance to satisfaction relationship: A causal analysis of stimulating and nonstimulating jobs. *Organizational Behavior and Human Performance*, 1978, *22*, 350–365.

Ivancevich, J. M. High and low task stimulation jobs: A causal analysis of the performance-satisfaction relationship. *Academy of Management Journal*, 1979, *22*, 206–222.

Jacobs, R., & Solomon, T. Strategies for enhancing the prediction of job performance from job satisfaction. *Journal of Applied Psychology*, 1977, *62*, 417–421.

Jones, A. P., James, L. R., Bruni, J. R., & Sells, S. B. Black-white differences in work environment perceptions and job satisfaction and its correlates. *Personnel Psychology*, 1977, *30*, 5–16.

Kabanoff, B. Work and nonwork: A review of models, methods, and findings. *Psychological Bulletin*, 1980, *88*, 60–77.

King, N. Clarification and evaluation of the two-factor theory of job satisfaction. *Psychological Bulletin*, 1970, *74*, 18–31.

Kraut, A. I., & Ronen, S. Validity of job facet importance: A multinational, multicriteria study. *Journal of Applied Psychology*, 1975, *60*, 671–677.

Kunin, T. The construction of a new type of attitude measure. *Personnel Psychology*, 1955, *8*, 65–77.

Landy, F. J. An opponent process theory of job satisfaction. *Journal of Applied Psychology*, 1978, *63*, 533–547.

Landy, F. J., & Trumbo, D. A. *Psychology of work behavior* (rev. ed.). Homewood, Ill.: Dorsey Press, 1980.

Lawler, E. E. *Pay and organizational effectiveness: A psychological view.* New York: McGraw-Hill, 1971.

Locke, E. A. What is job satisfaction? *Organizational Behavior and Human Performance*, 1969, *4*, 309–336.

Locke, E. A. The nature and causes of job satisfaction. In M. D. Dunnette (Ed.), *Handbook of industrial and organizational psychology.* Skokie, Ill.: Rand McNally, 1976.

London, M., Crandall, R., & Seals, G. W. The contribution of job and leisure satisfaction to quality of life. *Journal of Applied Psychology*, 1977, *62*, 328–334.

Lorenzi, P. A comment on Organ's reappraisal of the satisfaction-causes-performance hypothesis. *Academy of Management Review*, 1978, *3*, 380–384.

McCabe, D. J., Dalessio, A., Briga, J., & Sasaki, J. The convergent and discriminant validities between the IOR and the JDI: English and Spanish forms. *Academy of Management Journal*, 1980, *23*, 778–786.

McCormick, E. J., & Ilgen, D. R. *Industrial psychology* (7th ed.). Englewood Cliffs, N.J.: Prentice-Hall, 1980.

Mikes, P. S., & Hulin, C. L. Use of importance as a weighting component of job satisfaction. *Journal of Applied Psychology*, 1968, *52*, 394–398.

Miller, H. E., & Terborg, J. R. Job attitudes of part-time and full-time employees. *Journal of Applied Psychology*, 1979, *64*, 380–386.

Mirvis, P. H., & Lawler, E. E. Measuring the financial impact of employee attitudes. *Journal of Applied Psychology*, 1977, *62*, 1–8.

Mobley, W. H. Intermediate linkages in the relationship between job satisfaction and employee turnover. *Journal of Applied Psychology*, 1977, *62*, 237–240.

Mobley, W. H., Horner, S. O., & Hollingsworth, A. T. An evaluation of precursors of hospital employee turnover. *Journal of Applied Psychology*, 1978, *63*, 408–414.

Mobley, W. H., & Locke, E. A. The relationship of value importance to satisfaction. *Organizational Behavior and Human Performance*, 1970, *5*, 463–483.

Moch, M. K. Racial differences in job satisfaction: Testing four common explanations. *Journal of Applied Psychology*, 1980, *65*, 299–306.

Muchinsky, P. M. Employee absenteeism: A review of

the literature. *Journal of Vocational Behavior*, 1977, *10*, 316–340.

Muchinsky, P. M. Age and job facet satisfaction: A conceptual reconsideration. *Aging and Work*, 1978, *1*, 175–179.

Muchinsky, P. M., & Morrow, P. C. A multidisciplinary model of voluntary employee turnover. *Journal of Vocational Behavior*, 1980, *17*, 263–290.

Muchinsky, P. M., & Tuttle, M. L. Employee turnover: An empirical and methodological assessment. *Journal of Vocational Behavior*, 1979, *14* 43–77.

Near, J. P., Rice, R. W., & Hunt, R. G. Work and extra-work correlates of life and job satisfaction. *Academy of Management Journal*, 1978, *21*, 248–264.

Nicholson, N., Brown, C. A., & Chadwick-Jones, J. K. Absence from work and job satisfaction. *Journal of Applied Psychology*, 1976, *61*, 728–737.

Nord, W. R. Job satisfaction reconsidered. *American Psychologist*, 1977, *32*, 1026–1035.

Odewahn, C. A., & Petty, M. M. A comparison of levels of job satisfaction, role stress, and personal competence between union members and nonmembers. *Academy of Management Journal*, 1980, *23*, 150–155.

Opinion Research Corporation. *Strategic planning for human resources: 1980 and beyond*. Princeton, N.J.: Arthur D. Little, 1981.

O'Reilly, C. A., & Roberts, K. H. Job satisfaction among whites and non-whites: A cross-cultural approach. *Journal of Applied Psychology*, 1973, *57*, 295–299.

Organ, D. W. A reappraisal and reinterpretation of the satisfaction-causes-performance hypothesis. *Academy of Management Review*, 1977, *2*, 46–53.

Orpen, C. Work and nonwork satisfaction: A causal-correlational analysis. *Journal of Applied Psychology*, 1978, *63*, 530–532.

Porter, L. W. Job attitudes in management: I. Perceived deficiencies in need fulfillment as a function of job level. *Journal of Applied Psychology*, 1962, *46*, 375–384.

Porter, L. W., & Steers, R. M. Organizational, work, and personal factors in employee turnover and absenteeism. *Psychological Bulletin*, 1973, *80*, 151–176.

Ronen, S. A comparison of job facet satisfaction between paid and unpaid industrial workers. *Journal of Applied Psychology*, 1977, *62*, 582–588.

Salancik, G. R., & Pfeffer, J. An examination of need satisfaction models of job satisfaction. *Administrative Science Quarterly*, 1977, *22*, 427–456.

Sauser, W. J., & York, C. M. Sex differences in job satisfaction: A reexamination. *Personnel Psychology*, 1978, *31*, 537–547.

Schaffer, R. H. Job satisfaction as related to need satisfaction in work. *Psychological Monographs*, 1953, *67*, (304).

Schneider, B., & Dachler, H. P. A note on the stability of the Job Descriptive Index. *Journal of Applied Psychology*, 1978, *63*, 650–653.

Schriesheim, C. A. Job satisfaction, attitudes toward unions, and voting in a union representation election. *Journal of Applied Psychology*, 1978, *63* 548–552.

Seybolt, J. W. Work satisfaction as a function of the person-environment interaction. *Organizational Behavior and Human Performance*, 1976, *17*, 66–75.

Sheridan, J., & Slocum, J. W. The direction of the causal relationship between job satisfaction and work performance. *Organizational Behavior and Human Performance*, 1975, *14*, 159–172.

Slocum, J. W., & Strawser, R. H. Racial differences in job attitudes. *Journal of Applied Psychology*, 1972, *56*, 28–32.

Smith, F. J. Work attitudes as predictors of attendance on a specific day. *Journal of Applied Psychology*, 1977, *62*, 16–19.

Smith, P. C., Kendall, L. M., & Hulin, C. L. *The measurement of satisfaction in work and retirement*. Skokie, Ill.: Rand McNally, 1969.

Smith, P. C., Smith, O. W., & Rollo, J. Factor structure for blacks and whites of the Job Descriptive Index and its discrimination of job satisfaction. *Journal of Applied Psychology*, 1974, *59*, 99–100.

Steers, R. M., & Rhodes, S. R. Major influences on employee attendance: A process model. *Journal of Applied Psychology*, 1978, *63*, 391–407.

Vroom, V. H. *Work and motivation*. New York: John Wiley & Sons, 1964.

Wanous, J. P. A causal-correlational analysis of the job satisfaction and performance relationship. *Journal of Applied Psychology*, 1974, *59*, 139–144.

Wanous, J. P., & Lawler, E. E. Measurement and meaning of job satisfaction. *Journal of Applied Psychology*, 1972, *56*, 95–105.

Weaver, C. N. Negro-white differences in job satisfaction. *Business Horizons*, 1974, *17*, 67–72.

Weaver, C. N. Relationships among pay, race, sex, occupational prestige, supervision, work autonomy, and job satisfaction in a national sample. *Personnel Psychology*, 1977, *30*, 437–445.

Weaver, C. N. Black-white correlates of job satisfaction. *Journal of Applied Psychology*, 1978, *63*, 255–258. (a)

Weaver, C. N. Job satisfaction as a component of happiness among males and females. *Personnel Psychology*, 1978, *31*, 831–840. (b)

Weaver, C. N. Sex differences in the determinants of job satisfaction. *Academy of Management Journal*, 1978, *21*, 265–274. (c)

Weaver, C. N. Job satisfaction in the United States in the 1970s. *Journal of Applied Psychology*, 1980, *65*, 364–367.

Weaver, C. N., & Holmes, S. L. A comparative study of the work satisfaction of females with full-time employment and full-time housekeeping. *Journal of Applied Psychology*, 1975, *60*, 117–118.

Weiner, N. Determinants and behavioral consequences of pay satisfaction: A comparison of two models. *Personnel Psychology*, 1980, *33*, 741–757.

Weiss, D. J., Dawis, R. V., England, G. W., & Lofquist, L. H. *Manual for the Minnesota Satisfaction Questionnaire* (Minnesota Studies on Vocational Rehabilitation, vol. 22). Minneapolis: University of Minnesota, Industrial Relations Center, Work Adjustment Project, 1967.

Weiss, H. M., & Shaw, J. B. Social influences on judgments about tasks. *Organizational Behavior and Human Performance*, 1979, *24*, 126–140.

Wiggins, R. L., & Steade, R. D. Job satisfaction as a social concern. *Academy of Management Review*, 1976, *1*, 48–55.

Yeager, S. J. Dimensionality of the Job Descriptive Index. *Academy of Management Journal*, 1981, *24*, 205–212.

# chapter 10

# WORKER MOTIVATION

Motivation was one of the first topics researched in psychology. Some of the most grand (if not grandiose) theories have been theories of motivation. Psychologists such as Hull, Skinner, and Tolman proposed explanations of why people behave as they do. These theories were broad and limited in explaining the motivation of industrial workers. Consequently, a second set of theories was developed by I/O psychologists to explain the behavior of employees in a work setting. These are more limited; they deal with human motivation in a refined context. Work motivation is but a subset of the larger construct of human motivation. What we do at work is related to how we behave in our personal lives. However, theoretical constructs may be modified to explain behavior in the two domains.

Within the work world, there is no shortage of pat explanations for behavior. Various levels of performance are "explained" by such comments as "she's just lazy," "he's a real hustler," or "people will do anything if you pay them enough." Unfortunately, human behavior is not so simple. Motivation is one of the most complex phenomena. People are motivated by many factors, and the same person can be motivated by different factors in different situations. In this chapter, we will look at several theories of motivation. As will be seen, they offer fairly complex explanations for work behavior.

# ABILITY, PERFORMANCE, AND MOTIVATION

Consider this conversation:

Supervisor: George just isn't motivated!
Foreman: How can you tell?
Supervisor: His productivity has fallen off by more than 50 percent.

This conversation reflects a stereotypical misconception about motivation. Motivation is a hypothetical construct: its existence has to be inferred from observation. In this case, based on the worker's behavior (productivity), the supervisor infers his level of motivation. However, motivation and performance are not the same. A highly motivated person may not perform very well. The reason is that, in theory, performance is the product of motivation times ability. Ability is the individual's capabilities for performing certain tasks. They are necessary but not sufficient precursors of performance. Motivation is the individual's *desire* to demonstrate the behavior and reflects willingness to expend effort. When someone has either (1) no ability or (2) no motivation, performance will be poor. I have no musical ability, so all the motivation in the world will not make me a good musician. People perform best if they have the needed abilities and the desire to perform a task well. Poor performance is not always caused by low motivation. It can also be caused by a decay in the abilities needed. Motivation, therefore, mediates between ability and performance.

# DEFINITION OF WORK MOTIVATION

Steers and Porter (1975) identified three major components of motivation. The first is *energizing*—a force within the person that arouses behavior. The second involves *direction:* people may direct their efforts to certain situations and not others. A good motivation theory should explain why these choices are made. Finally, motivation involves *maintenance*. People will persevere in some tasks; other activities may be over quite quickly. Theories of work motivation concern the behavior of workers over an extended time (e.g., a career). Thus, maintenance is a particularly important component. Work motivation can be defined as "*conditions which influence the arousal, direction, and maintenance of behaviors relevant in work settings*," [italics added] (Steers & Porter, 1975).

**Two perspectives of motivation**

**Trait theory.**   Motivation has traditionally been viewed from one of two perspectives. The first is motivation is an enduring characteristic; some people have it and some don't. People are presumed to be born with a certain level, and this level remains stable. Accordingly, highly motivated people never "lose" it, and people with low motivation never become highly motivated. If you are a manager who wants highly motivated workers, the strategy you would use is to hire people who are judged to possess this trait. Thus, you would assess a person's motivation just as you would any other attribute, such as typing ability, physical strength, or mechanical aptitude. Many practitioners subscribe to this theory. You might therefore think that there are many tests to assess "how much" motivation a person has, just as intelligence or ability is measured. Such is not the case, however. Only a few tests of this kind were developed. One was designed by Wherry and South (1977). The test contained 70 items. Responses were on a 5-point scale from 1 (I almost never feel that way) to 5 (I almost always feel that way). Examples of items are shown in Table 10–1. Wherry and South administered the test to 240 workers in 35 organizations and correlated the scores with criterion measures, such as job satisfaction, salary, and job level. High scores on the motivation test were related to greater satisfaction, higher salary, and higher job level. Thus, there is evidence that differences in motivation can be quantified. We can differentiate poorly from highly motivated people. These types of tests are not as popular as intelligence and aptitude tests, conceivably because responses can be faked. With an aptitude test, there is one correct answer per question (e.g., "What is the square root of 64?") In contrast, we don't know whether a person is truthful when he or she says "I like to expend a lot of energy." Furthermore, we don't know their frame of reference. If a motivational test were given for personnel selection, applicants could respond in a way they thought would make them look highly motivated. This is especially true when the most desirable response is obvious. Though some tests (like the MMPI) have a built-in scale to detect faking, most do not. It would be nice if we could develop "fake-proof" questions to accurately assess motivation. To date, we have not been very successful.

**Environmental theory.** The second perspective is that situational or environmental factors determine motivation: given the right set of circumstances, people can be "made" to be motivated. Rather than believing that

**Table 10–1**          **Some items from Wherry and South's work motivation scale**

Desire promotion based on ability rather than seniority.
Spend much of my free time in self-improvement.
Like to keep my output at a high level.
Would rather work than loaf.
Like to expend a lot of energy.
Come to work early and stay late as a rule.
Believe in setting goals and achieving them.
Want to work my way to the top eventually.

SOURCE: R. J. Wherry and J. C. South, "A Worker Motivation Scale," *Personnel Psychology* 30 (1977), pp. 613–36.

**FRANK AND ERNEST**

*Reprinted by permission. © 1979 NEA, Inc.*

some people are highly motivated and some aren't, this view assumes that all people can become highly motivated if the necessary factors are present in the environment. Consequently, attention is given to understanding what these "motivation inducing factors" are and how they affect human behavior. Research from this perspective has sought to determine to what degree motivation is enhanced by attributes of the work that is performed, an individual's relationship with co-workers, and by rewards made contingent upon performance.

Both perspectives have some merit. Some people are indeed more motivated than others. However, the world is not divided into sloths and dynamos. Rather than "some have it and some don't," "some have more of it than others" is more realistic. The second perspective is quite exciting for those interested in designing effective organizations. If motivation can be improved, organizations need not be passive, only hoping to "find" motivated workers. Research has found factors that induce motivation. Therefore, a *balanced* perspective of motivation is most reasonable. There are differences in people and in environments which account for variation in motivation.

**Role of theory**

Most of this chapter is devoted to six theories of work motivation. The concluding section will attempt to integrate and synthesize the research on motivation, underscoring areas of convergence as well as divergence. The reader will undoubtedly be struck by the multitude of ways that work motivation has been conceptualized. Perhaps no other area of I/O psychology has produced such a differing array of perspectives on the same topic. One might also view the number of different theoretical perspectives as implicit testimony to the complexity (and our limited understanding) of work motivation as a construct. As McCormick and Ilgen (1980) say, the many orientations are "a blessing and a curse." They are a blessing in that they expand our understanding. Yet they also make the likelihood of a simple, unified theory quite remote. It would be futile to determine which theory is "right"; they all have strengths and weaknesses. Understanding the theories and their empirical support can help in designing personnel policies and work that encourage desirable behavior.

Each of these theories will be presented in three sections. A *statement of the theory, empirical tests,* and an *evaluation.*

## MOTIVATION THEORIES

### Need hierarchy theory

**Statement of the theory.**   One of the major theories of motivation was developed by psychologist Abraham Maslow. It is called the need hierarchy theory. Most of Maslow's writing was *not* concerned with work motivation. Only later in his career did Maslow become interested in applications of his theory. Most uses of his theory were derived by other researchers examining its relevance for industrial organizations.

According to Maslow (1954, 1970), the source of motivation is certain needs. Needs are biological or instinctive; they characterize humans in general and have a genetic base. They often influence behavior unconsciously. What causes people to behave as they do is the process of satisfying these needs. Once a need is satisfied, it no longer dominates behavior, and another need then rises to take its place. Need fulfillment is never ending. Life is thus a quest to satisfy needs.

Much of Maslow's theory identifies needs, but the second component explains how the needs relate to each other. Maslow proposes five types of needs: physiological, safety, social, self-esteem, and self-actualization. *Physiological* needs are the most basic; their fulfillment is necessary for survival. They include the need for air, water, and food. *Safety* needs are freedom from threat, danger, or deprivation. They involve self-preservation. Today, most of our safety needs are met. But people experiencing disasters like hurricanes or riots have had their safety needs threatened. *Social* needs include the desire for association, belonging, companionship and friendship.[1] These involve an individual's ability to exist in harmony with other people. *Self-esteem* needs include self-confidence, recognition, appreciation, and the respect of one's peers. Satisfaction of these needs results in a sense of adequacy; thwarting them produces feelings of inferiority and helplessness. The last type of need is *self-actualization;* it is the best known and least understood in Maslow's scheme. Self-actualization is the desire to realize one's full potential. In Maslow's words, "to become more and more what one is, to become everything that one is capable of becoming."

As mentioned, the second part of the theory concerns how these needs relate. According to Maslow, they exist in a *hierarchy.* At the base are the physiological needs which must be met first and continuously. The remaining needs are placed in order, culminating with the highest need, self-

---

[1] Some authors also refer to social needs as love or belongingness needs.

actualization. The need hierarchy theory is presented graphically in Figure 10–1. Physiological and safety needs are referred to as *basic;* the social, self-esteem, and self-actualization needs are *higher-order* needs.

Maslow proposed several points regarding the need hierarchy.

1. Behavior is dominated and determined by those needs which are unfulfilled.
2. An individual will systematically satisfy his needs, starting with the most basic and then work up the hierarchy.
3. Basic needs take precedence over all those higher in the hierarchy.

The first proposition is fundamental. Once a need is fulfilled, it no longer motivates behavior. A hungry person will seek food. Once the hunger is satisfied, it will not dominate behavior. The second proposition involves *fulfillment progression.* This means that a person will progress through the needs in order, moving on to the next one only after the former has been fulfilled. We all spend our lives trying to fulfill these needs because, according to Maslow, only a small percentage of people have fulfilled the self-actualization need. Maslow also says this need can never be fully satisfied. The third proposition stresses that the needs basic to survival always have a higher priority.

There are several implications of the theory for work behavior. When pay and security are poor, employees will focus on those aspects of work necessary to fulfill their basic needs. As conditions improve, the behavior of supervisors and their relationship with the individual take on increased importance. Finally, with a much improved environment, the role of the

**Figure 10–1**      **Maslow's need hierarchy**

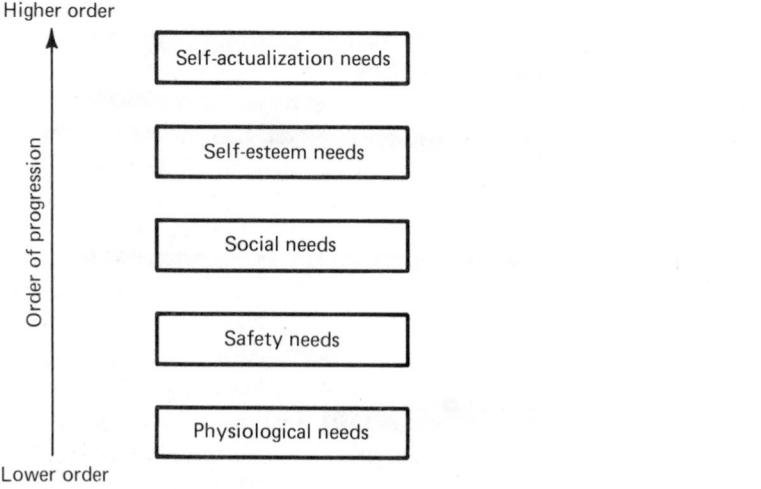

SOURCE: A. H. Maslow, *Motivation and Personality*, 2d ed. (New York: Harper & Row, 1970).

supervisor diminishes and the nature of the work reemerges. However, work is now important in self-actualization and not in fulfilling basic needs.

The theory also predicts that, as people move up in the management levels, they will be motivated by higher and higher level need; thus, managers at various levels should be treated differently. Additionally, employees can be expected to always want more. The organization can never give enough in terms of individual growth and development. It is the nature of the self-actualization need that once activated and satisfied, it stimulates an even greater desire for satisfaction. Thus, it is a continuing source of motivation (Miner, 1980).

**Empirical tests of the theory.**   The ultimate test of any theory is empirical support. But a problem with Maslow's theory involves measuring the variables. Because he did not provide operational definitions of his variables, measuring the variables and testing the theory has fallen to other researchers.

Research has focused mainly on the existence of the five needs and whether they exist in a hierarchy. Porter (1961) developed a need satisfaction questionnaire to assess the degree of fulfillment and the importance of the five needs. Using a seven-point scale, Porter asked people to indicate (1) how much of a given need is present in their life now, (2) how much there should be of this need, and (3) how important the need is. By subtracting the second variable from the first, Porter obtained a measure of "relative deficiency"—the difference between what people have and what they want. Using this method, Lawler and Suttle (1972) sampled a group of lower-level managers at two points in time separated by six months. The median stability (test-retest reliability) of the need measures over this six-month period was found to be only .38. This is evidence that either the managers' needs changed over the six months, or the measurement is fairly unreliable. Lawler and Suttle also found that needs exist in a two-level hierarchy (as opposed to the five Maslow proposed). The basic biological needs are on the bottom and all other needs on the top.

Mitchell and Mougdill (1976) assessed the needs of several samples of accountants and engineers in Canada using a questionnaire similar to Porter's (1961). Again the results did not support a five-level hierarchy. Their data suggested that security needs were distinct from the others, while the remaining needs clustered as a group. The authors did not totally reject the five-level hierarchy. But the data clearly did not support it.

Finally, Wahba and Bridwell (1976) reviewed all earlier research on Maslow's theory. They concluded that the theory has received little clear or consistent support. Some of Maslow's propositions were totally rejected; others received mixed or questionable support. Most support is for the importance of the basic needs; the least evidence is for the higher-level needs. The number of needs appears questionable, as does the idea of fulfillment progression.

**Evaluation of the theory.**   It is tempting to dismiss most of Maslow's theory given the lack of support. But there are a few points that suggest a more positive verdict. It is not a "theory" in the usual sense. Maslow did not propose testable hypotheses. As Wahba and Bridwell (1976) said, "Maslow's need hierarchy theory is almost a nontestable theory" (p. 234). It was based on logical and clinical insights into the nature of humans, rather than on research findings. Furthermore, Maslow did not discuss any guides for empirical tests on his theory. Many questions remain about the theory, and the way they are tested is open to interpretation. For example, what is the time span for the unfolding of the hierarchy? Is there relationship between age and the need we are trying to satisfy? How does the shift from one need to another take place? Do people also go down the hierarchy? These questions are very important; they affect how we would use the theory in the work environment.

The vagueness of the theory also leaves some nagging issues unanswered. According to Maslow, we systematically progress from one need in the hierarchy to the next. Yet we all need to eat, drink, and breathe every day. We never really have our physiological needs satisfied. People try to fulfill their self-esteem needs even though their social needs are not fully satisfied. Rather than going through the hierarchy in stages, perhaps we attempt to satisfy all needs concurrently. This speculation was not dealt with by Maslow.

Maslow's theory, a highly abstract statement about mankind, is far more philosophical than empirical. But Maslow's notion of self-actualization is well ingrained in the way we think about our mission in life. His writing (or philosophy) has generated a great deal of thought about the nature of mankind in general. While Maslow's theory is deficient to explain day-to-day behavior at work, his contributions to the field of psychology as a whole should not be ignored.

## ERG theory

**Statement of the theory.** A second major theory based on needs was proposed by Alderfer (1969, 1972). Its name is ERG theory which stands for three types of needs: existence, relatedness, and growth. Alderfer defined them as follows:

1. Existence needs: These are material and are satisfied by environmental factors, such as food, water, pay, fringe benefits, and working conditions.
2. Relatedness needs: These involve relationships with significant other people, such as co-workers, superiors, subordinates, family, and friends.
3. Growth needs: These involve the desire for unique personal development. They are met by developing whatever abilities and capabilities are important to an individual.

Alderfer proposed ERG in response to the shortcomings of Maslow's theory. His theoretical variables also involve specific measures. Alderfer's theory differs from Maslow's on three important dimensions.

**Table 10–2**                              **Comparison of Maslow's needs to Alderfer's needs**

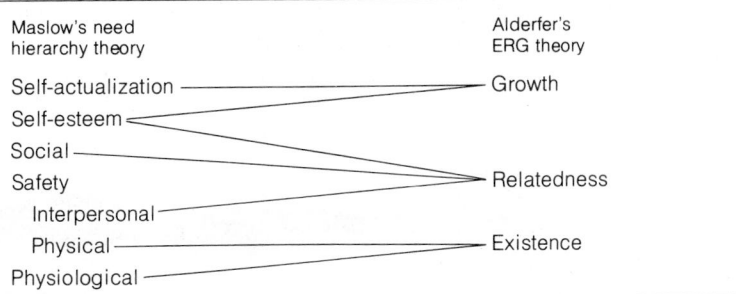

1.   He proposed three need categories, while Maslow proposed five need classes. The correspondence between the two is shown in Table 10–2.
2.   Alderfer arranged his needs along a continuum; Maslow placed his in a hierarchy. The continuum, as shown in Figure 10–2, is concreteness. Existence needs are the most concrete, growth needs the most abstract.
3.   According to Maslow, a person only moves up the need hierarchy (fulfillment progression). Alderfer allowed for "movement" back and forth on the continuum. Moving toward fulfillment of the growth and relatedness needs was also called fulfillment progression by Alderfer. Moving back toward the fulfillment of more concrete needs was referred to as *frustration regression*. Alderfer meant that if a person became frustrated in satisfying higher needs, he or she would regress toward fulfilling lower needs.

The two theories also differ on need fulfillment. This centers around the motivating properties of unfulfilled needs. According to Maslow, the less social needs (for example) are satisfied, the more they will be desired. To Alderfer, the less relatedness needs are satisfied, the more existence needs will be desired. The same relationship holds for growth needs. If not satisfied, they will be supplanted by relatedness needs. Again, this is the concept of frustration regression, which permits a person to seek fulfillment of more concrete needs if the more abstract needs are not satisfied.

**Empirical tests of the theory.**   Because ERG theory is relatively new, there are few tests. One study testing Maslow's theory (Hall & Nougaim, 1968) reported results which became the basis (in part) for Alderfer's theory. Hall and Nougaim found that the more a need is satisfied, the more

**Figure 10–2**                             **Alderfer's continuum of ERG needs**

| Existence needs | Relatedness needs | Growth needs |
|---|---|---|
| Most concrete | Continuum of concreteness | Least concrete |

important it becomes. Maslow's theory would predict that satisfaction at one level would correlate positively with importance at the next level.

Another study by Wanous and Zwany (1977) provided strong support for ERG theory, especially the existence of the three needs. They also found that the three were relatively independent of each other and could be measured reliably. The authors found support for the notion that people progress through the three needs as Alderfer proposed. Wanous and Zwany concluded that there was some hope for using Alderfer's theory in management. According to Maslow, a satisfied need is not a motivator. Therefore, "today's successful motivator becomes obsolete tomorrow" (p. 96). However, Wanous and Zwany found the opposite. Both relatedness and growth needs can become *more* (not less) important when highly satisfied. This is obviously encouraging for organizations seeking to motivate employees.

**Evaluation of the theory.** Alderfer's ERG theory received more support than Maslow's need hierarchy theory. But many of the same problems plague both. Exactly what a need is, is still unclear, especially its psychological and/or physiological basis. People also engage in behavior that is seemingly unrelated to need fulfillment. Campbell and Pritchard (1976) stated that Alderfer's definition of needs is "as slippery as ever and . . . represents no major conceptual breakthrough" (p. 77). In addition, needs are quite amorphous. Can managers "instill" certain needs to motivate employees? Are employees trying to satisfy existence needs less productive than employees striving to fulfill growth needs? Needs are nebulous for counseling an employee on improving performance. We don't have much advice to offer on changing from existence to relatedness needs as a basis for behavior.

Alderfer's theory, while less general than Maslow's, is also quite removed from reality. Wanous and Zwany (1977) concluded that need theories may be of little value in day-to-day management. This might explain why relatively little research has been done on ERG Theory.

## Equity theory

**Statement of the theory.** Adams (1965) proposed a theory of worker motivation drawn from the principle of social comparison. How hard a person is willing to work is a function of comparisons of the effort of others. The theory has perceptual and social bases since motivation is a function of how a person sees himself or herself in comparison to other people. Adams has suggested that motivation has a social, not biological, origin.

Equity theory has four major parts.

1. Because equity theory is a perceptually based theory, an individual perceives himself or herself in comparison to others. The person who does the perceiving is called *Person*.
2. It is postulated that Person compares himself or herself to another individual. This other person is called *Other*.

3. All of the assets Person brings to the job comprise the third component of the theory, and they are collectively referred to as *Inputs*. Inputs can include Person's education, intelligence, experience, skill, seniority, effort level, health, and so on. Inputs are anything of perceived value or importance Person brings to the job.

4. All benefits Person derives from the job are the fourth component. They are collectively referred to as *Outcomes*. Outcomes can include pay, benefits, working conditions, status symbols, seniority benefits, etc. Outcomes are those factors Person perceives as being derived from employment.

The theory states that Person forms a ratio of his or her inputs to outcomes and compares this ratio to perceptions of Other's input/outcome ratio. Adams assumes that people can quantify both their inputs and outcomes into common scale units. For example, Person will consider all the inputs she brings to the job; let's say they total 50. Person will also assess her outcomes in the same manner, and again let's assume they total 50 units. Person's ratio is therefore 50/50. Person then compares her ratio to what she perceives Other is putting into his or her job, and what Other is deriving in outcomes from the job. Let's assume Person assesses Other's inputs to be 50 units and outcomes to be 50 units. We now have two ratios as assessed by Person:

| *Person* | *Other* |
|---|---|
| *50/50* | *50/50* |

Because the ratio's are perceived to be equal by Person, this represents *equity* (which literally means "fair"). If Person perceives Other as deriving 100 units of outcomes from their job (due to more pay, higher status), but also contributing 100 units of inputs (due to greater education, more experience), this would also represent equity to Person. Other is getting more out of the job but is also putting more in (than Person). That is, 50/50 equals 100/100. However, what happens if Person's ratio is different from Other's ratio? What if Person's ratio is 50/50, while Other's ratio is perceived to be 50/75? Both Person and Other are perceived as contributing the same amount of inputs (50 units), but Other is deriving more outcomes (75 units). According to Adams, this situation would represent *inequity*, or unfairness. It is unfair in the sense that Other is perceived to be getting more out of the job than Person, while both people are perceived by Person as contributing the same amount of inputs.

Feelings of inequity cause tension according to Adams, and Person will become motivated to reduce this tension. The greater the inequity between Person and Other, the greater is the tension, and the greater will be the motivation to reduce the tension. Thus, for Adams, the source of motivation in people is feelings of tension caused by perceived inequity. Feelings of inequity are necessary for motivation to occur, for if Person perceives himself as being in an equitable relationship with Other, Person will not be motivated.

Adams proposed two types of inequity. *Underpayment* refers to when Person perceives himself as deriving *less* outcomes from a job than Other when both contribute comparable inputs. An example of underpayment inequity would be:

| Person | Other |
|--------|-------|
| *50/50* | *50/75* |

*Overpayment* refers to when Person perceives himself as deriving *more* outcomes from a job than Other when both contribute comparable inputs. An example of overpayment inequity would be:

*The Person* → *Person*      *Other* ← *who he compares himself with*
         *50/75*          *50/50*

Adams felt that people could alter their motivation level as a way to bring feelings of inequity back into line. The drive to reduce the tension caused by inequity would manifest itself in more or less effort being put into a job, which is a form of input. Adams said that how inequity was reduced would be a function of the method of payment used to compensate an employee. Adams considered two methods of payment: hourly (wages determined per unit of time, such as $3 per hour) and piece rate (wages determined per unit of production, such as 25 cents per object). Most of the research done on equity theory was conducted in laboratory or field experimental paradigms. In order to test the theory, feelings of overpayment and underpayment had to be induced in the subjects. Such inducements were created by the following types of manipulations. The experimenter, posing as a manager or supervisor of some fictitious company, would place an ad in a local newspaper announcing part-time jobs with the company. At the employment interview, subjects (who did not know this was a psychology experiment) were told the job paid a certain hourly rate (as $3 per hour) or piece-rate (as 25 cents per object produced). They then started work at this rate. After a few days, the experimenter would say: "We just received a large contract from the government, and we now can pay you more money. Starting tomorrow, you will make $5 per hour (or 40 cents per object)." This manipulation was meant to induce feelings of overpayment. Subjects would be paid more for doing the same job. To induce feelings of underpayment, the experimenter would say: "We have just experienced a major cutback in financial support due to the loss of a contract. Starting tomorrow we can pay you only $2 per hour (or 15 cents per object)." These experimental instructions would be selectively given to some subjects and not others. Thus, some people would work at the "new" rate, while others would continue to work under the original rate. The initial few days of employment were designed to set base rate expectations about the job. After a few days, the amount of compensation for the same work either went up (in the overpayment condition) or down (in the underpayment condition). The question to be answered was what would these people do following feelings of inequity. Given two types of inequity (underpayment and overpayment) and two compensation systems (hourly and piece-rate), four different sets of hypotheses were proposed as to how feelings of inequity would be reduced by Person.

*Overpayment—hourly.* In this condition, it is predicted that subjects would try to reduce the inequity caused by overpayment by working harder or expending more effort. By increasing their inputs (effort level), feelings of inequity would be reduced. The increased effort was predicted to manifest itself in increased quantity or quality of production.

*Overpayment—piece rate.* In this condition, subjects are being paid more for every object produced. Therefore, to reduce feelings of inequity, it was predicted they would work harder as a means of increasing their inputs. However, if their increased effort resulted in a greater *quantity* of output, the feelings of inequity would be magnified even more. Thus it was predicted that the subjects in this condition would produce fewer objects but of higher quality than before.

*Underpayment—hourly.* In this condition, subjects are now being paid less than they were before. As a means of reducing inequity, it was predicted that subjects would lower their effort to accommodate their decrease in outcomes. Decrements in product quantity and quality were predicted.

*Underpayment—piece rate.* In this condition, subjects are now being paid less for every object produced than before. In order to compensate for this loss in pay, it was predicted that subjects would produce more in quantity (to offset the decreased rate) but of appreciably lower quality.

**Empirical tests of the theory.** A fairly large number of studies have tested some or all of the predictions made by equity theory. In an early study, Adams and Rosenbaum (1962) used both payment systems in studying the effects of inequity on performance in the job of an interviewer. Certain groups of subjects were made to feel over- or underpaid; others were made to feel they were paid equitably. For the most part, the data supported the theory. Overpaid subjects conducted significantly more interviews only when paid by the hour. The quality of the interviews (measured by completeness and detail) was higher for those overpaid when a piece-rate system was used. A study by Pritchard, Dunnette, and Jorgenson (1972) also supported the theory in that overpaid subjects tended to process more catalogue orders than equitably paid subjects.

Most studies found that equity predictions hold up best in the underpayment conditions. Also, the results of studies using hourly payment are stronger than those with piece-rate payment. These findings have important implications which we will discuss shortly.

The original theory proposed that people expend more or less effort to reduce inequity. Later research showed that feelings of inequity can be resolved in ways other than changing motivation. In fact, in addition to many *behavioral* ways of reducing inequity, there are *cognitive* ways. These are listed in Table 10–3. As mentioned, one way to reduce inequity is to adjust the level of effort expended—changing one's inputs as the theory postulates. A second behavioral mode of reducing inequity would be to

*Read*

| Table 10–3 | **Modes of reducing inequity** |
|---|---|

Behavioral modes of inequity reduction:
1. Change inputs.
2. Change outcomes.
3. Get Other to change inputs or outcomes.
4. Quit job for more equitable one.

Cognitive modes of inequity reduction:
1. Distort own inputs or outcomes.
2. Distort Other's inputs or outcomes.
3. Change comparison Other.

alter one's outcomes, such as by asking for a raise if you felt underpaid. A third technique would be to get Other to change his inputs or outcomes; the use of peer pressure to get a co-worker to work faster or slower. Finally, if all else fails, Person can always quit a job if it is perceived to be too inequitable.

Three cognitive ways of reducing inequity are also available. By cognitive, we mean a person doesn't have to "do" anything; rather, inequity is reduced through mental processes. One way is for Person to distort views of his or her inputs or outcomes. For example, Person could think, "I'm not really working that hard. After all, I spent a fair part of my day just talking to my friends." Outcomes could be distorted in a similar way. A second technique is for Person to distort Other's inputs or outcomes. As an example, "She really has to put up with a lot from her supervisor that I don't have to take." Finally, if a particular Other makes Person feel inequitable, Person could always find a new Other for comparison. Equity theory does not state who Other has to be.

Most experiments on equity theory have supported the predictions made. Problems occur not because the theory is "wrong," but because hypotheses and predictions are not very precise. There are several ways of reducing inequity, and the theory does not specify which will be chosen. A second problem involves time. Many of the experiments studied behavior for short periods—from 10 minutes to 30 days. As with any motivation theory, we are interested in the long term effects on behavior. Some of the implications of this will be addressed in the next section.

**Evaluation of the theory.** A number of authors (Pritchard, 1969; Goodman & Friedman, 1971) have expressed concern with both the substance and implications of the theory. To date, the research on equity theory has addressed itself to the outcome of financial compensation. Yet financial compensation is but one of many outcomes derived from a job. We know very little about the effects of manipulating other outcomes on motivation. The results of most of the studies have found fairly strong support for the underpayment prediction but less support for the overpayment predictions. One of the consequences of inequity caused by underpayment is an increase in job dissatisfaction. If a person feels dissatisfied at work, we know such feelings are associated with increased absenteeism and turnover. We will have accomplished very little in the work force if, in the name of increased motivation, we make people feel underpaid, only to have them turn around and be absent from work and/or quit. In theory, feelings of overpayment will cause a person to work harder to produce more or higher-quality products. However, research has shown that feelings of overpayment don't last very long (Carrell & Dittrich, 1978). People seem to have a very high threshhold for overpayment (i.e., it takes a large increment for people to feel overpaid) but a low threshhold for underpayment (i.e., it doesn't take a large decrement for people to feel underpaid). Given that feelings of overpayment don't last long, an organization that doubled the wages of its employees every two months to make them feel consistently overpaid would soon be bankrupt. Finally, the whole issue of organizations deliberately manipulating its employees to feel inequitable has serious moral and ethical issues. Few employees would like working for an organization that willingly makes them experience inequity.

On the positive side, the notion of equity is important. As a motivation theory, however, it has some practical limitations. Notions of equity are of great concern with compensation. Organizations strive to keep *external* equity (salaries and wages comparable to those in other companies in the area and industry) and *internal* equity (salaries and wages comparable within the company). A major problem in industry today is that many recent college graduates command starting salaries above those offered by a company. Organizations have to remain financially competitive if they are to hire new employees, yet they also have to be fair to existing employees. An interesting paradox is that in compensation administration *equity* in salaries and wages must be maintained; in equity theory, it is necessary to maintain *inequity* for motivation.

Despite the problems, it is established that people expend effort in relation to the effort of others in the work force (Middlemist & Peterson, 1976). Social comparison is valid; what we do is in part a product of what others around us do. The theoretical origins of equity are both justified and accurate, in that there is a social component to motivation. Equity theory should be lauded for its attempt to consider this phenomenon as a basis for work motivation. Unfortunately, the path from the scientific statement of equity theory to the practice of motivation in the day-to-day work world is strewn with large boulders instead of small pebbles.

## Expectancy theory

**Statement of the theory.** Expectancy theory originated in the 1930s, but at that time, it was not related to work motivation. Georgopoulos, Mahoney, and Jones (1957) were the first to apply the theory in a work environment. However, it was a book by Vroom (1964) that catapulted expectancy theory into the arena of motivation research. In the last 20 years, expectancy theory has been the most popular and prominent motivation theory in I/O psychology. Since Vroom's formulation, several other researchers have proposed modifications (Graen, 1969; Porter & Lawler, 1968). We will not examine all of the variations but will focus on key elements.

This is very much a cognitive theory. Each person is assumed to be a rational decision maker who will expend effort on activities that lead to desired rewards. Individuals are thought to know what they want from work and understand that their performance will determine whether they get the rewards they desire. A relationship between effort expended and performance on the job is also assumed.

There are five major parts of the theory: job outcomes, valence, instrumentality, expectancy, and force.

*Job outcomes.*    Job outcomes are things an organization can provide for its employees. Examples include pay, promotions, vacation time, etc. There is no theoretical limit to the number of outcomes. They are usually thought of as rewards or positive experiences, but they need not be. Being fired could be an outcome, as could being transferred to a new location. Outcomes can also refer to intangibles like feelings of recognition or accomplishment.

*Valence.*    Valence is the employee's feelings about the outcomes provided. They are usually defined in terms of attractiveness or anticipated satisfaction to the individual. Valences are generated by the employee. That is, he or she could rate the anticipated satisfaction from (e.g., ascribe a valence to) each outcome considered. Rating is usually done on a $-10$ to $+10$ scale. The individual can indicate whether an outcome has positive or negative valence. If the employee anticipated that all outcomes would lead to satisfaction, varying degrees of positive valence would be given. If the employee anticipated that all outcomes would lead to dissatisfaction, varying degrees of negative valence would be assigned. Last, if the employee felt indifferent about the outcomes, a valence of zero would be given. The employee would generate as many valences as there were outcomes.

*Instrumentality.*    Instrumentality is defined as the perceived degree of relationship between performance and outcome attainment. This perception exists in the mind of the individual. Instrumentality is synonymous with the word "conditional," and literally means the degree to which the attainment of a certain outcome is conditional upon the individual's performance on the job. For example, if a person thought that increases in pay were totally conditional on their performance, the instrumentality associated with that outcome (a pay raise) would be very high. If a person thought that whether they were transferred or not was totally unrelated to their job performance, the instrumentality associated with that outcome (a transfer) would be very low. As with valences, instrumentalities are generated by the individual. He or she would evaluate the degree of relationship between their performance and outcome attainment on the job. Instrumentalities are usually thought of as a probability (which therefore ranges between 0 and 1.0). An instrumentality of 0 means the attainment of that outcome is totally unrelated to job performance, while an instrumentality of 1 means the attainment of that outcome is totally conditional upon job performance. Just as there are as many valences as there are outcomes, there are as many instrumentalities as there are outcomes.

*Expectancy.* Expectancy is the perceived relationship between effort and performance. In some jobs, there may not seem to be any relationship between how hard you try and how well you do. In others, there may be a very clear relationship—the harder you try the better you do. Expectancy, like instrumentality, is scaled as a probability. An expectancy of 0 means that there is no probability that an increase in effort will result in an increase in performance. An expectancy of 1 means that with certainty an increase in effort will be followed by a corresponding increase in performance. As with the valence and instrumentality components, the individual generates the expectancy for his or her job. After thinking about the relationship between effort and performance on the job, the individual would make an assessment (ascribe an expectancy) of that relationship. Unlike the previous terms in the theory, there is usually only *one* expectancy value generated by the person reflecting the effort-performance relationship on the job.

*Force.* The last component is force. Force is the amount of effort or pressure within a person to be motivated. The larger the force, the greater the hypothesized motivation. Mathematically, force is the product of valence, instrumentality, and expectancy, as expressed by the following formula:

$$\text{Force} = E \left( \sum_{i=1}^{n} V_i I_i \right)$$

This formula can better be explained with the aid of the information in Figure 10–3. It shows the components that comprise expectancy theory. Job outcomes ($O$), rated valences, instrumentalities, and expectancy are

**Figure 10–3**          **An example of Vroom's expectancy theory with four job outcomes**

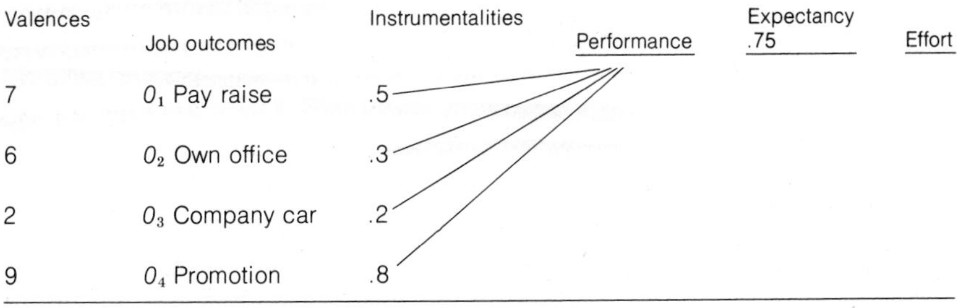

| Valences | Job outcomes | Instrumentalities | Performance | Expectancy .75 | Effort |
|----------|--------------|-------------------|-------------|----------------|--------|
| 7 | $O_1$ Pay raise | .5 | | | |
| 6 | $O_2$ Own office | .3 | | | |
| 2 | $O_3$ Company car | .2 | | | |
| 9 | $O_4$ Promotion | .8 | | | |

presented for a hypothetical employee. To compute this individual's force, we multiply the valence for an outcome times its corresponding instrumentality and then sum these numbers. Therefore:

$$(7 \times .5) + (6 \times .3) + (2 \times .2) + (9 \times .8) = \sum_{i=1}^{4} V_i I_i = 12.9$$

We then multiply 12.9 by the listed expectancy of .75, which yields a force score of:

$$E \left( \sum_{i=1}^{4} V_i I_i \right) = .75 \, (12.9) = 9.7$$

This product (9.7) represents the amount of force within the person to be motivated. It is the end product of the information on valence, instrumentality, and expectancy.

Now that we have this force score, what do we do with it? You can think of it as a predictor of how motivated a person is. As with any predictor, the next step is to correlate it with some criterion. Because the force score predicts effort, the criterion must also measure effort. What are some measures of effort? The most common one is a subjective assessment, usually a rating. Either the individual renders a self-assessment of how hard she is trying, the individual's supervisor makes the judgment, or in some cases, peer assessments of effort have been used. In trying to predict the motivation of students, the number of hours spent studying each week has been used as a measure of effort. In one type of validation paradigm of expectancy theory, force scores are calculated for a group of people. Criterion measures of effort are also obtained for these people. If the theory is valid, the greater the person's force score, the greater should be the effort. The validity of theory is typically assessed by correlating the force scores with the criterion of effort. High correlations between the two variables would substantiate the theory, while low correlations would disconfirm the theory. We will examine the validation process more closely in the next section.

Expectancy theory provides a rich rational basis for understanding motivation in a given job. Each component is a framework for analyzing the motivation process. First, we should consider the outcomes provided and their rated valence. If a person feels indifferent about the outcomes (they have a low valence), there is no reason to work hard for their attainment. Expectancy theory therefore says that the first ingredient for motivation is desired outcomes. Second, the person must believe that there is some relationship between job performance and outcome attainment (instrumentalities must be high). If a person wants the outcomes but doesn't see performance as a means of getting them, there is no link between what they do and what they want. Reward practices and the role of the supervisor are crucial in establishing high instrumentalities. If a supervisor says, "Your performance has been very good lately; therefore, I will reward you with a raise (or promotion)," the individual would see that the attainment of a pay raise or a promotion is conditional (instrumental) on good performance. Conversely, if a supervisor says, "We don't give pay raises or promotions on the basis of performance; we grant them only on the basis of seniority," the individual would not be motivated to perform well to attain these outcomes. Perhaps the only motivation would be to work hard enough not to be fired, so that these outcomes would eventually be attained through increased service with the organization. When outcomes are made contingent on performance and the individual understands this outcome-performance relationship, expectancy theory predicts job performance will be enhanced.

Finally, the notion of expectancy is crucial. The person must see a relationship (an expectancy) between how hard they try and how well they perform. If expectancy is low, it will make no difference to the individual whether he or she works hard, as effort and performance seem unrelated. When I first started college, I was a chemistry major. I desired certain outcomes (e.g., good grades, a sense of accomplishment). I also realized attaining these outcomes was conditional on my performance in classes. I had both high valences for the outcomes and perceived high instrumentalities. However, after three agonizing semesters, my expectancy was near zero. It didn't seem to matter how hard I tried; I just couldn't alter my (low) performance in chemistry classes. My overall motivation fell dramatically along with my performance, and I eventually chose a new major. In retrospect, I realize I lacked the abilities to perform well as a chemist. All the motivation I could muster would not lead to good performance.

The idea of expectancy also explains why some jobs seem to create high or low motivation. On assembly lines, performance level is determined by the speed of the line. Even if a person works hard, he or she cannot produce any more until the next object moves down the line. Employees soon learn that they only have to keep pace with the line. There is no relationship between individual effort and performance of the line. Alternatively, sales jobs are characterized by high expectancy. Sales people who are paid on commission realize that the harder they try (the more sales calls they make), the better their performance (sales volume). Expectancy theory would predict that motivation is greatest in jobs with high expectancies.

In summary, expectancy theory is very good at diagnosing the components of motivation. It provides a rational basis to understand the effort expenditure of people. In the next section, we will examine some of the research that has empirically tested the theory.

**Empirical tests of the theory.**    Implicit in expectancy theory is a measurement issue. The theory revolves around the relationship of valences, instrumentalities, and expectancy. Thus, measuring them with a high degree of reliability is important. A second issue is what to do with these concepts after we have measured them. Various studies have dealt with both issues.

Research on reliability of the valence, instrumentality, and expectancy measures is quite positive (Mitchell, 1974). Reliability estimates in the .70s and .80s are not uncommon for valence and instrumentality. This is taken to mean that preferences for outcomes (valences) and perceptions of outcome-performance relationships (instrumentalities) are fairly stable. Reliability of expectancy is somewhat lower; these coefficients cluster in the .50 to .60 range. This suggests some variability in perception of the extent that increasing effort leads to increasing performance. Perhaps situational factors (like feedback from supervisors) induce variation in perceptions of this concept. While some studies (e.g., Dachler & Mobley, 1973; DeLeo & Pritchard, 1974) have reported lower reliabilities for these components, on par it seems that the stability of the measurements is not a major problem.

Expectancy theory further states that the components should be multiplied to yield a force score. Before numbers can be multiplied, they should have ratio scale properties. The three components of the theory have only interval scale properties at best, and in some research designs, they are measured in a way as only to have ordinal scale properties. Schmidt (1973) stated that the multiplication of these components not only violates the principles of measurement, but may also yield spurious results. Schmidt feels that until we can measure these components with more precision, we should not be multiplying them together. However, Arnold and Evans (1979) countered Schmidt's argument by developing a statistical procedure which permits the multiplication of these terms even though they are not measured on a ratio scale.

The measurement issue is significant because we multiply these components together to enhance prediction of the criterion. By violating measurement assumptions, we may delude ourselves about the predictive power of the theory. Some research (e.g., Mitchell & Knudsen, 1973; Muchinsky & Taylor, 1976) showed that equally good predictions can be made by eliminating a component (as valence) from the theory or by simply *adding* rather than multiplying the components. Thus, on theoretical grounds, we should measure all the components and multiply them; but on empirical grounds, comparably good predictions can be made with alternative procedures. Research on this aspect of the theory suggests that the three components do not add unique information (similar to the finding on weighting the facets of job satisfaction by their importance), so reduced theoretical formulations have comparable predictive power. Limitations in our ability to measure the components may cause empirical findings to deviate from the postulations made by the theory.

Research has also been done on the specific predictions the theory tries to make. Two approaches have been taken. One assumes the theory tries to distinguish the "most motivated" from the "least motivated" people in a group. With one force score derived for each person, supposedly the person with the largest force score is most motivated, while the person with the smallest score, least. This type of approach is called an *across-subjects* design, because predictions are made across people. The second approach tests the theory differently. It is assumed that each person is confronted with many tasks, and the theory then tries to predict on which tasks the person will work the hardest and on which he or she will expend the least effort. The theory is expanded to derive a force score for each task under consideration, and a criterion of effort is obtained for each task. For *each* person, a correlation is computed between predictions of effort made by the theory and actual amounts of effort expended on the tasks. This type of approach is called a *within-subjects* design; predictions are made for each individual separately.

Validation studies generally find better predictions for the within-subjects design than the across-subjects design. Average validity coefficients for an across-subjects design are usually in the .30s to .40s (e.g., Lawler & Porter, 1967; Pritchard & Sanders, 1973). Average validity coefficients for within-subjects designs are usually in the .50s to .60s (Matsui, Kagawa, Nagamatsu, & Ohtsuka, 1977; Muchinsky, 1977). The theory seems better at predicting various levels of effort an individual will expend on different tasks than at predicting gradations of motivation across different people. These validity coefficients are quite impressive; they are generally higher than those reported for other motivation theories.

In a major study on incentive motivation techniques, Pritchard, DeLeo, and Von Bergen (1976) reported that, if properly designed, a successful program to motivate employees will have many of the attributes proposed by expectancy theory. Among the conditions they recommend for a successful program are:

1. Incentives (outcomes) must be carefully sought out and identified as highly attractive.
2. The rules (behaviors) for attaining the incentives must be clear to those administering the system and to those actually in the system.
3. People in the system must perceive that variations in controllable aspects of their behavior will result in variations in their level of performance and, ultimately, their rewards.

In somewhat different words, these three conditions for an effective incentive motivation program reflect the concepts of valence, instrumentality, and expectancy, respectively. The importance of having desired incentives is another way of stating that the outcomes should have high valence. The clarity of the behaviors needed to attain the incentives is reflective of the strength or magnitude of the instrumentalities. The ability to control levels of performance through differential effort expenditure is indicative of the concept of expectancy. In short, expectancy theory contains the key elements needed for a successful incentive system as derived through empirical research. While not all research on expectancy theory is totally supportive, in general, the results tended to confirm the theory's predictions.

**Evaluation of the theory.**    Expectancy theory is a highly rational and conscious explanation of human motivation. People are assumed to behave in a way that maximizes expected gains (attainment of outcomes) from performing certain job behaviors and expending certain levels of effort. To the extent that behavior is not directed toward maximizing gains in a rational, systematic way, the theory will not be upheld. Whenever unconscious motives deflect behavior from what a knowledge of conscious processes would predict, expectancy theory will not be predictive (Miner, 1980). Research suggests that people differ in the extent that their behavior is motivated by rational processes. This was quite apparent in a study by Muchinsky (1977). I examined the extent that expectancy theory predicted the amount of effort college students put into each course they were taking. With a within-subjects design, the average validity of the theory for all students was .52; however, validity coefficients for individual students ranged from −.08 to .92. Thus, the theory very accurately predicted the effort expenditure of some students, and was unable to predict the effort of others. This supports the idea that some people have a very rational basis for their behavior (and thus the theory works well for them); others appear to be motivated more by unconscious factors (thus the theory does not work well for them).

Additional research (Broedling, 1975; Lied & Pritchard, 1976) showed that there are some personality correlates of expectancy theory. Individuals for whom the theory is most predictive have an internal, as opposed to external, locus of control. Such people believe that events in their lives are largely subject to their own influence. Individuals with an external locus of control see themselves as largely at the mercy of fate. Given the rational emphasis of expectancy theory, it is not surprising that individuals with an internal locus emerge as more strongly motivated according to the theory.

While problems still exist with the measurement of the components, in general, empirical support for the theory is quite strong. Expectancy theory also has limitations in terms of applicability to different types of people. Despite these problems, the prevailing consensus is that it is the dominant motivation theory in I/O psychology today. While other motivational theories also show promise for explaining selected aspects of behavior, probably none has received the consistent support and has the generalizability of expectancy theory.

**Reinforcement theory**

**Statement of the theory.**    Reinforcement theory is one of the older approaches to motivation; what is novel is its application to industrial workers. It is also referred to as operant conditioning and behaviorism. The origins go back to the research of B. F. Skinner and his work on the conditioning of animals. It was not until the 1970s that I/O psychologists began to see some potential application of reinforcement theory to the motivational problems of employees.

The theory has three key variables: stimulus, response, and reward. A *stimulus* is any variable or condition that elicits a behavioral response. In an industrial setting, a *response* would be some measure of job performance like productivity, absenteeism, or accidents. A *reward* is something of value given to the employee on the basis of the elicited behavioral response, since the reward is meant to reinforce the occurrence of the desired response. Most attention has been paid to the response-reward connection. Based on research with animals, four types of response-reward connections or contingencies were found to influence the frequency of the response:

*Fixed interval.* The subject is rewarded at a fixed time interval, such as every hour. Those paid on an hourly basis can be thought of as rewarded on a fixed interval basis.

*Fixed ratio.* The subject is rewarded as a function of making a fixed number of responses. For example, a real estate salesperson who gets a commission after each sale is rewarded on a fixed ratio schedule. In this case, the reward schedule is said to be *continuous*.

*Variable interval.* The subject is rewarded at some time interval, but the interval varies.

*Variable ratio.* Reward is based on behavior, but the ratio of reward to response is variable. Using the example of the salesperson again, the person might sometimes be paid after each sale; at other times, payment would be made after two or three sales. The person would be paid on the basis of the response (i.e., making a sale), but the schedule of payment would not be constant.

Advocates of reinforcement theory believe that magnitude of the subjects' motivation to respond can be shaped by manipulating these reinforcement schedules.

A number of authors (e.g., Jablonsky & DeVries, 1972; Nord, 1969) discussed the potential benefits and liabilities of using reinforcement theory as a basis to motivate employees. Nord (1969) said that it entails placing the control of employee motivation in the hands of the organization since organizations can "regulate" the energy output of employees by manipulating reinforcement schedules. Nord thinks most people would like to feel in control of their own lives, rather than being manipulated into certain patterns of behavior by the organization. The issue of responsibility for controlling behavior is very sensitive because there are ethical considerations regarding employee welfare. If an employee works himself to exhaustion through mismanagement of his own efforts, he is responsible for his own actions. However, the employee who is manipulated into expending excessive effort has been victimized by a force beyond his control, and the organization should be held responsible for his condition. Issues of ethical responsibility for behavior are not central to the theory, but they are important when the theory is applied in daily life. Whenever anything is "done" to someone by an outside agent, *whose* values (the individual's or the agent's) are being optimized must be questioned.

**Empirical tests of the theory.** Empirical tests of reinforcement theory have involved determining which schedule of reinforcement has the greatest effect on increasing the occurrence of the desired behavioral response. In a series of studies involving tree planters, Yukl and Latham (1975) and Yukl, Latham, and Pursell (1976) compared the effectiveness of various schedules of reinforcement. Some planters were paid on a fixed interval schedule (hourly pay); others were paid based on how many trees they planted. Employees paid on a ratio schedule were significantly more productive (planted more trees). Pritchard, Leonard, Von Bergen, and Kirk (1976) examined the effect of different payment schedules on employees' ability to pass self-paced learning tests of electrical knowledge. Some employees were paid a flat hourly wage, others according to the number of tests they passed. Two types of ratio payment schedules were used, fixed (the employee was paid after passing every third test) and variable (the employee was paid after passing a variable number). The results of the study are shown in Figure 10–4. Employees paid contingently (i.e., based on their performance) passed 60 percent of the tests, those paid by the hour passed about 40 percent. Results also showed no difference in test performance between fixed and variable ratio reinforcement schedules. A

**Figure 10–4**        **Percent of tests passed under different schedules of reinforcement**

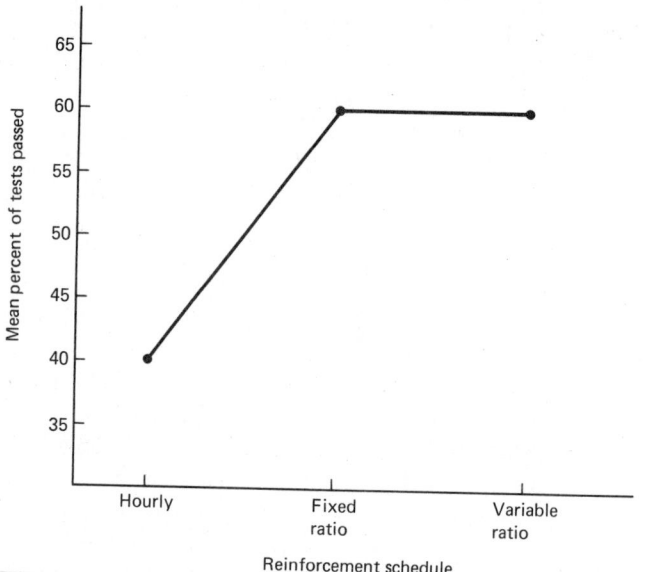

Source: R. D. Pritchard, D. W. Leonard, C. W. Von Bergen, and R. J. Kirk, "The Effect of Varying Schedules of Reinforcement on Human Task Performance," *Organizational Behavior and Human Performance* 16 (1976), pp. 205–30.

later study by Pritchard, Hollenback, and DeLeo (1980) confirmed that ratio schedules were more effective than interval schedules. However, there is no apparent difference among the different types of ratio schedules.

Research on reinforcement theory is not limited to measures of productivity. Pedalino and Gamboa (1974) described how the theory could be used to decrease absenteeism. The authors devised a plan whereby every employee who came to work on time was dealt one card from a poker deck. Each day, the attending employees were dealt a new card. At the end of the week, the employee with the best poker hand won $20. In this case, the desired response (attendance) was reinforced through money reward. Attendance under this plan was greater than before the program was introduced.

**Evaluation of the theory.**   Research clearly indicates that the principles of reinforcement theory do "work." However, the theory suffers from some limitations in industrial settings. As Mawhinney (1975) noted, current applications of reinforcement theory tend to ignore individual differences in what people value as rewards. In the Pedalino and Gamboa study, for example, it was assumed that all the employees were interested in playing poker and would respond positively to a gambling/lottery situation. Vast individual differences in preferences would preclude the success of any such program. Second, reinforcement has been primarily limited to studies of quantity of production. We don't know very much about how *quality* of performance is affected, the long-term effects of various reinforcement schedules, or people's attitudes toward such incentive methods. As Heiman (1975) commented, reinforcement theory seems fairly limited in applicability.

A second major issue involves ethics, values, and acceptability of the procedures advocated by reinforcement theory. How ethical is it for an organization to use a payment system that increases productivity but may cause adverse side effects? As Landy and Trumbo (1980) report, in Sweden piece-rate payment schedules have been condemmed because they cause tension and ultimately damage the mental and physical well-being of workers. There is also evidence that workers in short-cycle, monotonous jobs prefer hourly rates to piece rates. They complain that piece-rate systems "control" them (or at least their behavior), which is exactly the intent of the system. Indeed Pritchard et al. (1980) reported that subjects paid by the hour were most satisfied with their work. At the core of reinforcement theory is the assumption that people's behavior can be molded, shaped, or manipulated by tactical operations (e.g., methods of payment) used on them. It is one thing to use reinforcement theory to mold the behavior of rats in a maze; it is quite another to use it to mold the behavior of responsible, intelligent humans. The principles are the same, but the ethical responsibilities of the "controller" differ. Some authors are optimistic about using reinforcement theory in the work force (Schneier, 1974; Potter, 1980); others (Whyte, 1972) are more pessimistic for either operational or ethical reasons. What is clear from the research is that with certain types of tasks, piece-rate or ratio payment schedules induce more productivity than hourly or interval payment schedules. Ethical issues aside, this suggests that human motivation can be enhanced by using certain reward contingencies. However, there is not much apparent support for the use of reinforcement theory as a broadly generalizable theory of motivation applicable to a wide range of work behavior.

## Goal setting

**Statement of the theory.** Goal setting is a motivation theory based on the assumption that people behave rationally and consciously. The crux of the theory rests on the relationship between conscious goals, intentions, and task performance. The basic premise is that conscious ideas regulate a person's actions. Goals and intentions are what the individual is consciously trying to do, particularly as related to future objectives.

According to Locke (1968), goals have two major functions. They are a basis for motivation, and they direct behavior. A goal provides guidelines for deciding how much effort to put into work. Goals are intended behaviors; in turn, they influence task performance. However, two conditions must be met before goals can positively influence performance. First, the individual must be aware of the goal and know what must be accomplished (McCormick & Ilgen, 1980). Second, the individual must *accept* the goal as something he or she is willing to work for. Goals can be rejected because they are seen as too difficult, too easy, or because the person doesn't know what behaviors are needed for goal attainment. Acceptance of the goal implies the individual intends to engage in the behavior needed for goal attainment.

Locke's theory of goal setting states that more difficult goals lead to higher levels of job performance. Locke believed that commitment to a goal is proportional to its difficulty, so more difficult goals engender more commitment to their attainment (Steers & Porter, 1974). Goals can vary in specificity as well as difficulty. Some goals are general (to be a good biology student), while others are more specific (to get an A on the next biology test). The more specific the goal, the more concentrated the individual's effort in its pursuit. Goals direct behavior; the more specific the goal, the more directed the behavior (Terborg, 1977). It is also important for the person to receive feedback about task performance; this guides an individual as to whether he or she should work harder or continue at the same pace.

Therefore, according to goal setting theory, the following factors and conditions would induce high motivation and task performance. Goals are behavioral intentions that channel our energies in certain directions. The more difficult and more specific the goal, the greater will be our motivation to attain the goal. Feedback on our performance in pursuit of the goal tells us if we are "on target" in our efforts. The source of motivation, according to goal setting, is the desire and intention to attain the goal; this must be coupled with the individual's acceptance of the goal. Rather than being motivated by innate needs, feelings of inequity, or schedules of reinforcement, goal setting assumes people set acceptable target objectives and then channel their efforts in pursuit of them.

**Empirical tests of the theory.** For the most part, empirical tests of the theory are quite supportive. Latham and Yukl (1975a) reviewed over 25 field studies of goal setting, and nearly all substantiated the theory. As an example, Latham and Baldes (1975) studied truck drivers hauling logs to lumber mills. Performance was studied under two conditions. First, drivers were told only to "do their best" in loading the trucks. After a time, they were told to set a specific and rather hard goal of loading their trucks up to 94 percent of the legal weight limit. (The closer to the legal limit, the fewer trips were needed.) Each truck driver got feedback via a loading scale indicating tonnage. Figure 10–5 shows performance of the drivers over a 48-week period. At the onset of goal setting, performance improved greatly. However, the cause is not clear-cut. One explanation may be due to the effects of goal setting. Another could be a sense of competition among the drivers as to who would load the truck closest to the legal limit. In any

**Figure 10–5**        **The effect of specific hard goals on productivity**

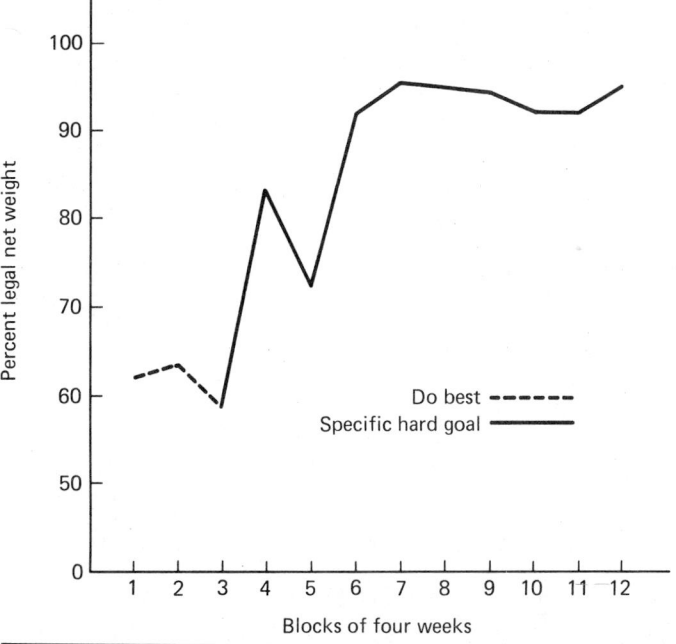

SOURCE: G. P. Latham and J. J. Baldes, "The Practical Significance of Locke's Theory of Goal Setting," *Journal of Applied Psychology* 60 (1975), pp. 122–24.

case, the study clearly showed that performance under goal setting was superior to the "do your best" condition.

In another study, Latham and Yukl (1975b) compared effectiveness of three types of goal setting on the performance of logging crews. One method of goal setting was simply to tell the crew members to "do their best." The second was for goals to be designated or assigned to the crew members; with the third, the loggers participated in setting their own goals. The results showed participation produced better performance and more frequent goal attainment. The average goal level set by the loggers was greater than the goal level set in the assigned group, which suggests that the performance difference was due in part to greater goal difficulty in the participative condition. Also, goal attainment was highest with participation despite more difficult goals. This suggests that goal acceptance was increased by participation.

While goal setting has been found to be effective in reaching certain levels of task performance, some research shows that groups differ in their acceptance of goals and in the behavior they see as related to goal attainment. Ivancevich and McMahon (1977) compared black and white technicians in a goal-setting program. Blacks were found to want more feedback and participation in the goal setting process, while whites wanted more difficult goals. Thus, there appear to be race-linked differences in acceptance of goal setting, and additional moderating differences may be found in future research. While variation does exist in terms of task behaviors and acceptance of goal setting, research indicates goal setting produces better performance than the absence of goals or very general goals.

**Evaluation of the theory.**    You should be struck by the elegance and simplicity of goal setting theory. There are no references to innate needs, perceived instrumentalities, or comparison others: the theory is not based on abstract concepts or hypothetical constructs. The theory states that the most effective task performance is obtained by intentionally channeling one's efforts in pursuit of a desired objective or goal. Difficulty and specificity of the goal influence performance. So do the amount and nature of feedback. There are some differences in performance if goals are assigned or self-selected. Different types of people also prefer different types of goals. But it is clear that goal setting elicits better performance.

Goal setting seems to be generalizable as a theory of motivation. It is not limited in applicability to highly rational people, though it does assume that people consciously follow through with their intentions. The theory has a cognitive basis: employees must think about the goals they want to pursue; they must decide whether the goal is acceptable; they must understand what behaviors they have to exhibit to attain the goal; and they must know how to evaluate feedback on their progress. Research on feedback (e.g., Erez, 1977; Kim & Hamner, 1976) showed that feedback is critical for optimal performance; but people differ in their ability to use the information provided. There is also evidence that goal setting is effective for groups as well as individuals. Thus, a work group can set a goal to decrease their scrap rate, for example, or to increase their productive output. Group goals can be more difficult to attain, however, in that in many cases, success of the group is more than just the success of individual members. A basketball team may set a goal of winning so many games a season, but team success will be determined by more than just the number of points scored by each player. Member coordination and integration must also be considered. One player might help the team by passing, another by rebounding, while the others might best serve as shooters.

Certain situational factors must also be present. A production worker can't increase the speed of an assembly line to be more productive. In some cases, effort or desire alone may not be enough for goal attainment. Reasonable opportunity must be provided. Perceptions of this opportunity may be a deciding factor in whether a person accepts a goal.

The concept of goal setting underlies management by objectives (MBO), a management technique meant to increase performance through goal setting (McConkie, 1979). There are many variations of MBO. In principle, a worker and his or her supervisor set objectives for the worker's future performance. By allowing the worker to take part in the goal setting process, it is thus thought that the worker's commitment to the goal will be greater. Though it is beyond our scope to fully discuss MBO, it is an actual management tool derived from empirical research on goal setting. Whenever industry adopts a procedure developed through scientific investigation, it is a fair indication that the procedure does indeed "work" outside the laboratory. Research on MBO, and on goal setting in general, is quite supportive. We are not totally clear on causal relationships, and more research must be done on issues relating to goal setting. But I/O psychologists are convinced that goal setting is a way of increasing task performance. Landy and Trumbo (1980) feel that the diverse findings should be placed in coherent framework general enough to embrace many work behaviors. Then goal setting may be the most reasonable approach to work motivation.

## Intrinsic motivation

**Statement of the theory.** Although it is not a complete theory, Deci (1975) proposed that people expend effort due to intrinsic as well as extrinsic motivation. If extrinsically motivated, people perform tasks because of the external rewards (e.g., money) such behavior will provide. If intrinsically motivated, they perform tasks for the inherent pleasure derived from engaging in those behaviors. Deci believed that people like to be responsible for their own actions, as opposed to believing something (external) is done to them. When people are made to behave in certain ways through punishment or rewards, they lose control over their actions. Deci believes jobs should be created so people get feelings of competence and pleasure. At the same time they should feel they are in control of their actions. These conditions would induce intrinsic motivation. In theory, an intrinsically

A vivid example of goal attainment. Winning a marathon requires a high degree of motivation (and a lot of ability).

*Wide World Photos*

motivated person will be more satisfied and committed to a task than a person who is extrinsically motivated.

Most researchers believe that motivation is additive. People will make an effort because a task is enjoyable (intrinsically motivating) and because they are externally rewarded (extrinsically motivating). Deci does not share this belief. He feels that when external rewards are tied directly to performance, intrinsic motivation declines. Thus, Deci suggests that paying someone for doing a task he or she also likes will decrease their intrinsic motivation. The issue becomes one of a changing locus of causation. If a person is paid for performing the task, their behavior is caused by the external reward. As the locus of control for the individual's actions shifts to something in the environment, the individual loses intrinsic motivation because the task is no longer performed for the feelings of competence and self-control. Deci argues that externally rewarding people for doing tasks they enjoy will, in the long run, decrease motivation.

**Empirical tests of the theory.** Deci derived most of the support for his theory in laboratory studies involving puzzles and games. For example, Deci (1972) conducted a study in which subjects were paid hourly or contingently for working on a puzzle they found enjoyable. Contingently paid subjects were rewarded for every puzzle they correctly solved. After the session, the subjects were given a chance to keep working on the puzzles for no pay. Deci discovered that subjects who were paid contingently spent less time working on the puzzles in the nonpay period than those subjects who were paid hourly to work on the puzzles. He concluded that when external rewards (money) are tied directly to performance (contingent payment), intrinsic motivation (desire to work on an enjoyable task) decreased.

Deci conducted other, similar studies. The paradigm was consistent. People were paid to perform a pleasurable task either contingently or not. Contingently rewarded subjects spent less time performing the same task in a "free period." Several others investigated the extent that external rewards decreased intrinsic motivation. The majority of these studies (e.g., Hamner & Foster, 1975; Phillips & Lord, 1980) did not clearly support Deci's contention that contingent pay decreases intrinsic motivation. People may not believe that contingent payment means their actions are being controlled by external forces. Or the effect of contingent payment may not be strong enough to diminish intrinsic motivation. These studies did not replicate Deci's findings. But they challenged the assumption that intrinsic and extrinsic motivation is additive. These studies did show that Deci was correct in stating that motivation is not simply additive (Pritchard, Campbell, & Campbell, 1977). If a person performs a task for sheer pleasure, paying him or her won't necessarily add to their motivation to perform the task. This research shows that external rewards can enhance motivation for certain, but not all, tasks.

**Evaluation of the theory.** Theories of intrinsic motivation suffer from many theoretical, methodological, and practical problems. On the theoretical side, there is confusion about what is meant by "intrinsic"—to the individual or the task (Scott, 1976)? If I find a task boring but you find it interesting, what is "intrinsic" seems to be within the individual. If many people find one task (a puzzle) fun but another (sorting cards) dull, what is "intrinsic" seems to be within the task. Whether theories of intrinsic motivation relate to differences in people or in jobs is unclear. What is intrinsic and what is extrinsic is also unclear (Dyer & Parker, 1975). What one person sees as extrinsic (the pay increase associated with a promotion), another might see as intrinsic (the gratification of accomplishment). The failure to clearly differentiate intrinsic from extrinsic rewards greatly undermines the basis of Deci's contentions.

Intrinsic motivation is dominated by laboratory research. Mawhinney (1979) and others feel the theory should be tested under field conditions as well. Problems with methodology underscore problems with the theory itself. Usually researchers have to carefully sort through an array of potential tasks to find one that subjects uniformly believe is interesting. If such "intrinsically motivating" tasks are so hard to come by, one can question the applicability of the theory. Also the time subjects spend working on the task in the free period (the typical dependent variable in such studies) is usually measured in *seconds* or *minutes*. If a person spends five extra minutes putting a puzzle together, broad conclusions are drawn on the generalizability of the findings. Obviously, for industrial applications, such generalizations are absurd. We are interested in the persistence of behavior over months and years, not minutes. The limitations of laboratory studies testing intrinsic motivation, as with equity theory, are particularly acute.

Finally we can ask about the practical implications of intrinsic motivation. We don't seem to have firm guidelines as to what an organization can do to pay people for jobs they find intrinsically motivating. Deci would contend they be paid noncontingently; other researchers are not so certain. How long an intrinsically motivating task will remain so is also debated. A puzzle may lose its appeal if a person has to work it eight hours a day, five days a week. We can conclude that some people find some tasks enjoyable (at least for short periods); when they are paid to perform these tasks contingently, such tasks lose some of their appeal. (At least the person's desire to perform the task decreases). There are anecdotes about people who like their jobs so much they would do them for little or nothing, but the average worker is not in that position. It seems that theories of intrinsic motivation have not been much help in explaining work motivation. Perhaps the research indicates that recreational pursuits (doing puzzles) should be intrinsically appealing if they are to sustain interests; but if it weren't for jobs that paid external rewards, people wouldn't have the time or money to pursue such activities.

## OVERVIEW AND SYNTHESIS OF WORK MOTIVATION THEORIES

Integrating theories of work motivation is an awesome task. At this stage of development, it is probably impossible. We can step back and view these theories from a broad perspective, highlighting major points of divergence and convergence. Landy and Trumbo (1980) make the astute observation that theories of work motivation are often more complex than the behavior they try to explain. The preceding sections dealt with each of these complex theories in detail; we will now attempt to simplify the perspectives.

The six theories discussed roughly reflect three different views of motivation. Need theories and the theory of intrinsic motivation presume that people are motivated by internal factors. These are either innate needs causing us to seek fulfillment or feelings of pleasure and self-control from performing tasks we find enjoyable. Expectancy theory and goal-setting theory presume that people are rational. After carefully considering our wants and the relationship between behavior and attaining desired outcomes or goals, we make an effort to maximize the chances of obtaining what we want. Equity theory and reinforcement theory presume we are motivated by external factors. With equity theory, our perceptions of what others are giving and getting is involved. With reinforcement theory, motivation is a product of a schedule of rewards.

We are left with diverse theoretical perspectives: either motivation springs from within us due to unconscious forces; it is a product of rationally calculating what we must do to get what we want; or it is a product of things that are "done" to us.

Which perspective is most defensible? There is some research support for all of them. But some theories received more confirmation than others. This is, in part, what makes motivation so intriguing. No theories are absolutely "wrong." But no theory to date has received so much support that it can be declared *the* theory of motivation. Even those receiving most research support make different predictions. Probably the two best theories of work motivation are expectancy theory and goal setting theory. Expectancy theory advocates setting easy goals to maximize motivation—the probability of effort resulting in attainment is very high. Goal setting advocates the opposite—setting difficult goals. Perhaps the theories differ on this point only in regard to time. Easier goals should first be set so people can build up confidence (expectancy) that effort will result in performance, which will lead to outcome attainment. As expectancy grows, progressively harder goals could be set, which could lead to even greater attainment. Goal setting theory stresses the difficulty of the goal; expectancy theory stresses the perceived relationship between effort, performance, and outcome attainment. Thus, predictions made by each theory need not be contradictory.

If we could distill the best of each of the six theories, we would arrive at the following: Need theory reminds us that individual differences are important and that our efforts will always first be channeled toward survival before social fulfillment. Different people have different needs and desires; any good theory of motivation must allow for this. Equity theory emphasizes that what we do is in part a product of what people around us do. We are social creatures; we do not exist in a vacuum. What we eat, how we dress, and how hard we work are all determined to some degree by other people in our environment. Expectancy theory raises motivation to a conscious choice. We deliberately choose how hard to work based on the gains we expect to receive from our efforts. If we don't see any benefit from our

**Table 10–4**                    **Summary and evaluation of six theories of work motivation**

| Theory | Source of motivation | Empirical support | Industrial applicability |
|---|---|---|---|
| 1. Need theory | Unconscious, innate needs. | Weak<br>Little support for proposed relationships among needs. | Very limited<br>Theory lacks sufficient specificity to guide behavior. |
| 2. Equity theory | The drive to reduce feelings of tension caused by perceived inequity. | Mixed<br>Good support for underpayment inequity, weak support for overpayment inequity. | Limited<br>Social comparisons are made, but feelings of inequity can be reduced through means other than increased motivation. |
| 3. Expectancy theory | The relationship among desired outcomes, performance-reward and effort-performance variables. | Moderate-strong<br>Theory is more strongly supported in within-subject than across-subject experiments. | Strong<br>Theory provides a rational basis for why people expend effort, although not all behavior is as consciously determined as the theory postulates. |
| 4. Reinforcement theory | The schedule of reinforcement used to reward people for their performance. | Moderate<br>Ratio reinforcement schedules evoke superior performance compared to interval schedules, but little difference exists among various ratio schedules. | Moderate<br>Contingent payment for performance is possible in some jobs, although ethical problems can be present in an organization's attempt to shape employee behavior. |
| 5. Goal setting theory | The intention to direct behavior in pursuit of an acceptable goal. | Moderate-strong<br>Performance under goal setting conditions is usually superior to conditions under which no goals are set. | Strong<br>The ability to set goals is not restricted to certain types of people or jobs. |
| 6. Intrinsic motivation theory | Feelings of competence and self-control that come from performing enjoyable tasks. | Mixed<br>Extrinsic and intrinsic rewards do not seem to be purely additive, but extrinsic rewards do not always decrease intrinsic motivation. | Very limited<br>Little evidence that intrinsically motivating tasks remain intrinsically motivating for long periods of time. |

efforts, we will not be motivated. Goal setting theory stresses that motivation is maximized by setting specific target objectives; such goals can prevent an ineffective diffusion of effort. Reinforcement theory states that when people are rewarded on units of performance as opposed to units of time, motivation is greater. Finally, intrinsic motivation theory suggests that people prefer to expend effort on tasks that enhance feelings of personal control and competence. A composite theory of motivation, drawing on the strengths of existing theories, would ideally include these findings as established by research. A general summary of all the motivation theories is presented in Table 10–4.

To what extent have these theories improved understanding of motivation in the work force? Any manager who adopted one theory (to the exclusion of the others) would probably not be very successful. Motivation is very complicated, and no one theory always "works." Pinder (1977) makes the point that when practitioners ask "How do I motivate my employees?" the researcher's answer should indeed be tentative. There are no automatic solutions to problems of worker motivation. If there were, you wouldn't have read about six different theories. As Pinder states, given the degree of empirical support, total application of a theory in industry is simply premature. We don't know enough to offer pat solutions—simple answers rarely serve complex problems. What you should learn from this chapter is that many approaches exist, and an understanding of all of them is necessary to appreciate the intricacies and dynamics of motivation in the work force.

# CASE STUDY

Joe Collins, production manager of York Tool and Die Company, tapped Harry Simpson on the shoulder. "Harry," Collins said, "I'd like to talk to you in my office."

"Right now?" asked Simpson.

"Right now," Collins replied.

Simpson took off his safety goggles and put them on the rack. He was a line foreman, and it was unusual to be called away from his line. He figured it had to be something big, otherwise Collins would have waited until break.

"Hey Willie," Simpson yelled at his lead man, "cover for me, will you? I've got to talk to Joe."

Simpson walked into Collins' office and sat down. The look on Collins' face told him it wasn't going to be good news.

"Harry, I've known you for eight years," Collins began. "You've always kept your nose to the grindstone. You've been conscientious and diligent. I've had fewer problems with you than with most of the other foremen. But lately things have been different. You've come to work late five times in the past month. You've been late turning in your weekly production sheets. The scrap rate of your line has been going up, too. I was also told that Willie had to spend a lot of time breaking in the two new guys. That's your job. What's going on, Harry?"

Simpson shuffled his feet and cleared his throat. "I didn't realize these things were happening."

"You didn't know you were late?!" Collins was incredulous. "You've been coming to work at 7:30 for eight years. When you punch in at 7:45, you're late, and you know it."

"I don't know, Joe, I just haven't felt 'with it' lately," Simpson explained. "Doris says I've been moping around the house a lot lately, too."

"I'm not here to chew you out, Harry," Collins replied. "You're a valuable man. I want to find a way to get you back in gear. Anything been bugging you lately?"

"Well, I've finally figured out I'm not going to make it to supervisor. At least not in the near future. That's what I've been working for all along. Maybe I've hit my peak. When Coleman made it to supervisor, I figured I'd be the next one up. But it never happened. I'm not sore—Coleman is a good man, and he deserved it. I just feel kind of deflated."

"You're well respected by management, Harry, and your line thinks you're great, too. You've set a tough example to live up to. I want you to keep it up—we need people like you."

"I know I have an important job," said Simpson, "but I figure I can't get ahead anymore, at least not on how well I do my job. I guess it boils down to luck or something."

"What if I give you a new line to run?" Collins asked. "Would that give you a new challenge?"

"No, I wouldn't want that, Joe," replied Simpson. "I like my line, and I don't want to leave them."

"Alright Harry, but here's the deal," Collins stated. "I want you to cut back on the lateness, pronto. Get your production reports in on time, and watch the scrap. With the price of copper going up, we've got to play it tight. Oh, and give Willie a break. He's got enough to do. Does this sound okay to you?"

"Yeah," Simpson said, "You're only telling me to do what I'm supposed to be doing."

"Keep at it, Harry," Collins said with a smile. "In two more years, you'll get a 10-year-pin."

Simpson got up to leave. "It won't pay the rent, but I'd like to have it."

Simpson walked back to the line. Willie looked up and saw him coming.

"What'd Joe want?" Willie asked.

"Oh, nothing much," Simpson replied.

Willie knew Simpson was hiding something, and Simpson figured Willie knew what it was.

Questions

1. Which theory of motivation do you feel best explains the recent behavior of Simpson?
2. What would equity theory have predicted about Simpson's behavior following the promotion of Coleman?
3. In the terms of expectancy theory, how would you describe Simpson's valence for a promotion and its instrumentality?
4. What psychological needs did Collins appeal to in talking to Simpson?
5. How might you use reinforcement theory to shape the behavior of Simpson in the areas needing attention?

# REFERENCES

Adams, J. S. Inequity in social exchange. In L. Berkowitz (Ed.), *Advances in experimental social psychology* (Vol. 2). New York: Academic Press, 1965.

Adams, J. S., & Rosenbaum, W. B. The relationship of worker productivity to cognitive dissonance about wage inequities. *Journal of Applied Psychology*, 1962, *46*, 161–164.

Alderfer, C. P. An empirical test of a new theory of human needs. *Organizational Behavior and Human Performance*, 1969, *4*, 142–175.

Alderfer, C. P. *Existence, relatedness, and growth: Human needs in organizational settings.* New York: Free Press, 1972.

Arnold, H. J., & Evans, M. G. Testing multiplicative models does *not* require ratio scales. *Organizational Behavior and Human Performance*, 1979, *24*, 41–59.

Broedling, L. A. Relationship of internal-external control to work motivation and performance in an expectancy model. *Journal of Applied Psychology*, 1975, *60*, 65–70.

Campbell, J. P., & Pritchard, R. D. Motivation theory in industrial and organizational psychology. In M. D. Dunnette (Ed.), *Handbook of industrial and organizational psychology.* Skokie, Ill.: Rand McNally, 1976.

Carrell, M. R., & Dittrich, J. E. Equity theory: The recent literature, methodological considerations, and new directions. *Academy of Management Review*, 1978, *3*, 202–210.

Dachler, H. P., & Mobley, W. H. Construct validation of an instrumentality-expectancy task-goal model of work motivation: Some theoretical boundary conditions. *Journal of Applied Psychology*, 1973, *58*, 397–418.

Deci, E. L. The effects of contingent and noncontingent rewards and controls on intrinsic motivation. *Organizational Behavior and Human Performance*, 1972, *8*, 217–229.

Deci, E. L. *Intrinsic motivation.* New York: Plenum Press, 1975.

DeLeo, P. J., & Pritchard, R. D. An examination of some methodological problems in testing expectancy valence models with survey techniques. *Organizational Behavior and Human Performance*, 1974, *12*, 143–148.

Dyer, L., & Parker, D. F. Classifying outcomes in work motivation research: An examination of the intrinsic-extrinsic dichotomy. *Journal of Applied Psychology*, 1975, *60*, 455–458.

Erez, M. Feedback: A necessary condition for the goal setting-performance relationship. *Journal of Applied Psychology*, 1977, *62*, 624–627.

Georgopoulos, B. S., Mahoney, G. M., & Jones, N. W. A path-goal approach to productivity. *Journal of Applied Psychology*, 1957, *41*, 345–353.

Goodman, P. S., & Friedman, A. An examination of Adams' theory of inequity. *Administrative Science Quarterly*, 1971, *16*, 271–288.

Graen, G. Instrumentality theory of work motivation: Some experimental results and suggested modifications. *Journal of Applied Psychology Monograph*, 1969, *53*(2).

Hall, D. T., & Nougaim, K. E. An examination of Maslow's need hierarchy in an organizational setting. *Organizational Behavior and Human Performance*, 1968, *3*, 12–35.

Hamner, W. C., & Foster, L. W. Are intrinsic and extrinsic rewards additive: A test of Deci's cognitive evaluation theory of task motivation. *Organizational Behavior and Human Performance*, 1975, *14*, 398–415.

Heiman, G. W. A note on "Operant conditioning principles extrapolated to the theory of management." *Organizational Behavior and Human Performance*, 1975, *13*, 165–170.

Ivancevich, J. M., & McMahon, J. T. Black-white differences in a goal-setting program. *Organizational*

*Behavior and Human Performance*, 1977, *20*, 287–300.

Jablonsky, S. F., & DeVries, D. L. Operant conditioning principles extrapolated to the theory of management. *Organizational Behavior and Human Performance*, 1972, *7*, 340–358.

Kim, J. S., & Hamner, W. C. Effect of performance feedback and goal setting on productivity and satisfaction in an organizational setting. *Journal of Applied Psychology*, 1976, *61*, 48–57.

Landy, F. J., & Trumbo, D. A. *Psychology of work behavior* (rev. ed.). Homewood, Ill.: Dorsey Press, 1980.

Latham, G. P., & Baldes, J. J. The practical significance of Locke's theory of goal setting. *Journal of Applied Psychology*, 1975, *60*, 122–124.

Latham, G. P., & Yukl, G. A. A review of research on the application of goal setting in organizations. *Academy of Management Journal*, 1975, *18*, 824–845. (a)

Latham, G. P., & Yukl, G. A. Assigned versus participative goal-setting with educated and uneducated wood workers. *Journal of Applied Psychology*, 1975, *60*, 299–302. (b)

Lawler, E. E., & Porter, L. W. Antecedent attitudes of effective managerial performance. *Organizational Behavior and Human Performance*, 1967, *2*, 122–142.

Lawler, E. E., & Suttle, J. L. A causal correlational test of the need hierarchy concept. *Organizational Behavior and Human Behavior*, 1972, *7*, 265–287.

Lied, T. L., & Pritchard, R. D. Relationship between personality variables and components of the expectancy-valence model. *Journal of Applied Psychology*, 1976, *61*, 463–467.

Locke, E. A. Toward a theory of task motivation and incentives. *Organizational Behavior and Human Performance*, 1968, *3*, 157–189.

Maslow, A. H. *Motivation and personality*. New York: Harper & Row, 1954.

Maslow, A. H. *Motivation and personality* (2nd ed.). New York: Harper & Row, 1970.

Matsui, T., Kagawa, M., Nagamatsu, J., & Ohtsuka, Y. Validity of expectancy theory as a within-person behavioral choice model for sales activity. *Journal of Applied Psychology*, 1977, *62*, 764–767.

Mawhinney, T. C. Operant terms and concepts in the description of individual work behavior: Some problems of interpretation, application, and eval-

uation. *Journal of Applied Psychology*, 1975, *60*, 704–712.

Mawhinney, T. C. Intrinsic X extrinsic work motivation: Perspectives from behaviorism. *Organizational Behavior and Human Performance*, 1979, *24*, 411–440.

McConkie, M. L. A clarification of the goal setting and appraisal processes in MBO. *Academy of Management Review*, 1979, *4*, 29–40.

McCormick, E. J., & Ilgen, D. R. *Industrial psychology* (7th ed.). Englewood Cliffs, N.J.: Prentice-Hall, 1980.

Middlemist, R. D., & Peterson, R. B. Test of equity theory by controlling for comparison worker's efforts. *Organizational Behavior and Human Performance*, 1976, *15*, 335–354.

Miner, J. B. *Theories of organizational behavior*. Hinsdale, Ill.: Dryden Press, 1980.

Mitchell, T. R. Expectancy models of job satisfaction, occupational preference, and effort: A theoretical, methodological, and empirical appraisal. *Psychological Bulletin*, 1974, *81*, 1053–1077.

Mitchell, T. R., & Knudsen, B. W. Instrumentality theory predictions of students' attitudes towards business and their choice of business as an occupation. *Academy of Management Journal*, 1973, *16*, 41–51.

Mitchell, V. F., & Mougdill, P. Measurement of Maslow's need hierarchy. *Organizational Behavior and Human Performance*, 1976, *16*, 334–349.

Muchinsky, P. M. A comparison of within- and across-subjects analyses of the expectancy-valence model for predicting effort. *Academy of Management Journal*, 1977, *20*, 154–158.

Muchinsky, P. M., & Taylor, M. S. Intrasubject predictions of occupational preference: The effect of manipulating components of the valence model. *Journal of Vocational Behavior*, 1976, *8*, 185–195.

Nord, W. Beyond the teaching machine: The neglected area of operant conditioning in the theory and practice of management. *Organizational Behavior and Human Performance*, 1969, *4*, 375–401.

Pedalino, E., & Gamboa, V. U. Behavior modification and absenteeism. *Journal of Applied Psychology*, 1974, *59*, 694–698.

Phillips, J. S., & Lord, R. G. Determinants of intrinsic motivation: Locus of control and competence information as components of Deci's cognitive evaluation theory. *Journal of Applied Psychology*, 1980, *65*, 211–218.

Pinder, C. C. Concerning the application of human motivation theories in organizational settings. *Academy of Management Review*, 1977, *2*, 384–397.

Porter, L. W. A study of perceived need satisfaction in bottom and middle management jobs. *Journal of Applied Psychology*, 1961, *45*, 1–10.

Porter, L. W., & Lawler, E. E. *Managerial attitudes and performance*. Homewood, Ill.: Richard D. Irwin, 1968.

Potter, B. A. *Turning around: The behavioral approach to managing people*. New York: American Management Association, 1980.

Pritchard, R. D. Equity theory: A review and critique. *Organizational Behavior and Human Performance*, 1969, *4*, 176–211.

Pritchard, R. D., Campbell, K. M., & Campbell, D. J. The effects of extrinsic financial rewards on intrinsic motivation. *Journal of Applied Psychology*, 1977, *62*, 9–15.

Pritchard, R. D., DeLeo, P. J., & Von Bergen, C. W. A field experimental test of expectancy-valence incentive motivation techniques. *Organizational Behavior and Human Performance*, 1976, *15*, 355–406.

Pritchard, R. D., Dunnette, M. D., & Jorgenson, D. O. Effects of perceptions of equity and inequity on worker performance and satisfaction. *Journal of Applied Psychology*, 1972, *56*, 75–94.

Pritchard, R. D., Hollenback, J., & DeLeo, P. J. The effects of continuous and partial schedules of reinforcement on effort, performance, and satisfaction. *Organizational Behavior and Human Performance*, 1980, *25*, 336–353.

Pritchard, R. D., Leonard, D. W., Von Bergen, C. W., & Kirk, R. J. The effect of varying schedules of reinforcement on human task performance. *Organizational Behavior and Human Performance*, 1976, *16*, 205–230.

Pritchard, R. D., & Sanders, M. S. The influence of valence, instrumentality, and expectancy on effort and performance. *Journal of Applied Psychology*, 1973, *57*, 55–60.

Schmidt, F. L. Implications of a measurement problem for expectancy theory research. *Organizational Behavior and Human Performance*, 1973, *10*, 243–251.

Schneier, C. E. Behavior modification in management: A review and critique. *Academy of Management Journal*, 1974, *17*, 528–548.

Scott, W. E. The effects of extrinsic rewards on "intrinsic motivation." *Organizational Behavior and Human Performance*, 1976, *15*, 117–129.

Steers, R. M., & Porter, L. W. The role of task-goal attributes in employee performance. *Psychological Bulletin*, 1974, *81*, 434–452.

Steers, R. M., & Porter, L. W. (Eds.). *Motivation and work behavior*. New York: McGraw-Hill, 1975.

Terborg, J. R. Validation and extension of an individual differences model of work performance. *Organizational Behavior and Human Performance*, 1977, *18*, 188–216.

Vroom, V. H. *Work and motivation*. New York: John Wiley & Sons, 1964.

Wahba, M. A., & Bridwell, L. B. Maslow reconsidered: A review of research on the need hierarchy theory. *Organizational Behavior and Human Performance*, 1976, *15*, 212–240.

Wanous, J. P., & Zwany, A. A cross-sectional test of need hierarchy theory. *Organizational Behavior and Human Performance*, 1977, *18*, 78–97.

Wherry, R. J., & South, J. C. A worker motivation scale. *Personnel Psychology*, 1977, *30*, 613–636.

Whyte, W. F. Skinnerian theory in organizations. *Psychology Today*, April 1972, *5*, 66–68.

Yukl, G. A., & Latham, G. P. Consequences of reinforcement schedules and incentive magnitudes for employee performance: Problems encountered in an industrial setting. *Journal of Applied Psychology*, 1975, *60*, 294–298.

Yukl, G. A., Latham, G. P., & Pursell, E. D. The effectiveness of performance incentives under continuous and variable ratio schedules of reinforcement. *Personnel Psychology*, 1976, *29*, 221–232.

# chapter 11

# LEADERSHIP

When you think of leadership, many ideas come to mind. Your thoughts might relate to power, authority, and influence. Maybe you think of actual people—Washington, Lincoln, Churchill, Napoleon—or what effective leaders do. In short, the concept of leadership evokes a multitude of thoughts, all of which in some way address causes, symptoms, or effects of leadership.

In this chapter, we will examine how I/O psychologists have tried to grapple with the multifaceted concept of leadership, particularly as it relates to behavior in the world of work. Research on leadership has followed the path of diversity, as various investigators have approached the concept from different perspectives. Some research has examined what strong leaders are like as people—demographic variables, personality traits, types of skills, etc. Without *followers* there can be no leaders, so accordingly, some research has examined leader-follower relations. Presumably strong leaders accomplish things (which earn them the label of "strong") that weak leaders do not, so another area of research is on the *effects* of leadership. An interesting question addresses contextual effects in leadership, e.g., is the leadership of a prison more demanding than the leadership of a business organization? Thus the *situation* in which leadership occurs has recently attracted much attention. Other areas of interest within the domain of leadership research have also been investigated. In the course of this chapter, we will examine the research on many of these leadership perspectives. Unlike the area of worker motivation, which encompasses multiple theories all aimed at explaining why and how people expend effort, the area of leadership is characterized by varying topics of investigation. While such diversity of interest expands our basis of understanding, it also creates ambiguity as to exactly what leadership is all about (Pfeffer, 1977).

Interest in leadership concerns the I/O practitioner as well as the scientist. In fact, leadership is one of the richer areas of interplay between the two—it has had a healthy influx of ideas from both camps. Identifying and developing leaders is a major concern of industry today. Companies often train their higher-level personnel in skill areas (interpersonal relations, decision making, planning) which directly affect their performance as leaders. In Greensboro, North Carolina, there is an organization called the Center for Creative Leadership whose purpose is to enhance the leadership abilities of key industrial and business personnel who are sent to the center for such training. Not surprisingly, the military is also greatly concerned with leadership. They sponsor a wide variety of research projects that have the potential to contribute to our understanding of leadership. In summary, balance between the theory and practice of leadership is fairly even as a result of this dual infusion of interest.

## MAJOR SUBSTANTIVE TOPICS OF INTEREST IN LEADERSHIP RESEARCH

Because of the many facets of leadership, researchers have focused on selected areas (Barrow, 1977). We can group these studies into five major categories.

**Positional power**

Some investigators view leadership as exercise of positional power. The higher the position in the organizational hierarchy, the more power that position has. As discussed before, there are several kinds of power. In the leadership context, we are most concerned with legitimate power—the formal power given to a position. The positional power of a company president exceeds that of a manager; in turn, the manager has more power than a secretary. Viewing leadership in terms of positional power separates the person from the role. Little attention is given to individuals' attributes; most is aimed at the use of positional power. Organizational theorists speak of such terms as *the power of the presidency* and *administrative clout*, issues not really related to the people in such positions. Sometimes history judges leaders on their inability to use all the power their position gives them. Other leaders try to exceed the power granted their positions. In some countries, leaders emerge by seizing power through military or political coups. Leadership, according to this perspective, is inherent in an organizational position based on the concept of power.

Kipnis and his associates (Kipnis & Cosentino, 1969; Wilkinson & Kipnis, 1978) have studied the tactics used by organizations to influence other organizations and people. Kipnis and Cosentino (1969) found that military supervisors rely more on direct attempts to change subordinate behaviors through corrective power (e.g., punishments); industrial supervisors rely more on persuasive power (e.g., diagnostic talks). In a study of interorganizational relations, Wilkinson and Kipnis (1978) found that leaders use both strong and weak influence tactics depending on the perceived power of the organization they are trying to influence. When the target organization is seen as more powerful than the initiating one, the latter will use gentle tactics like persuasion and ingratiation to exert influence. When the target is seen as less powerful, leaders will resort to stronger tactics (as threats of ending relationships and legal action).

In the total spectrum of leadership research, a relatively small number of studies have been done on positional power. Many I/O researchers find it hard to separate leadership itself from the characteristics of people in leadership positions. But research on positional power has shown that some leadership issues transcend individual differences.

**The leader**

Characteristics of individual leaders has been one of the most researched areas of leadership. Most leadership theories are based on understanding personal traits and behaviors and the importance of their differences. This is almost the opposite of emphasis on positional power, which minimizes individual differences. Many early studies leaned toward demographic and personality variables. Others studied what behaviors individual leaders exhibit that influence the judgment of whether they are strong or weak leaders. Statements like "strong leaders radiate confidence" or "weak leaders are indecisive" reflect the school of thought that stresses the importance of the leader in examining the leadership process. Research has been done on the *selection* of people into leadership positions, while other research has been devoted to *training* people to enhance their leadership skills. Both the leader's sex (e.g., Bartol & Wortman, 1975) and the leader's race (e.g., Bartol, Evans, & Stith, 1978) have been examined as variables. Research has also been done on how the behavior of individual leaders affects subordinate motivation (e.g., Klimoski & Hayes, 1980). The significance is that the focus is on leader characteristics or behavior and how this influences others. This is a classic I/O psychology perspective and it is the most popular in leadership research literature.

**The led**

An area which is becoming of increasing interest is on the characteristics of the followers or the led. This is quite a shift in emphasis from the preceding area, in that leadership is construed more in terms of who is led than who does the leading. Casual observation suggests that some people are easier for leaders to work with than others. Military leaders have long known that some groups of recruits are more responsive, cohesive, or productive. Teachers have noted variations among different student classes. Industrial training directors have found this among various trainee groups. We thus have evidence that a leader's performance is not the same across different groups of followers. Studies by Lowin and Craig (1968) and Greene (1975) showed that certain traits of subordinates (most notably performance) can cause changes in leader behavior. We might label this class of studies "followership" research.

As an example, consider the case of a high school science teacher. The material may remain fairly constant over time, but the teacher's behavior may vary depending on the students. One year the teacher may have a class of bright, motivated students who quickly grasp the material. The teacher may respond by offering the class more advanced knowledge, laboratory experiments, or field trips. In another year, the teacher could have students who have difficulty learning the material. The teacher may have to instruct at a slower pace, use more examples, and hold help sessions. Other variables include class size, disciplinary problems, and the backgrounds of the students. Thus attributes of the led (e.g., the students) as indexed by their intelligence, motivation, number, interpersonal harmony, and background would be examined as factors affecting the behavior of the leader (e.g., the teacher).

We do not know as much about followers as we do about leaders. Studying followers usually involves studying groups (as opposed to individuals), and groups are far more variable and difficult to study. Viewing the leadership process from the perspective of those who are led is fairly new in I/O psychology, but we are learning that followers can influence leaders just as we have long known the converse to be true.

**Influence process**

Rather than focusing on either the leaders or the led, some researchers have found it instructive to examine the relationship or link between the two parties, particularly as they influence each other. In this line of research, attention is given to the dynamics of this relationship, although characteristics of both the leader and the followers may also be considered. In a general sense, what leaders "do" to a group is to influence them in pursuit of some goal. Research on the influence process examines how this process is enacted.

The concept of influence entails how one person's actions affect those of another. As Cartwright (1965) notes, there are several methods of influence. Parties can try to influence each other through (1) coercion, (2) manipulation, (3) authority, and (4) persuasion. *Coercion* involves modifying behavior by force. *Manipulation* is a controlled distortion of reality as seen by those affected. People are allowed to see only those things which will evoke the kind of reaction desired. In *authority*, agents appeal to a mutual decision giving them the right to influence. *Persuasion* is displaying judgment in such a way that those exposed to it accept its value. Researchers study how these methods are used in leader-follower relations.

As an example, Greene and Schriesheim (1980) studied two types of leader behavior: instrumental and supportive. In instrumental leadership, a leader clarifies the group's goals. A supportive leader is friendly and considerate of others' needs. Various work groups were classified by size (large or small) and length of formation (new or long standing). The results showed that small and newly formed groups were most influenced by a supportive leader. Instrumental leadership worked better in larger and newly formed groups (perhaps because it brings order and structure to the group).

As this study shows, research on influence process tends to be fairly complex. It usually involves analysis of several variables. Perhaps more than in any other leadership perspective, this research has shown the intricacies and many facets of leader-group relations.

## The situation

Leadership research has also been directed at the situation or context in which leader-group relations occur. These factors can greatly affect the types of behaviors a leader has to exhibit to be effective. Imagine the leader of a boy scout troop, the supervisor of a production crew, and the warden of a prison. Each faces a different situation. Research on situational factors has tried to identify how various contexts differ and what effect they have on leader behavior.

Fiedler (1964) was one of the first researchers to acknowledge the importance of the context in which leadership occurs. One factor he considered important was leader-group relations—how the two get along. Some leader-group relations are friendly and positive, some are indifferent, and others may be hostile. Fiedler says it's easier to be a leader where there are friendly relations, while it would be difficult in a hostile atmosphere. He also proposed some other factors which differentiate leadership situations.

Depending on the context in which leadership occurs, different types of leader behavior will be called for. As an example, Green and Nebeker (1977) studied two types of leadership situations, one favorable and one unfavorable. In the favorable situation, leaders emphasized interpersonal relations and were supportive of the group members. However, in the unfavorable situation, the leaders became more task oriented and more concerned with goal accomplishment than interpersonal relations. Green and Nebeker were able to show that different situations evoke different styles of leadership behavior. In summary, researchers interested in situational leadership factors attempt to explain leadership behavior in the context in which it occurs.

## Overview

Leadership researchers do not limit their studies or theories to just one of these five areas. A researcher interested in influence processes might consider in what situations influence attempts will be successful. Interest in leader traits may also include consideration of follower traits. My pur-

**Table 11–1**                                    **Topics and associated issues in leadership research**

| Topic | Unit of analysis | Variables of interest | Research questions |
|---|---|---|---|
| 1. Position power . . . . . . . | Organizational roles and positions | Influence tactics; use of power | Under what conditions will organizations resort to strong influence attempts? |
| 2. The leader . . . . . . . . . . | Individual leaders | Personality characteristics; leader behaviors | What traits and/or behaviors differentiate effective versus ineffective leaders? |
| 3. The led . . . . . . . . . . . . . | Work groups and subordinates | Group size; experience of subordinates | What types of subordinates desire close supervision? |
| 4. Influence process . . . . | Superior-subordinate interface | Receptivity to influence; nature of influence attempts | Under what conditions are leaders most susceptible to subordinate influence attempts? |
| 5. The situation . . . . . . . . | Environment or context in which leadership occurs | Situational effects on leader behavior; Factors defining favorable situations | How do various situations modify leader behavior? |

pose in describing these areas is to highlight major categories of leadership research and acknowledge their different units of analysis while realizing the areas are not mutually exclusive. Table 11–1 summarizes the five major research areas and lists the types of topics and questions each area tends to address.

# THEORIES OF LEADERSHIP

Over time, researchers have proposed various leadership theories as they did with motivation theories. Motivational theories were distinct from each other; the newer theories rarely included concepts from the older ones. However, leadership theories have a cumulative effect. Some of the newer ones include concepts or principles first developed in previous theories. This is a healthy development in theory evolution since theorists do not have to begin at square one each time.

A second feature of leadership theories is their growing complexity. The early theories were quite simplistic—they tried to explain leadership on the basis of a few variables. The newer theories are far more complex in that they include a variety of elements. The profusion of empirical studies on diverse areas of leadership parallels the extent to which theory developers have tried to incorporate their findings. Some of the newer leadership theories are among the most complex in all of I/O psychology.

We will look at six leadership theories in this chapter. Five are classified primarily as *descriptive*. They try to describe the leadership process. Four focus on the leader. The newer theories also address the followers as well as the situation. The fifth theory takes a different tact. It examines leadership mainly from the perspective of influence. The final theory is classified as *normative*—it tries to prescribe (as opposed to describe) the leader's behavior. We will explore each theory and its supporting research.

## Trait theory

Though not a full-fledged "theory" in terms of stated hypotheses and postulates, the oldest approach to leadership is called trait theory. It views leadership solely from the perspective of the leader. In particular, it identifies personal traits associated with leader effectiveness, such as physical features and personality characteristics of the leader.

A three-step process is used to identify the traits associated with leader effectiveness:

1. Identify effective and ineffective leaders through some external criterion such as a subjective judgment of the leaders' effectiveness.
2. Measure both types of leaders on demographic and personality variables. Demographic variables could be age, height, weight, sex, and race. Personality variables could be ambition, authoritarianism, dominance, judgment, and self-confidence.
3. Determine if effective leaders could be identified from the ineffective on the basis of one or more of these traits. Such a trait, if found, would be called a critical leadership trait.

Stogdill (1948) and Hollander and Julian (1969) reviewed trait literature and found little or no connection between personal traits and leader effectiveness. Even if it were consistently found, other problems would ensue. There are too many variables and there is no rational guide to selecting them. It is "shotgun empiricism' in its worst form. Also, many personality scales have very low reliability. Last, trait theory gives no basis to explain *why* the critical leadership traits work as they do. What if effective leaders were found to be tall, heavy, and dominant? How would those variables account for variation in effectiveness?

Brown (1954) observed: "The longer and more comprehensive the list of qualities, the more obvious it must be that their possession would be of no use as a junior leader in industry, for he would inevitably be in demand elsewhere as a Prime Minister, or maybe as an Archangel" (p. 219). But, the myth of the trait approach to leader identification pervades. Famous

World War II leader General Douglas MacArthur was described as "some-one who just looks like a leader." But his associate General Omar Bradley had features and a general demeanor that prompted some people to question his face validity as a leader. Yet despite their different physical structures and personalities, both men were among the most effective military leaders in our nation's history.

Dissatisfaction with trait theory gave birth to the second major theory in leadership research—behavior theory.

## Behavior theory

Behavior theory, like trait theory, studies leadership by looking at the leader. But unlike trait theory, it sees leadership in terms of what leaders *do,* not what traits they have. According to behavior theory, effective leaders can be differentiated from ineffective leaders on the basis of their performing different behaviors. The research strategy behind the behavioral approach is: First, people in leadership positions are studied by direct observation and survey questionnaires. This determines the types of work behaviors they show. One example might be a supervisor who publically reprimands an employee for poor job performance. Another could be a supervisor who shows a new employee how to use certain equipment. Next, these behaviors are placed into categories on the basis of similarity. These categories are then put into a checklist or other type of classifying scheme. The checklist is used to evaluate behavior—does the leader follow this behavior on the job (yes or no) or how often does this behavior occur (as on a five-point scale). Last, leader effectiveness is judged, usually in terms of work group productivity, absences, turnover, or morale. If certain leader behaviors systematically relate to these effectiveness indices, we then have a solid empirical basis to judge leadership. The behavioral approach is far more fruitful in explaining leadership than the trait approach.

The most famous of all the behavioral studies of leadership were conducted at Ohio State University. They started in the early 1950s and continued for many years. They had such a dominant impact on leadership research that they have come to be known collectively as the Ohio State studies. They are probably best known for two major contributions to the leadership literature: first, they provided a number of questionnaires to measure leadership; second, they identified two dimensions of leadership later found to be highly reliable and valid.

The researchers began by developing many questionnaire items on what supervisors do in their leadership roles. Such questionnaires as "He knows about it when something goes wrong" and "He calls the group together to talk things over" are examples of these items. The items were placed into such general categories as domination, evaluation, and communication. Then they were given to a wide variety of people in leader-group relations, as in military, business, industrial, and school organizations. The leaders' behavior was described by their subordinates on each of the categories. The results showed there was overlap in these descriptions across the categories. Using a procedure called *factor analysis*, which reduces a large number of questionnaire items to a smaller number of factors based on similarity of content, two factors were found to underlie leader behavior. These factors were labeled *consideration* and *initiating structure*.

Fleishman and Harris (1962) define these factors as follows:

> *Consideration.* Includes behavior indicating mutual trust, respect, and certain warmth and rapport between the supervisor and his group. This does not mean that this dimension reflects a superficial "pat-on-the-back, first-name calling" kind of human relations behavior. This dimension seems to emphasize a deeper concern for group members' needs, and includes such behavior as allowing subordinates more participation in decision making and encouraging more two-way communication.
>
> *Structure.* Includes behavior in which the supervisor organizes and defines group activities and his relation to the group. Thus, he defines the role he expects each member to assume, assigns tasks, plans ahead, establishes ways of getting things done, and pushes for production. This dimension seems to emphasize overt attempts to achieve organizational goals (pp. 43–44).

Several questionnaires were developed to assess the content of leader behavior as reflected by these two factors. The first, the Leader Behavior Description Questionnaire (LBDQ), is completed by a *subordinate* who describes how the leader behaves in various situations. A second questionnaire, the Leader Opinion Questionnaire (LOQ), is completed by a *supervisor* and deals with questions on ideal methods of supervision. Sample items from the LBDQ and the LOQ are presented in Tables 11–2 and 11–3.

Over time, many studies were made of the psychometric properties of these questionnaires. Schriesheim and Kerr (1974) and Schriesheim and Stogdill (1975) found clear support for the value of LBDQ in studying leadership, while LOQ appears to have lesser value. About 80 percent of leader behavior variance can be explained by the consideration and initiating structure factors (Hemphill, 1950; Stogdill & Coons, 1957). Cross-cultural studies (e.g., Tscheulin, 1973) also supported the existence of these factors.

In terms of the *validity* of these dimensions, studies have correlated scores on the leadership questionnaires with such organizational criteria as

**Table 11–2**      **Sample items from the Leader Behavior Description Questionnaire**

| Structure | Consideration |
|---|---|
| 1. He schedules work to be done. | 1. He is friendly and approachable. |
| 2. He emphasizes the meeting of deadlines. | 2. He makes group members feel at ease when talking to them. |
| 3. He lets group members know what is expected of them. | 3. He does little things to make it pleasant to be a member of the group. |

| Table 11–3 | Sample items from the Leader Opinion Questionnaire |

| Structure | Consideration |
|---|---|
| 1. Put the welfare of your unit above the welfare of any person. | 1. Give in to your subordinates in your discussions with them. |
| 2. Encourage after-duty work by persons of your unit. | 2. Back up what persons under you do. |
| 3. Try out new ideas in the unit. | 3. Get approval of persons under you on important matters before going ahead. |

productivity, turnover, satisfaction, and grievances (Korman, 1966; Kerr & Schriesheim, 1974). These findings indicate that variations in leader behavior are significantly related to performance of the work group. But the relationships are not simple. In particular, they seem to be moderated by other variables. For example, Schriesheim and Murphy (1976) investigated the relationship between leader consideration and initiating structure and subordinate job satisfaction. They found that leader initiating structure was positively related to subordinate satisfaction in larger work units but negatively related in smaller units. The opposite pattern was found with the consideration-satisfaction relationship. The findings suggest that structure may aid in group integration for larger units, increasing subordinate satisfaction, while consideration may be more conducive to the maintenance of satisfaction for smaller, more intimate units. Therefore, subordinate satisfaction with leader behavior depends upon the size of the work group. Other moderating variables relating to subordinates (e.g., experience), supervisors (e.g., upward influence), and the task (e.g., the stress involved) have also been identified (Kerr, Schriesheim, Murphy, & Stogdill, 1974).

A study by Fleishman and Harris (1962) revealed that even the two leadership factors can interact in their effect on subordinate behavior. The authors examined to what degree the leader's consideration and initiating structure influenced the grievance rate of subordinates. The results of this study are shown in Figure 11–1. Leaders low in consideration incurred the greatest grievance rates, while those high in consideration incurred the lowest. For those leaders medium in consideration, degree of structure determined the grievance rate. Leaders low in structure incurred few grievances, but those high in structure incurred many. In short, the grievances of subordinates were determined by the combination or the interaction of the leader's consideration and initiating structure. The results from these types of studies showed that the leader's behavior does indeed influence the work group on a number of factors. But the relationship between the two is not simplistic.

In viewing a leader's behavior as measured by consideration and initiating structure, it becomes apparent on the basis of the validation studies that certain behaviors result in more desirable outcomes than others. That is, some research shows highly considerate leaders incur low grievance rates

**Figure 11-1**    **Interaction of consideration and structure relating to grievance rate**

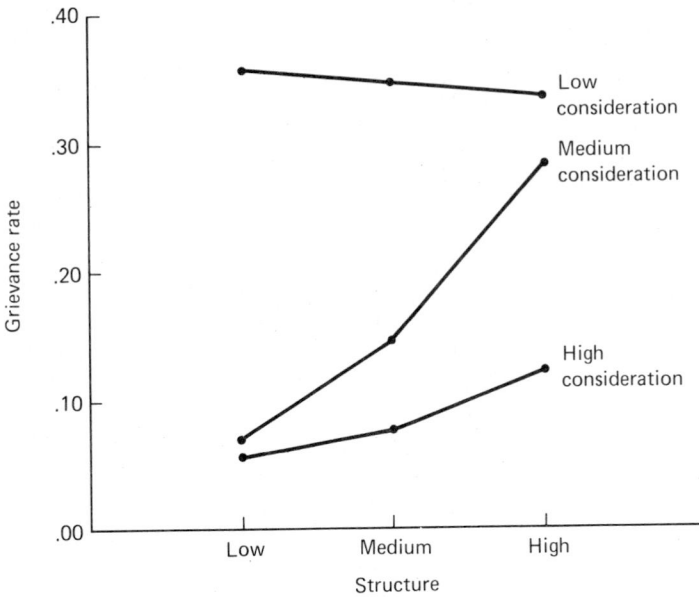

SOURCE: E. A. Fleishman and E. F. Harris, "Patterns of Leadership Behavior Related to Employee Grievances and Turnover," *Personnel Psychology* 15 (1962), pp. 43–56.

(Fleishman & Harris, 1962), while other research has shown leaders demonstrating high structure have highly productive work groups (e.g., Schriesheim, House, & Kerr, 1976). The relationship *between* consideration and initiating structure is important because both factors have been found to influence other variables. If the relation between them is negative, a high score on one factor would be paired with a low score on the other. If the correlation is positive, scores on both factors would covary positively. If the correlation were zero, a wide range of combinations of consideration and initiating structure would be possible. It was originally proposed that the two factors were independent or unrelated to each other. However, later empirical work has shown that the two factors are rarely independent (Weissenberg & Kavanagh, 1972). Some studies (e.g., Larson, Hunt, & Osborn, 1976) report correlations in excess of .70. These findings suggest that subordinates who describe their leader's behavior see these two factors as being related. Thus leaders who are described as exhibiting low feelings of consideration for their subordinates are also frequently seen as providing little guidance for goal attainment. Not all desirable organizational outcomes (e.g., low turnover, high satisfaction) are associated with high scores on these variables. Sometimes low scores are desirable, and in many cases, the relationships are moderated by other variables. It would be best for the organization if these two leadership dimensions were unrelated to each other. That would allow for the greatest flexibility in leader behavior. However, research indicates that subordinates see these aspects of leader behavior as positively related to each other, thus diminishing the likelihood of the desired flexibility in leader style.

**Overview of behavior theory.**    The behavioral approach to leadership is a big advance over the trait approach. Effective leadership became transformed into what leaders *do* as opposed to who they *are*. Emphasizing behaviors focuses attention on *training* leaders to be more effective. Behaviors are far less ambiguous than traits. It is far more useful to describe a leader as one who "never gives subordinates a chance to voice their feelings" than saying the leader is "highly dominant."

The Ohio State studies exemplified the behavioral approach to leadership. They provided reliable means to measure leader behavior. The identification of consideration and initiating structure, factors which account for the majority of variance in leader behavior, was a major advance in understanding leaderhip. While later approaches to leadership have added to our knowledge, probably no other theoretical perspective has advanced the discipline as much as the behavioral approach.

## Fiedler's contingency theory

The next phase in the evolution of leadership theory was Fiedler's contingency theory. His major contribution was the recognition that leader effectiveness depends on the situation in which the leader operates. The origins of Fiedler's thesis stemmed from some research he did on clinical therapists. Fiedler (1951) discovered that effective therapists viewed their patients as being similar to themselves, while ineffective therapists viewed their patients as being dissimilar to themselves. So the therapists' effectiveness was not independent of the situation in which they worked. Fiedler extended his findings and developed a theory of leader effectiveness applicable to a broad range of leader-group situations.

There are three major parts to Fiedler's theory. We will examine each part separately. The first part of the theory addresses individual differences among leaders. Leaders can differ from each other on many dimensions (intelligence, personality, experience, and so on). Fiedler did not find these factors to be particularly useful, so he developed a new method to identify types of leaders—a paper-and-pencil measure called the Least Preferred Co-worker (LPC) scale. The scale uses a series of bipolar adjectives to describe someone's personality (pleasant-unpleasant, friendly-unfriendly, etc.). There are eight scale points between the adjectives. Fiedler instructs the leader to think of the one person he or she would least like to work with, i.e., the least preferred co-worker. The leader then rates or describes this person on the LPC scale. The positive ends (pleasant, friendly) of the scale have high numerical values; the low ends (unfriendly, unpleasant), low values. The total score is called the LPC score. A leader with a high LPC score can differentiate a person's competence from their personality. A high

LPC score is an accepting description of the least preferred co-worker's personality; e.g., "You're incompetent as a coworker, but you are a pleasant person". A low LPC score is a rejecting description; e.g., "You're incompetent as a coworker, and you also have an unpleasant personality."

Fiedler (1967) says that a leader's LPC score reflects his or her style of leadership. Low LPC leaders are more task oriented, are more controlling in their leadership role, and tend to score higher on initiating structure variables from the Ohio State leadership scales. High LPC leaders are more relationship oriented, are more permissive in their leadership role, and tend to score higher on consideration variables from the Ohio State leadership scales. LPC scores are also related to cognitive complexity. Low LPC leaders tend to be cognitively simple; they do not differentiate judgments of personality from competence. High LPC leaders tend to be cognitively complex; they can differentiate judgments of personality from competence. We will examine the empirical research on LPC scores a bit later, but suffice it to say for the moment that they are the means by which Fiedler identifies different types of leaders.

The second part of Fiedler's theory involves how he measures differences in situations where leadership occurs. Fiedler thinks it is easier to be a leader in some situations than others. He proposed three variables to account for this. Each factor has two levels. The first factor, *leader-group*

Four presidents of the United States. What leader behaviors and characteristics would describe these individuals?

*Wide World Photos*

*relations,* deals with how well the leader and the group get along. When leader-group relations are good, the leader is accepted, the group members are loyal, and the leadership job is much easier. When leader-group relations are poor, the leader is rejected, and there is hostility between the leader and the group.

The second factor, *task structure,* is the clarity of the steps needed to complete a task. Some tasks have high structure: the task is straightforward, steps involved are clear cut, and everyone knows how to get the job done. Other tasks have low structure: what has to be done is not as clear, and roles are ambiguous.

The third factor, *leader position power,* is the amount of legitimate authority and number of sanctions available to the leader. Some leadership positions have high power (a company president); others have low power (the social chairperson of a club).

After defining these three factors, Fiedler combined the two levels of each factor to yield eight ($2 \times 2 \times 2$) types of situations—what he calls *octants* (see Table 11–4). Note that the octants differ in their favorability. Octant 1 is the most favorable—good leader-group relations prevail, there is high task structure, and the leader has a lot of power. Octant 8 is the least favorable—poor leader-group relations prevail, there is low task structure, and the leader has little power. The most influential factor determining situational favorableness is leader-group relations. The four most favorable situations have high leader-group relations. Thus, this second part of Fiedler's theory is independent of the characteristics of the leader since it relates only to differences in situations.

In the final part of the theory, Fiedler integrates the first two parts and makes specific predictions about leader effectiveness. There are differences in leaders (as indexed by LPC scores) and in situations (as indexed by situational favorableness), and certain types of leaders are predicted to be

**Table 11–4**                         **Factors defining situational favorability according to Fiedler's contingency theory**

Factors determining situational favorability

| Leader-group relations | Good | Good | Good | Good | Poor | Poor | Poor | Poor |
|---|---|---|---|---|---|---|---|---|
| Task structure | High | High | Low | Low | High | High | Low | Low |
| Position power | High | Low | High | Low | High | Low | High | Low |

| Octants | 1 | 2 | 3 | 4 | 5 | 6 | 7 | 8 |
|---|---|---|---|---|---|---|---|---|

(High)                                                   (Low)

Situational favorability

more effective in certain types of situations. Fiedler proposed that low LPC leaders are more effective in highly favorable and highly unfavorable situations. High LPC leaders are more effective in moderately favorable situations. The basis for these hypotheses is as follows. Moderately favorable situations are characterized by considerable differentiation among the various factors—some are positive and some are negative insofar as leader control and influence are concerned. Because a high LPC leader is cognitively complex, he or she can differentiate factors in the environment. It's a good match to have a cognitively complex person in a highly differentiated environment. A low LPC leader does not differentiate among factors in the environment. He or she is better off in a highly favorable and highly unfavorable situations; i.e., all the factors are either high or low. Therefore a good match would be to have undifferentiated types of people in undifferentiated types of situations. Figure 11–2 illustrates Fiedler's best match between leaders and situations.

The ultimate test of any theory's validity is the extent to which it predicts the criterion of interest. With Fiedler's theory, the criterion is leader effectiveness, defined in terms of performance by the group in its major assigned task. The measure most often used is a rating of group performance.

On par, tests of Fiedler's theory have had mixed results. Most studies give some support (i.e., performance in some octants is more predictable than others); only a few give no support. Negative findings have been reported by Graen, Alvares, Orris, and Martella (1970) and Vecchio (1977). In defense of his theory, Fiedler (1971) argued that the results, while not as strong as he would like, exceed the levels dictated by pure chance. To his credit, Fiedler has responded to criticism (Ashour, 1973) and tried to modify the theory.

Most of the problems with his theory have been with the LPC measure.

**Figure 11–2**       **Proposed relationship between situational favorability and leader LPC score as they affect group performance**

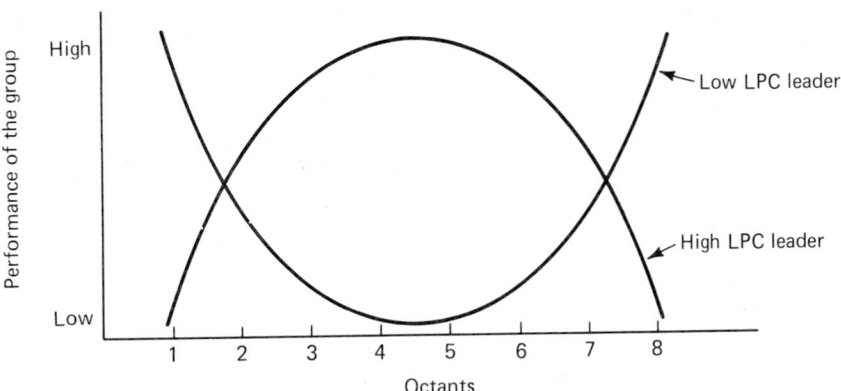

It is not clear what construct this scale really measures. Evans and Dermer (1974) said the scale more readily measures dogmatism than cognitive complexity. Sashkin, Taylor, and Tripathi (1974) found that LPC scores were not independent of the situation in which they were assessed. Stinson and Tracy (1974) and Rice (1978) reported problems with the scale's reliability and construct validity. Also, since the theory only covers high and low scores, what should be "done" with *average* LPC leaders? In short, there is room for improvement in the measure.

Recently, Fiedler took a further tact. He advocates social engineering (Fiedler, 1965)—restructuring the job (to make it more or less favorable) to fit the leader. Alternatively, the leader could be selected (high or low LPC) to fit the job (its degree of favorableness). Fiedler and his associates (Fiedler & Mahar, 1979a, 1979b) developed a self-paced learning program to train people to become more effective leaders. The training, called *Leader Match*, teaches leaders what they can do to change the favorableness of the situation to best match their LPC scores. For example, one way to increase a leader's control is to make more routine work assignments. Csoka and Bons (1978) compared two groups of student military leaders, one of which received the leadership training. The performance of the leaders was rated by peers and superiors. According to the authors, leaders who received Leader Match training performed better than the control leaders. In another test of Leader Match, Leister, Borden, and Fiedler (1977) studied two groups of naval officers; one received the training and one received no training. Superiors rated the performance of both groups before the training and again six months later. Table 11–5 shows changes in performance ratings. Though it would have been better if the control group had received placebo training, Leader Match does seem to improve performance.

Fiedler not only stressed the importance of the situation, he also devised a way to change the situation to fit the leader's style. This is the classic human factors approach to performance: assume the people are "fixed" and vary the environment. The Ohio State studies took the opposite approach: select or train leaders to fit the job.

**Overview of Fiedler's theory.** Some authors (e.g., Kerr et al., 1974) acknowledge that though Fiedler did not invent the contingent approach to leadership, he did elevate the importance of situational factors to the same level as leader characteristics. Fieldler changed the emphasis of lead-

**Table 11–5**          **Mean change in performance ratings for officers participating in Leader Match and controls**

|  | Experimental group (received training) | Control group (no training) |
|---|---|---|
| Naval air station officers | .53 | −.59 |
| Destroyer officers | .92 | −.18 |

SOURCE: A. Leister, D. Borden, and F. E. Fiedler, "Validation of Contingency Model Leadership Training: Leader Match," *Academy of Management Journal* 20 (1977), pp. 464–70.

ership research from just looking at the traits and behaviors of leaders to looking at both the leader and the context in which leadership occurs. It is also instructive to recognize the confluence of sources from which Fiedler developed his theory. His measure of leader position power reflects the importance some researchers place on positional power (as discussed earlier) in the role of leadership. His measure of the Least Preferred Co-worker draws on the importance of studying the leader in the leadership process. While what the LPC scale actually measures is a matter of debate, it seems to be associated to some degree with the perspective of examining personality factors and traits in leadership. His measure of situational favorableness is the prototype of leadership research that stresses the situation. Fiedler is less concerned with explicit leader behaviors, though research has shown that high and low LPC leaders do behave differently in their leadership roles.

Though not strongly supported (probably due to the LPC scale), Fiedler's theory has contributed a great deal to the field of leadership research. It has focused research in new directions. Some researchers proposed additional factors that contribute to situational favorability. Others modified the LPC scale. Yet other studies proposed new approaches to classifying situations. So even if Fiedler's theory is found totally lacking in validity, it still has been a catalyst for others. As a result of Fiedler's theory, when we are asked what makes for an effective leader, the answer is "it depends" (i.e., leader effectiveness is a contingent phenomenon). The course of leadership research changed after Fiedler's theory, and the contingency theme was magnified even more in the next major theory of leadership.

**Path-goal theory**     In the previous chapters, we have discussed job satisfaction, motivation, and leadership. These theories each address a limited aspect of human behavior. But in real life, how we feel about our boss, how motivated we are, and how satisfied we feel are not independent of each other. The following leadership theory integrates job satisfaction, motivation, and leadership. Though mainly a theory of leadership, it also explains subordinate motivation and job satisfaction.

Path-goal theory is a type of contingency theory. But it is more complex than Fieldler's theory because it includes a broader range of variables. Path-goal theory is relatively new, so it is still evolving and being tested. Proposed by House (1971) and House and Mitchell (1974), the theory mainly stresses the behaviors a leader has to exhibit in order for the subordinates to attain their goals. As a process theory, path-goal is loaded with links between variables. We will begin by examining the theory's two major postulates (House & Mitchell, 1974):

1.  Leader behaviors will be acceptable and satisfying to subordinates when the subordinates see the behavior as an immediate source of satisfaction or instrumental in obtaining future satisfaction.

2.  Leader behavior will increase subordinate effort expended when subordinates see effective performance as a means to satisfying important needs and when they see the leader as an aid in attaining effective performance.

These postulates are not simple. They involve subordinate perceptions of the leader's behavior, how the leader's behavior affects subordinate motivation, and to what degree the leader's behavior facilitates subordinate goal attainment. Path-goal theory has its roots in the expectancy theory of motivation. "Goals" are the outcomes that subordinates desire, and "paths" are the behaviors that have to be exhibited to attain these goals. In a nutshell, path-goal theory explains how the leader facilitates subordinate goal attainment. Note that path-goal theory shifts the focus from characteristics of the leader to how the leader affects subordinate motivation.

The theory states that a leader must be able to manifest four different styles of behavior. (These four styles come from previous research on work behavior.)

1.  *Directive leadership.* The leader provides specific guidelines to subordinates on how they perform their tasks. The leader should set standards of performance and provide explicit expectations of performance. This style reflects initiating structure from the Ohio State studies.
2.  *Supportive leadership.* The leader must demonstrate concern for the well-being of the subordinates and must be supportive of them as individuals. This style reflects the consideration factor from the Ohio State studies.
3.  *Participative leadership.* The leader must solicit ideas and suggestions from subordinates and invite their participation in decisions that directly affect them. The origins of this style of leadership stem from research on the value and importance of participative decision making (Likert, 1961).
4.  *Achievement-oriented leadership.* A leader must set challenging goals, emphasize improvements in work performance, and encourage high levels of goal attainment. This style of leadership is directly related to the findings from the goal setting theory of motivation and other approaches that stress achievement motivation.

Effective leaders need all four of these styles since each one produces different results. But when should a leader use which style? It depends on a number of situational factors. (Note the contingency basis here.) To date, two types of contingency factors have been identified.

Some of the factors relate to characteristics of the subordinates, others to environmental factors. Two subordinate characteristics are perceived ability and locus of control. Subordinates who believe they have a lot of ability are less accepting of the directive leadership style. They don't think they need much guidance and direction from their leader. Subordinates with an internal locus of control are more satisfied with the participative leadership style; those with an external locus of control favor the directive style. In short, internals like to be asked, externals like to be told. One environmental factor is the nature of the task being performed. The more dissatisfying and unpleasant the task, the more subordinates resent the directive leadership style. Leader behavior is motivating to the extent that it helps subordinates cope with environmental uncertainties, threats, or frustration.

What effect do these leader behaviors have? According to path-goal theory, the leader can influence the perceptions subordinates have of their jobs by (1) removing obstacles from the paths to desired goals, (2) rewarding subordinates for attaining their goals, and (3) helping subordinates clarify paths to valued goals. Thus, the leader is one who helps subordinates do the things that have to be done to obtain the desired rewards.

Finally, if the leader is successful, what will happen? First, subordinate job satisfaction will result since the job is seen as a vehicle for providing desired rewards. Second, the leader will be accepted by the subordinates. The leader will be seen as instrumental in helping the subordinates attain their desired rewards. Finally, subordinate motivation will be high since according to the postulates of expectancy theory, the leader provides feedback to show that effort leads to performance (expectancy) and that performance results in reward attainment (instrumentality). The entire path-goal theoy is presented graphically in Table 11–6.

Path-goal theory is an "organizational care package"—many good things are supposed to happen if the theory works. Indeed, the theory is quite imposing considering all that it purports to accomplish. Recently a number of tests have been made. But given the theory's complexity, only parts of

| Table 11–6 | **Path-goal theory of leadership** | | |
|---|---|---|

| Leader behavior | Contingency factors | Subordinate attitudes and behavior |
|---|---|---|
| 1. Directive | 1. Subordinate characteristics<br>   a. Locus of control<br>   b. Perceived ability<br>   c. Authoritarianism | 1. Job satisfaction;<br>   job → rewards |
| 2. Supportive | | 2. Acceptance of leader;<br>   leader → rewards |
| 3. Participative | | 3. Motivational behavior;<br>   effort → performance<br>   performance → rewards |
| 4. Achievement-oriented | | |
| | 2. Environmental characteristics<br>   a. Nature of the task<br>   b. Formal authority system<br>   c. Primary work group | |

it have been tested. Many tests looked at two of the four leadership styles (usually directive and supportive); others studied the results of using certain leadership styles (e.g., satisfaction, role clarity). Test results are indecisive. The theory can be judged on two dimensions: internal logic and empirical verifiability. The theory's logic seems sound—an effective leader should facilitate subordinate job satisfaction and motivation. But it is difficult to verify the theory's predictions. Like Maslow's theory, one major problem has to do with measurement. Concepts like path, goal, supportive leadership, directive leadership, etc., can be interpreted differently when put into operation.

Some results from empirical tests of path-goal theory are as follows. Hammer and Dachler (1975) found that subordinates of directive leaders saw path-goal instrumentalities as less clear than subordinates with less directive leaders—just the opposite of what the theory predicts. The authors felt the vagueness of the key theoretical concepts contributed to the negative results. A similar conclusion was drawn by Schriesheim and Von Glinow (1977) regarding the frequency of nonsupportive results due to poor variable operationalization. Other studies have reported mixed results. Both Stinson and Johnson (1975) and Downey, Sheridan, and Slocum (1975) found that the predicted results of supportive leadership were confirmed by data, but the predicted results of directive leadership were not. Downey, Sheridan, and Slocum (1976) and Schriesheim and Schriesheim (1980) reported weak support for the theory, but felt that unknown contingency factors may have contributed to the low level of support. As can be seen from these studies, there is no clear support for the theory, some mixed support, and a fair amount of nonsupport. But almost every author who disconfirms the theory does not point to faulty logic. They attribute the disconfirming evidence to poor operationalization of variables or the presence of additional contingency factors which moderate the results in unpredicted ways. It seems no one wants to junk the theory, though other theories of work behavior with such weak support usually fall out of favor. Path-goal theory has so much potential promise that researchers want more modification before they dismiss it.

A number of other issues have been raised. Greene (1979) conducted a study of path-goal theory which largely *supported* the predictions made. Yet he raised questions about causation among the variables. The theory states that leader behavior style causes certain subordinate attitudes and behavior. Yet Greene feels that the attitudes and behavior of the subordinates can cause changes in the style used by the leader. This reflects the school of thought that subordinates influence leaders just as leaders influence subordinates. Mawhinney and Ford (1977) have stated that because path-goal theory is based on expectancy theory, there is a tendency to view the theory from a cognitive, rational perspective. They argue that an operant interpretation of path-goal theory results is also plausible, that the behaviors of subordinates can be explained by the reinforcing behaviors of the leader. They support the logic of the theory but feel the operant perspective can explain the results as well as the cognitive perspective. Which perspective is more defensible depends on finding a condition where the two theories make opposite predictions. But such a test awaits further research.

**Overview of path-goal theory.** Path-goal theory is a confluence of many other theories. The four types of leader behavior styles were distilled most notably from the Ohio State studies. The perspective that leadership is a contingent phenomenon draws heavily on Fiedler's work. The hypothesis that a job provides desired rewards comes from existing theories of job satisfaction. The notion of a leader being instrumental for subordinate goal attainment has its roots in expectancy theory. Path-goal theory is the most complex of all the theories in I/O psychology. It is also the most comprehensive. We should not let the lack of supporting data sour us on its value. As a research strategy, it would be advisable to get better measures of the variables and continue to look for additional contingency factors. Usually, the more grounded a theory is, the more likely it is to be confirmed. When a theory is vague, lack of support can be attributed to poor tests of theory as well as the overall quality of the theory itself. Path-goal theory is a laudable model: it has tried to integrate three major areas of work behavior into a unified theory. While we cannot ignore problems with the theory, we would be ill-advised to retreat to the position of having a different theory for every nuance of human behavior. The theory needs a lot of further work, but nevertheless, it provides us with a rational basis for synthesizing our knowledge about work behavior which heretofore we have addressed in piecemeal fashion. While at this time the goals of the theory may be held in higher esteem than the theory itself, path-goal theory provides a strong basis for increasing our understanding of work behavior beyond just the topic of leadership.

## Mutual influence theory

As a departure from the progression of the last four leadership theories, some theories limit their view of leadership to the exchange of mutual influence between the leader and followers. As opposed to thinking in terms of leader characteristics or situational factors that moderate leader effectiveness, mutual influence theories focus on the dynamics of the leader-follower relationship, stressing the link between the two rather than either particular role.

Herold (1977) conceptualized leadership as a dyad and focused upon the relationship between the two partners. He discovered that through their own behavior each partner in a dyad, whether leader or subordinate, will affect the other's behavior and/or attitudes. So leadership is just a special case of this two-way influence process. However, in a typical situation, the leader has more power. Herold showed that while the influence process is reciprocal, powerful leaders affect subordinate behavior more than powerful subordinates affect leader behavior. Herold felt conceptualizing leadership as a *vertical dyad* (a superior and subordinate) would be the best unit of analysis.

Another researcher who used the mutual influence process in a dyad is Graen. Graen and his associates (e.g., Dansereau, Graen, & Haga, 1975) proposed what they call the *vertical dyad linkage model* of leadership. According to the theory, leaders differentiate their subordinates in terms of (1) competence and skill, (2) extent to which they can be trusted (especially when not being watched by the leader), and (3) their motivation to assume greater responsibility within the unit. The leader identifies those subordinates with these attributes, and they become members of what Graen calls the *in-group*. In-group members go beyond their formal job duties and take responsibility for completing tasks that are most critical to the success of the work group. In return, they receive more attention, support, and sensitivity from their leaders. Subordinates who don't have these attributes are called the *out-group;* they do the more routine, mundane tasks of the work group and have a more formal exchange with the leader. Leaders influence out-group members by using formal authority, though this is not necessary with in-group members. Thus, leaders and subordinates use different types and degrees of influence depending on whether the subordinate is in the in- or out-group.

Graen and Schiemann (1978) showed that in-group members agreed more with their leaders about work-related situations. The authors feel that leaders are closer to in-group members and are more likely to share common points of view. These findings raise some interesting questions about the validity of performance appraisals of in-group and out-group members. Since most performance appraisals involve supervisory evaluation, this theory may provide an additional basis for understanding the performance appraisal process. The vertical dyad linkage model can also be used to explain patterns of superior-subordinate communication, a topic we will examine in the next chapter.

Original formulations of the theory were based on studies of managers. However, the model also held for foremen (Liden & Graen, 1980). As before, in-group foremen were given greater responsibility by their supervisor than out-group foremen. In-group foremen received more job-related feedback, support, and personal sensitivity, all of which were the supervisor's way of rewarding them for their extra effort.

In addition to providing a new way of conceptualizing the leadership process, the vertical dyad linkage model underscores a major methodological issue in leadership research. Traditionally, perceptions of the leader (as in the LBDQ) are averaged across respondents to get a "typical" measure of the leader on some dimension. This model suggests that the leader-member exchange between a supervisor and each subordinate should be approached as unique. If a leader is very considerate of in-group members and very inconsiderate of out-group members, a statistical average will give a false picture. As opposed to thinking of 10 subordinates in a work group as one unit, the theory recommends that the leadership of this group be construed as 10 leader-subordinate dyads. This refinement may result in more accurate predictions.

In summary, the mutual influence theories focus on the linkage between superiors and subordinates and how both parties influence each other. Leadership is a special type of influence process, and what is special is the unequal nature of the power roles in the dyad. This view also transforms leadership from a purely independent variable to also a dependent variable. Thus leadership affects and is affected by other variables.

## Vroom-Yetton contingency theory

The final theory of leadership is quite different. First, it is normative—it tells leaders how they should behave. While Fiedler's contingency theory and path-goal theory also have some normative components (i.e., what behaviors a leader should exhibit is contingent on other factors), they are not nearly as prescriptive. Second, the Vroom-Yetton theory deals with only one aspect of leadership—decision making.

The essence of the Vroom-Yetton theory is the degree to which a leader allows subordinates to participate in the decision-making process. Depending on what the leader is trying to accomplish, certain leader behaviors (e.g., the degree of subordinate participation in decision making) produce certain outcomes. Vroom and Yetton (1973) developed a model of decision-making strategies for the leader to follow depending on certain aspects of the decision problem.

First, Vroom and Yetton outlined five types of leader behaviors and gave each a code number.

1. The manager solves the problem or makes the decision himself using information available at the time. (A1)
2. The manager gets the necessary information from subordinates and then decides on a solution. (A2)
3. The manager shares the problem with relevant subordinates individually, getting their ideas and suggestions without bringing them together as a group, and then makes the decision herself. (C1)
4. The manager shares the problem with subordinates as a group, gets their collective ideas and suggestions, and then makes the decision himself. (C2)
5. The manager shares the problem with subordinates as a group and is willing to accept any solution that has group support. (G2)

To help the manager select a certain decision-making strategy, Vroom and Yetton proposed a number of decision rules or criteria. These are (1) the *quality* of the decision, (2) the *acceptance* of the decision by the subordinates, and (3) the *time* needed to make a decision. These are the contingency factors in the Vroom-Yetton theory; which decision-making style the leader chooses is contingent upon these factors. In reviewing the five types of leader behaviors, you can see that some behaviors will need less time; others are more likely to produce greater subordinate acceptance of the decision.

Next, the authors use a *decision tree*, a graphic way to display various decision options. The "path" of the tree is determined by a yes or no answer to seven questions (see Figure 11–3). Depending on the answers to these seven questions, 14 different problem types can emerge.

With certain leader behaviors, less time is spent making the decision. However, time is not the only criterion in selecting a decision strategy. Group acceptance of the decision and the process of group development are also important. Table 11–7 shows three columns of variables. Column 1 shows the 14 problem types identified in Figure 11–3. The variables in column 2 indicate which of the five leader behaviors will result in the least amount of time being spent on the problems. Finally, the third column shows what ordering of the other leader behaviors would facilitate group development. A manager who uses one of these strategies might spend more time on the problem than necessary, but the trade-off is increasing amounts of group development. Moving to the right across the third column, time minimization is increasingly traded off against subordinate group development. The final behavior in column 3 is G2, letting the subordinates make the decision.

Most of the tests of the Vroom-Yetton theory have been comparisons of what the theory says managers should do versus what they actually do. We have less information on whether managers perform better when they follow the theory. Many of the subjects of these tests have been actual man-

| Table 11–7 | Feasible leader behaviors for each of 14 problem types | | | |
|---|---|---|---|---|
| Problem type | Behavior resulting in least time spent on problem | Behavior providing for increasing amounts of group development | | |
| 1 . . . . . . . . . . . . . . . . . A1 | | A2 | C1 | C2 | G2 |
| 2 . . . . . . . . . . . . . . . . . A1 | | A2 | C1 | C2 | G2 |
| 3 . . . . . . . . . . . . . . . . . G2 | | | | |
| 4 . . . . . . . . . . . . . . . . . A1 | | A2 | C1 | C2 | G2 |
| 5 . . . . . . . . . . . . . . . . . A1 | | A2 | C1 | C2 | G2 |
| 6 . . . . . . . . . . . . . . . . . G2 | | | | |
| 7 . . . . . . . . . . . . . . . . . C2 | | | | |
| 8 . . . . . . . . . . . . . . . . . C1 | | C2 | | |
| 9 . . . . . . . . . . . . . . . . . A2 | | C1 | C2 | G2 |
| 10 . . . . . . . . . . . . . . . . A2 | | C1 | C2 | G2 |
| 11 . . . . . . . . . . . . . . . . C2 | | G2 | | |
| 12 . . . . . . . . . . . . . . . . G2 | | | | |
| 13 . . . . . . . . . . . . . . . . C2 | | | | |
| 14 . . . . . . . . . . . . . . . . C2 | | G2 | | |

SOURCE: V. H. Vroom and P. W. Yetton, *Leadership and Decision-making* (Pittsburgh: University of Pittsburgh Press, 1973). Reprinted by permission of the University of Pittsburgh Press.

**Figure 11-3**  Decision tree for arriving at feasible leader behaviors for different problem types

Questions

| Step 1 | Step 2 | Step 3 | Step 4 | Step 5 | Step 6 | Step 7 |
|--------|--------|--------|--------|--------|--------|--------|
| Does the problem possess a quality requirement? | Do I have sufficient information to make a high-quality decision? | Is the problem structured? | Is acceptance of the decision by subordinates important for effective implementation? | If I were to make the decision by myself, is it reasonably certain that it would be accepted by my subordinates? | Do subordinates share the organizational goals to be attained in solving this problem? | Is conflict likely in preferred solutions? |

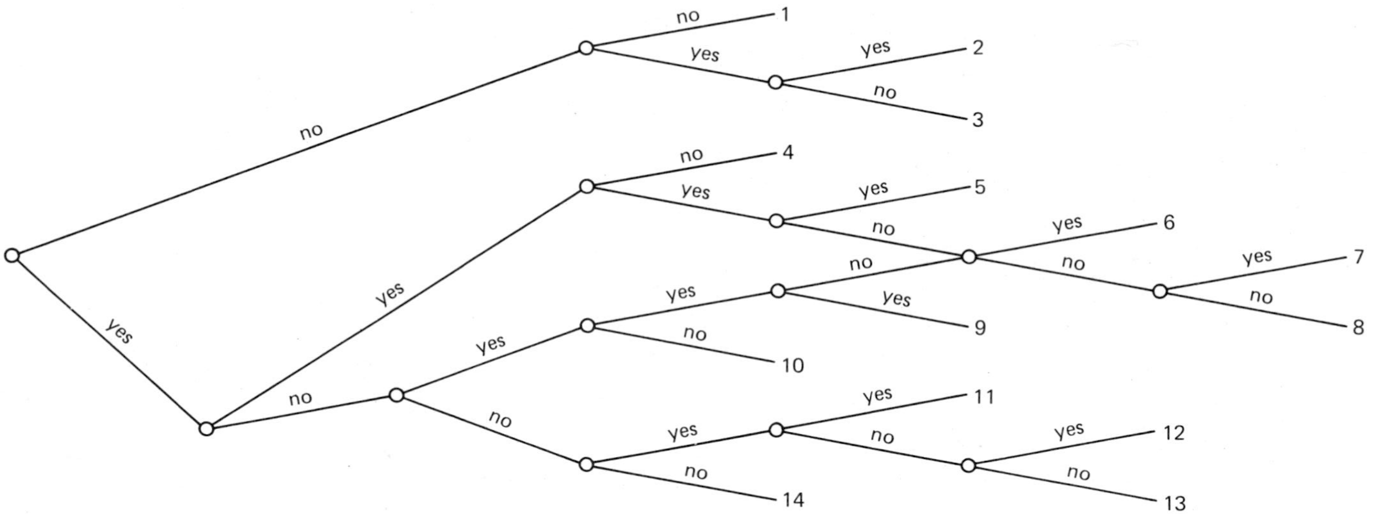

SOURCE: Adapted from V. H. Vroom and P. W. Yetton, *Leadership and Decision-making* (Pittsburgh: University of Pittsburgh Press, 1973). Reprinted by permission of the University of Pittsburgh Press.

agers who report how they deal with a particular problem. Research shows that managers share decision-making responsibilities when they feel their subordinates can be trusted. When Jago and Vroom (1977) studied managers at four organizational levels, they found greater use of participative methods at higher levels. Hill and Schmitt (1977) found that leaders apparently do make decisions based on the problem attributes (i.e., quality, time, acceptance). These decisions are fairly consistent with the theory's predictions, especially with regard to the time criterion. The authors also confirmed that some leaders are more concerned with decision quality and others with decision acceptance. Vroom and Jago (1978) reported that use of the theory enhanced decision acceptance, while lesser gains were made in decision quality. Nevertheless, Field (1979) has criticized these tests on the grounds that almost all the variables are assessed through self-reports of managers. Some external measures of these variables would result in a stronger test.

There seems to be fair empirical support for the Vroom-Yetton theory. Leaders can manipulate decision time, quality, and acceptance by using various decision-making styles or behaviors. But there is always a trade-off; the most expedient behaviors do not always result in acceptable or high-quality decisions. Conversely, decision strategies aimed at producing high group acceptance can take a long time. However, as a theory of leadership, the Vroom-Yetton model is narrow in scope. While decision making is an important aspect of leadership, it is by no means the *only* aspect. The Vroom-Yetton model is not on the same level as Fiedler's theory or path-goal theory in terms of inclusiveness of leadership issues. Though empirically supported, the theory will have to be expanded to be a comprehensive theory of leadership. But as limited as the theory is, it is imbued with the contingency flavor that has so dominated leadership research in the past 15 to 20 years.

## EVALUATION OF LEADERSHIP RESEARCH

As Davis and Luthans (1979) have observed, leadership is one of the most heavily researched areas in the field of work behavior. Leadership has been studied from such widely different perspectives as power, reciprocal influence, leader traits, leader behaviors, and situational properties. Researchers have also tried to explain leadership from cognitive and operant theoretical viewpoints. The explanations for leadership are as diverse as those for motivation.

The research on leadership can be condensed into "partial truths." The leadership process draws heavily on power and influence, yet there is more to it than just these concepts. While the trait approach to leadership has not been very fruitful, such measures as Fiedler's LPC (despite its problems) suggest there are some individual constructs that influence leader effectiveness. The behavioral approach has given some insight, yet we know the same leader behaviors won't produce the same results in all situations. The currently fashionable contingency approach shows that effective leadership does indeed *depend on* a number of factors, yet the list of factors seems to grow with each new study. It would be helpful to find a specific set of core contingency factors to account for most of the variance in leader effectiveness, but to date we have not been successful.

This chapter has documented the approaches taken by I/O psychologists in their pursuit of understanding leadership. Yet new approaches are unfolding all the time. Kerr and Jermier (1978) have asked what it is that organization members need to maximize in seeking organizational and personal outcomes. They conclude that employees seek both guidance and good feelings from their work settings. Guidance usually comes from role or task structuring; good feelings may stem from any type of recognition. Though the authors feel these factors must be present, they do not necessarily have to come from a superior. While a leader may provide guidance and recognition, other sources may also provide these factors. In those cases where guidance and recognition are strongly provided by other sources, the need for formal leadership is diminished. The authors reference *substitutes* for leadership and highlight the point that a leader is merely a vehicle for providing these services. Indeed, recently some organizations have experimented with abandoning foremen and supervisory positions, leaving such traditional leadership positions in the hands of the employees organized into special work teams. Such operating procedures are implicit testimony to the practical feasibility of having substitutes for formal leaders. While all leadership positions have not been abandoned in these organizations, there is evidence that the concept of leadership does not have to be vested in a formal position.

Leadership has traditionally been studied in terms of the characteristics of people, roles, and/or situations. But leadership can also be thought of as a series of processes or functions to facilitate organizational and personal effectiveness. The future may see a movement away from the *content* of leadership (i.e., what it is) and its traditional view as an independent variable to an emphasis on organizational practices that produce functional or dysfunctional consequences. That is, leadership may be more of a means than an end. In any case, the leadership process is so deeply imbedded in work behavior that it will remain a viable research topic for many years to come.

# CASE STUDY

Michael Harstrom, president of the New England Petroleum Company, was addressing a meeting of the company's executive officers. Harstrom was due to retire in less than a year, and he was concerned with the future of the company after his departure. Even though it was not his responsibility to choose his successor, he had some thoughts he wished to share with his associates.

"As you all are aware, within the next year I will retire from the company. While I greet this decision with mixed emotions, I feel compelled to share with you some concerns I have for the future of this company with regard to my successor. I feel the business world is tougher today than ever before, and I believe the trend will continue. I do not envy the decision before you, nor do I covet the tasks and responsibilities that await you in the years ahead.

"I have witnessed many changes in my 40 years in the petroleum industry. Furthermore, the rate of change is accelerating, so I advise you to seek a person who is adaptive, flexible, and has the foresight to anticipate problems, not just react to them. With the growing problems of taxation, petroleum import regulations, alternative means of home heating, as well as the changing composition of the work force, my successor will need a level of leadership ability unparalleled in the company's history. Perhaps my successor will be drawn from those in attendance here today. Such a person would be familiar with the strengths and weaknesses of the company, but I wonder if they would possess the desired degree of detached objectivity needed for analytic insight into our problems. Alternatively, we might look to bring in someone from one of our competitors. They may have some fresh ideas to chart new directions for the company. Finally, we may look to an industry totally unrelated to petroleum, perhaps manufacturing, sales, or finance. The problems of running a business are not unique to us. Maybe we are at a point in our history where a clean break with past tradition would be most advantageous."

Harstrom felt a tinge of relief knowing *he* would not have to cope with his problems much longer. He continued: "Today the work force is unlike any other time I have known. People are motivated by different things than before. They want more challenge and stimulation from their work. While they are as ambitious as ever, their ambition takes a form unlike that in my contemporaries. We have many more younger workers, minority workers, and dual-income families than ever before. Our employees have more formal education than those in the past, and they want job responsibilities commensurate with their education. My successor will have to demonstrate the leadership skills needed to address these issues. I would also recommend a more formalized mentoring program for our rising young executives. Perhaps if I had been more successful in training our staff to assume leadership positions in the company, I would view the problem of executive succession with less trepidation. I don't know if effective leaders are found or made, but I feel it would be wise to vigorously pursue both courses of action."

"I leave you with this charge. The successful leader of this company will have to possess a balanced mix of technical knowledge, interpersonal ability, foresight, analytic decision making skills, and acute sensitivity to an ever changing environment. The business problems of tomorrow will be increasing in intensity, severity, and magnitude. The choice you make will directly affect the welfare of this company for many years to come. I implore you to exercise good judgment. I've dedicated my career to this company, and I want to know my collective accomplishments will be resting in the hands of a skilled leader."

Questions

1. In terms of the topics that leadership researchers address, what topics does Harstrom refer to as particularly important?
2. Does Harstrom view leadership effectiveness as a contingent phenomenon? If so, what are some of the contingency factors he sees as relevant?
3. Which theory or theories of leadership does Harstrom subscribe to as the senior executive officer of the company?
4. Does Harstrom give equal weight to the consideration and initiating structure dimensions of leadership in his view of his successor?
5. Think of Fiedler's situational favorableness continuum. Is Harstrom describing the leadership situation his successor will face as primarily favorable or unfavorable? Depending on your answer, what type of leader would you recommend for this situation?

# REFERENCES

Ashour, A. S. The contingency model of leader effectiveness: An evaluation. *Organizational Behavior and Human Performance*, 1973, 9, 339–355.

Barrow, J. C. The variables of leadership: A review and conceptual framework. *Academy of Management Review*, 1977, 2, 231–251.

Bartol, K. M., Evans, C. L., & Stith, M. T. Black versus white leaders: A comparative review of the literature. *Academy of Management Review*, 1978, 3, 293–304.

Bartol, K. M., & Wortman, M. S. Male versus female leaders: Effects of perceived leader behavior and satisfaction in a hospital. *Personnel Psychology*, 1975, 28, 533–547.

Brown, J. A. *The social psychology of industry.* New York: Penguin Books, 1954.

Cartwright, D. Influence, leadership, control. In J. G. March (Ed.), *Handbook of organizations.* Skokie, Ill.: Rand McNally, 1965.

Csoka, L. S., & Bons, P. M. Manipulating the situation to fit the leader's style: Two validation studies of Leader Match. *Journal of Applied Psychology*, 1978, 63, 295–300.

Dansereau, F., Graen, G., & Haga, W. A vertical dyad linkage approach to leadership in formal organizations. *Organizational Behavior and Human Performance*, 1975, 13, 46–78.

Davis, T. R., & Luthans, F. Leadership reexamined: A behavioral approach. *Academy of Management Review*, 1979, 4, 237–248.

Downey, H. K., Sheridan, J. E., & Slocum, J. W. Analysis of relationships among leader behavior, subordinate job performance and satisfaction: A path-goal approach. *Academy of Management Journal*, 1975, 18, 253–262.

Downey, H. K., Sheridan, J. E., & Slocum, J. W. The path-goal theory of leadership: A longitudinal analysis. *Organizational Behavior and Human Performance*, 1976, 16, 156–176.

Evans, M. G., & Dermer, J. What does the Least Preferred Coworker scale really measure? A cognitive interpretation. *Journal of Applied Psychology*, 1974, 59, 202–206.

Fiedler, F. E. A method of objective quantification of certain counter-transference attitudes. *Journal of Clinical Psychology*, 1951, 7, 101–107.

Fiedler, F. E. A contingency model of leadership effectiveness. In L. Berkowitz (Ed.), *Advances in experimental social psychology* (Vol. 1). New York: Academic Press, 1964.

Fiedler, F. E. Engineer the job to fit the manager. *Harvard Business Review*, 1965, 43 (5), 115–122.

Fiedler, F. E. *A theory of leadership effectiveness.* New York: McGraw-Hill, 1967.

Fiedler, F. E. Validation and extension of the contingency model of leadership effectiveness: A review of empirical findings. *Psychological Bulletin*, 1971, 76, 128–148.

Fiedler, F. E., & Mahar, L. The effectiveness of contingency model training: A review of the validation of LEADER MATCH. *Personnel Psychology*, 1979, 32, 45–62. (a)

Fiedler, F. E., & Mahar, L. A field experiment validating contingency model training. *Journal of Applied Psychology*, 1979, 64, 247–254. (b)

Field, R. H. A critique of the Vroom-Yetton contingency model of leadership behavior. *Academy of Management Review*, 1979, 4, 249–258.

Fleishman, E. A., & Harris, E. F. Patterns of leadership behavior related to employee grievances and turnover. *Personnel Psychology*, 1962, 15, 43–56.

Graen, G., Alvares, K., Orris, J. B., & Martella, J. A. Contingency model of leadership effectiveness: Antecedent and evidential results. *Psychological Bulletin*, 1970, 74, 285–296.

Graen, G., & Schiemann, W. Leader member agreement: A vertical dyad linkage approach. *Journal of Applied Psychology*, 1978, 63, 206–212.

Green, S. G., & Nebeker, D. M. The effects of situational factors and leadership style on leader behavior. *Organizational Behavior and Human Performance*, 1977, *19*, 368–377.

Greene, C. N. The reciprocal nature of influence between leader and subordinate. *Journal of Applied Psychology*, 1975, *60*, 187–193.

Greene, C. N. Questions of causation in the path-goal theory of leadership. *Academy of Management Journal*, 1979, *22*, 22–41.

Greene, C. N., & Schriesheim, C. A. Leader-group interactions: A longitudinal field investigation. *Journal of Applied Psychology*, 1980, *65*, 50–59.

Hammer, T. H., & Dachler, H. P. A test of some assumptions underlying path goal model of supervision: Some suggested conceptual modifications. *Organizational Behavior and Human Performance*, 1975, *14*, 60–75.

Hemphill, J. K. *Leader behavior description.* Columbus: Ohio State University Personnel Research Board, 1950.

Herold, D. M. Two-way influence processes in leader-follower dyads. *Academy of Management Journal*, 1977, *20*, 224–237.

Hill, T. E., & Schmitt, N. Individual differences in decision making. *Organizational Behavior and Human Performance*, 1977, *19*, 353–367.

Hollander, E. P., & Julian, J. W. Contemporary trends in the analysis of the leadership process. *Psychological Bulletin*, 1969, *71*, 387–397.

House, R. J. A path-goal theory of leader effectiveness. *Administrative Science Quarterly*, 1971, *16*, 321–338.

House, R. J., & Mitchell, T. Path-goal theory of leadership. *Journal of Contemporary Business*, 1974, *3*, 81–98.

Jago, A. G., & Vroom, V. H. Hierarchical level and leadership style. *Organizational Behavior and Human Performance*, 1977, *18*, 131–145.

Kerr, S., & Jermier, J. M. Substitutes for leadership: Their meaning and measurement. *Organizational Behavior and Human Performance*, 1978, *22*, 375–403.

Kerr, S., & Schriesheim, C. A. Consideration, initiating structure, and organizational criteria—an update of Korman's 1966 review. *Personnel Psychology*, 1974, *27*, 555–568.

Kerr, S., Schriesheim, C. A., Murphy, C. J., & Stog-dill, R. M. Toward a contingency theory of leadership based upon the consideration and initiating structure literature. *Organizational Behavior and Human Performance*, 1974, *12*, 62–82.

Kipnis, D., & Cosentino, J. Use of leadership powers in industry. *Journal of Applied Psychology*, 1969, *53*, 460–466.

Klimoski, R. J., & Hayes, N. J. Leader behavior and subordinate motivation. *Personnel Psychology*, 1980, *33*, 543–555.

Korman, A. "Consideration," "initiating structure," and organizational criteria: A review. *Personnel Psychology*, 1966, *19*, 349–361.

Larson, L. L., Hunt, J. G., & Osborn, R. N. The great hi-hi leader behavior myth: A lesson from Occam's razor. *Academy of Management Journal*, 1976, *19*, 628–641.

Leister, A., Borden, D., & Fiedler, F. E. Validation of contingency model leadership training: Leader Match. *Academy of Management Journal*, 1977, *20*, 464–470.

Liden, R. C., & Graen, G. Generalizability of the vertical dyad linkage model of leadership. *Academy of Management Journal*, 1980, *23*, 451–465.

Likert, R. *New patterns of management.* New York: McGraw-Hill, 1961.

Lowin, A., & Craig, J. R. The influence of level of performance on managerial style: An experimental object lesson in the ambiguity of correlational data. *Organizational Behavior and Human Performance*, 1968, *3*, 441–458.

Mawhinney, T. C., & Ford, J. D. The path goal theory of leader effectiveness: An operant interpretation. *Academy of Management Review*, 1977, *2*, 398–411.

Pfeffer, J. The ambiguity of leadership. *Academy of Management Review*, 1977, *2*, 104–112.

Rice, R. W. Construct validity of the Least Preferred Coworker (LPC) score. *Psychological Bulletin*, 1978, *85*, 1199–1237.

Sashkin, M., Taylor, F. C., & Tripathi, R. C. An analysis of situational moderating effects on relationships between least preferred co-worker and other psychological measures. *Journal of Applied Psychology*, 1974, *59*, 731–740.

Schriesheim, C. A., House, R. J., & Kerr, S. Leader initiating structure: A reconciliation of discrepant research results and some empirical tests. *Orga-*

*nizational Behavior and Human Performance,* 1976, *15,* 297–321.

Schriesheim, C. A., & Kerr, S. Psychometric properties of the Ohio State leadership scales. *Psychological Bulletin,* 1974, *81,* 756–765.

Schriesheim, C. A., & Murphy, C. J. Relationships between leader behavior and subordinate satisfaction and performance: A test of some situational moderators. *Journal of Applied Psychology,* 1976, *61,* 634–641.

Schriesheim, C. A., & Stogdill, R. M. Differences in factor structure across three versions of the Ohio State leadership scales. *Personnel Psychology,* 1975, *28,* 189–206.

Schriesheim, C. A., & Von Glinow, M. A. Tests of the path-goal theory of leadership: A theoretical and empirical analysis. *Academy of Management Journal,* 1977, *20,* 398–405.

Schriesheim, J. F., & Schriesheim, C. A. A test of the path-goal theory of leadership and some suggested directions for future research. *Personnel Psychology,* 1980, *33,* 349–370.

Stinson, J. E., & Johnson, T. W. The path-goal theory of leadership: A partial test and suggested refinement. *Academy of Management Journal,* 1975, *18,* 242–252.

Stinson, J. E., & Tracy, L. Some disturbing characteristics of the LPC score. *Personnel Psychology,* 1974, *27,* 477–485.

Stogdill, R. M. Personal factors associated with leadership. *Journal of Psychology,* 1948, *25,* 35–71.

Stogdill, R. M., & Coons, A. E. (Eds.). *Leader behavior: Its description and measurement.* Columbus: Ohio State University Bureau of Business Research, 1957.

Tscheulin, D. Leader behavior measurement in German industry. *Journal of Applied Psychology,* 1973, *57,* 28–31.

Vecchio, R. P. An empirical examination of the validity of Fiedler's model of leadership effectiveness. *Organizational Behavior and Human Performance,* 1977, *19,* 180–206.

Vroom, V. H., & Jago, A. G. On the validity of the Vroom-Yetton model. *Journal of Applied Psychology,* 1978, *63,* 151–162.

Vroom, V. H., & Yetton, P. W. *Leadership and decision-making.* Pittsburgh: University of Pittsburgh Press, 1973.

Weissenberg, P., & Kavanagh, M. The independence of initiating structure and consideration: A review of the literature. *Personnel Psychology,* 1972, *25,* 119–130.

Wilkinson, I., & Kipnis, D. Interfirm use of power. *Journal of Applied Psychology,* 1978, *63,* 315–320.

# chapter 12

ORGANIZATIONAL COMMUNICATION

Organizational communication is somewhat of an enigma. It is not nearly as heavily researched as job satisfaction, motivation, or leadership; in fact, I/O psychologists have only begun systematic studies in the last 5 to 10 years. One explanation for this general lack of research (until recently) is that communication is more an organizational (as opposed to industrial) topic. In the gradual movement to study more $O$ topics, communication has acquired a new sense of recognition and importance in the discipline. Organizational communication is a vitally important topic because communication is central to the concept of an organization. The following quotes illustrate the esteem in which communication is held by organizational scholars:

"The first executive function is to develop and maintain a system of communication" (Barnard, 1938).

"When communication stops, organized activity ceases to exist. Individual uncoordinated activity returns" (Hicks, 1967).

"The communication system serves as the vehicle by which organizations are embedded in their environments" (Guetzkow, 1965).

As Rogers and Agarwala-Rogers (1976) have noted, a major reason for studying organizational communication is that it occurs in a highly structured context. An organization's structure can greatly affect the communication process—communication from a subordinate to a superior is quite different from communication between peers.

Communication is the lifeblood of an organization. It pervades an organization's activities. It is a valuable means through which individuals understand their organizational roles, and it integrates organizational subunits. Communication is a means for making decisions, obtaining feedback, and pursuing organizational goals. It is the thread that holds the various interdependent parts of an organization together. If we can learn a lot about communication within an organization, we will have learned a lot about that organization.

## DEFINITION OF COMMUNICATION

Probably no other concept has as many definitions as "communication." Dance (1970) identified over 95 definitions of communication that have been used by researchers. For our purposes, we can define communication as "the exchange of information between a sender and receiver and the inference of meaning between participants (O'Reilly & Pondy, 1979). While all communication does not occur in an organizational context, such a context does produce a more restrictive consideration of communication. These restrictions may result from organizational roles (superior versus subordinate), norms (what can and can't be discussed), and structure (lines of authority). Given a typical organizational structure, there are at least three major levels in which organizational communication can occur:

1.  Communication between a sender and a receiver, as a superior and subordinate (interpersonal communication).
2.  Communication between groups or subunits of the organization, such as between the production and the sales departments (*intra*organizational communication).
3.  Communication between organizations, such as between an organization (a chemical company) and a federal regulatory agency (the Environmental Protection Agency) (*inter*organizational communication).

Roberts, O'Reilly, Bretton, and Porter (1974) noted that organizational communication may be viewed from any or all of these levels. In a more general sense, Farace and MacDonald (1974) have defined organizational communication as the process by which organizationally relevant information is transmitted and received. Organizational communication is a subset of communication in general, a process which is affected by, and in turn affects, all the defining properties of an organization.

# PURPOSES OF COMMUNICATION

Communication in organizations has many purposes. It is involved in such processes as leadership, influence, control, planning, and decision making. Behind each of these are functions that communication serves to enhance. Scott and Mitchell (1976) have proposed four such functions of communication:

1. Control, to clarify duties and establish authority and responsibility.
2. Information, to provide the basis for decision-making.
3. Motivation, to elicit cooperation and commitment to organizational objectives.
4. Emotive, to express feelings.

A performance appraisal interview between a superior and subordinate may manifest all four of these functions. The superior may review a subordinate's goals and objectives as a basis for establishing an evaluative framework, clearly a control function. The subordinate can discuss problems on the job, which may serve as a basis for deciding how the job might best be restructured. If the superior and subordinate reach agreement on mutual goals for the future, the motivational properties of such communication can elicit greater commitment to goal attainment. Finally, the subordinate can air feelings of pleasure and displeasure about various aspects of the job. Likewise, other organizational practices are reflective of these functions, though some may have a more narrowly defined purpose. Shortly, we will examine several organizational practices and constructs, and how communication is centrally related to each.

# A MODEL OF COMMUNICATION

There are four major components in the communication process—the source, message, channel, and receiver. This is referred to as the S-M-C-R model of communication (Berlo, 1960). Though probably oversimplified, it is a useful framework for analyzing the communication process. The model in Figure 12–1 shows the four major components (S, M, C, R) plus two others, effects and feedback.

**1. Source.** The *source* is the originator of the message. It may be an individual or an institution. The source has the main responsibility for preparing the message.

**2. Message.** The *message* is the stimulus that the source transmits to the receiver. The message is what the process of communication is primarily about; it is the idea that is communicated.

Messages may be language symbols (words), nonverbal symbols (facial

**Figure 12–1**               **The S-M-C-R model of communication**

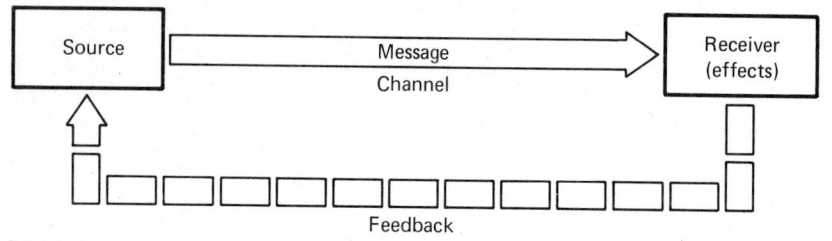

SOURCE: David K. Berlo, *The Process of Communication: An Introduction to Theory and Practice.* Copyright © 1960 by Holt, Rinehart, and Winston, Inc. Reprinted by permission of Holt, Rinehart, and Winston, CBS College Publishing.

gestures, etc.) or pictures. *Meanings* are references, such as ideas, images, and thoughts, that are commonly shared between the source and the receiver. Without these shared meanings, communication cannot occur. Many communication failures are due to mistaken assumptions by the source or the receiver about the meaning of a symbol they have exchanged. Berlo stated, "Meanings are in people, not in the message." He meant that words have no meanings in themselves: their meanings are assigned by the source and the receiver.

3.  **Channel.**   A channel is the means by which a message travels from a source to a receiver. It is the path through which the message is physically transmitted. Channels can be classified into mass media or interpersonal channels. Mass media channels enable a source to reach many receivers (newspapers, books, radio, and TV). Interpersonal channels usually involve a face-to-face exchange between a source and a receiver.

4.  **Receivers.**   Receivers are the recipients of the message. They are often ignored by the source, which results in a failure to communicate. Some sources are source-oriented—textbook authors sometimes write for their colleagues and go over the heads of their student readers. Some other sources are message-oriented. The sources know a great deal about the topic but cannot express it meaningfully to their receivers. Other sources are channel-oriented. They are preoccupied with one channel of communication (writing memos instead of calling a staff meeting). Effective communicators must be receiver-oriented because the receivers are the object of the communication.

5.  **Effects.**   Communication effects are the changes in receiver behavior that occur as a result of transmitting the message. "Effective communication" is communication that results in those changes in receiver behavior that were intended by the source. There are three major types of communication effects: changes in receiver *knowledge, attitude,* and *overt behavior.* Normally, but not always, these effects occur in sequence; a change in knowledge (e.g., a new company policy) precedes a change in

attitude (e.g., attitude toward tardiness), which precedes a change in overt behavior (e.g., coming to work on time).

**6. Feedback.** Feedback is a response by the receiver to the source's message. The source may take account of feedback in modifying subsequent messages. *Positive feedback* informs the source that the intended effect of a message was achieved; *negative feedback* informs the source that the intended effect of a message was *not* achieved.

For example, I am the source of this communication. The message is the content of I/O psychology. The channel that is used is the printed medium, in this case a book. College students are the primary receivers of the message. The effects of the message are hopefully a change in receiver knowledge and possibly a change in attitude (about I/O psychology) and overt behavior (perhaps seeking employment in the field of psychology). Negative feedback from instructors and students will cause me to make revisions in the next edition.

The S-M-C-R model is a useful way to understand the process of communication. Failures to communicate can be caused by "breaks" in any or all of the model's components. Research on organizational communication has also shown some interesting correlates of each component. We will examine these findings later in the chapter.

## COMMUNICATION IN WORK BEHAVIOR

Communication is basic to an organization's functioning since it pervades many aspects of work behavior. We will discuss five topics (selection, job performance, performance appraisal, training, and organizational climate) in terms of their relevance to communication. But keep in mind that communication affects (directly or indirectly) probably every substantive area in I/O psychology.

**Selection.** The applicant's ability to communicate a desirable impression is of fundamental importance in personnel selection. Applicants have been known to be denied employment on the basis of their poor written communication skills relating to the selection instrument being used. Levine and Flory (1975) have noted that some applicants hurt their chances by not listing full details on an application blank. Some application blanks require the applicant to explain why they would like to have the job. The answers are sometimes so disjointed and illogical that the applicants are not hired due to their deficient written communication skills. Letters of recommendation are another type of selection device heavily influenced by written communication. Referees are sometimes unable to describe the applicant adequately for the prospective employer. I have received hundreds of letters of recommendation written for applicants to graduate school. One of the more memorable ones contained this sentence: "If you knew Ralph as I know Ralph, you would think of Ralph as I think of Ralph." Was this an endorsement or a condemnation of Ralph? Obviously the message was distorted between the source (the referee) and the receiver (me).

Effective oral communication skills are critical when the selection instrument is an interview. This holds for both the interviewer and the applicant. The interviewer attempts to foster a positive image of the company as an attractive employer. The applicant tries to impress the interviewer with his or her credentials. The verbal and nonverbal behavior of both parties can have a great bearing on the outcome of the selection interview (Schmitt, 1976). Inarticulation, reticence, verbosity, and redundancy all contribute to lower evaluations. People who cannot express themselves verbally suffer negative judgments of their capabilities, particularly in jobs that require a high degree of oral communication.

A growing body of literature has also underscored the importance of nonverbal communication in the selection interview. Factors such as eye contact, posture, facial expressions, and hand gestures do correlate with selection decisions. Knowingly or unknowingly, interviewers are influenced by applicants' nonverbal communication. Research (e.g., Ekman, 1965; Hall, 1966) has shown that applicants who use a moderately high degree of positive, nonverbal communication signals are seen as much more enthusiastic, motivated, self-confident and pleasant. Proxemics (distance between discussants) of four to five feet seems most comfortable for many North Americans. Greater distance is perceived as aloofness. However, nonverbal communication modes cannot be understood in isolation (Baskin & Aronoff, 1980). They relate to each other and especially to accompanying verbal communication. Sometimes the two types of modes complement each other (an applicant keeps close eye contact and says she is interested in the job). Other times, the two modes yield conflicting messages (an applicant yawns while saying the job sounds interesting). In summary, personnel selection is closely tied to communication. Verbal and nonverbal communication are both important in the selection interview. Written communication is evident in application blanks and letters of recommendation. Many seemingly qualified applicants never get their foot in the door because they can't communicate their skills and abilities effectively.

**Job performance.**    For some jobs, communication ability (written or oral) is not crucial to job success (as in some kinds of manual labor). However, the ability to communicate is an important dimension of success for many jobs. For some jobs, in fact, it may be the dominant dimension. Jobs that require interpersonal skills need someone with communication ability. Major corporations responding to a survey said that ability to communicate was the prime requisite of a promotable executive (Randle, 1956). Given the highly technical nature of many businesses today, clarity in written communication is particularly important. Fielden (1964) noted that many managers can't write. He suggests using a written performance inventory to evaluate managers' writing skills on four factors: readability, correctness, appropriateness, and thought. Fielden also contends that managers can be trained to write better once their deficiencies are identified.

Oral communication skills are also related to job performance. Wilcox (1959) said that if a person doesn't understand a *written* report, the person may reread it, refer back or ahead, or even consult other sources. But *oral* communication disappears into thin air. Therefore, to aid understanding, voice and language skills must be developed. In an empirical study, Pace (1962) demonstrated that differences between effective and ineffective sales representatives were due to differences in oral communication skills. Less-effective representatives were deficient in using special types of persuasive communication.

Though most educational and training programs stress knowledge, they rarely teach how to communicate that knowledge to others, even when it is a vital part of the person's job. Many business and educational leaders make comments like: "It's really too bad about Mr. (or Professor) Jones—he knows his material, but he just can't communicate it to his subordinates (or students). Effective communication skills are trainable and we will discuss communication training shortly.

**Performance appraisal.**  In Chapter 7, we discussed the importance of the performance appraisal interview. Superiors should communicate to the subordinate what performance objectives are being reviewed and how well the subordinate is performing on these objectives. A number of studies have revealed several communication correlates of employee satisfaction with the appraisal interview. Nemeroff and Wexley (1977) found that the proportion of time the subordinate spoke in the interview was positively correlated with subordinate satisfaction. Burke, Weitzel, and Weir (1978) reported that subordinates who were allowed to communicate their ideas about planning improvements in their performance subsequently performed better on the job. While the performance appraisal interview is but one avenue of superior/subordinate communication (Jablin, 1979), the content and process of this communication are related to both subordinate satisfaction and performance.

Other research has studied how employees learn about how well they are performing their jobs. Greller and Herold (1975) identified five sources from which employees receive information about their job performance: the formal organization; superior; co-workers; the task itself; and personal thoughts and feelings. The authors proposed that the informativeness of these sources for providing appraisal information increased as one moved from psychologically distant sources (i.e., the formal organization) to psychologically nearer sources (i.e., personal thoughts and feelings). A later study by Hanser and Muchinsky (1978) confirmed the validity of these sources of information. They found that the nearer sources (the task and personal thoughts and feelings) communicated more information to employees than the more distant sources. Finally, Hanser and Muchinsky (1980) showed that how much trust employees have in their superiors is related to how accurate and reliable they perceive appraisal information to be. Thus, appraisal information is communicated to employees from several sources. How believable the information is (especially from superiors) is related to interpersonal trust and affect. The value of performance appraisal information depends on the source it comes from.

**Training.**  Communication is important in developing and implementing a training program. The goals of the program should be clearly explained along with the actual content of the training material. If the employees don't understand the message, there will be a very limited opportunity for skill acquisition. Because many training programs are in highly technical areas (e.g., use of computers), there is a tendency for trainers to lapse into using jargon they understand, but may be quite foreign to the trainees. As an occasional trainer myself I have been guilty of this oversight. A company will hire me to train supervisors on how to appraise their employees' performance. At first, I would use expressions like "criterion-related validity," "freedom from contamination," "a minimum of halo error," and so on. Blank stares from the supervisors communicated (nonverbally) to me that I was not communicating (verbally) with them. *I* knew what I was saying, but I was not getting my message to them given their level of education and experience. I learned to translate "criterion-related validity" into "the ratings of performance have to be related to how well people are doing their job."

Companies also train their employees directly in how to communicate. Rogers and Farson (1969) described a procedure designed to help people listen, the first step in helping people to understand. Listening is a skill, and like most other skills, it can be acquired with practice. After hearing a message, the trainee paraphrases it. The differences in what people hear (and see) are amazing—a phenomenon that exasperates police trying to obtain eyewitness testimony about a crime (Woocher, 1977). Oral communication skills can be enhanced by using videotape and other transcription methods. Company executives can go through such communication training, particularly when they are under public scrutiny (Powell, Heimlich, & Goodin, 1980). Written communication skills can be enhanced through workshops and other training methods (e.g., Fielden, 1964). Recently, certain types of businesses (as the insurance business) have come under fire for issuing documents (e.g., policies) that the average person can't understand. The ability to communicate can be enhanced through training, and it is becoming an increasingly common area of training.

**Organizational climate.**  Organizational climate is the combined perceptions of individuals that are useful in differentiating organizations according to their procedures and practices. One climate factor relates to organizational communication. That is, organizations can be differentiated in part on the basis of their communication practices. Sims and LaFollette (1975) identified a climate factor they called Openness of Upward Communication; it involved communication between employees and management. Specific items covered managers' willingness to accept and act on subordinate's ideas and management's career counseling of subordinates. Some organizations have receptive climates for communication—open-door policies that encourage employee contact with superiors. Other organizations have more formal communication structures—employees communicate only through channels of authority. Organizations can greatly shape communication behavior by supporting open communication or suppressing it.

Some communication climates are better than others for pursuing certain organizational goals. Muchinsky (1977b) correlated several communication variables with measures of both climate and job satisfaction. The perceived accuracy of communication and employee satisfaction with communication were related to the interpersonal atmosphere in the organization, perceptions of management, and judgments about organizational practices. Employees who were dissatisfied with communication and who felt that most communication was inaccurate did not like the interpersonal atmosphere, felt poorly toward management, and were critical of the way the organization conducted itself. In addition, employees who felt communication was accurate and were satisfied with it were generally satisfied with their work, their supervision, and their co-workers. Perceptions of organizational communication are vital if a company wants to foster positive feelings in their employees.

## TECHNIQUES OF COMMUNICATING IN ORGANIZATIONS

There are many ways that parts of the organization can communicate with each other and a lesser number of ways that the organization can communicate with other organizations. We will examine some of the more widely used techniques and comment on their particular purposes. We will classify the techniques on the basis of whether they are used mostly for downward communication (i.e., from sources high in the structure to receivers in lower-level positions) or for upward communication (i.e., from sources in lower-level positions to receivers high in the structure).

**Downward communication**

**Letters, meetings, and the telephone.** Before sending any message downward, senders must know what audience they want to reach and how to reach it most effectively. Three of the most common techniques of organizational communication are group meetings, phone, and written letters or memos. Oral media (phone and meetings) provide personal interchange, are highly adaptable to a wide variety of situations, and can be used when time is crucial. Written communication, on the other hand, is required when the action called for is complex and must be done in a precise way.

The written word is not distortionproof, but it has less distortion than its oral counterpart. Written communication provides a permanent form of record-keeping, which is often desirable. It's also easier to reach 100 people with a single letter than to make 100 phone calls or schedule a time for 100 people to meet. However, each of these techniques can lose effectiveness if overused. A distinguished visitor from Europe once said that Americans spend too much time in meetings and on the phone. There is certainly no shortage of paperwork that crosses my desk on matters ranging from the crucial to the irrelevant. The sheer volume of junk mail I receive each week makes the truly valuable correspondence of special significance. Between lecturing to my classes, talking with students, reading correspondence, attending staff meetings, and answering the phone, there are days when seemingly all I do is engage in varieties of organizational communication.

One source of job-related stress (e.g., Gupta & Beehr, 1979) involves the anxiety produced by excessive communication at work. A second consequence (less severe) is communication *overload;* i.e., people receive more information than they can process. We will examine communication overload in greater detail later in the chapter.

**Manuals.**   Company manuals are another technique of downward communication. A manual is an integrated system of long-term instructions, brought together between covers, classified, coded, indexed, and otherwise prepared to maximize its reference value (Redfield, 1953). Manuals have a high degree of authority and are highly formal. They are prepared by the company and intended for a limited audience. Manuals mostly deal with policy, procedure, or organization. A typical supervisors' manual focuses on institutional policy and procedure, personnel administration, and organization structure and interdepartmental relationships. Figure 12–2 is a sample page from an office manual dealing with payroll procedures. Manuals are usually loose-leaf notebooks so they can be easily revised. Because manuals are technical and complex, employees should be *trained* in how to use them. A 300–500-page technical manual can be quite imposing to a new employee. It will probably collect dust if the employee is simply told "here it is in case you ever need it."

**Handbooks.**   Handbooks are usually less authoritative, less formal, less rigidly controlled, and generally apply at lower organizational levels. Handbooks are also smaller than manuals. The employee handbook is the most popular type; it outlines the duties and privileges of the individual worker. Figure 12–3 shows a sample page from an employee handbook. Handbooks have a low-key, friendly, and personal approach. In fact, many of the most stringent company rules may be shown in cartoons. A handbook can simplify material from the manual so it is more appropriate to a new audience. In one organization, the handbooks were so much more practical that even higher-level supervisors used them instead of their manuals. This was

**Figure 12–2**      **Sample page from an office manual**

EXAMPLES OF VARIOUS USES OF TIMECARDS

To pay an "E" base employee overtime hours above the regular monthly salary paid per "E" base appointment:

1.     Submit hours to be paid over eighty (80) in a two week overtime pay period as overtime hours on a timecard marked as "E Base Overtime".

2.     Rate indicated in the rate box should be regular hourly rate for the "E" base salary.

3.     Hours in the overtime box will be automatically calculated and paid at one and one-half times the regular rate indicated on the timecard in the rate box.

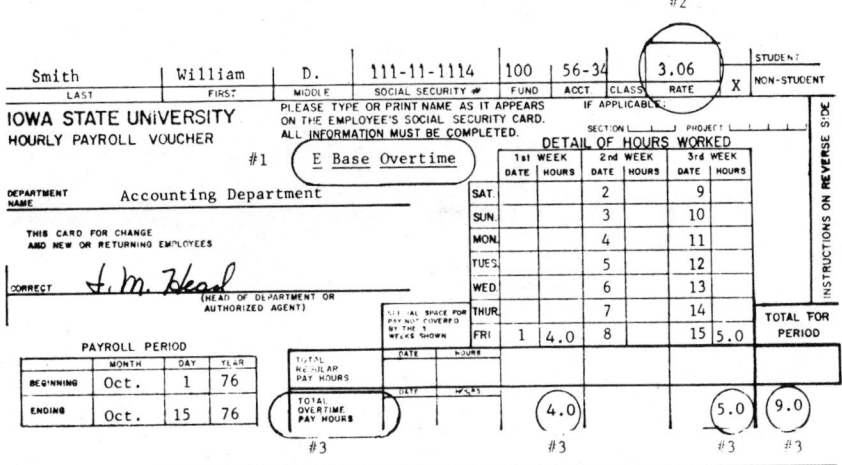

SOURCE: Ames, Iowa: Iowa State University.

unfortunate, since the manuals were much more authoritative and comprehensive. Handbooks are revised, though not as often as manuals. Because they are written at a more general level, they don't become outdated as quickly.

**Newsletters.** Company newsletters are usually issued biweekly or monthly. Informal and rarely technical, they are a means to disseminate information to a large number of employees. Newsletters might contain stories about employees cited for perfect attendance or superior job performance, announcements of company social functions, questions and answers about employment issues, etc. Newsletters are morale boosters—they help make employees in diverse jobs feel that they are part of the whole. Unlike a manual, which communicates specific, job-related information, a newslet-

**Figure 12–3**      **Sample page from an employee handbook**

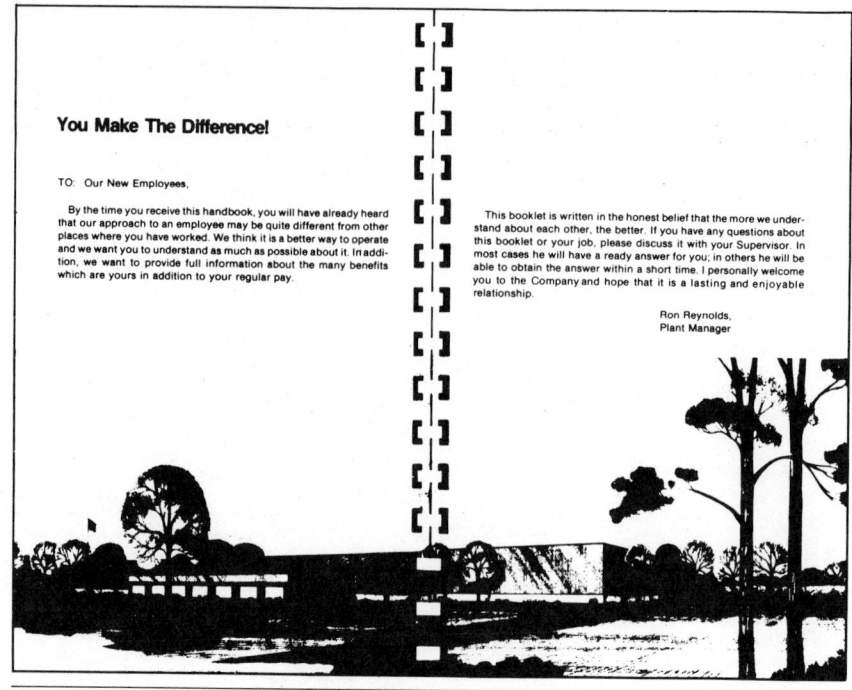

SOURCE: Young Radiator Company, Centerville, Iowa.

ter has a mix of personal, social, and work-related information. An example of a newsletter is shown in Figure 12–4.

**Upward communication**

Three techniques are used particularly in upward communication.

**Suggestion systems.** A suggestion system is a procedure where employees can submit ideas or suggestions for improving company effectiveness. The suggestions are then evaluated by a panel of managers, and the valuable ones are acted on. The initiator of the idea usually gets a cash award (the amount depends on how useful the suggestion is to the company). Large organizations today often award employees over $1 million a year for their suggestions. Some companies use letters of commendation, certificates of merit, and insignia in place of cash, though financial awards are still the most prevalent. Actual suggestion boxes may serve as receptacles for the ideas, or the suggestions may be forwarded through administrative channels. Many companies use printed forms (see Figure 12–5). The rationale behind suggestion systems is that employees are in the best position to contribute ideas to make their jobs more effective. The suggestion system is thus a way to communicate such ideas to the organization. Though some have alleged there is inequity between the suggestion's value

**Figure 12–4**  **Sample page from an employee newsletter**

non-academic

# staff newsletter
iowa state university

Address communications to Information Service, 109 Morrill Hall

VOL. VII, No. 32
June 19, 1981

AN EYEWITNESS ACCOUNT of life in Nicaragua will be given by a recent University of Iowa College of Medicine graduate Monday, June 22. Dr. Leighton Berryhill will speak on "Nicaragua After the Revolution" at 8 p.m. in the Memorial Union's Pioneer Room. She will report on current conditions, including health and cultural aspects, based on her experiences working in several health clinics after the fall of Anastasio Somoza. She also traveled to the Central American country before the 1979 revolution, working with a volunteer vaccination program. Her talk is sponsored by the Committee on Lectures.

CANCER RESEARCH SCIENTIST Dr. Rosalie Bertell will discuss "Health Hazards of Low Level Radiation" Wednesday, June 24, at 8 p.m. in the Memorial Union Gallery. Bertell, a member of the Grey Nuns of the Sacred Heart, is research director for the Ministry of Concern for Public Health, a group of scientists and health professionals who work to inform citizens and decision makers about scientific findings. She has studied environmental causes of leukemia at a national cancer research center, specializing in radiation-related health effects. Bertell's talk is sponsored by the Committee on Lectures.

321 Beardshear
## STAFF CONCERNS

Question: Many universities offer tuition assistance programs as a fringe benefit for their employees. Is there any way to make this suggestion to ISU?

Answer: The P & S Council and the Staff Council have a joint committee presently studying tuition assistance programs. Suggestions or questions may be directed to the chairperson of either council.

SOURCE: Staff Newsletter (Ames, Iowa: Iowa State University, June 19, 1981).

**Figure 12–5**  **A typical suggestion blank**

EMPLOYEE SUGGESTION SYSTEM
No. 160

I suggest _____

_____

_____

I believe my idea will:

| | | |
|---|---|---|
| Increase production ☐ | Improve service ☐ | Improve methods ☐ |
| Reduce costs ☐ | Prevent waste ☐ | Improve quality ☐ |
| Prevent accidents ☐ | | |

to the company and the size of the cash award, the system is a long-standing practice of upward communication.

**Grievances.** As discussed in Chapter 3, grievances are formal written complaints submitted by employees regarding alleged unfair treatment on the job. Grievances can cover almost any topic—working conditions, promotions, pay, disciplinary action, supervision, and work assignments. There are usually several steps in the grievance process. In the first step, the grievance is reviewed by the employee's immediate supervisor. If the grievance cannot be resolved, the next step might be to appeal the grievance to a work unit superintendent. Other steps might involve the company's industrial relations office or use of an outside mediator. The grievance process is more formal in a unionized company, an issue we will discuss in greater detail in Chapter 14.

The grievance process is an established system for allowing employees to air their complaints. The receivers of these messages are usually responsible people who have the power to make changes if they are justified. Without such a system, an employee could channel dissatisfaction in counterproductive ways, such as lowering productivity, increased absenteeism, drug dependence, sabotage, or turnover. Employees do sometimes resort to these when company officials repeatedly ignore grievances or refuse to act on them. Grievances are more than just blowing off steam—they are a way for employees to communicate feelings of injustice in the workplace. Organizations should always have a formal grievance process since grievances are as important as suggestions for upward communication.

**Attitude surveys.** Attitude surveys are probably *the* classic form of upward communication. They are often conducted annually or bi-annually. The organization uses the survey to learn about employees' feelings and attitudes on many employment issues. The surveys are usually administered by an outside consultant. Responses are anonymous, so employees can speak their minds without fear of identification or reprisal. The employees either complete the surveys at their work stations or in groups in the company cafeteria or meeting rooms. Figure 12–6 shows sample questions from an attitude survey. Some surveys deal strictly with opinions or attitudes; others add some factual questions to assess employees' knowledge about company benefits. The results are tabulated and a report is prepared. The company then acts on the information provided. If the employees lack knowledge about the company retirement plan, for example, the company might explain it in more detail. If many employees are dissatisfied with a certain area, such as working conditions, the company should either make improvements or explain why they can't. The company must respond to the results of the survey, or no one will take it seriously. Furthermore, employees will resent being surveyed if the company doesn't act on their feelings. Attitude surveys can give potent and sometimes surprising information. Employees may admit to doing things differently than the company handbook suggests. Management may find such "discrepancies"

**Figure 12–6**         **Sample questions from an employee attitude survey**

1. Do you feel free to discuss problems or complaints with your supervisor?
   - a. Always
   - b. Usually
   - c. Sometimes
   - d. Seldom
   - e. Never

2. Are your suggestions for changes in the methods of doing your work, which allow you to work more effectively, carefully considered?
   - a. Always
   - b. Usually
   - c. Sometimes
   - d. Never
   - e. Have not made any suggestions

3. How useful are the bulletin boards as a means of communication?
   - a. Very useful
   - b. Useful
   - c. Of some use
   - d. Of no use
   - e. I don't read the bulletin boards

4. Compared to other companies in the area, how do you rate the company's dental insurance program?
   - a. Better than other companies
   - b. About the same
   - c. Not as good

5. State in your own words what you like best about working for the company.

annoying or embarrassing, but they would be foolish to ignore them. Attitude surveys can be of tremendous value if employees answer them honestly and management acts on the information they provide.

# METHODS OF STUDYING ORGANIZATIONAL COMMUNICATION

Organizational communication has been studied with field and laboratory methods. Questionnaires, interviews, observation, and experimental paradigms have all been used (Greenbaum, 1974). In fact, Porter and Roberts (1976) commend the diversity of research methods used in this area. However, a number of research methods are used exclusively or primarily in the study of organizational communication. We will examine four of these methods in some detail.

**Activity sampling**

Activity sampling is a field technique where the investigator records and analyzes communication in process at many points in time. Generalizations are then made from these samples. For example, a group of interviewers might ring a bell and then immediately ask each person how they were communicating when the bell rang (face-to-face and phone conversations, letters being written or read, purpose of the communication, and so on). Multiple samples can be taken on several consecutive days to get a communication data base. While the method has been used in a number of studies, it needs a lot of cooperation between the researchers and the subjects. Studying communication can disrupt work, so it lacks unobtrusiveness.

## Sociogram

The sociogram was first developed by sociologists to study group formations. In communication, a sociogram is a graphic portrayal of who communicates with whom in a group. During a set period of time (as a day), an investigator records interpersonal communication patterns in a work group using a tally sheet or some other coding device. The sociogram in Figure 12–7 shows a seven-person work group. Person 1 communicates with everyone in the group except person 7. Person 1 is probably (but not necessarily) the group leader. He or she is called a "star," a person who communicates with almost everyone else in the group. Persons 2, 3, and 4 form a triad; they communicate with each other as well as person 1. Persons 5 and 6 form a dyad; they communicate only between themselves and with person 1. No one communicates with person 7, the "isolate." The sociogram is often combined with other methods to get a global perspective of communication patterns. A sociogram does not show the nature of the communication; this has to be collected by another method.

## Ecco analysis

Ecco analysis is a questionnaire-based method developed by Davis (1953). *Ecco* is derived from the words "*e*pisodic *c*ommunication *c*hannels in *o*rganization." The basic purpose of the method is to find out when each person first received a certain piece of information. Employees answer the same questionnaire at the same time. The results show the pattern of how information spreads through the organization. For example, Mike and Lorraine said they first got the information from Nick, who said he got it from Ben. The pattern is therefore Ben to Nick to Mike and Lorraine.

**Figure 12–7**                    **A sociogram showing communication patterns in a seven-person work group**

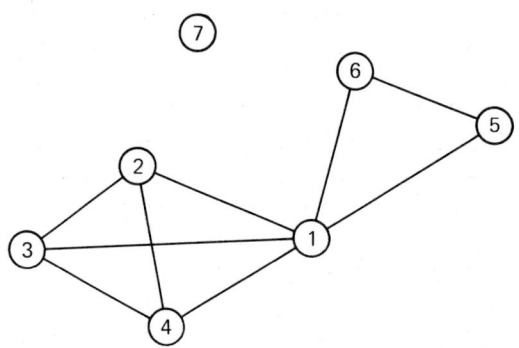

In practice, the researcher selects an event or piece of information which is the subject of the investigation. The event might be that a major company official is going to quit to take another job. The questionnaire, for example, might consist of the sentence, "Jim Link is leaving Fleischman's soon to enter the banking business in Norwalk." Each employee will receive this questionnaire, which might be distributed at the start of the workday. The accompanying instructions ask, "By noon yesterday did you know the information below or any part of it?" The employees then respond by indicating which part of the information they knew, who first told them the information, and the medium by which the information was communicated.

Davis (1953) says ecco analysis has a dynamic quality because it portrays a sequence of communications about an event. It shows the spread of a piece of information from its origin to all persons in the organization who knew it at the cutoff hour (e.g., noon). In an empirical test, Davis showed that information was communicated to others at the same job level who worked in the same job function. Relatively few people spread the information; most were only passive receivers. In general, ecco analysis has adequate reliability and validity and is most useful for studying the flow of information in an organization.

## Flesch index

Flesch (1948) developed a method to study written communication that has been used for over 30 years. His quantifiable method for calculating the reading ease of written material is based upon two factors: (1) the number of syllables per 100 words; and (2) the average length of a sentence in words. Using regression analysis he derived the following equation:

$$\text{Reading ease} = 207 - .846 \text{ (word length)} - 1.015 \text{ (sentence length)}$$

The derived reading ease score puts a piece of writing on a scale between 0 (practically unreadable) and 100 (easy for any literate person). We can find the reading ease of this book by subjecting a sample of my writing (first paragraph of Chapter 1) to Flesch's formula.

First, count out a 100-word sample of writing. Our sample concludes with the word *image* in the sixth sentence of the first paragraph. Next, count the number of syllables in this 100-word passage. That total comes to 177. Then, compute the average number of words in the sentences used in the 100-word sample. That figure (including the complete sixth sentence) is 17.5 words based on 105 words in six full sentences. Therefore, the reading ease score of this book based upon the first paragraph of Chapter 1 is:

$$\text{Reading ease} = 207 - .846 \,(177) - 1.015 \,(17.5) = 39.5$$

Flesch's normative standards for gauging reading ease are shown in Table 12–1. As can be seen, the writing style associated with a reading ease

**Table 12–1**    **Pattern of reading ease scores**

| Description of style | Average sentence length | Averate number of syllables per 100 words | Reading ease score | Estimated school grades completed | Estimated percent of U.S. adults |
|---|---|---|---|---|---|
| Very easy | 8 or less | 123 or less | 90 to 100 | 4th grade | 93 |
| Easy | 11 | 131 | 80 to 90 | 5th grade | 91 |
| Fairly easy | 14 | 139 | 70 to 80 | 6th grade | 88 |
| Standard | 17 | 147 | 60 to 70 | 7th or 8th grade | 83 |
| Fairly difficult | 21 | 155 | 50 to 60 | Some high school | 54 |
| Difficult | 25 | 167 | 30 to 50 | High school or some college | 33 |
| Very difficult | 29 or more | 192 or more | 0 to 30 | College | 4–5 |

SOURCE: R. Flesch, *The Art of Readable Writing* (New York: Harper & Row, 1974).

score of 39.5 is "difficult." The classification of "high school or some college" (Table 12–1) does indeed describe the nature of this book.

Flesch's formula is relevant for many areas of organizational communication. It is a way to gauge if the written message is suitable for the intended audience. Manuals, handbooks, memoranda, etc., can be written over the heads of their readers. Reading ease scores can also be associated with levels of education. Some paper-and-pencil selection tests have been "written" for the college graduate level, yet the job requires only a high school diploma. In such a case, the test must be rewritten to coincide with the job's educational requirements. Because Flesch's method is a quantitative way to assess readability, it is a useful diagnostic device.

# THE EFFECTS OF ORGANIZATIONAL STRUCTURE ON COMMUNICATION

The structure of an organization is its anatomy and how all the parts interrelate in pursuit of the organization's goals. Structure can influence communication in the organization by limiting and guiding its flow. In fact, some authors (e.g., Roberts & O'Reilly, 1978) think of differences among organizations in terms of differences in communication structure. Within an organization, a main purpose of communication is to help maintain *coordination* among the parts. Depending on the organization's structure, communication can enhance coordination among the parts in different ways. We will examine how three dimensions of organizational structure influence communication.

**Size**

Perhaps the most obvious structural factor is the organization's size. In a small organization, formal communication rarely exceeds face-to-face interactions. Four or five employees of a gas station can communicate with each other and with customers without letters, memoranda, staff meetings, and phone conversations.

However, what are the communication needs of the large oil company that controls the local gas station (and many others)? The company may have hundreds or thousands of retail dealerships. They might also be involved in oil exploration, refining, and transportation as well as other petroleum-related products, such as chemicals. An organization of this size couldn't survive on just face-to-face communication; it would need the full gamut, particularly written communication. Speed of communication is obviously much slower than in the local gas station. Though all the station's employees need to be equally informed of job-related matters, not all the parent company's employees need to be. Employees in the credit card department don't need to know about problems in the refinery. Thus, communication in a large organization is far more selective and limited (otherwise, the employees would suffer from overload). But, the *need* for communication in the parent company is much more acute. There are more parts to coordinate, and thus more chances for information to be omitted or distorted. The organization's structure limits possible interactions among group members (O'Reilly & Roberts, 1977a). Its size is a major structural determinant of group interactions and thus a major determinant of the nature and frequency of communication.

## Centralized/ decentralized shape

In a highly centralized organization, vertical (upward and downward) communication is stressed, and there is a lot of "distance" between the top and bottom levels. Communication flows between levels along established lines of authority. How much the organization is mechanized can also influence the amount of vertical communication. Simpson (1959) found that with low mechanization, vertical communication (as indexed by the need for close supervision) was high because supervisors had to continually monitor the work of subordinates. Under conditions of medium mechanization (a typical assembly line), the need for vertical communication was far less since the line set the pace of work. Under conditions of high mechanization (highly automated plants), the need for vertical communication was again high to deal with frequent and serious machine breakdowns.

In a decentralized organization, there are fewer levels of authority. The work units are distributed more horizontally (along similar functional lines). There is a greater emphasis on horizontal communication (among similar work units). Horizontal communication is aimed more at resolving problems and coordinating the work-flow; vertical communication is aimed more at issues of control. In a centralized organization, there is a more desire to maintain control through formal lines of authority. In a decentralized one, there is a more need for integration among interdependent parts. Vertical communication is based on power relationships (e.g., superior/subordinate); horizontal stresses cooperation among parties with equal levels of power. Employees in highly centralized organizations often say that "everything is done by the book" (heavy emphasis on policies and procedures). Employees in highly decentralized organizations say that communication is informal and that they must "get along with each other" to accomplish their objectives.

Centralized/decentralized shape is not an either/or phenomenon—most companies have some attributes of both. But the shape of the organization influences the use of certain types of communication, which in turn are based on power relationships. That is, the link between shape and communication is strong but not direct. Managers transferred from corporate headquarters to a regional office notice the difference in the way things get done. Power-based, vertical communication is often the norm at headquarters but may not suffice in a regional office. People notice the same thing when they leave the military for other jobs. Shape, like size, limits the types of communication an organization uses.

## Degree of uncertainty

Some organizations must deal with changes in technology, labor markets, and the availability of raw material. In this complex environment, uncertainty threatens the organization's ability to survive and attain its goals. Galbraith (1973) has stated the basic effect of uncertainty is to limit the organization's ability to preplan or to make decisions about activities in advance of their execution. O'Reilly and Pondy (1979) think that uncertainty requires increased communication among members if the organization is to be effective. In support of this position, Tushman (1978) reported that the more complex the task in a research lab, the greater the amount of technical communication required. Bacharach and Aiken (1977) found that the more routine the task in a work group, the less the employees communicated. Other studies have supported the relationship between uncertainty and communication.

The more uncertainty an organization faces, the greater is its need to communicate. The investment industry is a prime example. In this highly uncertain environment, no person or organization has yet found the key to predicting the stock market. So investment companies continually need to communicate about financial matters.

The ability to reduce uncertainty through communication is directly related to the effectiveness of the organization. For some companies, it is the difference between adequate and superior performance; for others, between survival and demise. A company that tried to buy and sell stocks at last week's prices would soon be out of business.

## COMMUNICATION STRUCTURE VARIABLES

When we think of structural variables, we tend to think of *organizational* structure. But there are a number of variables that pertain to *communication* structure. Alone or in concert with organizational structure variables, they influence and control the flow of information. We will examine three communication structure variables.

## Communication networks

A communication network refers to the accessibility of channels of communication among people. Some networks are restrictive—one person communicates with one other person. Other networks, far more flexible, allow communication among large numbers of people. Most of the research on communication networks was done using laboratory methods and typically examined a network of a certain size, such as five people. By using an intercom or allowing subjects to pass messages through partitions, an experimenter could control who communicates with whom. Several possible five-person networks are shown in Figure 12–8.

A typical study involved giving the subjects a problem to solve collectively so they had to share information. (For example, each subject is given a card with five symbols on it, and the group must find out which symbol is common to all cards.) Measures of performance included the accuracy (correctness) of the group's decision and how much time it took to reach it. The subjects also had to assess group morale in the network.

In terms of problem-solving efficiency, when the task was simple (symbol identification), the centralized wheel, chain, and Y networks (see Figure 12–8) were superior to the circle and all-channel networks (Leavitt, 1951). For more complex problems (as in human relations), the decentralized all-channel and circle networks were faster, made fewer errors, and exchanged more ideas. Similar findings occurred for group morale—the decentralized networks had higher morale than the centralized ones (Shaw, 1964).

What do the findings mean? Though generalizing from the laboratory to the organization should be viewed with caution (Burgess, 1968), there are some meaningful implications. First, for a relatively simple task (as in automated production), the company does not need a system for all employees to communicate with each other. Such a decentralized communication structure may only confuse matters. However, if an organization is faced with complex problems (as many are), a more decentralized communication structure is desirable. A more rapid exchange of ideas is possible with an all-channel network. An organization can hurt its own cause by forcing members to communicate only through centralized channels of authority; a more open and interconnected system is better. Likewise, forcing people to communicate with each other through strict parlimentary procedure (i.e., all communication must flow through a central person) fosters low morale. In general, research indicates that a decentralized communication network is preferable (except as noted). The supervisor or manager who has an open-

**Figure 12–8**     **Various five-person communication networks**

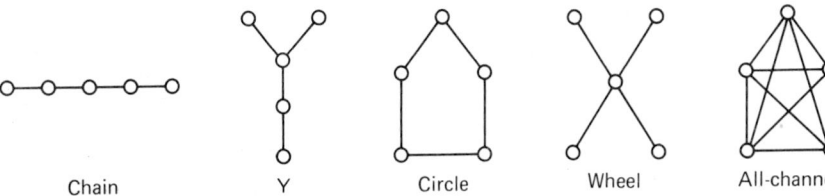

Chain     Y     Circle     Wheel     All-channel

door policy in effect produces an all-channel network. The findings from these studies suggest that the most efficient communication structure may not match the company's organizational structure.

## Communication roles

The research on communication networks revealed the importance of *communication roles*—the communication function that a person serves within the network. People in central positions within the network are normally more active in communicating and subsequently more satisfied. They have more potential power, both to pass on or withhold information and to introduce new information into the network. We will examine two communication roles: (1) people in positions to control information ("gatekeepers"); and (2) people in positions to bring new information into a group ("liaisons").

**Gatekeepers.** To some extent, everyone is a gatekeeper because they can decide what information to pass on to others. However, some jobs have more opportunity for gatekeeping than others. Secretaries and administrative assistants are gatekeepers when they decide what matters get to the their bosses' attention (O'Reilly & Pondy, 1979). The role of a gatekeeper has considerable power.

Research on gatekeeping shows that the power to control information flow is indeed a good way to affect certain outcomes. For example, Pettigrew (1972) described a study in which a company was contemplating buying an expensive computer system. One person within the company was able to control the timing and substance of information sent to the decision-making group. This control allowed the individual to orchestrate the purchase decision. Many administrators tell subordinates "only the information they need to know." But opinions differ over what subordinates need to know. Most employees complain that their superiors withhold too much information rather than not enough.

Gatekeeping occurs in both upward and downward communication. Subordinates sometimes screen out information they think is not important enough for their superior's attention (upward). Superior's sometimes limit the flow of information to their subordinates (downward). Gatekeeping is a double-edged sword. Failure to gatekeep at all results in information overload; receivers get more information than they can process. Too much gatekeeping results in lack of communication; employees are kept in the dark on matters they feel they should know.

**Liaisons.** In many organizations, liaisons keep groups informed of each other's activities. Usually, the groups involved do not interact often, so the liaison transmits and receives information between groups. The need for liaisons is greater in organizations with highly differentiated work groups or departments. While these groups normally work independently, occasionally they must communicate with each other. This is where the liaison's role is important. Figure 12–9 shows a liaison's role in work groups.

**Figure 12–9**                    **Communication structure among three work groups**

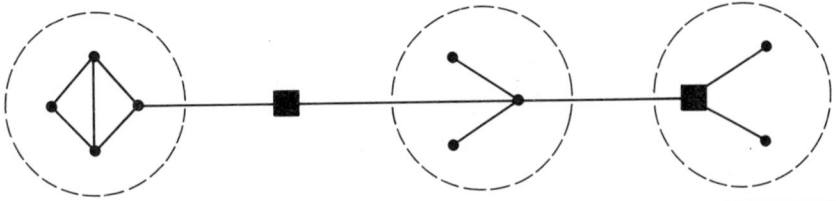

Note: The dashed lines represent extant work groups, squares represent liaison role persons, solid circles are nonliaison role persons, and the solid lines represent frequent interpersonal contacts. The liaison role person at the left is not a member of any existing work group, while the liaison role person at the right is a member of a work group.

In a study of the plastics industry, Lawrence and Lorsch (1967) found companies that used liaisons to link highly differentiated departments were more successful than firms that didn't. Who serves as a liaison? Schwartz and Jacobson (1977) studied communication in a university and found that liaisons had a legitimate responsibility to involve themselves in the operations of various work groups. Such people were usually administrators who served on various academic committees. Liaisons are welcome in complex organizations because they let the right hand know what the left hand is doing. Liaisons facilitate coordination among groups, and their ability to make these links may be vital to the organization's effectiveness.

**Communication modalities**

Communication modalities are the means by which information is communicated between individuals. Face-to-face communication is the most general means of communication throughout an organization. Oral communication is the most effective for exchanging ideas, concepts, or information that needs clarifying. Clarification and elaboration are not possible with written communication. People prefer face-to-face interactions to communicate. Muchinsky (1977b) found that frequency of face-to-face communication was positively correlated with work satisfaction; frequency of written communication was negatively correlated with work satisfaction.

But there are many occasions where face-to-face communication is not enough to meet the organization's needs. The more formal the communication, the greater is the need to put it in writing. Technical material is best communicated in writing so it can be studied and used later as a reference. It's also more efficient to communicate standard information (e.g., an orientation program for new employees) in a handbook rather than repeating it orally to each employee. In many cases, a combination of oral and written modes is used. Ideas can be exchanged at a meeting and later transcribed into minutes. With the growing trend to hold corporations accountable for their actions, many companies have had to document their communication

In the contemporary world of work we can communicate through four modalities—telephone, written, face-to-face, and computer graphics.

for future reference. Due to increased litigation, companies have resorted to "paper trails" of documents so they can defend their actions in court.

Communication modes are also misused. I get stacks of letters and memos on matters that could more effectively be handled by a meeting or a phone call. I attend meetings on matters that could more effectively be handled in writing. Some communicators are "channel-bound;" use one channel to solve all their communication needs. But while certain modes are more effective in certain cases, the final choice can be partly determined by cost (phone rates and postage costs are rising).

## COMMUNICATION PROCESS VARIABLES

In this section, we will discuss those variables that directly affect communication between individuals—*communication process variables*.

### Accuracy

Accuracy refers to the correctness of the message transmitted from the source to the receiver. Most of the research on accuracy deals with *perceived* accuracy—the extent to which the receiver perceives the information as correct. In a sense, the accuracy of information can be thought of as its validity. But again, don't confuse validity with reliability. Some sources are reliable (they give consistent and predictable messages), yet the messages are not accurate. The Soviet newspaper *Pravda* consistently reports news favorable to the Communist party, but Western countries question its accuracy.

What factors contribute to perceived accuracy of information? O'Reilly and Roberts (1976) studied the relationship between perceived accuracy and credibility (believability) of the information source. General trustworthiness and expertise of the source was positively correlated with perceived accuracy of the information. People who are trusted for their honesty and those with expertise are perceived to supply accurate information.

Two other correlates of perceived accuracy have been identified. Roberts and O'Reilly (1974) found that superiors with a great deal of influence in the organization were seen as providing accurate information. One reason may be that influential superiors have clout due to their referent power, which has a basis in knowledge and information. Hanser and Muchinsky (1980) reported that trust in the superior also contributed to perceptions of accurate information. Superiors who were trusted by their subordinates were perceived as supplying more accurate performance appraisal information. In short, perceptions of accurate information are related to three factors: the credibility of the source; the influence of the source; and the amount of trust in the source.

## Openness

Open communication means a free flow of information and feelings between two or more people. Some people are very guarded; they choose their words carefully. Diplomats are well-known for this (and what they say often has to be "translated" into more comprehensible language).

Research on communication openness is limited, but we do know a few of its correlates. O'Reilly and Roberts (1976) reported that a source's credibility is associated with how uninhibited the communication is perceived to be. Research shows that people have more contacts (both job-related and social) in a group where communication is seen to be open. The results suggest that individuals tend to minimize contact with information sources that provide guarded and stilted communication. Guarded communication is a way of maintaining role distance; a lack of candor in communication serves to prevent the parties from becoming psychologically "close." Guarded communication occurs more often in situations where different role status exists. Someone in a higher status role may refuse to communicate with someone in a lower status role as a means of maintaining the status differential. The willingness of the higher status person to be candid varies directly with the magnitude of the discrepancy in role status.

## Distortion

Information distortion is the incorrect reproduction of objectively correct information. It can be caused by either unconscious or deliberate alteration. All too often in an organization, the same message is not received by all parties. After people "exchange notes" on a particular message, there are often subtle differences in content (e.g., "Well, the way I heard it was

. . ."). Somewhere along the communication network distortion had occurred.

What causes distortion? A study by O'Reilly (1978) showed several correlates of information distortion. Senders suppress important unfavorable information sent to superiors and accent favorable information about themselves. Subordinates often screen information before sending it upward to avoid upper-echelon overload, but deliberate distortion can have a negative affect (Athanassiades, 1973). This is especially true when important but unfavorable information is suppressed, while irrelevant but favorable information is sent. Superiors may lose the ability to discriminate between the relevant and irrelevant with a consequent loss in decision-making performance. O'Reilly also found that low trust in the receiver results in much more suppression by senders, especially when the information reflects unfavorably on the sender. While distortion also occurs in the downward direction (e.g., O'Reilly & Roberts, 1974), it appears that downward communication is less susceptible to the suppression of unfavorable information and the magnification of favorable information. Downward communication is seemingly marked more by gatekeeping (the withholding of certain information) than the alteration or distortion of information. That is, senders passing information downward screen out information not perceived to be relevant for subordinates' tasks.

## Overload

Information overload occurs where there is more information than can effectively be processed. The converse of overload is underload—an inadequate amount of information present. Overload is more prevalent than underload. Most of the research on overload deals with its consequences, though an interesting line of research would address what conditions cause overload. Meier (1963) studied overload in a library. As requests for library service increased beyond the system's capacity, employee stress and confusion increased and service broke down.

Overload and underload are difficult to define precisely. The terms deal both with an amount of information as well as a person's ability to process the information. Individual differences exist—the same amount of information may be an overload for one person and an underload for another. Therefore, these terms deal more with subjective appraisals than objective measures. In a study on the effects of overload, O'Reilly (1980) found the volume of information in an environment affects individual satisfaction and performance differently. Overloaded people were more satisfied with communication than those who were underloaded. But overloaded people performed worse on the job. Individuals seem to want more information than they can use; and they feel more confident about their decisions when they have it even though their decisions may actually be of lower quality. Rather than getting more information, they might make better use of existing information. The research on overload rebuts the contention that "more is better."

Miller (1960) reports several individual responses to overload—most of them negative. These responses include: (1) omission—failing to process some of the information; (2) error—processing information incorrectly; (3) filtering—separating out less significant and less relevant information; (4) approximation—categorizing input and using a blanket response; and (5) escaping—avoiding the information. Some of these methods are more effective than others. The appropriateness of a response is determined by the task involved and the feedback received after using it. Chronic and excessive overload can cause psychological stress and tension. Using Miller's terms, I use a combination of filtering and approximation responses to deal with information overload. I sort my mail into first and third class letters (filtering), and all third class letters I throw away—unopened (approximation). My rationale is that if the letter wasn't worth being sent first class, it wasn't worth reading. To date, I have not (knowingly) lost any golden opportunities.

## THE OUTCOMES OF COMMUNICATION

If communication in organizations is truly important, it should relate directly to important outcomes, such as performance and satisfaction (O'Reilly & Pondy, 1979). These relationships do indeed exist.

**Performance**

We can view performance on a number of levels including individual task performance, group productivity, and the effectiveness of entire organizations. Research shows that communication does influence performance. We have long known (e.g., Arps, 1920) that knowledge of results and feedback facilitate performance. Whether the feedback comes from the organization, a supervisor, co-workers, or the task itself (Greller & Herold, 1975), it has both informational and motivational components. Feedback focuses attention on relevant aspects of the task and gives direction as to which behaviors are most desirable or relevant. Feedback improves job performance in many tasks ranging from visual search (Mudd & McCormick, 1960) to complex decision making (Schmitt, Coyle, & Saari, 1977). While excessive feedback can cause information overload and decreased performance (Ilgen, Fisher, & Taylor, 1979), with no feedback, behavior is directionless and random.

At the group level, communication is associated with effectiveness. Zand (1962) found in a laboratory study that groups with higher levels of trust and more open communication were better able to solve problems and deal with conflict. O'Reilly and Roberts (1977b) studied 43 U.S. Navy work teams and found that more effective work teams had more open and accurate communication. Special police units (SWAT teams) trained in assault tactics feel that intragroup communication is basic to the efficiency of their unit.

While we know less about the relationship between communication and performance at the organization level, evidence shows (Lawrence & Lorsch, 1967) that more effective organizations have more information flow across subunits. Research has also shown that well-developed employee orientation programs can quickly socialize a new employee with a minimum of disruption in the company's work procedures (Marion & Trieb, 1969). Since clear and informative manuals enhance efficiency, many companies hire professionals to write them. While O'Reilly and Roberts (1977a) showed that accuracy of communication is related to individual performance, it also enhances performance of the entire organization.

Because there are so many facets to communication, researchers must specify what dimensions of communication they feel will enhance performance. Some indices of communication may be more related to performance than others. For example, Muchinsky (1977a) suggested there may be no correlation at all between the *frequency* of communication and subordinate performance. Two employees may engage equally in upward communication but for different reasons. One employee may be giving advice and service to a supervisor, whereas the other may need constant guidance and direction. Obviously, the communication differs in content and purpose. Thus the *nature* of upward communication may correlate with individual performance, while its frequency may not.

In summary, variations in individual, group, and organizational performance can be identified on the basis of variations in communication. Increasing amounts and types of communication enhance performance up to the point of overload.

## Satisfaction

Much evidence links communication with satisfaction. O'Reilly (1978) reported that people who felt they were the victims of distorted communication had feelings of low satisfaction. O'Reilly (1980) found that people who experienced information overload were satisfied with their jobs even though the extra information hindered their performance. Individuals who experienced underload were all dissatisfied. Dissatisfaction is also associated with deliberate omission or distortion.

Muchinsky (1977b) identified several communication correlates of job satisfaction. Perceived accuracy of information correlated positively with both facet and overall job satisfaction. Gatekeeping negatively correlated with satisfaction (employees do not like to have information withheld from them). Similar to other studies, Muchinsky found high job satisfaction is associated with the opportunity to initiate face-to-face interactions. Finally, satisfaction with communication was positively correlated with all aspects of job satisfaction. These relationships are shown in Figure 12–10.

People like to be informed and knowledgeable about work-related information. They don't like to be excluded or to have messages altered en route. People want more information than they can effectively process. Perhaps lack of information breeds insecurity, while overabundance allows

**Figure 12–10**          **Communication correlates of job satisfaction**

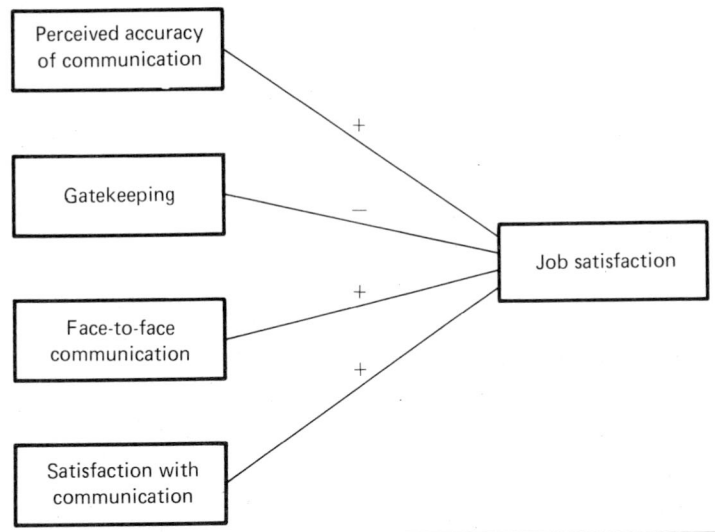

SOURCE: P. M. Muchinsky, "Organizational Communication: Relationships to Organizational Climate and Job Satisfaction," *Academy of Management Journal* 20 (1977), pp. 592–607.

the receiver to choose what information to process. Information and the ability to communicate it are forms of power. Power can aid goal attainment, or it can be misused. Failure to communicate is a failure to exercise power adequately.

The inability to communicate can be due to problems with the source, receiver, message, or channel. Many factors have to work in harmony for communication to occur. In the course of this chapter, we discussed these factors and how they are influenced by a number of extraneous variables.

# SUMMARY

Communication is a pervasive characteristic of organizations. Indeed, without communication in some form, organizations would cease to exist. Communication is the "glue" that holds the parts together. The ability to communicate effectively is extremely important. People with well-developed oral and written communication skills are highly valued by organizations. Communication process variables such as gatekeeping, openness, distortion, and overload contribute to individual satisfaction and job performance. An organization's structure (size, shape) affects its communication patterns. In turn, individual behavior and attitudes are related to the use of communication patterns.

# CASE STUDY

The pop machine in the lunchroom of the Conover Radiator Company flashed the message "Exact Change Only." Wanda Gilman turned to the woman next to her and asked if she had change for a quarter. Patty Sniezek handed her two dimes and a nickel, and Gilman deposited twenty cents in the machine.

"You new here?" Gilman asked of Sniezek.

"Yes" Sniezek replied, "I just started work last Monday. I'm over in the Molding Department. The only thing I've figured out so far is how to find the bathroom, lunchroom, and time clock."

"You'll get used to it," Gilman said, as she headed for a table. "Sit down, and I'll fill you in."

Both women opened their lunches. "The first thing you got to know," Gilman began, "is who to talk to and who to avoid. If you're in Molding, get to know Connie Rosini. Whatever is happening, Connie knows about it first, and it's usually straight. By the time it gets passed around the floor, people get it all twisted around. I used to be in Molding, and Connie would give me the lowdown."

"How about Phil Tesatore?" Sniezek asked. "He's my foreman, and he was the one who explained my job to me."

"Tesatore? Are you kidding?" Gilman mockingly asked. "He's bucking for a management job. He'll tell you the party line but only what he wants you to hear. Half of what he tells you is wrong, and the other half is old. I bet you won't see much of him any more. After he does his bit breaking in the new people, he takes off. They call him the 'phantom.' He's probably greasing up somebody for a promotion right now."

"They told me in Personnel that he would answer any questions I might have," Sniezek stated.

Gilman shook her head in disbelief. "Look," she said, "about six months ago they changed the parking assignments in the lot. Tesatore whipped up a memo to explain it to everyone in the department. By the time he made his big announcement, everybody already knew about it. Connie got the word and spread it around first. Tesatore gave some line about 'less congestion' in the lot when we leave work, but we figured the real reason was so the foremen and supervisors could park closer to the door."

"And another thing," Gilman cautioned, "if your machine jams, go ask Red Martin what to do. If he can't fix it himself, he'll know who to contact. If you go through channels, it could be hours. And then they'll hold you responsible for catching up on what you missed."

"They did give me a manual to read on my machine," Sniezek explained. "They said it wasn't tough to figure out, but I really don't understand it."

"Don't worry about it," Gilman said. "Nobody reads those damn things anyway. They must have been written a hundred years ago."

"There is one thing maybe you could help me with," Sniezek asked. "Do you know where I can get a good babysitter? They told me to check the bulletin board and the newsletter for announcements, but I can't find any."

"The bulletin board and newsletter usually tell you things like who got the highest score in bowling last month. Big deal! See Betty Felice over in the Crating Department. I hear her sister takes in a lot of kids. Maybe she can help you."

"Speaking of bowling," Gilman added, "do you bowl?"

"A little," Sniezek answered.

"Do you want to get on the team for the summer league?" asked Gilman.

"I'd like to," Sniezek said. "They told me the sign-up announcement would come out in a few weeks."

"By the time the sign-up sheets come out, the team will already be filled. If you want in, I'll get you on today," Gilman instructed.

Sniezek nodded her head. Gilman tapped another woman on the shoulder, said something inaudible, and motioned her head toward Sniezek.

The woman looked up at Sniezek and said, "What's your name?"

Questions

1. How does Gilman assess the credibility of the formal channels of communication?
2. How would Gilman evaluate Rosini and Tesatore in terms of such factors as openness and distortion of communication?
3. Will Sniezek's job satisfaction and performance be affected by her exposure to Gilman? If so, in what ways?
4. In Chapter 8, we discussed the topic of roles. What roles do Rosini and Gilman fill in the organization?
5. Do you feel the discrepancies between what is communicated formally versus informally are inevitable in a large organization? What factors might contribute to the size of the discrepancy?

# REFERENCES

Arps, G. F. Work with knowledge of results versus work without knowledge of results. *Psychological Monograph*, 1920, *28*, (3, Whole No. 125).

Athanassiades, J. The distortion of upward communication in hierarchical organizations. *Academy of Management Journal*, 1973, *16*, 207–226.

Bacharach, S. B., & Aiken, M. Communication in administrative bureaucracies. *Academy of Management Journal*, 1977, *20*, 365–377.

Barnard, C. I. *The functions of the executive*. Cambridge, Mass.: Harvard University Press, 1938.

Baskin, O. W., & Aronoff, C. E. *Interpersonal communication in organizations*. Santa Monica, Calif.: Goodyear Publishing, 1980.

Berlo, D. K. *The process of communication*. New York: Holt, Rinehart & Winston, 1960.

Burgess, R. L. Communication networks: An experimental re-evaluation. *Journal of Experimental Social Psychology*, 1968, *4*, 324–337.

Burke, R. J., Weitzel, W., & Weir, T. Characteristics of effective performance review and development interviews: Replication and extension. *Personnel Psychology*, 1978, *31*, 903–919.

Dance, F. E. The "concept" of communication. *Journal of Communication*, 1970, *20*, 201–210.

Davis, K. A method of studying communication patterns in organizations. *Personnel Psychology*, 1953, *6*, 301–312.

Ekman, P. Differential communication of affect by head and body cues. *Journal of Personality and Social Psychology*, 1965, *2*, 726–735.

Farace, R. V., & MacDonald, D. New directions in the study of organizational communication. *Personnel Psychology*, 1974, *27*, 1–19.

Fielden, J. "What do you mean I can't write?" *Harvard Business Review*, May–June 1964, *42*, 144–148, 151–152, 154, 156.

Flesch, R. A new readability yardstick. *Journal of Applied Psychology*, 1948, *32*, 221–233.

Flesch, R. *The art of readable writing*. New York: Harper & Row, 1974.

Galbraith, J. *Designing complex organizations*. Reading, Mass.: Addison-Wesley Publishing, 1973.

Greenbaum, H. H. The audit of organizational communication. *Academy of Management Journal*, 1974, *17*, 739–754.

Greller, M. M., & Herold, D. M. Sources of feedback: A preliminary investigation. *Organizational Behavior and Human Performance*, 1975, *13*, 244–256.

Guetzkow, H. Communication in organizations. In J. G. March (Ed.), *Handbook of organizations*. Skokie, Ill.: Rand McNally, 1965.

Gupta, N., & Beehr, T. A. Job stress and employee behaviors. *Organizational Behavior and Human Performance*, 1979, *23*, 373–387.

Hall, E. T. *The hidden dimension*. New York: Doubleday Publishing, 1966.

Hanser, L. M., & Muchinsky, P. M. Work as an information environment. *Organizational Behavior and Human Performance*, 1978, *21*, 47–60.

Hanser, L. M., & Muchinsky, P. M. Performance feedback information and organizational communication: Evidence of conceptual convergence. *Human Communication Research*, 1980, *7*, 68–73.

Hicks, H. G. *The management of organizations*. New York: McGraw-Hill, 1967.

Ilgen, D. R., Fisher, C. D., & Taylor, M. S. Consequences of individual feedback on behavior in organizations. *Journal of Applied Psychology*, 1979, *64*, 349–371.

Jablin, F. M. Superior-subordinate communication: The state of the art. *Psychological Bulletin*, 1979, *86*, 1201–1222.

Lawrence, P. R., & Lorsch, J. W. *Organization and environment: Managing differentiation and integration*. Boston: Harvard University Graduate School of Business, 1967.

Leavitt, H. J. Some effects of certain communication patterns on group performance. *Journal of Abnormal and Social Psychology*, 1951, *46*, 38–50.

Levine, E. L., & Flory, A. Evaluation of job applications—a conceptual framework. *Public Personnel Management*, November/December 1975, 378–385.

Marion, B. W., & Trieb, S. E. Job orientation: A factor in employee performance and turnover. *Personnel Journal*, 1969, *48*, 799–804, 831.

Meier, R. Communication overload: Proposals from the study of a university library. *Administrative Science Quarterly*, 1963, 7, 521–544.

Miller, J. G. Information input, overload and psychopathology. *American Journal of Psychiatry*, 1960, *116*, 367–386.

Muchinsky, P. M. An intraorganizational analysis of the Roberts and O'Reilly organizational communication questionnaire. *Journal of Applied Psychology*, 1977, *62*, 184–188. (a)

Muchinsky, P. M. Organizational communication: Relationships to organizational climate and job satisfaction. *Academy of Management Journal*, 1977, *20*, 592–607. (b)

Mudd, S. A., & McCormick, E. J. The use of auditory cues in a visual search task. *Journal of Applied Psychology*, 1960, *44*, 184–188.

Nemeroff, W. F., & Wexley, K. N. Relationships between performance appraisal interview characteristics and interview outcomes as perceived by supervisors and subordinates. Paper presented at the meeting of the National Academy of Management, Orlando, Fla., 1977.

O'Reilly, C. A. The intentional distortion of information in organizational communication: A laboratory and field approach. *Human Relations*, 1978, *31*, 173–193.

O'Reilly, C. A. Individuals and information overload in organizations: Is more necessarily better? *Academy of Management Journal*, 1980, *23*, 684–696.

O'Reilly, C. A., & Pondy, L. R. Organizational communication. In S. Kerr (Ed.), *Organizational behavior*. Columbus, Ohio: Grid, 1979.

O'Reilly, C. A., & Roberts, K. H. Information filtration in organizations: Three experiments. *Organizational Behavior and Human Performance*, 1974, *11*, 253–265.

O'Reilly, C. A., & Roberts, K. H. Relationships among components of credibility and communication behaviors in work units. *Journal of Applied Psychology*, 1976, *61*, 99–102.

O'Reilly, C. A., & Roberts, K. H. Communication and performance in organizations. *Proceedings of the Academy of Management*, 1977, 375–379. (a)

O'Reilly, C. A., & Roberts, K. H. Task group structure, communication, and effectiveness in three organizations. *Journal of Applied Psychology*, 1977, *62*, 674–681. (b)

Pace, R. W. Oral communication and sales effectiveness. *Journal of Applied Psychology*, 1962, *46*, 321–324.

Pettigrew, A. Information control as a power resource. *Sociology*, 1972, *6*, 187–204.

Porter, L. W., & Roberts, K. H. Communication in organizations. In M. D. Dunnette (Ed.), *Handbook of industrial and organizational psychology*. Skokie, Ill.: Rand McNally, 1976.

Powell, J. D., Heimlich, K. T., & Goodin, E. H. Training executives for today's communication challenges. Paper presented at the meeting of the National Academy of Management, Detroit, 1980.

Randle, C. W. How to identify promotable executives. *Harvard Business Review*, May–June 1956, *34*, 122–134.

Redfield, C. E. *Communication in management*. Chicago: University of Chicago Press, 1953.

Roberts, K. H., & O'Reilly, C. A. Failures in upward communication: Three possible culprits. *Academy of Management Journal*, 1974, *17*, 205–215.

Roberts, K. H., & O'Reilly, C. A. Organizations as communication structures: An empirical approach. *Human Communication Research*, 1978, *4*, 283–293.

Roberts, K. H., O'Reilly, C. A., Bretton, G., & Porter, L. W. Organizational theory and organizational communication: A communication failure? *Human Relations*, 1974, *27*, 501–524.

Rogers, C. R., & Farson, R. E. Active listening. In R. C. Huseman, C. M. Logue, & D. L. Freshley (Eds.), *Readings in interpersonal and organizational communication*. Boston: Holbrook Press, 1969.

Rogers, E. M., & Agarwala-Rogers, R. *Communication in organizations*. New York: Free Press, 1976.

Schmitt, N. Social and situational determinants of interview decisions: Implications for the employment interview. *Personnel Psychology*, 1976, *29*, 79–101.

Schmitt, N., Coyle, B. W., & Saari, B. B. Types of task information feedback in multiple cue probability learning. *Organizational Behavior and Human Performance*, 1977, *18*, 316–328.

Schwartz, D., & Jacobson, E. Organizational communication network analysis: The liaison communication role. *Organizational Behavior and Human Performance*, 1977, *18*, 158–174.

Scott, W. G., & Mitchell, T. R. *Organizational theory: A structural and behavioral approach*. Homewood, Ill.: Richard D. Irwin, 1976.

Shaw, M. E. Communication networks. In L. Berkowitz (Ed.), *Advances in experimental social psychology*. New York: Academic Press, 1964.

Simpson, R. L. Vertical and horizontal communication in formal organizations. *Administrative Science Quarterly*, 1959, *4*, 188–196.

Sims, H. P., & LaFollette, W. R. An assessment of the Litwin and Stringer organization climate questionnaire. *Personnel Psychology*, 1975, *28*, 19–38.

Tushman, M. Technical communication in research and development laboratories: The impact of project work characteristics. *Academy of Management Journal*, 1978, *21*, 624–645.

Wilcox, R. P. Characteristics and organization of the oral technical report. *General Motors Engineering Journal*, 1959, *6*, 8–12.

Woocher, F. D. Did your eyes deceive you? Expert psychological testimony on the unreliability of eyewitness identification. *Stanford Law Review*, 1977, *29*, 969–1030.

Zand, D. D. Trust and managerial problem solving. *Administrative Science Quarterly*, 1972, *17*, 229–240.

# The work environment

# chapter 13    JOB DESIGN AND ORGANIZATION DEVELOPMENT

Organizations constantly try to maximize the "fit" between worker and workplace. The better the fit, the more likely the organization will be effective and smooth running. Thus far, our discussion of increasing the fit (what we called "person/environment congruence" in Chapter 8) centered on the worker. Using the peg and the hole as an analogy, we discussed finding new pegs that fit existing holes (personnel selection), or reshaping existing pegs for better fit (personnel training). However, the problem of fit can be approached by trying to change the shape of the hole. It is possible to change the workplace instead of, or besides, changing the worker. The overall purpose is increasing organization effectiveness. This may show itself in greater productivity, less cost, increased satisfaction, less turnover, and so on.

In this chapter, we will examine two approaches to changing the workplace. One focuses on changing a *job* and is called *job design*. The other has a larger scope and involves more than just a job. It is called *organization development*. The two approaches are not unrelated; some authors consider job design part of organization development. However, organization development usually involves reorganizing many components of the workplace; job design has a more narrow scope.

## ALTERING THE WORKER OR THE WORKPLACE?

The choice of changing worker or workplace is not easy. It is also not strictly an either/or choice; efforts to change the work environment may be made at the same time that workers are changed. Usually, though, there is more emphasis on changing one or the other. There is no magic formula telling the I/O psychologist which side most deserves attention. This is a matter of professional judgment, best guided by the psychologist's experience with the organization. The history of the organization's problems is usually the best place to begin. If a company has been successfully manufacturing a product or providing a service, it would be better to replace a few workers who don't perform well than revamp the entire organization. If large parts of the work force have difficulty adjusting to work demands, personnel training may be the best method of raising skill levels to match organization needs. However, when problems reappear seemingly independent of *who* performs the work, thought must be given to altering the workplace. As a rule, it is more difficult to alter the workplace than the workers. Usually changing one part of an organization will have effects (intended and unintended) on the rest of the organization.

Because organizations are designed to have interchangeable human parts, the life span of an organization can exceed the (working) life span of its employees. The complexities of personnel selection, placement, and training notwithstanding, the workplace is less changeable than the work force. Successful organizations learn to alter both as conditions demand. In this chapter, we will look at ways of changing the workplace, recognizing that the constant search for good "fit" warrants giving attention to both sides of the relationship.

## JOB DESIGN

**Historical overview**

Job design originated in the early years of this century. Frederick Taylor, a founder of industrial psychology, believed that efficiency could be improved by carefully designing work to increase productivity. Taylor advocated structuring jobs for simplification and standardization. Simplification meant breaking jobs into small tasks and having each worker then perform a small part of a total operation. A worker does this task repeatedly, thus resulting in extreme specialization. For example, a job might be connecting two pieces of metal with a bolt. This is one part of an entire operation and it might be repeated over 100 times every hour. Other workers perform similar specialized tasks, until the entire product is finally produced through the total efforts of all workers. The work process is also standardized, i.e., the sequence of activities performed is the same.

This approach did improve productivity. Workers were able to produce more goods. Also, the skill levels needed for these specialized tasks was less, as was the time needed to train workers.

In the short run, this approach resulted in economic efficiency. In Taylor's time, economic conditions were not good, jobs were relatively scarce, and people were grateful for whatever work they could get. However, this approach also produced problems. Workers rebelled at highly specialized, routine jobs. Monotony produced boredom, which, when coupled with lack of challenge and a sense of depersonalization, lead to dissatisfaction (Dunham, 1979). The behavioral consequences of work simplification and standardization are presented in Figure 13–1.

We know that dissatisfaction shows itself in ways that *detract* from efficiency—lateness, absenteeism, turnover, stress, drug use, and sabotage. Over time, the problem was exacerbated by changing populations of workers. At the turn of the century, workers were relatively uneducated and jobs were scarce: workers were not very critical of the jobs. As the education of workers increased and more jobs were available, workers were no longer content with jobs that provided income and little else. The economic gains of increased efficiency were offset by reactions to the simplified jobs. The pendulum swung back. Companies realized that efficiency could be enhanced by designing jobs that were gratifying. This has been called the "humanization" of work. Research on job design describes attempts to make jobs "better" by making them more meaningful and rewarding.

## Job enlargement and job enrichment

In the 1940s and 1950s, organizations began to realize that the structure of jobs must be changed from specialization to work satisfying employee needs. During this time, two "job change" strategies became popular. They were called *job enlargement* and *job enrichment*. In theory, the two are different. In practice, they have a lot in common. *Job enlargement* is increasing the number and variety of tasks a worker performs. *Job enrichment* is increasing worker control of the planning and performance of a job and participation in setting organization policy (Lawler, 1969). Job enlargement involves expanding the scope of a worker's job duties. An example might be a production worker being responsible for assembling several parts (as opposed to one) of a piece of equipment. Job enrichment involves giving the worker more autonomy and decision-making power in when and

**Figure 13–1**        **Behavioral consequences of work simplification**

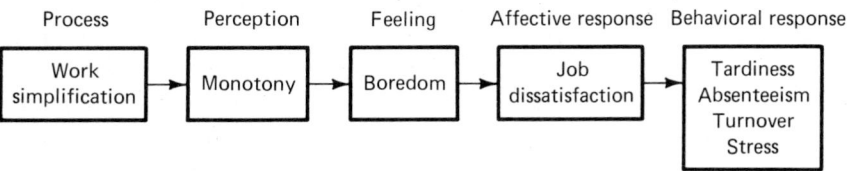

how work operations are performed. At the core of both programs was the belief that motivation would be better if workers had more sense of achievement in their work.

Many early studies examined the effects of job enlargement/enrichment on worker behavior and attitudes. One can think of these as field studies; on-site performance before and after job change was compared. Several studies reported increases in either attitude or performance as a result of job-design changes. However, the research was not of the best quality since control groups were rarely used. A company would often introduce new technology along with changes in work operations. It was thus impossible to tell whether the changes in performance and attitude were due to changes in technology or job-design changes. Despite the methodological problems, some authors reported major gains in efficiency. Paul, Robertson, and Herzberg (1969) and Ford (1969) reported improvements in satisfaction, turnover, and production after introduction of job-change programs. However, not all reports were positive. Maher and Overbagh (1971) reported short-term improvements in satisfaction and performance. But after one year, these variables returned to preprogram levels. There was thus some evidence that reported changes in worker response were due more to a Hawthorne Effect.

The incomplete research designs and inability to determine causes for change led people to question the value of job enrichment and enlargement. It seemed that they produced changes in worker response, but the reasons for the changes were not clear. And the changes were often for a limited time. As a result, attention was focused on the specific parts of jobs that were altered and how these specific changes affected behavior and attitudes. More research was directed at explaining why job design succeeded or failed. There were fewer large-scale job-enlargement/enrichment programs. Researchers began to identify the structure of jobs, and how changing this structure would lead to changes in performance.

## Task attributes

As the name suggests, research on *task attributes* was meant to identify characteristics of jobs (composed of tasks) that influence worker behavior. In an early study, Turner and Lawrence (1965) identified six task attributes they thought related to satisfaction and attendance. They were: variety, autonomy, required interaction, optional interaction, knowledge and skill required, and responsibility. They conducted interviews and made field observations of these six attributes for 47 different jobs. Each attribute was scaled, yielding a score reflecting "how much" of these attributes were present in each job. Jobs that scored high on these variables were positively correlated with high worker satisfaction and attendance. Yet a curious finding also emerged. This relationship held only for workers from factories in small towns, not for urban workers. Turner and Lawrence concluded that worker reactions to task attributes were influenced by cultural factors. This gave impetus to investigating what "types" of people respond most positively to redesigned jobs. The findings from such studies will be discussed shortly.

Following the Turner and Lawrence study, other researchers investigated how certain task attributes influence performance. Hackman and Lawler (1971) identified four *core dimensions* of jobs: variety, autonomy, identity, and feedback. They concluded that jobs high on these core dimensions, performed by individuals desiring satisfaction of higher-order needs (in the Maslow sense of achievement, recognition, etc.), had the greatest satisfaction, motivation, attendance, and performance. A later study by Brief and Aldag (1975) repeated the findings.

It was apparent that motivation was influenced by job structure. Further, it seemed possible to design jobs to increase motivation. Research by Steers and Porter (1974), Steers (1975), and Steers and Spencer (1977) produced evidence that jobs providing variety, autonomy, identity, and feedback increased motivation among some employees. The increased motivation manifested itself in increased organizational commitment and job involvement, as well as in increased attendance and job satisfaction.

However, it also became apparent that not *all* people responded in the same way. Why people differed in responses to jobs with comparable task attributes had to be explained. Researchers focused on the role of *human needs* in determining the "type" of job a person would want. It was thought that people trying to satisfy *higher-order* needs would want more stimulating jobs. They would thus respond more positively to enriched jobs. Jobs providing high levels of certain task attributes seemingly satisfied such needs.

Several scales were developed to identify those who would want an enriched job and would respond positively to (be more motivated by) such work. Hackman and Oldham (1975) developed one such scale—the *Higher-Order Need Strength Measure B*. Sample items are presented in Figure 13–2. The relative strength of growth needs is reflected in the choice of jobs characterized by opportunities for decision making, using a variety of skills and abilities, freedom and independence, and challenge over jobs characterized by high pay, fringe benefits, job security, and friendly coworkers (Aldag & Brief, 1979). Results of studies testing the effect of these needs suggest that people with strong higher-order needs do derive more satisfaction from enriched jobs (Hackman & Lawler, 1971). Similarly, both Wanous (1974) and Oldham, Hackman, and Pearce (1976) found that differences in higher-order need strength moderated the relationship between job characteristics and feelings of satisfaction. However, not all research is supportive. Stone, Mowday, and Porter (1977) reported little difference in the attitudes and behavior of people with high versus low growth needs. It appears that an individual's desire (need) to be challenged at work does affect reactions to an enriched job, but this alone does not account for all variance in these reactions.

**Figure 13–2**                **Sample items from the Higher Order Need Strength Questionnaire B**

INSTRUCTIONS

People differ in what they like and dislike in their jobs. Listed below are several pairs of jobs. For each pair, you are to indicate which job you would prefer. Assume that everything else about the jobs is the same—pay attention only to the characteristics actually listed for each pair of jobs.

If you would prefer the job in the left-hand column (Column A), indicate how much you prefer it putting a check mark in a blank to the left of the neutral point. If you prefer the job in the right-hand column (Column B), check one of the blanks to the right of neutral. Check the neutral blank only if you find the two jobs equally attractive or unattractive. Try to use the neutral blank rarely.

Column A

1. A job which offers little or no challenge.

Strongly prefer A          Neutral          Strongly prefer B

Column B

A job which requires you to be completely isolated from co-workers.

2. A job where the pay is very good.

Strongly prefer A          Neutral          Strongly prefer B

A job where there is considerable opportunity to be creative and innovative.

3. A job where you are often required to make important decisions.

Strongly prefer A          Neutral          Strongly prefer B

A job with many pleasant people to work with.

4. A job with little security in the somewhat unstable organization.

Strongly prefer A          Neutral          Strongly prefer B

A job in which you have little or no opportunity to participate in decisions which affect your work.

5. A job in which greater responsibility is given to those who do the best work.

Strongly prefer A          Neutral          Strongly prefer B

A job in which greater responsibility is given to loyal employees who have the most seniority.

SOURCE: J. R. Hackman and G. R. Oldham, "Development of the Job Diagnostic Survey," *Journal of Applied Psychology* 60 (1975), pp. 159–70.

## Job characteristics model

Clearly, there was no one theoretical explanation of why and how task attributes affect workers. The way jobs influence motivation could be (partially) explained by several existing theories, including Maslow's need hierarchy, Herzberg's two-factor theory, and expectancy theory (Steers & Mowday, 1977). To integrate and synthesize much of the literature on this topic, a model was proposed by Hackman and Oldham (1976) to explain how jobs influence attitudes and behavior. It is called the job characteristics model and is probably the most researched explanation of job enrichment.

According to Hackman and Oldham, any job can be described by five core dimensions:

1. *Skill variety.* The degree a job requires a variety of activities, involving a number of different skills and talents.
2. *Task identity.* The degree a job requires completion of a whole, identifiable piece of work—that is, doing a job from beginning to end, with visible results.
3. *Task significance.* The degree a job has an impact on the lives or work of other people, whether within or outside the organization.
4. *Autonomy.* The degree a job provides freedom, independence, and discretion in scheduling work and determining procedures used in doing it.
5. *Task feedback.* The degree that carrying out the activities required results in direct and clear information about the effectiveness of performance.

The five core job dimensions stem from considering what the authors call *implementation concepts.* Szilagyi and Wallace (1980) describe these as follows:

1. *Combining tasks.* This is a movement away from high specialization by combining specialized tasks in one larger work module. A combination of tasks affects both *task variety* and *task identity.*
2. *Forming natural work units.* This focuses on "ownership" of a job, giving a worker continuing responsibility for an identifiable body of work. A sense of *task identity* and *task significance* is thus provided.
3. *Establishing client relationships.* The worker can gain a new perspective on work by establishing direct relationships with clients. For example, a shipping supervisor may be concerned about the condition of a product when the customer receives it. Giving the supervisor the opportunity to talk directly with the client or to visit the customer's plant increases *variety, autonomy,* and *feedback.*
4. *Vertical loading.* Like job enrichment, this concerns greater latitude and responsibility. It directly affects *autonomy, variety, task identity,* and *significance* of the job.

5. *Opening feedback channels.* Providing more *feedback* helps employees learn whether or not their performance is improving. Most feedback channels focus on information given an employee by a supervisor. Another method is learning about performance directly from the job.

The second part of the model deals with the effect of the core job dimensions on the individual. They are said to influence three critical *psychological states*. The *experienced meaningfulness of work* is high when the job involves skill variety, task identity, and significance. The *experienced responsibility for work outcomes* is influenced mainly by amount of autonomy. *Knowledge of results of work activities* is a function of feedback. According to the theory, high levels of the critical psychological states will lead to favorable personal and work outcomes. These include high internal motivation, high work performance, high satisfaction, and low absence and turnover (Dunham, 1979).

The final part of the Hackman and Oldham model is an individual difference variable called growth need strength (GNS); it reflects a desire to fulfill higher-order needs, as discussed. As had others, Hackman and Oldham felt that people with high needs for personal growth and development should respond more positively to jobs high on the core dimensions. Only people with high GNS should strongly experience the critical psychological states associated with such a job. The entire job characteristics model is portrayed in Figure 13–3.

Hackman and Oldham developed an equation to index the potential of a job to motivate its holder. The equation is based on the five core dimensions. Hackman and Oldham refer to their index as the *motivating potential score* (MPS) and define it as:

$$\text{MPS} = \frac{\text{Skill variety} + \text{Task identity} + \text{Task significance}}{3} \times \text{Autonomy} \times \text{Feedback}$$

The first three core dimensions are averaged because they all contribute to the experienced meaningfulness of work, the first critical psychological state. The other two dimensions, autonomy and feedback, reflect the remaining critical states, so they are not averaged.

The motivating potential of a job will be very high when each component of the formula is high. Because the components are multiplied, low scores on any one will yield a low motivating potential score. In the extreme, a score of zero (e.g., a job completely lacking in autonomy) on any of the major components reduces the MPS to zero; the job has no potential to motivate incumbents.

Finally, as shown in Figure 13–3, the entire effect of the job characteristics model is moderated by the strength of growth need. Only those em-

**Figure 13–3**      **The Job Characteristics Model**

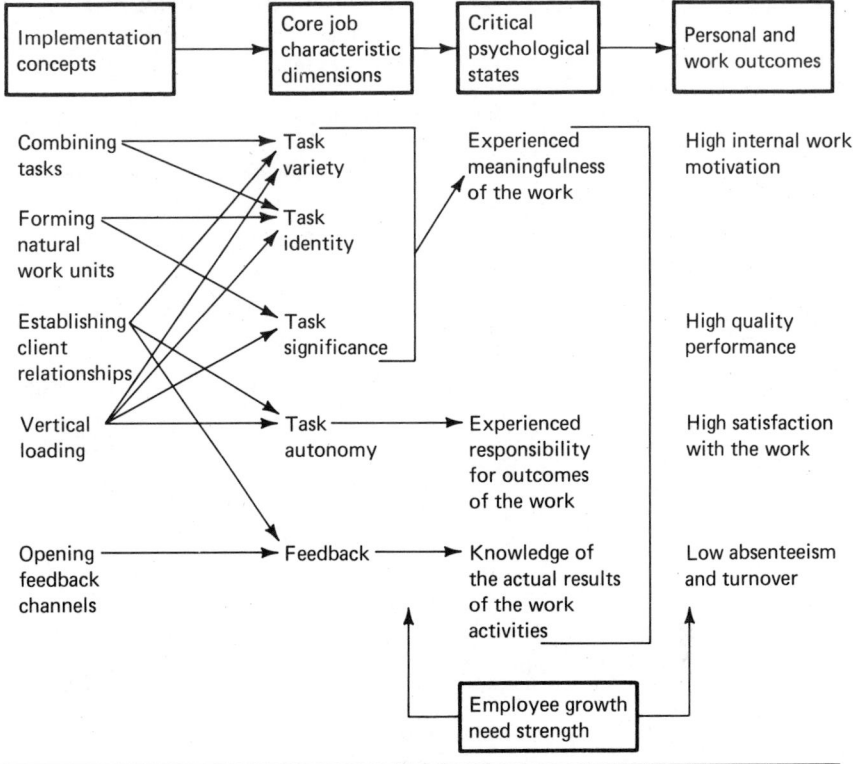

SOURCE: J. R. Hackman, G. R. Oldham, R. Janson, and K. Purdy, "A New Strategy for Job Enrichment," *California Management Review*, 17, no. 4 (1975), pp. 57–71.

ployees trying to satisfy higher-order needs will respond favorably to a job high in motivating potential.

**Empirical tests of the model.** A number of studies tested the relationships and predictions of the model. Empirical support is mixed. Certain parts of the model are substantiated more than others.

Hackman and Oldham (1976) provided validation evidence for their own theory. In general, the results were moderately supportive:

1. The core job dimensions relate to the critical psychological states. Skill variety, task identity, and task significance combined to predict the level of experienced meaningfulness. The authors were thus able to identify those factors contributing to "meaningful work," a frequent desire of employees.

2. The three critical psychological states related to selected personal and work outcomes. In particular, high levels were associated with satisfaction and internal motivation.

3. Individual differences in GNS have a moderate effect, as Hackman and Oldham suggested. In particular, high GNS employees were more likely to have favorable personal and work outcomes after experiencing the critical psychological states.

However, not all findings were supportive:

1. The core dimensions of autonomy and feedback were not clearly related to the corresponding critical psychological states of experienced responsibility and knowledge of results. Some of the other dimensions predicted these states as well or better.
2. The critical psychological states were only weakly related to absence and performance.

In general, the results showed that jobs high on the core job dimensions were associated with high levels of personal and work outcomes. Individuals with high GNS responded most favorably to these types of jobs. The importance of the intervening critical psychological states was not strongly supported.

Two other studies tested the validity of the job characteristics model. Evans, Kiggundu, and House (1979) reported mild support for GNS as a moderator of the core job dimensions–psychological states relationship. As with research on expectancy theory, validity and superiority of multiplying the parts of the MPS formula were not supported. It seems that a simpler model (perhaps adding the parts) would yield equally good or better predictions. Another study by Arnold and House (1980) reached similar conclusions. They also found GNS was a better moderator of the core dimensions–psychological states relationship than the relationship between psychological states and job outcomes.

While the research on the job characteristics model is not totally supportive of its validity, several points should be kept in mind. First, the model is quite new. As with all explanatory models, modifications will probably be made as empirical tests warrant. Second, the model incorporates a broad range of variables. It proposes relationships among jobs (core dimensions), intervening constructs (psychological states), and work behavior (personal and work outcomes), all moderated by individual differences (GNS). Given such an array, some problems with validity should be expected. A few researchers (e.g., Roberts & Glick, 1981) also feel that some research does not directly follow the relationships proposed in the model. If the model has indeed been "misinterpreted," it is not surprising that results are less than fully supportive. Finally, as always in I/O psychology and science in general, accuracy of measurement is crucial. Many of the concepts are not particularly easy to measure. Thus, accuracy of the model is weakened in proportion to weaknesses in assessing the variables. Problems and issues in measuring job-design variables are discussed in the next section.

## Measurement of job design variables

It is virtually impossible to get pure, objective measures of task characteristics. The variety and autonomy present in a job are usually best ascertained by asking incumbents. In the final analysis, what is important is how workers perceive their jobs, for it is on the basis of these perceptions that workers develop feelings about their jobs. Therefore, many measurement issues involve the extent that workers see common dimensions in their jobs.

When Hackman and Oldham (1976) proposed the job characteristics model, they also developed a questionnaire, the *Job Diagnostic Survey* (JDS). This assessed the variables in the model. Hackman and Oldham (1975) felt the JDS would be a reliable and valid assessment of core dimensions, critical psychological states, and strength of individual growth needs. Perhaps the most critical issue was the number and nature of core job dimensions, for it is these dimensions that supposedly are the basis for enriched and meaningful work. Hackman and Oldham proposed five core job dimensions; other researchers tried to confirm the existence of these dimensions.

In testing the validity of the JDS, Dunham (1976) could find little difference in the measures of variety and autonomy. This suggests the two dimensions are not as distinct as Hackman and Oldham proposed. Dunham also felt that all five dimensions could be subsumed in a single dimension reflecting *job complexity* without losing the meaning of enriched work. That is, an enriched job is simply more complex than a routine job. In another study of the JDS, Dunham, Aldag, and Brief (1977) found the concept of enriched work could be defined in terms of two, three, four, and sometimes five factors, depending upon the nature of the jobs. The five core factors proposed by Hackman and Oldham did not appear every time. I/O psychologists seem to agree that certain key factors define enriched work, but there does not seem to be agreement about what or how many factors there are. There has also been research on other instruments useful in job design (e.g., Sims, Szilagyi, & Keller, 1976). But exactly what factors we should measure in designing jobs is also debatable. Sims et al. (1976) identified six core job factors using an instrument they called the Job Characteristics Inventory. As did Hackman and Oldham, they identified variety, autonomy, feedback, and task identity as four core job factors. However, they also identified two factors unique to their study, dealing with others and friendship.

In summary, attempts to determine the important variables in job design have been only moderately successful. In a general way we know the types of variables critical to enriched work. Precisely what these variables are for different types of jobs is not consistent. While measurement problems persist, it will be difficult to develop a verifiable model or theory that will help in job design. Limitations in our ability to generalize for different jobs necessitates a situation specific approach. This will not prevent "reshaping holes," but it will certainly not make our job any easier.

## How to redesign jobs

Given some understanding of what constitutes an enriched job, the next step is actually changing a job to make work more stimulating. The process of job redesign is by no means simple or routine; many factors must be considered. Aldag and Brief (1979) recommend the following procedures for redesigning a job:

1. Assessment of need is the first step. Presumably there is a reason to alter a job, like unsatisfactory turnover, absence, performance, or accident levels. If such a need exists, the job should meet the following criteria:

a. It should be simple, demanding a low skill level and short-cycle completion sequences. Such jobs are often seen as monotonous.

b. Altering production methods and procedures is economically feasible. If redesign entails huge new capital investments (for equipment and facilities), the expected gains in performance might not offset the costs of technology.

c. Job holders accept and are ready for job redesign. This means seeing increased variety, autonomy, etc., as desirable. The incumbents must also have (or be capable of learning) the aptitudes, skills, and abilities needed to perform the work after redesign.

2. If a job meets these criteria, a committee or task force should be formed to further investigate the prospects. The task force should include management and labor, as well as outsiders as needed. Those holding the job in question are ideal candidates. The main responsibility of the task force is intently studying the job in question, particularly the tasks performed on the job. The best source of information is a structured job analysis, which may have already been done for another reason, like personnel selection, performance appraisal, or training. The task force should identify exactly the activities that contribute to perceptions of task attributes like autonomy, variety, and feedback. Since the job was chosen because it is seen as monotonous, efforts should be made to understand what about the job produces lack of autonomy, task identity, feedback, and so on. The task force should focus on the link between activities performed and reactions holders have to the job along core task dimensions.

3. The task force should then plan some possible redesign aimed at improving the job in terms of task attributes. That is, what changes can be made in how work is performed to increase feelings of autonomy, variety, feedback, and task identity? Perhaps different changes would contribute to each task attribute. The goal of this phase is coming up with new procedures which allow workers to get their job done and also result in stronger perceptions of the task attributes. The changes may involve expanding the scope of job duties, new sequences of work procedures, or developing a new production system.

4. The task force should choose the criteria used to judge whether redesign has succeeded. Many factors would be included—employee atti-

tudes; objective individual indexes like absence, turnover, and performance; and organization indexes like cost efficiency. These factors will be the "scorecard" judging the redesign program. Changes should then be made, and performance of holders monitored closely. If the efforts were successful, thought might be given to expanding the program to other jobs. The entire job redesign strategy is presented in Figure 13–4.

Job redesign takes a fairly long time to plan, execute, and monitor—months or years rather than days or weeks. Rigid standards for evaluating

**Figure 13–4**          **Strategy for redesigning jobs**

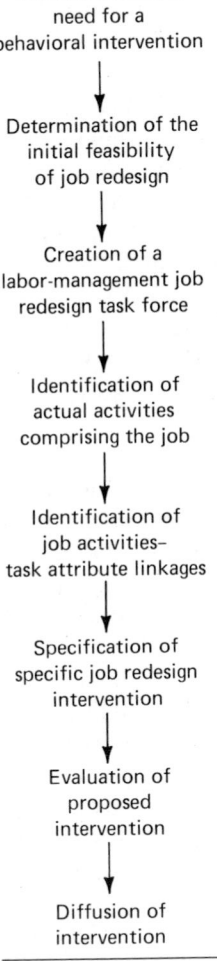

SOURCE: R. J. Aldag and A. P. Brief, *Task Design and Employee Motivation* (Glenview, Ill.: Scott, Foresman, 1979). Copyright © 1979, Scott, Foresman and Company. Reprinted by permission.

the program are also necessary. Organizations must be sure that job redesign is truly "worth it" before undertaking major changes. If the changes are attributable only to a Hawthorne Effect, the organization would be wise to tread softly. That is, organizations should be sure that changes in attitudes or behavior are not due simply to the novelty of new ways of working. Intelligent decisions can only be made by using good information; this necessitates using appropriate evaluation procedures.

Finally, it is not uncommon for changes in one area to have repercussions through the whole organization. Job redesign is not done in a vacuum. We will shortly examine how job redesign can have "ripple effects."

## Effectiveness of job redesign programs

Does job redesign "work"? Does it produce the intended positive outcomes? We are just beginning high-quality research on the effectiveness of job redesign, taking a hard look at whether it succeeds.

Umstot, Bell, and Mitchell (1976) conducted a field experiment comparing the attitudes (e.g., satisfaction) and performance of workers in both enriched and unenriched jobs. The job in question involved identifying and coding land with appropriate zoning codes. The five core dimensions (task attributes) of the job characteristics model were experimentally manipulated to create enriched work (high in autonomy, skill variety, etc.) or unenriched work (low in the dimensions). Both male and female employees were represented in both conditions. After two days, employee attitudes and performance were assessed. Those with enriched work were more satisfied, but there were no differences between groups in productivity. In the second phase of the study, the routine work was redesigned. Following this, satisfaction increased significantly, but level of performance did not. Umstot et al. (1976) concluded that job redesign was effective in producing more satisfying work but not in increasing productivity.

A study with quite different results was done by Locke, Sirota, and Wolfson (1976). The authors conducted a carefully controlled field experiment involving clerical jobs in a federal agency. A redesign program was introduced after careful diagnosis of the work situation; both experimental and control groups were used to evaluate effectiveness. In this study, behavior (productivity and absence) of those with enriched jobs improved significantly, but there were no differences in satisfaction. However, the authors were skeptical about the real cause for the change in worker behavior. They believed that rather than because of enriched work, productivity increased because of more efficient use of manpower while absenteeism decreased because employees expected to be rewarded for better attendance. When the employees discovered there were no rewards (promotions or raises) for improved performance, they became very angry and bitter. Locke et al. (1976) concluded that employees value enriched work not because it is more stimulating or pleasing, but only because it is seen as a way of increasing rewards.

The final study we will discuss was done by Hackman, Pearce, and Wolfe (1978). A number of clerical jobs in a bank were redesigned because of technological innovation, which thus gave the authors a chance to assess the effects of the changes on employees. Some jobs became more complex and challenging, some less so, while others were unchanged. Measures of attitudes and work behavior were collected before and after the changes. Results showed that job satisfaction was directly related to changes in job characteristics; changes in performance and absence depended on employee growth needs. In general, the results supported both the job characteristics model and the concept of job enrichment. The changes in employee attitudes and behavior were as predicted.

What can we conclude about the effectiveness of job redesign? Probably the safest conclusion is that results vary widely, and we cannot simply assume such programs will have a common outcome. Most studies report mixed findings (improvements in some areas but not others), but total failures have also been cited (Frank & Hackman, 1975). Job redesign is complex; it is hard to generalize findings across diverse situations. Differences can exist not only in redesign techniques, but also in employees (age, experience, education, skill level) and workplace (differences in jobs, organizations, union status). In trying to improve the worker/workplace fit by changing the workplace, we should exercise the same caution and concern used in evaluating workers. Just as we know that a given test is not valid for hiring many different kinds of workers, we should also realize that a given job redesign technique will not always work for different jobs. Unfortunately, there are no universal procedures for selecting or modifying pegs or for reshaping holes. While research on job redesign is still in its infancy, we are just beginning to understand what determines its effectiveness.

## Organizational implications of job redesign

As discussed in Chapter 8, organizations are complex systems composed of interdependent parts. If you alter one part of an organization, changes (often unanticipated) in other parts will likely ensue. As a simple example, suppose job redesign was successful in increasing the output of a production department. The organization would have to accommodate the growing supply of manufactured goods—a warehousing and space problem. Pressure would likely be brought to increase the sale of these goods as the stockpile increased. If the sales department was successful, responsibility of the accounting and bookkeeping departments would be increased. Thus, changes in production have implications for the rest of the organization. "Ripple effects" are not at all uncommon, and organizations often don't understand the consequences of making changes in selected areas.

Dunham (1977) reported a study illustrating this point. He found that jobs characterized by higher scores on the core job dimensions were also associated with higher aptitude levels and higher pay. When an organization wants to make jobs more challenging, it should realize that people with more talent and ability must perform the restructured jobs. Further, increased employee talent will also demand more pay—more talented people are worth more. These types of relationships have often been overlooked in job-design literature. An organization cannot hope to simply make work more interesting without affecting anything else in the organization. To the extent that "secondary effects" are anticipated and beneficial, change strategies like job redesign can be of great value to an organization. However, if how the changes will affect the entire organization are not fully comprehended, intervention may do little more than exchange a headache for an upset stomach.

## ORGANIZATION DEVELOPMENT

In the first part of this chapter, we discussed job design—changing jobs to make them more interesting and meaningful for the worker. Job design is one way of improving organization effectiveness, but by no means the only way. Sometimes the problems facing organizations require solutions beyond a *job* as the unit of change. The topic of *organization development*, often referred to simply as *OD*, concerns how organizations can grow, change, and develop to function more effectively. In this part of the chapter, we will examine OD.

### What is OD?

As a formal subdiscipline of I/O psychology, OD is a new area. It is diverse and rapidly evolving; thus, there is no single definition encompassing OD. Perhaps one of the best definitions was supplied by the American Society for Training and Development (1975). OD is "an effort planned, organization-wide, managed from the top, to increase organization effectiveness and health through planned intervention in the organization using behavioral science knowledge." There are five key parts to this definition. (1) OD is a *planned* activity since it involves diagnosing problems, implementing a plan, and mobilizing resources to carry out the plan. (2) OD efforts affect the entire *organization*, though the total organization may not be the focal point of the effort. (3) OD effects must be managed and supported from the *top*. Like personnel training as discussed in Chapter 6, without support and commitment from top management, OD will fail. (4) OD programs are meant to improve the *health and effectiveness* of the organization. Organization health is like individual health. Healthy entities can perform at high levels; lack of health precludes this. (5) Goals flow from deliberate *interventions;* procedures may range from altering physical layout to sensitivity training for certain organization members.

As this suggests, OD is broad based, intentionally designed to facilitate

Automation has simplified many jobs, but the work often becomes monotonous—the case of postal workers verifying ZIP codes. How would you enrich this job?

*Courtesy United States Postal Service*

the well-being of the organization. As we will soon see, there are many issues to be considered in an OD program.

**Why the need for OD?**

Why must organizations be "developed" periodically? It is not characteristics of the organization per se that cause this need, but rather rapidly changing environments (technological, social, political, etc.) in which organizations exist. Changing environments exert pressure on the organization; to perform effectively (sometimes just survive), organizations must change to cope with environments. There are few creatures in life durable and adaptable enough *not* to change over time and still survive. Organizations have a greater need to change now than ever before for at least three major reasons (Huse, 1980).

**1. The knowledge explosion.** For centuries, the amount of knowledge remained at a fairly constant level. From 1600 to 1800, the amount of knowledge doubled. That figure was again doubled by 1900. As a culture, we now double our knowledge far more often (now estimated at every 50 years) because of tremendous advances in medicine, communication, and technology, etc. As a result, knowledge quickly became obsolete. Organizations dependent on such knowledge can become obsolete just as quickly.

**2. Rapid product obsolescence.** As new knowledge is acquired, old knowledge and products quickly become obsolete. With growing emphasis on research and development, products are quickly replaced by newer versions or models. The design of automobiles, medical instruments, and hand-held calculators are three examples of revolutionary changes. Only flexible organizations are likely to compete successfully in such a dynamic market and to continue providing jobs for their workers.

**3. The changing composition of the labor force.** The types of people filling jobs are rapidly changing. Today's work force is better educated, and educated people want more from a job than did their relatively uneducated counterparts 60 years ago. There are more women and racial minorities in the work force, and they are assuming jobs that they typically did not hold earlier. Two-career families are not uncommon, and many people hold more than one job. Organizations must find ways to cope with the changing work force because people are the life blood of any organization.

Given the pressures from legislation, foreign competition, the domestic economy, and social concerns, there is a growing need for organizations to learn to change. Inability to change can have serious implications. Since OD involves organization change, and the need to change is increasingly necessary, OD will probably increase in importance.

**Three basic concepts**

Three concepts are invariably apparent in all OD literature. Each has been the subject of extensive investigation; each is also an integral part of any OD effort. Collectively, they are the ingredients of all OD programs.

**1. The change agent.** The change agent (sometimes referred to as the *interventionist*) is the person who initiates the change. This is usually someone outside the organization (a hired consultant), but occasionally it may be a person in the organization. The agent is usually involved in diagnosing and classifying problems, identifying courses of action, recommending change procedures, and in some cases actually implementing the changes.

Glickman (1974) proposed that effective change agents possess the following qualities: diagnostic ability, basic knowledge of behavioral science, empathy, knowledge of the theories and methods of the consultant's own discipline, goal-setting ability, and problem-solving ability. The agent must strive to build trust among organization members; he or she must be seen as someone sincerely concerned with improving the well-being of the organization. Without this trust, organization members will resist attempts at change.

Also, as Harrison (1970) observed, the agent must intervene only to the extent required for an enduring solutions to the problem at hand. If the agent's role is to help the organization diagnose problems and plan strategies for improvement, he or she should not impose predetermined "solutions" with supposed "guaranteed" results. The change agent should never try to exceed the limits of his or her role; these should be mutually agreed on at the start of the program.

**2. The client.**  The client is the recipient of the change effort. This may be an individual, a group, or possibly the entire organization. You might not think it would be a problem, but sometimes exactly who the client is, is not clear. For example, an organization may at first hire a consultant to diagnose why an important manager suffers from excessive role overload. It is also agreed that the consultant may offer strategies for alleviating the problem. In diagnosing the problem, the consultant discovers that the manager had assumed more and more responsibility because his or her subordinates are seen as incompetent. Rather than overseeing a poor job, the manager gradually assumes responsibility for doing it. At this point, there are three parties (besides the consultant) involved. There is the manager, the subordinates, and the organization employing these people.

As French and Bell (1978) stated, to help people, an agent must interact with and influence them. If the agent's authority doesn't extend to interacting with subordinates, the real problem probably won't be resolved. Perhaps the truth in the situation described is incompetent subordinates, but it could also be a manager who has false views of the quality of subordinates' work. Perhaps the manager is not good at delegating, irrespective of the merits of subordinates. In this case, how can the consultant help the client, and who in fact is *the* client? In practice, there may be more than one client. The manager is the *key* client, but there are various ancillary clients, all part of the total organization. In some cases, helping one client may conflict with enhancing the well-being of another. The agent must decide how the organization can best be helped, realizing that this is not always an easy decision.

**3. The intervention.**  Intervention is what the change agent does on behalf of the client. The change agent can engage in a broad range of activities. French and Bell (1978) described the major types, including:

a.  *Diagnostic activities:* fact finding to ascertain the state of the system, the status of a problem, the "way things are."

b.  *Intergroup activities:* activities to improve effectiveness of interdependent groups.

c. *Education and training activities:* activities to improve skills, abilities, and knowledge.

d. *Coaching and counseling activities:* working with people to help them (1) define learning goals; (2) learn how others see their behavior; (3) learn new behavior to see whether it improves goal achievement.

e. *Life- and career-planning activities:* activities that enable individuals to focus on life and career objectives and how they might achieve them.

Each of these includes many activities and exercises. They all use conceptual material and actual experience with the phenomenon studied. Some are directed toward specific targets, problems, or processes. For example, intergroup activities are directed toward work teams, life-planning activities toward individuals. In general, interventions are structured activities in which selected units (target groups or individuals) engage in a series of tasks directed toward organization improvement.

## Generalized models of change

How do organizations change? Are there any guidelines to help consultants see consistencies in the change process? Researchers have tried to formulate theories explaining change; there seem to be repeatable patterns in the process. Since there are so many types of change, it seems impossible to generate an exact and precise "theory" to which all change efforts rigidly conform. As such, they are more "conceptual guidelines" and are referred to as *generalized models* of change.

One of the simplest and oldest was proposed by the eminent social psychologist Kurt Lewin. He saw change as a three-step process:

$$\text{Unfreezing} \rightarrow \text{Change} \rightarrow \text{Refreezing}$$

*Unfreezing* is weakening the structural support of the system needing change—getting the system to "open up." *Change* is moving the system in a new direction. *Refreezing* is reinforcing the changes made, providing support and stability to prevent the system from slipping back to its previous form. While this three-step process is abstract, it is the basis for virtually all successful OD programs.

At a lower level of abstraction, two models of change are endorsed. Again, these models are nothing more than the rationale behind a change agent's efforts. Both try to facilitate change, but each has distinctive characteristics.

**Planned change.** The first model is referred to as *planned change* and closely mirrors Lewin's model. It was first developed by Lippitt, Watson, and Westley (1958), and has since been modified and refined. The basic concept is the dynamic seven-step process shown in Figure 13–5. The figure also shows Lewin's original notion of unfreezing, change, and refreezing superimposed on the more refined model of planned change. The seven-step process consists of: scouting, entry, diagnosis, planning, action, eval-

**Figure 13–5**                **Model of planned change and Lewin's concept of change**

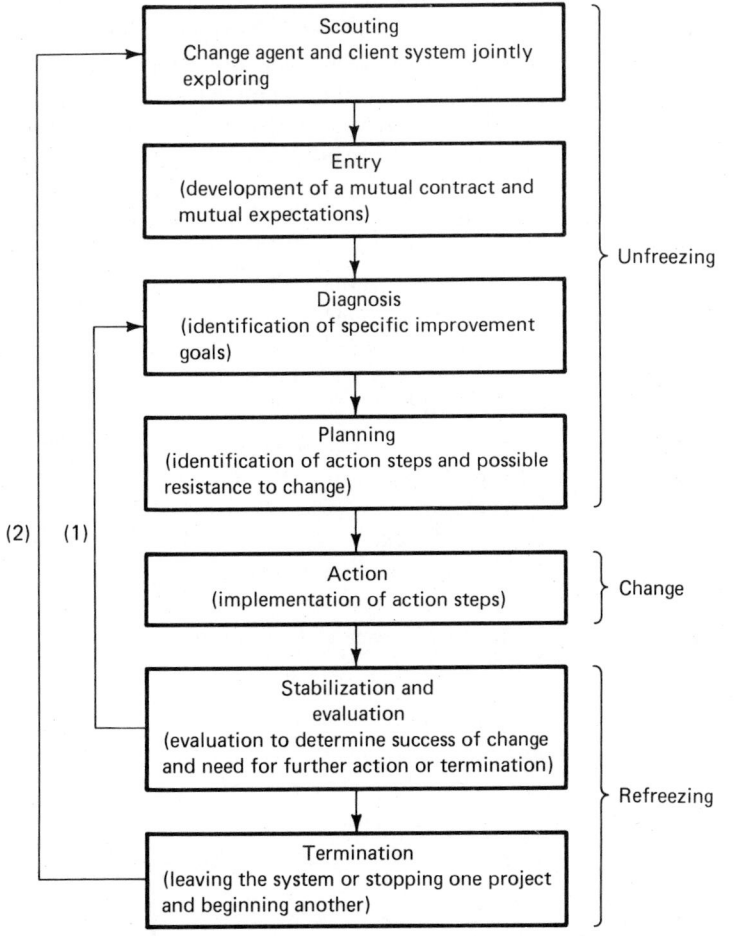

uation, and termination. In the process, consultant and client may change strategies and modify approaches based on continuing diagnosis of the client's problems. This rediagnosis and reformulation is reflected by the feedback arrow marked "1" in Figure 13–5. If the consultant terminates one program but indicates that other problems needing further work have been identified, the consultant-client relationship may begin anew, as indicated by feedback arrow "2."

The planned change model has strengths and weaknesses. It does not emphasize the diagnosis and problem-identification of OD; but it quite strongly emphasizes using specific changes to solve specific problems (Sashkin, Morriss, & Horst, 1973). This approach is often based on using a planned intervention strategy (like sensitivity training). Other change models are more flexible; strategy evolves from problem diagnosis. Some intervention strategies are widely applicable, but it is not always advisable to select a solution before thoroughly analyzing the problem. This is like the personnel training situation in which a training technique is selected before ascertaining the organization's training needs.

**Action research.**    Action research is a second model of change. Unlike planned change, which *may* have feedback or cyclical properties, action research is based on a cyclical process. The model emphasizes data gathering and preliminary diagnosis before planning and implementing action, and developing *new* behavioral science knowledge which can be applied in other organization settings. The concept was originally proposed by Lewin, but has since been expanded by others (e.g., Frohman, Sashkin, & Kavanagh, 1976).

Figure 13–6 is a model of action research. While the model seems to have many parts, in fact, there are only seven major components, repeated cyclically.

1. *Identification of problem(s)*. This begins when a key person senses one or more problems that might be alleviated by a change agent.

**Figure 13–6**                    **A diagrammatic model of action research**

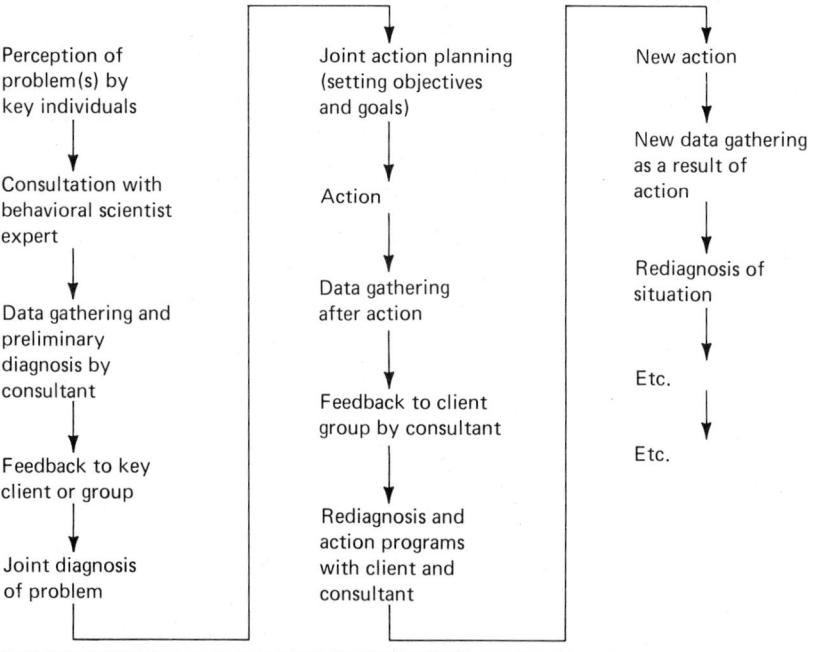

SOURCE: W. French, "Organization Development: Objectives, Assumptions and Strategies," *California Management Review* 12, no. 2 (1969), pp. 23–34.

2. *Consultation with an expert.* The change agent and client establish an atmosphere of trust and openness, and establish a collaborative relationship.

3. *Data gathering and preliminary diagnosis.* This is usually done by the consultant to assess the current status of the organization. The most common methods are interviews, observation, questionnaires, and organization performance data.

4. *Feedback to key client.* The results of data gathering are given to the client; this is the change agent's attempt to tell the client about itself. Usually the change agent is concerned with helping the client determine strengths and weaknesses of the unit in which the change agent is working.

5. *Joint diagnosis of problem(s).* At this point, the change agent and the client discuss the feedback and try to define the real problems that need change. The change agent does *not* "tell" the client what the problem is, as a doctor would do with a patient, but helps the client determine what it is.

6. *Planning and action.* The change agent and client agree on action to be taken. This begins the unfreezing process, as the client starts to move to a different equilibrium.

7. *Data gathering after action.* Since action research is cyclical, data must also be collected to assess the effects of action taken. These new data are again fed back to the client; in turn, this leads to rediagnosis and new action. The entire process is repeated until the consultant-client relationship is ended.

Action research emphasizes evaluation of results, which is why it is called action *research*. Results are evaluated as a basis for further collaborative efforts with the client in the cyclical process of diagnosis, action, and rediagnosis. The method also generates new knowledge which can be used elsewhere. One strength of action research is its emphasis on diagnosis; problems are analyzed from many perspectives. This is especially attractive when problems are not clearly understood or are interdependent. A second advantage is the emphasis on evaluation. Strategies are selected based on the success of preceding strategies. However, one drawback is the model's painstaking approach to problem resolution; this can greatly extend the total change process and can create client dependency on the change agent. At some point, the client must be "cured" enough for the change agent to leave the system. It is particularly difficult to end a consultant-client relationship when the client is deeply enmeshed in a cycle.

A few points should be added about planned change and action research. First, not all change agents prefer one or the other. Some agents may favor one approach, but both may be used. Second, certain problems may lend themselves more to one approach than the other. In fact, while each model has distinguishing characteristics, they are not totally different strategies of change. Finally, these are general models, not unyielding operating standards. Depending on the nature of the problem, there may be deviation and certain steps may be more heavily emphasized. In any case, planned change and action research are two rational approaches to OD.

## Typology of OD intervention

Change agents deal with different kinds of clients (individuals, groups, total organizations), fill different roles, and direct their efforts to different problems. Consequently, researchers have tried to integrate the various OD interventions into a *typology*. A typology is a classification of types of things, usually in graphic form, used to better understand relationships among the types studied. In OD, typologies have classified interventions on such factors as role of the change agent, type of client, types of problems addressed, kinds of interventions, and so on. I developed a typology of OD interventions based on the research of previous authors, notably Blake and Mouton (1976) and White and Mitchell (1976). I chose to present my hybrid typology (as opposed to those of the original authors) because I think it will be more useful in understanding OD interventions. That typology is shown in Figure 13–7.

A cube is created from the three dimensions of OD interventions. The

**Figure 13–7**            **Typology of organization development interventions**

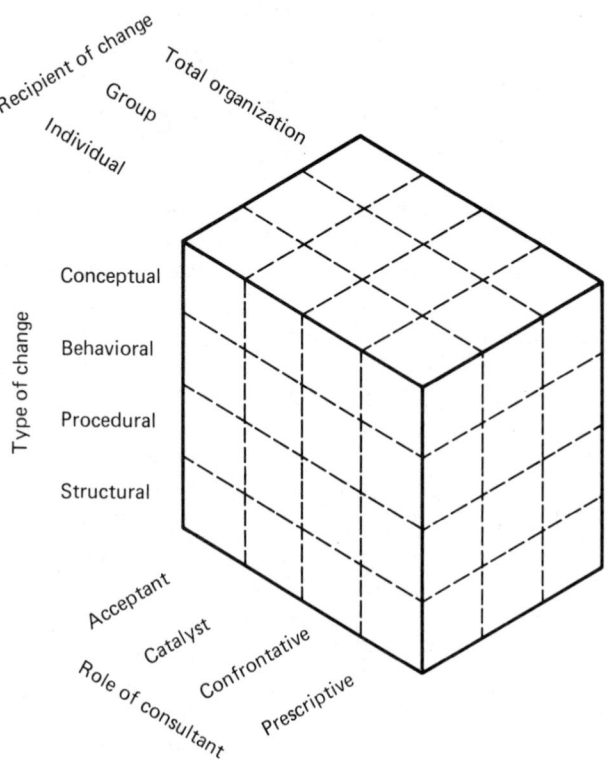

first dimension is the recipient of the change effort—the client. Basically, agents try to change either selected *individuals, groups* of workers, or *entire organizations.* The second dimension is level or nature of change. This can be *conceptual* (new information or knowledge), *behavioral* (new skill), *procedural* (new policy or practice), or *structural* (including organization reporting relationships). Finally, four roles of the change agent are presented. In an *acceptant* role, the consultant offers passive support permitting clients to explore problems and feelings in the presence of an accepting outsider. In a *catalyst* role, the consultant stimulates self-examination by providing feedback on the client's problems; in general, the agent functions as a catalyst for change. The consultant challenges client attitudes or procedures in the *confrontative* role by asking probing questions, presenting discrepant data, and proposing alternatives which motivate clients. Finally, with the *prescriptive* role, the consultant serves as an expert, controls the situation, and prescribes what should be done.

As researchers have commented, a change agent's intervention will not fit neatly into one of the boxes in the cube. In an intervention, the key client may be an individual, but that person's relationship to a subgroup may also become an issue. Especially with the action research model, changes may be sequential and incremental, and may affect the way work is performed. Finally, during the intervention, a consultant may support, stimulate, challenge, or direct the client, depending on the problem and stage of intervention. Nevertheless, a typology is often helpful in ordering the dimensions of a concept. The reader may find that Figure 13–7 serves such a purpose, recognizing that it is only a graphic representation, and not a mirror of reality.

**Major OD interventions**

As noted, there are many intervention strategies a consultant may draw on. It is beyond our scope to describe all or even most of them. However, three OD interventions deserve explication.

1. **Process consultation.**    Process consultation was proposed by Schein (1969) as a means for groups to understand the process of interacting with each other. The recipient is the work group. In fact, in the majority of OD interventions, the work group is probably the client. In process consultation, there is an almost exclusive focus on diagnosis and management of interpersonal and group processes. The consultant's role is observing groups in action, helping them diagnose the nature and extent of their problems, and helping them better solve their own problems.

According to Huse (1980), process consultation focuses on several types of activities. In each case, the consultant's job is providing feedback to the group about its conduct, and in so doing, tendencies that retard the group's effectiveness may be revealed. One area is communication within the group. The consultant observes a group meeting and notes such factors as who does most of the talking, whether people are cut off or are invited to speak, and discrepancies between verbal and nonverbal messages. Another activity concerns the roles of group members. Some members may find themselves presenting factual information, others may provide judgments (e.g., "I don't like that idea"), while others may verify or refute comments. The consultant may videotape a meeting to study members' roles. In many cases, the same people fill the same roles over many meetings. What is fascinating is that the members are rarely (if ever) formally *assigned* these roles; they are *assumed* as a result of the group dynamics. Yet another activity involves group norms. As discussed in Chapter 8, norms are group standards of behavior. The consultant can assist the group in identifying its own norms and understanding whether those norms are helpful.

In many cases, members are so immersed in the group that they fail to "see" communication patterns, role prescriptions, and norm development. For this reason, an independent outsider (the consultant) is brought in. Group members are often surprised at what the consultant observes. Many factors influencing group behavior are subtle. The consultant identifies these influences, describes how they affect interaction, and then allows the group to decide whether changes are warranted. A good process consultant has to be very sensitive and aware of group dynamics. The consultant can feed back only what has been observed; like all skills, observation has to be well developed before it can be effective.

2. **Team building.** Organizations require the cooperation of many people if work is to be done effectively. Consequently, groups or teams come together permanently or temporarily to accomplish work. The primary purpose of a team is problem solving. However, in many cases problems are ill defined and dependent on other organizational problems and issues. The problem-solving effectiveness of groups can be lowered by many factors, including role conflict and ambiguity, confusion about assignments, and lack of imagination and motivation. An OD consultant may then be called in to strengthen the effectiveness of the team. The name given to this intervention strategy is *team building*.

Beer (1976) describes a twofold role in team building: (1) the immediate barriers to group effectiveness must be removed; and (2) the group must develop self-sufficiency in managing future processes and problems. The consultant's main job is increasing cohesiveness and synchronization, from which benefits follow. Team building relies on diagnosis by the group and setting goals providing unity of purpose. In most team-building activities, groups spend time examining and finding ways to improve how they structure their approach to work. In many cases, work groups are concerned with effective time use. The group may examine present planning methods, introduce better ones, and identify ways of more effectively using skill and knowledge. As the group develops, it becomes more aware of the need for action about specific problems or tasks, as well as for better self-diagnosis of the processes used to accomplish tasks (Huse, 1980).

Team building is one of the more challenging intervention strategies.

There are many forces (temporal and longitudinal) limiting a group's problem-solving ability. Team building is a generic strategy in that different groups have problems for very different reasons. The consultant must be adept at having team members diagnose these problems and develop plans for dealing with them. Team building is not a one-shot process—it usually involves many follow-up interventions (Beer, 1976). The factors contributing to group ineffectiveness are usually not static; thus, team-building strategies may be continual. The importance of the group and the severity of its problems influence the nature and extent of a consultant's efforts.

**3. Survey feedback.** A widely used intervention strategy involves systematically collecting data and feeding it back to individuals and groups at all levels. The recipients' task, facilitated by the consultant, is analyzing and interpreting the data and developing corrective action based on the results. These activities are called *survey feedback* (French & Bell, 1978). There are two major components: use of attitude surveys and feedback workshops. Survey feedback may be used as part of team building; but it generally serves a much broader purpose.

Many organizations use attitude surveys to assess current feelings; survey feedback involves more than administering attitude surveys. Most attitude surveys have limited value for improving organization effectiveness. The survey feedback approach is potentially a very powerful intervention strategy. French and Bell (1978) compared the two uses of attitude surveys—traditional and survey feedback—as presented in Table 13–1. As can be inferred, survey feedback requires more "work," but the benefits are also greater.

Neff (1966) stated that for change to take place, three things must happen. First, the work group must accept the data as *accurate*. People often resist data about their organization, claiming "employees really don't feel that way—they were just letting off steam." This defensiveness must be overcome. Second, the work group must *accept responsibility* for its part in the problems identified. There can be a tendency to shirk this responsibility, saying, in effect, that dealing with the problem rests with someone else. Third, the work group must commit itself to *solving problems*. It is not enough to identify problems; steps must be taken to resolve them when possible. Not all problems can be solved. For example, although most employees may be unhappy because a plant is located 20 miles from their home town, the plant cannot be moved to decrease commuting. However, other steps might be taken, like company-sponsored car pools. If *some* of the problems are not dealt with, employees will regard the attitude survey as a farce and treat it as such. The leaders of each work group guide feedback, discussion, diagnosis of problems, and action to solve the problems. The consultant's role is working with leaders, acting as a resource and facilitator.

Survey feedback has been shown to be an effective change technique in OD. Bowers (1973) reported that it is more effective then process consul-

**Table 13–1**                    **Two approaches to the use of attitude surveys**

|  | Traditional approach | Survey feedback or OD approach |
|---|---|---|
| Data collected from ........... | Rank and file, and maybe supervisors | Everyone in the system or subsystem |
| Data reported to .............. | Top management, department heads, and perhaps to employees through newspaper | Everyone who participated |
| Implications of data are worked on by ........... | Top management (maybe) | Everyone in work teams, with workshops starting at the top (all superiors with their subordinates) |
| Third-party intervention strategy .......... | Design and administration of questionnaire, development of a report | Obtaining concurrence on total strategy, design and administration of questionnaire, design of workshops, appropriate interventions in workshops |
| Action planning done by .................... | Top management only | Teams at all levels |
| Probable extent of change and improvement ..... | Low | High |

SOURCE: W. L. French and C. H. Bell, *Organization Development: Behavioral Science Interventions for Organization Improvement,* 2d ed. (Englewood Cliffs, N.J.: Prentice-Hall, 1978). Copyright © 1978. Reprinted by permission of Prentice-Hall, Inc.

tation or sensitivity training. Further, Solomon (1976) found that survey feedback is seen as most effective when the information is negative. Positive information per se does not inspire or direct movement; negative information suggests that movement is desirable and the direction is implied. Solomon feels that survey feedback is particularly useful if an organization is having many problems and the need for change is particularly acute.

**A case study**                My own experience as an OD consultant may help the reader understand the OD process. About 25 years ago, a man developed a new storm door. He found that some people in his town needed it. Because he was mechanically inclined, he built the doors himself. Each morning, he would build two storm doors by hand; in the afternoon, he would install the doors. Soon word spread about his doors, and he got more orders than he could fill. He then rented out a small building and hired two people to assist him in the production of doors, while he retained the responsibility for hanging the doors and keeping the company records. As business grew, he was forced to move to a larger building, take on more help, distribute his products over a wider area, and maintain more records. He discovered there was also a market for storm windows, and he began producing them. Business continued to grow. He opened a second production facility and put his son in charge. Business grew to the point where today there are four production facilities and several warehouse distribution centers, along with a total work force of close to 200. The founder and his son felt they could move into more product lines and newer markets; but because they were each working about 70 hours a week, they didn't know where they would get the time or energy. At this point, I was called in as a consultant.

I began with lengthy discussions with key people. I discovered that top management was suffering from role overload; there was simply too much to do and not enough time to do it. I learned that, as the business grew, top management took on more and more responsibility and rarely delegated. The company president did such things as: (1) maintaining the financial records; (2) hiring all personnel; (3) developing new sales territory; (4) designing new products (with a drafting board and pen); (5) responding to all salespeople that called on the company; (6) ordering material needed. It was hardly surprising that there was no time left for planning and growth (typical responsibilities of top management). The two top people literally did just about everything but physically stand on the production line. I asked why they took on such wide responsibilities. They told me this was how the company started; the system "worked" (the company grew and prospered), so why tamper with success? The president and his son were reluctant to give up what they had been doing for years. It was only after I collected data revealing that employees were not satisfied with their treatment by top management that there was an impetus for change. Employees complained they only had five minutes of contact with the boss a day. (They felt they needed more guidance). This was not surprising given top management's workload. The major impetus for change occurred when I convinced management that only *they* could decide to expand the company (which they wanted to do). If they didn't do it, it would never get done. Obviously, something had to give. I got them to see the need for hiring several key people to assume some of their duties. This included a product design engineer, a personnel manager, a sales manager, and a comptroller. By giving up some self-imposed duties, the two top people had more time for activities that led to further growth and development.

Let's review some of the text material in the context of this case. The client in this case was the total organization, but the focal point of my intervention was top management. Decisions made later affected many other people in the organization. My role was to first diagnose the *cause* of the problems and then help top management see the need for change. Once the need was recognized, I proposed various alternatives. They would not give up some duties, others they would consider. I couldn't tell them what to do, but I did explain the consequences for them and the company of the courses of action selected. Once decisions were made, other issues had to be addressed. New jobs had to be created, the right people had to be hired, and the people had to be trained. I would also add that all the changes did not occur overnight. It was almost two years from when I was first contacted to when the last major person was hired (and the company was thus reorganized). Change is still taking place as new markets and products are found. Both the company and I learned from this that change is (1) necessary, (2) difficult, (3) slow, and (4) continuous. OD facilitates change, and for that reason, it is a valuable tool for the I/O psychologist. However, there is nothing mystical about organizational change. It is based on careful deliberation and insight, and not magic wands or snake oil.

## Research on OD

As White and Mitchell (1976) observed, in recent years the *practice* of OD has far surpassed *research* on the subject. With any method or technique we must ask whether the method works, to what degree, and whether it is cost effective. Answers can only be provided through research, and OD research is still embryonic. It may be tempting to castigate I/O psychologists for this lack of development, but it is often very difficult to do high-quality OD research. In the case study I reported, it would have been virtually impossible to find a second company of the same size, technology, history, etc., for a control. Yet it is such things as sample size, use of control groups, random assignment of people to experimental conditions, and so on which define "good" research. Given the difficulties in an OD context, it is not surprising that the quality of OD research is not as high as, for example, personnel selection research. Nevertheless, we still must determine the adequacy of our interventions, recognizing that this is sometimes difficult.

The relatively small amount of OD research indicates, not surprisingly, that our methods sometimes succeed, sometimes fail, and often are mixed. Porras and Berg (1978) reviewed the results of 35 empirical studies of OD activities; results were mixed. Among the findings were that worker satisfaction does not always increase following intervention; change more often affects *outcomes* (what gets done) than *processes* (how it is done); and *individuals* are more likely to change than are *groups*. White and Mitchell (1976) asked whether many of the positive changes brought about by OD interventions might be due to a Hawthorne Effect. This question is unanswerable without appropriate research. It does seem very possible that changes in organization effectiveness might result from any number of strategies, rather than from just the one used in a given case. However, this would not totally discount the value of OD. It suggests that OD is

Table 13–2 | **Average methodology/design scores for OD studies classified by outcome**

| OD outcome | Number of studies | Average score |
|---|---|---|
| Uniformly positive | 35 | 2.66 |
| Mixed | 12 | 3.25 |
| Uniformly negative | 5 | 4.80 |

SOURCE: D. E. Terpstra, "Relationship between Methodological Rigor and Reported Outcomes in Organization Development Evaluation Research," *Journal of Applied Psychology* 66 (1981), pp. 541–43.

effective as a change method; but we may be fooling ourselves about the respective merits of a given OD strategy. Of course, if changes are short lived, we face a far more serious situation. In such a case, we have a classic Hawthorne Effect, and both the effectiveness of a given strategy and the entire OD process would be suspect. Again, answers can be derived only through rigorous research; to date, this has not often been forthcoming. As White and Mitchell (1976) stated, if OD is to advance as a science (instead of a belief), the answers must be ascertained.

Terpstra (1981) reported an interesting study directly addressing the relationship between quality of OD research and reported outcomes of intervention. Terpstra evaluated 52 OD studies on such variables as sample size, use of control groups, and sampling strategy. After "scoring" each study on quality of research design, he examined whether the study produced (1) uniformly positive findings, (2) uniformly negative findings, or (3) mixed results. The results are shown in Table 13–2. The higher the average methodology/design score, the better the research. Uniformly positive findings are associated with the lowest quality research, uniformly negative findings with the highest quality research. Terpstra's results indicate that we should be careful in concluding that OD interventions are effective when we have not rigorously determined whether such a conclusion is warranted.

It would be misleading and unfair to leave the reader thinking that OD interventions don't succeed or only represent Hawthorne Effects. Many organizations reported big gains in effectiveness following OD interventions. However, psychologists deal with not only the practice of OD, but also its scientific status. In reality, the science and practice are not independent. As is true of many areas in I/O psychology, the *science* needs to shorten the gap with the *practice*. As discussed in Chapter 2, the whole profession will be helped by a close relationship between science and practice.

## Values and ethics in OD

It is appropriate to end the discussion of OD with a comment on values and ethics. Whenever change is deliberate, someone's values and beliefs are being acted on. The act of change itself is based on a value (i.e., change is good or necessary). OD is saturated with values. Sometimes they are implicit, sometimes explicit, and sometimes there is a clash of values (Connor, 1977). Among the values operative in OD are that cooperation is preferable to conflict, openness preferable to suppression, and the level of trust and support is lower than necessary or desirable in most groups and organizations. Psychologists have long known that behavior manifests values. The behavior of the change agent and client in an OD intervention is also guided by values. All parties involved should discuss their values before discussing possible choices. Some conflicts over strategies occur because participants disagree about fundamental values. Many times agreement is assumed, when, in fact, this is not the case. A manager I knew preferred creating a feeling of competition among his subordinates to see who would come up with the "best idea" for a project. It would have been foolish to engage in team building to enhance intragroup cooperation, when that value was not endorsed by the manager.

The issue of ethics is also vitally important to the OD consultant. As any professional working with people's lives, the OD consultant must have integrity. Conflicts can arise which directly involve ethical issues. One of the toughest decisions for a change agent is when to end a consultant-client relationship. On the one hand, the consultant liks to "be there" to help; on the other hand, there comes a point when the client must break free of the consultant. If the consultant leaves the system too soon, the client may not have the internal resources to solve problems. If the consultant prolongs the relationship (all the while being paid a fee), the consultant may create a situation where he or she is "needed" by the client to survive. When to end a relationship is a matter of professional judgment. No formula will provide the answer. While ethical matters are rarely a case of black or white, they are the substance of the consultant's professional character.

## SUMMARY

Seldom in life are we dealt a "pat hand"—a set of circumstances so right that changes are never needed. Such is also true in the work world. Forces affecting work necessitate changes. These forces may come from the workers, the job, or the organization's environment. It is thus necessary to change the workplace to cope with these forces. In this chapter, we looked at two general methods of changing work. Job design involves altering a person's job, usually to make it more satisfying and rewarding. The second method is organization development, a much broader approach. Job design may be considered one part of organization development; in many cases with OD, the unit of change is much greater than a job.

In trying to improve the fit between worker and job, it is necessary to modify either the "pegs" or the "holes." This chapter reviewed the theories, methods, and results of changing the "holes" to fit the "pegs." Ultimately, the fit between the two is product of knowing when and how to change both.

# CASE STUDY

The Verplanck Adhesive Company had been in business about three years. The firm manufactured industrial glues and adhesives and employed a staff of about 200. The president was a research scientist who had worked for an international chemical firm. He quit to form his own company. The company was growing, new positions were being created, and new markets were discovered. Bill Verplanck knew a lot about chemistry, but he was quite unenlightened about "people problems." He hired Warren Miller to handle these matters and gave him the title of Personnel Director. Verplanck was genuinely more interested in chemical bonding than in staff maintenance and development. Accordingly, Verplanck gave Miller a free hand in running that part of the business. However, it was becoming difficult to convince Verplanck to invest resources in his employees. Miller was increasingly sensitive to employee unrest, while Verplanck continued to have a deaf ear.

Miller heard grumbling about inadequate orientation programs, raises smaller than were given elsewhere, complaints about tools and equipment, and poorly trained supervisors. Miller didn't know how widespread the feelings were. It could be a few malcontents, or it might really reflect a pervasive problem. He felt if the extent of the problem wasn't ascertained quickly, the company could face some serious problems—and Verplanck would hold him accountable.

While washing his hands in the rest room, Miller noticed some graffiti on the mirror above the sinks. A few were obscenities aimed at anonymous supervisors, but one read, "Verplanck can take his glue and stick it." Miller felt the graffiti was symptomatic of many underlying problems. It wasn't just attitude, either. Recently, waste and spillage, turnover, and lateness had increased. Someone had posted a union flyer by the water cooler. Written in the margin was "How about it folks?"

Verplanck seemed oblivious to what Miller thought were blatant signals. Miller decided to ask Verplanck about hiring a consultant to administer an attitude survey. He wanted the consultant to find out what was going on and to take some action. From his experience in personnel, he knew that some problems were in the minds of employees, others were legitimate and real. Some problems can be resolved, others cannot. However, all employee concerns should be identified and dealt with. Survey feedback would be a basis for a plan to deal with these matters. At the very least, they would find out just what the perceived problems were.

Miller caught Verplanck leaving a conference room. "Bill," said Miller, "I've got to talk to you about. . . ." Before Miller could finish, Verplanck shot back a jubilant "I've got to talk to you, too. You'd better hire three more salespeople. Looks like we've made some inroads in a new market, and I couldn't be happier!" Verplanck strode away whistling.

Miller stared at the floor. Short of knocking Verplanck over the head, he didn't know how to get his attention. However, if he didn't do it soon, getting three new salespeople would be the least of his problems.

Questions

1.  If you were Miller, how would you get Verplanck to understand the seriousness of the problems facing the company?
2.  One of the principles of organization development is that the need for change is understood and desired. Is it important for this need to be felt throughout the entire organization before change can occur? Why or why not?
3.  Besides survey feedback, are there other diagnostic and change strategies that Miller might consider? What would they be?
4.  Do you feel the chances for change are *improved* or *retarded* because the company is relatively new? Why?
5.  What would some of the limitations be if Miller conducted an attitude survey himself instead of calling in an outside consultant?

# REFERENCES

Aldag, R. J., & Brief, A. P. *Task design and employee motivation.* Glenview, Ill.: Scott, Foresman, 1979.

American Society for Training and Development. *Characteristics and professional concerns of OD practitioners.* Madison, Wis.: American Society for Training and Development, 1975.

Arnold, H. J., & House, R. J. Methodological and substantive extensions to the job characteristics model of motivation. *Organizational Behavior and Human Performance,* 1980, *25,* 161–183.

Beer, M. The technology of organization development. In M. D. Dunnette (Ed.), *Handbook of industrial and organizational psychology.* Skokie, Ill.: Rand-McNally, 1976.

Blake, R., & Mouton, J. *Consultation.* Reading, Mass.: Addison-Wesley Publishing, 1976.

Bowers, D. G. OD techniques and their results in 23 organizations: The Michigan ICL study. *Journal of Applied Behavioral Science,* 1973, *9,* 21–43.

Brief, A. P., & Aldag, R. J. Employee reactions to job characteristics: A constructive replication. *Journal of Applied Psychology,* 1975, *60,* 182–186.

Connor, P. E. A critical inquiry into some assumptions and values characterizing OD. *Academy of Management Review,* 1977, *2,* 635–644.

Dunham, R. B. The measurement and dimensionality of job characteristics. *Journal of Applied Psychology,* 1976, *61,* 404–409.

Dunham, R. B. Relationships of perceived job design characteristics to job ability requirements and job value. *Journal of Applied Psychology,* 1977, *62,* 760–763.

Dunham, R. B. Job design and redesign. In S. Kerr (Ed.), *Organizational behavior.* Columbus, Ohio: Grid, 1979.

Dunham, R. B., Aldag, R. J., & Brief, A. P. Dimensionality of task design as measured by the Job Diagnostic Survey. *Academy of Management Journal,* 1977, *20,* 209–221.

Evans, M. G., Kiggundu, M. N., & House, R. J. A partial test and extension of the job characteristics model of motivation. *Organizational Behavior and Human Performance,* 1979, *24,* 354–381.

Ford, R. N. *Motivation through the work itself.* New York: American Management Association, 1969.

Frank, L. L., & Hackman, J. R. A failure of job enrichment: The case of change that wasn't. *Journal of Applied Behavioral Science,* 1975, *11,* 413–436.

French, W. L. Organization development: Objectives, assumptions and strategies. © 1969 by the Regents of the University of California. Reprinted from *California Management Review,* volume XII, no. 2, pp. 23 to 24 by permission of the Regents.

French, W. L., & Bell, C. H. *Organization development* (2nd ed.). Englewood Cliffs, N.J.: Prentice-Hall, 1978.

Frohman, M., Sashkin, M., & Kavanagh, M. Action-research as applied to organization development. *Organization and Administrative Sciences,* 1976, *7,* 129–142.

Glickman, B. Qualities of change agents. Paper presented at Boston College, Chestnut, Mass., 1974.

Hackman, J. R., & Lawler, E. E. Employee reactions to job characteristics. *Journal of Applied Psychology,* 1971, *55,* 259–286.

Hackman, J. R., & Oldham, G. R. Development of the Job Diagnostic Survey. *Journal of Applied Psychology,* 1975, *60,* 159–170.

Hackman, J. R., & Oldham, G. R. Motivation through the design of work: Test of a theory. *Organizational Behavior and Human Performance,* 1976, *16,* 250–279.

Hackman, J. R., Oldham, G. R., Janson, R., & Purdy, K. A new strategy for job enrichment. *California Management Review,* 1975, *17* (4), 57–71.

Hackman, J. R., Pearce, J. L., & Wolfe, J. C. Effects of changes in job characteristics on work attitudes and behaviors: A naturally occurring quasi-experiment. *Organizational Behavior and Human Performance,* 1978, *21,* 289–304.

Harrison, R. Choosing the depth of organizational intervention. *Journal of Applied Behavioral Science,* 1970, *6,* 181–202.

Huse, E. F. *Organization development and change* (2nd ed.). New York: West Publishing, 1980.

Lawler, E. E. Job design and employee motivation. *Personnel Psychology,* 1969, *22,* 426–435.

Lippitt, R., Watson, J., & Westley, B. *The dynamics of planned change.* New York: Harcourt Brace Jovanovich, 1958.

Locke, E. A., Sirota, D., & Wolfson, A. D. An experimental case study of the successes and failures of job enrichment in a government agency. *Journal of Applied Psychology,* 1976, *61,* 701–711.

Maher, J. R., & Overbagh, W. B. Better inspection performance through job enrichment. In J. R. Maher (Ed.), *New perspectives in job enrichment.* New York: Van Nostrand Reinhold, 1971.

Neff, F. W. Survey research: A tool for problem diagnosis and improvement in organizations. In A. W. Gouldner & S. M. Miller (Eds.), *Applied sociology.* New York: Free Press, 1966.

Oldham, G. R., Hackman, J. R., & Pearce, J. L. Conditions under which employees respond to enriched work. *Journal of Applied Psychology,* 1976, *61,* 395–403.

Paul, W. J., Robertson, K. B., & Herzberg, F. Job enrichment pays off. *Harvard Business Review,* March–April 1969, *47,* 61–78.

Porras, J. I., & Berg, P. O. The impact of organization development. *Academy of Management Review,* 1978, *3,* 249–266.

Roberts, K. H., & Glick, W. The job characteristics approach to task design: A critical review. *Journal of Applied Psychology,* 1981, *66,* 193–217.

Sashkin, M., Morriss, W., & Horst, L. A comparison of social and organizational change models: Information flow and data use processes. *Psychological Review,* 1973, *80,* 510–526.

Schein, E. *Process consultation: Its role in organization development.* Reading, Mass.: Addison-Wesley Publishing, 1969.

Sims, H. P., Szilagyi, A. D., & Keller, R. T. The measurement of job characteristics. *Academy of Management Journal,* 1976, *19,* 195–212.

Soloman, R. J. An examination of the relationship between a survey feedback OD technique and the work environment. *Personnel Psychology,* 1976, *29,* 583–594.

Steers, R. M. Effects of need for achievement on the job performance-job attitude relationship. *Journal of Applied Psychology,* 1975, *60,* 678–682.

Steers, R. M., & Mowday, R. T. The motivational properties of tasks. *Academy of Management Review,* 1977, *2,* 645–658.

Steers, R. M., & Porter, L. W. The role of task-goal attributes in employee performance. *Psychological Bulletin,* 1974, *81,* 434–452.

Steers, R. M., & Spencer, D. G. The role of achievement motivation in job design. *Journal of Applied Psychology,* 1977, *62,* 472–479.

Stone, E. F., Mowday, R. T., & Porter, L. W. Higher-order need strength as a moderator of the job scope—job satisfaction relationship. *Journal of Applied Psychology,* 1977, *62,* 466–471.

Szilagyi, A. D., & Wallace, M. J. *Organizational behavior and performance* (2nd ed.). Santa Monica, Calif.: Goodyear Publishing, 1980.

Terpstra, D. E. Relationship between methodological rigor and reported outcomes in organization development evaluation research. *Journal of Applied Psychology,* 1981, *66,* 541–543.

Turner, A. N., & Lawrence, P. R. *Industrial jobs and the worker: An investigation of response to task attributes.* Cambridge, Mass.: Harvard University Press, 1965.

Umstot, D. D., Bell, C. H., & Mitchell, T. R. Effects of job enrichment and task goals on satisfaction and productivity: Implications for job design. *Journal of Applied Psychology,* 1976, *61,* 379–394.

Wanous, J. P. Individual differences and reactions to job characteristics. *Journal of Applied Psychology,* 1974, *59,* 616–622.

White, S. E., & Mitchell, T. R. Organization development: A review of research content and research design. *Academy of Management Review,* 1976, *1* (2), 57–73.

# chapter 14    UNION/MANAGEMENT RELATIONS

Over the years, I/O psychologists have been involved in a broad range of topics relating to work. Strangely enough, one *not* often addressed is union/management relations. This area can't be dismissed as "tangential" to work; for many organizations, union-related issues are among the most crucial. Many authors (i.e., Dubno, 1957; Stagner, 1961; Shostak, 1964) observed that there is a great imbalance in I/O psychologists' interest in union and management problems. The two are not mutually exclusive, but I/O psychology seems more aligned with management as a client. Just listing some of the professional activities of I/O psychologists testifies to this: managerial consulting, management development, using assessment centers to identify those with management ability, determining the criteria of managerial success, and so on. However, I/O psychology has not spurned the advances of unions or has been unreceptive to them. The relationship was described by Shostak (1964) as "mutual indifference." Unions appear reluctant to approach I/O psychology in solving their problems. Rosen and Stagner (1980) think this is caused partly by the belief that I/O psychologists are not truly impartial, and partly by reluctance to give outsiders access to union data.

The reasons for this are not totally clear. One explanation is the development of industrial psychology is closely tied to the work of Frederick

Taylor. Criticisms of "Taylorism" were raised by union workers; they opposed exploiting workers to increase company profits. There can be an adversary relationship between unions and management—a "we/them" perspective. Unions may still see I/O psychology as a partner of "them"—management. Also, some factors may operate which place I/O psychologists more in the management camp. I/O psychologists are often placed in management-level positions. It is also invariably *management* that sees the need for a consultant, explains problems to the consultant, and pays the consultant. In short, I/O psychology has been more involved with management than with unions (to the point that some authors refer to I/O psychology as a "management tool"). This is most apparent in the conspicuous absence of psychological research on unions.

However, in the past several years interest in unions has increased. Whether the "thaw" will continue and grow remains to be seen. I suspect current interest stems from the realization that worker/workplace problems need not be dealt with from an either/or perspective. Unions and management can benefit from solving problems which affect them jointly. If our discipline is successful in overcoming its "promanagement" image, we can and will make greater inroads in understanding unions. Current research suggests that such changes are beginning.

In this chapter, we will examine the nature of unions, factors influencing union/management relations, recent research on unions, and how unionization affects many topics discussed earlier.

## WHAT IS A UNION?

According to Tannenbaum (1965), "unions are organizations designed to promote and enhance the social and economic welfare of their members" (p. 710). Basically, unions were created to protect workers from exploitation. Unions originally sprang from the abysmal working conditions in this country 75 to 100 years ago. Workers got little pay, had almost no job security, had no benefits, and perhaps most important, worked under degrading and unsafe conditions. Unions gave unity and power to the employees. This power forced employers to deal with workers as a group, thereby providing a basis for improvements in welfare. It should also be realized that federal laws were passed forcing employers to stop certain activities (such as the employment of children) and engage in others (such as social security contributions). Collectively, labor unions and labor laws brought about many changes in the workplace. While the problems facing the North American worker today are not as severe as they were 75 years ago, unions continue to give a sense of security and increased welfare to their members, just as they did many years ago.

Why do workers join unions? What can unions accomplish? According to several authors, unions have consistently contributed to attaining certain outcomes. Bok and Dunlop (1970) feel unions made the following contributions to worker welfare:

1. They increased wages. When this happens, employers raise the wages of some nonunion workers, as well.
2. They bargained for and got benefits such as pensions, insurance, vacations, and rest periods which also improved the lot of employees.
3. They provided formal rules and procedures for discipline, promotion, wage differentials, and other important job-related factors. This led to less arbitrary treatment of employees.

Sherman (1969) adds the following reasons for joining unions: they provide better communication with management, better working conditions, increased employee unity, and higher morale. Other authors cite social reasons like belonging to a group with which workers can share common experiences and fellowship. Thus, there are both economic and personal reasons.

## UNIONS AS ORGANIZATIONS

According to Glueck (1974), approximately 20 million U.S. citizens belong to labor unions, representing about 25 percent of the nonagricultural work force. In Canada, membership is over 2 million. The largest labor union is the American Federation of Labor–Congress of Industrial Organizations (AFL-CIO). Of all union members, 83 percent belong to an AFL-CIO affiliate. Other large unions include the United Auto Workers and the International Brotherhood of Teamsters. While unions are strongest in blue-collar jobs, some white-collar workers (particularly government employees and teachers) are also being unionized as witnessed by the growth in American Federation of State, County, and Municipal Employees. There has been a recent trend away from unionization as the number of service jobs increases and manufacturing jobs decline.

Each union has a headquarters, but the strength of a union is its many "locals." A local may represent members in a geographic area (e.g., all tollbooth collectors in Philadelphia) or a particular plant (e.g., Amalgamated Beef Packers at the Dubuque, Iowa, slaughterhouse of Armour Meats). The local elects officials. If the union is large enough, some officials have full-time jobs running the local. Other officials are full-time employees but may get time off for union activities. The *shop steward* or union steward has a union position equivalent to that of the supervisor for the company. The steward represents the union on the job site; he or she handles grievances and discipline. Usually the steward is elected by members for a one-year term.

A union represents an organization (e.g., a labor organization) within another organization (the company). The local depends on the company for existence; without a company and jobs, there would be no labor union. Large companies often have a multiunion labor force, thus creating multiple organizations within an organization. In this case, the employer must deal with several collectively organized groups, for example, production workers, clerical workers, and truck drivers. Each union negotiates separately, trying to improve the welfare of its members. A large, multiunion employer is a vivid example of how organizations are composed of interdependent parts. Each union has a certain degree of power, and that power can influence the behavior of the total organization.

Union members pay membership dues. The union would have no resources without member support. The union can also collect money for a strike fund—a pool members can draw from if they are on strike and don't get paid. (More about strikes shortly.) Unions use their funds to offer members such things as special group automobile insurance rates or union-owned vacation facilities. Unions are highly dependent on their members. Increased membership gives a union more bargaining clout, generates more revenue, and provides a greater range of services for members. If a union has no members, it cannot exist. Indeed, declining membership threatens the survival of some unions.

## THE FORMATION OF A UNION

When employees want to consider joining a union, a standard procedure is followed. The first step involves inviting representatives to solicit union membership. Federal law allows organizers to solicit membership as long as this does not endanger safety or performance of the employee. Solicitations usually occur over lunch or at break time. It is illegal for employers to physically threaten, interfere with, or harass organizers. It is also illegal to fire employees for prounion sentiments.

Both the union and the company will typically mount campaigns on behalf of their positions. The union will stress how it can improve the workers' lot. The company will mount a counter-campaign stressing how well off the employees already are, the costs of union membership, and loss of freedom. A federal agency, the National Labor Relations Board (NLRB), is involved. The NLRB sends a hearing officer to oversee the union campaign and monitor further developments.

Employees are asked to sign cards authorizing a union election. If less than 30 percent sign the authorization cards, the process is ended. If 30 percent or more sign, the next step is an election to determine whether a union will represent the employees. The NLRB officer must determine which employees are eligible to be in the union and thus eligible to vote. Management personnel (supervisors, superintendents, and managers) are excluded. The hearing officer schedules the election, provides secret ballots and ballot boxes, counts the votes, and certifies the election. If more than 50 percent of the voters approve, the union is voted in. If the union loses the election, the entire process can be repeated at a later date. A union would probably do so if it lost a close election.

Brief and Rude (1981) proposed that deciding to accept or reject a union is not unlike other choices facing an individual. An employee will support a union to the extent that it is seen as a way of getting outcomes important to the individual without prohibitive costs. Bakke (1945) stated this most eloquently:

> The worker reacts favorably to union membership in proportion to the strength of his belief that this step will reduce his frustrations and anxieties and will further his opportunities relevant to the achievement of his standards of successful living. He reacts unfavorably in proportion to the strength of his belief that this step will increase his frustrations and anxieties and will reduce his opportunities relevant to the achievement of such standards (p. 38).

DeCotiis and LeLouarn (1981) developed a model of the determinants of unionization shown in Figure 14–1. The work context includes employee reactions to work, organization climate, perceived organization structure, and supervision. Personal characteristics include age, sex, and race, as well as feelings of job satisfaction. The work context and personal characteristics determine union instrumentality, i.e., the extent that a union is seen as improving the employee's welfare. Instrumentality affects the employee's attitude toward unions; in turn, this affects the employee's intent to vote for a union. The actual vote is determined by the sequence shown in the

**Figure 14–1**        **A model of the determinants of the unionization process**

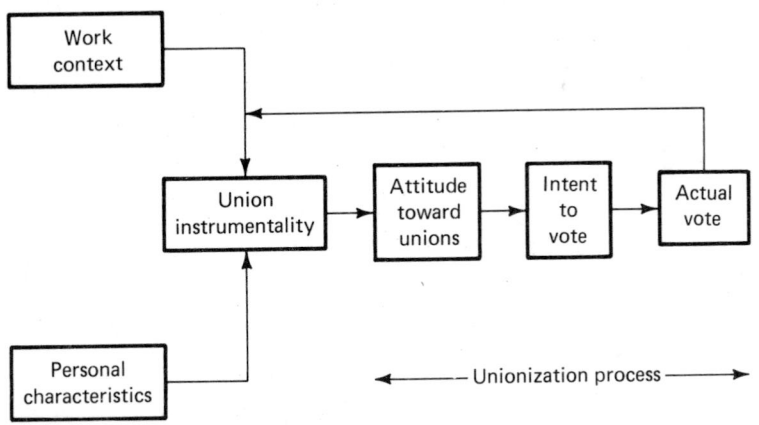

SOURCE: T. A. DeCotiis and J. Y. LeLouarn, "A Predictive Study of Voting Behavior in a Representation Election Using Union Instrumentality and Work Perceptions," *Organizational Behavior and Human Performance* 27 (1981), pp. 103–118.

model. DeCotiis and LeLouarn were able to explain over 54 percent of the variance in perceptions of union instrumentality on consideration of the concepts in their model.

## THE LABOR CONTRACT

Once a union is recognized, its officials are authorized to negotiate a labor contract. This is a formal agreement between union and management specifying conditions of employment over a set period.

Both sides prepare a preliminary list of what they want included; the union presents its demands, and the employer its offers. The union tends to ask for more than it knows it can get; management tends to offer less. While both sides seek a satisfactory agreement, they often resort to bombast, which is a hallmark of such negotiations. Union officials may claim management is making huge profits and taking advantage of workers. Management may claim that malicious union leaders have duped the good workers, and that their policies may force the company into bankruptcy. Over time, both sides usually come to an agreement; the union often gets less than it wanted and management gives more. When agreement is not reached (an *impasse*), other steps are taken, as will be discussed.

Contract negotiations take place between two teams of negotiators. The union side is typically local union officials, shop stewards, and perhaps a representative of the national union. Management usually fields a team of a few personnel and production managers, who follow guidelines set by top management. The contract contains many articles; there are also many issues to bargain over. The issues can generally be classified into five categories:(1) compensation and working conditions; (2) employee security; (3) union security; (4) management rights; and (5) contract duration (Glueck, 1974). Table 14–1 gives examples of these and the position typically taken by each side.

In the process, each bargaining team will check with its members to see whether they will compromise on initial position. Each side may be willing to yield on some points but not others. Eventually, a tentative agreement is reached. Union members then vote on the contract. If members approve it, the contract is *ratified* and remains in effect for the agreed upon time (typically two-to-three years). If members reject the contract, further negotiation is necessary.

What determines whether a contract will be ratified? Typically: (1) industry practices, (2) community practices, and (3) recent trends. If the union represents truck drivers, and a critical issue is wages, the union will collect data needed to judge the proposals. What other companies in the industry pay truck drivers, what other companies in the community pay them, and whether prices and wages are rising or falling will be considered. Stagner and Rosen (1965) refer to the area of compromise as the *bargaining zone*;

| Table 14–1 | **Typical bargaining issues and associated positions taken by union and management** | | |
| --- | --- | --- | --- |
| | Issue | Union's position | Management's position |
| | 1. Compensation and working conditions ........ | Higher pay, more fringe benefits, cost-of-living adjustments. | Limit company expenditures by not yielding to all union demands. |
| | 2. Employee security ........ | Seniority is the basis for promotions, layoffs, and recall decisions. | Merit or job performance is the basis for these decisions. |
| | 3. Union security ............ | A union shop in which employees must join the union when hired. | An open shop in which employees can choose to join the union. |
| | 4. Management rights ........ | Union wants more voice in setting policies and making decisions which affect employees. | Management feels certain decisions are their inherent right, and does not want to share them with the union. |
| | 5. Contract duration ........ | Shorter contracts. | Longer contracts. |

this is presented in Figure 14–2. Both parties must move toward a compromise without exceeding their tolerance limit; this is the point beyond which the contract is unacceptable. If both parties reach a compromise within their expectations, there is agreement. If, however, one side exceeded its tolerance limit, the proposed contract would not be acceptable.

Both sides will use whatever external factors are available to influence the contract in their favor. If there is high unemployment and the company could replace workers who go on strike, management has an advantage. If the company does much of its business around Christmas, the union may choose that time to negotiate a contract, knowing the company could ill afford a strike then. Each side looks for factors that will bolster its position.

**Collective bargaining and impasse resolution**

Whether the bargaining process runs smoothly is often due to the approach of the parties to bargaining. Walton and McKersie (1965) distinguish *distributive* and *integrative* bargaining postures. Distributive bargaining is predominant in the United States. This assumes a win-lose relationship; whatever the employer gives the union, the employer has lost, and vice versa. Because both sides are trying to minimize losses, movement toward a compromise is often painful and slow.

The alternative is integrative bargaining. Both sides work to improve

**Figure 14–2**                    **Desires, expectations, and tolerance limits that determine the bargaining zone**

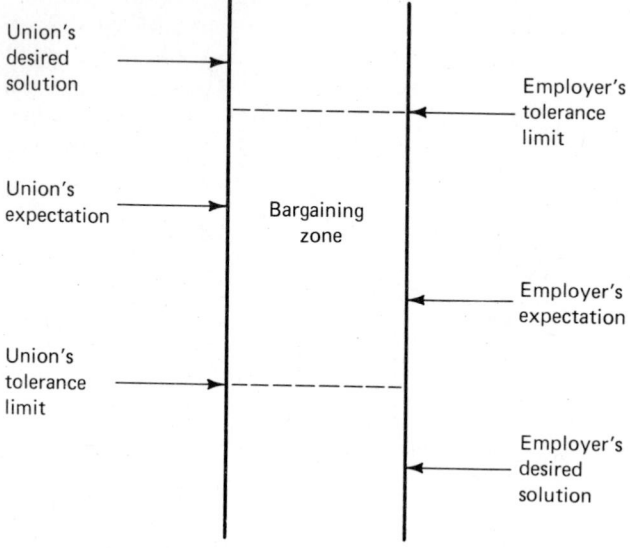

SOURCE: R. Stagner and H. Rosen, *Psychology of Union-Management Relations* (Belmont, Calif.: Wadsworth, 1965), p. 96. Reprinted by permission of the publisher, Brooks/Cole Publishing Company, Monterey, California.

the relationship while the present contract is in effect. Contract renewal is not seen as the time and place for confrontation. Instead, both parties seek to identify common problems and propose acceptable solutions that can be adopted when the contract expires.

These bargaining postures are not formally chosen. Rather, they are implied by behavior in the workplace. While it is not always a strictly either/or decision, it appears that distributive bargaining is far more characteristic of union/management relations than integrative bargaining.

What happens if the two parties cannot reach an agreement? In some cases, the labor contract may stipulate what will be done if an impasse is reached. In other cases, union and management must jointly determine how to break the impasse. In either case, there are three options, all involving third parties.

**Mediation.** According to Kochan (1980), mediation is the most used, yet the most informal third-party option. A neutral third party (a mediator) assists union and management to reach voluntary agreement. A mediator has no power to impose a settlement; rather, he or she facilitates bringing both parties together.

Where do mediators come from? The Federal Mediation and Conciliation Service (FMCS) provides a staff of qualified mediators. An organization contacts FMCS for the services of such a person. The mediator need not be affiliated with FMCS, as any third party acceptable to labor and management may serve. Generally, however, both parties prefer someone with training and experience in labor disputes, so FMCS is often called on.

*How* a mediator intervenes is not clear-cut. Mediation is voluntary; thus, no mediator can function without the trust, cooperation, and acceptance of both parties. Acceptance is important since the mediator must obtain confidential information which the parties have withheld. If the information is used indiscriminately, the party's bargaining strategy and leverage could be weakened. The mediator tries to reduce the number of disputed issues; ideally, he or she reaches a point where there are no disputes at all. The mediator encourages information sharing to break the deadlock. Without a mediator, it is often difficult for parties to "open up" after assuming adversary roles. The mediator facilitates the flow of information and progression toward compromise. If the mediator is unsuccessful, both parties may engage in the next phase, fact-finding.

**Fact-finding.** Fact-finding is more formal than mediation. A qualified mediator may also serve as a fact finder, but his or her role will change. In fact-finding, the third party reviews the facts, makes a formal recommendation to resolve the dispute, and makes the recommendation public. It is presumed that if the recommendation is public, pressure will be brought on the parties to accept the recommendation or use it for a negotiated settlement. However, according to Kochan (1980), fact-finding has not produced the desired pressure. Public interest is apparently aroused only when a strike threatens or actually imposes direct hardship on the public.

Fact-finding may be most useful when one party faces internal differences and needs recommendations from an expert to overcome opposition to a settlement. There appears to be a difference in the effectiveness of fact-finding for private and public-sector employers. Fact-finding in the public sector has met with limited success. Parties learn that rejecting a fact-finding recommendation is not politically or economically costly, so they are unlikely to value the opinion of the fact finder. In the private sector, fact-finding could be helpful primarily because the final technique of settlement (arbitration) is strongly opposed by unions and management. However, in general, fact-finding is not used very often in the private sector.

**Arbitration.** Arbitration is the final and most formal settlement technique. Both parties *must* abide by the decision of the neutral third party. "Final and binding" is usually associated with arbitration. It is the *final* step in the resolution process. The outcome of arbitration is *binding* on both parties. Use of arbitration may be stipulated in the labor contract; it may also be agreed upon informally. This is called *interest* arbitration, as it involves the interests of both parties in negotiating a new contract.

Arbitrators must have extensive experience in labor relations. The American Arbitration Association (AAA) maintains the standards and keeps a list of qualified arbitrators. Arbitrators listed by AAA often also serve as mediators listed by FMCS. The same skills are needed for an effective mediator, fact finder, or arbitrator. What distinguishes the services is the clout of the third party.

There are many forms of interest arbitration. With *voluntary* arbitration, the parties *agree* to arbitration. It is most common in the private sector in settling disputes arising while a contract is still in effect. *Compulsory* arbitration is legally *required*. It is most common in the public sector. There are other types of arbitration. With *conventional* arbitration, the arbitrator creates the settlement he or she deems appropriate. In *final offer* arbitration, the arbitrator must select the proposal of either union or management; no compromise is possible. For example, the union demands $8 per hour, while the company offers $7. In conventional arbitration, the arbitrator could decide on any wage but will probably split the difference and decide on $7.50. In final offer arbitration, the arbitrator must choose between the $7 and $8. An additional variation also holds for final offer arbitration. The arbitrator may make the decision on a *total package;* he or she must choose the complete proposal of the employer or the union on all issues. The decisions may also be made on an *issue by issue* basis. In this case, the arbitrator might choose the employer wage offer, but select the union offer on vacation days. Decisions on voluntary versus compulsory arbitration, conventional versus final offer arbitration, and total package versus issue by issue resolution are determined by law for public sector employers, or by mutual agreement in the private sector.

Interest arbitration is more common in the public sector. The private sector has been historically opposed to outside interference in resolving labor problems that are "private" affairs. Thus, private sector employers will readily seek the *advice* of a mediator, but shun strategies which *require* certain courses of action. The public sector, however, is quite different. Strikes in the public sector (e.g., police) can have devastating effects on the general public. They are often prohibited by law. Therefore, other means of settlement (fact-finding, arbitration) are provided. Some public sector employees have gone on strike (sometimes legally, usually illegally); but strikes are more often the outcome of impasses in the private sector. We will next consider the options available if no settlement is reached through standard procedures.

## Responses to impasse

Consider the situation when union and management cannot resolve their disputes. They may or may not have used a mediator. Assume the private sector is involved because mediation, fact-finding, and arbitration might be required in the public sector. What happens if the two parties cannot agree?

Collective bargaining entails realizing that both sides can take action if they are not pleased with the outcome. The actions both sides can take are weapons to bring about favorable settlements. What the union can do is to strike. Union members must vote for a strike. If members support a strike and no settlement is reached, at a particular time the employees will stop work. That point is typically the day after the current contract expires. Taking a strike vote during negotiations brings pressure on management to agree to union demands; management knows the employees will strike if their demands are not met. The right to strike is a very powerful tool. The losses from a long strike may be greater than the concessions made in a new contract. Unions are also skilled in scheduling their strikes (or threatening to do so) when the company is particularly vulnerable (as around Christmas for the airline industry). If employees do strike, the company is usually closed down completely. There may be limited production if management performs some jobs. It is also possible to hire workers to replace those on strike. These replacements are called "scabs." Given the time it takes to recruit, hire, and train new workers, replacements will not be hired unless a long strike is predicted.

A strike hurts management; but it isn't pleasant for the workers, either. Since they are not working, they don't get paid. The employees may have contributed to a strike fund, but such funds are usually only a fraction of regular wages. A strike is the price employees pay to get their demands. It sometimes also limits their demands. By the time a union faces a strike it is usually confronted with two unpalatable options. One is to accept a contract it doesn't like; the other is to strike. Employees may seek temporary employment while they are on strike; but such jobs are not always available. Labor economists studied the costs of strikes to both the employees and the company; it is safe to say that strikes rarely benefit either party. Sometimes the company suffers the most, in other cases, the union. There are rarely any "winners" in a strike. Stagner and Rosen (1965) illus-

"Management and labor are going to be even further apart by tomorrow. Management is going to Jamaica until the strike is over."

Reprinted courtesy of The Register and Tribune Syndicate.

Figure 14–3    **Illustration of union and company alternatives and related consequences**

Company                                Union

*Alternative 1*

Perceived consequences of giving in to    Perceived consequences of accepting
   union demands:                           company counteroffer:
1. Lessening of investor return.        1. Loss of membership support.
2. Loss of competitive standing.        2. Loss of status within union move-
                                           ment.
3. Setting bad precedent.               3. Setting bad precedent.
4. Avoiding costly strike.              4. Avoiding costly strike.
5. Avoiding government and public ill    5. Avoiding government and public ill
   will.                                   will.

*Alternative 2*

Perceived consequences of refusing to    Perceived consequences of sticking to
   accede to union demands:                  original demands:
1. Due to potential strike, loss of inves-   1. Prove strength and determination of
   tor return.                             union to members.
2. Due to potential strike, loss of com-   2. Due to potential strike, loss of mem-
   petitive standing.                      ber income.
3. Loss of government and public good    3. Due to potential strike, loss of mem-
   will.                                   ber support.
4. Maintenance of company preroga-      4. Loss of government and public good
   tives.                                  will.
5. Breaking union power.                5. Teach company a "lesson."

SOURCE: R. Stagner and H. Rosen, *Psychology of Union-Management Relations* (Belmont, Calif.: Wadsworth, 1965), p. 103. Reprinted by permission of the publishers, Brooks/Cole Publishing Company, Monterey, California.

trate the consequences for both union and management in accepting each other's alternatives, particularly as they relate to a strike. That is shown in Figure 14–3.

A recent study examined some of the dynamics associated with strikes. Stagner and Eflal (1982) looked at the attitudes of unionized automobile workers at several times, including when contracts were being negotiated, during an ensuing strike, and seven months after the strike ended. The authors found that union members on strike (*a*) had a higher opinion of the union and its leadership than before the strike; (*b*) evaluated the benefit package more highly after the strike; (*c*) became more militant about the employer during the strike; and (*d*) reported more willingness to engage in union activities. The results of this study support predictions based on theories of conflict and attitude formation.

However, management is not totally defenseless in case of a strike. If a strike is anticipated, production might be boosted beforehand to stockpile goods. Most public sector employees perform services, and services cannot be stockpiled. This is one reason strikes are illegal in some parts of the public sector. Sometimes a strike uncovers information about the quality of the work force. When one company replaced strikers with temporary help, new production records were set. In this case, the strike revealed a weakness in the employees.

A strike is not the only option available to the union. Work *slowdowns* have also been used. Workers operate at lower levels of efficiency. They may simply put out less effort and thus produce less, or they may be absent to reduce productivity. Since strikes are illegal in the police force, police officers dissatisfied with their contracts have called in sick *en masse* with what has become known as the "blue flu." Such tactics can exert great pressure on management to yield to union demands.

*Sabotage* is another response to impasse in negotiations. Stagner and Rosen (1965) describe a situation where production in a factory increased from 2,000 to 3,000 units per day by modifying a drill press. However, wages were not increased, and workers resented it. They found that bumping the sheet metal against the drill would eventually break the drill. The employee would have to wait idly for a replacement. By some curious accident, average production continued around 2,000 units per day. Management got the "message." While sabotage is not a sanctioned union activity like a strike, it is a way of putting pressure on management to accept demands.

Management also has a major tactic to get the union to acquiesce. It is called a *lockout* and is considered the employer's equivalent of a strike. The company threatens to close if the union doesn't accept its offer. Employees can't work; they "pay" for not accepting the employer's offer. A threatened lockout may put the pressure of a majority of workers on a minority holding out against a contract issue. Like strikes, lockouts are costly to both the company and the union, and they are not undertaken lightly. They are management's ultimate response to an impasse.

Before we leave the area, note that strikes, slowdowns, sabotage, and lockouts are failures in the collective bargaining process. Because a settlement was not reached, these actions are taken. Like most responses to frustration, in the long run they are rarely beneficial. Some unions may want to "teach the company a lesson"; some companies want to break a union; but both parties have a symbiotic relationship. A company can't exist without employees, and without a company, employees have no jobs. Collective bargaining reflects the continual tussle for power; but neither side can afford to be totally victorious. If a union exacts so many concessions that the company goes bankrupt, it accomplished nothing. As Estey (1981) put it, "Labor does not seek to kill the goose that lays the golden eggs; it wants it to lay more golden eggs, and wants more eggs for itself" (p. 83). If management drives employees away by not making enough concessions, it won't have a qualified work force. Industrial peace is far more desirable for all parties than warfare. Conflict can provide opportunities for change and development; if conflict gets out of hand, it can be devastating. Union/management relations are not all typified by infighting and power plays. Nothing unites opposing factions faster than a common enemy. Because the United States is losing some economic battles to foreign competition, some union/management relations have become far more *integrative*. For example, in 1982, unions in the auto industry gave up some previous concessions before the present contract expired. The company, in turn, used the money saved to become more competitive. By remaining solvent, the company continued to provide jobs. Both management and labor could pursue some common goals. Collective bargaining is a delicate process. Neither side can lose sight of the total economic and social environment, even though short-term, narrow issues are often at the heart of disputes.

**Disputes over contract interpretation**

Collective bargaining is mainly directed toward resolving disputes over new labor contracts; however, disputes also occur over the contract currently in effect. No matter how clearly a labor contract is written, there are invariable disagreements over meaning or extent. Developing a clear and precise contract involves writing skills in their highest form. Despite the best intentions of those involved, events occur that are not clearly covered in a labor contract. For example, companies often include a contract clause stating that sleeping on the job is grounds for dismissal. A supervisor notices that an employee's head is resting on his arms and his eyes are closed. The supervisor infers the employee is asleep and fires him. The employee says he wasn't sleeping; he felt dizzy and rested for a moment, rather than risk falling down. Who is right?

If the supervisor dismissed the employee, the employee would probably file a *grievance*. A grievance is a formal complaint. The firing decision can be appealed through a grievance procedure, which is usually a provision of a labor contract (Ash, 1970). First, the employee and supervisor try to reach an understanding. If they don't, the shop steward represents the employee in negotiating with the supervisor. This is often done whether or not the steward thinks the employee "has a case." The steward's job is representing union members. If not resolved, the case may then be taken to the company's director of industrial relations. This person will hear testimony from both sides and issue a verdict. This may be a compromise—the employee keeps his job but is on probation. The final step is calling in an arbitrator. This person is given the labor contract, hears testimony, and renders an opinion. This is called *rights* or *grievance* arbitration; it involves the rights of the employee. Usually, the labor contract specifies that union and management share the cost of arbitration; this may be $1,000 per hearing. This is done to prevent all grievances from being routinely pushed to arbitration. Each side must believe it has a strong case before calling in an arbitrator.

The arbitrator must be acceptable to both sides; this means being seen as neither prounion nor promanagement. The arbitrator may decide in favor of one side or issue a compromise decision. The decision is final and

Striking employees can make a public display of their position in labor disputes by picketing.

Wide World Photos

binding. If an arbitrator hears many cases in the same company and repeatedly decides in favor of one side, he or she may become unacceptable to the losing side. Articles of the labor contract that are repeated subjects of grievance (due mainly to ambiguous language) become prime candidates for revision in the next contract.

A few studies examined the grievance process. Thayer and McGehee (1977) describe an episode involving plant supervisors' understanding of a labor contract. Many grievances are supposedly filed because labor contracts are not understood; thus, the authors planned a training program to improve such understanding. A test was constructed measuring knowledge of the contract; the company president offered a steak dinner to the supervisor who got the best score. Informal bets were placed among the supervisors. With a sense of competition, motivation to do well was very high. Because all of the supervisors wanted to do well, they studied the contract in detail. The test was then given to the 75 supervisors in the plant. There were 75 perfect or near-perfect scores, so the president ended up hosting a steak dinner for all supervisors. The company accomplished its goal, but the dynamics of learning were not what the authors had anticipated.

A number of studies examined determinants of grievance. The most common are characteristics of grievants, personality of the union steward, and the nature of the environment in which grievances are filed. Several studies (e.g., Eckerman, 1948, Sulkin & Pranis, 1957) tried to ascertain the "type" of person who submits a grievance. The design usually calls for comparing grievants and nongrievants on a variety of factors. Using this method, Sulkin and Pranis (1957), for example, reported that grievants had more education, were more active in the union, had a higher absence rate, and received lower wages with fewer net increases. The characteristics of grievants seem stable within a given company; characteristics across companies are not consistent (Kissler, 1977).

Dalton and Todor (1979) examined the relationship between personality characteristics of the union steward and propensity to file a grievance. The union steward is instrumental in the grievance process. Dalton and Todor discovered wide differences in the conduct of stewards toward grievances. Some stewards never tell an employee not to file a grievance; others try to resolve problems on the plant floor to keep them from becoming formal grievances. Further, the more dominant the personality of the steward, the more likely he or she is to file a grievance in an employee's behalf.

Dalton and Todor (1982) presented a model of the grievance process, emphasizing the role of the union steward. This is shown in Figure 14–4. Some incident occurs which is seen as a possible grievance. A management representative may try to reduce grievances by resolving the problem informally with the union steward's consent. If the employee wants to pursue a grievance (has a positive propensity), the steward might discourage this, but would probably support the action. If a worker has a negative propensity to file a grievance, the steward may encourage the individual or may file in the name of the union without the worker's consent. Finally, the bottom link in the model shows a steward could bypass any worker propensities (positive or negative) and file a grievance in the name of the union.

**Figure 14–4**             **Model of the grievance process**

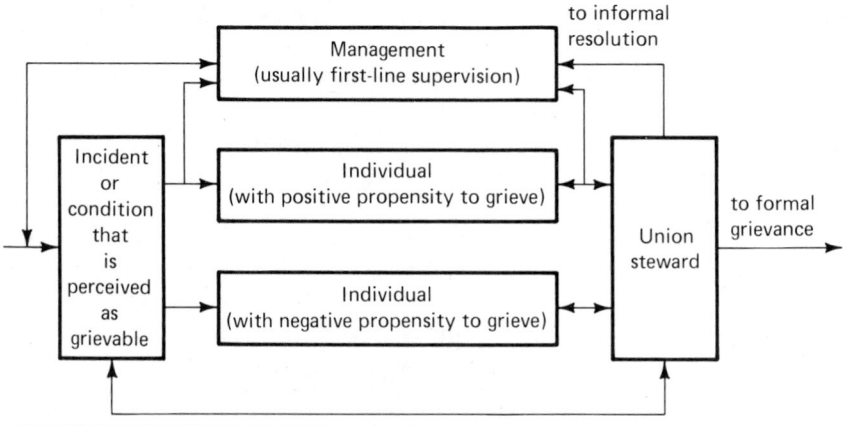

SOURCE: D. R. Dalton and W. D. Todor, "Antecedents of Grievance Filing Behavior: Attitude/Behavioral Consistency and the Union Steward," *Academy of Management Journal* 25 (1982), pp. 158–69.

In such a case, it is the propensity of the steward alone which determines the action. Dalton and Todor feel the union steward holds a key role in the union member–grievance relationship, a role which until recently has not been well understood.

A few studies examined the extent that the work environment contributes to number and types of grievances. Ronan (1963) studied grievance activity over a five-year period in two plants manufacturing heavy equipment. He found the plant did have a significant effect on number of grievances; however, the kind of work did not. Employees at both plants submitted grievances for similar reasons and seemed to follow the same pattern in terms of rate. Muchinsky and Maassarani (1980) found that depending on the type of work, certain articles of a contract are more likely to be grieved. Public employees who work as prison guards and attendants in state mental hospitals were more likely to file grievances about their own safety and disciplinary actions than were employees in a transportation department. On the other hand, transportation department employees filed more grievances about hours of work and wages. Thus, allegations are directly related to type of work. The most "sensitive" aspects of work are likely to differ from organization to organization.

One may think of grievances as an index of the quality of union/management relations. When the working relationship is good, grievances will be fewer. The soundness of the labor contract cannot be ignored, however; a poorly written or inconsistently interpreted contract invites grievances (Werther, 1974). There can be much grievance activity in a recently unionized organization; employees will use grievances to "test" management's knowledge of the labor contract (Muchinsky & Maassarani, 1981). Particularly in the public sector where collective bargaining is relatively new, public officials are expected to act as "management" although they have little or no training in dealing with labor (Redenius, 1976). Such an imbalance contributes to errors in contract administration. There is much publicity about strike-related issues, but members feel the union's highest priority should be better ways of handling grievances (Kochan, 1979). Unions serve many purposes; however, it seems the most pressing need they fill is ensuring fair treatment in employment. Of course this is a prime reason unions appeal to workers.

# INFLUENCE OF UNIONS ON NONUNIONIZED COMPANIES

Even though they don't have unionized employees, companies are still sensitive to union influence. Companies unresponsive to the needs of employees invite unionization. A nonunion company that wants to remain so must be receptive to the ideas and complaints of its workers. If a company can satisfy employees' needs, a union is not necessary. Said another way, the company voluntarily does what would be forced on it by a labor union.

In a given community or industry, there is often a mix of union and non-union companies. If unionized employees get concessions from management on wages, benefits, hours, etc., these become reference points for nonunionized employees. Thus, a nonunion company may feel compelled to raise wages, for example, to remain competitive. If a labor contract calls for formal grievance procedures, a nonunion company may well follow suit. Workers are aware of employment conditions in other companies. They have a frame of reference for judging their own employment conditions. If a company does not offer comparable conditions, employees may see a union as a means of improving their welfare. This is not to say that nonunion companies must offer *identical* conditions. There are costs associated with a union (e.g., dues); a nonunion company might set wages slightly below those paid in a unionized company so the net effect (higher wages minus dues) is comparable. What economists call the "union/nonunion wage differential" has been the subject of extensive research.

While a prudent nonunion employer will keep abreast of employment conditions in the community and the industry, a company cannot act to keep a union out "at all costs." There is much labor relations legislation. Many laws (like the National Labor Relations Act) were enacted to prohibit unfair practices on both sides. For example, an employer cannot fire a worker just because he or she supports a union. The history of labor relations is full of cases of worker harassment by unions or management to influence attitudes toward a union. But both sides can suffer for breaking the law.

## BEHAVIORAL RESEARCH ON UNION/MANAGEMENT RELATIONS

Thus far, we examined the structure of unions, collective bargaining, and various issues in union/management relations. For the most part, we didn't discuss psychological issues; with the exception of grievances, there is little behavioral research on union/management relations. However, over the past few years, interest in this area has increased. We are beginning to see an interdisciplinary approach to topics which were historically treated with parochialism (Brett, 1980). In the next few pages, we will examine research on union/management relations with a strong behavioral thrust.

A number of studies dealt with why employees support a union, particularly with regard to personal needs and job satisfaction. Feuille and Blandin (1974) sampled the attitudes of over 400 college professors about unionization at a university experiencing many financial and resource cutbacks. The items measured were satisfaction with areas like fairness of the university in making personnel decisions, adequacy of financial support, representation of faculty interests in the state legislature, and salary. The professors were also asked to rate their inclination to accept a union. Professors dissatisfied with employment conditions were much more likely to support a union. Respondents also were consistent in their attitude toward a union and perception of its impact and effectiveness. Those who favored a union saw it as an effective way of protecting employment interests and as having a positive impact. In general, results indicated that unionization is attractive as employment conditions deteriorate.

Using a similar research design and sample, Bigoness (1978) correlated measures of job satisfaction, job involvement, and locus of control with disposition to accept unionization. Bigoness also found that feelings of dissatisfaction related to acceptance of unionization. In particular, dissatisfaction with work, pay, and promotions each correlated .35 with attitude toward unionization. Additionally, unionization was more appealing to people less involved in their jobs and with an external locus of control. Combining all independent variables in a multiple regression equation, Bigoness accounted for over 27 percent of the variance in attitudes toward unionization.

Studies by Hamner and Smith (1978) and Schriesheim (1978) were already discussed. But both merit a brief review. Hamner and Smith (1978) examined union activity in 250 units of a large organization. In half the units, there had been some union activity; in the other half, no activity was reported. Using an immense sample of over 80,000, the authors found that employee attitudes were predictive of level of unionization activity. The strongest predictor was dissatisfaction with supervision. Schriesheim (1978) found that prounion voting in a certification election was positively correlated with dissatisfaction; dissatisfaction with economic facets were also more predictive than dissatisfaction with noneconomic factors. A similar finding was reported by Allen and Keaveny (1981). Faculty member dissatisfaction with economic factors and administration of rewards accounted for most of the variance in support for a union at a university.

What the five studies discussed have in common is they all show that dissatisfaction with employment conditions are predictive of support for unionization. The more satisfied workers are, the less likely they are to think a union is necessary, or that it will improve their welfare. These results are not surprising. They do reveal the facets of dissatisfaction associated with a disposition toward unions. Some authors tout the social benefits of unions (e.g., association with similar people). But it is mainly the perceived economic (not social) advantages that give unions their appeal. However, not all support for unions is based on dissatisfaction with economic conditions. Hammer and Berman (1981) found that faculty at one college wanted a union mainly because they distrusted administrative decision making and were dissatisfied with work content. Prounion voting was motivated by a faculty desire for more power in dealing with the administration.

One myth about unions is that they appeal mostly to blue-collar workers. White-collar employees supposedly have more needs met on the job; thus they are not disposed to unionization. The fallacy of this is evident in the growing number of white-collar employees, mainly in the public sector, becoming unionized. Bass and Mitchell (1976) also provide evidence to refute this. A sample of business managers was asked to rate on a nine-point scale the felt need for unionization among scientists in their organization. The managers' average rating was 2.8; they didn't think scientists would be positive about a union. Yet the scientists' average rating was 5.8, reflecting a moderately strong need. The managers clearly believed the myth that scientists (among other professionals) are not interested in unionization. The data indicate that scientists, like other groups, will accept unions if they are seen as improving employment conditions. *Degree* of support for unions may vary for different occupations; but no group seems categorically opposed to unions.

One alleged fear of college administrators is that faculty unionization will affect organization effectiveness. A recent study by Cameron (1982) dealt with this in 41 colleges. Faculty in 18 colleges were unionized, in 23 they were not. Cameron proposed nine indexes of effectiveness for a college involving student academic development, faculty and administrator satisfaction, and ability to acquire resources. Nonunion colleges were significantly more effective on three of the nine indexes; unionized colleges were not significantly more effective on any. Cameron also collected attitude data from faculty members on five factors relating to their work. These results are presented in Figure 14–5. Faculty power and red tape were seen as increasing since unionization; collegiality was seen as decreasing. The study revealed some major differences in effectiveness of union and nonunion colleges; however, the cause was not determined. Unionization may "cause" colleges to be less effective, which would be a strong argument against unions. However, the less effective colleges may turn to unions to improve. This is obviously an argument supporting unionization in some

**Figure 14–5**              **Perceptions of the effects of faculty unionization**

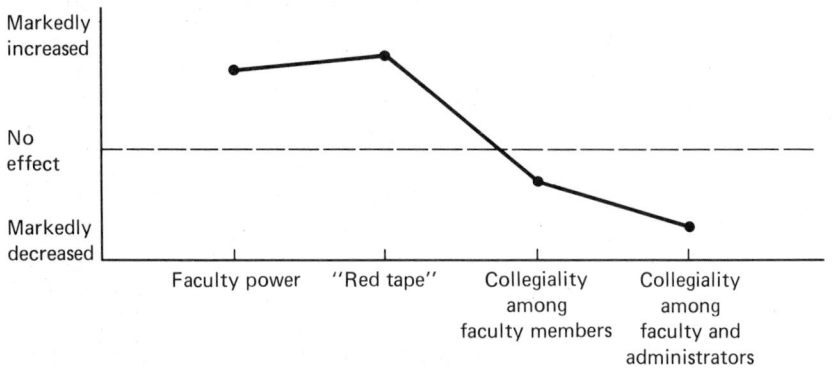

SOURCE: K. Cameron, "The Relationship between Faculty Unionism and Organizational Effectiveness," *Academy of Management Journal* 25 (1982), pp. 13.

| **Table 14–2** | **Elements defining the union/management relationships scale** |
|---|---|

| Element number | Statement wording |
|---|---|
| 1 ............ | Both labor and management fully accept the importance of collective bargaining. |
| 2 ............ | The union is strong enough to create a balance of power between labor and management. |
| 3 ............ | Although each party identifies most strongly with its own interests, they know and respect each other's goals. |
| 4 ............ | The parties recognize that they have certain goals in common. |
| 5 ............ | Management has a strong, well-organized labor relations program. |
| 6 ............ | Communication between parties, other than negotiations, is highly developed. |
| 7 ............ | Negotiations are carried out with intelligence, preparation, and a sincere desire to achieve results. |
| 8 ............ | The contract is understood and effectively administered in good faith by both parties. |
| 9 ............ | The grievance procedure is comprehensively structured with a binding final step. |
| 10 ............ | Both parties continually evaluate the effectiveness of their relationship with the other party. |
| 11 ............ | Employees feel a sense of participation in their general welfare as a result of collective bargaining. |

SOURCE: L. L. Biasatti and J. E. Martin, "A Measure of the Quality of Union-Management Relationships," *Journal of Applied Psychology* 64 (1979), p. 388.

colleges. As discussed in Chapter 2, causality is difficult to determine. In this context, the union/effectiveness question awaits more research.

With the interest in measuring work-related variables, it is not surprising that there has been I/O research on the quality of union/management relations. Biasatti and Martin (1979) identified 11 elements common to the union/management relationship. The authors developed a survey measuring the quality of this relationship. The 11 elements are shown in Table 14–2. Union and management officials were asked whether these elements were present in their relationship. The scale was found to have high internal consistency reliability, and the correlation between the way management and the union perceived their relationship was .83. Biasatti and Martin felt their scale may help parties identify problems in their relationship that could be improved on by mutual effort.

In the last chapter, we discussed job enrichment, and added there are always organization costs of enriching jobs. Giles and Holley (1978) examined how often union workers wanted contract negotiations to involve five issues: pay, fringe benefits, working conditions, job security, and job enrichment. Employees at two plants, one manufacturing, the other food processing, were asked to indicate their preferences. The results are shown in Table 14–3.

Job enrichment received the lowest mean rating at both plants. This

**Table 14–3**

**Perceptions of the time representatives should devote to certain issues of union members at two plants**

| Negotiation issue | Plant A | Plant B |
|---|---|---|
| Fringe benefits | 28% | 17% |
| Pay | 24 | 47 |
| Job security | 18 | 14 |
| Working conditions | 16 | 13 |
| Job enrichment | 13 | 9 |

SOURCE: W. F. Giles and W. H. Holley, "Job Enrichment versus Traditional Issues at the Bargaining Table: What Union Members Want," *Academy of Management Journal* 21 (1978), p. 728.

suggests that members don't particularly want unions to actively bargain for job enrichment. It is not that union workers are absolutely *uninterested* in enriched jobs; but compared to other issues, job enrichment is relatively unimportant. In both plants, traditional economic issues of pay and fringe benefits got higher ratings than the noneconomic issues of working conditions, job security, and job enrichment. An alternative explanation is that job enrichment is not seen as a legitimate union function, so union employees did not give it a high rating. Indeed, Holley, Feild, and Crowley (1981) reported that union members expressing a strong preference for job enrichment also indicated a strong preference for more union-management cooperation in addressing work problems. Some union members seem supportive of job enrichment, but they look to joint union-management participation to attain it.

Hammer (1978) proposed the strength of a union (indexed by the wages of members) related to members' views of various work-related outcomes. Studying 17 unions, Hammer found that the stronger the union was measured to be, the more likely members felt they would be promoted, held secure jobs, and received good pay. In stronger unions, workers collaborated more with each other (e.g., sought co-worker's advice on problems, accepted supervisor's advice) than in weaker unions. In general, Hammer felt the strength of a union influences worker's motivation, performance, and satisfaction. Hammer developed a model showing the union's role in shaping attitudes and behavior; this is shown in Figure 14–6. Understanding of motivation, performance, and satisfaction is evidently improved by knowledge of union characteristics. For example, unions can affect the ease with which employees perform their jobs by offering special training, requiring apprenticeships, or giving members leadership experience in union activities. Through labor contracts, amount of work (such as flight hours per month for airline pilots), speed (controlling the assembly line), overtime per worker, or kinds of tasks an employee can perform (production workers can't repair broken equipment) can also be restricted. Hammer's model clearly indicates that unions play a significant role in topics traditionally studied by I/O psychologists; to date, this has rarely been acknowledged.

Finally, a major study by Gordon, Philpot, Burt, Thompson, and Spiller (1980) is the latest and perhaps strongest invitation for I/O psychologists to engage in union research. The goal was investigating worker commitment to the union. Employees differ in this; the study sought to unravel some determinants of union commitment. The focus of this study parallels organization commitment, discussed in Chapter 8.

The authors developed a questionnaire measuring commitment; this was completed by more than 1,800 union members. Responses were factor analyzed. "Union commitment" is actually composed of four dimensions: (1) loyalty, (2) responsibility to the union, (3) willingness to work for the union, and (4) belief in unionism. The research had at least two major benefits for unions. First, the questionnaires could be used by unions to assess the effect of their actions and estimate solidarity, especially before negotiations. Second, the research revealed the importance of socializing new union members. The authors felt union commitment is increased when formal and informal efforts are made to involve a member in union activities soon after joining. Co-worker attitudes and willingness to help are crucial to the socialization process. Improving socialization of new members improves their commitment, which is one index of union strength.

The Gordon et al. (1980) study is particularly significant in that it was not "authorized" by management to improve understanding of unions. The

**Figure 14–6**         **The union's role in a motivation-performance-satisfaction model**

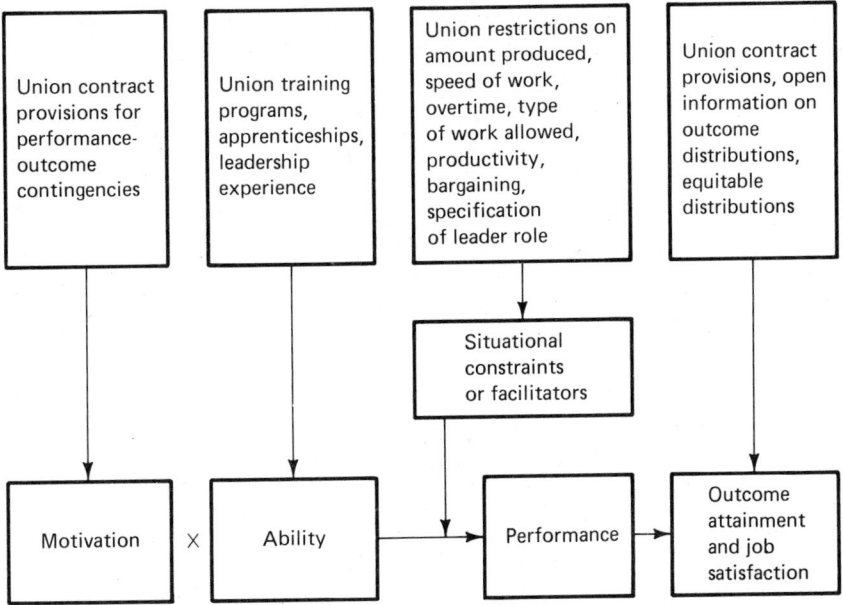

SOURCE: T. H. Hammer, "Relationships between Local Union Characteristics and Worker Behavior and Attitudes," *Academy of Management Journal* 21 (1978), p. 573.

study is a sincere effort of I/O psychologists to examine unions from the union perspective, and, in the long-run, help the union. The studies reviewed in this section are encouraging and refreshing in that I/O research does not always involve *management* problems. The balance in examining problems from union and management perspectives will enhance the value of I/O research. The studies discussed suggest that I/O psychology is moving toward more balance.

## UNIONS AND THE CONTENT OF I/O PSYCHOLOGY

This book is organized around areas of I/O psychology. At the start of this chapter, we said that unions have a strong influence on the work world. It is thus instructive to examine some of the ways unions affect the areas of I/O psychology. While this presentation is not intended to be exhaustive, it will reveal there is a pervasive union influence upon the substantive topics addressed by I/O psychology.

**Personnel selection**

In union and nonunion companies, management determines the knowledge, skills, and abilities needed to fill jobs. The personnel office usually determines fitness for employment in lower-level jobs. For higher-level jobs, responsibility is spread through various units of the company. However, in a union company, the labor contract may stipulate that those hired for jobs represented by the union *must* join the union. This is a *union shop;* the employee has no choice about joining.[1] In other unionized companies, the employee has the *choice* of joining a union. That is an *open shop.* However, considerable pressure can be brought on an employee to join. In many cases, it is also to the employee's advantage to join the union for the benefits and protection it affords.

Union influence in personnel selection can affect both applicant and company. Those who don't endorse unions (or who are uncertain of them) may not apply for jobs in union companies. Obviously, the applicant pool for unionized companies is reduced if such feelings are common. The extent of this problem will vary with antiunion sentiment and availability of other jobs.

Union influence can also work in reverse. One company I know of prides itself on remaining nonunionized. They believe unionization is encouraged by employees with prior union experience. They therefore carefully screen applicants for union membership. Those who have been members are not considered. (However, they are not told why). The company wants applicants with the talent needed for the job; but they place a higher priority on avoiding unionism. Whether the company can continue this without

---

[1]However, some states have "right-to-work" laws prohibiting union shops.

adversely affecting the quality of the work force depends on the jobs for which applicants are considered, and the number of applicants seeking employment with the company. Thus, from the perspectives of the applicant and the company, unions can and do ultimately influence who gets hired.

## Personnel training

One area in which unions have direct and significant influence is in personnel training. One of the oldest forms of training is apprenticeship, and unions have a long history of this kind of training, especially in trades and crafts. Apprenticeship is governed by law and, at the national level, it is administered by the U.S. Department of Labor. The Bureau of Apprenticeship and Training works closely with unions, vocational schools, state agencies, and others. According to the Department of Labor (1977), there are over 425 apprenticed occupations employing over a quarter of a million apprentices. Apprentices go through a formal program of training and experience. They are supervised on the job and are given the facilities needed for instruction. There is a progressive schedule of wages over the course of an apprenticeship, which normally lasts several years. Upon completion of apprenticeship, the individual is well versed in all aspects of the trade. Some authors (e.g., Franklin, 1976) think apprenticeship training is unnecessarily long; but there is little doubt that such programs turn out highly-skilled artisans.

Most apprentice programs are in heavily unionized occupations (construction, manufacturing, transportation); thus, unions work closely with the Bureau of Apprenticeship and Training. For example, Figure 14–7 shows the cooperation among various organizations and agencies in the carpentry trade. Not all unions are involved in apprentice programs; but the link between unions and apprenticeship is one of the oldest in the history of American labor.

## Performance appraisal

A labor contract might specify the dimensions of job performance that will be evaluated. Management may prefer certain aspects, like attendance, while the union may feel that quality of work is salient. Together, they decide which aspects will be appraised and the uses of appraisal information. Usually, raises are based on merit and seniority; the union may negotiate the contribution of merit in the wage decision. It is of obvious benefit to the union to appraise the "relevant" aspects of work (particularly to supply workers with feedback on performance); but union and management may not agree on the relevant aspects. As with all disputes, disagreements over performance appraisal must be negotiated.

## Job satisfaction

We have already discussed at some length research showing that worker dissatisfaction is associated with a disposition toward unions. Other re-

**Figure 14–7**

**Illustration of the cooperation between unions, industry, and government in the apprenticeship system of the carpentry trade**

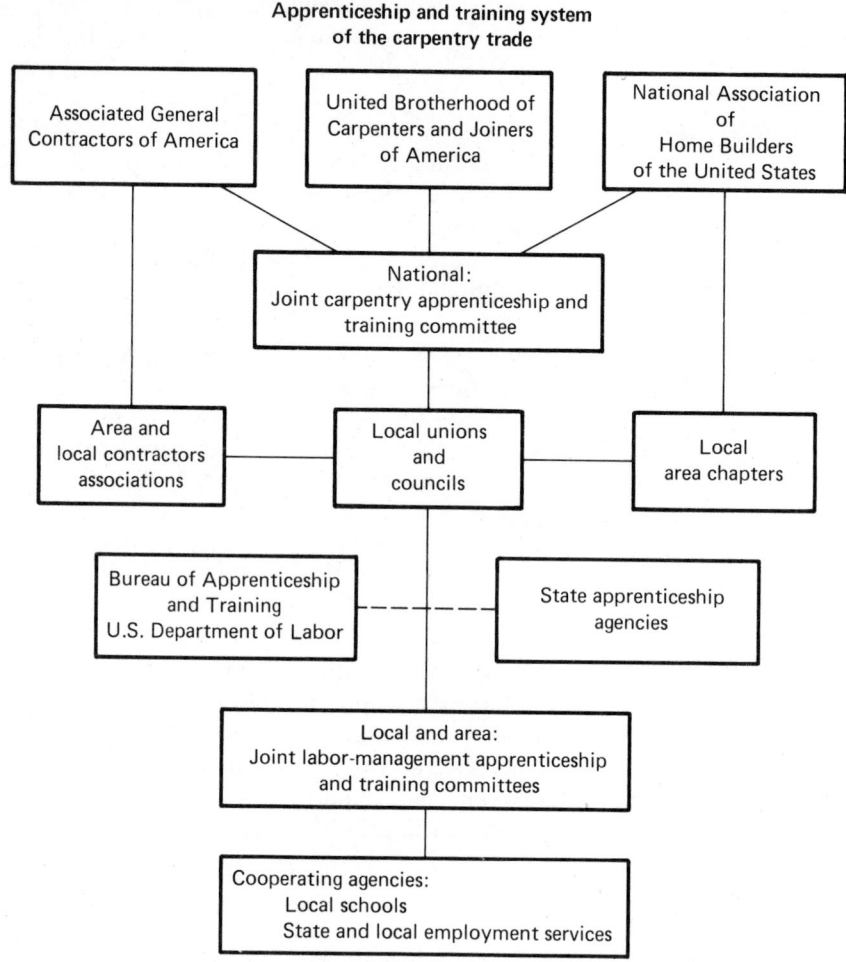

**Apprenticeship and training system of the carpentry trade**

SOURCE: U.S. Department of Labor, *Apprenticeship: Past and Present* (Washington, D.C.: U.S. Government Printing Office, 1977), p. 25.

search, most notably by Hammer (1978), showed that satisfaction with pay, working conditions, and security is associated with union status. Unions are seen as *instrumental*. (They help employees attain certain outcomes.) Thus, these findings are not surprising. In fact, if better pay, fringe benefits, job security, etc., were *not* related to union status, it is unlikely that unions would survive.

There are no studies definitely showing whether unionized employees are more or less satisfied. Differences in personal characteristics, type of company, strength of the union, and many other factors would probably moderate this relationship. It should also be recalled that job satisfaction is multifaceted. Union workers may feel more satisfied with certain aspects (like job secuirty) but less satisfied with others (like autonomy). Satisfaction is influenced by unions. Dissatisfaction with conditions invites unionization; workers dissatisfied with their unions can vote to expel them. This is union *decertification*.

## Motivation

From various theoretical perspectives, unions should influence motivation. The direction of influence (more or less) is debated. According to need theory, unions should fill basic or existence needs; this allows employees to seek fulfillment of higher-order needs. According to expectancy theory, unions are instrumental in attaining desired outcomes like good pay, job security, fringe benefits, and so on. The union enhances instrumentality. According to the theory, this provides for greater motivation.

Some authors think unions suppress motivation. For example, to the extent that unions enhance group solidarity, the strength of a group norm to limit productivity may be greater than in a nonunion company. One can think of limiting production as an artificial restriction in outputs, which is a component of the equity theory approach to motivation. However, the norm of production limitation has been observed in both union and nonunion companies; we can't conclude that unions per se "cause" production limits.

One allegation of administrators is unionization of college professors would decrease intrinsic motivation. Professionals are supposedly intrinsically motivated by love of their work; it is feared that unions will weaken this and lower output. To date, there is little evidence that professors are any less (or more) productive after unionization. If we infer motivation from productivity, research suggests that unionization does not have an appreciable effect on the motivation of college professors. Whether unions *cause* increases or decreases in motivation must be solved by complex, longitudinal research. No definitive *empirical* study has answered this question. From a *theoretical* perspective, unions should influence motivation.

## Leadership

There is little research on how leadership is affected by unions. As part of the validation of the Leader Behavior Description Questionnaire from the Ohio State leadership studies, Fleishman and Harris (1962) showed that the amount of consideration and initiation of structure supervisors demonstrated did influence the turnover and grievances of unionized employees. However, these findings probably would be replicated irrespective of union status.

Other areas are ripe for investigation. Union members vote for shop stewards and officials representing them in collective bargaining. Union members seem to believe certain characteristics are more effective in bargaining. They vote for those who best exemplify these characteristics (Stagner, 1956). There are differences in elected union leaders: some unions favor more outspoken, militant types; others, more experienced and diplomatic types. Management also seeks certain "types" of leaders they feel can deal with a union, especially during contract negotiations. In short, there is little doubt that certain characteristics are desired by both union and management in dealing with each other; the exact nature has yet to be studied empirically.

## Organizational communication

Unions influence communication within organizations. One of the major reasons employees accept a union is better communication with management. Management must formally direct its communication to the aggregated work force if the latter is organized.

Grievances are a major channel of communication in an organization. Workers communicate formal complaints, and management must respond. Some authors contend that grievances are partially meant to "keep management on their toes" and keep it aware of the union. Another major form of union-inspired communication is contract negotiation and administration. Communication is particularly intense during negotiation; but even day-to-day interpretation and administration of the contract can involve continuous union-management communication. One of the major duties of the shop steward is communicating employees' cases to management. Other examples of union-based communication include union newsletters, union/management committees, interactions between the local and national union, and solicitation of new members. In keeping with the concept of a union as "an organization within an organization," union communication can be classified as intraorganizational (communication within the local union), interorganizational (communication with management), and extraorganizational (communication with the national union). Communication is clearly a dominant thread in the union/management fabric.

## SUMMARY

We have examined a topic long neglected by I/O psychologists. Whatever the legitimate or illegitimate reasons, the tide appears to be turning. It is hoped that interest in research on unions over the past five years will continue. While I/O psychologists profess interest in human problems in the work world, we simply cannot ignore the impact of unions in this environment. Indeed, as Gordon and Nurick (1981) stated, knowledge of organization behavior is incomplete without understanding union influence.

The first part of this chapter reviewed union/management relations. Most of this material is not psychological; it is of great importance in understanding unions, collective bargaining, and union/management relations. Next we examined some recent research on unions. In this area, psychology is beginning to make a contribution. Finally, we reviewed how unions influence the basic areas of I/O psychology. Employee selection, training, performance appraisal, motivation, satisfaction, and communication are all affected by unions.

# CASE STUDY

Carl Dwyer and Ann Stovos were faculty members at Springdale College. The college had been in existence for about 30 years, and Dwyer had been on the staff almost since the beginning. Stovos was a relative newcomer, just completing her third year as a faculty member. For the past two years, there had been talk about unionizing the faculty. Much of the interest was sparked by two events. First, the college had experienced financial cutbacks due to low enrollment. Without tuition revenue, the college was facing hardships paying the faculty. As a result, six teaching positions had been eliminated. The faculty understood the college's financial problems, but they felt cutbacks should be made in other areas, like eliminating some administrative positions. The faculty was also critical of how the college determined which teaching positions were eliminated.

The other event was that for the third year in a row, the faculty were given only a 5 percent raise. Other colleges in the state were giving bigger raises, and some of the Springdale faculty felt they were getting the short end of the stick.

Various union representatives had been on campus; there was enough support for a representation election to be held in about a month. The faculty really seemed divided. Some openly supported a union, some were openly opposed, but the majority didn't voice their sentiments. Carl Dwyer was opposed to the idea of collective bargaining, while Ann Stovos supported it. Since they were office mates, the topic came up quite often. On this particular day, they were discussing whether the goals of unions were compatible with the goals of higher education.

Dwyer began the conversation. "I just don't think there is any place in a college for burly picketers carrying placards and threatening to beat up anyone who crosses the picket line. A college is a place for quiet scholarly thought, an opportunity to teach interested students, and to contemplate some of the deeper values. I've been here since we had only five buildings and a staff of 20. I don't want to see this place turned into a playground for skull crushers."

"You've been watching too many movies, Carl," Stovos replied. "No one is going to turn Springdale into a battlefield. I want the same things you do. I didn't come here to be physically intimidated. I wouldn't like that any more than you do. But I also want to be treated fairly by the administration. I'd like some security from arbitrary decisions. There's nothing immoral about that, is there?"

"Do you think a union can prevent layoffs and get us 25 percent yearly raises?" Dwyer asked facetiously.

"No I don't," Stovos countered, "but a union can force the drafting of fair and equitable policies if layoffs have to occur. And if everyone else is getting 10 percent raises, maybe they can help us there, too. A union won't work miracles, but it can help to prevent injustice."

"You don't understand, Ann. A college is not a factory. Different ideals run a college. It's not profit, but scholarship. We have to foster a climate for inquisitive minds, learning, and personal growth. If I were only interested in making a buck, I wouldn't have become a college professor," Dwyer replied.

"Whether you like it or not, Carl, we are employees like all other working people. What's wrong with trying to ensure fair treatment at work? We have bills to pay and families to support, just like everyone else. I don't understand why a college is somehow 'different' from all other employers," Stovos rejoined.

"That's the problem in a nutshell," Dwyer added. "A college is not just an *employer,* and we just don't have *jobs.* We have *careers,* and the success of our career depends on an environment which supports what we are trying to do. Union organizers, picket lines, labor contracts, and mediators have no place in a college."

"I don't see why a college is somehow 'immune' from having to treat its employees fairly like every other employer. What makes a college so special?" Stovos asked.

"Twenty years ago—10 years ago even—the very thought of a union would have been absurd. The fact that we're now considering one is just proof the quality of education in this country is going downhill. I can just see it now. 'Sorry class, this is our last meeting. I'm going on strike Monday,' " Dwyer fumed. He got up from his desk, grabbed his coat and hat, and headed off for a meeting.

Stovos shot back: "I suppose you'd feel better if you met you class for the last time because *you* were one of the ones whose position got eliminated."

Dwyer didn't answer, but he slammed the door on the way out.

Questions

1. Do you feel that Dwyer is correct in believing a union would interfere with the goals of higher education?
2. What benefits does Stovos see from unionization?
3. Do you believe that some organizations, because of their purpose and goals, should not have unionized employees? If so, which ones and why?
4. Do you think the respective lengths of time that Dwyer and Stovos have spent at the college have any relationship to their attitudes? Why or why not?
5. When you think of unions, what thoughts come to mind? Why do you feel as you do?

# REFERENCES

Allen, R. E., & Keaveny, T. J. Correlates of university faculty interest in unionization: A replication and extension. *Journal of Applied Psychology*, 1981, *66*, 582–588.

Ash, P. The parties to the grievance. *Personnel Psychology*, 1970, *23*, 13–37.

Bakke, E. W. Why workers join unions. *Personnel*, 1945, *22*, 37–46.

Bass, B. M., & Mitchell, C. W. Influences on the felt need for collective bargaining by business and science professionals. *Journal of Applied Psychology*, 1976, *61*, 770–773.

Biasatti, L. L., & Martin, J. E. A measure of the quality of union-management relationships. *Journal of Applied Psychology*, 1979, *64*, 387–390.

Bigoness, W. J. Correlates of faculty attitudes toward collective bargaining. *Journal of Applied Psychology*, 1978, *63*, 228–233.

Bok, D., & Dunlop, J. *Labor and the American community*. New York: Simon & Schuster, 1970.

Brett, J. M. Behavioral research on unions and union management systems. In B. M. Staw & L. L. Cummings (Eds.), *Research in organizational behavior*. Greenwich, Conn.: JAI Press, 1980.

Brief, A. P., & Rude, D. E. Voting in a union certification election: A conceptual analysis. *Academy of Management Review*, 1981, *6*, 261–267.

Cameron, K. The relationship between faculty unionism and organizational effectiveness. *Academy of Management Journal*, 1982, *25*, 6–24.

Dalton, D. R., & Todor, W. D. Manifest needs of stewards: Propensity to file a grievance. *Journal of Applied Psychology*, 1979, *64*, 654–659.

Dalton, D. R., & Todor, W. D. Antecedents of grievance filing behavior: Attitude/behavioral consistency and the union steward. *Academy of Management Journal*, 1982, *25*, 158–169.

DeCotiis, T. A., & LeLouarn, J. Y. A predictive study of voting behavior in a representation election using union instrumentality and work perceptions. *Organizational Behavior and Human Performance*, 1981, *27*, 103–118.

Dubno, P. The role of the psychologist in labor unions. *American Psychologist*, 1957, *12*, 212–215.

Eckerman, A. C. An analysis of grievances and aggrieved employees in a machine shop and foundry. *Journal of Applied Psychology*, 1948, *32*, 255–269.

Estey, M. *The unions: Structure, development, and management* (3rd ed.). New York: Harcourt Brace Jovanovich, 1981.

Feuille, P., & Blandin, J. Faculty job satisfaction and bargaining sentiments: A case study. *Academy of Management Journal*, 1974, *17*, 678–692.

Fleischman, E. A., & Harris, E. F. Patterns of leadership behavior related to employee grievances and turnover. *Personnel Psychology*, 1962, *15*, 43–56.

Franklin, W. S. Are construction apprenticeships too long? *Labor Law Journal*, 1976, *27*, 99–106.

Giles, W. F., & Holley, W. H. Job enrichment versus traditional issues at the bargaining table: What union members want. *Academy of Management Journal*, 1978, *21*, 725–730.

Glueck, W. F. *Personnel: A diagnostic approach*. Plano, Tex.: Business Publications, 1974.

Gordon, M. E., & Nurick, A. J. Psychological approaches to the study of unions and union-management relations. *Psychological Bulletin*, 1981, *90*, 293–306.

Gordon, M. E., Philpot, J. W., Burt, R. E., Thompson, C. A., & Spiller, W. E. Commitment to the union: Development of a measure and an examination of its correlates. *Journal of Applied Psychology*, 1980, *65*, 479–499.

Hammer, T. H. Relationships between local union characteristics and worker behavior and attitudes. *Academy of Management Journal*, 1978, *21*, 560–577.

Hammer, T. H., & Berman, M. The role of noneconomic factors in faculty union voting. *Journal of Applied Psychology*, 1981, *66*, 415–421.

Hamner, W. C., & Smith, F. J. Work attitudes as predictors of unionization activity. *Journal of Applied Psychology*, 1978, *63*, 415–421.

Holley, W. H., Feild, H. S., & Crowley, J. C. Negotiating quality of worklife, productivity, and traditional issues: Union members' preferred roles of their union. *Personnel Psychology*, 1981, *34*, 309–328.

Kissler, G. D. Grievance activity and union membership: A study of government employees. *Journal of Applied Psychology*, 1977, *62*, 459–462.

Kochan, T. A. How American workers view labor unions. *Monthly Labor Review*, 1979, *102*(4), 23–31.

Kochan, T. A. *Collective bargaining and industrial relations*. Homewood, Ill.: Richard D. Irwin, 1980.

Muchinsky, P. M., & Maassarani, M. A. Work environment effects on public sector grievances. *Personnel Psychology*, 1980, *33*, 403–414.

Muchinsky, P. M., & Maassarani, M. A. Public sector grievances in Iowa. *Journal of Collective Negotiations*, 1981, *10*, 55–62.

Redenius, C. Public employees: A survey of some critical problems on the frontier of collective bargaining. *Labor Law Journal*, 1976, *27*, 588–599.

Ronan, W. W. Work group attributes and grievance activity. *Journal of Applied Psychology*, 1963, *47*, 38–41.

Rosen, H., & Stagner, R. Industrial/organizational psychology and unions: A viable relationship? *Professional Psychology*, 1980, *11*, 477–483.

Schriesheim, C. A. Job satisfaction, attitudes toward unions, and voting in a union representation election. *Journal of Applied Psychology*, 1978, *63*, 548–552.

Sherman, V. C. Unionism and the non-union company. *Personnel Journal*, 1969, *48*, 413–422.

Shostak, A. B. Industrial psychology and the trade unions: A matter of mutual indifference. In G. Fisk (Ed.), *The frontiers of management psychology*. New York: Harper & Row, 1964.

Stagner, R. *Psychology of industrial conflict*. New York: John Wiley & Sons, 1956.

Stagner, R. Implications of psychology in labor-management relations: Comments on the symposium. *Personnel Psychology*, 1961, *14*, 279–284.

Stagner, R., & Eflal, B. Internal union dynamics during a strike: A quasi-experimental study. *Journal of Applied Psychology*, 1982, *67*, 37–44.

Stagner, R., & Rosen, H. *Psychology of union-management relations*. Belmont, Calif.: Wadsworth, 1965.

Sulkin, H. A., & Pranis, R. W. Comparison of grievants with non-grievants in a heavy machinery company. *Personnel Psychology*, 1957, *10*, 27–42.

Tannenbaum, A. S. Unions. In J. G. March (Ed.), *Handbook of organizations*. Skokie, Ill.: Rand McNally, 1965.

Thayer, P., & McGehee, W. On the effectiveness of not holding a formal training course. *Personnel Psychology*, 1977, *30*, 455–456.

U.S. Department of Labor. *Apprenticeship: Past and present*. Washington, D.C.: U.S. Government Printing Office, 1977.

Walton, R. E., & McKersie, R. B. *A behavioral theory of labor negotiations*. New York: McGraw-Hill, 1965.

Werther, W. B. Reducing grievances through effective contract administration. *Labor Law Journal*, 1974, *25*, 211–216.

# chapter 15    WORK CONDITIONS

People work under a broad array of conditions. For example, most work indoors, some outdoors. Some jobs require exposure to intense heat, cold, and noise; the conditions in others are temperate. Many people work from 8:00 A.M. to 5:00 P.M., but other hours are also common. Some jobs involve a high risk of injury or illness; others are low risk. How do these different conditions affect attitudes and behavior? What have I/O psychologists learned about responses to variations in working conditions? This chapter is devoted to how work conditions affect the employee.

Before we begin, it should be acknowledged that research in this area has been conducted in a wide range of professions. Though I/O psychology has made many contributions to the area, so have engineering, physiology, and medicine. Engineers have designed tools, equipment, and work procedures to minimize employee stress and fatigue. Physiologists have studied the effect of heat, cold, and noise (and other forms of physical stress) on the human body. Physicians studying industrial medicine examine the relationship between certain illnesses and types of work, like black lung disease among coal miners and cancer among asbestos workers. Thus, research on working conditions and employee behavior is interdisciplinary. Many of the questions addressed extend beyond I/O psychology; but our profession is a primary contributor to the area.

534

# STRESSORS IN THE WORKPLACE

As discussed in Chapter 8, stress is highly complex and multifaceted. In the approach of Beehr and Newman (1978), the causes of stress include work demands and characteristics, role pressures, and organization characteristics. We discussed how role pressures contribute to stress in Chapter 8. In this chapter, we will examine how work demands (noise, heat, and cold) and some organization characteristics (most notably work hours) contribute. There are wide individual differences associated with perception of stress. That is, one person may feel stressed by a hectic schedule, another may enjoy the challenge and variety. Any stimulus (e.g., work pace, noise, role pressure) that elicits a stress response is a *stressor*. We will now examine several stressors associated with the physical conditions of work; for the most part, they elicit fairly consistent stress responses. However, the *degree* of stress is often moderated by individual differences.

**Noise**

Before we examine the effects of noise on performance, we must understand the characteristics of sound. Two physical characteristics are *frequency* and *intensity;* their psychological counterparts are *pitch* and *loudness.* Sound emanates in waves. If the sound is "pure" (like a tuning fork), a graph of the wave looks like a sine (sinusoidal) wave. Low-frequency sounds have fewer wave repetitions per unit of time than high-frequency sounds. In fact, the number of waves per second is the frequency. Frequency is usually measured in cycles per second (cps), or Hertz (Hz). Impure sounds have more complex wave patterns because they are composed of differing frequencies. The psychological analogue of frequency is pitch; we recognize this by saying that a tenor has a different pitch than a soprano.

Intensity of sound is usually measured in decibels (dB) and reflects differences in sound energy. Differences in frequency are represented by differences in waves per second; differences in intensity are represented by differences in the height of the waves. "Loud" sounds have more intensity than "soft" sounds. Figure 15–1 shows various sounds and associated decibel values.

It is difficult to say definitely what effect noise has on performance since "performance" has been examined in many contexts. Some aspects of performance are more affected by noise than others. Early research on noise stress (e.g., Broadbent, 1957) suggested that only when levels exceeded 90 decibels was there an appreciable decrease in performance. However, later research indicates that much lower levels can disrupt certain dimensions of performance. In particular, Cohen (1968) found that tasks requiring concentration are more likely to be adversely affected by noise.

Additional research added to our knowledge of how noise affects people, and reveals the complexity of this relationship. Fiedler and Fiedler (1975)

**Figure 15–1** | **Decibel levels for various sounds**

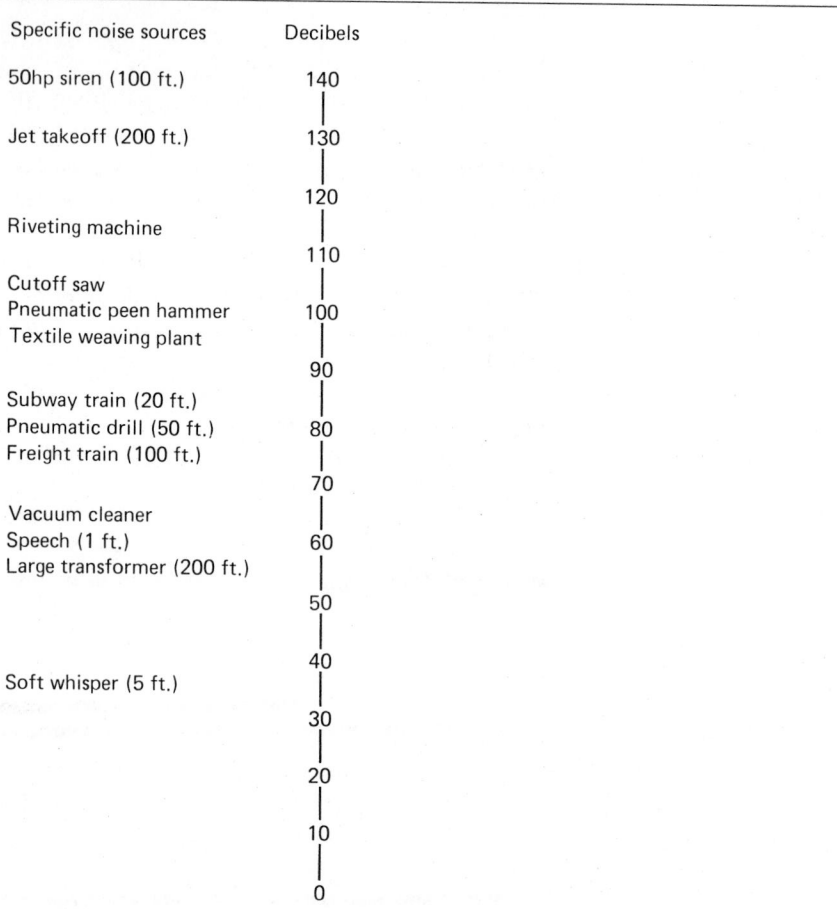

| Specific noise sources | Decibels |
|---|---|
| 50hp siren (100 ft.) | 140 |
| Jet takeoff (200 ft.) | 130 |
| | 120 |
| Riveting machine | 110 |
| Cutoff saw | |
| Pneumatic peen hammer | 100 |
| Textile weaving plant | |
| | 90 |
| Subway train (20 ft.) | |
| Pneumatic drill (50 ft.) | 80 |
| Freight train (100 ft.) | |
| | 70 |
| Vacuum cleaner | |
| Speech (1 ft.) | 60 |
| Large transformer (200 ft.) | |
| | 50 |
| | 40 |
| Soft whisper (5 ft.) | |
| | 30 |
| | 20 |
| | 10 |
| | 0 |

SOURCE: A. P. Petersen and F. E. Gross, *Handbook of Noise Measurement,* 8th ed. (New Concord, Mass.: GenRad, 1978).

compared the verbal and behavioral reactions of people living near a large airport and those in communities out of the airport's noise range. In general, people who lived near the airport developed ways of coping with, adjusting to, or ignoring the noise. There were few differences between the two groups in such variables as headaches or nervousness, disruption of social lives, and the length of residence. This indicates that some people, at least, can adjust to noise. The authors also found wide individual differences in noise tolerance. Some people complained of noise-induced headaches, irritability, and sleeplessness even though they lived in areas free of aircraft-related noise or noise from heavy highway traffic. The proportion of people complaining about noise was equivalent in the two groups. The results suggest that aircraft-related noise did not systematically affect many lives.

Finkelman et al. (1977) examined the extent that noise adversely affects driving. Drivers were asked to follow a course marked with pylons, driving as fast as possible without knocking any down. The noise stressor was 93 dB bursts of white (undifferentiated) noise from a speaker in the rear of the car. The noise came in 3-, 6-, and 9-second bursts, with 3, 5, and 7 seconds of silence, all in random order. Performance was compared with and without noise. Though noise increased driving time through the course, for most drivers it decreased accuracy (more pylons were knocked over). Drivers seem willing to increase the risk of accident rather than sacrifice driving time. Similar to Cohen's (1968) findings, these authors found performance requiring concentration can be impaired by noise.

Weinstein (1978) studied sensitivity of college students to noise in a dormitory. A sample of college freshmen completed a self-report measure of noise sensitivity before they arrived on campus. Two groups were created based on the scores: a noise-sensitive and a noise-insensitive group. Performance of both groups on a number of variables was monitored during freshmen year. Sensitive students were much more bothered by dormitory noise and became increasingly disturbed by noise over the year. They also had less academic ability, felt less secure socially, and had a greater desire for privacy. Unlike those in the airport study, college students couldn't adjust to or ignore dormitory noise. The results suggest that colleges might consider providing noise-sensitive students with special housing so they can adjust to a typically noisy environment.

It should be apparent that there are no simple relationships between noise and human performance. Noise adversely affects performance of some tasks but not others. Additionally, some people are more sensitive to noise than others. To the extent that I/O psychologists can (1) identify tasks where noise impairs performance, and (2) identify people sensitive to noise, steps can be taken to improve the worker/workplace fit. Headphones and sound-proofed construction material can be used in jobs prone to interference from noise. People can be hired based on sensitivity to noise. As we stated, with differences in jobs and differences in people, the I/O psychologist's job is getting as good a match as possible between abilities and work requirements.

**Hearing loss from work.**   Employees exposed to intense noise over long periods of time usually lose a portion of their hearing. If the noise is of a particular frequency, partial or complete hearing loss to tones of that frequency is quite possible. Employees exposed to intense noises over the full spectrum of frequencies may suffer a general decrease.

A study by LaBenz, Cohen, and Pearson (1967) provides empirical evidence of work-related hearing loss. Hearing capacity was examined for earth-moving equipment operators repeatedly exposed to noise levels ranging

**Figure 15–2**     **Mean hearing loss of three groups of earth-moving equipment operators varying in years of exposure**

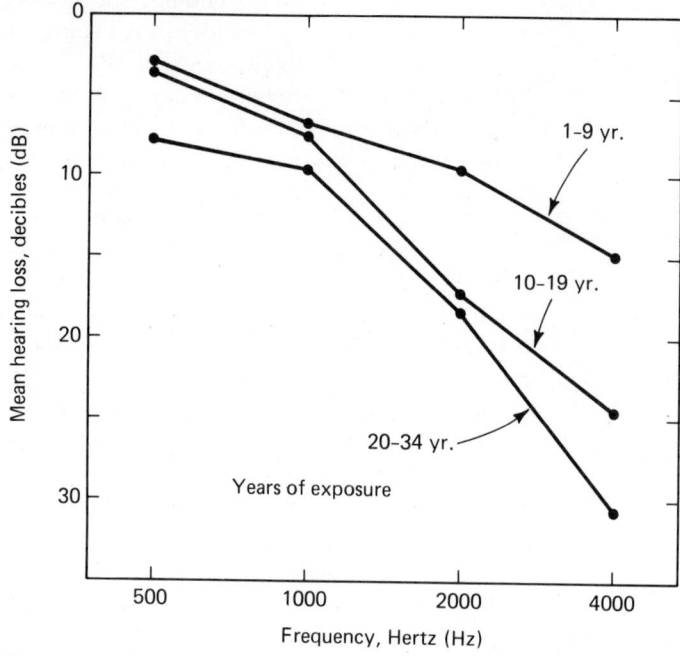

SOURCE: P. LaBenz, A. Cohen, and B. Pearson, "A Noise and Hearing Survey of Earth-Moving Equipment Operators," *American Industrial Hygiene Association Journal* 28 (March–April 1967), pp. 117–28.

from 90 to 120 dB. Hearing tests were given and results compared with estimates of hearing loss typical for individuals of comparable age. Figure 15–2 shows the respective losses for three groups of operators differing in years of exposure, corrected for the age. The hearing loss is particularly acute at higher frequencies for more experienced workers.

To protect workers in noisy jobs (like airline ground employees, construction workers, and data processors) from hearing loss, companies provide headphones or earplugs. Many labor contracts specify that not wearing such safety equipment is grounds for dismissal. Some companies also approach the problem of noise stress via personnel selection, hiring partially or totally deaf people for noisy jobs.

Noise stress is a major concern for some companies. Noisy equipment may have to be reengineered or housed in certain areas to lessen disruptive influences. Special ear protection has been devised, eliminating the intensity of unwanted noise, but not preventing communication among workers. Employees suffering from work-related hearing impairment are eligible for special compensation from employers; some victims of hearing loss have sued employers for not providing safe working conditions. Fortunately, risk of hearing impairment is slight in most jobs, but in jobs where it is a problem, corrective measures are necessary.

**Heat**

Discomfort from heat is due not only to high temperatures. Adjustment to heat is a function of three variables: air temperature, humidity, and air flow. High temperatures, high humidity, and a lack of air flow are most uncomfortable. Some research (e.g., Pepler, 1958) indicated that humidity may be the most important variable in determining discomfort. With high temperature and humidity, rapid air movement can make the situation tolerable. Because the sensation of heat cannot be adequately measured by simply recording air temperature, other indexes have been developed. One used in enclosed environments is the wet-bulb globe temperature (WBGT). This takes into account the effects of humidity in combination with air temperature. The WBGT is a more sensitive index of discomfort than simple air temperature.

Heat stress is a problem not only for those who work outdoors, but also for people working around furnaces, boilers, dryers, and other heat-producing equipment. Heat stress can greatly impair productivity of those doing strenuous work. Workers lose stamina because their bodies are taxed by the combination of heat and physical exertion. However, heat stress can also impair performance in tasks requiring little physical effort, even those limited to mental skills. For example, Fine and Kobrick (1978) compared performance of individuals working on cognitive tasks under different heat-stress conditions. The treatment group worked under 95° F and 88 percent humidity, while two control groups worked under 70° F and 25 percent humidity. Performance was monitored for seven hours. Results are shown in Figure 15–3. The number of errors made by the treatment group was considerably greater, and the extent of the difference became greater over time.

Organizations are aware of the effects of heat and expend a lot of money to cope with the problem. Central air conditioning is a standard feature of most new office buildings. Dehumidifiers are installed where humidity may affect performance or damage sensitive equipment (like computers). Industrial fans are often installed to draw off the heat (and noxious fumes) associated with some types of manufacturing. However, in many cases, the climate cannot be controlled or modified, as in outdoor work. In such cases, workers may be allowed more rest breaks or may be relieved by other crews. Given rising energy costs, it is increasingly expensive to maintain ideal climates. Recent federal laws specify thermostat levels to limit energy consumption. Although I am not aware of formal research on the effects of allowing greater heat stress, workers are probably more uncomfortable, become more irritable, and become tired quicker.

**Figure 15–3**

**Mean percent of errors in cognitive tasks over a seven-hour period for a group working under heat and for two control groups**

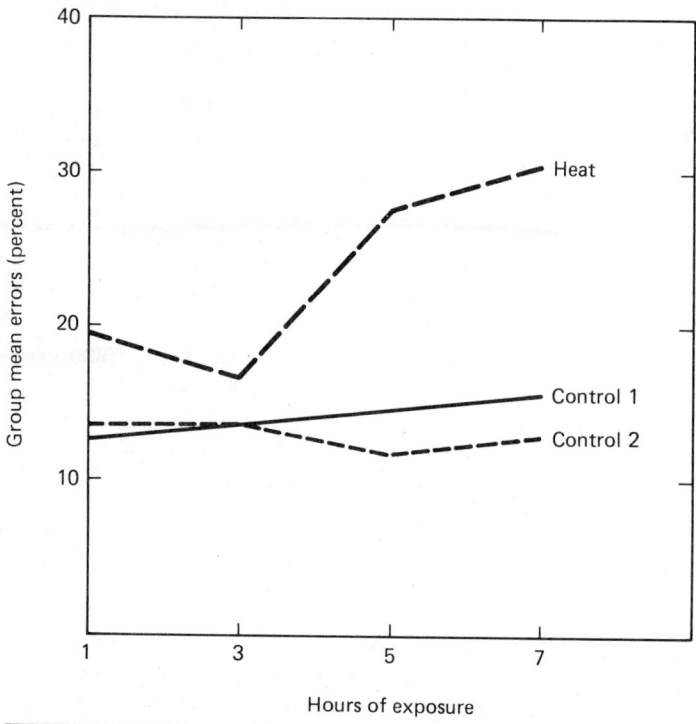

SOURCE: B. J. Fine and J. L. Kobrick, "Effects of Altitude and Heat on Complex Cognitive Tasks," *Human Factors* 20 (1978), pp. 115–22. Copyright 1978 by The Human Factors Society, Inc., and reproduced by permission.

## Cold

Both mental and physical tasks are affected by cold; however, there is evidence that people can adapt to cold over time (Teichner & Kobrick, 1955). Prolonged exposure constricts blood vessels, which reduces blood flow to the skin surface and reduces skin temperature. Under such conditions, exposed skin and extremities (fingers and toes) become numb. Under more extreme conditions, total body temperature will be lowered. Manual performance is adversely affected by lowered body temperature, even when hands are kept warm (Lockhart, 1966). Similar results have been reported for tasks requiring concentration (Poulton, Hitchings, & Brooke, 1965). In attempting to explain this, Fox (1967) suggested that cold causes other stimuli to compete for the individual's attention. Cooling of the extremities and threat of injury distracts the worker from the task at hand. Performance is impaired. Cold also increases the pain of many minor injuries.

Relatively few indoor industrial jobs involve cold exposure. However, outdoor jobs may entail prolonged exposure, so steps must be taken to ensure workers' safety. Special clothing and footwear have been designed,

Many companies provide their workers with special
protective equipment and clothing to guard against injury
in hazardous jobs.

*Courtesy Norton Company, Safety Products Division*

and hand warmers and space heaters have been used. Some workers receive extra compensation for working in cold.

**Multiple stressors**     Stressors need not exist in isolation. If they exist jointly, a worker must contend with their *additive* or *interactive* effects. For example, if the noise level decreases performance by 10 percent and the heat level decreases it by 10 percent, the combined effect of a hot, noisy workplace may reduce performance 20 percent. These two stressors have an additive effect. However, in some cases, stressors have an *interactive* effect, and their combined effect may exceed the sum of the independent effects.

I recall an episode from a job analysis that illustrates the effect of multiple stressors. A construction worker described his job in the summer as being "hot and noisy." I wanted to observe him at work. He was using a pneumatic air drill to remove street pavement, and the temperature was 90° F. However, the heat radiating off the pavement made the temperature at street level over 110° F. The noise from a pneumatic drill (at a range of about 15 feet) was over 100 decibels. After observing this worker for about five minutes and taking notes on his job duties, the effect of the heat and noise made me feel faint and nauseated. While the construction worker could perform under those conditions, I couldn't. I found the noise worse than the heat, but the combined effect made me abandon my efforts. I also learned that simple descriptive phrases like "hot and noisy" mean different things to different people.

From a practical standpoint, stressors occurring in combination create a far more dangerous work environment than stressors occurring in isolation. Attempts to minimize the effects of one stressor may compound the effects of the other. While protective headgear can reduce noise, the extra covering can increase the effects of heat. Headgear protecting a worker from cold may also affect hearing and may cause accidents. Action taken to minimize stressor effects must not make the worker vulnerable to other potential hazards.

## FATIGUE

Fatigue is quite elusive, yet it is a major symptom associated with poor worker-workplace fit. There are several kinds of fatigue, and they all have physiological and psychological characteristics. The I/O psychologist studies fatigue not to understand its physiological basis, but to eliminate as many of its effects, particularly in performance and satisfaction, as possible (Blum & Naylor, 1968).

The symptoms of fatigue include: tiredness, diminished willingness to work, and boredom. However, fatigue is not synonymous with being bored or tired; such feelings may be short-lived and can be "cured" by a diversion or a night's sleep. Fatigue is more generalized and enduring. Also, distinguishing various kinds of fatigue is difficult because of interrelated effects. Several authors (e.g., Grandjean, 1968) attempted to isolate different kinds of fatigue; there seem to be four major varieties. The most distinct type is *muscular* fatigue, caused by prolonged and demanding physical activity. This is associated with biochemical changes and is an acute pain in the muscles. *Mental* fatigue is more closely aligned with feelings of boredom associated with monotonous work. *Emotional* fatigue results from intense stress, and is generally characterized by a dulling of emotional responses. Finally, *skills* fatigue is associated with a decline in attention to certain tasks. With skills fatigue, standards of accuracy and performance become progressively lower (McFarland, 1971). The decline is thought to be a major cause of accidents, particularly involving automobiles and airplanes.

I/O psychologists are concerned with all four types of fatigue, though their response to each is different. Muscular fatigue is best dealt with through new work procedures so people will not overexert themselves. It may involve redesigning a piece of equipment or finding other, less strenuous ways to perform the task. Mental fatigue is addressed through job redesign attempting to make work more stimulating and challenging. However, as we saw in Chapter 13, individuals differ widely in what they think is boring. Emotional fatigue is usually caused by factors external to the workplace, but many organizations provide counseling services for employees. Companies are doing this because performance can be affected by problems in either the workplace or the home. Skills fatigue is a major concern for those in jobs with a small margin for error. For a pilot or air traffic controller, the consequences of lower standards can be severe and tragic. Such employees are continually monitored for skills fatigue, and are given time off when necessary.

People differ in susceptibility to fatigue and jobs differ in inducing fatigue. I/O psychologists still have much to learn about fatigue, particularly treatment and prediction. Muscle fatigue is easier to remedy than mental fatigue, at least on a long-term basis. We can better predict the type of person who will be fatigued on a *group* basis. Fatigue is the product of a poor match between talents, skills, and abilities and environmental demands. As our work world becomes increasingly complex, problems of fatigue probably will not abate.

## SAFETY AND ACCIDENTS

Industrial safety and accidents are among the oldest topics in I/O psychology, dating back to the turn of the century. One of the first responsibilities of psychologists was developing safer working conditions. Engineers also contribute greatly, particularly in equipment design and plant layout. While we have made big strides in improving work safety, industrial accidents still are a major concern. The National Safety Council published some alarming statistics:

1.  Approximately 1 million productive person years are lost annually through work accidents.
2.  Accidents cost the nation at least $51.1 billion in lost wages, medical expenses, property damage, and insurance costs.

3. Injuries to U.S. workers each year have the same economic impact as if the nation's entire industrial community shut down for one full week.
4. In the United States, loss of life from accidents during this century far exceeds that from wars, earthquakes, floods, tornadoes, and other natural catastrophies *combined* (DeReamer, 1980).

Researchers in different disciplines address the problem of industrial accidents from many perspectives, but all are concerned with reducing frequency and severity. I/O psychologists focus on individual characteristics associated with accidents, and investigate various traditional approaches (personnel selection, work design, and training) in accident reduction. Industrial hygienists view occupational diseases as consequences of recurring events or accidents. Safety engineers see accidents as results of a sequence of acts or events with "undesirable" consequences like personal injury, property damage, or work interruption.

Accidents and injuries are not synonymous. Injury is the consequence of an accident, but many "no-injury" accidents also occur. Though psychologists are concerned with accidents whether or not they result in injury, those accidents producing injuries generally get more attention.

**Safety legislation**

There are state and federal laws to protect the welfare of the worker. The major one is the Occupational and Safety Health Act (OSHA). OSHA became effective in 1971; it was meant to integrate federal and state legislation under a federal program establishing uniform codes, standards, and regulations. The purpose of the act is "to assure, as far as possible, every working woman and man in the nation safe and healthful working conditions, and to preserve our human resources." To accomplish this, there are provisions for safety and health standards, research, information, and education and training in occupational safety and health (DeReamer, 1980).

OSHA is comprehensive, covering such things as record-keeping, inspection, compliance, and enforcement of safety standards (Nothstein, 1981). The law lists over 5,000 safety and health standards. Standards are specified ranging from density of particles in the air to the height at which a fire extinguisher is to be mounted. Some critics suggest that OSHA is too concerned with "Mickey Mouse" standards which burden employers without really protecting workers. Others consider OSHA one of the most important and influential pieces of legislation ever enacted. The law provides for safety inspections and fines for noncompliance. Over 100,000 inspections are conducted annually by trained officers. Companies can be fined for maintaining improper safety records, and for the willful violation of safety standards. In 1978, financial penalties totaling $228,700, the largest sum ever levied against an employer, were proposed against a large petroleum company for having 137 safety violations.

Other laws involving safety (e.g., Workers' Compensation) exist, but none of them has the far-reaching impact of OSHA. OSHA made the whole realm of occupational safety and health more visible. It has given new status and responsibility to safety and health practitioners. OSHA has increased concern among employers and unions over safety and health problems, as well as compliance with safety regulations. However, whether OSHA has reduced industrial accidents is unclear. The system for documenting accidents was changed by the act; data comparing the situation before and after the act are inadequate.

**The causes of accidents**

Many people do believe that "accidents just happen." They have been attributed to bad luck and "acts of God." In truth, accidents are explainable, though the causes are sometimes difficult to discern. Safety programs are based on the belief that (1) accidents have rational causes, (2) steps must be taken to prevent them, and (3) accidents will recur if corrective action is not taken.

What causes accidents? Two major factors are unsafe conditions and unsafe acts; these usually occur jointly. Unsafe conditions include poorly designed equipment, improperly assembled or situated equipment, hazardous physical situations (ice on an airport runway or water spilled on a floor), and worn-out or damaged facilities. Unsafe acts cover improper use of equipment (using a chisel to open a can of paint), improper conduct (running with a sharp object), and horseplay. DeReamer (1980) presented a diagram of the anatomy of an accident, which is shown in Figure 15–4 and illustrates the following points:

1. The supervisor's safety performance and the physical and the mental condition of the worker are the main sources of unsafe acts and unsafe conditions.
2. Not all unsafe acts and unsafe conditions result in accidents; but all accidents result from unsafe acts and conditions, usually in combination.
3. All work accidents delay production and cause spoilage or waste.
4. Some accidents cause injuries; in a small percentage of cases, the injury is disabling.

There is little doubt that individual behavior (unsafe acts) is a major cause of accidents. Products, equipment, and facilities can be designed to be safe. In the final analysis, the individual has to accept and comply with the safety features. Human errors contribute to a disproportionately high percentage of all accidents. For example, many drivers do not use seat belts. Workers remove or fail to use safety guards.

In general, safety has rarely generated much enthusiasm or interest. Why? Bird (1974) suggested that people want their safety needs met (a la Maslow); but other needs (and thus behaviors) conflict. These conflicting

**Figure 15–4**                    **A flowchart of the anatomy of an accident**

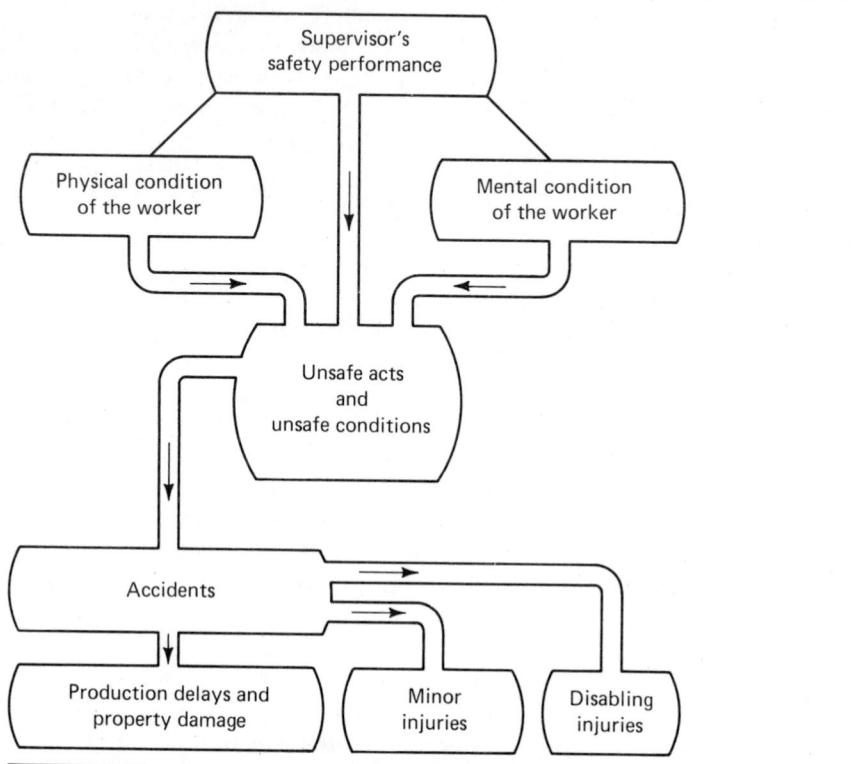

SOURCE: R. DeReamer, *Modern Safety and Health Technology* (New York: John Wiley & Sons, 1980).

needs are presented in Table 15–1. Safety needs are secondary to many factors. The desire to save time, save effort, to be more comfortable, to attract attention, to assert independence, and to gain acceptance most often conflict with the desire to work safely. Coupling a lack of conviction about safety with the feeling that "it won't happen to me," people often take chances. Viewing unsafe behavior as a learned response and not a whim, psychologists can offer behavior-change strategies to reduce the frequency. This is more constructive than attributing all accidents to unsafe conditions (which is not true) or irrational behavior (which is also not true). Shortly, we will examine what psychologists have offered in identifying individual differences contributing to unsafe behavior and in efforts to change this behavior.

**Accident proneness.**   For many years, one of the more popular "theories" was accident proneness. This is a combination of abilities and characteristics that make a person have accidents regardless of the environment.

The concept originated with the discovery that a small percentage of the

| Table 15-1 | **Common needs which conflict with safety needs** |
|---|---|

1. *Safety versus saving time:* If the safe way takes more time than an unsafe way, some people will choose the unsafe way to save time.
2. *Safety versus saving effort:* If the safe way requires more work than the unsafe way, some people will choose the unsafe way to save the effort.
3. *Safety versus comfort:* If the safe way is less comfortable than an unsafe way, some people will choose the unsafe way to avoid discomfort.
4. *Safety versus getting attention:* If an unsafe way attracts more attention than the safe way, some people will choose the unsafe way.
5. *Safety versus independence:* If an unsafe way gives greater freeedom from authority than the safe way, some people will choose the unsafe way simply to assert their independence.
6. *Safety versus group acceptance:* If an unsafe way has greater group approval than the safe way, many people will choose the unsafe way to get or maintain group acceptance.

SOURCE: F. E. Bird, *Management Guide to Loss Control* (Santa Monica, Calif.: Institute Press, 1974).

population had a high percentage of accidents. These people were labeled "accident-prone." It is true that some people have more accidents than others; however, the concept of accident proneness is not needed to explain this. Statistical probability based on a normal or random distribution would make a similar prediction. Consider the data in Table 15–2. The left-hand column shows a distribution of actual injuries in a sample of 10,964 workers. The number of injuries per worker ranged from a low of 0 to a high of 11, shown in the middle column. Because a total of 90 workers each had five or more injuries it is tempting to label them accident-prone because of the high rate. However, the right-hand column of the table is a distribution of injuries derived from a statistical equation of the normal distribution based on the sample size. On the basis of chance alone, 79 workers would be predicted to have five or more injuries. The difference between the actual and theoretical distributions is extremely small; the distribution of real injuries closely approximates a chance distribution. The difference between the 90 actual cases of 5 or more injuries and the predicted 79 cases of 5 or more can be explained by such factors as changes in working conditions, changes in mental or physical condition of the workers, quality of supervision, and so on. The 11 cases that exceed chance expectation out of a sample of over 10,000 workers hardly constitute a strong case for accident proneness.

The theory of accident proneness is based on identifying *individuals* who have certain characteristics. The theory would have validity if the *same* individuals *repeatedly* had large numbers of accidents. Some people do fall in this category, but we don't need a theory of accident proneness to identify them. For example, alcoholics and drug addicts often have higher accident rates. Thus, alcoholism and drug addiction are valid predictors of accidents, and we can reduce accidents by identifying and treating these

**Table 15–2**          **Distributions of actual injuries and theoretically predicted injuries for a sample of workers**

| Number of workers: actual injuries | Number of injuries per worker | Number of workers: theoretically predicted injuries |
|---|---|---|
| 8,189 | 0 | 8,256 |
| 1,834 | 1 | 1,698 |
| 550 | 2 | 594 |
| 212 | 3 | 237 |
| 89 | 4 | 100 |
| 43 ⎫ | 5 | 44 ⎫ |
| 26 ⎪ | 6 | 19 ⎪ |
| 14 ⎪ Total of | 7 | 9 ⎪ Total of |
| 3 ⎬ 90 workers | 8 | 4 ⎬ 79 workers |
| 3 ⎪ | 9 | 2 ⎪ |
| 0 ⎪ | 10 | 1 ⎪ |
| 1 ⎭ | 11 | 0 ⎭ |
| 10,964 | | 10,964 |

SOURCE: R. DeReamer, *Modern Safety and Health Technology* (New York: John Wiley & Sons, 1980).

conditions. However, on the basis of *group* data, it is fruitless to attempt to identify high-accident-rate *individuals* without any other information.

Despite rather convincing statistical data that accident proneness is not a very useful concept for explaining accidents, the notion has an appeal. Studies by Arbous and Kerrich (1951) and Whitlock, Clouse, and Spencer (1963) refuted accident proneness. Yet many people cling to the myth. DeReamer (1980) reports that in a survey of personnel executives, nearly two thirds of the companies represented try to identify "accident-prone" employees. Only one personnel representative in the group said, "There is no such thing as an accident-prone employee." Myths are sometimes very slow to die, even among people who should know better.

**Biorhythms and accidents.**    Another "theory" of accidents is based on biorhythms. Human behavior is supposedly characterized by three cycles called *biological rhythms* or *biorhythms*. The three cycles are a 23-day

## Frank and Ernest

I'M ACCIDENT-PRONE AND I WANT YOU TO FIND OUT WHY, BALDY.

THAVES 11-17

*Reprinted by permission. © 1980 NEA, Inc.*

physical cycle, a 28-day emotional cycle, and a 33-day intellectual cycle. The physical cycle influences physical tasks, the emotional cycle situations of high emotional content, and the intellectual cycle pursuits requiring awareness and judgment.

The biorhythm cycles are curves with a positive phase, a negative phase, and a zero or "critical point," when the curve crosses the axis from positive to negative or vice versa, as shown in Figure 15–5. Although negative days are regarded as less favorable than positive days, it is the critical days (the dots in Figure 15–5) occurring six times a month that are considered most important. Accidents are most likely to occur during the critical days.

A few studies examined the validity of biorhythms for predicting industrial accidents; the results are negative. Carvey and Nibler (1977) examined 150 work-related vehicular accidents and 210 on-the-job accidents in which the worker was responsible. Each accident was analyzed to determine whether or not it occurred on a critical day. The results showed no systematic relationship between critical days and accidents. In another study, Wolcott, McKeeken, Burgin, and Yanowitch (1977) examined the extent biorhythms predicted aviation accidents. Biorhythms were calculated for over 4,000 pilots involved in accidents in one year. Exact dates and times of the accidents were recorded, and they were separated into two groups: those in which the pilot was at fault and those in which the pilot was not. The results showed no relationship between biorhythms and accidents.

The results suggest that biorhythms are not a useful explanation for accidents. Their value for explaining other events also seems questionable (e.g., Floody, 1981). If biorhythms have any value in reducing accidents, it may be that during negative or critical days, people will be more cautious and thus act in a safer manner.

**Figure 15–5**          **The biorhythmic 23-day physical cycle, 28-day emotional cycle, and 33-day intellectual cycle**

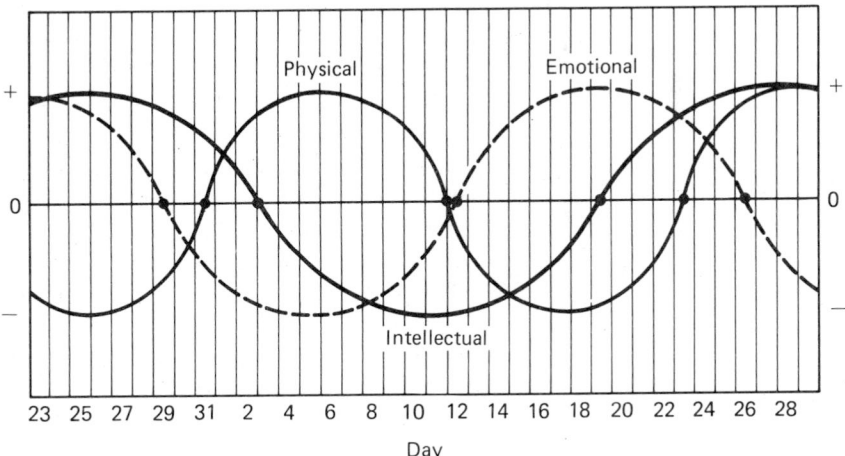

**Psychological approaches to accident reduction**

Throughout this book, we stressed three approaches to achieving a better fit between worker and workplace. The first is based on individual differences and involves selecting people who have the characteristics thought necessary or desirable for specified work demands. This is the personnel selection approach, the analogue of finding the "right pegs" to fit the "holes." The second approach is training people in the necessary skills, knowledge, or attitudes needed. This is the personnel training approach, the analogue of "reshaping the pegs" to fit the "holes." The third approach is modifying the workplace to provide a better match with abilities and characteristics. This is the engineering psychology or work design approach, the analogue of "reshaping the holes" to fit the "pegs." These approaches are all used to reduce industrial accidents where the criterion of interest is creating a safer work environment. We will now examine in some detail I/O research to achieve this objective.

**Personnel selection approach.**   The personnel selection approach is the search for individual differences predictive of accidents. Usually scores on some measure (e.g., a test) are correlated with frequency of accidents for the test sample. This method is used by insurance companies in deciding whom they will insure and at what price. Based on data for hundreds of thousands of drivers, insurance companies learned that certain characteristics are associated with frequency of accidents. For example, younger drivers have more accidents. Men (especially young men) have more accidents than women. Because the insurance business is highly competitive, insurance companies are always looking for ways to attract more customers; thus, they also reduce rates for certain types of people. For example, some companies found that nonsmokers have fewer accidents; reduced rates are thus offered to nonsmokers. Similarly, some companies offer reduced rates to students with a B average in school, as research indicates such students are better drivers.

This approach is called *actuarial* prediction; it is based on statistical analysis of group data. Some people feel this is unjust, saying things like, "Just because I'm under 25 I have to pay a higher premium than my older brother, and neither of us ever had an accident." Making predictions about accidents is not so refined that everyone can have a personally tailored premium rate based on a long list of personal characteristics. Insurance companies are always looking for individual variables that further differentiate people within coarse groups (male/female, young/old); but they still must set insurance rates on *group* characteristics. Some may feel "their group" does not fairly represent them as a person; because of the inexact nature of prediction, decisions about individuals will still be made on aggregate behavior.

Apart from insurance research, other studies have tried to identify individual differences predictive of accidents. This research dealt with a range of variables predictive of accidents. The results are mixed. Kephart and Tiffin (1950) investigated the relationship between visual skills and accidents for those in 11 different job classes. The authors found that employees who met the visual standard had fewer accidents in 10 of the 11 jobs. The results of a similar study on vision and accidents for a sample of machine operators are shown in Figure 15–6.

A number of studies examined differences in perceptual skill and accidents. Ability to perceive a figure or object embedded in a complex background was assessed. Differences in ability were then related to accident data. Barrett and Thornton (1968) found that this was predictive of the number of accidents and near accidents with pedestrians in a simulated driving situation. Those better at finding the hidden figure had fewer accidents. Mihal and Barrett (1976) reported similar findings. They also found that better drivers select certain specific information cues while other drivers try to process all available information. Williams (1977) also found that three-dimensional or stereoscopic perceptual tests predict accidents.

Findings are less positive with other variables. A few studies reported that certain vocational interests (Kunce, 1967) and personality factors (Spangenberg, 1968) predict accidents. Generally, there does not appear to be a strong relationship between personal, emotional, and attitudinal factors and accidents (Goldstein, 1964). Differences in visual and perceptual skills seem to bear directly on accidents. Identifying other types of variables has not been very successful.

In keeping with the personnel selection approach, it should be apparent that variables predictive of accidents could be used to hire people for jobs where accidents are important. People can be hired for transportation jobs (e.g., chauffeurs, bus drivers, pilots) and jobs having a high risk factor (e.g., handling of hazardous chemicals) on their likelihood of having accidents.

**Engineering psychology approach.** Engineering psychology approaches accident reduction by modifying the workplace. It involves careful analysis of the workplace including design of equipment, tools, and machinery, as well as physical layout, to diagnose unsafe conditions. As Adams (1972) stated, engineering psychologists are not interested in machines, per

**Figure 15–6**          **Relationship between vision and frequency of serious accidents among machine operators**

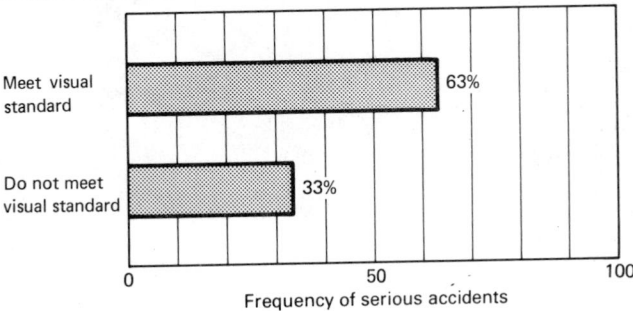

se. They are interested in human behavior and performance, like all psychologists; they use the person/machine interface as a focal point.

It is beyond our scope to present a complete discourse on engineering psychology. The interested reader should refer to McCormick (1970) and Chapanis (1976) for more detail. Designing a safer work environment is one of the oldest and most prominent objectives of engineering psychologists. We will review a few examples of their work.

Yoder, Lucas, and Botzum (1973) faced the problem of workers developing muscle fatigue and a condition called tenosynovitis (inflammation of tendons) because the pliers they used were not well suited for the task. The work consisted of cutting molded plastic parts used in a pharmaceutical plant. The existing pliers depended on primary use of the third and fourth fingers, which caused muscle fatigue, and holding the pliers at an angle, which produced the wrist injury. The authors redesigned the pliers to be more compatible with the limitations of the human hand and wrist. The new pliers utilized a greater proportion of the muscles from all fingers and changed the wrist position needed to perform the task. Figure 15–7 shows (a) the original and (b) and (c) redesigned pliers. The authors feel that other tools can be redesigned to minimize muscle fatigue and work-related injuries.

Voevodsky (1974) described a study that tried to reduce the number of

**Figure 15–7**          **Original pliers (A) and redesigned pliers (B and C) as developed to reduce muscle fatigue and injury**

| A | B | C |
|---|---|---|
| 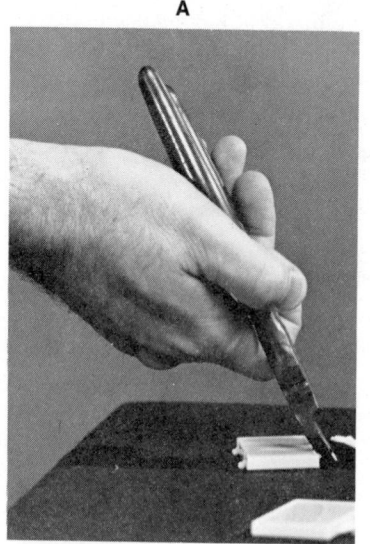 | 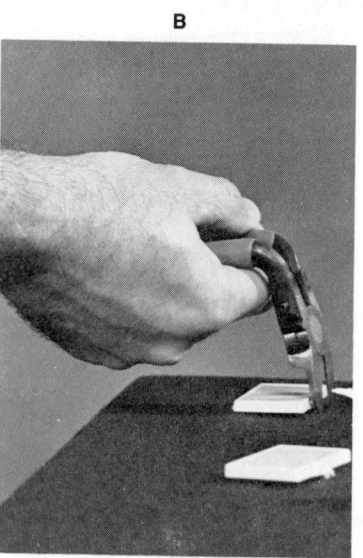 | 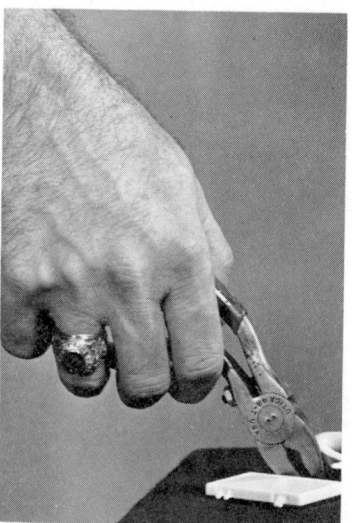 |

*John P. May, photographer*

SOURCE: T. A. Yoder, R. L. Lucas, and G. D. Botzum, "The Marriage of Human Factors and Safety in Industry," *Human Factors* 15 (1973), pp. 197–205.

times taxi cabs are struck in the rear. Cab drivers often stop fast, and those cars following don't anticipate it. Voevodsky installed yellow warning lights on the trunks of 343 cabs. These lights began to blink when the cab slowed down. The rate of blinking was proportional to the rate of deceleration; faster blinking implied more rapid deceleration. A control group of 160 cabs were not fitted with the lights.

After 10 months, accident statistics on the two groups of cabs were compared. On three major performance dimensions (number of rear-end collisions, cost of repairs necessitated, and injuries to cab drivers) the experimental cabs outperformed the control cabs. The size of the difference was also very impressive; accidents were reduced by over 60 percent. The statistics on the control cabs were unchanged during the study. To see whether the differences were not due simply to drivers of experimental cabs being more careful, comparisons were made of *front-end* collisions. No significant differences were found between experimental and control cabs. The author thus concluded that cab drivers did not change their driving, but the motorists behind them did.

Both studies are good examples of the engineering psychology approach to safety. The researchers modified the equipment used, and the changes resulted in fewer accidents and injuries. Engineering psychology showed that performance can be improved by designing the workplace to complement human skills, be it in terms of muscle usage or reaction time.

**Personnel training approach.** As discussed in Chapter 6, personnel training involves more than selecting a method to improve skills. It also involves creating an atmosphere in which training is supported and trained persons are rewarded for improvement. The personnel training approach to safety involves everything we discussed about other types of training, and represents a major approach to accident reduction. As is the case in all training, employees must be motivated. With safety training, there must be a reason for employees to behave safely. As Bird (1974) commented, there are many reasons employees would *not* want to behave safely. Training is thus directed toward making safety a desirable outcome.

All training programs are conducted within a climate that places some degree of importance on training. In some organizations, training may be highly valued, while in others, it may be treated with only mild indifference. Three studies have examined the degree that organization influences relate to safety behavior. Zohar (1980) developed a questionnaire to assess organizational climates regarding safety. Employees at 20 companies rated their perceptions of the safety climate. A team of four experienced safety inspectors evaluated each organization on safety practices and accident-prevention programs. Scores on the questionnaire were then compared with inspectors' judgments. The results revealed that management's commitment to safety is a major factor in the success of safety programs. Organizations with a strong safety climate have job-training programs, give executive authority to safety officials, have high-level managers on safety committees, and consider safety in job design. Zohar feels that attempts to improve safety, like new regulations or poster campaigns, without management commitment will probably not succeed. As we stated in Chapter 6, the role of management is critical to any training program, and safety training is no exception.

Dunbar (1975) conducted a study again revealing the importance of management in fostering positive attitudes about safety. The author investigated the extent that employee attitudes about their managers related to their perception of who is responsible for safety. Dunbar thought when employees felt their managers were very supportive, employees would have greater feelings of personal responsibility for their own safety. If employees did not have strong feelings of personal responsibility, they would be dependent on managers to make the work environment safe. Dunbar asked a sample of employees to rate how supportive their managers were; they were also asked who they felt was ultimately responsible for a safe workplace. The results revealed that managers can exert a strong influence with regard to safety. Employees who felt their managers supported them also believed they were responsible for their own safety behavior; employees who felt little support shifted responsibility to their managers. Dunbar's findings support the idea that management influences employee awareness of responsibilities for safe behavior.

Butler and Jones (1979) also investigated how perceptions of a leader's behavior related to accidents in hazardous work environments. The authors related views of officers among enlisted personnel aboard U.S. Navy ships to accident occurrence. In work environments characterized as recognizably hazardous, behavior of the leader was not highly related to injury-producing accidents. However, when hazards were less evident, the behavior of the leader was related to accidents. Butler and Jones recommend that in highly hazardous environments, accident prevention might most effectively involve direct reduction of equipment hazards, mechanically or through training. In less hazardous environments, leadership that involves clarity in defining tasks, structuring work activities, and clarity in job demands appears important.

These studies attest to the importance of an environment conducive to safety training. Employees quickly pick up cues on the importance of safety. Scrap or waste on the floor, unprotected wires, and workers not wearing hard hats contradict bulletin board posters saying "Safety First." Organization attitudes toward safety are conveyed by what people do. The studies show that management behavior and attitudes relate to employee feelings about safety and to accidents.

In terms of actual safety training, Komaki and associates showed the efficacy of goal setting, positive reinforcement, and feedback. Komaki, Barwick, and Scott (1978) studied employees in two departments of a food manufacturing plant: production (makeup) and wrapping. After analyzing the jobs in both departments, the authors identified safe and unsafe behavior.

Slides showing safe and unsafe behaviors were made. Workers saw two slides per task, and discussed safe and unsafe behavior. After reviewing their current accident rate, employees in both departments set goals for safe behavior. The goals were plotted on a large graph conspicuously displayed at the work site. The researchers then observed behavior, provided feedback and encouragement, and plotted behavior on the graph.

The results are shown in Figure 15–8. In the wrapping department, the baseline of safe behaviors jumped from 70 percent to 95 percent after training; in the makeup department, the percentage increased from 77 to 99 percent. After termination of the program, safe behavior reverted to its pretraining levels. Komaki et al. (1978) reported that worker motivation was very high throughout the study, and pressure was put on co-workers not to "ruin the graph." The results clearly indicate that safe behavior can be enhanced through training aimed at increasing motivation and sensitivity. The findings also indicate that safe behavior requires continual atten-

**Figure 15–8**　　　　**Percentage of safe behavior of employees in two departments of a food manufacturing plant during a 25-week period**

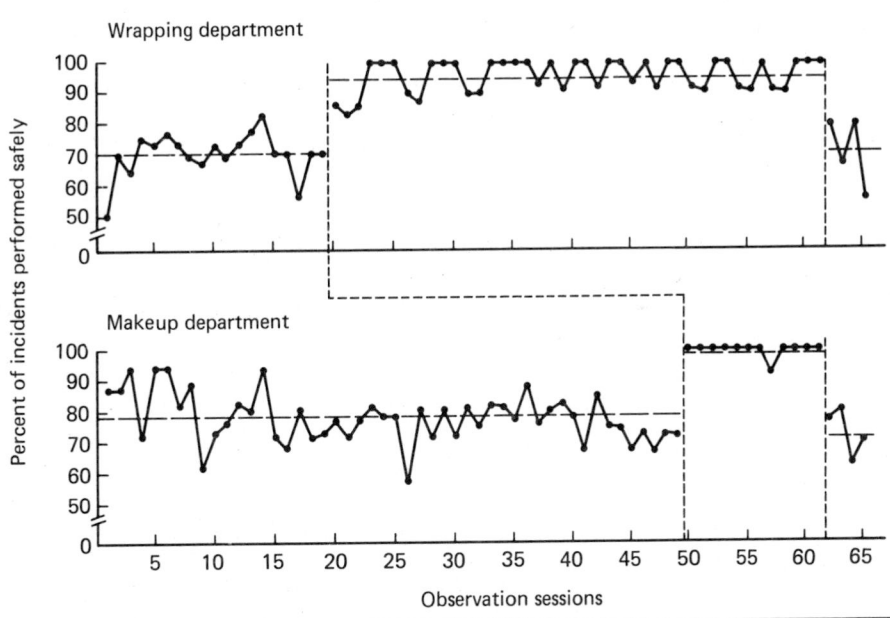

SOURCE: J. Komaki, K. D. Barwick, and L. R. Scott, "A Behavioral Approach to Occupational Safety: Pinpointing and Reinforcing Safe Performance in a Food Manufacturing Plant," *Journal of Applied Psychology* 63 (1978), pp. 434–45.

tion; unsafe behavior returned to its base rate *immediately* following the end of the program (labeled "Reversal" in the figure).

In a later study, Komaki, Heinzmann, and Lawson (1980) again showed the effectiveness of training and feedback in accident reduction. They made 165 observations of worker performance in a city's vehicle maintenance department over a 45-week period. As in the previous study, safe and unsafe behavior was identified, and slides were made. The employees set goals for improving safety; their behavior was observed and posted on a graph. The research design involved five stages. First, baseline behavior was observed and recorded for about 10 weeks. The second stage involved seeing the slides of safe and unsafe behavior, and discussing them. The third phase was again seeing the slides, followed by feedback on performance as recorded on the graph. Stages four and five were replications of stages two and three. The results showed that performance did improve somewhat during training (slide viewing and discussion); but the major gains occurred when feedback was provided. The researchers concluded that training alone is not enough to improve and maintain performance. *Feedback* (in this case, a graph) is necessary. The results of both Komaki et al. (1978, 1980) studies are strong support for the value of training programs in promoting safe behavior.

## Overview

Organizations need not limit themselves to one approach to reducing accidents. In fact, the prudent organization would adopt a comprehensive program using all three approaches together. Each approach has its own merits; when used in combination, they improve the likelihood of reducing accidents. Research indicates that people differ in their tendency to have accidents. To the extent that these differences can be reliably predicted, we can staff organizations with people who exhibit safe behavior. The engineering psychology approach entails modifying the tools, equipment, and machinery to avoid unsafe conditions. Machines must be designed to complement human skills and limitations. The training approach is based on the belief that, like all skills, safety skills can be improved through training. This approach stresses the importance of a conducive safety environment and acquiring the knowledge and skills needed to reduce accidents. Each method approaches safety from a different perspective; but all three were proved effective in reducing accidents.

# WORK SCHEDULES

## Shift work

As stated earlier, not all employees work 8:00 A.M. to 5:00 P.M., five days a week, Monday through Friday. The nature of the services performed necessitates other schedules. Police officers, fire fighters, and telephone operators provide 24-hour-a-day service. In industrial manufacturing, some technology requires constant monitoring and operation. It isn't practical to shut off furnaces, boilers, and chemical process operations at 5:00 P.M. just because the workers went home. In those cases, it is advantageous to run them continually by having different shifts work around the clock. About 25 percent of all working hours in the United States are estimated as "nontraditional" (Dunham, 1977). Psychologists have become interested in how different hours (shift work) affect employee attitudes and behavior.

There are no uniform shift-work hours; various companies use various shifts. Usually a 24-hour day is broken into three 8-hour work shifts, like 7:00 A.M.–3:00 P.M. (day shift), 3:00 P.M.–11:00 P.M. (swing or afternoon shift), and 11:00 P.M.–7:00 A.M. (night shift). Some companies have employees work just one shift; but workers generally don't like the swing and night shifts, so many firms rotate the shifts. Employees may work two weeks on the day shift, two weeks on the swing shift, and then two weeks on the night shift. A shift workweek need not be Monday to Friday. Also, there may be an uneven number of days off between shifts, like two days off after the swing shift and three after the night shift. Psychologists have investigated to what degree workers cope with these changes in work time.

Research has focused on employee performance, satisfaction with shift work, physiological adjustments to shift work, and social/cultural adjustment. We will briefly examine some of the findings.

**Performance.** Malaviya and Ganesh (1976, 1977) examined individual and group productivity of weavers who alternated between day and swing shifts in an Indian textile mill. Half of the weavers worked 13 days on the day shift followed by 12 days on the swing shift; the sequence was reversed for the other half of the sample. The results revealed that, for the *group*, productivity was superior during the day shift. However, there were differences in performance of individual weavers over the two shifts. Some produced more during the day shift, others during the swing shift, while for others there was no difference over the two shifts.

**Satisfaction.** Many people prefer traditional hours; but some are quite satisfied with aspects of shift work. In a study by de la Mare and Walker (1968), the following was reported about preference in work schedules:

| Preference | Percent |
|---|---|
| Permanent day work | 61% |
| Rotating shift work | 12 |
| Permanent night work | 27 |

In this study, workers favored permanent day work; others report positive preferences for shift work. For example, Wedderburn (1978) reported the following responses from British steel workers to the question "On the whole, how do you feel about working shifts?"

| Response | Percent |
|---|---|
| I like it very much | 18% |
| I like it more than I dislike it | 29 |
| I neither like it nor dislike it | 22 |
| I dislike it more than I like it | 23 |
| I dislike it very much | 8 |

There is large variability in individual worker attitudes. In the same study, Wedderburn obtained responses about perceived advantages and disadvantages of shift work in a number of specific areas. These are reported in Table 15–3. Advantages and disadvantages are seen with each shift. On par, however, it seems that more disadvantages are associated with the night shift, and the findings reported by Wedderburn are representative of other such studies.

**Adjustment problems.** Shift workers experience many problems in physiological and social adjustment. Most physiological problems are associated with interruptions of the *circadian rhythm;* that is, our bodies are

**Table 15–3**          **Reported perceptions of steel mill workers regarding shift work**

| Descriptive item | Percentage of "yes" responses about* | | |
|---|---|---|---|
| | Day shift | Afternoon shift | Night shift |
| Quickly over | 84 | 38 | 29 |
| Seems a longer shift | 12 | 40 | 64 |
| Gives me indigestion | 7 | 4 | 21 |
| Tiring | 58 | 15 | 80 |
| Disturbs my sleep | 36 | 2 | 52 |
| More friendly atmosphere | 48 | 51 | 21 |
| Makes me irritable | 25 | 18 | 48 |
| Peaceful | 49 | 62 | 58 |
| More responsibility at work | 28 | 16 | 24 |
| More independent | 35 | 26 | 42 |
| Good for family life | 73 | 19 | 17 |
| Gives me more spare time | 88 | 15 | 49 |
| Wastes the day | 10 | 68 | 55 |
| Starts too early | 53 | 7 | 20 |
| Restricts my social life | 17 | 79 | 77 |
| Sexless | 13 | 11 | 44 |

*Responses were to the question: "Think of work on _____ shift. How well does each of the above words describe what it is like for you on _____ shift?"
SOURCE: A. A. Wedderburn, "Some Suggestions for Increasing the Usefulness of Psychological and Sociological Studies of Shiftwork," *Ergonomics* 21 (1978), pp. 827–33.

"programmed" for a certain time cycle (Aschoff, 1978). Because shift work interrupts the cycle of eating, sleeping, and working, workers often experience physiological problems. They complain of lack of sleep, fatigue, constipation, irritability, and appetite loss. Meers, Maasen, and Verhaagen (1978) reported that the health of a sample of shift workers declined during the first six months of shift work; the decline became more pronounced after four years.

Because most people work during the day and sleep at night, shift workers also have social problems. Difficulties with children, marital relationships, and recreation are often experienced. Frost and Jamal (1979) reported that shift workers experience less need fulfillment, are more likely to quit their jobs, and participate in fewer voluntary organizations. Jamal (1981) reported similar findings; workers on fixed work schedules are better off than workers on rotating schedules in terms of mental health, job satisfaction, and social participation. Shift workers are a relatively small proportion of the population; they are thus forced to work their schedules around the rest of society. Dunham (1977) makes the interesting point that many social problems would be alleviated by *increasing* shift work. Society would then make more concessions to the needs of shift workers. Changes might be made in such things as hours of television broadcasting, restaurant service, recreational services, and hours of business operation (banks, supermarkets, gas stations, etc.).

Research indicates that shift work has a strong influence on the lives of people who perform such work. As long as certain industries require 24-hour-a-day operations, psychologists will continue searching for ways to improve this particularly difficult person/environment fit. Social problems may be lessened by changing some existing patterns in the community. However, physiological problems will be more difficult to overcome. At least one major source of physiological difficulty is the rotation of workers across shifts. If workers were assigned to a *fixed* shift (day, swing, night), their behavior would be consistent, which would help in adjusting to the circadian rhythm. Some people *prefer* to work afternoons or nights; part of the solution may be personnel selection. Workers could choose a shift; if enough workers of the appropriate skill level were placed in each shift, both the individual and organization needs would be met. We will probably see more attention paid to the needs and problems of shift workers in the future.

## Shorter workweek

Employees traditionally worked 8 hours a day, five days a week, for a 40 hour workweek. However, in the past 10 years, many organizations adopted a different schedule. Some employees now work 10 hours a day for four days. This is popularly known as the "4/40." Poor (1970) estimated that five organizations per day are converting to 4/40.

There are several obvious advantages to a four-day workweek for the individual and organization. Individuals have a three-day weekend which gives them more recreation time, the chance to work a second job, more time for family life, and so on. Organizations have fewer overhead costs because they are open one day less per week. However, there are also possible drawbacks; these include fatigue, fewer productive hours, and more accidents.

There is not much empirical evidence on the subject; several studies have been reported. A few examined worker acceptance of the four-day week. Nord and Costigan (1973) and Goodale and Aagaard (1975) reported favorable reaction. In both studies, over 80 percent of the workers favored the new system; acceptance remained high after the 4/40 had been in effect for a year. The findings also indicated that workers grew more tired toward the end of the day; there were also some adjustment problems in their family lives. Dunham and Hawk (1977) found that support for 4/40 often comes from younger workers with low-level jobs, low income, and relatively low job satisfaction. They felt 4/40 may be supported when it is seen as a partial reprieve from the negative aspects of work.

Fottler (1977) found that continued acceptance of 4/40 is in large part determined by perceptions of changes in jobs. Employees in an urban hospital voted for 4/40. The change was made; six months later, the employees were asked about their jobs and attitudes toward 4/40. Those who felt the new workweek increased status and responsibility continued to be supportive. Those who saw the least upgrading following the switch were most negative.

Ivancevich conducted two of the few studies of changes in actual job performance with 4/40. Ivancevich (1974) reported gains in production, employee effectiveness as team members, and overall job performance 13 months after inception of 4/40. This is positive support for improvements under the shorter workweek. However, Ivancevich and Lyon (1977) presented disconcerting findings in a later study. The results from the 1974 study were replicated over another 13-month period with a different sample; but 25 months later all differences in performance between the five-day and four-day workweeks *disappeared*. The later study indicates that gains with 4/40 may be a Hawthorne Effect. However, with so few studies, we don't have a large enough data base to draw any firm conclusions. Even if there are no *gains* in productivity, the four-day workweek may provide benefits in other areas like increasing satisfaction and decreasing turnover and absence. We clearly need more research before we evaluate the four-day workweek.

We should add that conversion to 4/40 is not simply a matter of worker preference. Organizations are limited in altering their work schedules by the services they provide and other factors. For example, Goodale and Aagaard (1975) feel 4/40 is not viable if customer service is provided five days a week. Success of organizations providing services partially depends on accessibility. If an organization cannot do the same business volume in four 10-hour days, conversion to 4/40 is counterproductive. Internal factors may not favor the shorter workweek. Goodale and Aagaard suggest if employees work in groups and supervisors must be available during all working hours, 4/40 may not be applicable.

We will undoubtedly see more research on shorter workweeks in the future. Organizations prematurely rushing to 4/40 may encounter more problems than anticipated. Research to date revealed some advantages; but we clearly need answers to many more questions.

## Flexible working hours

Another variation in work schedules is flexible working hours, popularly known as *flextime*. According to one report, approximately 13 percent of private sector organizations have adopted a form of flextime since it was introduced in the early 1970s (Nollen & Martin, 1978). According to Ronen (1981b), the main objective of flextime is creating an alternative to the traditional, fixed working schedule by giving workers some choice in arrival and departure times. The system is usually arranged so that everyone must be present during certain designated hours ("coretime"), but there is latitude in other hours ("flexband"). For example, coretime may be 9:00 A.M. to 3:00 P.M. However, flexband may range from 6:00 A.M. to 6:00 P.M. Some employees may start working at 9:00 A.M. (and work until 6:00 P.M.), some may end at 3:00 P.M. (by starting at 6:00 A.M.), or any combination in between. Problems with family commitments, recreation, second jobs, commutation, and stress may be alleviated by flexible working hours. Lateness is virtually eliminated, since the workday begins with arrival. Workers can only be late if they arrive during coretime. Flexible working hours are relatively new, and psychologists are just beginning to understand their effect.

While there is not yet much research on flextime, the results appear quite positive. At least, no very adverse effects have yet been reported. The variables examined include satisfaction, productivity, absence, and turnover. Some studies report more positive results than others. Golembiewski and Proehl (1978) summarized findings of several studies on flextime; they reported that worker support for adoption or continuation of flextime across nine samples of workers ranged from 80 to 100 percent. It thus appears that many employees are highly receptive to the idea.

Hicks and Klimoski (1981) found that employees did *not* become more satisfied with their work after flextime was adopted. Nevertheless, they reported other benefits like easier travel and parking, less interrole conflict, more feelings of control in the work setting, and more time for leisure activities. The findings on flextime's effect on productivity are mixed, but only a few studies dealt with this issue. Schein, Maurer, and Novak (1977) examined the degree that performance of clerical employees improved under flextime. Out of five production units, performance increased in two and remained unchanged in the others. Schein et al. (1977) were cautious in saying that flextime *increased* productivity; they were confident that it did not lower performance. Kim and Campagna (1981) found that performance over four months of flextime increased in three out of four divisions of a county welfare agency. The authors also reported that flextime had a very positive impact in reducing short-term, unpaid absence (leave without pay for two hours or less a day). Ronen (1981a) reported that in a sample of government workers in Israel, lateness was much less with flextime. After beginning flextime, late arrivals decreased from an average of 6 to 0.67 times per worker per month.

A number of points should be made about the effect of flextime. First, we don't really have much data. Definite conclusions about its effectiveness would be premature. Second, reported gains in productivity may be Hawthorne Effects. As with the Ivancevich and Lyon (1977) study on 4/40, it may take up to two years for Hawthorne Effects to dissipate. Third, even if productivity gains are Hawthorne Effects, this is not necessarily an indictment of flextime. Organizations should state what they hope to gain with flextime; gains in productivity may not be a main objective. As Hicks and Klimoski (1981) reported, employees seem to benefit from flextime. Only in utopia will organization changes have uniformly positive effects—increasing productivity and satisfaction, decreasing absence, lateness, and turnover, and increasing contentment with aspects of nonwork lives. Trade-offs must always be made; thus, organizations must set priorities. Finally, flextime may have negative effects on teamwork and superior/subordinate relationships. If employees must work as a team, flextime, with continual coming and going, may not be viable. Also, if workers must be closely supervised, supervisors must be on the job for the full flexband period. If supervisors can't work 12-hour days, other supervisors may have to be hired, which would create other problems. As with 4/40, more research must be done in the future. For the present, however, flextime appears to be beneficial and workable in certain organizations.

## SUMMARY

This chapter examined many factors relating to work conditions. Things like stress caused by physical conditions, accidents, and work schedules all directly affect work lives. I/O psychologists have responded to this by trying to improve the fit between human needs and work demands. Instead of adopting a strict personnel selection approach (searching for the "right people" to fit a static work environment), recent advances like the 4/40 workweek and flextime hours show that it is possible to modify the workplace to accommodate the worker. I/O psychologists constantly seek to reduce unnecessary demands in the workplace and to select and train people to better cope with demands that cannot be changed. People and work demands are constantly changing; thus, searching for ways to improve the worker/workplace fit will be an ongoing responsibility for I/O psychology.

# CASE STUDY

Janet Ryder sat at her kitchen table reading the entertainment section of the local newspaper. A movie was playing that she had heard a lot about, and she was hoping it would stay in town for at least two weeks. Her husband, Mark, had recently changed jobs and was now working for St. Regis Aluminum, a large manufacturer of lightweight metal products. The company worked shifts, and Mark was starting a two-week stint on the night shift. Neither Janet nor Mark had any previous experience with shift work, and the switch from conventional hours was difficult for both of them.

Janet tried to plan their family life around Mark's changing hours, but she couldn't get the hang of it. Little things kept cropping up which had never been a problem before. For example, the boy next door had been taking trumpet lessons for about two months. He would practice after school. Janet heard the straining notes from the trumpet, but after a while the sounds seemed to blend in with the rest of the neighborhood noise, and she could ignore them. When Mark was sleeping in the afternoon, the noise of the trumpet often woke him up. They had had two arguments about whether they should call the boy's mother and ask that he practice at another time.

Yesterday, there had been a sale on roast beef, which was one of their favorite dinners. Janet liked to fix a fancy dinner when there was something special to eat. However, with Mark's schedule, she had to "time" special meals when he worked the day shift. While Mark might be ready to sit down to a full meal at 7:00 A.M. after working the night shift, Janet couldn't quite handle either fixing it or eating it after just getting up. The roast beef sits in the freezer, waiting for a time when they both can enjoy it.

It was also pretty awkward for their friends. They had been in a biweekly poker club which met on Friday nights. They got together with some other couples at 8:00, and the party would break up around midnight. When Mark worked afternoons, there was no way they could play. When he worked the night shift, they would have to leave at 10:00, just when things were going great. Only when he worked the day shift could they make it. Now they played in the poker club about once every two months, and their friends got another couple to sub for them.

Janet started to be guilty about feeling sorry for herself. It had been no bargain for Mark, either. The weekend the long-awaited Custom Boat and Trailer Show arrived in town, Mark was working the swing shift. He got to visit the show for about a half hour before he had to leave for work. It seemed that on Saturdays and Sundays just when he found something he liked to do, it was time to go to the plant.

Their 10-year-old son Billie wandered into the kitchen. Billie was holding a Little League schedule in his hand. "Mom" he said, "in three weeks there's the regional tournament in Union City. Will you and dad make it to my game?"

Janet got up and checked Mark's work schedule, which was posted on the cupboard. "I can make it, Billie, but dad will be working the afternoon shift that week," Janet said.

Billie looked downcast. "I never get to see dad very much any more," he said, as he slowly walked out of the kitchen.

Questions

1. Think of Chapter 9 on job satisfaction. Do you see any relationship between work and nonwork satisfaction for shift workers?
2. What other disruptions in family life might you predict for the Ryder family as a result of shift work?
3. Are there things the St. Regis Aluminum Company could do to alleviate some of the problems of shift workers? What might they be?
4. Are there things the community might do to make life easier for shift workers? What might they be?
5. How long would you guess it takes for a family to get into the "rhythm" of shift work?

# REFERENCES

Adams, J. A. Research and the future of engineering psychology. *American Psychologist*, 1972, *27*, 615–622.

Arbous, A. G., & Kerrich, J. E. Accident statistics and the concept of accident-proneness. *Biometrics*, 1951, *7*, 340–432.

Aschoff, J. Features of circadian rhythms relevant to the design of shift schedules. *Ergonomics*, 1978, *21*, 739–754.

Barrett, G. V., & Thornton, C. L. The relationship between perceptual style and driver reaction to an emergency situation. *Journal of Applied Psychology*, 1968, *52*, 169–176.

Beehr, T. A., & Newman, J. E. Job stress, employee health, and organizational effectiveness: A facet analysis, model, and literature review. *Personnel Psychology*, 1978, *31*, 665–699.

Bird, F. E. *Management guide to loss control*. Santa Monica, Calif.: Institute Press, 1974.

Blum, M. L., & Naylor, J. C. *Industrial psychology: Its theoretical and social foundations*. New York: Harper & Row, 1968.

Broadbent, D. S. Effect of noise on behavior. In C. M. Harris (Ed.), *Handbook of noise control*. New York: McGraw-Hill, 1957.

Butler, M. C., & Jones, A. P. Perceived leader behavior, individual characteristics, and injury occurrence in hazardous work environments. *Journal of Applied Psychology*, 1979, *64*, 299–304.

Carvey, D. W., & Nibler, R. G. Biorhythmic cycles and the incidence of industrial accidents. *Personnel Psychology*, 1977, *30*, 447–454.

Chapanis, A. Engineering psychology. In M. D. Dunnette (Ed.), *Handbook of industrial and organizational psychology*. Skokie, Ill.: Rand McNally, 1976.

Cohen, A. Noise effects on health, production, and well-being. *Transactions of the New York Academy of Sciences*, May 1968, Series II, *30*, 910–918.

de la Mare, G., & Walker, J. Factors influencing the choice of shift rotation. *Occupational Psychology*, 1968, *42*, 1–21.

DeReamer, R. *Modern safety and health technology*. New York: John Wiley & Sons, 1980.

Dunbar, R. L. Manager's influence on subordinate thinking about safety. *Academy of Management Journal*, 1975, *18*, 364–369.

Dunham, R. B. Shift work: A review and theoretical analysis. *Academy of Management Review*, 1977, *2*, 626–634.

Dunham, R. B., & Hawk, D. L. The four-day/forty-hour week: Who wants it? *Academy of Management Journal*, 1977, *20*, 644–655.

Fiedler, F. E., & Fiedler, J. Port noise complaints: Verbal and behavioral reactions to airport-related noise. *Journal of Applied Psychology*, 1975, *60*, 498–506.

Fine, B. J., & Kobrick, J. L. Effects of altitude and heat on complex cognitive tasks. *Human Factors*, 1978, *20*, 115–122.

Finkelman, J. M., Zeitlin, L. R., Filippi, J. A., & Friend, M. A. Noise and driver performance. *Journal of Applied Psychology*, 1977, *62*, 713–718.

Floody, D. R. Further systematic research with biorhythms. *Journal of Applied Psychology*, 1981, *66*, 520–521.

Fottler, M. D. Employee acceptance of a four-day workweek. *Academy of Management Journal*, 1977, *20*, 565–668.

Fox, W. F. Human performance in the cold. *Human Factors*, 1967, *9*, 203–220.

Frost, P. J., & Jamal, M. Shift work, attitudes and reported behavior: Some association between individual characteristics and hours of work and leisure. *Journal of Applied Psychology*, 1979, *64*, 77–81.

Goldstein, L. G. Human variables in traffic accidents: A digest of research. *Traffic Safety Research Review*, 1964, *8*, 26–31.

Golembiewski, R. T., & Proehl, C. W. A survey of the

empirical literature on flexible workhours: Character and consequences of a major innovation. *Academy of Management Review*, 1978, 3, 837–853.

Goodale, J. G., & Aagaard, A. K. Factors relating to varying reactions to the 4-day workweek. *Journal of Applied Psychology*, 1975, 60, 33–38.

Grandjean, E. Fatigue: Its physiological and psychological significance. *Ergonomics*, 1968, 11, 427–436.

Hicks, W. D., & Klimoski, R. J. The impact of flexitime on employee attitudes. *Academy of Management Journal*, 1981, 24, 333–341.

Ivancevich, J. M. Effects of the shorter workweek on selected satisfaction and performance measures. *Journal of Applied Psychology*, 1974, 59, 717–721.

Ivancevich, J. M., & Lyon, H. L. The shortened workweek: A field experiment. *Journal of Applied Psychology*, 1977, 62, 34–37.

Jamal, M. Shift work related to job attitudes, social participation and withdrawal behavior: A study of nurses and industrial workers. *Personnel Psychology*, 1981, 34, 535–548.

Kephart, N. C., & Tiffin, J. Vision and accident experience. *National Safety News*, 1950, 62, 90–91.

Kim, J. S., & Campagna, A. F. Effects of flexitime on employee attendance and performance: A field experiment. *Academy of Management Journal*, 1981, 24, 729–741.

Komaki, J., Barwick, K. D., & Scott, L. R. A behavioral approach to occupational safety: Pinpointing and reinforcing safe performance in a food manufacturing plant. *Journal of Applied Psychology*, 1978, 63, 434–445.

Komaki, J., Heinzmann, A. T., & Lawson, L. Effect of training and feedback: Component analysis of a behavioral safety program. *Journal of Applied Psychology*, 1980, 65, 261–270.

Kunce, J. T. Vocational interest and accident proneness. *Journal of Applied Psychology*, 1967, 51, 223–225.

LaBenz, P., Cohen, A., & Pearson, B. A noise and hearing survey of earth-moving equipment operators. *American Industrial Hygiene Association Journal*, March–April 1967, 28, 117–128.

Lockhart, J. M. Effects of body and hand cooling on complex manual performance. *Journal of Applied Psychology*, 1966, 50, 57–59.

Malaviya, P., & Ganesh, K. Shift work and individual differences in the productivity of weavers in an Indian textile mill. *Journal of Applied Psychology*, 1976, 61, 774–776.

Malaviya, P., & Ganesh, K. Individual differences in productivity across type of work shift. *Journal of Applied Psychology*, 1977, 62, 527–528.

McCormick, E. J. *Human factors engineering* (3rd ed.). New York: McGraw-Hill, 1970.

McFarland, R. A. Understanding fatigue in modern life. *Ergonomics*, 1971, 14, 1–10.

Meers, A., Maasen, A., & Verhaagen, P. Subjective health after six months and after four years of shift work. *Ergonomics*, 1978, 21, 857–859.

Mihal, W. L., & Barrett, G. V. Individual differences in perceptual information processing and their relation to automobile accident involvement. *Journal of Applied Psychology*, 1976, 61, 229–233.

Nollen, S. D., & Martin, V. H. *Alternative work schedules, part I: Flexitime*. New York: AMACOM, 1978.

Nord, W. R., & Costigan, R. Worker adjustment to the four-day week: A longitudinal study. *Journal of Applied Psychology*, 1973, 58, 60–66.

Nothstein, G. Z. *The law of occupational safety and health*. New York: Free Press, 1981.

Pepler, R. D. Warmth and performance: An investigation in the tropics. *Ergonomics*, 1958, 2, 63–88.

Petersen, A. P., & Gross, F. E. *Handbook of noise measurement* (8th ed.). New Concord, Mass.: GenRad, 1978.

Poor, R. *Four days, forty hours: Reporting a revaluation in work and leisure*. Cambridge, Mass.: Bursk & Poor, 1970.

Poulton, E. C., Hitchings, N. B., & Brooke, R. B. Effect of cold and rain upon the vigilance of lookouts. *Ergonomics*, 1965, 8, 163–168.

Ronen, S. Arrival and departure patterns of public sector employees before and after the implementation of flexitime. *Personnel Psychology*, 1981, 34, 817–822. (a)

Ronen, S. *Flexible working hours: An innovation in the quality of working life*. New York: McGraw-Hill, 1981. (b)

Schein, V. E., Maurer, E. H., & Novak, J. F. Impact of flexible working hours on productivity. *Journal of Applied Psychology*, 1977, 62, 463–465.

Spangenberg, H. H. The use of projective tests in the selection of bus drivers. *Traffic Safety Research Review*, 1968, 12, 118–121.

Teichner, W. H., & Kobrick, J. L. Effects of prolonged exposure to low temperature on visual-motor performance. *Journal of Experimental Psychology*, 1955, *49*, 122–126.

Voevodsky, J. Evaluation of a deceleration warning light for reducing rear end automobile collisions. *Journal of Applied Psychology*, 1974, *59*, 270–273.

Wedderburn, A. A. Some suggestions for increasing the usefulness of psychological and sociological studies of shiftwork. *Ergonomics*, 1978, *21*, 827–833.

Weinstein, N. D. Individual differences in reactions to noise: A longitudinal study in a college dormitory. *Journal of Applied Psychology*, 1978, *63*, 458–466.

Whitlock, G. H., Clouse, R. J., & Spencer, W. F. Predicting accident proneness. *Personnel Psychology*, 1963, *16*, 33–44.

Williams, J. R. Follow-up study of relationships between perceptual style measures and telephone company vehicle accidents. *Journal of Applied Psychology*, 1977, *62*, 751–754.

Wolcott, J., McKeeken, R., Burgin, R., & Yanowitch, R. Correlation of general aviation accidents with biorhythm theory. *Human Factors*, 1977, *19*, 283–294.

Yoder, T. A., Lucas, R. L., & Botzum, G. D. The marriage of human factors and safety in industry. *Human Factors*, 1973, *15*, 197–205.

Zohar, D. Safety climate in industrial organizations: Theoretical and applied implications. *Journal of Applied Psychology*, 1980, *65*, 96–102.

# AUTHOR INDEX

Note: Page numbers in italic indicate that citation is in chapter references.

# SUBJECT INDEX

## A

Ability, 113–116, 358
Absenteeism, 82–83, 130, 250, 340–341
Accident proneness, 546–548
Accidents
  approaches to reduction, 550–556
  causes of, 545–549
  description of, 83, 130, 251
Accuracy of communication, 452–453
Achievement-oriented leadership, 414
Across-subjects design, 377
Action research, 486–488
Activity sampling, 443–444
Actuarial prediction, 550
Adjustment problems of shift workers, 558–559
Adverse impact, 107, 186–187
Affirmative Action, 185–186
AFL–CIO, 503
Age differences in job satisfaction, 331–332
American Arbitration Association (AAA), 509
American Psychological Association (APA), 3–5, 58, 106, 227
Apprentice training, 208–209, 525
Arbitration
  interest, 509–510
  rights, 514–517
*Army Alpha* test, 16
*Army Beta* test, 16
*Army General Classification Test* (AGCT), 20
Assessment centers, 271–275
Attitude centers, 271–275
Attitude surveys, 442–443, 491–492
Audiometer, 113
Audiovisual material, 209–210
Authority, 400
Autonomy, 471

## B

Bargaining zone, 506–508

Base rate, 157–158
Behavioral checklists and scales
  behavioral observation scales, 261–263
  behaviorally anchored rating scales, 259–261
  critical incidents, 258–259
  mixed standard scale, 263–264
  weighted checklist, 259
Behavioral criteria, 228
Behavioral expectation scales; *see* Behaviorally anchored rating scales
Behavioral observation scales, 261–263
Behavioral role modeling, 219–220
Behaviorally anchored rating scales (BARS), 259–261
*Bennett Test of Mechanical Comprehension*, 111
Bimodal distributions, 47
Bingham, Walter, 17–18, 20
Biographical information (biodata), 124–127
Biorhythms, 548–549
Bureau of Apprenticeship and Training, 525–526
Business games, 217–218

## C

Cattell, James, 18
Center for Creative Leadership, 398
Central tendency errors, 255
Centralized/decentralized shape, 447–448
Certification election, 504–505
Certification of psychologists, 11–12
Channel, 432
Circadian rhythm, 558–559
Civil Rights Act, 23, 107
Classification, 183–185
Client, 483
Coercion, 400
Coercive power, 292
Cold stress, 540–541
Collective bargaining, 10–11, 507–510

Communication
  definition of, 430
  downward, 437–440
  effects of organizational structure on, 446–448
  methods of studying, 443–446
  modalities, 451–452
  model of, 431–433
  networks, 449–450
  outcomes of, 455–457
  press variables, 452–455
  purposes of, 431
  training, 436
  union influence on, 528
  upward, 440–443
  in work behavior, 433–437
Comparison process theory, 322–323
Composite criteria, 87–88
Computer-assisted instruction, 215–217
Conclusions from research, 57–58
Concurrent criterion-related validity, 100, 167–168, 187
Conferences, 210–211
Confidentiality, 106–107
Content validity index, 178
Content validity ratio, 178
Contrast effects, 121
Correlation
  multiple, 142–144
  simple, 52–57
Cost-effectiveness, 195
Credibility, 275, 453
Criterion (criteria)
  actual, 68–70
  composite, 87–88
  contamination, 71–72, 249, 274
  cutoff, 157–161
  deficiency, 70–72, 249
  development of, 72–75
  distal, 73
  multiple, 88–89
  proximal, 73
  relationships among, 85–87

*This book has been set VIP, in 10 and 9 point Caledonia, leaded 2 points. Section numbers are 12 and 30 point Avant Garde demi-bold; section titles are 16 point Avant Garde demi-bold. Chapter numbers are 12 and 36 point Avant Garde Book, and chapter titles are 18 point Avant Garde Book. The overall size of the type page is 36½ by 47½ picas.*

$$3 \overline{)73}$$

24

3.8
2.5
20

7 3

5 )65
2.1
6 5
20
2.5
20